RELIGION, POLITICAL CULTURE
AND THE EMERGENCE
OF EARLY MODERN SOCIETY

STUDIES
IN MEDIEVAL AND
REFORMATION THOUGHT

EDITED BY

HEIKO A. OBERMAN, Tucson, Arizona

IN COOPERATION WITH

THOMAS A. BRADY, Jr., Eugene, Oregon
E. JANE DEMPSEY DOUGLASS, Princeton, New Jersey
GUILLAUME H.M. POSTHUMUS MEYJES, Leiden
DAVID C. STEINMETZ, DURHAM, North Carolina
ANTON G. WEILER, Nijmegen

VOLUME L

HEINZ SCHILLING

RELIGION, POLITICAL CULTURE
AND THE EMERGENCE
OF EARLY MODERN SOCIETY

RELIGION, POLITICAL CULTURE AND THE EMERGENCE OF EARLY MODERN SOCIETY

Essays in German and Dutch History

BY

HEINZ SCHILLING

E.J. BRILL
LEIDEN • NEW YORK • KÖLN
1992

ISSN   0585-6914
ISBN   90 04 09607 8

CONTENTS

PART THREE

THE NETHERLANDS — THE PIONEER SOCIETY
OF EARLY MODERN EUROPE

PREFACE

The essays collected in this volume were written during the last
one and a half decades. Most of them were originally published
in German periodicals or symposium volumes, while one (No.
9) appears for the first time in print here. The collection
reflects discussions within the younger generation of German
Early Modernists on urban and Reformation history, on
confessionalization and early modern modernization, as well as
on social structure and social change within Old European
societies in general. Heiko A. Oberman, University of Arizona,
first suggested that they be collected and translated. I am very
much obliged to him and to E.J. Brill, publishers at Leiden, for
encouraging me to bring my research to a broader audience of
English-speaking readers. As the collection brings together for
the first time articles that originally appeared in a variety of
places, the book will also be of use for those readers who are
familiar with one or another of the original German articles.
Funding for the translation was generously provided by the
Hessische Minister für Wissenschaft und Kunst as a part of the
project *"Politische und konfessionelle Identitäten in Europa"*
within the research program *"Nationale und kulturelle Identität"*. The translations were done by Dr. Stephen G. Burnett,
Lincoln, Nebraska. I have revised each article, in some cases
rewriting parts of them, and have updated the notes. Although
Dr. Burnett did his very best to transform the complex German
syntax, especially sophisticated in my early articles of the
1970's, into readable American English, the teutonic flavor is
still present. I hope very much that the English speaking reader
will accept this generously──as an expression of the specific
"charm" of German scholarship.

All the typing, technical arrangements and copy editing,
including the production of camera-ready copy, were the work
of a team in Giessen. I wish to thank especially Frau Ruth
Ludwig and Holger Gräf, M.A., as well as Ute Lotz, Heike
Scherneck, M.A. for their commitment in undertaking this
formidable task.

PLACES OF FIRST PUBLICATION:

Article 1: Gab es im späten Mittelalter und zu Beginn der Neuzeit in Deutschland einen städtischen "Republikanismus"? Zur politischen Kultur des alteuropäischen Stadtbürgertums, in: H. Koenigsberger (ed.), Republiken und Republikanismus im Europa der Frühen Neuzeit, München 1988, 101-143.

Article 2: Die politische Elite nordwestdeutscher Städte in den religiösen Auseinandersetzungen des 16. Jahrhunderts, in: W.J. Mommsen (ed.), Stadtbürgertum und Adel in der Reformation, Stuttgart 1979, 232-308.

Article 3: Wandlungs— und Differenzierungsprozesse innerhalb der bürgerlichen Oberschichten West— und Nordwestdeutschlands im 16. und 17. Jahrhundert, in: M. Biskup/K. Zernack (eds.), Schichtung und Entwicklung der Gesellschaft in Polen und Deutschland im 16. und 17. Jahrhunderts, Wiesbaden 1983, 121-173.

Article 4: Die deutsche Gemeindereformation. Ein oberdeutsch-zwinglianisches Ereignis vor der "reformatorischen Wende" des Jahres 1525?, in: Zeitschrift für Historische Forschung 14 (1987), 325-333.

Article 5: Die Konfessionalisierung im Reich—Religiöser und gesellschaftlicher Wandel in Deutschland zwischen 1555 und 1620, in: Historische Zeitschrift 246 (1988), 1-45.

Article 6: Die "Zweite Reformation" als Kategorie der Geschichtswissenschaft, in: H. Schilling (ed.), Die reformierte Konfessionalisierung in Deutschland.—Das Problem der "Zweiten Reformation", Gütersloh 1986, 387-437.

Article 7: Die Geschichte der nördlichen Niederlande und die Modernisierungstheorie, in: Geschichte und Gesellschaft 8 (1982), 475-517.

Article 8: Religion und Gesellschaft in der calvinistischen Republik der Vereinigten Niederlande—"Öffentlichkeitskirche" und Säkularisation; Ehe und Hebammenwesen; Presbyterien und politische Partizipation, in: F. Petri (ed.), Kirche und gesellschaftlicher Wandel in deutschen und niederländischen Städten der werdenden Neuzeit, Köln/Wien 1980, 197-250.

Article 9: Published for the first time in this volume.

INTRODUCTION

The three sections of the present volume represent the topics in early modern European history that interest me most. *First*: urban society mainly in northern Germany and the Netherlands from the fifteenth to the early nineteenth centuries, with regard to its specific social structure and social dynamism but also the religion, mentality, political culture, and political thinking of the burghers and the rising early modern "bourgeoisie." *Second*: confessionalization as a fundamental process of social change within Old European society and the confessional era as a decisive phase within early modern modernization, discussed primarily with examples from Calvinist regions. *Third*: the Dutch Republic of the United Netherlands as the great successful republican and "bourgeois" alternative to the predominantly noble and princely world of Old Europe—a specific type of early modern society which is fascinating because of its economic success and multicultural profile as well as its function as a forerunner society and model for early modern modernization in such large centralized national states as England and France, and in several of the German territorial states, especially Brandenburg-Prussia.

The *first section* on "Urban Society and Reformation" begins with a more recent article which summarizes several earlier case studies on urban uprisings and the political culture of the German middle class.[1] At the same time it extends the

---

1 These case studies are: H. Schilling, Bürgerkämpfe in Aachen zu Beginn des 17. Jahrhunderts. Konflikte im Rahmen der alteuropäischen Stadtgesellschaft oder im Umkreis der frühbürgerlichen Revolution?, in: Zeitschrift für historische Forschung 1 (1974), 175-231; idem, Aufstandsbewegungen in der Stadtbürgerlichen Gesellschaft des Alten Reiches. Die Vorgeschichte des Münsteraner Täuferreichs, 1525-1534, in: H.-U. Wehler (ed.), Der Deutsche Bauernkrieg 1524-1526, Göttingen 1975, 193-238; idem, Reformation und Bürgerfreiheit. Emdens Weg zur calvinistischen Stadtrepublik, in: B. Moeller (ed.), Stadt und Kirche im 16. Jahrhundert, Gütersloh 1978, 128-161. (English version in: H. Schilling, Civic Calvinism in Northwestern Germany and the Netherlands, Kirksville, Mo, 1991.) H. Schilling, Dortmund im 16. und 17. Jahrhundert—Reichstädtische Gesellschaft, Reformation und Konfessionalisierung, in: G. Luntowski and N. Reimann (eds.), Dortmund—1100 Jahre Stadtgeschichte, Dortmund 1982, 151-202; idem, The Reformation in the Hanseatic Cities, in: The Sixteenth Century Journal 14 (1983), 443-456.

area under consideration from the northern and western parts of Germany to the entire Empire, discussing civic republicanism as the specific contribution of the medieval and early modern burghers to the political culture of Germany. A product of the Middle Ages, civic republicanism remained strong well into the seventeenth century. Except in the imperial cities it was weakened decisively by the ultimate victory of the princes and their territorial states. The triumph of princely absolutism not only limited the economic opportunities of the middle class, but it was also a blow to their self-confidence and a setback for the political culture of German society in general. I have placed this article first on the advice of my translator Dr. Burnett. He suggested that "beginning students should start with this article before reading either 'Urban Elites and the Religious Conflicts' or 'The Rise of Early Modern Burgher Elites,' because 'Civic Republicanism' contains such a clear explanation of both the structure of city governments and the assumptions that lay behind them. The former articles essentially assume a working knowledge of the contents of 'Civic Republicanism.' Instead of being a 'tough nut to crack' I found it a fascinating article to translate."[2]

The next two articles are concerned with the political and social elites of the cities and towns of the Hansa region. The first one (No. 2) focuses on the behavior of elites during the religious, political, and social conflicts of the Reformation era, looking for commonly held positions and the reasons they were adopted. Like the lesser nobility the urban elites had powerful "primary inhibitions" that hindered them from supporting the Reformation. These inhibitions grew out of their deep involvement in the existing social and ecclesiastical order. But in the course of events, which were shaped by a three-cornered struggle between the citizenry, urban regime, and territorial rulers, the urban elites as a rule broke through these barriers and joined the majority of the citizens in their pro-Lutheran attitude. The new urban consensus, based upon the communalization of the town church, strengthened the position of the cities considerably against their princely overlords. On the whole this article can be read as a parallel to Bernd Moeller's theses on the upper German imperial cities, but it modifies Moeller's findings in two important respects: by emphasizing

---

2 Letter from January 9, 1991, to the author.

the communal character of North German non-imperial towns
and by pointing out the communal nature of Lutheranism,
which retained its character as a civic ideology well into the
second half of the sixteenth century, at least within the Hanseatic cities under consideration. The second article on urban
elites (No. 3) discusses the social changes and shifts in mentality within the political elites from the late Middle Ages to the
end of the Thirty Years' War, resulting from demographic,
economic, political, and—last but not least—religious and
ecclesiastical developments. Prosopographical analyses of a
variety of town councils show that in the course of these
developments the medieval type of Hanseatic-city-elite was
supplanted by the early modern type of urban elite or—more
correctly—by two types of early modern burgher elites, an
urban one, focusing on the traditional values of urban communalism and republicanism, and a territorial one, becoming an
early modern "bourgeoisie" which sought to take advantage of
the opportunities provided by the rise of the early modern territorial state and its bureaucracy.

In certain respects the final essay in the urban history and
Reformation section (No. 4) grows out of the findings discussed in the first three articles.[3] It enters the debate over
Peter Blickle's brilliant thesis concerning the communal
character of the Reformation, pointing out that the communal
nature of the urban Reformation has been well established in
German Reformation research for decades. I have also drawn
attention to problems that arise from several additional asser-
tions of Professor Blickle concerning the structural identity of
urban and rural communalism, the alleged fundamental importance of the year 1525 as the turning point in German history,
and finally and most confusing, the contrasting view of a
communal upper German Zwinglian and a non-communal

---

3 And in the following publications: H. Schilling, Konfessionskonflikt und
Staatsbildung. Eine Fallstudie über das Verhältnis von religiösem und sozialem
Wandel in der Frühneuzeit am Beispiel der Grafschaft Lippe, Gütersloh 1981;
idem, Aufbruch und Krise. Deutsche Geschichte von 1517 bis 1648, Berlin 1988;
idem, Bürgerkämpfe (note 1); idem, Reformation und Bürgerfreiheit (note 1);
idem, Konfessionskonflikte und hansestädtische Freiheit im 16. und frühen 17.
Jahrhundert, in: Hansische Geschichtsblätter 97 (1979), 36-59; idem, Dortmund
(note 1); idem, The Reformation in the Hanseatic Cities (note 1); idem, Vergleichende Betrachtungen zur Geschichte der bürgerlichen Eliten in Nordwestdeutschland und in den Niederlanden, in: H. Schilling und H. Diederiks (eds.),
Bürgerliche Eliten in den Niederlanden und in Nordwestdeutschland, Köln/Wien
1985, 1-32.

lower German Lutheran Reformation, which contradicts the
findings of almost all of the research done on northern German
urban history for at least the last generation.

The *second section* of this collection consists of two articles
on confessionalization—one on the Reformed or Calvinist type
(No. 5), the other on the paradigm in general and its application to German history (No. 6).[4] The "confessionalization"
paradigm is a product of both German history and German
historiography. It stems from German history because more
than any other European country, early modern Germany was
shaped by distinct state-church-systems which strongly influenced political, social, intellectual, and cultural developments.
It is a product of German historiography because the paradigm
arose out of the debates over the reconstruction of German
historiography after the Second World War along the lines of
social and societal history (*Gesellschaftsgeschichte*). The specifically German contribution to this type of new history was
an emphasis upon both legal and constitutional history and on
religious and ecclesiastical history as indispensable and necessary for any good societal history of Old Europe.[5]

Meanwhile the "confessionalization" paradigm has been
adapted outside of Germany too, and has provoked one of the
key debates on early modern history, encompassing the whole
spectrum of social, political, cultural, and intellectual developments in early modern Europe. At the same time, this debate
signals a remarkable shift in the definition of historical
periods. German historians of the Reformation period have
broadened their purview to include the second half of the
sixteenth and the early seventeenth centuries, those decades of

---

4 The European context is discussed in: H. Schilling, Nation und Konfession in
der frühneuzeitlichen Geschichte Europas. Zu den konfessionsgeschichtlichen
Voraussetzungen der frühmodernen Staatsbildung, in: K. Garber (ed.), Nation
und Literatur im Europa der frühen Neuzeit, Tübingen 1989, vol. 1, 87-107; idem,
Nationale Identität und Konfession in der europäischen Geschichte der Neuzeit,
in: B. Giesen (ed.), Nationale und kulturelle Identität in der europäischen Neuzeit, Frankfurt 1991; idem, Konfessionalisierung und Formierung eines internationalen Systems während der frühen Neuzeit, forthcoming in H. Guggis-
berg/G.Kroedel (eds.), Papers of the VRG/SRG Symposium, September, 1990, in
Washington, D.C..

5 On the historiography of "confessionalization" cf. H. Schilling,
Konfessionsbildung, Konfessionalisierung und konfessionelles Zeitalter-ein
Literaturbericht, in: Geschichte in Wissenschaft und Unterricht (42) 1991, 447-
463; and the most recent and excellent review-article B. Rüth, Reformation und
Konfessionsbildung im städtischen Bereich. Perspektiven der Forschung, in: Zeit-
schrift der Savigny-Stiftung für Rechtsgeschichte KA 77 (1991), 197-282.

accelerated social change which are the focus of this book. To scholars working in the field of western European history, there is nothing especially novel about this change since they have always paid special attention to this later period. But it is a new departure for German historiography, which has been primarily interested in the early Reformation for centuries. This attitude was reinforced during the sixties and seventies by the Marxist paradigm of an "Early Bourgeois Revolution" (*Frühbürgerliche Revolution*) and by the subsequent claim that the year 1525 was the decisive turning point in German history. Consequently, the following decades, especially the second half of the sixteenth century, were denigrated as a "dull period and boring interlude," even by historians who have written important books on this period.[6] This new focus upon the decades at the end of the sixteenth century will strengthen the comparative approach in German historiography. In so doing, it will make an important contribution to the rewriting of German history from a European perspective, which is one of the most urgent and honorable tasks of German historiography at the end of the twentieth century.

The three articles of the *third section* of the present volume represent a field of reseach that I have been interested in since the very beginning of my historical writing.[7] In contrast to the case studies on Groningen which have recently appeared in

---

6 B. Vogler, Le monde germanique et helvétique à l'époque des Réformes, 1517-1618, vol. 2, Paris 1981, 251. Similar, W. Schulze, in: Zeitschrift für Historische Forschung 10 (1983), 253.

7 H. Schilling, Niederländische Exulanten im 16. Jahrhundert. Ihre Stellung im Sozialgefüge und im religiösen Leben deutscher und englischer Städte, Gütersloh 1972; idem and W. Ehbrecht (eds.), Niederlande und Nordwestdeutschland, Studien zur Regional- und Stadtgeschichte Nordwestkontinentaleuropas im Mittelalter und in der Neuzeit, Franz Petri zum 80. Geburtstag, Köln/Wien 1983; idem and H. Diederiks (eds.), Bürgerliche Eliten in den Niederlanden und in Nordwestdeutschland. Studien zur Sozialgeschichte des europäischen Bürgertums im Mittelalter und in der Neuzeit, Köln/Wien 1985; idem, Der Aufstand der Niederlande: Bürgerliche Revolution oder Elitenkonflikt?, in: H.-U. Wehler (ed.), 200 Jahre amerikanische Revolution und moderne Revolutionsforschung, Göttingen 1976, 177-231; idem, Calvinistische Presbyterien in Städten der Frühneuzeit—eine kirchliche Alternativform zur bürgerlichen Repräsentation? (Mit einer quantifizierenden Untersuchung zur holländischen Stadt Leiden), in: W. Ehbrecht (ed.), Städtische Führungsgruppen und Gemeinden in der werdenden Neuzeit, Köln/Wien 1980, 385-444; idem, Innovation through Migration: The Settlements of Calvinistic Netherlanders in Sixteenth- and Seventeenth-Century Central and Western Europe, in: Histoire sociale-Social History 16, Nr. 31 (May 1983), 7-33; idem, Die Republik der Vereinigten Niederlande—ein bewunderter und beargwöhnter Nachbar, in: H. Duchhardt (ed.), In Europas Mitte. Deutschland und seine Nachbarn, Bonn 1988, 20-28.

English,[8] the articles presented here are more concerned with macro-historical analysis. They examine the structures and the specific dynamism of a whole society, the society of the United Republic of the Northern Netherlands. The focus of the first article (No. 7) is the problem of early modern societal change and its continuity or discontinuity with the great transformation from the *ancien régime* to the modern world since the end of the eighteenth century. The second one (No. 8) traces in more detail the religious and cultural component of these structures and changes, whereas the third (No. 9) discusses the meaning of the proto-liberal theory of Dutch Regent republicanism within its historical context and its place in European political thinking during the early modern period. These articles grow out of the Weberian perspective on early modern development, but—as I have argued in length in No. 7—present specific variations and modifications that make it suitable for historical analysis of the early modern period. At the same time it is a rather traditional approach since European history should always be written from a comparative perspective.[9]

---

8 In H. Schilling, Civic Calvinism (note 1).

9 Brilliant examples of this approach include works by the Dutch historian Jan Romein, Historische lijnen en patronen. Een keuze uit de essays, Amsterdam 1971; idem and A. Romein-Verschoor, Aera van Europa. De Europese geschiedenis als afwijking van het algemeen menselijk patroon, 2nd ed. Leiden 1986. Cf. also K. Davids, J. Lucassen and J. Luiten van Zanden, De Nederlandse geschiedenis als afwijking van het algemeen menselijk patroon. Een aanzet tot een programma van samenwerking, Amsterdam 1988.

PART ONE

URBAN SOCIETY AND REFORMATION

CHAPTER ONE

CIVIC REPUBLICANISM IN LATE MEDIEVAL AND EARLY MODERN GERMAN CITIES

The absence of explicitly republican political theories in late medieval and sixteenth century German cities will hardly surprise experts on German urban history.[1] The idea of a universally applicable, self-consistent political theory ran counter to the mentality of the urban citizenry and its conception of a well-ordered society. The city itself as a concrete entity was still the point of reference for the political thought of its citizens during these centuries. And even the concept of order implicit in a city's constitution was very seldom articulated or formulated as an internally consistent, sophisticated system of ideas that could properly be called a "political theory." The citizens had clear ideas regarding the political workings of the civic order in its internal affairs and also in its relations with external powers. But these ideas must be inferred both from the forms of legal argumentation that they used when dealing with specific problems of daily political life and from their actions.

In this essay I will attempt to describe the concept of political order held by citizens of German cities, illustrating its components with a whole series of different urban events and contexts. In so doing I hope to demonstrate that the essential foundation stones of a republican understanding were present despite the lack of a political theory of republicanism.[2] (102)

---

1 This essay was written for the conference "Republics and Republicanism in Early Modern Europe", organized by H.G. Koenigsberger at the Historisches Kolleg in Munich in spring of 1985. On the idea and the scope of the topic see: H.G. Koenigsberger, Schlußbetrachtung. Republiken und Republikanismus im Europa der frühen Neuzeit aus historischer Sicht, in: H.G. Koenigsberger (ed.), Republiken und Republikanismus im Europa der frühen Neuzeit, München 1988, 285-302.

2 I have referred to the problem in several of my earlier articles, where the older literature is given in the notes. See H. Schilling, Aufstandsbewegungen in der Stadtbürgerlichen Gesellschaft des Alten Reiches. Die Vorgeschichte des Münsteraner Täuferreiches, 1525-1534, in: H.-U. Wehler (ed.), Der deutsche

I will focus on the Empire and will refer to the Netherlands[3] only for the purpose of comparison. I will concentrate on cities in the Hanseatic region and in the adjoining areas further to the South and Southwest, that is, the Rhineland, Hesse, and part of Thuringia. My argumentation and conclusions, however, can be considered valid in their essentials for the Empire as a whole.

The main axiom of political theory for cities between the thirteenth and seventeenth centuries can be expressed in a single sentence: "Each city possessed a constitution in the eyes of its citizens." This "constitution"[4] was partly unwritten and partly expressed in documents such as privileges, contracts, and

Bauernkrieg 1524-1526, Göttingen 1975, 193-238; idem, Bürgerkämpfe in Aachen zu Beginn des 17. Jahrhunderts. Konflikte im Rahmen der alteuropäischen Stadt-gesellschaft oder im Umkreis der frühbürgerlichen Revolution?, in: Zeitschrift für Historische Forschung 1 (1974), 175-231; idem, Die politische Elite nordwest-deutscher Städte in den religiösen Auseinandersetzungen des 16. Jahrhunderts, in: W. J. Mommsen (ed.), Stadtbürgertum und Adel in der Reformation. Studien zur Sozialgeschichte der Reformation in England und Deutschland, Stuttgart 1979, 235-308 (English translation below p. 61-134); idem, The Reformation in the Hanseatic Cities, in: The Sixteenth Century Journal XIV, 4 (1983), 443-456; idem, Konfessionskonflikte und Hansestädtische Freiheiten im 16. und frühen 17. Jahrhundert. Der Fall "Lemgo contra Lippe", in: Hansische Geschichtsblätter 97 (1979), 36-59; idem, Konfessionskonflikt und Staatsbildung. Eine Fallstudie über das Verhältnis von religiösem und sozialem Wandel in der Frühneuzeit am Bei-spiel der Grafschaft Lippe, Gütersloh 1981.—The most important studies that have appeared since the publication of this article are: E. Isenmann, Die deutsche Stadt im Spätmittelalter, 1250-1500, Stuttgart 1988; M. Stolleis (ed.), Recht, Verfassung und Verwaltung in der frühneuzeitlichen Stadt, Köln/Wien 1991 (esp. the contribution of G. Schmidt, Städtetag, Städtehanse und frühneuzeitliche Reichsverfassung); V. Press, Die Reichsstadt in der altständischen Gesellschaft, in: J. Kunisch (ed.), Neue Studien zur frühneuzeitlichen Reichsgeschichte, Berlin 1987, 9-42; M. Neugebauer-Wölk, Reichsstädtische Reichspolitik, in: Zeitschrift für historische Forschung 17 (1990), 27-48; G. Schwerhoff, Bürgerlicher Konflikt in Köln, 1608-1610, in: Jahrbuch des Kölnischen Geschichtsvereins 60 (1989), 31-75; W. Schmitz, Verfassung und Bekenntnis. Die Aachener Wirren im Spiegel der kaiserlichen Politik (1550-1614), Frankfurt 1983; M. Prak, Civil Disturbance and Urban Middle Class in the Dutch Republic, in: Tijdschrift voor sociale geschie-denis 15 (1989), 165-173.—Recent works on urban conflicts at the end of the early modern period include the essays of K. Gerteis and K. Müller in H. Berding (ed.), Soziale Unruhen in Deutschland während der Französischen Revolution, Göttingen 1988.

3 For a more detailed discussion of the Dutch sources see: H. Schilling, Cal-vinismus und Freiheitsrechte. Die politisch-theologische Pamphletistik der ost-friesisch-groningischen "Patriotenpartei" und die politische Kultur in Deutsch-land und in den Niederlanden, in: Bijdragen en Mededelingen Betreffende de Geschiedenis der Nederlanden 102 (1987), 403-434 (English translation in: idem, Civic Calvinism, Kirksville 1991).

4 We do not, however, interprete the Old European city constitutions as direct forerunners of modern constitutionalism, as historians of the nineteenth century did.

Rezesse. The latter were formal settlements or compromises between the city council and the citizens. These documents were expressions of statute law, ordinances written in response to immediate problems, which constituted in their totality the city's "entire common polity" (*gantze gemeine politie*), as a burgher committee in Hildesheim described it in 1589.[5] This "constitution" regulated the legal and political relations of the city with political entities outside of the city, including the Emperor and territorial prince. It also governed political organization within the city itself, including the scope of magisterial responsibility and the communal right of participation, whether through representatives of the citizenry and/or by a direct right of co-determination in particular questions. The burghers regarded it as one of their fundamental rights that the content of this "constitution" should be known by all citizens. It was not to be treated as an *arcane* subject for specialists on the city council or within a small circle of the political elite.[6] (103)

For a variety of reasons during the late Middle Ages it became more and more difficult for burghers to maintain this knowledge and thereby to secure the basis of the civic communal constitution. These reasons included an increase in political and administrative differentiation, a trend toward the centralization of power in the hands of city councils, and a social narrowing of the elite who held political office. The citizens feared that the political elite would deprive them of their rights and would "betray" the city's rights of autonomous authority through accommodation with the territorial authorities. Instances of both kinds of accusations have been preserved for both territorial and imperial cities.[7] The commune attempted to counter these threats by demanding—mostly during periodic uprisings—that the civic privileges and *Rezesse* regularly be read aloud to the citizenry on occasions such as the annual appointment of the city council or periodically, when the

---

5 Joachim Brandis des jüngeren Diarium ergänzt aus Tilo Brandis Annalen. 1528-1609, ed. M. Buhlers, Hildesheim 1902, 265.

6 See for instance the critique of the burgomasters by the burgher movement in Brunswick given by H. J. Querfurth, Die Unterwerfung der Stadt Braunschweig im Jahre 1671. Das Ende der Braunschweiger Stadtfreiheit, Braunschweig 1953, 189s.; similarly see M. Meyn, Die Reichsstadt Frankfurt vor dem Bürgeraufstand von 1612 bis 1614. Struktur und Krise, Frankfurt/Main 1980, 60ss.; Schilling, Bürgerkämpfe (note 2), 198.

7 Hildesheim: Brandis, Hildesheim (note 5), 115; Aachen: Schilling, Bürgerkämpfe (note 2), 191, 197.

commune swore its oath of allegiance to the new prince, and
the prince, for his part, confirmed the privileges of his estates
and subjects.

What were the principal elements of these "civic constitutions?" I will try to answer this question in three steps: first, I
will discuss the internal principles of civic order (I), and then
the burgher conception of the status of their cities within larger political units, i. e. the territories and the Empire (II).
Finally, I will attempt to categorize the political thinking of the
German urban burghers within the history of European political theory (III).

I

The internal civic order rested upon four pillars: the existence
of "fundamental rights and personal liberties" (I,1), the demand that all city residents should participate equally in fulfilling civic obligations and duties (I,2), the legal claim of the
burgher commune for participation in the exercise of political
power (I,3), and finally the oligarchic and egalitarian structure
of the burgher political elite (I,4).

1. The history of civic "fundamental rights and personal
liberties" has been summarized convincingly by Werner Holbeck, using the important example of fifteenth century Cologne
(1396-1517). His interpretation, however, is incorrect in two
respects because he allowed his analysis to be "guided by present day fundamental rights." Proceeding from this false
assumption he wrongly concluded that the city of Cologne was
unique in its respect for the personal and fundamental rights of
its citizens. Also his thesis that "the liberties of that time were
limited, serving only to dispose of specific disadvantages" is at
very least a misunderstanding of the sources and historical
circumstances.[8] It is true that in contrast to modern fundamental law civic (104) liberties in medieval and early modern
European cities were not based upon natural law, and that they
were established by each individual city for itself.
Nevertheless, the principle of personal liberty was an essential
part of Old European civic life and was also fundamental to

---

8 W. Holbeck, Freiheitsrechte in Köln von 1396 bis 1513, in: Jahrbuch des kölnischen Geschichtsvereins 41 (1967), 31-95; quotations: 31, 92. See also E. Ennen,
Erzbischof und Stadtgemeinde in Köln, in: F. Petri (ed.), Bischofs- und Kathedralstädte, Köln/Wien 1976, 27-46, here 45s.

the western concept of urban citizenship. Both "personal liberty" and security under the law as protection from the arbitrary actions of others were functional necessities of civic life, making it possible for burghers to lead a predictable life, that is to pursue their trades and commercial activities. As in Cologne, fundamental rights and personal liberties were legally guaranteed by statute law in a whole series of other cities in the course of the Middle Ages.

The protection of burghers against *arbitrary arrest*, for example, was widely recognized.[9] How deeply this right was rooted in the civic mentality and in the urban concept of political order can be inferred from a corruption trial in Hildesheim. When the city council and commune pressed corruption charges against thirteen citizens of Hildesheim, including several former city councillors, neighboring cities felt compelled to remind the magistrates of the defendants' right to protection against arbitrary governmental acts.[10]

After the mid-fifteenth century these fundamental rights increasingly came under attack. This occurred not only because of the ambitions of city councils to accrue more power for themselves, but also as a result of the great structural changes that were taking place. These included territorial state-building, the centralization of urban power in the hands of the magistrates, rapidly advancing economic changes and increased social differentiation. The internal urban conflicts that resulted from these processes, and also the Reformation which occurred somewhat later, were accompanied repeatedly by numerous arrests that the citizenry or individual groups of burghers regarded as arbitrary. These conflicts resulted in a dangerous situation, imperilling the "fundamental consensus" between the city council and the citizenry that was crucial for the functioning of Old European civic society. At the same time these conflicts served to sharpen the burghers ideas concerning the fundamental meaning of their liberties. Therefore we can formulate a general thesis on the basis of this first point which the following arguments will only substantiate further: The

9 Examples: Schilling, Bürgerkämpfe (note 2), 193; idem, Aufstandsbewegungen (note 2), 208. On Hamburg see J. Bolland, Senat und Bürgerschaft. Über das Verhältnis zwischen Bürger und Stadtregiment im alten Hamburg, Hamburg 1954, 8s.; W. Jochmann and H.-D. Loose (eds.), Hamburg. Geschichte der Stadt und ihrer Bewohner, vol. 1: Von den Anfängen bis zur Reichsgründung, Hamburg 1982, 124; R. Postel, Die Reformation in Hamburg, Gütersloh 1986.
10 Brandis, Hildesheim (note 5), 15.

confrontation between city councils and citizenries at the end
of the Middle Ages and the beginning of the modern period
did not weaken communal and corporate ideas in the cities but
rather strengthened them.

In principle it did not matter which crime the prisoners were
charged with—in Hamburg during 1410 it was an offense
against the Duke of Lauenburg and the breach of a promise for
safe-conduct, and in Münster during 1527 it was disturbing the
episcopal court.[11] Structural friction between city council and
commune was clearly the reason for most of these arrests,
perceived by the latter to be arbitrary. (105) A typical source
of conflict involved burgher claims to communal rights of use
in the city or in rural and wooded areas under the city's jurisdiction. Such rights of use had gradually been abrogated as a
result of an increasingly oligarchic ruling elite, the centralization of ruling authority within the city council, and a growing
trend toward certain kinds of economic individualism. When
burghers tried to exercise what they considered to be their
rights, arrests ensued. After 1520 religious conflicts became the
reason for an increasing number of arrests.[12] At the beginning
of the seventeenth century burghers were forced to defend
their personal liberties particularly against the assaults of territorial princes. One of the chief causes for the rebellion of the
city of Emden against the Counts of East Friesland in 1595,
according to the city's published legal justification, was civic
outrage over the practices of territorial magistrates, including
their "taking pleasure in throwing burghers into jail, pressuring
them, and placing them in abject servitude." When the Counts
of East Friesland without any hesitation repeatedly jailed representatives of the city in reaction to the "Emden Revolution," the burghers regarded this as an *exempel Pharonis*, the
act of a tyrant who scorned the law.[13]

The right to free and unrestricted use of property was a

---

11 Hamburg: Jochmann/Loose (eds.), Hamburg (note 9), 124; Münster: Schilling, Aufstandsbewegungen (note 2), 20.

12 See the examples in the articles given above in note 2, especially in Schilling,
Bürgerkämpfe, 193; idem, Konfessionskonflikt, 254s.; idem, Dortmund im 16. und
17. Jahrhundert—Reichsstädtische Gesellschaft, Reformation und Konfessionalisierung, in: G. Luntowski and N. Reimann, Dortmund—1100 Jahre Stadtgeschichte, Dortmund 1982, 151-202.

13 Apologia, Das ist / Vollkommene Verantwortung / so Bürgermeister und
Rath / samt ... der gantzen Bürgerschaft der Stadt Embden, zu entdeckung ihrer
unschuld mussen ausgeben, Groningen 1602, 97, 128, 155; Beilagen zur Apologie,
Groningen 1602, 91s., 95ss.—The quotation is from the Apologia, 97.

second focal point of the civic concept of fundamental rights. This was, of course, related to the Old European corporate and communal concept of civic privileges which linked the authority to levy taxes with the right to property. Within the urban context, however, this Old European concept was developing into a modern, individualistic one. It was concerned with property owned and used by individual persons and not—as in rural areas—the pre-modern type of property rights on land that were divided between landlords entitled to *dominium directum* and peasants entitled to *dominium utile*. It was this urban individualistic type of property rights, further developed by the Dutch regent republicans in the mid-seventeenth century, which became a generally applicable, fundamental law in the modern sense, including within its purview the inhabitants of rural areas who were not bound to landlords. At the same time the Dutch regents asserted that it was a structural feature of a free republic.[14]

Burghers defended this right to property internally, against the city council, and externally, against the territorial prince and the Emperor. Burgher unrest or even revolts occurred again and again because of the fiscal policies pursued by city councils, either because they were fraudulent or because they were secretive. It was a fundamental rule that the magistrate was dependent upon the approval of communal representatives, if not the agreement of an assembly of citizens, in every situation which called for higher public spending and thus would bring with it a new financial burden for the individual burgher. (106) This fundamental law was frequently codified in statute law, similar to the protection against arbitrary arrest.[15]

---

14 H. Schilling, Der libertär-radikale Republikanismus der holländischen Regenten. Ein Beitrag zur Geschichte des politischen Radikalismus in der frühen Neuzeit, in: H.-Ch. Schröder (ed.), Politischer Radikalismus im 17. Jahrhundert, Göttingen 1984, 498-533.—For an interesting discussion of Dutch civil disturbances in the framework of "Civic Republicanism"/"Corporatism" see Prak, Disturbance (note 2).

15 Hamburg: Bolland, Senat (note 9), esp. 12; Jochmann/Loose (eds.), Hamburg (note 9), 127, 220ss., 278; H. Reincke, Hamburg. Ein Abriß der Stadtgeschichte von den Anfängen bis zur Gegenwart, Bremen 1926, 62-63; Th. Schrader, Bürgerliche Unruhen, in: idem (ed.), Hamburg vor 200 Jahren. Gesammelte Vorträge von Th. Schrader, U. Jacoby, U.J.W. Wolters, O. Rüdiger and R. Ehrenberg, Hamburg 1892, 299-316, here: 304.—Lübeck: J. Asch, Rat und Bürgerschaft in Lübeck 1598-1669, Lübeck 1961, 85, 151; M. Hoffmann, Geschichte der freien und Hansestadt Lübeck, Lübeck 1889, 1st fascicle, 144-147, 2nd fascicle, 20ss., 79ss.; F. Endres, Geschichte der freien und Hansestadt Lübeck, Lübeck 1926, 76ss.; G. Korell, Jürgen Wullenwever. Sein sozial-politisches Wirken

Even at the end of the eighteenth century imperial publications
considered the confirmation of fiscal decisions by burgher
committees to be characteristic of an urban regime, which by
that time had come to mean the regime of an "imperial city"
and was *expressis verbis* understood to be republican in
character.[16]

As the early modern state pursued its financial and taxation
claims against the cities, the burghers had to defend their civic
property rights more and more frequently against attacks from
outside of the city. Usually conflicts flared up over very specific taxes and payments, such as excise taxes. Accordingly, the
legal argumentation used by burghers to oppose princely taxation varied from city to city and from case to case, depending
upon the privileges and legal guarantees that they were able to
draw upon. As a rule princely financial claims were not in
principle rejected. The issues contested usually concerned a
form of burgher co-determination in approving and particularly in levying taxes. The burghers felt that their property
rights were protected only if the city council, and indirectly
also the communal burgher community or its representatives,
had agreed to the tax and if civic agencies installed by the
community or at least by the civic council, but not by princely
authorities, raised it. After the failure of the "Common Penny"
(*Gemeine Pfennig*) tax, the imperial cities experienced hardly
any fundamental problems in the area of taxation. Territorial
cities, however, were pressed harder and harder by the growing
tax demands of their overlords. The burghers of these cities
stoutly opposed these demands, not primarily for economic
reasons but for constitutional ones. They feared that they
would lose their property rights and become an object of arbitrary, despotic taxation, that is to say, taxation without the
consent of taxpayers. Accordingly the urban magistrates step-

in Lübeck und der Kampf mit den erstarkenden Mächten Nordeuropas, Weimar
1980, 39-57; A. Grassmann (ed.), Lübeckische Geschichte, Lübeck 1988.—Brunswick: W. Spieß, Geschichte der Stadt Braunschweig im Nachmittelalter. Vom
Ausgang des Mittelalters bis zum Ende der Stadtfreiheit (1491-1671) 1st fascicle,
Braunschweig 1966, 31, 36-43; idem, Die Ratsherren der Hansestadt Braunschweig 1231-1671, Braunschweig, 2nd ed. 1970, 34s.—Aachen: Schilling, Bürgerkämpfe (note 2), 196.—Frankfurt: Meyn, Frankfurt (note 6), 65ss.; G. Soliday, A
Community in Conflict. Frankfurt Society in the Seventeenth and Early Eighteenth Centuries, Hanover, N.H. 1974, 107ss.—Hildesheim: Brandis, Hildesheim
(note 5), 13ss.

16 E.g. J.F. Malblank, Abhandlungen aus dem Reichsstädtischen Staatsrechte,
Erlangen 1793.

ped forward with a fiscal instrument called the *Aversum*, the payment of taxes by a lump sum, the imposition of which would remain solely in the hands of the city government. The motive behind this policy was certainly the wish of the city councils to hinder the territorial prince from gaining a clear idea of the economic and (107) military power of the cities. At the same time it was a reflection of the civic concept of fundamental property rights described above. This too was clearly expressed during the revolution of 1595 in Emden. On the list of offenses committed by the Count of East Friesland against the fundamental rights of Emden's citizens, used as a form of political propaganda to portray him as a tyrant, the second offense was his attempt to "rob the burghers of their property."[17]

2. The second pillar of internal civic republicanism, the ideal—based upon the oath of citizenship—that all burghers should participate equally in bearing civic obligations and duties, was a corollary to the principle of personal liberties and fundamental rights. This equality of obligations covered a wide range of civic responsibilities, including the payment of taxes and other fees, communal labor such as aiding in the construction of city walls, and the commitment of life, goods, or special knowledge and abilities, such as those possessed by doctors and lawyers, for the defense of the city or in other emergencies. City councillors and burgomasters were not exempt from this and sometimes had to risk more than their time and property, particularly in the diplomatic service of the city. Differences in wealth and political influence were accepted features of the urban social order. However, if a burgher attempted to evade his responsibilities, or if he claimed personal exemption from civic duties or other privileges in order to set himself above the commune, then his fellow burghers turned on him without mercy. This was graphically illustrated by the case of Peter Eigen, alias von Argun, a citizen of medieval

17 Emder Apologie (note 13), 97. Further examples of tax conflicts: Schilling, Konfessionskonflikt (note 2), 156ss., 226ss.; Spieß, Geschichte (note 15), 105ss., 144ss.; J. Schildhauer, Soziale, politische und religiöse Auseinandersetzungen in den Hansestädten Stralsund, Rostock und Wismar im ersten Drittel des 16. Jahrhunderts, Weimar 1959, 15-20; H. Langer, Stralsund 1600-1630, Weimar 1970, 178ss., 180ss., 200ss.; H. Heuer, Lüneburg im 16. und 17. Jahrhundert und seine Eingliederung in den Fürstenstaat, Hamburg 1969, 68-71; W. Ehbrecht, Hanse und spätmittelalterliche Bürgerkämpfe in Niedersachsen und Westfalen, in: Niedersächsisches Jahrbuch für Landesgeschichte 48 (1976), 77-105, here 80ss.

Augsburg.[18] Similar cases were reported in northern German cities during the sixteenth and seventeenth centuries.

The political and social concept of civic republicanism was practically defined by this principle of equality in fulfilling civic obligations, which served at the same time to distinguish it from the non-civic concept of social and political order. The burghers demanded, with increasing stridency, that other groups who lived within the city but were not themselves citizens should recognize the principle that there were no gradations of responsibility for meeting city obligations and duties. This claim was an inexhaustible source of anti-clericalism in German cities during the Middle Ages. Consequently during the urban Reformation one of the most important demands was a redefinition of the social status of the clergy. They were to become burghers who could no longer claim exemption from city obligations on the basis of social privileges; all forms of clerical exemption from civic duties were to be abolished. Later in the course of the sixteenth century (108) the burghers made the same demand of a new social group that was alien to the corporate world of the cities, namely the officials of the territorial bureaucracy, who preferred to live in old urban centers but claimed—as the medieval clerics had done—exemption from taxation on the basis of their occupational status. In numerous cities this question sparked a fundamental social and legal confrontation between factions espousing conflicting conceptions of public order—the communal and corporate model of civic republicanism on the one hand, and the new authoritarian model of the princely state on the other.[19] In those cases where the civic principle of equal obligation was also applied to a territory, affecting the nobility and commoners alike, more than a first step had been made toward modern republicanism. We will return to this point in part II of this essay.

Characteristically enough the expression *res publica*, refer-

---

18 H. Boockmann, Spätmittelalterliche deutsche Stadt-Tyrannen, in: Blätter für deutsche Landesgeschichte 119 (1983), 73-91, here 78ss.

19 Dicussed in detail in Schilling, Konfessionskonflikt (note 2), 266ss., 271ss.; idem, Wandlungs- und Differenzierungsprozesse innerhalb der bürgerlichen Oberschichten West- und Nordwestdeutschlands im 16. Jahrhundert, in: M. Biskup and K. Zernack (eds.), Schichtung und Entwicklung der Gesellschaft in Polen und Deutschland im 16. und 17. Jahrhundert. Parallelen, Verknüpfungen, Vergleiche, Wiesbaden 1983, 121-173 (English translation below p. 135-187). See also Brandis, Hildesheim (note 5), 169s. (1580).

ring to a specifically urban form of commonwealth, was used by burghers in discussions concerning the responsibility of non-burgher groups to help meet civic obligations. In the city of Hamburg for example it was said of the cathedral chapter that "the priests want to live here but don't want to do anything" while the "city council and burghers are obliged to risk their lives and property *pro Republica* on land and sea." Similarly in Münster the Jesuits were advised that their attempt to claim exemption from the jurisdiction of city courts, to which all inhabitants of the city were subject, was "improper in a free republic."[20]

3. A third core element of the civic mentality and concept of political and social order was the *demand for political participation*. In contrast to the "property rights and personal liberties" discussed at the outset, political participation was not an individual right but a communal one, exercised by the commune as a corporation bound together by oath. Urban historians have regularly praised this form of political participation. During the nineteenth century it was considered to be a forerunner of constitutionalism, while at present it is studied especially in connection with burgher movements.[21] We must assess the extent to which this communal and corporate participation can be considered a building block for republican political theory. (109)

A specific example illustrates the problem and its correlation with the principle of property rights discussed earlier: In 1531, when an audit of the finance office records in the city of Hildesheim revealed a series of irregularities in the use of funds, the regular guild and communal representatives refused to co-

---

20 "De pfaffen wolten da wonen, und nichts dar zu thun" whereas "Rat und Burger sullen zu lande und wasser ir leff und gudt pro Republica wagen" (City Archives Hamburg, Senat C 1 I, Lit 06 No. 3, Fas. 2 fol. 94). See R. Postel, Obrigkeitsdenken und Reformation in Hamburg, in: Archiv für Reformationsgeschichte 70 (1979), 169-200, here 193.—"In libera Republica nit gburen wolte" (City Archives Münster AII, 20 RP, vol. 34 Pol. 140, 17.5.1602). On the situation in general see R. Po-chia Hsia, Society and Religion in Münster, 1535-1618, New Haven 1984.

21 See K. Schreiner, "Kommunebewegung" und "Zunftrevolution". Zur Gegenwart der mittelalterlichen Stadt im historisch-politischen Denken des 19. Jahrhunderts, in: F. Quarthal and W. Setzler (eds.), Staatsverfassung—Verfassungsstaat—Pressepolitik. Festschrift für E. Naujoks, Sigmaringen 1980, 139-168; L. Schorn-Schütte, Stadt und Staat. Zum Zusammenhang von Gegenwartsverständnis und historischer Erkenntnis in der Stadtgeschichtsschreibung der Jahrhundertwende, in: Die Alte Stadt 10 (1983), 228-266.

operate with the city council any longer in dealing with the
matter. It was, in the words of the diarist Joachim Brandis, "an
important matter which affected the city as a whole, and hence
they (the guild and communal representatives) were not willing
to confer behind their (fellow citizens') backs. They demanded
that the commons participate in making the decision." The city
council called a burgher assembly—"unwillingly" as the diarist
comments—that checked the register and documents and took
part in the interrogation of the accused through the dispatch of
representatives from district corporations (*Burschaftsvertreter*).
Only after the commune (*meine stat*) had ended its investigation and had authorized the city council together with the
regular burgher representatives "to deal with the matter further
in a correct manner" could the magistrate again act autonomously on a renewed basis of legitimacy, but had to be prepared for further communal oversight at every point.[22] The
perspective—articulated by the communal representatives of
Hildesheim, recognized by the city council, and reported by
the chroniclers without any special emphasis—that matters
affecting every burgher directly were to be discussed "by the
entire city" and were to be dealt with by the magistrates only
by using measures approved by the commons, was one of the
fundamental principles of political organization in the cities of
the region under discussion. Dozens of other examples can be
mentioned where similar events took place, mostly at the insis-
tence of the citizenry but often through the prudent foresight
of the city council itself.[23] In cases where the citizenry was
denied the right to participate in decisions concerning the most
important matters (110), they regularly took measures to secure
this right, if necessary by force. From the burghers'
perspective these were not acts of rebellion but steps taken to
protect their political rights that were guaranteed by the "city
constitution," which the magistrate had broken.[24]

---

22 Brandis, Hildesheim (note 5), 14s.

23 Braunschweig: Spieß, Geschichte (note 15), 31ss., 167ss., 221ss.; J. Walter,
Rat und Bürgerhauptleute in Braunschweig 1576-1604, Braunschweig 1971, 47ss.;
Schilling, Elite (note 2), 249ss., 259ss., 273ss., 296.—See also: Heuer, Lüneburg
(note 17), 77, 105s.; Schilling, Bürgerkämpfe (note 2), 190-194; Jochmann/Loose
(eds.), Hamburg (note 9), 132, 271ss., 283; Bolland, Senat (note 9), 5ss.; Langer,
Stralsund (note 17), 180-190, 192ss., 205-207.—On the legal institution of
"Bursprake" see J. Hoppe, Das Bürgerbuch der Stadt Lemgo von 1506-1866,
Detmold 1981, XI; Bolland, Senat (note 9), 6; Jochmann/Loose (eds.), Hamburg
(note 9), 120; Schildhauer, Auseinandersetzungen (note 17), 26.

24 Discussed in detail in Schilling, Aufstandsbewegungen (note 2), here 230-

These burgher uprisings are particularly instructive for our theoretical context because they display most clearly the communal and corporate principles of civic republicanism—not only in words but by deeds and political and symbolic actions. Despite great differences in their causes and historical circumstances, these uprisings followed a common pattern, which included particular activities[25] that historians of the Annales school often describe as "public rituals." At least for German cities, the symbolic legal content of these activities must be considered their most important characteristic. These burgher movements were symbolic expressions of the political viewpoint that motivated them. I do not think it too daring to suggest that the burghers acted as if they and the city had reverted to a communal and corporate original state (*gemeindlich-genossenschaftlichen "Urzustand"*) after and because the magistrate had violated the constitution. In this situation the communal and corporate political ideal, now threatened with extinction by early modern state-building and its new conception of sovereign, authoritarian power, was thought to have unlimited validity. "The convent . . . is superior to the abbot;"[26] this is how the leader of one such burgher movement (111) tellingly expressed the fundamental principle of late medieval and early modern civic republicanism. At the same time he was obviously drawing upon the conceptual world of conciliarism. In this original state (*Urzustand*) political power

---

236.

25 Most important are the contributions of W. Ehrbrecht, Bürgertum und Obrigkeit in den hansischen Städten des Spätmittelalters, in: W. Rausch (ed.), Die Stadt am Ausgang des Mittelalters, Linz 1974, 275-312, esp. 278-280; idem, Zu Ordnung und Selbstverständnis städtischer Gesellschaft im späten Mittelalter, in: Blätter für deutsche Landesgeschichte 110 (1974), 83-103, 97ss.; idem, Hanse (note 17), 83.—Also important are the following studies: R. Barth, Argumentation und Selbstverständnis der Bürgeropposition in Städtischen Auseinandersetzungen des Spätmittelalters, Lübeck 1404-1408—Braunschweig 1374-1376—Mainz 1444-1446—Köln 1396-1400, Köln/Wien 1974; E. Maschke, Deutsche Städte am Ausgang des Mittelalters, in: W. Rausch (ed.), Stadt (o.c.), 1-44. Schilling, Bürgerkämpfe (note 2); idem, Aufstandsbewegungen (note 2); idem, Konfessionskonflikt (note 2), esp. 139-144, 73-97, 252-259; Ch. R. Friedrichs, 'Citizens or Subjects?' Urban Conflict in Early Modern Germany, in: M. Usher Chrisman and O. Gründler (eds.), Social Groups and Religious Ideas in the Sixteenth Century, Kalamazoo 1978, 46-58; idem, German Town Revolts and the Seventeenth-Century Crisis, in: Renaissance and Modern Studies 26 (1982), 27-51.—More recently, see P. Blickle, Unruhen in der ständischen Gesellschaft, München 1988.

26 "Der convent is uber dem Abt", quoted in Schilling, Bürgerkämpfe (note 2), 226.

was again in the hands of the commune. This was reflected in
the behavior of the burghers. They would run to the market
square—frequently to the tolling of church bells—weapons in
hand, and would swear an oath together, reconstituting the
burgher commune as a corporation for mutual protection,
bound together by oath. The commune would then summon
communal and corporate representative bodies. *Burgher
committees*, acting in the name of the commune, represented it
before the magistrate, the territorial prince, or the Emperor
and were mentioned in connection with practically every
burgher movement. The *communal original state* finally ended
when the burgher commune confirmed or restored the regular
power of the city council by acknowledging its renewed
legitimacy, as occurred in the Hildesheim example mentioned
above. City government could pass—partially or completely
—into the hands of a new group within the political elite or
even to *homines novi* as a result.[27]

In addition to alleviating specific grievances, the most
important goal of such burgher revolts was to place restrictions
upon the magistrate in its political dealings so that it acknowledged the will of the commune. This meant resistance to the
emergence of a non-civic mentality in early modern cities since
the revolts served to remind the city councillors and their
office holders, particularly the city clerk and the *syndici* whose
political and administrative principles were shaped by Roman
law, of the communal and corporate roots of their power. In
the Westphalian and lower Saxon cities as well as in the coastal
cities—in imperial cities and territorial cities alike—the
burghers very early attempted to give their communal right of
co-determination an institutional expression. This resulted in a
specific type of urban constitution that ensured communal participation by means of a "double-stemmed" structure for the
city's ruling institutions. This can be illustrated by the urban
constitutions present in Lemgo and Münster:[28] (112)

---

27 These social changes within the political elite of the cities are analyzed and
discussed in the two following chapters of this volume.

28 The Lemgo diagram is taken from Schilling, Konfessionskonflikt (note 2), 87
and the diagram of Münster's government is based on "Die Wiedertäufer in
Münster". Katalog einer Ausstellung im Stadtmuseum 1.10.1982 - 30.1.1983, 107,
and "Münster 800-1800, 1000 Jahre Geschichte der Stadt", Stadtmuseum Münster 21. Sept. 1984 - 30. Juni 1985, 59. Similar patterns of organisation existed in
many other cities in the Hanseatic region, among them the imperial city of Dortmund, see Luntowski/Reimann (eds.), Dortmund (note 12), 180.

Lemgo Governmental Structure according to the
Regimentsnottel of 1491

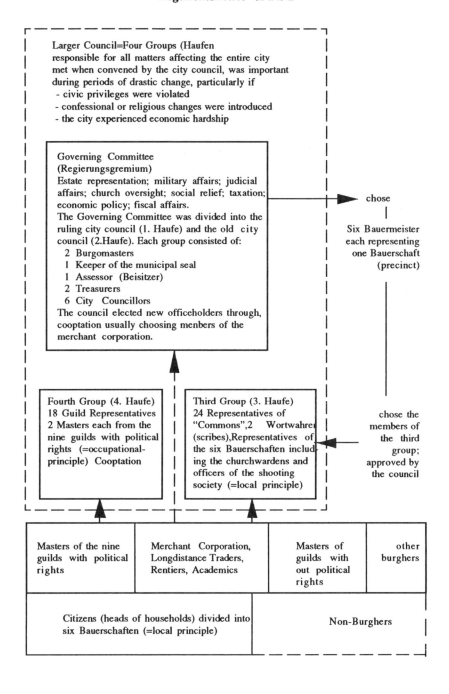

Larger Council=Four Groups (Haufen
responsible for all matters affecting the entire city
met when convened by the city council, was important
during periods of drastic change, particularly if
- civic privileges were violated
- confessional or religious changes were introduced
- the city experienced economic hardship

Governing Committee
(Regierungsgremium)
Estate representation; military affairs; judicial
affairs; church oversight; social relief; taxation;
economic policy; fiscal affairs.
The Governing Committee was divided into the
ruling city council (1. Haufe) and the old city
council (2.Haufe). Each group consisted of:
  2 Burgomasters
  1 Keeper of the municipal seal
  1 Assessor (Beisitzer)
  2 Treasurers
  6 City Councillors
The council elected new officeholders through,
cooptation usually choosing menbers of the
merchant corporation.

chose

Six Bauermeister
each representing
one Bauerschaft
(precinct)

Fourth Group (4. Haufe)
18 Guild Representatives
2 Masters each from the
nine guilds with political
rights (=occupational-
principle) Cooptation

Third Group (3. Haufe)
24 Representatives of
"Commons",2   Wortwahrer
(scribes),Representatives of
the six Bauerschaften including the churchwardens and
officers of the shooting
society (=local principle)

chose the
members of
the third
group;
approved by
the council

Masters of the nine guilds with political rights	Merchant Corporation, Longdistance Traders, Rentiers, Academics	Masters of guilds with out political rights	other burghers
Citizens (heads of households) divided into six Bauerschaften (=local principle)		Non-Burghers	

Governmental Structure in Münster

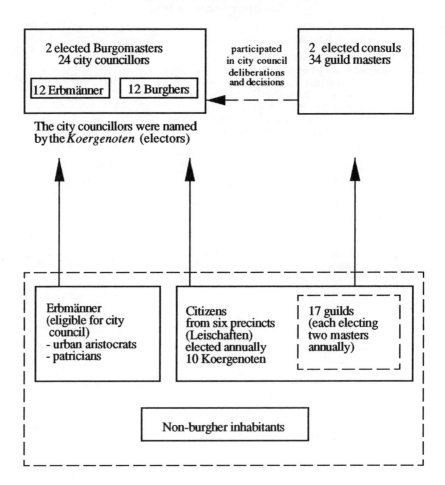

Besides the actual city council, which consisted of two bodies, alternately serving for one year as the "ruling" and "older" (non-ruling) city council, there were regular communal representative committees, composed of burgher representatives of the guilds and the "commons" (*Gemeinheit*). The latter men represented burghers who were not members of guilds and those from district corporations. In contrast to the situation in Italy,[29] "clan structures" were not particularly important in northern German cities. Instead the district corporations emerged (113) relatively early as participants in the exercise of public authority.[30] The district corporations were called *Viertel*, *Klucht*, *Laischaft*, *Bauerschaft*, or *Burschaft* (in lower German *Nabûrschop*—neighborhood). They and the other communal and corporate neighborhood groupings gave the city government a specific political character in the sense of a broad foundation of public power, if not of real political participation.

The burgher communal branch in the Westphalian episcopal city of Münster was especially strongly developed and invested with far-reaching responsibilities. Here we find an extreme form of communal participation in that the burgher commune was involved in the annual election of the city council through its *Laischaften*, the district corporations that elected the electors (*Wahlmänner*) whose task it was to elect the twelve burgher councillors. This semi-democratic procedure is all the more remarkable because cooptation was the rule in most Old European city councils, and even communal representatives were seldom chosen directly by the citizenry. (114)

In normal times even the electoral process in Münster produced an oligarchic city council. But the Münster constitution offered members of the communal and corporate movements—once they had seized control—simpler and quicker access to the city council than was usually the case where the principle of cooptation (the common method of election in most other cities) was practiced, as the events

---

29 S. Bertelli, Elites et pouvoir dans la ville-état de la Renaissance, in: Koenigsberger, Republiken (note 1), 27-40.

30 B. Scheper, Frühe bürgerliche Institutionen nordwestdeutscher Hansestädte, Köln 1975; idem, Über Ratsgewalt und Gemeinde in nordwestdeutschen Hansestädten des Mittelalters, in: Niedersächsisches Jahrbuch für Landesgeschichte 49 (1977), 87-108; J. Schultze, Die Stadtviertel. Ein städtegeschichtliches Problem, in: Blätter für deutsche Landesgeschichte 92 (1956); 18-39; K. Schwarz, Kompanien, Kirchspiele und Konvente in Bremen 1605-1814, Bremen 1969.

between 1525 and 1533 attest.[31] The few cities of our area which had no permanent institutions for communal representation at the end of the Middle Ages developed them in the course of the Reformation.[32] Among the best known examples is the *Oberaltenkollegium* of Hamburg. The constitution of Emden represents a later phase of this kind of constitutional development. In the second half of the sixteenth century a burgher committee was formed which organized the "Revolution" of 1595 against the city council, which had been appointed by the princely ruler, and then became the *Committee of Forty (Vierziger Kollegium)* structured according to the pattern of the medieval committees described above as a permanent communal representative body alongside of the princely city council. Even after Emden had won its autonomy from the territorial ruler in 1595 and an independent burgher city council was installed, the *Committee of Forty* was retained to serve as a counterbalance to the magisterial power of the city council.

The particular causes giving rise to demands for communal participation and also the political and legal matters for which such participation was demanded differed greatly. Most commonly they included financial questions, public building activities, foreign policy issues, particularly military undertakings and the formation of alliances, and, of course, basic changes in the "city constitutions" (*Stadtkonstitutionen*) such as the uniting of city boroughs which had hitherto been legally and politically autonomous.[33] New political demands could become the focus

---

31 Described in Schilling, Aufstandsbewegungen (note 2). On the political elite: idem, Elite (note 2); idem, Wandlungs- und Differenzierungsprozesse (note 19).

32 Schilling, Elite (note 2), 294-302 (Hamburg, Lippstadt, Emden, Göttingen); O. Mörke, Rat und Bürger in der Reformation. Soziale Gruppen und kirchlicher Wandel in den welfischen Hansestädten Lüneburg, Braunschweig und Göttingen, Hildesheim 1983; Postel, Hamburg (note 9).

33 Meyn, Frankfurt (note 6), 35-94 (privileges, finances); Schilling, Bürgerkämpfe (note 2), 196, 197 (foreign policy, finances); Brandis, Hildesheim (note 5), 53, 200 (foreign policy, unification of the old with the new part of the city); Walter, Rat (note 23), 76s. (statutes of the city); Jochmann/Loose (eds.), Hamburg (note 9), 220s. (foreign policy, finances); Mörke, Rat (note 32), 65-75 (Lüneburg: finances, foreign policy); Langer, Stralsund (note 17), 169, 171, 184, 195 (finances, visitation of church property, corporative rights of use); Ehbrecht, Hanse (note 17), 83-89 (Magdeburg: finances; Osnabrück: foreign policy); Ehbrecht, Bürgertum (note 25), 278-280 (jurisdiction, economic policy); Ehbrecht (note 25), Ordnung, 97 (Erfurt: foreign policy), 98, 100ss. (finances: Augsburg, Brunswick, Lübeck, Nordhausen, Cologne).

of burgher aspirations to political participation at any time since there was no fixed legal canon.

Between Luther and the outbreak of the Thirty Years' War religious and confessional questions occupied center stage. This has become clear to us from intensive research on urban history during the Reformation era. This was the case not only in southern German imperial cities, but also in western and northwestern German cities and even, in a weakened form, in some eastern German cities. (115) Indeed heightened burgher participation, expressed by burgher movements, burgher committees, burgher assemblies, and public disputations, were characteristic of more than the narrow phase of the Reforma-tion.[34] During the latter part of the sixteenth century burghers claimed repeatedly that a city's official confession could not be changed without their consent. This was particularly important during the Interim crisis and again at the end of the sixteenth and early seventeenth centuries, when territorial princes attempted to subjugate many of the hitherto autonomous city churches to their territorial churches.[35] The "Emden Revolution," already referred to several times, should be included in the latter category. The Calvinist burgher commune wished to maintain their own religious position against a Lutheran territorial prince "who . . . wished to rob (them of) their religion," as they stated in the third and final point of the city's list of the prince's tyrannical acts.[36] On account of the linkage of

---

34 On the theme of "city and Reformation" see the collective review of Kaspar von Greyerz, Stadt und Reformation: Stand und Aufgaben der Forschung, in: Archiv für Reformationsgeschichte 76 (1985), 6-63; H.-Ch. Rublack, Is there a "New History" of the Urban Reformation?, in: E.J. Kouri and T. Scott (eds.), Politics and Society in Reformation Europe (G. Elton Festschrift), London 1987, 121-141.—On the disputations see B. Moeller, Zwinglis Disputation. Studien zu den Anfängen der Kirchenbildung und des Synodalwesens im Protestantismus, 1st part, in: Zeitschrift der Savignystiftung für Rechtsgeschichte, kanonistische Abteilung 56, 87 (1979), 275-324; 2nd part, in: Zeitschrift der Savignystiftung für Rechtsgeschichte, kanonistische Abteilung 60, 91 (1974), 213-364; O. Scheib, Die Reformationsdiskussion in der Hansestadt Hamburg 1522-1528. Zur Struktur und Problematik der Religionsgespräche, Münster 1976. Overviews of the long term development include: O. Mörke, Integration und Desintegration. Kirche und Stadtentwicklung in Deutschland vom 14. bis 17. Jahrhundert, in: La ville, la bourgeoisie et la genèse de l'état moderne, Paris 1988, 297-321; E. Schubert, Stadt und Kirche in Niedersachsen vor der Reformation, in: Jahrbuch der Gesellschaft für niedersächsische Kirchengeschichte 86 (1988), 9-39.

35 J. Regula, Die kirchlichen Selbständigkeitsbestrebungen der Städte Göttingen, Nordheim, Hannover und Hameln in den Jahren 1584-1601, in: Zeitschrift der Gesellschaft für niedersächsische Kirchengeschichte 22 (1917), 123-152.

36 Emder Apologie (note 13), 97.

confessionalization and territorial state-building this was at the same time an early round in the fight between the early absolutist princely state and the autonomy of the Old European estates, a subject which will be addressed in the next section.

Accordingly, the view held by many Reformation historians that communal and corporate ideas were extinguished during the sixteenth century—possibly due to the Lutheran Reformation—is incorrect. The distinction between a "passion for liberty" emerging with western European Calvinism and a "passion for obedience" promoted by the Lutherans—a memorable phrase first coined by Troeltsch—has caused a good deal of confusion. The idea that the southern German urban Reformation was theologically Reformed/Zwinglian and hence communal, and the northern German urban Reformation was by contrast imposed from above because it was Lutheran, has by now become a tenaciously defended cliché. By contrast, historical reality shows that until well into the seventeenth century Lutheranism in the German cities was also driven by a "passion for liberty," a type of liberty, however, determined by corporative not individualistic principles. This qualification holds true also for Reformed or Calvinistic cities: even the "Emden Revolution," regarded as the greatest accomplishment of Calvinism on German soil, was an expression of civic corporate principles rather than modern libertarian ones.

Within this corporate sphere the demand of burgher communes for political participation did not abate until the outbreak of the Thirty Years' War. (116) It was in fact articulated more strongly and more passionately rather than less. This later phase of the burgher demand for political participation has been continually overlooked in German urban historical research, as it has been in general history, because historical studies have tended to focus upon the victors, i. e. the rising territorial states. Of course their historical success is just as indisputable as the superiority of their legal tools and the state theory that they used against the cities. Their claims did not, however, remain unopposed. On the contrary there was practically a renaissance of communal and corporate thought within urban burgher circles in response to the governmental absolutist offensive during the decades before the great war. And it was the cities of the lower German region who defended their autonomy most energetically and for the longest time. Although these cities had never possessed imperial autonomy and usually never aspired to it, they were able to resist territorial princes of middle-sized and smaller states because of their economic and political power. The princes, who often had less fiscal and military power than their cities, did not have the means to contest this until the seventeenth century.

We see in this conflict for the most part a confrontation between the early modern territorial state and the Old European ideal of urban liberty. The renaissance of communal and corporate thought provoked by the aggressive advance of the territorial states, however, meant at the same time a new apogee for the claim to internal political participation by the commune and for its resistance to the oligarchic tendencies of the city councils. This can be demonstrated by such important examples as the cities of Lüneburg and Brunswick in the territories ruled by the Welfs and by the large port city of Stralsund. Other examples include middle-sized territorial cities such as Lemgo and Paderborn and smaller towns such as Höxter.[37] However, apart from a few exceptions, this was also the final phase of the history of Old European civic republicanism in these territorial cities. The relationship between commune and city council came to be ordered according to the new principles which were introduced when their city was integrated into the territorial state, a process that they could not stop. In addition no fundamentally new arguments were advanced to support burgher claims for a right of participation in the course of this discussion within the territorial cities.

The situation was different in the *imperial cities*. There it was indispensable that the relationship between the city council and citizenry be clarified in a fundamental way. For, in the case of the imperial cities, the new doctrine of sovereignty, was not an exterior challenge, a threat to their liberty made by territorial princes, but an interior one, which affected the urban constitution, especially the relationship between magistracy and burgher commune. At the beginning of the seventeenth century in a number of imperial cities located in our region conflicts over fundamental principles broke out, pitting the oligarchic claims of the city councillors and the demands of the communes for participation. In Cologne and Aachen, for example, these conflicts were linked with confessionalization, a

---

37 Mörke, Rat (note 32), 251ss.; Heuer, Lüneburg (note 17), 105ss.; Langer, Stralsund (note 17), 180ss.; Schilling, Bürgerkämpfe (note 2), 176s. and note 2.

situation typical for this era. In Frankfort and Hamburg the
problem of minorities played a significant part in triggering
conflicts. (117) Similar, if less spectacular, struggles took place
in Lübeck and Dortmund.[38] The constitutional discussion
within the imperial cities, sparked by these circumstances,
continued in some cases well into the eighteenth century, so at
this point I will have to devote some attention to a period
outside of the strict chronological limits of my topic. The
burghers of the fifteenth and sixteenth centuries had a pragmatic understanding of politics that was expressed on a case-
to-case basis without theoretical reflection. By the eighteenth
century this process of deductive reasoning had resulted in
voluminous collections of precedents. Consequently, the
burghers were forced to change their method of legal argumentation, since they pressed their demands for participation
under different historical and political conditions than those
presupposed by the corporate concepts of political order which
informed the demands of communes in the territorial and
imperial cities of the fifteenth and sixteenth centuries. In addition their demand for participation had to be upheld against
the newer arguments for state sovereignty and constitutional
theory.

In this context it should be noted that during the late seventeenth century the imperial cities reached a turning point similar to the situation of territorial cities during the sixteenth and
early seventeenth centuries. As a result of political and economic differentiation, perhaps only a dozen of them retained
any genuine political importance after 1650.[39] In our region
these important cities included especially Frankfort and Hamburg, and to a lesser extent Aachen, Lübeck, and Cologne.
Consequently the discussions about political theory that took
place in these cities deserve particular attention. Otto Brunner,

---

38 On the early 17th century burgher movements in Cologne see: Revolutionen
in Köln 1074-1918, Katalog zur Ausstellung im Historischen Archiv der Stadt
Köln 25. April - 13. Juli 1973, ed. by. T. Diederich, Köln 1973, 58; Schwerthoff,
Konflikt (note 2); Aachen: see Schilling, Bürgerkämpfe (note 2), esp. 191ss.; in
Frankfort: Meyn, Frankfurt (note 6); Hamburg: Jochmann/Loose (eds.), Hamburg
(note 9), 220ss.; in Lübeck: Asch, Rat (note 15), 56-59, 92ss.—Meanwhile Volker
Press has published a penetrating essay on the imperial cities: V. Press, Die
Reichsstadt in der altständischen Gesellschaft, in: J. Kunisch (ed.), Neue Studien
zur Reichsgeschichte, Berlin 1987, 9-42.

39 In 1667 Samuel Pufendorf thought that only a few imperial cities had any
chance of preserving their independence: De statu Imperii Germanici, chapter 2, §
13.

who has exhaustively analyzed social and constitutional conflicts in early modern imperial cities,[40] based his work particularly upon Hamburg sources. An episode in the conflict
over the renewal of the residency agreement with the Portuguese Jewish community during 1618 is particularly instructive
for our investigation. At the height of the confrontation between the Hamburg city council, which was convinced that it
ruled by the grace of God, and the burgher commune whose
desire for participation was just as fervent, a leader of the
commune demanded a written statement from the city council
de statu huius reipublicae, an sit aristocraticus, an democraticus.
Burgomaster Vincent Moller, a jurist experienced in legal and
constitutional questions, rejected these alternatives as useless
scholastic wrangling. He argued that among the cities of their
day there was not a single example of a government that was
either a pure aristocracy or a pure democracy but that all city
governments were based (118) much more on a mixed constitution.[41] This was a theoretical determination of the constitution
of imperial cities which during the same period gained acceptance in other imperial or autonomous cities, as, for example, in
Aachen where the Catholic city council defined "the entire
republic" as "the city council and the commune," during its
confessional conflicts[42] or in Danzig whose form of
government was described in the mid-seventeenth century as
an "aristocracy, although tempered by democracy."[43]

When in the end a generally acknowledged solution for the
constitutional problems of imperial cities throughout the

---

40 O. Brunner, Souveränitätsproblem und Sozialstruktur in den deutschen
Reichsstädten der frühen Neuzeit, in: idem, Neue Wege der Verfassungs- und
Sozialgeschichte, Göttingen 1968, 315-377.

41 Jochmann/Loose (eds.), Hamburg (note 9), 270; Brunner, Souveränitätsproblem (note 40), 314ss. Quotation from H. Reincke, Große Hamburger Juristen aus
fünf Jahrhunderten, Hamburg 1954, here 20s. See also F. Voigt, Bedenken der
Oberalten gegen Sätze im zweiten Teil der Origines Hamburgenses Petri
Lambecii, 1661, in: Mitteilungen des Vereins für Hamburgische Geschichte 35
(1915), 213-219, here 216.

42 The council argued that its policy was legal because it was based on the
declaration of the Emperor of 1598, which had been approved by the "gantze
Respublica, ein Rath unnd die gemeinde" (City Archives Aachen, Akten betr.
Religionsunruhen fol. 197r).

43 "Aristokratisch, wiewohl mit der Democratia temperirt". M. Zeiller,
Topograhia Prussiae et Pommereliae (1652); quotation from P. Baumgart (ed.),
Ständetum und Staatsbildung in Brandenburg-Preußen. Ergebnisse einer inter-
nationalen Fachtagung, Berlin/New York 1983, 144.—Similarly, see Langer,
Stralsund (note 17), 197.

Empire emerged, it was structured along these lines of a mixed
constitution and not according to the extreme theory of *deo
gratia potestas*, set forth in the early seventeenth century by
the rigidly oligarchic faction in the Hamburg city council just
mentioned.[44] In Hamburg and even more in Lübeck, however,
the entire seventeenth century was characterized by fierce
struggles and by fundamentally irreconcilable formulations of
the positions held by both commune and city council. The traditionally authoritarian Lübeck city council was especially loath
to compromise with the citizenry. There was a fierce constitutional discussion in Lübeck during the first years of the seventeenth century—at about the same time as the events in Hamburg took place—occasioned by a rigid governmental interpretation of the oath of citizenship adopted by the magistrate.[45]
The city council accused the burgher committees of wishing to
overthrow the *status aristocraticus in democratiam*, while the
burghers understood themselves to be defenders of the *status
aristocraticus et liberae Reipublicae*, in their eyes a mixed constitution. The guilds of Lübeck (119) used exactly the same
words, *aristocratico-democratice mixta Respublica*, during the
renewed and particularly fierce constitutional conflicts of the
1660's. Elements of modern political theory appear to have
entered the political discussions in Lübeck quite early on both
sides of the line—the council based its argumentation on
Bodin's concept of sovereignty, whereas the citizens refered to
the doctrine of the monarchomachians, especially as expressed
by Johannes Althusius, concerning the popular origin of state
power.[46]

   Finally a solution was achieved here as well. In Hamburg it
was even established in a manner similar to a fundamental law:
The first article of the *Rezess* of 1712 reads as follows: "The
Kyrion or the highest law and power," consists in "an insepa-
rable bond (*inseparabili nexu conjunctim*) between the noble

---

44 "Wann schon (that is: Even if) eine Avericheit gottlos, tyrannisch und gitzig
iß, so gehoret dennoch den Unterdahnen nicht, dat se sick darjegen uplehnen und
thowedder setten, sundern schölen datsulve velemehr vor ene straffe des All-
mechtigen erkennen, so de Underdahnen mit eren Sünden vorwircket hebben!".
Quoted in Reincke, Juristen (note 41), 20; N.A. Westphalen, Geschichte der
Hauptgrundgesetze der Hamburgischen Verfassung, vol. 1, Hamburg 1844, 158-
187, esp. 165, 175ss.
   45 Asch, Rat (note 15), 83ss.
   46 This is the opinion of Asch, Rat (note 15), 139ss. This problem needs further
research.

city council and the hereditary commune and may not be freely exercised by one party or the other alone."[47] This article was by no means an expression of a specifically "Hanseatic" republicanism as local historians of Hamburg often claim. It reflects much more the usual development of constitutional theory in the imperial cities that was valid for the eighteenth century in general.

When assessing the impact of this kind of civic republicanism on German history, however, we must keep in mind that its limitation to imperial cities was only established during the late sixteenth century, whereas there had been no strict distinction between imperial and territorial cities in the earlier period, at least with respect to civic republicanism. By contrast it was characteristic of the communal and corporate burgher movements of the late Middle Ages and the beginning of the modern period that they drew no distinction between imperial and non-imperial cities when considering their internal political order.

Furthermore the internal conflicts of the late seventeenth and eighteenth centuries and the accompanying political theory debates within the imperial cities, particularly within northern and northwestern Germany, were tied more closely with imperial politics and imperial constitutional law than they were during the Middle Ages. It was no accident that imperial commissions were usually active in mediating the quarrels between city councils and citizenries during this period. Even the Hamburg *Rezess* of 1712 resulted from such a mediation. There is as yet no synthetic study of the role played by such imperial commissions and the Emperor himself in the constitutional and political history of the imperial cities during the seventeenth and eighteenth centuries. By the end of the Holy Roman Empire it was in any case a commonplace in the legal literature of the *Reichspublizistik* that even in an aristocratic constitution "the city council does not itself possess an autonomous the right to sovereignty or the right to represent the city in impe-

---

47 "Das Kyrion oder das höchste Recht und Gewalt (liegt) bey Einem Edlen Rath und der Erbgesessenen Bürgerschaft inseparabili nexu conjunctim und zusammen, nicht aber bey einem oder andern Theil privative." Unwiderrufliches Fundamental-Gesetz-Regimentsform oder Hauptrezess der Stadt Hamburg ... mit einer Einleitung, ed. by Ludwig v. Hess, Hamburg 1781.—See Jochmann/Loose (eds.), Hamburg (note 9), 269ss.; Bolland, Senat (note 9), 17; Westphalen, Verfassung (note 44).

rial diets; (120) these are rather the possession of the entire commune and the citizenry."[48]

4. The corporate burgher movements of the late Middle Ages and the early modern period were not egalitarian in their political aims. This is a qualitative difference between civic republicanism of the Old European period and modern republicanism since the French Revolution, a distinction that cannot be glossed over when Old European structures and intellectual traditions are analyzed historically. The *normative* restriction of the city council to the will of the commune and the *addition* of communal offices to the magisterial branch of the city council's government by the guilds and commons did not represent modern democratic demands for the direct or indirect exercise of power through representatives by the citizenry. The communal and corporative understanding of political order, described in the preceding paragraphs, presumed that the "corporate original state" (*genossenschaftliche Urzustand*), which gave legal power to the commune, was only transitory. In principle it was never questioned that the commune would return governmental power to the city council. Frequently the city council never quite lost such power even during civil uprisings. The resulting oligarchic tendencies of Old European urban society were an expression of the principle of availability (*Abkömmlichkeit*) as it was defined by Max Weber.

Communal and corporate ideas of civic order were compatible with the existence of an oligarchic city council elite rather than contradicting it; indeed they practically presuppose such an elite. It was generally accepted that the *libera Respublica*, as defended by the guilds of Lübeck at the turn of the sixteenth and seventeenth centuries, could and should possess an "aristocratic status."[49] In any case it is important for the present analysis to note that both the citizenry and the members of the councillor elite laid down certain requirements for the recruitment and character of the urban political elite. It had to be open to newcomers, or at least relatively so, and had to be marked by *collegiality* and *equality*. Permanent domination of the rest of the council by a single group, or worse by a single

---

48 "Daß die Landeshoheit und Reichsstandschaft einem Reichsstädtischen Magistrat auch in einer Aristokratischen Verfassung nicht als ein eigenes Recht zustehe, sondern auf der ganzen Gemeinheit und Bürgerschaft haftet". Malblank, Abhandlungen (note 16), 38.

49 See above note 45.

person, was diametrically opposed to the political culture of German cities.

Social openness varied from place to place and from region to region but also varied considerably over time within individual cities and regions. The composition of city councils changed repeatedly during periods of accelerated social change within political elites. In the region that we are considering, and in the Empire as a whole, political elites were more open to newcomers during the late fifteenth and early sixteenth centuries than during the seventeenth and eighteenth centuries.[50] During this period of pronounced social change "qualifications" in a modern sense, particularly "accomplishments," became a more important consideration in recruiting the urban political elite (121), joining the otherwise crucial Old Europeanan qualification of birth.

The *collegiality* of city government was inherent within the structure of city councils itself. Although during the period under consideration the council as a collective organ lost genuine political power in favor of the burgomaster and magistrates, the top positions—especially the office of burgomaster—were held by at least two incumbents. The determination of city council oligarchies to ensure political and social *equality* within their own ranks is convincingly attested by the defeat of late medieval city tyrants.[51] Many cities—southern German as well as northern German and Dutch—had proper systems of regimentation and ordinances that were intended to enforce equality upon the burgher oligarchy, even to the extent of prescribing norms for burial, epitaphs, and images of the deceased.[52] Powerful families and individuals active in these cities frequently endangered this equality.

The ideals of internal political order held by the burghers of German cities amounted to an oligarchic government that was obligated to follow the collective will of the citizenry in the

---

50 For more detail see Schilling, Elite (note 2); idem, Wandlungs- und Differenzierungsprozesse (note 19); idem, Vergleichende Betrachtungen zur frühneuzeitlichen Geschichte der bürgerlichen Eliten in Nordwestdeutschland und in den Niederlanden, in: H. Diederiks and H. Schilling (eds.), Bürgerliche Eliten in den Niederlanden und in Nordwestdeutschland. Wandlungs- und Differenzierungsvorgänge vom 15. bis zum 20. Jahrhundert, Köln/Wien 1985, 1-32.

51 Boockmann, Stadt-Tyrannen (note 18), esp. 88s.

52 R. and T. Wohlfeil, Nürnberger Bildepitaphien. Versuch einer Fallstudie zur historischen Bildkunde, in: Zeitschrift für Historische Forschung 12 (1985), 129-180, esp. 130, 142s., 174ss.

sense described above and was supplemented by communal
offices which shared in the task of governing. We are inclined
to regard, with modern democratic eyes, the reality of oligarchic rule by the city council as traditional and contradictory
to progressive forms of political organization. However, I think
that it is reasonable to evaluate even this oligarchic principle as
a part of the Old European tradition of civic republicanism,
especially in light of the relative value that urban political
elites attached to professional accomplishment as a qualification
for recruitment, and also their egalitarian structure. By
contrast, the monarchic-princely principle of one-person-rule,
based upon dynastic descent, that was predominant during the
early modern period did not value these ideals.

II

Let us now turn to the burghers' ideas of the relationship between cities and exterior political systems. First, we will discuss
the fundamental pattern of urban autonomy and the cities'
claims to civic liberty (II,1), and then consider the consequences of early modern state formation guided by the modern
concepts of *superioritas territorialis* and sovereignty (II,2).
Finally we will discuss more closely the political theory used to
justify the "Emden Revolution" of 1595 (II, 3), because it is
commonly considered to be the earliest manifestation of
modern liberal political theory on German soil, overcoming the
limitations of Old European civic republicanism. (122)

1. To consider the fundamental pattern of the principle of
urban autonomy we must look back to the fifteenth and sixteenth centuries when the process of territorialization, that is,
the emergence of the territorial states and the formation of the
early modern *Reich* as a specific political system, had not yet
taken place. Consequently there was no clear distinction between cities of imperial and territorial status either in the eyes
of their citizens or in the laws of the Empire. How the
burghers viewed the position of their cities within the overarching political system of developing territorial states and the
Empire is no less revealing for our topic of civic republicanism
than their understanding of the internal order. In any case we
must dispense with a rash definition of "republican" as "anti-
monarchical." Instead we must examine those elements within
the legal concepts and political thinking of the citizens which

explicitly or implicitly postulate an urban political order that differed from the political ideals and the political praxis of the nobility and princes. The authors of such legal formulations sought to distance the cities from the monarchic system of the advancing princely state and strove to place them beyond the reach of princely-monarchical claims of sovereignty.

In principle, keeping monarchical authority at bay was a problem for all cities whether they were under direct rule of the Emperor or a territorial ruler; one needs only remember the conflicts of the imperial cities of Aachen with Jülich and Wetzlar with Hesse.[53] In both cases the authority of territorial rulers or the Emperor threatened civic autonomy although the political and legal contexts differed. Because of limited space, however, I will restrict myself to cities that did not possess imperial freedom, the situation of most cities in the region under investigation. After the end of the fifteenth century these cities were threatened by early modern state-building in the territories, and thus they were forced to confront the monarchical principle represented by the princes directly and repeatedly. The internal disagreements between city councils and communes can be disregarded in this context, because the protection of civic autonomy itself was almost never an issue.

Nearly every important city of our region had a concept of independence and autonomy that remained vibrant until the moment when they were more or less violently integrated into princely states during the late sixteenth and the seventeenth centuries. Originally the cities' claim to urban autonomy did not in principle involve distancing themselves from the terri-tories in the sense of striving for imperial status. Similarly they did not reject their princely or noble overlords out of hand in the way that a radical, anti-monarchical form of republicanism would. Instead the cities defended their traditional status within the medieval land before its reshaping into an early

---

53 Schilling, Bürgerkämpfe (note 2). Wetzlar: V. Press, Wetzlar—Reichsstadt und Reich im Spätmittelalter und in der Frühen Neuzeit, in: Mitteilungen des Wetzlarer Geschichtsvereins 31 (1985), 57-101. Goslar: W. Hesse, Der Haushalt der freien Reichsstadt Goslar im 17. Jahrhundert (1600-1682), Goslar 1935, 3; W. Werner, Goslar am Ende seiner reichsstädtischen Freiheit unter besonderer Berücksichtigung der Reformen von J.G. Siemens, Goslar 1967, 26.—For general discussions of the problem see K. Fritze, E. Müller-Mertens and W. Stark (eds.), Autonomie, Wirtschaft und Kultur der Hansestädte, Weimar 1984; and G. Vogler, Bürgertum und Staatsgewalt in der Epoche des Übergangs vom Feudalismus zum Kapitalismus, in: Jahrbuch für Geschichte des Feudalismus 1 (1977), 305-331.

modern territorial state, (123) based upon their traditional
liberties. The legal argumentation of the cities was as a result
historical, and it took the form of statutory rather than natural
law. Its points of reference were the medieval type of local
overlord and his territory in the form of a medieval land.
During the period of foundation and early consolidation from
the twelfth to the early fifteenth centuries nearly all towns and
cities of the Hanseatic region had had positive experiences with
their local overlords. This sprang from an alliance of interests
between burghers and rulers who wanted to augment their
power through the flourishing cities. Since the cities were
usually the dominant party in this partnership they were able
to gain certain advantages during the late Middle Ages. Step by
step the cities accumulated rights to exercise certain kinds of
authority autonomously, but without ever questioning the
authority of the overlord in principle. As a result by the end of
the Middle Ages they possessed a strong legal position vis à vis
the princes, not to speak of their economic and financial
superiority. This development was bolstered by independent
economic policies that crossed territorial boundaries and their
far-reaching cultural and legal relationships through the
Hanseatic League. In reality and especially in their self-
conception these Hanseatic cities were free, largely autonomous
communes that can appropriately be described as "city states"
even though they belonged to the territories.

Of course there were great differences between individual
cities in terms of the kind of privileges that they had accumulated and the extent of their autonomy, just as the cities
themselves differed in their economic and political power. This
becomes obvious by comparing the economic and political roles
played by larger Hanseatic cities such as Soest, Brunswick,
Lüneburg, Wismar, Stralsund, and Rostock with those played
by middle-sized Hanseatic cities such as Wesel, Lemgo, Göttingen, and Greifswald and smaller towns such as Attendorn,
Brilon, or Waldeck in the Sauerland-Hessian region. Regardless
of these differences, however, there is a common pattern for
these cities, both in their dealings with territorial authorities
and in the argumentation they used to represent their own
position. The citizens regarded their episcopal or princely territorial rulers not as authorities with sovereign statutory or
executive power but as contract partners who were in principle
equal to themselves. The diverse legal agreements that burgher

representatives of cities had made with their overlords through
the course of the Middle Ages were seen as agreements and
contracts that were binding for both partners and consequently
could not be changed or revoked by the authoritarian decisions
of the ruler. In principle it did not matter whether this concerned the bestowal of a broad range of privileges or only the
right to autonomy in particular instances, a right which was
acquired under specific circumstances, often in return for providing a loan or directly obtained through purchase. These
liberties and privileges were confirmed by every new ruler
when he received homage, partially—as in the case of Brunswick—in the form of a "written statement of duties and obligations."[54] In their totality these agreements were understood
to be a series of contracts which governed the city's relations
with other political units (124) in the manner of a constitution
and were a core element of the city constitution in the sense
described at the beginning of this essay.

2. In the wake of early modern state-building these conceptions and the claims associated with them were increasingly
called into question, since it contradicted the raison d'être of
modern princely power to accept other powers within a territory as contract partners. In addition the integration of towns
and cities into the territory was a question of political and
financial survival for the territorial states, particularly for the
smaller ones. Questions of taxation and especially the Reformation and confessionalization were major areas of contention
between city and territorial state just as they were within the
cities themselves. As I have already described such problems in
detail in my book on the relations between the County of
Lippe and the city of Lemgo from the end of the fifteenth to
the early seventeenth centuries, I can restrict my remarks here
to the more general, essential elements.[55]

To understand the significance and pertinence of republican
elements in German urban history correctly, it is crucial to
recognize that the entire epoch from the end of the Middle
Ages until the eve of the Thirty Years' War was characterized
by contradictory tendencies. From a long-term perspective, the
Reformation and the rise of the territorial state marked a sur-

---

54 "Schriftliche Verpflichtung und Obligation". See the detailed legal discussion in City Archives, Braunschweig BIII Vol. 14, quotation from fol. 2 (report of
the Saxonian Councilor Hieronymus Schurff).

55 Schilling, Konfessionskonflikt (note 2).

render to the princely interpretation of the legal relationship
between city and territory in imperial constitutional law. The
Religious Peace of Augsburg in 1555 was a widely-recognized
milestone on this road. Most importantly a theoretical instrument emerged in the doctrine of the *superioritas territorialis*
and later through Bodin's concept of sovereignty which undermined the traditional constitutional argument of the citizens
and their claim of exemption from state interference with the
postulate of a unified state power. In lower Germany, however,
for some decades actual events ran counter to this general development. As a consequence of the powerful urban Reformation movements cities there often gained power at the
expense of the territories during the 1530's and 1540's. This in
turn fueled an increasing desire for liberty and independence,
supported not least by the communal and corporate currents
within the community that were revitalized by the communal
Reformation. Urban communes in our region perceived themselves throughout the period as autonomous in their relations
with territorial princes and their sense of independence grew
stronger during the entire Reformation period and in the decades following until the Thirty Years' War.

The cities were fully aware of the danger inherent for them
in both the territorialization of the Empire and in the new
legal and political theories, and they were on the look-out for
suitable political and theoretical countermeasures. The first
significant period in this search encompassed the Interim crisis
(125) and the negotiations leading up to the Peace of Augsburg.
In a number of cities furious confrontations took place between
the citizenries and territorial princes in conjunction with the
Interim since the princes were more willing to comply with
imperial demands both for political and legal reasons. Their
wishes clashed with the willingness of the Protestant communes
to offer resistance.[56] Some interesting triangular relationships
between cities, territorial princes and the Emperor resulted

---

56 W.D. Hauschild, Zum Kampf gegen das Interim in niederdeutschen Hansestädten, in: Zeitschrift für Kirchengeschichte 84 (1973), 60-81; F. Petri, Karl V.
und die Stadt im Nordwestraum während des Ringens um die politisch-kirchliche
Ordnung in Deutschland, in: Jahrbuch des Vereins für Westfälische Kirchengeschichte 71 (1978), 7-21; O. Mörke, Landstädtische Autonomie zwischen den
Fronten.—Göttinger Ratspolitik zwischen Bürgerbewegung, Landesherrschaft und
Reichspolitik im Umfeld des Augsburger Interims, in: W. Ehbrecht and H. Schilling (eds.), Niederlande und Nordwestdeutschland im Mittelalter und in der
Neuzeit. Festschrift für Franz Petri, Köln 1983, 213-214.

whose political significance and implications for political theory have still not been examined adequately. From the example of Brunswick one receives the impression that some cities sought to solidify their threatened autonomy through an appeal to the Emperor.[57] But an alliance between the Hanseatic cities and the Emperor, which would have opened up completely new possibilities for imperial rule in northern Germany, was never a practical possibility because the Hapsburgs had so decisively chosen the side of Catholicism and the Counter Reformation.

The Hanseatic cities sought to have an article of their own accepted in the Religious Peace during the Augsburg negotiations of 1555, not least because of their experiences during the Interim crisis. This was primarily a tactic of confessional policy designed to allow those evangelical Hanseatic cities, such as Osnabrück or Paderborn, which were ruled by Catholic territorial princes or bishops to evade the principle of *cuius regio eius religio*. The argumentation employed by the lawyers of the Hanseatic cities, however, had important implications at the same time for constitutional law and thus are relevant for political theory. Had the Hanseatic cities succeeded in the negotiations, their claim to be free cities with their own status and not ordinary territorial cities would have been recognized in imperial law. This clearly did not happen. Nonetheless their efforts were in a sense successful. As records of the negotiations show, the article of the Hanseatic cities foundered on the confessionally based resistance of King Ferdinand and the three ecclesiastical Electors. The secular Electors, by contrast, advanced the citys' argumentation as their own: The representative of Electoral Saxony argued during the decisive meeting of September 2, 1555, (126) that King Ferdinand's reference to the inclusion of imperial cities did not make the article of the Hanseatic cities extraneous, because "the others (that is Hanseatic cities) are not actually subject to the Empire itself but rather to the authority of a ruler." In the eyes of the Saxon politicians and jurists this fact did not, however, justify their subjugation under the *ius reformandi* of the territorial princes, for the cities were "not unconditionally oriented toward and subject to their overlords." According to the supporting argu-

---

57 The report quoted in note 54 argues that the ruler has only limited power over Brunswick, because he is "inferior a principe, caesare scilicet" (City Archives Braunschweig BIII, 1 Vol. 14, fol. 10v).

ment advanced by Electoral Brandenburg, the Hanseatic cities
were "for the most part organized in such a way that, although
they recognize an overlord they nevertheless have their own
regime." There was, however, a further argument which the
princes obviously emphasized strongly. Such an article would
be indispensable for a lasting peace because the coastal cities
were inclined to unrest, as was well-known, and they would
refuse to submit to the Religious Peace of Augsburg. Furthermore, they would find support among their princely co-con-
fessionalists, "and thus a new commotion (*newe lerm*) could
arise on their account."[58]

This "new commotion" did in fact break out. However, it
did not spread any further and become an Empire-wide religious war—as the Electors thought it would in 1555. Even in
northern and northwestern Germany the system of imperial
peace and territorialization was maintained, supported by a
solidarity among the territorial rulers that crossed confessional
lines. It was the individual princes who felt the full impact of
the "new commotion" present within the Hanseatic cities when
they attempted to integrate the local, home-grown, Protestant
city churches into their territorial churches according to the
principle of *cuius regio eius religio*. The religious confrontation
was especially fierce during the confessional age, and the
princes used it to break the medieval freedom and autonomy
enjoyed by the cities and to replace it with the unified authority and sovereignty of the early modern state. At the same time
there were more confrontations over purely secular titles to
authority, such as the right to taxation, military authority, and
legal jurisdiction. These disputes became most frequent in the
two decades before the outbreak of the Thirty Years' War.[59] In

---

58 The cities of the Hanseatic league were "nit so eigentlich dem Reich,
sondern aber einer obrigkeit unterworffen," but "nit indeterminante etlichen
Herren zugewendet und unterthenig". Brandenburg argued that, on the contrary,
they were "den mehren theil also geschaffen, ob wol sie einen Herrn recognoscie-
ren, das sie dennoch ir eigen regiment haben". Vienna Imperial Archives, Haus-,
Hof- und Staatsarchiv, Mainzer Erzkanzlerarchiv, Reichstagsakten Fz. 38 fol.
766r-767v, 2. September 1555.—G. Pfeiffer, Der Augsburger Religionsfrieden und
die Reichsstädte, in: Zeitschrift des Historischen Vereins für Schwaben 61 (1955),
213-321, esp. 245ss., 257ss.

59 On this wave of burgher movements see Schilling, Bürgerkämpfe (note 2),
177, note 2; Friedrichs, Town (note 25), 40-49; H. Schilling, The European Crisis
of the 1590s: The Situation in German Towns, in: P. Clark (ed.), The European
Crisis of the 1590s, London 1985, 135-156, here 151ss. Cities on the Baltic Sea:
Langer, Stralsund (note 17), 161-166, 200, 215s.; H. Bei der Wieden, Rostock
zwischen Abhängigkeit und Reichsunmittelbarkeit, in: R. Schmidt (ed.), Pom-

addition to the *cuius regio eius religio* principle and the resultant claims that city churches should be subordinate to the
territorial church, the diffusion of the doctrine of sovereignty
and the idea of state power as formulated by Jean Bodin and
Justus Lipsius gave a new edge to the argumentation employed
by princes. Bodin's concept of sovereignty forced above all a
fundamental clarification of the position of cities within overarching political systems—both the territorial state and the
Empire—in terms of state law, as it did for the relationship
between city council and citizenry within imperial cities. (127)

The cities fought back, defending their autonomous position.
With respect to the question of church constitutions, which had
been settled decisively in favor of the princely states in the
legal decisions of 1555, city legal experts developed the theory
of a "secondary church authority" in the hands of the city
councils, based upon the maintenance of the traditional legal
rights of medieval bishops.[60] Here, as at other points, they
followed a traditional pattern of argumentation. Against the
claim that the territorial prince was the highest, undivided
authority in the state (*Superioriteit und hohe Obrigkeit*), and
that he was superior to both statutory law and traditional law
in disputed cases, the representatives of cities advanced the
traditional idea of contracts, with the implication that both
partners were equally obliged to observe such agreements. In
individual cases this legal strategy was successful and the validity of this legal perspective was further substantiated during
the seventeenth century by newly concluded agreements in
which cities and territorial princes appeared together as parties
to the contract. Examples of such legal agreements include the
contract between Brunswick and its Welfish overlords in 1615
and that of Lemgo with the Counts of Lippe in 1617.[61] Taking

mern und Mecklenburg, Köln/Wien 1981, 111-132. Korbach: W. Medding, Die
Geschichte einer hessischen Stadt, Korbach 1955, 203-210. The following cities
were involved in such disputes: Emden (1595-1603), Wismar (1595-1600), Lübeck
(1598-1605), Paderborn (1600-1604), Höxter (1600-1604), Schwäbisch-Hall
(1601-1604), Brunswick (1603-1604), Greifswald (1603-1618), Hamburg (1607),
Donauwörth (1608-1610), Cologne (1608-1614), Aachen (1609-1617), Lemgo
(1612-1616), Frankfort/Main (1612-1616), Stralsund (1613-1616), Worms (1613-
1616), Wetzlar (1613-1615), Brunswick (1613-1623), Korbach (1615-1624), Stet-
tin (1616).
60 Schilling, Konfessionskonflikt (note 2), 118, note 209; 295-303;
315.—Regula, Selbständigkeits-bestrebungen (note 35), 123-152; Langer, Stralsund (note 17), 200ss.
61 Braunschweig: Querfurth, Unterwerfung (note 6), 24; Spieß, Geschichte

up the argumentation advanced at the negotiations for the Peace of Augsburg, legal experts of the Hanseatic cities elaborated the theory that the northern German cities were *civitates mixti status*, or simply *civitates mixtae*, which held a status between that of imperial cities and ordinary territorial cities.[62]

From a long-term perspective, however, the cities were unable to uphold the principles of autonomy and independence from territorial authorities with this argumentation that, on the one hand, recognized territorial state formation, but on the other demanded a legal framework that was fundamentally incompatible with it. The special status of an autonomous *Landstadt* secured by contract, as represented by Brunswick until 1671, by Rostock until the eighteenth century, and by Lemgo even into the nineteenth century, quickly became an anachronistic legal exception. The experience of most Hanseatic cities was subjugation to the territorial principle. As a result the *civitas mixta* theory became obsolete because it could be applied only to a dwindling number of cities. Moreover it was opposed to early modern imperial law, which aimed to provide clarity and was oriented toward the territorial structure of the Empire that had triumphed so decisively during the sixteenth century. Consequently, in contrast to the Middle Ages, early modern imperial law drew a clear distinction between imperial cities and territorial cities. The larger territorial Hanseatic cities such as Rostock, Stralsund, Osnabrück, and Münster, which still pursued an aggressive policy of civic autonomy in the mid-seventeenth century, (128) adjusted themselves to the changed legal circumstances. They no longer claimed the status of *civitates mixtae* but tried to achieve the clear status of imperial cities. All of these attempts, however, were doomed to failure.[63]

(note 15), 175s.; Lemgo: Schilling, Konfessionskonflikt (note 2), 352ss.; Langer, Stralsund (note 17), 204.

62 W. Ebel, Die Hanse in der deutschen Staatsrechtliteratur des 17. und 18. Jahrhunderts, in: Hansische Geschichtsblätter 65/66 (1940/41), 145-169; F. Frensdorff, Das Reich und die Hansestädte, in: Zeitschrift der Savignystiftung für Rechtsgeschichte, germanistische Abteilung 20 (1899), 115-163; G. Fink, Die rechtliche Stellung der deutschen Hanse in der Zeit ihres Niedergangs, in: Hansische Geschichtsblätter 61 (1936), 122-137; Schilling, Konfessionskonflikte (note 2), esp. 50ss., 57ss.

63 On Eger, Erfurt, Magdeburg, Munich, Münster, Osnabrück, Rostock, Stralsund, Hamburg see Acta Pacis Westphalicae, Serie III, Abt. A, Protokolle vol. 6: Die Beratungen der Städtekurie Osnabrück 1645-1649, ed. by G. Buchstab, Münster 1981, XL. Idem, Reichsstädte, Städtekurie und Westfälischer Friedens-

3. There was no direct road leading from the model of civic republicanism present in medieval and early modern cities to the modern, democratic republicanism of the nineteenth and twentieth centuries. This was almost certainly because the middle-sized and smaller Hanseatic cities lost their independent economic and financial dynamism as a result of the Thirty Years' War. No less important, however, was the fact that civic republicanism and its demand for autonomy was decisively defeated by the territorialization of the Empire and by the absolutistic theory of a sovereign state. The cities had no adequate countermeasures to oppose these legal theories. They referred repeatedly to the *iura naturalia defensionis*.[64] As a result they remained within their traditional framework of argumentation. As far as I know the politicians and lawyers of these territorial cities[65] made no use of the new monarchomachian, natural law political theory developed especially in western Europe since the final third of the sixteenth century, as a direct response to the state theory of the princely, all-powerful state.

I will now consider some important exceptions to this general development: the political discussions which took place in the context of the so-called "Emden Revolution" of 1595 and during the conflicts between the city of Korbach and the Counts of Waldeck in the Hessian region.[66] (129)

The events in the East Frisian port city of Emden, discussed in the first part of this article concerning the internal meaning of civic republicanism, are particularly significant for its external significance as well. In Emden the principle of urban autonomy achieved its most telling and spectacular success

---

kongreß, Münster 1981.

64 Examples from the sixteenth century: see the reports in the City Archives of Braunschweig quoted above note 54, esp. fol. 5v. For examples from the early seventeenth century see: Schilling, Konfessionskonflikt (note 2), 302s.

65 As we know, the situation was different in the case of imperial cities (see above, note 45).

66 Emden: Schilling, Calvinismus (note 3); H. Schmidt, Politische Geschichte Ostfrieslands, Leer 1975; M. Smid, Ostfriesische Kirchengeschichte, Pewsum 1974; H. Wiemann, Die Grundlagen der landständischen Verfassung Ostfrieslands. Die Verträge von 1595 bis 1611, Aurich 1974; idem, Materialien zur Geschichte der ostfriesischen Landschaft, Aurich 1982; H. Schilling, Reformation und Bürgerfreiheit. Emdens Weg zur calvinistischen Stadtrepublik, in: B. Moeller (ed.), Stadt und Kirche im 16. Jahrhundert, Gütersloh 1978, 128-161 (English translation in Schilling, Calvinism, note 3).—Waldeck: G. Menk, Rechtliche und staatstheoretische Aspekte im Waldeckischen Herrschaftskonflikt 1588-1624, in: Geschichtsblätter für Waldeck 72 (1984), 45-74.

among all of the numerous conflicts between cities and early
modern princely states at the very end of the sixteenth century.
In his Hamburg dissertation submitted in 1950, Ulrich Wangerin developed the thesis that the "spiritual background" of the
revolution was characterized by the acceptance of a modern
political theory developed in western Europe and based on
natural law and its specific legitimation of resistance. According to Wangerin the Emden Revolution was a product of "the
ideals of western European Calvinism that had an effect in this
one place on German soil!"[67] From this perspective Emden's
struggle for liberty and autonomy, culminating in 1595 and the
following decades, was based largely upon a political theory
that was imported from outside of the Empire and for which
no point of contact could be found within German tradition, at
least not in the framework of civic political culture. If this
interpretation were correct, the "Emden Revolution" would not
be of any interest for the present article on the autochthonous
tradition of civic republicanism in German cities. The same
would apply to the case of Korbach's opposition to the Counts
of Waldeck where the political and legal justification, according to Gerhard Menk, was decisively influenced by the western
European Calvinism taught in the nearby university or *Gymnasium Illustre* of Herborn.

Without wishing to dispute the role of Calvinist monarchomachian political theory in principle or to deny the connections
of Emden and Korbach with western European Protestantism
through Herborn, the Rhenish Palatinate, Nassau, and the
Netherlands, I think that it is also necessary to consider the
influence of traditional civic republicanism, characterized by
communal and corporate principles, in contrast to the modern
natural rights theory. In doing so I will concentrate upon
Emden, but the results are relevant for Korbach as well,
because in this old Hanseatic city the medieval tradition of
autonomy, civic rights, and privileges was much stronger than
in the case of Emden. (130)

I have described elsewhere in detail how Emden, a city
which at the end of the Middle Ages had almost no urban
identity, developed a strong sense of burgher identity over the
course of the sixteenth century in conjunction with a long eco-

---

67 U. Wangerin, *Der geistige Hintergrund der Auseinandersetzung Emdens und
der ostfriesischen Stände mit der Grafschaft zur Zeit der Emder Revolution 1595*,
phil. Diss., Hamburg 1950, (typescript, Hamburg university library), 181.

nomic expansion and a powerful stream of immigrants from
the Netherlands, and how finally the burghers gradually built
up organs for self-representation.[68] The logical conclusion of
these developments was the complete overthrow of the non-
civic city council, which was "non-civic" because it was
appointed by the Count. Emden's city council was transformed
by the revolution of 1595 into a communal and corporate institution and thus into an urban city council in a real sense. It
was in no way exceptional that the rise of a civic city council
was closely connected with the rise of a civic church organization, independent of the princely territorial church. On the
contrary, it conforms to the thesis advanced in the first part of
this article that the German Reformation strengthened the
communal and corporate spirit within the cities. In the case of
Emden the only difference was the confessional label, not
Lutheranism as in the case of the urban Reformation of the
1520's and 1530's, but Calvinism. The swift constitutional
changes in Emden were an expression of the fact that the
conceptions of political order of Old European urban burghers
had entered Emden, or were decisively strengthened, through
rapidly increasing economic contacts with the older Hanseatic
cities and through the settlement of immigrants from urban
centers in Groningen, Friesland, Holland, Brabant, and Flanders.

It is evident that the victory of civic republicanism in
Emden was part of the communal and corporate renaissance of
the "long sixteenth century" described in the previous section
of this essay. The uniqueness of Emden, from my perspective,
can be seen in the confluence of the stream of traditional civic
republicanism originating from the German Hanseatic region
with currents from the Netherlands and France and thus with
the modern natural rights theory of western Europe. Unfortunately the sources are not adequate to provide a clear answer to
the question of which influence was dominant: did the traditional civic republicanism of the Hanseatic cities decisively
strengthen the communal and corporate elements within the
Dutch Revolt or was it the other way around, with the new

---

68 Schilling, Calvinism (note 3).—See also Ch. Lamschus, Emden unter der
Herrschaft der Cirksena. Studien zur Herrschaftsstruktur der ostfriesischen Resi-
denzstadt 1470-1527, Hildesheim 1984; B. Kappelhoff, Die Reformation in
Emden, in: Emder Jahrbuch 57 (1977), 64-143 and 58 (1978), 22-67.

monarchomachian elements of the Dutch Revolt providing the
ultimate legitimization for the Emden Revolution?

At the same time when civic republicanism triumphed
within the city, Emden won its external autonomy from the
territorial prince and the territorial state. In so doing it
followed the characteristic pattern of urban "foreign policy" in
the lower German region, even in its political strategy and
political argumentation. The burghers of medieval Hanseatic
cities step by step acquired liberties and privileges in the form
of agreements and contracts concluded with the territorial
prince, which, when taken together, formed the fundamental
basis in statutory law for a city constitution. It was precisely
this traditional type of "constitutional" and legal argumentation
(131) which Emden used to justify resistance to a treaty-
breaking territorial prince. Monarchomachian or other impulses
originating in natural law theory are unnecessary to explain
this, or at least are not necessary prerequisites. Traditional civic
republicanism was the legitimizing political ideology of
Emden's magisterial justification as it appeared in a pamphlet
entitled the *Emden Apology,* written by Ubbo Emmius.[69]
Menso Alting, the fierce Calvinist minister of Emden's town
church, also argued consistently according to the pattern of
civic republicanism when he described the uprising in a letter
to his Basel colleague Johann Jacob Grynaeus as a legal action
taken by the commune against arbitrary changes made in the
city constitution by the Counts in both ecclesiastical and
secular questions (*ut pro libidine sua omnia sacra et prophania
tam in urbe quam in agro mutare praesumeret*).[70] That the
preacher Alting played a decisive role in preparing the way for
the burgher uprising also reflects a familiar pattern present in
other German cities during the Reformation and the
confessional era.

Finally the Emden Revolution ended no differently than the
uprising of Lemgo against the Counts of Lippe or that of
Brunswick against the Welfish dukes. The Delfzijler Agreement
of 1595 and the Territorial Concord of 1599 provided new
agreements in the form of statutory law which renewed con-

---

69 See the long speech of the Emden burgomaster Gerhard Bolardus inserted
into the pamphlet in: Emder Apologie (note 13), 95-98.

70 Letter from March 16, 1596, Church Archives of the Reformed Church
Wuppertal, Manuscripts of H. Klugkist-Hesse. See also Wangerin, Hintergrund
(note 67), 183s.

stitutional relationships between the city and its local overlord.[71] As in Brunswick and Lemgo, from now on the major emphasis of Emden's foreign policy was to secure its legal status by means of power politics.[72] Like Brunswick and Lemgo Emden sought the help of the Estates General of the neighboring Netherlands, which was even more valuable for the East Frisian port and border city than it was for either of the inland cities. Eventually Emden achieved the same status of independence and autonomy which most of the other Hanseatic cities had considered their inherent right for generations. Although the Count, even on the day of the revolution, thought that he could order the Emdeners "to refrain from using the title Republic any longer," the city secretary Caspar Moller signed the Delfzijler agreement as a representative of the *Respublica Emdana*.[73] With this self-designation, which all of the large territorial cities of the Hanseatic region (132) used during the sixteenth century,[74] the East Frisian territorial city, whose political culture only a century before was closer to that of Frisian villages than medieval cities, finally entered the circle of the *civitates mixtae* that claimed a special political and legal status within their territories. Nothing unusual occurred here either from the perspective of legal and constitutional history or with respect to contemporary political ideals. Even the point in time at which this improvement in status occurred seems noteworthy only to an historian looking back. Given the strong spirit of autonomy and resistance to territorialization

---

71 Wiemann, Grundlagen (note 66).

72 Wangerin, Hintergrund (note 67), 138.

73 Letter of the Count from March 18, 1595, Territorial Archives Aurich Rep 4, BIV,e, 187, fol. See H. de Buhr, Die Entwicklung der Stadt Emden in der zweiten Hälfte des 16. Jahrhunderts, Hamburg 1967, 121.— The Delfzijl treaty was edited by Wiemann, Grundlagen (note 66), 136. On "Respublica Emdana" and S.P.Q.E. see e.g. City Archives Emden, I Registratur XVII, 740 (Requisitoriales; Promotoriales et Intercessionales in Prozeß-Sachen), March 16, 1596: "Nos Consules et Magistratus Reipublicae Emdanae in Frisia orientali". A similar conflict broke out at the beginning of the 18th century: MS 105, letter of Count Georg Albrecht from September 29, 1716; Library of the Große Kirche Emden, Katalog, Juridica No. 488, anonymous treatise of 1728 on the tradition of Emden's "libera Respublica"-title.

74 There is no comprehensive study on the abbreviation S.P.Q.X. Some evidence is given by G. Wells on Antwerp, in: idem, Emergence and Evanescence: Republicanism and the Res Publica at Antwerp before the Revolt of the Netherlands, in: Koenigsberger, Republiken (note 1), 155-168. On Groningen, Emden's neighboring city, see O. Feith, De vervolging der Hervormden te Groningen 1566-1570, in: Bijdragen tot de Geschiedenis en Oudheidkunde inzonderheid van de provincie Groningen, vol. 8, Groningen 1871, 241-291, here 254s.

that cities everywhere demonstrated at the beginning of the
seventeenth century, contemporary observers could hardly have
predicted that within a generation the larger and more independent Hanseatic cities such as Stralsund, Lüneburg, Münster,
Osnabrück, and Brunswick would lose their special status.

Along with these parallels, the comparison between Emden
and the autonomous Hanseatic cities also illustrates two important differences between medieval burgher movements and the
"Emden Revolution" that can largely be explained by differences in the early modern context. First, Emden's policy of
autonomy was closely tied to the struggle over the division of
power between the prince and the estates within the rising
early modern state, and secondly the Emperor participated in
the peace settlement between the Count and city, as was typical
in the early modern period. As a result, the contracts made
between Emden and its territorial prince were from the very
beginning based on the territorial principle of the early modern
Empire and the system of imperial peace.[75]

It was at this juncture that the Emdeners pursued a new line
of development by (133) abandoning the traditional policy of
urban autonomy and civic republicanism. After the conclusion
of the Concord of 1599 it quickly became apparent that the
contracts were being used by the gifted territorial chancellor,
Thomas Franzius, to stabilize and even to expand the territorial
state, in sharp contrast to the aims of Emden. In the long run
this state of affairs would necessarily have endangered the
city's recently won autonomy.[76] The political strategies that
were employed by the citizens to protect the autonomy of
Emden sought to fend off this threat by using two remarkable
new lines of argumentation. The first was an historical mythology of liberty worked out by the Humanist philosopher and
historian Ubbo Emmius which had overtones of natural law.
The second was an attempt to go beyond the theory of
contracts composed purely of concrete legal stipulations and to
replace statute law contract theory with a new doctrine of

---

75 See the imperial mandate from February 2, 1589, and the declarations of the
East Frisian Estates from 1590 and 1593 and the imperial mandate from January
21, 1595, all edited in E.R. Brenneysen, Ost-Friesische Historie und Landes-Ver-
fassung, vol. 2, Aurich 1720. On the events themselves see H. Schmidt, Geschichte
(note 66).

76 On Thomas Franzius (1591-1597) see Wiemann, Grundlagen (note 66), 43,
note 50; idem, Materialien (note 76), 150-160. On the Concord of 1599 see
Schmidt, Geschichte (note 66), 222s.; Wangerin, Hintergrund (note 67), 138ss.

contracts based on natural law. Such contracts could, in turn, call statutory law agreements into question when these contradicted the abstract claims to liberty advanced by the citizenry.

In his writings Emmius, an historian and legal thinker who for a time served as a political advisor to the "revolutionary" Emden city council, moved beyond the theory of contracts in the form of statutory law which served as the legal foundation for the urban constitution. Instead he espoused the doctrine of medieval Frisian liberty, actually an historical myth of freedom that only superficially argued on groundd of statute law. This new type of republican theory was more dynamic than traditional claims for autonomy that were based upon concrete solutions to legal disputes, because the myth of Frisian liberty could, in principle, call any contemporary framework of order into question by making reference to an historical "original state."

Not surprisingly the arguments based upon reason and natural law, justifying the action taken by Emden according to ratio and aequitas, the reasonable norms of justice, emerged at the same time as this historical argument for utopian liberty. The recourse to reason and natural law first appeared in two letters of Ubbo Emmius to the new Emden city council, providing them with a suitable political theory shortly after the outbreak of the Emden Revolution.[77] In these letters, however, the new elements of natural law are mentioned only in passing. The actual breakthrough occurred in the *Emden Apology*, particularly in its second part, largely written by Emmius and published in 1602.[78] A few years before, in the struggle over the Delfzijler Agreement of 1595 which had been called into question by Count Edzard (134), the Emdeners had still assumed the unconditional validity of contracts once they were concluded. Now the second part of the *Apology* sharply attacked the Concordat of 1599. The focus of criticism was the legal form of the document. It was not—as it should have been according to the standards of civic republicanism discussed above—"a treaty and agreement of *two* contending *parties*," but was "a decree or order enacted *by the Count* to harm the poor

---

77 Briefwechsel des Ubbo Emmius, ed. by H. Brugmans and F. Wachter, vol. 1, Aurich 1911, No. 39 and 40, p. 71-76; Wangerin, Hintergrund (note 67); J.J. Boer, Ubbo Emmius en Oost-Friesland, Groningen 1935.

78 Emder Apologie (note 13), 335-572.

people."[79] The content of the contracts in the eyes of the citizens violated "the traditional privileges, liberties, and justice" of the East Frisian estates at numerous points. The citizens feared that the Count of East Friesland would enhance his own authority at the expense of Frisian traditions of law and liberty so that he would become an equal of "the other Electors and princes of the Empire of the German Nation."[80] Fundamentally this criticism of the contract was directed against a decision on taxation made at the Diet of Aurich of 1601 that was detrimental to the burghers. It resulted in an inversion of the traditional statute law doctrine of contracts espoused by so many medieval and early modern burgher movements, since the argumentation used by Emden in 1602 to fend off this threat called into question the binding character of statutory law enacted by treaty.[81]

This new defense for civic autonomy was not, however, exclusively or even primarily based upon natural law. It resulted much more from a mixture of traditional and newer elements that characterized the political theory of the "Emden Revolution" in general. Abstract appeals to general "justice and equity" can be found together with references to irregularities and the use of force by the territorial prince as well as—remarkable for our topic—a *radically corporate* argument, that a treaty signed by representatives of the magistrate was invalid because it had been concluded without the knowledge or approval of the civic commune. The abandonment of a statutory law doctrine of contracts and the resulting radicalization of Emden's claims to autonomy were not consequences solely of the new argumentation based upon the historical mythology of Frisian medieval liberty or upon reason and natural law. This radicalization was clearly also related to traditional civic republicanism, based upon corporate and communal principles.

The political confrontations between Count and city show unmistakably that this communal and corporate traditional thought constituted an essential element of the burghers' civic

---

79 Ibid., 236: It was not a "Vertrag und Vereinbarung streitender Parteyen", but had been issued to the harm of "des armen Volcks ... als ein Decret oder befelch des Herrn Grafen".

80 Ibid., 238ss: Its content is "in nit wenig Puncten connivendo wider die Väterliche Privilegien, freyheit und Gerechtigkeit". By this the Count wanted to establish an authority equal to that of "anderer Chur- und Fürsten im Reich teutscher Nation".

81 Ibid., 395ss.

alternative to the princely model of a territorial state. In his attempt through personal intervention to convince the city to accept the decision of the diet of Aurich, Count Enno came to realize that the policy espoused by Emden during the summer of 1601 was made not by the city council but by the *Committee of Forty* (the burgher committee mentioned in part I), and by an assembly of the citizenry. This realization caused the territorial prince great consternation since it directly contradicted his own princely concept of order expressed in the territorial state. If he had to discuss political matters with a city at all, he wanted to do so with the city council and the magistrates, i.e., with an institution of authority, not with committees of the burghers or—even worse—with assemblies composed of ordinary citizens of the burgher community. Consequently Count Enno declared that "because the city council no longer ruled the citizens and could not force them to obey, he had to look for ways and means to force the rebellious citizenry into submissive obedience."[82] (135)

The radically corporate version of civic republicanism was close to becoming a qualitatively new theoretical concept since in the Emden propaganda writings, particularly the *Apology*, the doctrine of liberty was no longer restricted to the city but aimed at the territorial commonwealth of East Friesland as a whole. The course that had been set by the imperial constitution during the fifteenth and sixteenth centuries toward an early modern princely state was not to be instituted in East Friesland. The goal was to establish an corporative state (*Ständestaat*) according to the Dutch model in which the Counts would have played a role similar to that of the *stadhouders* of the House of Orange in the United Netherlands. And there can be no doubt that the Emden model of autonomy is reminiscent of the Dutch situation in one further respect: although the nobility and peasants were to be included in the communal and corporate republic, what Emden really sought was burgher domination, with the burghers of Emden playing a leading role. Advocates of this idea probably found their inspiration in the situation of neighboring Groningen rather than in the other Dutch provinces such as Holland. The civic flavor of this territorial model of liberty became more and

---

82 Ibid., 394: "Dieweil der Rath die Burger nit regieren, noch zu Gerhorsamb pringen könte, so müßte Er (d.h. der Graf) ... mittel und wege" suchen, die "Widerspenstigen ... zu unterthenigem Gehorsamb" zu bringen.

more apparent when, at the beginning of the seventeenth century, the nobility accepted the Concordat of 1599 and the
peasantry had little room for political maneuvering.

   This territorial model of a communal and corporate republic
was also rooted in the traditional type of civic republicanism.
By rejecting the ordinances passed during the diet of Aurich of
1601, which created a new alliance of interests between the
territorial prince and the knights on the basis of a far-reaching
exemption from taxation for the nobility, the *Emden Apology*
fundamentally questioned the privileges of the nobility. In their
place it advanced a principle well-known to us from the analysis of the internal structure of civic republicanism in the first
part of this essay, the principle of a strict correlation between
duties, obligations, and privileges, particularly concerning the
right to political participation.

> "He who seeks and allots for himself *honorem*, that is,
> honor from something must take upon himself *onera*,
> duties. Anyone who wishes to have *commodum* or advan-
> tage must also feel *incommodum*, or disadvantage, and
> should be mindful that he accept both in proportion and
> equal measure. The same is true of him who does not wish
> to accept the obligation—he should have no power to force
> others to take on the burden and because he will not do
> anything in such matters;—he shall also not have any voice
> in the decision."[83] (136)

The fundamental principle of a balance between rights and
duties which we have described in the first part of our essay
was applied here to an entire territory. The ideal of order

---

83 "Und wer honorem, die Ehr / aus einem dinge suchet und sich zumasset /
das der auch onera, die lasten / mit auff sich nehme / Wer das commodum oder
Vortheil / genießen wil / das er auch incommodum, oder den schaden / mit füh-
len / und also beyderseits die proportion und gleichmessigkeit in achtung nehmen
solle. Item / Wer keine last begert zu tragen / das der keine Macht habe andern
die last beyzuschauben / und das er in solchen sachen / darzu er nichts thun wil
/ keine Stirn haben sol". (Apologie (note 13), 405.)—Another anti-aristocratic
statement can be found on 440s.: "Diesem ihren wahn und einbildung (that is to
dominate the discussions of the Eastfriesian Diets) wollen Wir dis gewisse tieffge-
grundete fundament entgegen setzen / das auff der rechten vernunft und alge-
meiner erfahrung beruhet: Nemblich / das zu erhaltung der Natur und aller din-
gen nichts so nötig und nutze sey / als proportion und gleigmessigkeit: und das
dis mit der naturlichen Vernunfft sonderlich ubereinstimme / das wer den
grossesten schaden traget / das demselbigen das grosseste vortheil auch zu
gemessen geburt. Item / dem für andern / und am meisten an eine sach gelegen /
das derselbe die furnemste stim auch habe."

upheld by the nobility, which was rooted in the medieval feudal system and which continued to affect the early modern princely state in a weakened form, was opposed by the burgher principle of equal rights and obligations. From this position it was only one small step to the form of republicanism instituted by the Dutch regents, in principle both anti-noble and anti-princely.

This final step was never taken in Emden. Even the radically corporate movement described above was limited to a small group within the political elite of the city. Moreover, they were successful only for a short period of time. The Calvinist city-state as it finally emerged in the first years of the seventeenth century differed little in character from other autonomous territorial cities in early modern German history. Despite the many special conditions present in the northwestern corner of the Empire at the end of the sixteenth century that encouraged the civic autonomy movement, it was not possible to institute a republican polity in the full sense of the word. This is in part a consequence of the limited interest in East Friesland shown by the Estates General of the Netherlands, which precluded the possibility of any lasting and decisive external support for the radical party in Emden, much less for the city's inclusion in the Dutch Republic. It is also, however, a particularly striking testimony to the stability of the territorial structure of the early modern Empire and its legal mechanisms for maintaining peace, dominated as it was by the princely state.

In the course of the seventeenth century Emden continued to be a focal point for the history of political thought, because Johannes Althusius served as a *syndicus* for the city council from 1604 until his death in 1638.[84] Under his influence a particular political theory developed within the port city that was only indirectly connected with the urban setting and hence cannot be discussed in the present context. However, our discussion has shown that there were plausible links between the political theory of the great jurist and the older communal and corporate tradition of urban burghers which we have examined.

84 H. Antholz, Die politische Wirksamkeit des Johannes Althusius in Emden, Aurich 1955; more recently see the articles in K.W. Dahm, W. Krawietz and D. Wyduckel (eds.), Politische Theorie des Johannes Althusius, Berlin 1988.

III.

In my closing summary I will define the place of the communal
and corporate conceptions of participation and liberty espoused
by the German burghers in the history of European political
thought. (137)

1. During the late Middle Ages the burghers of German
cities developed a system of concepts concerning the form of
political order appropriate for both the internal affairs of a
city and its status within larger political entities, i.e. the territory and the Empire. This political thought was pragmatic in
character and expressed in the form of statutory law, rather
than philosophically and theoretically organized. Since, however, it was based upon commonly held fundamental principles,
it can rightly be called an implicit political theory. A city's
status according to imperial law, i.e., whether it was an imperial or a territorial city, originally played no major role in this
political theory in the northern and northwestern German area.
Hence the political model espoused by the burghers in this
region of the Empire was hardly less broadly based than in
urbanized northern Italy, Flanders, or Brabant until late in the
early modern period. In its content the German civic model of
state and society was informed by communal and corporate
ideals. Internal political order was dominated by three fundamental principles: *personal liberties* that were guaranteed for all
burghers without distinction; a correlation between *rights and
duties*, i. e. the participation of all burghers in meeting city
obligations and the direct responsibility of each individual to
strive for the common good; and finally the *communal participation* of the citizenry in the administration of their city, a
right which had to be protected whenever the city council or
another institution tried to establish an authoritarian regime. A
similar principle of constitutional order was espoused in
foreign policy. The relationship between city and territory—or
territorial prince—was regulated by treaty. In this relationship
as well the magistrate was only a representative of the
commune. Fundamental decisions had to be made by the
citizenry as a whole. This contractual relationship was renewed
by both territorial prince and commune through an oath
whenever a new prince assumed the throne and the city did
homage to him.

2. This civic political theory was not weakened during the first stage of state-building. In reaction to the authoritarian political theory advanced by the princes and their lawyers, a renaissance of communal and corporate thought took place during the sixteenth century, at least in northern and northwestern Germany. It was further empowered by strong impulses that were generated both by the urban Reformation and the resulting confessional identity of the commune. The early modern communal renaissance reached its climax in the decades before the outbreak of the Thirty Years' War. Burgher movements were formed in many cities during this period, which demanded a strengthening of corporate participation in internal affairs and external autonomy for the cities. Since authoritarian state formation, which opposed this communal and corporate renaissance, had gained considerable momentum in both political and theoretical terms after the mid-sixteenth century, these burgher movements for participation and autonomy confronted a new set of circumstances at the beginning of the seventeenth century. After its decisive victory enshrined in the fundamental laws of the Peace of Augsburg in 1555, the princely territorial state was practically uncontested, for it possessed a new political theory that undermined the demands for autonomy made by the communes, now precisely classified as territorial cities (*Landstädte*). Nevertheless it would be wrong to describe the period one-sidedly as a crisis for the cities and their corporate political theory. (138) The crisis of the early seventeenth century was much more a result of clashes between two powers—the communalism and corporatism of the cities and the territorialism of the princes—that had both been strengthened by the circumstances of the sixteenth century, even if their chances of victory varied considerably. The extent of this crisis and the scope of the burgher movement can be measured by the surge in the production of legal opinions, theoretical writings, and pamphlets that it evoked. In cities such as Brunswick, Emden, and Korbach the citizenry developed a type of political propaganda which in the two decades before the war fostered public opinion, a development reminiscent of Dutch circumstances.[85] In theoretical

---

85 At the same time the Hanseatic League started a propaganda offensive. See Schilling, Konfessionskonflikte (note 2), 50s.—In Stralsund the city councilor Balthasar Prütze wrote treatises, which combined the traditional statute law position of the urban political culture with elements of the new political theory.

terms the new situation was characterized by civic argumentation designed to parry the new legal and political theoretical
strategies of the princely states, and this was not at all limited
to those places, such as Emden and Korbach, exposed to Cal-
vinist-monarchomachian thought.

3. The changes that took place in the legal and political
framework during this period resulted in a new role for the
Emperor and the Empire in conflicts both within the cities
themselves and between the cities and territorial princes. This
does not contradict the well-known territorialization of the
Empire during the sixteenth century but rather was one of its
consequences. On the basis of the territorial structure and the
system of imperial peace, which was established in 1555 and
regulated the relationship between princes and cities, the
Emperor and the Empire were obliged to step forward as guar-
antors of this system. At first this meant protection for the
cities against the arbitrary measures of territorial princes. There
are even hints that the cities sought recourse to the Emperor
and the Empire in order to strengthen their own position. This
strategy could only bring tactical successes, however, since the
activities of the Emperor and Empire presupposed the territorial structure of Germany. In the long run they could only
have the effect of reducing the autonomous free cities to the
status of ordinary territorial cities. Similarly, the need for
peace and recourse to "the rule of law," which at first glance
would seem to offer considerable help to the cities, became a
disadvantage to them in the long run.

Characteristically, it was the burghers of Emden who were
able to develop a successful countermeasure since the city
lacked a tradition of medieval autonomy. Thus from the beginning the burghers could fight for urban autonomy using the
early modern imperial constitution as its legal foundation. With
the help of an historical-utopian claim to Frisian liberty, the
Emdeners were able to question the validity and scope of
princely and authoritarian territorialization in Germany—not in
principle, but with regard to the specific situation of East
Friesland. The fact that they cited imperial privileges in
defense of the specific, non-authoritarian status of Frisian territory was only a superficial paradox since the Emperor Char-

---

See Langer, Stralsund (note 17), 196ss.; idem, Die "Ungefehrliche Reformation
oder Regimentsordnung" des Stralsunder Ratsherrn Balthasar Prütze (1570-
1632), in: Stolleis, Recht (note 2).

lemagne, who allegedly had laid the foundations for Frisian liberty, was an early medieval ruler (139) and not the representative of the early modern imperial system.

In contrast to the territorial cities, the new system which led to intervention by the Emperor in case of internal conflicts strengthened the specifically civic structures of imperial city constitutions in the long-term. Outside intervention pushed the traditional communal and corporate elements further in the direction of a true early modern city-republic.[86] However because the number of dynamic imperial cities was so small, they were not able to compensate for the major weakening of the political culture of the urban middle class within the Empire, which occurred with the leveling of the communal and corporate traditions of the large territorial communes in northern and northwestern Germany.

Significantly enough in the long run the transformation of Old European civic republicanism into modern society was successful not so much in the southern German region dominated by imperial cities, but in the northwestern Hanseatic region, shaping the political culture especially of two present-day city-states: Hamburg and Bremen.[87] But compared with the wide scope of late medieval and sixteenth century civic republicanism present in hundreds of towns and cities these two city states of the nineteenth and the twentieth centuries are only isolated outposts or remnants. I thus share the judgement of Thomas A. Brady, Jr. that civic republicanism no longer had

---

86 See the definition of imperial cities in Nicolai Reusner, De Urbibus Germaniae Liberis sive Imperialibus Libri Duo (s.l. 1602), 24, as cities, "quae suis utuntur legibus ad morem Rerumpublicarum". See also Johann Stephan Pütter, Historische Entwicklung der heutigen Staatsverfassung Teutschen Reichs, 2. Theil von 1538-1740, Göttingen 1786, 208ss.; Malblank, Abhandlungen (note 16); Tobias Ludwig Ulrich Jäger, Juristisches Magazin für die deutschen Reichsstädte, Ulm 1790s.; Johann Jacob Moser, Teutsches Staatsrecht, Nürnberg 1737-54, vols. 39-43; idem, Von der Reichs-Städtischen Regimentsverfassung, Frankfurt/Leipzig 1712; idem, Neues teutsches Staatsrecht, vol. 18.—Literature: H. Conrad, Die verfassungsrechtliche Bedeutung der Reichsstädte im Deutschen Reich (etwa 1500-1806), in: Studium Generale 16 (1963), 493-500; R. Hildebrandt, Rat contra Bürgerschaft. Die Verfassungskonflikte in den Reichsstädten des 17. und 18. Jahrhunderts, in: Zeitschrift für Stadtgeschichte, Stadtsoziologie und Denkmalpflege 2 (1974), 221-241; Press, Reichsstadt (note 2).

87 On this tradition see H. Berding, Staatliche Identität, nationale Integration und politischer Regionalismus, in: H. Patze (ed.), Staatsgedanke und Landesbewußtsein in den neupreußischen Gebieten (1866), Marburg/Ulm 1985, 111-133, here 132 (also Blätter für deutsche Landesgeschichte 121, 1985); R. Postel, "Hanseaten". Zur politischen Kultur Hamburgs, Bremens und Lübecks, in: Hans-Georg Wehling (ed.), Regionale politische Kultur, Stuttgart 1985, 15-35.

"much significance for German society as a whole" after it had been confined to the imperial cities, whose influence with very few exceptions was declining rapidly.[88] However, I disagree with Professor Brady on the timing of this development. Based on the material discussed in this essay I do not think that civic republicanism was banished from territorial cities during the Reformation; this development only took place during the early seventeenth century, and accelerated during the Thirty Years' War. After fundamental changes had taken place during the three decades of martial chaos even large and politically powerful urban communes such as Brunswick, Erfurt, Münster, and Magdeburg were no longer able to resist their territorial overlords. Their defeat marked the end of the great tradition of civic republicanism within the urban centers of northern Germany which had shaped the political culture of German society for centuries.[89]

4. In order to determine the place of the communal and corporate model of political order espoused by German urban burghers within the history of European political theory and political culture, it is advisable to begin with the extraordinary success enjoyed by the Reformation in German cities from Constance to Schleswig and from Aachen to Danzig. After intensive and fruitful research we know (140) that its success was largely determined by the overall agreement between communal and corporate elements in the constitution of cities, which the citizenry understood to be a sacral community (*Heilsgemeinschaft*), and the fundamentals of the congregational concept of the Christian church displayed by the Reformation, both Zwinglian and Lutheran.[90] Even after the Reformation the demands of the cities for religious liberty were largely made on an corporate basis. The only exceptions to this were the movements generated by the "left wing" of the Reformation that were very important for long term changes, but were only minor episodes during the sixteenth century.[91]

88 Th. A. Brady, Patricians, Nobles, Merchants, in: M.U. Chrisman and O. Gründler (eds.), Social Groups and Religious Ideas in Sixteenth Century, Kalamazoo 1978, 38-45, here note 7, p. 159s.

89 For more detail see H. Schilling, Aufbruch und Krise. Deutsche Geschichte 1517-1648, Berlin 1988, 162-184, and idem, Höfe und Allianzen. Deutsche Geschichte 1648-1763, Berlin 1989, 207-211, 234-240.

90 H.-Ch. Rublack, Forschungsbericht Stadt und Reformation, in: Moeller (ed.), Stadt (note 66), 9-26; von Greyerz, Stadt (note 34).

91 On the failure of non-Lutheran alternatives in the early urban Reformation

There was no direct road leading from the demands of the Old European cities for religious self-determination, so strikingly expressed during the Reformation and confession-alization eras, to the modern freedom of religion and con-science for the individual. Continuing in the medieval tradi-tion, self-determination was understood to be a corporately legitimized self-determination of the civic commune as a whole, rather than a decision made by individual burghers. This was also true of Emden, since a Calvinist city church was organized there in 1595 which refused the city's Lutheran inhabitants, and of course the Catholic inhabitants as well, the right to religious self-determination. This fixation on the right of the commune to decide questions of conscience is all the more important since it affected the individual and the state of each person's soul in a far more powerful way than did fiscal, foreign, or military policy. This dialectical tension between medieval corporate thought and modern individualism marks not only the limits of the urban Reformation but also the limits of communal and corporate model of political and social order in general. It can be argued that because the corporate prin-ciple in medieval German cities was so strong and was further strengthened on a new foundation during the Reformation, it was very difficult for the German burghers of the seventeenth and eighteenth centuries to switch over from Old European civic republicanism or "communalism"—to use the term coined by Peter Blickle—to modern republicanism.

5. Despite this reservation, however, I think that to classify the political culture of the urban burghers as traditional and undynamic, in order to contrast it with the "genuinely" pro-gressive theories of natural law doctrine and/or monarcho-machianism—as has often been done by historians of political theory—is not only counterproductive for the history of polit-ical ideas but also incorrect. The relationship between these two theories was considerably more complex, as has been shown particularly by examining the ideology of the Emden Revolution. The communal and corporate renaissance of the sixteenth century could serve to prepare the ground for the adoption of the new ideas of natural law and at a later stage

see H. Schilling, Alternative Non-Lutheran Conceptions of the Reformation and the Compulsion to Lutheran Identity, in: S.C. Karant-Nunn and A. Fix (eds.), Germania illustrata. Essays presented to Gerald Strauss (working title), Kirksville 1991.

even of liberalism. These concepts seem to be one further step along a line that had already been present during the late Middle Ages rather than a change of direction. Indeed communal and corporate thought itself was obviously not incapable of absorbing these new ideas. (141)

It is true that such developments were exceptional and that discussions of both internal political participation and the autonomy of cities within the overarching political system ran along traditional lines in the vast majority of cities. Nevertheless I do not consider this to be a proof that the German urban middle classes were completely incapable of further developing their political culture. In Germany, particularly in the Hanseatic cities, the citizens had achieved remarkable success during the Middle Ages on the basis of their understanding of liberty. As a result of this positive experience, which even during the seventeenth century had not yet changed everywhere, few city communes felt the need for a new political theory.

Finally, I think it appropriate to ascribe greater importance to the urban burgher political tradition even if it was restricted to imperial cities during the seventeenth and eighteenth centuries. It is, of course, undisputed that the discussions in German cities never achieved the modern, profile of western European republicanism but continued to follow traditional Aristotelian paths. There was also no development of a pattern of participation that transcended the corporate burgher commune. These two aspects mark the principal limits of political discussion during the early modern period in German cities. Modern republican ideas first intruded upon the cities with the French Revolution and were only imposed with great difficulty because of the enduring vitality of corporate ideals of liberty. However, we must not overlook the fact that civic republicanism, despite these limitations, was an alternative model that opposed the prevailing authoritarian model of the princely state. It was distinguished by four structural elements:

—The principle of equality within the political elite and the radical rejection of one-person-rule.

—The "constitutionally" guaranteed participation of the burgher in the government and administration of his city as a member of the corporate and communal confederation of citizens.

—The public character of civic authority within the cities and its commitment to the general interest and the common good, a structural characteristic for any republic according to the modern type of republicanism developed by the Dutch regents in the middle of the seventeenth century.[92]

—Finally, in a continuation of the medieval norm that all fundamental decisions ought to be made in cooperation with the commune, the participation of the burgher commune in determining the "common good," or at very least its right to review such decisions.[93] I consider this to be the most important point of similarity between the model of corporate and communal constitutionalism of the Old European cities and the political culture of modern republics. Concerning this central point in political culture both stand in sharp contrast to the absolutist princely state, (142) where the "common good" was determined by the state and its officials in isolation from the society, even if their work was thought to be for its benefit.[94]

6. My statements concerning the renaissance of the communal and corporate spirit in German cities during the sixteenth century and my concluding thesis that the Old European culture of the urban middle classes was capable of accepting elements of the new political theory is surprising only with respect to German history. Within Dutch history the importance of the communal and corporate renaissance within the urban middle classes at the end of the sixteenth century is well known, as is the transformation of burgher political thought to modern forms, which grew beyond the urban context and which resulted in a modern individualistic type of republicanism. At the beginning there were evidently similarities in the political culture of Dutch and German cities. The reasons that they followed such different paths later during the seven-

92 Schilling, Republikanismus (note 14).

93 Stressed by Malblank, Abhandlungen (note 16), 99: "So wenig in der Regel einem Reichsstädtischen Magistrat die administratorische Gewalt in Ansetzung der Stadt-Einkünfte widersprochen werden kann; so gewiß ist es jedoch auch auf der anderen Seite, daß die Bürgerschaft eine Concurrent und Theilnehmung an dieser Gewalt begehren könne, sobald der Magistrat die Absicht der ihm ertheilten Vollmacht nicht ganz erfüllt, das gemeine Beste nicht vor Augen hat, überall nur seinen Privatvortheil beherzigt, die Finanzzweige für die Macht vernachläßigt, das Aerarium mit großen Schulden beschweret, und zu dessen Verfall den Weg bahnt."

94 Schilling, Republikanismus (note 14) and—with a wider scope—idem, Höfe (note 89), 74-77, 85-93, 443-447. See also the interesting observations on this subject by R. von Friedeburg, Der "Gemeine Nutz" als affirmative Kategorie, in: Zeitschrift des Vereins für Hessische Geschichte und Landeskunde 89 (1982/83), 27-49.

teenth and eighteenth centuries have yet to be clarified. The
fact that in the Netherlands it was possible to follow the path
toward an early modern republic while in Germany, even in
the areas that bordered on the Netherlands, such a development
was blocked, was not a consequence of the strength or
weakness of the political culture of the middle classes on one
side of the border or the other. It cannot even be explained
primarily in terms of confessional history, as a result of
Lutheran domination in the case of northern Germany or Calvinist domination in the Netherlands. The different paths taken
by political culture were mainly a consequence of differing
forms of political development, particularly in the area of constitutional law, which had occurred in the Burgundian provinces on the one hand and in the rest of the Empire on the
other after the end of the Middle Ages.

   This observation, in my opinion, can be applied to other
border areas of the medieval Empire as well. A comparison of
the history of other parts of Europe with our considerations
(especially in section III, 3) suggests that the strengthening of
urban autonomy movements and their further development into
sophisticated republican theories in upper Italy, Switzerland,
and the Netherlands was fostered to some extent because these
regions had drifted away from the Holy Roman Empire during
the late Middle Ages and consequently were no longer affected
by the early modern formation of the German imperial system
based on the principle of state formation in the territories.

   These observations concerning functional parallelism, however, underscore the significant distinction that has persistently
affected the modern history of political thought in Europe and
hence its historiography. I am referring to the fact that an
explicit political theory emerged first in Italian cities and that
it was further developed particularly in the Netherlands and in
England. The German cities developed a specific political culture during the late Middle Ages—as has been shown—and
this was expressed, among other ways, by a vibrant tradition of
city chronicles. They did not, however, elaborate an explicit
political theory. (143)

   7. This leads to my final point, the terminology and the
paradigm used to discuss the communal and corporate concepts
of participation and liberty espoused by urban burghers of the
late Middle Ages and the early modern period. The standard
expression in German urban historiography is "corporatism" or

"corporate idea" (*Genossenschaftsgedanke*). It has been used in older research on urban history which was primarily concerned with legal history, especially in the work of the legal historian Otto von Gierke.[95] This expression is problematic, however, because it does not correspond to the paradigms more commonly used in international discussions, particularly in the history of modern political theory. Peter Blickle, who first recognized this difficulty, has introduced the term "communalism."[96] Apart from the theoretical problem that this term creates by assuming the identity of urban and rural communal institutions, an issue which cannot be discussed here,[97] I am afraid that this concept could also be understood as an expression of the exceptional character of German history rather than an invitation for international comparisons. For this reason Koenigsberger's suggestion that the topic be discussed under the rubric of "republics and republicanism" seems particularly fruitful to me. Consequently in the present article I have used the term "civic republicanism" to characterize the political culture of urban corporations and urban communalism, although there was no elaborate, explicitly formulated theory of republicanism present in German cities during the period under investigation. The term "civic republicanism" seems to be particularly well suited to demonstrate that the conceptions of social and political order espoused by German urban burghers must be considered as part of that broad stream of Old European political thought from which both the early modern and modern forms of republicanism emerged.

---

95 See the magisterial work by Otto von Gierke, Das deutsche Genossenschaftsrecht, 4 vols., Leipzig 1868-1913, re-print Graz 1954. On Gierke and the older tradition of urban history in Germany see: L.Schorn-Schütte, Stadt und Staat. Zum Zusammenhang von Gegenwartsverständnis und historischer Erkenntnis in der Stadtgeschichtsschreibung der Jahrhundertwende, in: Die alte Stadt 10 (1983), 228-266 (especially literature note 25); eadem, Karl Lamprecht, Kulturgeschichtsschreibung zwischen Wissenschaft und Politik, Göttingen 1984 (index); cf. most recently the essay of G. Dilcher on the historiography of the notion "Genossenschaft" in: G. Dilcher and B. Diestelkamp (eds.), Recht, Gericht, Genossenschaft und Policey. Studien zu Grundbegriffen der germanischen Rechtshistorie, Berlin 1986.

96 P. Blickle, Deutsche Untertanen. Ein Widerspruch, München 1981; idem, Der Kommunalismus als Gestaltungsprinzip zwischen Mittelalter und Moderne, in: Gesellschaft und Gesellschaften. Festschrift für Ulrich Imhof, Bern 1982, 95-113.—Another plausible suggestion was made by Prak, Disturbance (note 2): "'early modern urban republicanism', or in a short form 'corporatism'" (166).

97 See the remarks in the chapter "Communal Reformation", below 189-201.

CHAPTER TWO

URBAN ELITES AND THE RELIGIOUS CONFLICTS OF THE SIXTEENTH CENTURY

I

When it comes to identifying the groups who supported the Reformation, there is hardly a city in northwestern Germany whose political elite could be named among its earliest supporters. In this region the Lutheran Reformation was in its origins a "popular movement," according to the well-known evaluation of Franz Lau,[1] which as a rule had to contend with resistance from both city councils and political elites. Although this assessment is certainly correct in its essentials, it is none the less worthwhile to examine the political elites of the cities when considering the social history of the Reformation. A one-sided concentration upon the "popular basis," as is the current trend among (236) social historians of the Reformation,[2] does

---

1 F. Lau, Der Bauernkrieg und das angebliche Ende der lutherischen Reformation als einer Volksbewegung, in: Luther-Jahrbuch 26 (1959), 109-134, reprinted in: W. Hubatsch (ed.), Wirkungen der deutschen Reformation bis 1555, Darmstadt 1967, 68-100. Recently B. Moeller, Deutschland im Zeitalter der Reformation, Göttingen 1977, 84, 112. See the review articles: H.-Ch. Rublack, Forschungsbericht Stadt und Reformation, in: B. Moeller (ed.), Stadt und Kirche im 16. Jahrhundert, Gütersloh 1978, 9-26; F. Kopitzsch, Bemerkungen zur Sozialgeschichte der Reformation und des Bauernkrieges, in: R. Wohlfeil (ed.), Der Bauernkrieg 1524-26. Bauernkrieg und Reformation, München 1975, 177-218, esp. 181ss., 199ss.

2 See the comments by A. Laube in: idem et al. (eds.), Illustrierte Geschichte der deutschen frühbürgerlichen Revolution, Berlin 1974; K. Czok, Revolutionäre Volksbewegung in mitteldeutschen Städten zur Zeit von Reformation und Bauernkrieg, in: L. Stern and M. Steinmetz (eds.), 450 Jahre Reformation, Berlin 1967, 128-145; H.-U. Wehler (ed.), Der deutsche Bauernkrieg, 1524-1526, Göttingen 1975; P. Blickle (ed.), Revolte und Revolution in Europa, München 1975; B. Moeller (ed.), Bauernkriegs-Studien, Göttingen 1975. For basic considerations on the problem of "social movements" within towns: W. Ehbrecht, Verlaufsformen innerstädtischer Konflikte in nord- und westdeutschen Städten im Reformationszeitalter, in: B. Moeller (ed.), Stadt (note 1), 27-47; E. Maschke, Deutsche Städte am Ausgang des Mittelalters, in: W. Rausch (ed.), Die Stadt am Ausgang des Mittelalters, Linz 1974, 1-32, esp. 20ss.

not offer sufficient insight into the processes of societal history
during the pre-modern era, particularly during the periods of
deepening crisis. Furthermore, the initial breakthrough phase
of the Reformation, which was strongly influenced by the
"popular movements," was not decisive for the long-term survival of the Protestant churches and the final form that they
assumed. The questions of when and in what form the political
elite was prepared to accept, or could accept, the religious
demands of the citizenry was decisive for the stabilization and
institutionalization of the new church.[3] Finally, it is instructive
to study the attitude of the political elite toward the Reformation because one can thus draw conclusions about the social or,
more inclusively still, societal implications of a religious
movement from the reservations expressed by outsiders and
from the reasons given by opponents for rejecting it. (237)

With regard to the northwestern German cities it seems
appropriate to define the term "political elite" in a broad
sense. It should refer not only to those persons who held
councillor positions at a given time, but should also include the
broader circle of all who on the basis of their prestige and
wealth could in principle seek a seat on the city council within
the setting of a given city constitution. This was especially the
case if such persons had already been invested with one of the
various communal offices outside of the city council. A
political elite so defined can be distinguished relatively easily
from the groups who were not considered eligible for the
council, without having to characterize it as homogeneous or as
representing a conformity of interests. Since it refers to social
function, the term "elite" is better suited, in my opinion, than
the concept of "ruling class" to convey the reality of an estate-
based leadership circle rather than one reckoned according to
class.[4]

I would like to begin by making several general observations

---

3 On political elites and Reformation see W. Jacob, Politische Führungsschichten und Reformation. Untersuchung zur Reformation in Zürich 1519-1528,
Zürich 1970; Th. A. Brady Jr., Ruling Class, Regime and Reformation at Strasbourg, 1520-1555, Leiden 1978; J. Bátori and E. Weyrauch, Die bürgerliche Elite
der Stadt Kitzingen. Studien zur Sozial- und Wirtschaftsgeschichte einer landesherrlichen Stadt im 16. Jahrhundert, Stuttgart 1978; D. Demandt und H.-C.
Rublack, Stadt und Kirche in Kitzingen. Studien zu Spätmittelalter und Reformation, Stuttgart 1978.

4 H. Stoob (ed.), Altständisches Bürgertum, vol. 2: Erwerbsleben und Sozialgefüge, Darmstadt 1978, IX.

about the urban Reformation, laying out a system of political and social coordinates against which our discussion of the conduct of the political elites of individual cities can be charted.

1. It is important to understand the Reformation in the cities as part of a general process of development in urban civic society and not only as a continuation of medieval conditions and conduct. The latter connections have received ample consideration in research thanks to the influential book of Bernd Moeller and, more recently, through the studies of Wilfried Ehbrecht on medieval and Reformation era civic uprisings.[5] However, the lines that run from the Reformation to the second half of the sixteenth century and into the seventeenth century are equally important for the history of cities and the urban burghers as well as for the rise of new types of burghers whose primary concern was no longer the city. This period has until now received little attention because the year 1555 has been considered the "classical" termination point for studies in Reformation history.[6] (238)

2. The most important elements of continuity with the Middle Ages can be found in the internal currents and conditions of cities. The Reformation represents one link in a long chain of conflicts, in the course of which the form of public life was disputed according to the particular needs of the urban citizenry. The medieval struggles, which urban society experi-

---

5 B. Moeller, Reichsstadt und Reformation, Gütersloh 1962; Ehbrecht, Verlaufsformen (note 2); idem, Zuordnung und Selbstverständnis städtischer Gesellschaft im späten Mittelalter, in: Blätter für deutsche Landesgeschichte 110 (1974), 83-103; idem, Bürgertum und Obrigkeit in den hansischen Städten des Spätmittelalters, in: Rausch, Stadt (note 2), 275-294.

6 Despite the article by F. Lau mentioned in note 1 and dozens of other articles showing that popular Reformation did not break down in the towns in 1525, there are still historians who hold the traditional view that the Reformation from below ended in the year 1525. See my article: H. Schilling, The Communal Reformation in Germany: An Upper German, Zwinglian Phenomenon before the "Turning Point of the Reformation" in 1525?, pp. 189-201 below. I have published several articles showing the continuity in urban history before and after 1525: see H. Schilling, Aufstandsbewegungen in der stadtbürgerlichen Gesellschaft des Alten Reiches: Die Vorgeschichte des Münsteraner Täuferreiches, in: Wehler, Bauernkrieg (note 2), 191-238, esp. 230-236; idem, Bürgerkämpfe in Aachen zu Beginn des 17. Jahrhunderts, in: Zeitschrift für Historische Forschung 1 (1974), 175-231; and idem, Reformation und Bürgerfreiheit. Emdens Weg zur calvinistischen Stadtrepublik, in: Moeller, Stadt (note 1), 128-161. Similar considerations have also been raised by Ch. Friedrichs, Citizens or Subjects? Urban Conflict in Early Modern Germany, in: M. Usher Chrisman and O. Gründler (eds.), Social Groups and Religious Ideas in the Sixteenth Century, Kalamazoo 1978, 46-58. More recently, see: H. Schilling, Civic Republicanism in Late Medieval and Early Modern German Cities, above pp. 3-60.

enced in different waves from the rise of the city in a legal
sense to the end of the fifteenth century,[7] were primarily
concerned with achieving a "proper" constitution and social
order. These problems continued to play an important role at
the beginning of the early modern period both before the
Reformation and during it, but, according to Erich Maschke,
the social and economic conditions of the common people
became the most important factors.[8] In my opinion, however,
the burgher movements of the 1520's and 1530's cannot be
explained simply by adding economic and social factors to the
older constitutional and political considerations. (239) The
characteristic feature of the burgher movements of the Reformation period, by which they can be distinguished from previous waves of burgher unrest, is their struggle for the
recognition of a new way to eternal salvation, more satisfactory
for the burgher mentality, and the related struggles to compel
the magistrates to make the legal, constitutional, and institutional changes necessary to accomplish it. That is to say, the civic
resistance movement advanced to the so-called "third stage,"
which was primarily concerned with a form of religion and
church organization adequate for the city and its citizenry after
the pre-Reformation struggles in which accommodating the
political and social systems of cities to the needs of their inhabitants had been the central feature.[9]

Of course when these burgher movements demanded religious and ecclesiastical changes they created at the same time a
whole series of new social and political problems since secular
and ecclesiastical matters were structurally linked in Old European society. In addition, the Reformation message was ideally
suited to activate or reactivate the communal principle within

---

7 It is well-known that there are two main waves before the Reformation which
must be distinguished: the "communal movement" of the high Middle Ages and
the "burgher movement" of the late Middle Ages: K. Czok, Zur Stellung der
Stadt in der deutschen Geschichte, in: Jahrbuch für Regionalgeschichte 3 (1968),
9-33; see also E. Ennen, Die europäische Stadt des Mittelalters, Göttingen 1972,
112ss., 120-138, 207; E. Maschke, Verfassung und soziale Kräfte in der deutschen
Stadt des späten Mittelalters, vornehmlich in Oberdeutschland, in: Vierteljahresschrift für Sozial- und Wirtschaftsgeschichte 46 (1959), 289-349, 433-476; idem,
"Obrigkeit" im spätmittelalterlichen Speyer und in anderen Städten, in: Archiv
für Reformationsgeschichte 57 (1966), 7-22.

8 Maschke, Städte (note 2), 1-44, esp. 20.

9 The three stages are the "communal movement" (Kommunebewegung) of the
high Middle Ages, the "civic or burgher movement" (Bürgerbewegung) of the late
Middle Ages and the urban Reformation of the sixteenth century.

the cities because its particular theology, especially its communal and congregational principle, was congenial to the communal institutions of the cities and the communal mentality of the burghers. For the early phase of the Reformation I will not distinguish between Lutheran and Reformed/Zwinglian movements in this respect since both could and did trigger burgher movements in favor of a communal Reformation. Consequently, a linkage easily occurred between religious and ecclesiastical claims and the general demands of the citizenry, based upon communal and corporate norms, which in turn brought about stronger demands for political participation as well as greater consideration of the social and economic concerns of the common people, i.e. those not eligible for the city council.

The ties that bind the events of the Reformation era with the period after 1555, by contrast, are more concerned with "foreign relations," that is the (240) relationship of city and citizenry with overarching political and societal units, with the territorial state and the Empire. Volker Press has recently drawn attention to the long-term impact of the urban Reformation in a study which is quite revealing, particularly with regard to social history. He has shown that civil servants who had come from upper German imperial cities exercised a considerable influence upon territorial confession-building and the erection of a territorial church.[10] In northwestern Germany similar interactions can be observed, although antagonism between city and territory, burghers and princes, was far more common in this region than agreement. Many examples show that in this area conflicts between city and territory, which had reached their first climax during the Reformation, had effects that endured until well into the seventeenth century. Occasionally even these later conflicts between cities and territories were triggered or influenced by confessional and ecclesiastical questions.[11] The simultaneity of internal and external problems

---

10 V. Press, Stadt und territoriale Konfessionsbildung, in: F. Petri (ed.), Kirche und gesellschaftlicher Wandel in deutschen und niederländischen Städten der werdenden Neuzeit, Köln 1980, 251-296; K. Wriedt, Universitätsbesucher und graduierte Amtsträger zwischen Nord- und Süddeutschland, in: W. Paravicini (ed.), Nord und Süd in der deutschen Geschichte des Mittelalters, Sigmaringen 1990, 193-201.

11 E.g. northern and central German towns such as Emden, Höxter, Lemgo, Marburg, Paderborn and Lüneburg must be mentioned (at the beginning of the seventeenth century), together with cities such as Münster (in the middle of the

affecting the cities as well as the new opportunities offered to burghers within the rapidly expanding princely bureaucracy are the two most important characteristics of urban history during the Reformation and the confessional period.

3. In essence the problems of urban external policy were concerned with the consequences of the rise of the early modern territorial state. They affected imperial cities[12] as (241) much as other cities. It must also be remembered that the distinction between the imperial cities which had the *ius reformandi* and the territorial cities which were considered to be part of a territory and thus at least in theory subject to the *cuius-regio-cuius-religio* principle, a distinction that was important for territorial law and territorial ecclesiastical law, was itself a result of the Reformation, not a precondition for it. However, the consequences and implications of territorial state-building were quite different for both types of cities, as were the attendant opportunities and dangers for their citizens. Since the course and outcome of the Reformation was an important factor in the development of territorial states, it had especially significant consequences in the case of the territorial cities, both for the political and social position of their citizens in general and for ruling groups in particular. In this respect it made no difference whether the territorial prince had chosen the old or the new faith. In cases where the Reformation triumphed, it had to be decided who should have control over the newly established city church and its attendant rights. Would it become a further addition to the autonomous communal

---

seventeenth century), Brunswick (at the beginning and in the second half of the seventeenth century), and Berlin (in the year 1615). See H. J. Querfurth, Die Unterwerfung der Stadt Braunschweig im Jahre 1671, Brunswick 1953; H. Schmidt, Politische Geschichte Ostfrieslands, Leer 1975, 195-256; M. Smid, Ostfriesische Kirchengeschichte, Leer 1974, 234-265, 345f.; L. Keller, Die Gegenreformation in Westfalen und am Niederrhein. Aktenstücke und Erläuterungen, 3 vols., 1881-1895; K. Honselmann, Der Kampf um Paderborn 1604 und die Geschichtsschreibung, in: Westfälische Zeitschrift 118 (1968), 229-38; K. Löffler, Zur Reformationsgeschichte der Stadt Höxter, in: Zeitschrift für vaterländische Geschichte und Altertumskunde 70 (1912), 250-271, also Keller, vol. 2, 631-698; Historischer Bericht, Der Newerlichen Monats Augusti zugetragenen Marpurgischen Kirchenhändel, Marburg 1605; H. Lahrkamp, Galens städtische Widersacher. Streiflichter zur Erhellung der münsterschen Opposition gegen den Fürstbischof Christoph Bernhard, in: Westfalen (1973), 238-253; E. Faden, Der Berliner Tumult von 1615, in: Jahrbuch für brandenburgische Landesgeschichte 5 (1954), 27-45.

12 E.g. the attacks of Brunswick-Wolfenbüttel upon the imperial city of Goslar in the first third of the sixteenth century and the government of Jülich's pressure upon the imperial city of Aachen at the end of the sixteenth century.

system, and hence a part of the "governing rights" of the burgher elite, or would it become a part of the centralized bureaucracy and thus a further element of territorial princely presence in the city as well as a tool that could be used to integrate the city into the territorial state? When considering "foreign policy," that is the relationship between a city and its overlord—the prince in the case of territorial cities and the Emperor in the case of imperial cities—it is necessary, in my opinion, to draw a typological distinction between the Reformation in the imperial cities and in territorial cities. Within the area under discussion the latter type can also be called the "Hanseatic city Reformation." [13]

For the sake of completeness it should be noted that I will not discuss those cases where ecclesiastical renewal within a city took place as part of a territorial Reformation by a territorial prince. This was the case mostly in smaller and very small towns which lacked the political strength and civic tradition necessary to take the initiative in religious reform or the ability to oppose it independently of the prince and the territorial state.[14] (242)

In principle there was no difference between the Reformation in territorial cities and in imperial cities from an internal perspective. The communal and corporate principle was one of the fundamental ideals of the medieval citizenry. There are even some indications that this ideal was particularly strongly expressed in the lower German area during the sixteenth century. Moeller's results, drawn largely from southern German imperial cities, can also be extended to the northern German territorial cities.[15]

---

13 The Hanseatic towns claimed a special legal status between the status of imperial cities and the status of territorial towns. See H. Schilling, Konfessionskonflikte und Hansestädtische Freiheiten im 16. und 17. Jahrhundert, in: Hansische Geschichtsblätter 97 (1979), 6-59; idem, Republicanism (note 6).

14 Caution is advisable when classing particular cities or even certain urban landscapes in this special type of "territorial-princely Reformation in the towns." It would be a mistake to place towns of eastern und central German territories which had strong rulers in this category. K. Blaschke has recently shown that even in Ernestine Saxony, a prototype of the Protestant territorial state, the Reformation movement started in the towns and that the movement had its strongest roots and most popular support in the towns. See K. Blaschke, Die Auswirkungen der Reformation auf die städtische Kirchenverfassung in Sachsen, in: Moeller, Stadt (note 1), 162-167, 178; for southern Germany see O. Mörke, Die Ruhe im Sturm—die katholische Landstadt Mindelheim unter der Herrschaft der Frundsberg im Zeitalter der Reformation, Augsburg 1991.

15 Ehbrecht, Verlaufsformen (note 2); E. Pitz, Wirtschaftliche und soziale Pro-

4. Territorial state-building affected not only the laws and
constitution of the cities; it also had a particular impact upon
the social position and economic opportunities of the urban
burghers. This affected artisans as well as the landed upper
stratum of the citizenry, whose economic opportunities dete-
riorated in the wake of changes such as the expansion of rural
manufacturing and the peasant protection policies of the
princes. The sources convey the impression that it was this
political change introduced by the rise of the early modern
state and its social consequences that deeply affected the confi-
dence of the inhabitants of northern German cities in each and
every social stratum during the sixteenth century. Other significant developments included the changes in long-distance trade,
the shift from an agricultural depression to an agricultural
boom, the emergence of rural manufacturing——in the lower
German area above all textiles, and the replacement of the
Hanseatic long-distance trader by a new type of merchant, or
by the cottage industry entrepreneur and the distributor of
rural manufactured goods. These economic changes were most
important when considering the objective framework of early
modern history. Within the subjective horizon and the mentality of contemporaries, however, these economic factors were
apparently of only secondary importance. They were experienced, in part, as a function of the political change.[16]
Nevertheless, these changes must be taken into account in a
structural analysis of the Reformation movements, whereby it
must be decided on a case to case basis (243) whether and to
what degree they had already affected each city at the beginning of the sixteenth century.

Political as well as economic change affected urban society
as a whole in each and every social stratum. For the broader
strata of society the decisive question was whether it would
result in a decline of urban prosperity and was a threat to their
wealth. To what degree this was indeed the case during the
Reformation era is difficult to say at present, for we still know
very little about the genuine economic condition of the cities as
well as the individual burgher groups. It appears, however, that

---

bleme der gewerblichen Entwicklung im 15./16. Jahrhundert nach hansisch-nie-
derdeutschen Quellen, in: C. Haase (ed.), Die Stadt des Mittelalters, vol. 3,
Darmstadt 1973, 137-176, esp. 145ss., 148.

16 This impression is based on the continuous reading of urban sources not on
a systematic investigation of the problem.

a general crisis or even a decline can no longer be assumed
within the Hanseatic region, and the situation must be clearly
differentiated from city to city. Above all, it remains to be
determined to what extent the 1520's and 1530's, as opposed to
the end of the fifteenth century, had not already ushered in a
period of economic growth.[17] In any event it is worth noting
that the social and economic problems which played an explicit
role in the Reformation movement resulted overwhelmingly
from changes in the rural (i.e. non-urban) situation as well as
from a short-term crisis of harvest and supply.

We can perceive the consequences that these changes had for
the political elite in the rise of new groups such as an upper
stratum of academics or entrepreneurial artisans and also in the
increasing reorientation of older patrician or semi-patrician
councillor families from mercantile trade to a *rentier* existence,
an agrarian noble life in the countryside, or toward the learned
professions within the city or in the territory. What occurred
here was a long-term shift from the Hanseatic urban elite of
the late Middle Ages to a territorial city elite of the early
modern period. It should be observed that in each city this
development had (244) a different character and its own
rhythm. Whether and to what degree this social process and the
urban Reformation reciprocally influenced each other is one of
the central questions of the following study.

5. The connection between ecclesiastical and territorial questions in the course of the Reformation of the territorial cities
caused an extension of the bi-polar opposition between city
council and citizenry that was common in the imperial cities to
a three-way struggle between the citizenry, the city council,
and the territorial prince/territorial state. In the following
discussion the political, social, and religious circumstances
within this triangle will be described and evaluated with reference to their significance for the political elite. It is clear that
the Protestant preachers, the Emperor[18] and the Empire as well

---

17 Such a thesis, which I tend to agree with for at least some towns, is supported by Pitz (note 15) and Ehbrecht, Verlaufsformen (note 2), 38. For opposing
views, see: J. Schildhauer, Soziale, politische und religiöse Auseinandersetzungen
in den Hansestädten Stralsund, Rostock und Wismar im ersten Drittel des 16.
Jahrhunderts, Weimar 1959; K. Fritze, Entwicklungsprobleme der Sozialstruktur
der Städte im Ostseeraum im Spätmittelalter, in: Entwicklungsprobleme des
Feudalismus und Kapitalismus in Ostseegebiet, Tartu 1972.

18 F. Petri, Karl V. und die Städte im Nordwestraum während des Ringens um
die politisch-kirchliche Ordnung in Deutschland, in: Jahrbuch für Westfälische

as the territorial estates, particularly the nobility, were further important factors. For our purposes, however, it is defensible to ignore them to a large extent. They usually participated in the struggle on behalf of one of the three principals, the preachers for the burghers and the Emperor and Empire, as well as the estates for the territorial prince or the territory.

The actual course of the Reformation within individual northwestern German cities[19] shows that only particular combinations of the numerous theoretically possible alliances and lines of confrontation within this triangle of forces actually occurred. Conceivable interactions between these parties, such as a burgher commune choosing to support Catholicism and to defend itself against the reforming tendencies of a city council or a princely government, did not in fact occur, at least not in the larger cities. There were also relatively few cases where the urban ruling elite maintained a firm Catholic alliance with the territorial prince to the point of a rupture with the urban commune. (245) The best-known example is probably Hanover.[20] Equally an early alliance between the burgher commune and the city council under the Protestant banner against a territorial prince loyal to the old faith, as occurred in Bremen,[21] must be regarded as exceptional. The same is true for an alliance between a Protestant citizenry and a Protestant territorial prince against a Catholic city council. Such a constellation seems to have appeared for a brief time in Lüneburg.

By far the most frequent case was a Protestant initiative on the part of the citizenry against a Catholic city council and a Catholic territorial prince during the early phase. Later the

---

Kirchengeschichte 71 (1978), 7-31.

19 A. G. Dickens, The German Nation and Martin Luther, London 1974, Chapter 8: Some Hanseatic Cities—and Erfurt; J. Schildhauer, Zum Charakter der Reformation in Norddeutschland und in den skandinavischen Ländern, in: M. Steinmetz and G. Brendler (eds.): Weltwirkungen der Reformation, Berlin 1969, 318-329.

20 W. Bahrdt, Geschichte der Reformation der Stadt Hannover, Hanover 1891; E. Sehling, Die evangelischen Kirchenordnungen des 16. Jahrhunderts, vol. VI/2, = Niedersachsen 1/2, Tübingen 1957, 940ss.; H. Plath, H. Mundhenke and E. Brix, Heimatchronik der Hauptstadt Hannover, Köln 1956, esp. 40ss.; most recently S. Müller, Stadt, Kirche und Reformation. Das Beispiel der Landstadt Hannover, Hanover 1987.

21 J. Iken, Die erste Epoche der Bremischen Reformation, in: Bremisches Jahrbuch 8 (1876), 40-113; B. Heyne, Die Reformation in Bremen 1522-1524. Am Vorabend—Der Beginn—Die Bahnbrecher, in: Hospitium Ecclesiae 8 (1973), 7-54; B. Moeller, Die Reformation in Bremen, in: Jahrbuch der Wittheit zu Bremen 17 (1973), 51-73.

fronts shifted, mostly in the direction of a (246) Protestant
alliance between the citizenry and the city council against the
Catholic territorial prince. This outcome was achieved either
because of a flexible accommodation to the position of the
citizenry by the political elite, as occurred in Osnabrück and
Brunswick, or by a more or less violent uprising, as was the
case in Soest and Göttingen, which left the councillors with
two alternatives: either they could vacate their offices and possibly also leave the city, or they could conform. A third phase,
in which all three participants were adherents of Protestantism,
was reached, if at all, relatively late as a rule. However, confessional harmony did not in any way guarantee freedom from
political and social tensions.[22] Osnabrück during the 1540's was
an exception to this generalization.

From this schematic survey two basic facts are clear. First,
only the citizenries and the territorial princes acted as
relatively autonomous powers, while the city councils and the
political elites rarely took the initiative. Usually they reacted to
and were forced to choose between the two fronts. Second,
there was clearly a pressure toward internal harmony and
equalization. It ran to the disadvantage of the councils and
ruling circles to the extent that——regardless of whether or not
the territorial prince was Protestant or Catholic——it had to
conform to the Protestant stance of the burghers over the
course of time. In the following discussion the status and
activity of the political elites during the Reformation of the
territorial cities will be described in more detail with the help
of a series of individual cases in order to find explanations for
their specific position within the urban Reformation
movements. Of particular importance is the extent to which an
early rejection of Protestantism by the political elite and a later
narrowing of differences was religiously or politically and
socially conditioned. Was the Reformation teaching in this
sense "class-specific," in that it addressed primarily the middle
and lower strata of the burghers and inhabitants, but was
rejected by the groups who bore political responsibility because
of its specific theological content? Or was it non-religious
factors that first hindered the advance of Protestantism into the
urban political elites, but then at a later phase encouraged it?

---

22 E.g. in the case of Protestant Lüneburg and its Protestant ruler Duke Erich.

II

I regard it as methodologically necessary, in view of the mani-
fold differences in the concrete sets of conditions affecting
each individual city Reformation, to begin with a detailed
description of one individual case and in a second step to draw
comparisons with other cities. Several generalizing theses will
then follow. (247)

    For the individual case I have chosen an example familiar to
me from my own archival work. It concerns the territorial city
of *Lemgo* in the Westphalian County of Lippe, whose Reformation history can be assigned to the pattern most frequently
encountered of those described above. Although in absolute
terms of its population size and economic power Lemgo was of
modest importance, it played a dominant role within the
County of Lippe as an intellectual and economic center as well
as a transportation junction and a political force.[23] Its mercantile citizenry, in whose hands lay the city government, had
supported the territorial prince again and again during the
Middle Ages with political counsel and financial help. In its
response to the Reformation the Lemgo elite displayed the
typical pattern of immobility, reaction, and political maneuvering between the fronts. During the decisive phase between
1525 and 1532 the Reformation was a burgher and communal
movement which had to open a road to ecclesiastical renewal
without any native theological leadership. This situation
changed after the burghers called a Protestant preacher to be
the pastor at the city's main church of St. Nikolai in the year
1528, and after the political and social status of the magistrate
had been severely weakened by numerous violent riots during
the summer of 1531. Although the leading Catholic group
within the council had to leave the city temporarily, the
burghers did not appoint new councillors. This can be attributed to, among other factors, the influence of Hessian
mediators.[24] Six months later, however, the regular election of

---

23The following is based on H. Schilling, Konfessionskonflikt und Staatsbildung. Eine Fallstudie über das Verhältnis von religiösem und sozialem Wandel in
der Frühneuzeit am Beispiel der Grafschaft Lippe, Gütersloh 1981; idem, The
Reformation in the Hanseatic Cities, in: The Sixteenth Century Journal 14
(1983), 443-456; idem, Between the Territorial State and Urban Liberty, in: R.
Po-chia Hsia (ed.), The German People and the Reformation, Ithaca 1988, 263-
283.

24 Landgrave Philipp of Hesse, who was feudal lord of the Counts zur Lippe

the city council, which as usual was performed by cooptation, i.e. the old members choosing new ones in the presence of all citizens, brought Protestants into both burgomaster offices. Under their direction the Lemgo city council changed its policy and actively supported the Reformation, working closely with the commune and a committee appointed by it.

When considering the causes and motives of the city council's opposition to the Reformation I would like to distinguish those of primary and secondary importance. Two factors can be identified as primary causes:

1. In Lippe until well into the 1520's there was traditionally a good relationship between the territorial prince and the estates, especially the political elite of Lemgo, the most influential representatives of the burgher estate within the territory. A sudden opposition movement that fundamentally opposed the Count's decision to support Catholicism would have been unusual, and would have brought Lemgo into conflict with the nobility and the smaller cities of the territory.

2. The urban elite, particularly that part which sat on the city council, was far more strongly involved with the old church system than the rest of the citizenry: through a series of benefices and endowed masses, through the Kaland brotherhood, in which the 24 city councillors had united with the city's 24 priests and 12 leading burghers, cultivating active social contacts, and through the supply of benefices offered by the Dominican convent of St Mary to their daughters, in addition to women from noble families and even from the princely dynasty of Lippe.[25] When the Lemgo city council actively supported the early countermeasures set in motion by the Paderborn diocesan administration, it was an expression of this traditional bond.

In addition to these original "limiting factors," a series of secondary reasons for rejection emerged, which resulted from the linkage of the Reformation with the burgher protest

together with the Bishop of Paderborn, intervened again and again in the 1520's and 1530's in the internal affairs of Westphalian territories, to support energetically the Reformation. See R. Wolf, Der Einfluß des Landgrafen Philipp des Großmütigen von Hessen auf die Einführung der Reformation in den westfälischen Grafschaften, in: Jahrbuch des Vereins für westfälische Kirchengeschichte 51/52 (1958/59), 27-149.

25 F. Gerlach, Der Archidiakonat Lemgo in der mittelalterlichen Diözese Paderborn. Unter Benutzung des städtischen Archivs und des Stadtarchivs von St. Maria zu Lemgo, Münster 1932.

movement. The longer the councillor families remained
opposed to the new doctrine, the more clearly the burgher
movement espousing ecclesiastical renewal had to identify itself
as a communal, corporate opposition movement which
questioned the authority of the city council and (249) the
legitimacy of the political elite. This began with civil
disobedience to the ban on attending worship services in
nearby Herford, which had been instituted by the city council
and territorial prince, and developed from the autonomous
appointment of the pastor at St. Nikolai to a fundamental
renunciation of their obedience to the ruling authorities,
because they opposed—as the preacher Peter Gossmann
expressed it from the pulpit—the "common good," i.e., the
purification of the church according to Protestant standards.[26]

What is important here is that demands for the application of
corporate and communal principles within the ecclesiastical
sphere had a direct effect upon the political and social system
of the city. The constitution of Lemgo had been newly established a generation before the Reformation. In theory it showed
a well-balanced combination of communal-corporative and of
authoritative-oligarchic elements which fostered cooperation
between the communal districts (the so-called *Bauernschaften*)
and guilds on the one hand, and the self-appointed city council
on the other hand. In reality power lay in the hands of a limited circle of councillor families. They can be characterized as
an *Honoratiorentum* (an elite of notables) on account of its
basic openness to newcomers, in contrast to a patrician group,
which is socially closed. This *Honoratiorentum* was composed of
long-distance merchants, who were at the same time land-
owners, and after the beginning of the sixteenth century
increasingly of academics, especially jurists.[27] Through the
power of cooptation this elite was able to hold the most
important offices in both the city council and in the town
government as a whole. At the same time they supervised the
recruitment of the guild and communal district
(*Bauernschaften*) representatives. The political rights of the

---

26 Gossmann is even said to have demanded that his audience, "die Obersten
auf den Markt zu bringen und ihnen den Kopf abzuschlagen" ("should bring the
councillors to the market place and cut off their heads") (Territorial Archives
Detmold, L 29, B 1, fol. 42, note of the Count's chancellery).

27 E. Geiger, Die soziale Elite der Hansestadt Lemgo und die Entstehung eines
ländlichen Exportgewerbes in Lippe und Ravensberg, Detmold 1976.

citizenry were limited to confirming (*Vollbort*) the annual
appointment of the city council, from which the same men
repeatedly emerged in rotations of two years.

The reactivation of the burghers' claim to direct participation constituted a great danger for the rule of this *Honoratiorentum*, which already showed oligarchic traits in common with
the tendencies generally found in late medieval cities. This was
all the more dangerous because the burgher committee, which
had been formed to further the religious demands of the citizenry, did not limit itself to ecclesiastical activities. During the
uprising, when the burghers demanded the election of "an
impartial committee of representatives," it was clear that they
no longer trusted and recognized their constitutionally sanctioned representatives from the guilds and commons. Because
of the Reformation movement a burgher committee did indeed
come into existence (250) which together with the city council
determined the policies of the city for years afterward.

Apart from these repercussions upon their freedom of political action, attacks on certain commercial practices of the
Honoratioren groups also resulted from the communal currents
of the Reformation. In a list of secular grievances,[28] assembled
at the same time as the ecclesiastical demands, the burghers
accused several councillor families of depriving the commune
of its rights for their own profit and of injuring the principle
of burgher solidarity. Individual charges included the privatization of communal rights to use of common land, favoritism
in the allocation of city property and privileges—such as wood
cutting and fishing—as well as grain hoarding and speculation
at the expense of burgher consumers. All of these were practices—some of them abuses of official authority—which the
circle of *Honoratioren* engaged in, in order to take advantage
of the agricultural boom of the sixteenth century that was just
beginning. The burghers demanded an end to these preferential
dealings, a restitution of the common right of use for all, a
method of allocation for the urban common land that also took
account of the interests of the common burghers, and finally
greater participation of the wealthy in meeting the general
obligations of the city.

It is easy to understand how this linkage of religious renewal
with demands for political and social restrictions upon the

---

28 Town archives Lemgo, Urkunde (Charter) No. 1008.

Honoratioren by the burgher corporation served to strengthen
the reservations of the city councillors against Protestantism.
Burgomaster Konrad Flörken, the most outstanding Catholic
representative, was a member of an old councillor family
which after starting out in long-distance trade had invested its
wealth increasingly in land. Flörken himself was a learned
jurist and experienced politician, but, as the burghers'
complaints illustrate, he was also involved in the private use of
city land. He stated plainly that the old church had to be
maintained on account of its hierarchical structure;
Lutheranism had to be opposed because it meant disorder and
the beginning of a general upheaval. He feared the
Reformation because he thought that it would lead to a general
weakening of the oligarchic and authoritative elements in
church and society.[29]

It is easy to suppose that if the urban elite had swiftly come
to an agreement with the territorial prince in this situation, the
burgher movement in Lemgo would have been quickly isolated
and defeated without any doubt. However, such a supposition
is based on a false premise. (251) The struggle for ecclesiastical
renewal in Lippe occurred at a time when the territorial
government first made a serious effort to establish an early
modern institutionalized territorial state. This meant, however,
that the traditional consensus between city and territory, the
territorial prince and the political elite of Lemgo, had been
fundamentally shaken. After the city of Lippstadt, a few decades older and at first of equal importance, had become an
exclave and was subject to the joint sovereignty of Lippe and
Kleve, Lemgo became the cornerstone of the domain of Lippe,
since it was the most important city of the medieval domain
that was located in the core area of the later territory. The
coalition between the dynastic family *zur Lippe* and the financially powerful merchant and artisan citizenry of Lemgo created the foundation for the quite exceptional rise of the ruling
family of Lippe out of numerous Westphalian dynasties to territorial rule and later to the status of imperial counts. Hence it
was only natural that representatives of the urban political elite
were continually recruited as influential advisors of the territorial prince during the Middle Ages. The provision of the so-

---

29 H. Hamelmann, Historia renati Evangelii in ecclesia urbis Lemgoviensis
comirarus Lippiae Westphalorum, in: E. C. Wasserbach (ed.), Opera genealogico-
historica, Lemgo 1711, 1057-1081, here 1060.

called "*pactum unionis*," which allowed the burgomasters of
Lemgo and Lippstadt to choose the Count's heir in the case of
a disputed succession and required the territorial nobility and
the smaller cities to endorse their decision,[30] is indicative of
the distribution of political power and social prestige within
the medieval territory of Lippe. For the County of Lippe the
erection of a unified territorial state meant in the first instance
an elimination of the "local autonomy" (*Punktherrschaft*)[31] of
Lemgo as well as the subjugation of its political elite under the
authority of the Count. Once the most important ally of the
medieval aristocratic lords of Lippe, Lemgo's citizenry had
become the chief opponent of the early modern imperial Count
of the Lippe territorial state. This threat of political and social
decline for the burgher elite of Lemgo was emerging at the
same time as the economic and political rise of the nobility,
who no longer subdivided all of their land into peasant holdings but started to build up large estates, managed by stewards.
After the mid-1530's the territorial estates were no longer
dominated by the political elite of Lemgo, but by the landed
nobility. Both developments could not continue without consequences for the position of the urban elite.[32] (252) Naturally it
would be wrong to attribute Count Simon V's choice to support
Catholicism directly to his interests as a territorial prince and
to the interests of the territorial state. However, once the decision was made—we can ignore the reasons here—it immediately became a factor of greatest importance within the confrontation between city and territorial state. Apart from the
dictates of his own conscience, it was for the Count a question
of territorial *raison d'état* to make his decision in favor of
Catholicism binding upon all his subjects, especially upon the
citizenry of Lemgo. The military subjugation of Lippstadt by
the Count together with the Duke of Kleve shows that the
Count was conscious of this.[33] At the same time the Lutheran

---

30 Urkunde (Charter) of the year 1368, in: Lippische Regesten, edited by 0.
Preuß and A. Falkmann, 4 vols., Lemgo and Detmold 1860-68, No. 1189.

31 This expression was coined by Heinz Stoob, Westfälische Beiträge zum Verhältnis von Landesherrschaft und Städtewesen, in: Westfälische Forschungen 21
(1968), 69- 97, here 96.

32 During the Middle Ages the nobility of Lippe lived within the towns. Only
at the beginning of the sixteenth century did the nobles leave the towns and live
on their estates. W. Meyer, Guts- und Leibeigentum in Lippe, in: Jahrbuch für
Nationalökonomie und Statistik, 3. Folge, vol. 12, 1896, 801-831, esp. 813ss.

33 Lippstadt was part of a co-dominion of the Counts of Lippe and the Dukes

Reformation became for Lemgo a sign of its independence and liberty.

The conflict was triggered by a series of concrete individual questions, particularly jurisdiction and arrangements for levying taxes and a delimitation of city and princely rights within the countryside surrounding Lemgo, the so-called *Feld-mark*. The Count sought to gain direct control over this rural district by settling his peasants there, by attempting to exercise direct administrative control over its use by the citizenry, and by seeking to remove it from municipal control in general. The citizenry of Lemgo as a whole, not only particular groups within it, began immediately to resist these policies. The commune and the guildsmen were the first to take the initiative in these secular controversies as they had in the religious question, and they forced the city council to take a firm stand. This situation, which can be found in other territorial cities at the beginning of the sixteenth century as well, shows that the broad social basis of urban burgher self-confidence and independence had not yet been shaken and that all burgher groups felt threatened by the advance of the territorial state. Obviously this was also the case even for the lower stratum and for non-burgher groups among the city's inhabitants.

Members of the political elite were particularly affected by this in so far as the independent, underived character of their authority as urban magistrates was now in jeopardy. In theory their authority as rulers was based upon medieval privileges given by the territorial lord. Since, however, they were no longer delegated by the prince directly, the authority of the city council was considered to be based upon the city's political autonomy. It was not (253) by accident that the Count of Lippe tried to gain direct influence upon the recruitment of the urban governmental bodies for the first time during the Reformation epoch. He began to exercise his formal right to grant permission for electing the city council, which he gave annually to the burghers of Lemgo, as a starting point for the subjugation of the urban elite under the supervision of the territorial state.[34] In spite of its sympathy with the religious

---

of Kleve. See H. Niemöller, Reformationsgeschichte von Lippstadt, der ersten evangelischen Stadt in Westfalen, Halle 1906; H. Klockow, Stadt Lippe-Lipp-stadt, Lippstadt 1964.

34 In the founding charter the ruler had granted that neither he nor his successors would appoint town councillors without the consent of the burgher com-

convictions of the Catholic Count and its own antipathy toward the burgher Reformation movement, the urban elite had to be careful, for its own sake, not to discredit in principle the demands of the commune for the right of autonomy in central questions that affected the citizenry as a whole. Thus the city council had to counter all the attempts of the territorial ruler to interfere directly in the internal affairs of the city, even if this would have supported their own religious and political position.

When faced with the decision of submitting either to a restriction of its internal authority by the burgher corporation or to closer supervision by the territorial prince, the city council finally divided into two factions. A smaller part of the elite, which, however, comprised the most important political leaders including both Catholic burgomasters, Konrad Flörken and Christian Kleinsorge, was clearly ready to ally itself with the Count in order to resist the demands of the burgher commune for an equal share in political power as well as to defend the old faith. When their willingness to make concessions to the Count in negotiations became public, it was interpreted by the citizenry as treason and constituted grounds for forcibly banishing the council from the city as mentioned above. Some individual councillors remained Catholic even after a compromise between the council and the citizentry had been negotiated by Philipp of Hesse, and they gave up their public offices. Flörken, one of the burgomasters dismissed from office, refused even to return to the city. He was by that time obviously completely committed to the territorial prince. Armed with all the necessary privileges he proceeded to develop a farm into an estate similar to that of a knight, clearly in order to lay the foundation for his family to live independently of the city. He was, however, unsuccessful. The Flörken "burgher-knightly" estate foundered in the course of the sixteenth century. Konrad's son Florinus, who became a burgomaster of Lemgo in 1537, was an adherent of the Reformation and played a decisive role in the task of organizing the new Lutheran city church.

It must be stressed that already before 1532, while the magistrate as an institution still pursued a clearly anti-Reformation policy, there was no consensus favoring a rejection of Protestantism among the city councillors, much less within the

---

munity. During the late Middle Ages the rulers had lost any influence on the recruitment of the town council.

wider elite circle.[35] It is noteworthy that the (254) barriers hindering acceptance of the new faith were easier to cross for members of the elite who were not invested with city councillor offices at that time. Some of them had not only become adherents of Lutheranism but were even apparently leaders of the Protestant burgher movement. By 1532 there were thus Protestants available from the traditional ruling circles who could take over the direction of the city council.

The changes introduced in connection with the Reformation led neither to a constitutional change nor a social change in the city's leadership. The urban constitution, written down in the so-called *Regimentsnottel* of 1491, which regulated entry to the city council, remained in force and unchanged. The government remained more or less in the hands of the old families, who were all Lutheran by the middle of the century at the latest. In so far as there was social displacement within the recruitment of the city council—such as the entry of members of the *Hökeramt*, the guild of grocers, or the increased influence of jurists—it represented a long-term change and played no decisive role for the Reformation, but it was also not interrupted by it.[36] The changes of personnel in the city leadership can best be described as an acceleration of the normal process of change and succession. The group of "fathers" who were in power and bore governing responsibility responded to the Reformation by temporizing or rejecting it; they were replaced by a group of "sons" who, while not excluded from power in principle, were excluded at that time and who quickly accepted the new faith.[37] That no Catholic family tradition could be built up is, from a long-term point of view, certainly connected with the fact that after the death of Simon V in 1536 the Reformation was also introduced in the territory, under the decisive influence of Philipp of Hesse who had raised the young Count of Lippe at his court.

The city and its citizenry emerged strengthened from the Reformation period and the first phase of acute confrontation with the territorial prince that accompanied it. Similar to a number of other lower German cities—Brunswick, Wesel, and

---

35 E.g. the treasurer Johannes Deiterding had already become Lutheran at the end of the 1520's: Hamelmann, Historia (note 29), 1059, 1060.

36 Geiger, Elite (note 27).

37 The burgomasters who entered office through the Reformation movement were young men at that time.

Emden to name a few—the proceedings in and around Lemgo do not fit the model of the so-called "princely Reformation," which unilaterally served the interests of the territorial princes and contributed to the building of territorial states, not least by subjugating the cities. The introduction of the Reformation in opposition to the territorial prince inevitably meant at the same time an increase in political independence. Attempts to integrate the city fully into the territory and to supervise it by a central administration (255) under the authority of the territorial prince had lost their basis for a long time to come. The situation was most clearly manifested in the fact that Lemgo, even after the end of the 1530's, when the Reformation had also triumphed in the remainder of the county, was able to avoid not only formal subordination under the territorial church and its ordinances,[38] but still in 1586 could set down in a statute book issued by the city council the comprehensive legal and administrative instructions necessary for an autonomous city church.

The major beneficiary of this development was, however, not the citizenry as a whole, but the political elite. These events in the sphere of ecclesiastical renewal, and particularly their organizational consequences, brought about, from a long-term perspective, an important consolidation and even an extension of its social and political predominance. Although the Protestant movement had obligated the city council to heed the will of the burgher commune, it had at the same time made the council's independence from the territorial prince more pronounced. When the polarized confrontation between the city council and the citizenry was resolved, the limitation of councillor authority by the burgher corporation, which forced it to uphold the common interests of the citizenry, became less and less important. What remained was a solidified claim to urban administrative and governmental authority which was not derived from another authority and which was not, in its origins, directly delegated by the territorial prince. Still more important was the establishment of the council's authority within the newly founded city church. Since the magistrate was now Prot-

---

38 Lemgo and the territory of Lippe introduced two different church ordinances. See J. F. G. Goeters, Die evangelischen Kirchenordnungen Westfalens, in: Westfälische Zeitschrift 113 (1963), 111-168, esp. 133ss.; R. Stupperich, Der Lemgoer Streit um die Glaubensgerechtigkeit, in: Lippische Mitteilungen aus Geschichte und Landeskunde 39 (1970), 33-85.

estant, nothing prevented it from doing so. As a result, the congregational beginnings of Lutheranism faded increasingly into insignificance. Since the administration of the church included also discretionary power over marital matters, the schools, and education in general, as well as poor relief and social welfare, it represented a considerable broadening, both quantitatively and qualitatively, of the authority of the political elite over the burgher commune when compared with the Middle Ages. To this was added control of church property, which the magistrate administered together with the so-called *Kirchendechen*, congregational representatives who were recruited overwhelmingly from city council families. This opened up new opportunities to provide well-endowed benefices for members of their own circle including, for example, grants for students. The right of appointment to parishes and Latin schools offered similar opportunities, (256) creating not only further support positions, but also extending the influence of the burgher elite into the educational and sacral spheres. This, together with the higher prestige enjoyed by the city council because of the broadening of its jurisdiction over the church, must have significantly solidified the social and political position of the urban burgher elite, even without a formal claim to authority by divine right.

The final decision in the confrontation between Lemgo and the territorial state of Lippe, which had been delayed by Lemgo's successful struggle for autonomy during the Reformation epoch, occurred during the seventeenth century. It can only be mentioned in passing that this confrontation took place within a legal framework and an historical climate which had substantially worsened for the territorial cities. Lemgo can be numbered among those cities where the second stage of the conflict also occurred under the confessional banner: Count Simon VI was an important ruler who, together with the territorial civil servants, whose number and influence had grown substantially since the first confrontation, had converted to Calvinism and sought to impose upon the city once and for all the principle of the territorial state together with the Second Reformation.[39] Lemgo and its citizenry rallied around Lutheranism to resist this policy. In the resulting conflicts I would

---

39 Discussed in detail in H. Schilling (ed.), Die reformierte Konfessionalisierung in Deutschland. Das Problem der "Zweiten Reformation", Gütersloh 1986.

like to trace only those social consequences that affected the political elite, because the social changes within the elite which had begun during the Lutheran Reformation reached their final stage here.

The conflict over the Second Reformation lay in the center of a renewed broad spectrum of conflict between city and territorial prince, whose focal points were partly the same as those at the time of the Lutheran Reformation.[40] On the level of internal city politics a burgher movement appeared once again. (257) The burghers now sought not to change but to preserve the ecclesiastical and religious status quo, that is, to defend the Lutheran city church against the introduction of Calvinism by the territorial prince. The independent city church and Lutheran confessional stance were potent symbols because they were the reminders of the historical accomplishment of the burgher corporation during the Reformation period. An important new social factor, which had as yet played no role in the Lutheran Reformation, was the struggle against the civil servants and the rising bureaucracy of the territorial state. Most of the territorial civil servants lived in Lemgo and were regarded as an alien element within the urban burgher world. With the rise of these groups, who gained importance as the early modern bureaucracy in Lippe expanded after the mid-sixteenth century, the situation of the Lemgo elite changed at the same time. Now a genuine alternative to an urban burgher existence was open to them in the form of a burgher life in the territory that was independent of the city, such as burgomaster Konrad Flörken had sought as an individual after his break with the Lutheran movement during the 1530's.[41] The middle stratum of the citizenry saw only danger in these social and political changes. For the members of the elite, by contrast, territorial state-building was a neutral phenomenon which could be either a threat or an opportunity because they had the chance to obtain an academic education. If the members of the urban elite were prepared to dispense with their traditional positions in the urban sphere and accept the new principle of the state, they could expect new leadership responsibilities within the territorial state and at the same time new economic

---

40 A. Falkmann, Beitrage zur Geschichte des Fürstentums Lippe nach archi-valischen Quellen, vols. 3-6: Graf Simon VI. zur Lippe und seine Zeit, 1554-1617, Lemgo and Detmold 1869-1902.

41 See above, pp. 79-80.

opportunities. The new type of academically trained lawyer or jurist, serving the territorial state and its bureaucracy, enjoyed a social prestige that was not inferior to that of the medieval urban burghers and his future prospects were doubtless better than those that a member of the traditional urban elite could anticipate.

The political elite of Lemgo came to a parting of ways in these years. Its members had to choose between the traditional urban system with its well-established political, social, and economic privileges and the modern territorial system with new legal and social standards, by which the authority of the political elite and also its prestige and power were no longer rooted in the principle of urban autonomy, but were derived from princely sovereignty. The result of this choice is indicated by the reaction of the members of the Lemgo elite to the Second Reformation. The city council divided into two factions, one oriented toward the urban burgher commune which defended Lutheranism and took over the leadership of the burgher resistance, as a result expanding its position within the urban system. The other party sided with the territory. The latter overwhelmingly converted to the Calvinist position of the territorial prince and took advantage of opportunities within the territorial bureaucracy. Generation after generation their families served as territorial civil servants, some of whom later rose into the nobility. What decided the matter for either side cannot be determined. The two elite factions cannot be distinguished either by their commercial (258) or entrepreneurial activities, their land holdings in the territory or the possession of a juristic-academic education. It can be said, however, that a shorter family tradition in Lemgo made it easier to side with the territorial prince.[42]

III

The conclusions reached through analysis of a single case must now be compared with the processes at work in other cities of the neighboring Westphalian and more distant lower-Saxon and northwestern German regions. It is not possible within the scope of this essay to compare them at every point, but such a comparison is even unnecessary for our approach to the prob-

---

[42] These are the results of a prosopographic analysis. See Schilling, Konfessionskonflikt (note 23).

lem.[43] I will restrict my analysis to the constellation of forces
within the three-way struggle, the situation of the political
elite resulting from it, its attitude toward Lutheranism and
especially the consequences of the Reformation for its composition and recruitment. The arguments employed by the individual burgher movements will be left out of consideration as
will the question of the connecting links between religious,
social, and political developments. What has been discussed in
the case of Lemgo can be regarded as an exemplar for these
points.

I will turn my attention first to the Welfish city of *Brunswick*,[44] whose early modern history shows some parallels with
Lemgo despite the fact that Brunswick was a much larger city.
The similarities are especially striking with respect to the conflict between the city and the territorial state. In the case of
Brunswick this conflict also started early in the sixteenth century, but was only decided during the seventeenth century,
though, in contrast the Lemgo, to the detriment of the city.[45]
While confessional questions (259) played no role in this conflict, problems of the church and ecclesiastical constitution no
doubt did, particularly the question of who would have authority over the Lutheran city church——the city council or the territorial ruler. In the case of Brunswick the social history of the
Reformation must also be seen within the context of a continuous time period of one and a half centuries.

The course of the Reformation can be characterized as comparatively peaceful when seen against a background of pre-
Reformation burgher unrest that was especially strongly
expressed in Brunswick for a final time during the years 1512-
1514 in the so-called "revolution of poverty" (*Aufruhr der
Armut*)[46] which forced a further adjustment of the constitution.[47] The city was completely spared from the uprisings of

---

43 The following argumentation is based on printed material.

44 O. Mörke, Rat und Bürger in der Reformation. Soziale Gruppen und kirchlicher Wandel in den welfischen Hansestädten Lüneburg, Braunschweig und Göttingen, Hildesheim 1983.

45 Querfurth, Unterwerfung (note 11).

46 W. Spieß, Geschichte der Stadt Braunschweig im Nachmittelalter, 1491 bis
1671, 2 vols., Brunswick 1966, here 36-42.; R. Barth, Argumentation und Selbstverständnis der Bürgeropposition in städtischen Auseinandersetzungen des Spätmittelalters, 2nd ed., Köln 1976.

47 The first dissemination of Lutheranism can be detected between the years
1521-1524; a Lutheran burgher movement formed in 1527; after May of 1528 the
Reformer Johannes Bugenhagen was active in the town; with the acceptance of

1525, although Lutheranism was already much stronger in
Brunswick than in places such as Münster and Osnabrück,
which had strong burgher movements in the year of the
Peasants' War. During the years 1527-1528, however, a strong
burgher movement espousing the Reformation was formed.
This independent activity of the burghers was already politically explosive since there was in Brunswick an explicit constitutional prohibition against autonomous assemblies of the
citizenry without the formal consent of the city council. This
protection of the civic magistrate against spontaneous expressions of burgher opinion, introduced during the fifteenth century and expanded in 1513 to cover also the regular representative bodies[48] of the commune, could not withstand the
religiously based claim to self-determination by the "Christian
commune."[49] Certainly in the present context (260) older communal and corporate ideals of the citizenry were reactivated.
The burghers did not rely upon their constitutionally sanctioned representatives, the twenty-eight guild masters from the
fourteen guilds with political rights and the twenty-eight *Bürgerhauptleute* as representatives of the community outside of
the guilds. They chose additional "appointees" (*Vorordnete*)
whose "duty was to press the religious cause upon the city
council."[50]

It is not easy to evaluate the role of this extraordinary
burgher committee. On the one hand the prevailing opinion
that it soon lost its function cannot be correct, for it appeared
in the year 1530—still or again?—as a party negotiating with
the city council about complaints of the burgher commune,
regarding both ecclesiastical affairs, such as the vestiges of

---

his church ordinance by the council and the community on September 5 the town
became officially Lutheran; in 1531 it joined the Schmalkadic League.

48 After 1513 the "Bürgerhauptleute", the representatives of the community
who were not guild members, were bound by oath not to come together without
the consent of the council (J. Walter, Rat und Bürgerhauptleute in Braunschweig
1576-1604, Brunswick 1971, 24). See W. Spieß, Die Ratsherren der Hansestadt
Braunschweig 1231-1671, 2nd ed., Brunswick 1970, especially the introduction on
the history of the constitution of the town.

49 In August of 1528 the smiths protested against the councils' view that it was
a revolutionary action: "Daraus ergibt sich aber noch nicht, daß Versammlungen,
von denen kein Aufruhr zu besorgen, schädlich ... seien; wieviel weniger denn
solche, darin man der Christenheit zum Frommen von der Wahrheit und Kraft
des Evangelii handelt". (Quoted in: L. Hänselmann (ed.): Bugenhagens Kirchenordnung für die Stadt Braunschweig, Wolfenbüttel 1885, LI.)

50 P. J. Rehtmeier, Antiquitates ecclesiasticae inclytae urbis Brunsvigae oder
Der berühmten Stadt Braunschweig Kirchen-Historie, part 3, Brunswick 1713, 33.

Catholicism, and secular ones, including the police ordinance
(*Polizeiordnung*) and city law.[51] On the other hand the regular
representatives of the commune had already gained ground
immediately after the appointment of the extraordinary committee. At the end of August, after the burgher commune had
agreed to the proposed church ordinance drawn up by Bugenhagen, the twenty eight guild masters and the twenty-eight
Bürgerhauptleute could once again claim to be the undisputed
spokesmen of the burghers.[52] However, when, on February 3,
1528, the first embassy around the reformer Heinrich Winckel
was dispatched, apart from a city councillor one of the
"appointees," Autor Sander, was also present. Yet in May,
when Johannes Bugenhagen was successfully called the call was
made exclusively by members of the city council or the magistrate.[53] (261)

The case was similar with respect to the political implications of the Reformation movement. Indeed, in Brunswick both
religious and secular complaints appeared together. The most
politically explosive part of the movement's program was its
protest against the prohibition of assemblies of the commune
without the formal consent of the city council. This protest was
lodged when the proposed church ordinance was to be formally
approved by the citizenry and it was supported by several
corporations, most decisively by the Smiths' Guild.[54] Despite
the activities of the burgher commune, the position of the city
council and the traditional elite group was never called into
question and was never in any serious danger. The situation
again became tense after the departure of Bugenhagen because
of the activities of "sectarian" preachers, probably Zwinglians.
However, in Brunswick neither the inter-Protestant antagonisms nor the removal of images of the saints, which in other

---

51 See Mörke, Rat (note 44).

52 See the introduction in Hänselmann, Bugenhagens (note 49); 0. Hesse, Ein
Beitrag zur Vorgeschichte von Bugenhagens Braunschweiger Kirchenordnung von
1528, in: Jahrbuch der Gesellschaft für niedersächsische Kirchengeschichte 64
(1966), 62-69.

53 Spieß, Geschichte (note 46), 57ss.; P. Tschackert, Autor Sander, der "große
Freund des Evangeliums". Ein Mitarbeiter an der Reformation zu Braunschweig,
Hildesheim und Hannover, in: Zeitschrift der Gesellschaft für niedersächsische
Kirchengeschichte 9 (1904), 1-21.

54 The statement of the smiths' guild quoted in note 49 continues: Assemblies
for the sake of evangelical truth and against "eingerissene Mißbräuche" are not a
revolt; "und solche Versammlungen zu halten, wollen wir Macht haben"
(Hänselmann). Their statement was unconvincing to the authorities.

places usually resulted in a general protest movement, provoked a political or social uprising against the city council in the true sense of the word. This attests to the remarkable flexibility of the Brunswick constitution. The institutionalized form of communal representation had served in such a way that the burgher movement, despite the appointment of an extraordinary committee, functioned more or less along constitutional lines. Above all the *Bürgerhauptleute*, the representatives of the commune outside of the guilds, maintained their loyalty to the city council during the Reformation period.[55] In addition, the burgher corporation and the magistrate were accustomed to solve their problems by negotiation, since the city council received the accumulated complaints of each precinct annually after the election of the *Bürgerhauptleute*.[56]

With regard to "foreign policy," Brunswick came into a sharp confrontation on account of the Reformation with Duke Heinrich the Younger of Brunschwick-Wolfenbüttel, the most important of the Welfish overlords of the city and a supporter of the old faith.[57] In contrast to Lippe, in the case of Brunswick these conflicts in the wake of the Reformation had already reached the second stage of the struggle to reshape the relationship between city and territory. After the defeat of Heinrich the Elder in the "Great City Strife" (*Grossen Stadtfehde*, 1491-94) his son Heinrich the Younger (1514-42/68) had had no other alternative, given the severe fiscal crisis of the Duchy, but to confirm all the (262) city's privileges without reservation and then to suspend all territorial encroachments upon them. Yet the situation changed again to Brunswick's disadvantage with the Duke's success in the "*Hildesheimer Stiftsfehde*," which took place between 1519-1523 and which augmented not only his territory, but also his reputation and power.[58] Although there were no direct confrontations, the citizens and the council were certainly aware that from the beginning of the 1520's the duke was again pursuing his

---

55 Walter, Rat (note 48), 10, 25. Only in the last quarter of the sixteenth century did the council and the Bürgerhauptleute oppose each other.

56 See Walter, Rat (note 48), 13ss.

57 The city of Brunswick was a condominium of all branches of the Welf dynasty. However, the most important of the rulers was the Duke of Brunswick-Wolfenbüttel, whose territory surrounded the town. See the maps in: Spieß, Geschichte (note 46), vol. 2.

58 Spieß, 47; E. Döll, Die Kollegiatsstifte St. Blasius und St. Cyriacus zu Braunschweig, Brunswick 1967, 59s.

father's ambition to erect an early modern territorial state[59] and that he would sooner or later also resume his attempts to integrate Brunswick, the most important of his cities, into the territorial system. Protection of internal civic peace and a defense or rebuilding of civic unity were the needs of the hour. This could only happen, as the internal situation after 1527 shows, if the city council adopted Lutheranism.

A further political consideration probably made this process simpler. Ducal rights over ecclesiastical institutions within the city[60] were a dangerous focal point for the expansion of princely influence. Heinrich sought zealously to establish his authority in ecclesiastical matters within the city. The majority of the city councillors became convinced that the Reformation was an ideal means for counteracting this threat. They realized this at the very latest when the discussions with Bugenhagen concerning the form and shape of the new Protestant church took place. The church ordinance that was finally passed silently ignored all the ecclesiastical rights of the territorial ruler within the city and transferred them into the hands of the city council.[61] Another aspect of the confrontation between the city and the duke concerned the countryside surrounding Brunswick: during the late Middle Ages the city had gained political and legal authority over several villages and law courts, but the duke wished to curtail this influence. During the Reformation period it soon became clear to the political elite that the city's presence in these areas could be further consolidated if it were able to extend Protestantism and the city council's ecclesiastical authority to these parts of the countryside.[62] This must have been of special interest to the land-owning city council families. And finally, the inclination of the elite toward Protestantism was strengthened by the fact that the independence of Brunswick could only be advanced if

---

59 See B. Krusch, Die Entwicklung der Herzogl. Braunschweigischen Central-behörden, Canzlei, Hofgericht und Consistorium bis zum J. 1584, in: Zeitschrift des Historischen Vereins für Niedersachsen 1893, 201-315; 1894, 39-179; and H. Samse, Die Zentralverwaltung in den südwelfischen Landen vom 15. bis zum 17. Jahrhundert, Hildesheim/Leipzig 1940.

60 Including most of the urban parish churches. See E. Sehling, Die evangelischen Kirchenordnungen des 16. Jahrhunderts, VI/1 Niedersachsen, Die welfischen Lande, Die Fürstentümer Wolfenbüttel und Lüneburg mit den Städten Braunschweig und Lüneburg, Tübingen 1955, 338ss.; E. Döll, Kollegiatsstifte (note 58), 60ss.

61 Sehling, Kirchenordnungen (note 60).

62 Spieß, 74ss., as well as the map in the appendix of the second fascicle, 789.

the city joined the Lutheran confession of the "distant" overlord in Lüneburg, to gain protection against their Catholic overlord in nearby Wolfenbüttel.[63] Thus in the case of Brunswick the decision in favor of Lutheranism was an attack by the city in the struggle against the threat to civic liberty posed by the territorial state of Brunswick-Wolfenbüttel.[64] The magistrate was able to advance this policy decisively by rejecting the Catholic demands of the Duke of Wolfenbüttel at the *Landtag* of Salzdahlum (at the end of February and the beginning of March 1531) and especially through Brunswick's entry into the Schmalkaldic League the following summer. A decade later the League expelled Duke Heinrich from his territory.[65]

A number of important preconditions for a comparatively quick and frictionless religious change were present in Brunswick. These included a relatively high external pressure to reach an internal consensus together with the opportunity to improve measurably the town's initial position for an unavoidable conflict with the territorial prince who sought expansion, a burgher Reformation movement without any clearly expressed points of contention with the political elite and the city council's practice of heeding burgher grievances. As a result the urban political elite, who at first rejected Lutheranism and then temporized, eventually came around to the Protestant position held by the majority of the burghers. The plausibility of the Reformation ethos of a Christian government and the prospect of (264) a far-reaching right of administration within the new church order probably supported this development, for they lowered the primary barriers which stood in the way of a quick acceptance of the new faith by the Brunswick city council families, who—like their peers in Lemgo—had close ties of interest, mentality, and religion with the medieval church.

Participation in this development by some of the clergy who were related to the burgher upper stratum is noteworthy.

---

63 ibid., 49s., 72.

64 Membership in the Schmalkaldic League was in some respects a new attempt to get rid of the ruler, similar to the late medieval attempt "to switch from the Welf dynasty to the bishops of Hildesheim" (Spieß, Ratsherren, note 48). At the beginning of the seventeenth century there was a similar political constellation through the city's alliance with the Netherlands.

65 In 1542 Duke Heinrich was expelled from his territory by the victorious Schmalkadic League; in 1547, after the victory of Emperor Charles V, he returned, but Brunswick was able to keep its independence.

During the 1520's the abbot of Ägidii, Magister Thiederich
Koch, probably a member of the city council family of that
name, had worked closely with the magistrate in the fight
against Lutheranism as presiding officer of a corporative
alliance of all higher clergy within the city, the so-called
Union. In 1533 he attended the University of Wittenberg and
afterwards worked as Protestant preacher in Brunswick until
his death. When the *Kreuzkloster*, the most important institution that provided benefices for the daughters of the upper
burgher stratum, was reformed in 1532, the abbess Gertrude
Holle, who was probably the daughter of a guild city council
family, was replaced by Adelheid von Lafferde, a patrician's
daughter.[66]

No changes in personnel within the political leadership
occurred in connection with the shift to a pro-Lutheran policy.
Although two religiously differing parties can be distinguished
between 1527 and 1529 (in Brunswick terms of office on the
city council lasted three years), the church ordinance presented
by Bugenhagen in September 1528 was made legally binding
through the "normal process of law making." The Catholic
party in the city council bowed to the will of the citizenry and
the majority of their colleagues. Consequences for the composition of the city council were only evident a year later in
November 1529 during the scheduled preparations, mandated
by the constitution, for the up-coming election of the city
council in January 1530.[67] Twenty-one city councillors were
forced to give up their offices because of their Catholic faith,
although all of them were reassured that their honor remained
"unblemished."[68] Of the 103 members of the larger council a
fifth was excluded on religious grounds. Four of these persons
belonged to the smaller council of 25, the actual governing
(265) committee, but were not among its political leaders.[69] In
the place of these Catholics and others who were excluded for
other reasons, thirty new city councillors took office, all convinced partisans of the Reformation.

To what degree did this replacement of persons represent a

66 Spieß, Geschichte (note 46), 48, 52, 55, 73, 65.
67 Lists of the councillors in: Spieß, Ratsherren (note 48), 36s.
68 Quoted from Spieß.
69 Bartold Lafferde, burgomaster of Altstadt, Hans van Vechelde, treasurer,
Ludeke van Peine, burgomaster of Hagen, and Tile Kalm, treasurer. All were
members of the patriciate.

change in the social composition of the city government? Two factors suggest a change. First, there is the fact that the greatest replacement of personnel took place in Altstadt and in Hagen, to the detriment of the patriciate[70] and the merchants.[71] Second, fifteen of the thirty newly-chosen Protestants came from families that had to this point never supplied a city councillor.[72] The first observation must, however, be qualified. The heavy losses suffered by the traditional elite[73] in Altstadt and in Hagen were made up for to some degree in the district of Altewiek.[74] What is more important is the fact that we can find—among the dismissed Catholics as well as among the new Protestant councillors, though in differing proportions—members of the patricians and old guild families.[75] The same is true for councillors whose families had not previously appeared in the city council nor did so afterwards,[76] and for a third group, that of (266) "families of rising prominence" who appeared in the city council in the first or second generation and consolidated their position within the circle of the political elite during the sixteenth century, some even forming family ties with the patriciate.[77] The reaction of the latter group, the persons of rising prominence, who either as members of especially profitable crafts or of the new type of merchants and retailers, had risen to wealth and prestige, is particularly noteworthy in my opinion. Here it is also evident that as a group this type of new elite saw its political and social interests and opportunities affected neither by a choice for the old nor for

---

70 The expression "patriciate" refers to members of the old Hanseatic merchant families.

71 In Altstadt and Hagen 14 Catholics withdrew and 20 new councillors were elected. In Neustadt, Altewiek und Sack the figures were: 2:3, 2:5, 4:2 (Spieß).

72 Spieß, Ratsherren (note 48), 36s. and 65ss. (lists of councillors).

73 See W. Spieß, Der Stand der Geschlechter und der Stand der weißen Ringe. Das Problem "Patriziat und Honoratiorentum" in der Stadt Braunschweig im 16. und 17. Jahrhundert, in: Braunschweigisches Jahrbuch 30 (1949), 65-80.

74 In Altewiek two Catholics from families without a tradition of council membership retired. Four of the five new councillors elected in this part of Brunswick belonged to families whose members had served on the council at least since the middle of the fifteenth century, some of them since the thirteenth century.

75 Thus it is misleading to call them "homines novi", as Spieß, Ratsherren (note 48), 36, does.

76 See Mörke, Rat (note 44).

77 Catholics: Hans Binder, Diderik Behre, Henrik Schrader the Elder, Hans Damman. Protestants: Dirk Binder, Henrik Schrader the Younger, Henning Damman, Frederik Vaders, Sander Bergmann (Spieß, 36s. and an alphabetical list, 63ss.)

the new faith. Members of the same families, even fathers and sons, can be identified on opposing sides in 1529 and 1530.[78] This is also true, incidentally, for members of old city council families.[79] The political and social significance of the city council purge is relativized by this finding, because only two of the Protestants who entered the city council in 1530 advanced into the smaller council, where they formed a small minority,[80] and because only two of the families succeeded in founding (267) significant political traditions.[81] Even after 1530 the crucial offices remained in the hands of the traditional elite, that is the patriciate and the guild *Honoratiorentum*. Of all the newly elected city councillors of 1530 it was the members of these groups who dominated the smaller council during the following decades and who were invested with the important burgomaster offices.[82] These families set the tone for the entire sixteenth century in the Brunswick city council, giving the impression that their position was strengthened rather than weakened by the Reformation.[83]

Despite the fact that even in Brunswick the dynamic for the Protestant movement was supplied by broad segments of the

78 Hans and Dirk Binder (brothers or cousins), Henrik the Elder and Henrik the Younger Schrader (father and son, see H. Schrader, Zur Geschichte des Braunschweigischen Stadt- und Ratsgeschlechtes Schrader, Mitteilungen des Familienverbandes Schrader e.V., No. 30, 1935), Hans and Henning Damman, Henning and Hans Lüders, Diderik and Hans Behre (Spieß).

79 Tile and Albert Kalm, Bodo III und Bodo IV Glümer (Spieß, Ratsherren, 114); Hans von Vechelde and his nephew Cort (W. Spieß, von Vechelde. Die Geschichte einer Braunschweiger Patrizierfamilie, Brunswick 1951, 56); Bartold II Lafferde left the council as a Catholic; in 1532 a niece of his, Adelheid von Lafferde, became the first Protestant abbess at the Kreuzkloster, which had just been reformed (Spieß, Geschichte, note 46, 65); his son Bartold III had studied in Wittenberg and was an admirer of Luther (K. von Laffert, Geschichte des Geschlechts von Laffert, Göttingen 1957, 44, 47ss.).

80 Hans Simon, who became Kleinbürgermeister already in 1530 and Großbürgermeister in 1542, and Hans Mygen, first treasurer, later burgomaster. Mygen remained the only member of his family in the council; of the members of the Simon family only one other person was elected councillor in the last quarter of the century.

81 These were the Vaders and Bergmann families. Of the 13 others elected as councillors for the first time, 8 remained the only council members of their families; the other 5 later on had some occasional successors, but these did not have any political influence.

82 See the careers of Tile Broitzem, Cort van Damm, Albert Kalm, and Henrik Bardenwerper.

83 This was only changed by the revolt of 1614. See W. Spieß, Die Braunschweiger Revolution von 1614 und die Demokratisierung der Ratsverfassung 1614-71, in: Jahrbuch des Braunschweiger Geschichtsvereins, 2nd series, 7 (1935), 55-71.

citizenry, above all by the artisans, the Reformation does not mark a significant social break either in the general history of the city or the composition of its political elite. There was no lasting change in the recruitment of the ruling elite. The numerical proportion of city council seats, unchanged since 1346, allotted to the individual guilds and to the non-guild burghers of the five precincts, who gave clear preference to the members of the five "aristocratic corporations,"[84] does not appear to have been called into question during the first third of the century. (268) Only the changes, especially economic ones, of the following decades caused a "striking incongruity between the economic weight of particular guilds or precincts and their representatives in the city council."[85] At the beginning of the seventeenth century this became the focus of burgher protests. As a consequence of the Revolution of 1614 a fundamental change occurred in the method of electing the city council.[86] The political elite committed itself to Lutheranism only after a clear delay and was divided into two camps. This division did not, however, signal a shift from one elite group to another. It seized patricians and old guild families in the same way as people of rising prominence from the new *Honoratiorentum* and, incidentally, the important special group of legally educated magisterial civil servants.[87] The division was an affair that lasted only a few years and had no significant political or social consequences for the recruitment of the political elite. It affected one generation and was the result of decisions made by individuals, not by families or family networks.

What influenced individual choices would have to be studied on a person-by-person basis. For example, the treasurer of the *Bruch* precinct, Tile Kalm, who was removed from his office

---

84 Spieß, Fernhändlerschicht und Handwerkmasse, 85; Walter, Rat (note 48), 27; chapter 11,1: "Der Verlust des ausgewogenen Verhältnisses zwischen wirtschaftlicher Macht und politischem Einfluß".

85 Walter, Rat (note 48), 27.

86 Walter identifies the Bürgerhauptleute as a pressure group of those members of the economic elite who did not belong to the city council. For the new members see the list in Spieß, Ratsherren (note 48), 47.

87 Among the leading Protestants we find Autor Sander, since 1533 elected syndic of Hanover (Spieß, Geschichte, note 46, 55ss., 725s.), and Levin van Emden, first syndic to the council of Brunswick (ibid., 55, 70, 726). The second syndic, Dietrich Prüsse, in contrast, belonged to the core of the Catholic group in the council (ibid., 55, 61). After the decision in favor of the Reformation he became Lutheran between 1532 and 1535 (ibid., 71, 75, 85).

during the Reformation, had already been removed from office
during the uprising of 1488, but was then accepted back into
the "reactionary city council."[88] Like burgomaster Flörken in
Lemgo,[89] he was one of the experienced city councillors who
valued order and authority very highly and hence must have
understood Lutheranism as nothing more than an inflammatory
ideology because of its connection with the "people's
movement." (269) However, among the Catholics and the
opponents of the Protestant burgher opposition there were also
other men with quite a different background than supporters of
law and order such as Kalm. Among them were Henrik
Schrader the elder, who was elected to the "revolutionary city
council" in 1488, and Bodo Glümer, who had served as a
spokesman for the commune while already a city councillor in
1513 during the "revolution of poverty."[90] Generalizations at
this level of individual psychology are hardly possible. However, it seems that age played a role. As a rule it was the older
city councillors who refused to accept the new doctrine.[91]
Younger members of the same elite stepped into their places,
in part their sons or relatives. How many of these new city
councillors had served previously in communal or guild offices
or had belonged to the leadership of the Reformation burgher
movement can only be established by further study.[92] Members
of the elite in the generation following the Reformation were
in any case Lutheran to a man.[93] Only after the end of the
sixteenth century were there a few Catholic city councillors
again, remarkably enough some of them descendants from
Lutherans of "the first hours."[94]

No report has been preserved that any of the city councillors
who were removed from office in 1529 because of their faith
turned their back on the Protestant city and acted against it in

88 Spieß, Ratsherren (note 48), 143.

89 See above, pp. 79-80, 83.

90 Spieß, Ratsherren (note 48), 210; H. v. Glümer, Die Familie Glümer. Ein
Beitrag zur Geschichte des Braunschweiger Patriziats, in: Braunschweigische
Heimat 24 (1933), 10-14.

91 Tile Kalm und Henrik Schrader the Elder were elected as councillors already
in the 1480's; Hans van Vechelde was an old man, too. See Spieß, Vechelde (note
79), 56.

92 See Mörke, Rat (note 44).

93 See, for example, the Vechelde family: Spieß, Vechelde (note 79), 56, 66.

94 For example, the members of the Schrader, Simon, Elers and Odelem families. See the list in: Spieß, Ratsherren (note 48).

the service of the Catholic territorial prince. From this it can
be deduced that the alternative of a "burgher" or noble life in
the territory, independent of the city, had hardly entered the
purview of the political elite in Brunswick during the Reformation epoch. The patriciate was also still heavily involved in
the grain trade and in financial dealings and remained clearly
bound to the urban economy and society.[95] Their land holdings, for some considerable, functioned to provide security for
these urban economic activities until the first third of the following century.[96] Because a large proportion of their landed
property was enfiefed (270) most of these families owed allegiance to the Welfs.[97] The suspicion of their fellow citizens
that they had thus alienated themselves from the interests of
the city[98] as "the Duke's men" finds no confirmation in the
course of the Reformation conflicts. Since the Brunswick
patriciate obviously attached little importance to a formal rise
to noble status,[99] they lacked this motive to ally themselves
with the territorial prince. And finally it appears that a career
in the territorial civil service offered few incentives to the
Brunswick patriciate. At the time of the Reformation clergy
councillors were still quite influential in the territorial administration of Wolfenbüttel—this included in part members of
monasteries and foundations within the city—and non-
residents were dominant among the councillors of the prince.[100]
Even when this finally changed the Brunswick patriciate
showed little interest in entering the service of the prince.[101]

In this respect the families of the *Honoratiorentum*,
emigrants from other cities or successful artisans from the city
itself who had risen in prominence after the end of the fifteenth century, may have acted somewhat differently. Among
individual examples it can be observed that some members of
such families were active as long-distance merchants and
financiers, exercising power in the city council in decisive

---

95 Spieß, Vechelde (note 79), esp. 69ss.; H. Mitgau, Ein patrizischer
Sippenkreis Braunschweigs um 1600, Brunswick 1976.

96 Spieß, Vechelde (note 79), 186.

97 The origin, the composition and the history of the feudal property of a
patrician family in Brunswick is described by Spieß, Vechelde (note 79), 171-189.

98 Ibid., Vechelde (note 79), 182.

99 Spieß, Stand (note 73), esp. 74ss.

100 Samse, Zentralverwaltung (note 59), 7, 21 , 42, 58 and table 53; 152ss., No.
10, 14, 15, 21.

101 This seems to be the case during the seventeenth century, too.

positions, while others, after studying law at a university, entered offices in the territorial service.[102] This phenomenon belongs, however, mainly to the post-Reformation period, and can be used to explain the territorial Reformation or confession-building,[103] but not the earlier Lutheran city Reformation.

In comparison with the developments in Brunswick it seems strange that in the neighboring city of *Lüneburg*, the political elite maintained its loyalty to the old faith for a long time and that the introduction of the Reformation occurred only with great difficulty, although Lüneburg was located in the territory of Ernst the Confessor (*der Bekenner*), one of the very first adherents of Luther among the German princes.[104] After a closer examination it becomes clear that behind this difference in confessional stance lies a very similar policy pursued by each of the political elites. The contrasting courses of the Reformation in the two Welfish cities show emphatically the degree to which the religious stance of the urban elite was influenced by the constellation of political and religious factors present in both the city and the territory. With respect to the early decision of Duke Ernst for Lutheranism the conservative ecclesiastical policy of the Lüneburg city council was, in the same way as the opposing confessional decision made by the elite of Brunswick, an attempt to oppose an expansionist territorial prince, who fought (272) with the city over a whole series of rights and privileges and who left no doubt that he wanted to tie the economically most important of his cities more closely to his territory.[105] It could not be expected that a swift acceptance of the religious decision of the territorial prince by the city would bring any relief, much less that it could resolve concrete political and economic disagreements. On the contrary, the city council had to fear that it would

---

102 E.g. the Schrader family which immigrated during the fifteenth century from a small town named Hadersleben and rose to prominence in Brunswick during the sixteenth century.

103 See Press, Stadt (note 10).

104 Moeller, Deutschland (note 1), 113. - On the Reformation in Lüneburg see Mörke, Rat (note 44). A. Wrede, Die Einführung der Reformation im Lüneburgischen durch Herzog Ernst den Bekenner, Göttingen 1887; G. Matthaei, Die Einführung der Reformation in Lüneburg vor 400 Jahren, Lüneburg 1930; K. Friedland, Der Kampf der Stadt Lüneburg mit ihren Landesherren, Stadtfreiheit und Fürstenhoheit im 16. Jahrhundert, Hildesheim 1953.

105 Friedland, Kampf (note 104), 43ss.

offer the duke the opportunity, if not to introduce a fully
developed ecclesiastical authority within the city, at least to
strengthen his presence measurably by securing a series of
ecclesiastical rights as well as through the takeover of property
previously owned by the autonomous medieval church.[106] In
contrast to those places where the cities led the way to Reformation, Lüneburg ran the risk of a "princely Reformation," in
which ecclesiastical renewal was introduced as an instrument of
territorial policy directed against municipal autonomy already
by the mid-1520's. The city council of Lüneburg recognized
this danger quite early on, as is apparent in an advisory report
in the form of a letter by the provost Johannes Coller, who as
a former magisterial office holder had an accurate picture of
the political situation of the city.[107] For the salt master
(*Sülfmeister*) patriciate, who alone were eligible for city councillor office in Lüneburg, the prospect that the duke could gain
influence over the salt trade through the secularization of
church property, the majority of which was salt-producing
property, was even more serious than such political consequences.[108] This would not only have affected the foundation
of the city's prosperity, but would have seriously weakened the
economic and social position of the *Sülfmeister* as well, and at
the same time would have called into question the monopoly of
city council positions that the *Sülfmeister* had enjoyed since
the late Middle Ages.

The experience of the Reformation as a demand made upon
the city by a territorial prince and his territorial state resulted
in the elite of Lüneburg not only maintaining its spiritual and
familial contacts with the medieval church[109] (273) but further
strengthening them. A particularly close and long-lasting
alliance was formed between the city council and the Catholic
clergy,[110] who had to work largely in secret after the rise of
the burgher Reformation movement.

As a result, in Lüneburg Lutheranism had to depend upon

---

106 Wrede, Einführung (note 104), 110ss., 146ss.

107 The letter, dated June 23, 1528, is adressed to the city council (Wrede,
Einführung, note 104, 111s.).

108 Coller's letter expressly points to this possibility.

109 W. Reinecke, Geschichte des Lüneburger Kalands, in: Jahresbericht des
Museums-Vereins für das Fürstentum Lüneburg, 1891-95, 1-54, esp. 39, 41, note
1; Matthaei, Einführung (note 104), 20.

110 Matthaei, Einführung (note 104), 32s.; Wrede, Einführung (note 104), 110-
162 passim.

the vehicle of the burgher movement even more than in other
cities. The character and course of this burgher movement
were, on the other hand, less suited to break down the barriers
that hindered acceptance of the new doctrine among the patriciate. Lüneburg had experienced comparatively little civic
unrest during the Middle Ages. In contrast to the majority of
northwestern German cities the commune had no formalized
representation.[111] Authority and administration lay completely
in the hands of the city council which at the beginning of the
sixteenth century was recruited on the basis of the principles
of cooptation and life-long tenure from the small and homogeneous circle of the salt masters, that is the leading entrepreneurs of salt production and salt trading. Within the context of
such a constitution the burgher movement supporting the
Reformation was a challenge to the ruling families, even if it
did not explicitly demand a fundamental change in the political
system. The absence of a constitutional representative body of
the commune[112] precluded any "legal" channel of expression.
The government and the "rebellious" burghers confronted each
other directly for a long period. For many years Lutheranism
retained the stigma of illegality and rebellion. The committee
of one hundred burghers and its narrower executive council,
organized by the citizenry during the years 1530-1532, was a
"revolutionary" government of the opposition with regard to
ecclesiastical politics. In the secularized St. Mary's convent
regular meetings took place, and soon all threads of the
burgher commune's religious policy ran together there.[113] The
alliance between (274) the city council and the Catholic clergy
corresponded to an alliance between the Protestant burgher
movement and the evangelical preachers which even the
moderate, government-oriented Lutheran Urbanus Rhegius
could not avoid. At times the burgher committee treated the
city council as a kind of executive body, existing to further
and impose the committee's decisions regarding ecclesiastical

---

111 W. Reinecke, Geschichte der Stadt Lüneburg, vol. 1, Lüneburg 1933; C.
Haase, Das Lüneburger Stadtrecht. Umrisse seiner Geschichte, in: U. Wendland
(ed.), Aus Lüneburgs tausendjähriger Vergangenheit, Lüneburg 1956, 67-86; H.
Heuer, Lüneburg im 16. und 17. Jahrhundert und seine Eingliederung in den
Fürstenstaat, phil. Diss. Hamburg 1969.
    112 Heuer, Lüneburg (note 111), chapter 2: "Gab es eine Bürgervertretung?",
73ss.
    113 Wrede, Einführung (note 104), 115ss., 145, 181, 193.

policies upon the clergy and the commune.[114] Its demands for
participation in the administration of secularized church property as well as the use of the municipal salt refinery[115] went
beyond the narrowly political sphere and were intended to
undermine not only the political hegemony of the salt patriciate, but also their dominant economic position. These
demands were all the more dangerous because they paralleled
the intentions of the territorial prince as has already been
described.

The political and social situation that the Lüneburg patriciate
saw itself forced into as a result of the Reformation problem—both within the city and in the rural areas under its control—must have enlarged the "primary barriers" which hindered any spontaneous, religiously-based union with Lutheranism. This was, however, only true for the short term. In
contrast to the case of Brunswick, the anti-Protestant policy of
containment instituted by the city council under the Catholic
banner was thoroughly defensive. At a certain point this policy
threatened to turn upon its supporters, since it no longer served
to protect either urban autonomy or the economic and social
interests of the political elite, but rather was perceived to be a
further danger to them. This point was reached when the possibility of an alliance between the Lutheran territorial prince
and the powerful Protestant burgher movement arose. The
forces which at first had worked to alienate the political elite
from Lutheranism were re-oriented at that point and the way
was cleared for the development of a Protestant religious
dynamic largely free from extra-religious barriers.

The attempts of the territorial prince at rapprochement with
the citizenry, its responses, the city council's turn toward the
ecclesiastical policy of the burgher committee, at first only
tactically but then increasingly religiously motivated, and the
growing confrontation over political and ecclesiastical issues
between the newly united evangelical city and its evangelical
territorial prince—these further developments cannot be
discussed here in detail. The result, however, is important: the
city council succeeded, with the support of the citizenry, in
preventing any expansion of the territorial prince's influence
within the city. (275) After the mid-1530's the religious con-

114 Wrede, Einführung (note 104), 181ss.
115 Wrede, Einführung (note 104), 145.

sensus in Lüneburg was reconstituted under the Lutheran banner. There were no political and social consequences in the sense of a constitutionally guaranteed end to the monopoly of authority enjoyed by the *Sülfmeister* patriciate. It is obvious, however, that the burgher commune had become more self-confident as a result of the Reformation and that the authorities considered it advisable that it should be more deeply and frequently involved in decision-making.[116]

Due to the lack of preparatory research it is difficult to judge the social background of this development more precisely. It can be assumed from the facts that the broad definition of an elite given at the beginning of this essay is not applicable to Lüneburg. Eligibility for councillor office was limited to a small group who shortly before the Reformation had become still more exclusive.[117] There was no wider circle of political leadership, as was present within many other cities, because the Lüneburg patriciate accepted new members only in exceptional cases, and there were no communal offices that could serve as the first step to full political rights. Further research is necessary to examine the degree to which the differing attitudes of the narrower and broader elite circles present in the other cities discussed in this study correspond to a similar phenomenon within the narrowly defined Lüneburg patriciate. In any case individual patricians could already be found among the Lutherans in the early years.[118] And after the victory of the Reformation could not be prevented any longer, some Catholic city councillors gave up their offices.[119] The decisive front, however, ran on another level. Instead of a recognizable division within the broader political elite and the swift acceptance of the Reformation by a leadership group within the city council, as occurred in the majority of the other cities, there was obviously a confrontation in Lüneburg between (276) the patriciate and groups of rising social prominence who were not eligible for the city council. Some facts[120]

116 Heuer, Lüneburg (note 111), 78ss.

117 Reinecke, Geschichte (note 111), vol. 1, 353, 378; E. Thurich, Die Geschichte des Lüneburger Stadtrechtes im Mittelalter, Lüneburg 1960, 23s.

118 Mörke, Rat (note 44); Wrede, Einführung (note 104), 144.

119 During the Reformation period of the years 1529-1533 there were six new appointments—an extraordinary high number for Lüneburg!

120 Examples of such men include Cort Jördens (Wrede, Einführung, note 104, 116) and Hans Polde (Heuer, Lüneburg, note 111, 76); Reinecke, Geschichte (note 111), vol. 1, 390.

suggest that the burgher committees supporting the Reformation were led by members of the burgher upper stratum who
had a claim to councillor office on the basis of their prestige
and wealth according to the general norms of urban burgher
life in Old Europe, but in Lüneburg were excluded from such
political participation.

When considering both the social and political factors that
influenced the reception of Lutheranism and the position of
the political elite within the Reformation movement, the
outcome in Lüneburg was comparable throughout with other
cities. Until now Lüneburg has been considered an exception
with regard to the social changes in the recruitment of the city
council. Because of the unbroken constitutional continuity, it
was thought that in the case of Lüneburg the Reformation had
no consequences for the social composition of the city council,
in contrast to almost all other northwestern German cities. Each
group won a religious victory, but neither of them a political
or social one. A study by Olaf Mörke on the personnel structure of the urban governmental bodies over a longer period of
time (from 1450 to 1599) now reveals clearly that in the time
immediately following the Reformation there was "more
frequent acceptance of city councillors who were 'non-patrician,' and not from among the masters of the salt trade, disre-
garding previous practice." These *homines novi* were recruited
from among the rising social groups, including long-distance
merchants from outside of the salt trade and manufacturing
concerns, particularly the brewers who were also advancing in
other cities as entrepreneurs of the "commercial crafts." The
burgomaster offices, however, and with them the key positions
of power, remained in the hands of the patriciate.[121]

Two further points are worth noting from the perspective of
social history. First, the fact that in Lüneburg the burgher
groups involved in manual labor were not unified in their
response to the Reformation. The salt workers, together with
the masons, carpenters, and bargemen, were plainly willing in
1533 to offer their support to the Catholic city council against
the burgher committee.[122] Second, it is worth noting that it was
in interest of the entire citizenry to maintain the city's autonomy. At a time when the council was still strongly resisting

---

121 Mörke, Rat (note 44).
122 Wrede, Einführung (note 104), 192ss.

the Reformation, the Protestant burgher committee rejected an agreement with the territorial (277) prince.[123] The readiness of the urban burghers to reach agreement, or to force agreement, which in other cities can be judged by the extent to which the city council accepted the demands of the burgher movement, is obviously characteristic of the burgher movement here as well. They were not prepared to impose their confessional demands to the detriment of the common good of the city. The urban burgher consensus was based especially upon the economic prosperity of the salt city which benefited all inhabitants, and which, it was believed, would be threatened by an advance of the territorial prince. The building of an independent Lutheran city church probably strengthened the consensus of the citizenry in Lüneburg as well. Only in the seventeenth century did an opposition appear that was not committed to the ideal of urban burgher solidarity.[124]

IV

The episcopal cities form a special category within the Reformation of the northwestern German territorial or Hanseatic cities. They can be represented by Osnabrück, Münster, and Paderborn, each of which showed remarkably different developments during the sixteenth century. With these examples we return to the region of Westphalia where the similarities with the case of Lemgo, already examined in some detail, are accordingly particularly numerous. Thus one constantly comes across burgher protests against the privatization of common rights and against the preferential allocation of communal lands to members of the political elite, but also against the authoritarian governing practices of the councils. It is worth noting that when considering the independence of the social and, in a more narrow sense, religious reform movements, these demands of the commune antedated the penetration of Lutheranism in Osnabrück and Münster, and even in Soest they were formulated relatively independently of the ecclesiastical demands. On account of the strong presence of ecclesiastical institutions, unrest in the episcopal cities had a clear anticlerical accent

---

123 Wrede, Einführung (note 104), 126; Heuer, Lüneburg (note 111), 77.

124 In 1637 Lüneburg was seized by the ruler and was given a new constitution two years later. On this problem and the conflicts within the city see Heuer, Lüneburg (note 111), 112ss.

which was not as strong in the previously discussed cases. The thesis that in Westphalia the burgher movements of the Reformation period were by and large narrowly anticlerical must, however, be rejected.[125]

The Reformation in *Osnabrück*[126] occurred in an unusually quiet fashion. In contrast to Brunswick the adjustment of city council policy to the Protestant initiative of the commune took over a decade rather than a few months. What is more remarkable is that there was almost no violence or unrest while the processes were under way. The so-called *"Oberg* uprising" of 1525 cannot be regarded as a part of the actual Reformation since evangelical demands appeared there only tangentially. When compared with other cities some characteristics of the "popular Reformation movement" in Osnabrück are striking. Lutheranism attracted the burgher commune not in one campaign, but after numerous attempts. After very superficial beginnings in the year 1525, the evangelical activities of Adolf Klarenbach followed in 1527/28, which, however, affected only a small circle. The preacher Dietrich Buthmann brought about the first significant progress in 1532. The decisive breakthrough occurred finally at the beginning of the 1540's. Between each of these waves of activity came a period during which the spread of the new doctrine stagnated or lost ground. Corresponding to this ebb and flow the activities of the burgher corporation directed toward a reshaping of the church organization were less decisive here than elsewhere. The year 1532 was an exception, when the individual parish congregations—surely not without central guidance from group fol-

---

125 The thesis that the Reformation in Westphalia was essentially an anti-clerical movement originates in the confessional historiography. See T. Legge, Flug- und Streitschriften der Reformationszeit in Westfalen 1523-1583, Münster 1933, 152. See my comments in: Wehler, Bauernkrieg (note 2), 209. The thesis is repeated by A. Schröer, Die Reformation in Westfalen, 2 vols., Münster 1983 and Dickens, Nation (note 19), 162s.

126 H. Stratenwerth, Die Reformation in der Stadt Osnabrück, Wiesbaden 1971; A. Spengler-Ruppenthal on the church ordinance of the territory and the city in: Sehling, Kirchenordnungen (note 60), vol. 7, 2nd half, 1st fascicle, Tübingen 1963; W. Berning, Das Bistum Osnabrück vor Einführung der Reformation (1543), Osnabrück 1940. See also L. Wiese-Schorn (now Schorn-Schütte), Von der autonomen zur beauftragten Selbstverwaltung. Die Integration der deutschen Stadt in den Territorialstaat am Beispiel der Verwaltungsgeschichte von Osnabrück und Göttingen in der frühen Neuzeit, in: Osnabrücker Mitteilungen 82 (1976), 29-59. Recently W. Ehbrecht, Köln-Osnabrück-Stralsund, in: Petri, Kirche (note 10), 23-63; H.-B. Meier, Unruhen und Aufstand in Osnabrück im 15. und 16. Jahrhundert, in: Osnabrücker Mitteilungen 89 (1983), 60-121.

lowing the itinerant preacher Buthmann—acted to enforce their claims by appointing Protestant preachers to every church in the city except the cathedral. (279) In so doing they violated not only the rights of the ecclesiastical institutions which were responsible for all pastoral appointments in Osnabrück, but they also opposed the religious policy of the city council which defended the old Catholic order until the beginning of the 1540's.[127] This did not result in a confrontation because of the sympathy toward Protestantism displayed by Franz von Waldeck, the territorial prince,[128] during these months and also because of the careful response of the city council. At first the council allowed the evangelical preachers to have their way and only forbade them to preach the following summer. As a result they had to leave the city within a few days. The burgher commune, which had acted so resolutely only a few months before, was now obviously unable to offer any serious resistance. In 1534 the city council was also able to defeat the nascent Anabaptist movement, supported by Münster, without any difficulty.

If an unsatisfactory source situation does not badly mislead, the linkage of the Reformation movement with the political and social demands of the burgher commune against the city council, commonly observed in other cities, was absent in Osnabrück after 1525. Only in 1532 did the itinerant preacher Buthmann question the general submissiveness with regard to religion.[129] However, no more extensive claims of the burgher commune grew out of this. It is true that immediately before the religious policy pursued by the government was changed in 1542, the Protestant movement again went on the offensive and religious pressure on the city council steadily increased, raising the possibility of a communal Reformation that would be imposed upon the political elite.[130] Nothing, however, indicated the danger of a political and social revolt. The rule of the political elite was not threatened for a moment, and it was not directly exposed to violent assaults. Obviously, after the end of

---

127 There is evidence that individual Lutherans were members of the city council at a much earlier time.

128 F. Fischer, Die Reformationsversuche des Bischofs Franz von Waldeck im Fürstbistum Münster, Hildesheim 1907.

129 Stratenwerth, Reformation (note 126), 76s.

130 Stratenwerth, Reformation (note 126), 106 (chronicle of Dietrich Lilie), 67ss., 81ss.

the 1530's, a Lutheran consensus had spread in Osnabrück from the burgher commune to the city council in a more or less hidden fashion, which could only have occurred after violent clashes in other places. In 1542 the magistrate took the initiative abruptly and led the city to the new faith within a few (280) months. Again one of the first steps was the choice of a suitable reformer. In contrast to many of the neighboring cities, representatives of the popular Reformation movement did not participate in the delegation dispatched for this purpose. It consisted of two city councillors. The way opened by the Protestant burgher movement had merged with the road of a magisterial Reformation, which nevertheless was eager to stress its legitimacy as an expression of the communal will.[131]

When considering the relations between city and territory[132] the cathedral chapter must be added in the case of a bishopric or an episcopal city to the three forces of the Reformation constellation mentioned earlier.[133] In contrast to the territorial estates in the case of the cities within secular territories, the first and most important of their estates, i.e. the cathedral chapter, cannot be left out of consideration because it had specific rights of administration and government in episcopal territories it and also had a special relationship with the prince bishop. In the case of Osnabrück the efforts made first by Erich II von Grubenhagen (1508-1532) and then by Franz von Waldeck (1532-1553) to establish an early modern territorial state with a centralized bureaucracy were directed primarily against the powers of the cathedral chapter, not against the cities.[134] In this respect the case of Osnabrück differed sharply from the neighboring episcopal territory of Münster. Consequently, the city of Osnabrück stayed out of the great constitutional and social battle for the institution of the early modern state. Indeed, it found itself in a favorable situation where it could wring important concessions from both contenders—the bishops and the chapter—by switching alliances. In 1532 when the cathedral chapter was faced with the election of a new

131 Sehling, Kirchenordnungen (note 60), 247.

132 C. Stüve, Geschichte des Hochstiftes Osnabrück, esp. vol. 2: Von 1508-1623, Osnabrück 1872, (repr.) Osnabrück 1970.

133 Stratenwerth, Reformation (note 126), 136-155; G. Christ, Selbstverständnis und Rolle der Domkapitel in den geistlichen Territorien des Alten Deutschen Reiches in der Frühneuzeit, in: ZHF 16 (1987), 257-328.

134 Stüve, Geschichte (note 132); M. Bär, Abriß einer Verwaltungsgeschichte des Regierungsbezirks Osnabrück, Hanover/Leipzig 1901.

bishop, and tried to prevent further advances by the territorial state, under which it had suffered during the time of Bishop Erich II, the city council took advantage of the situation and negotiated a treaty with the chapter in which the clergy made a series of concessions. The most important provisions were the restitution of communal land to the city and recognition by the chapter that the commune had the right to levy taxes upon property previously owned by burghers but now in the hands of the clergy.[135] The treaty concessions fulfilled several important demands of the citizenry which dated back to the Middle Ages. Such claims added momentum to the Reformation movements, especially in the episcopal cities (281) and had also been expressed in Osnabrück during the pre-Reformation uprising of 1525. The new authority won by the city council through this agreement with the cathedral chapter contributed in no small way to stabilizing the internal situation of the city.

On the other hand the city and its citizenry were regarded as potentially important allies by the bishop and his bureaucracy in their struggle with the cathedral chapter. In contrast to Lippe, the good relationship between the city and the territorial prince in Osnabrück, which had also been built up during the late Middle Ages, was not shattered at the beginning of the early modern period. It was further consolidated on a new basis. This was true both for the governing periods of Erich II and for the early years of Franz von Waldeck. This constellation was of direct importance for the urban Reformation, as Bishop Franz considered a plan for the Reformation of his bishopric at the beginning of the 1540's out of political and dynastic considerations. Both the city council and the territorial prince changed their policies at the same time and in close agreement, embarking on a course of ecclesiastical renewal, so that at this phase of the Osnabrück urban Reformation there was a convergence of the religious interests of the citizenry, the city council, and the territorial prince. This is an extremely unusual constellation in the northwestern German urban Reformation. The danger of an attack by the territorial state upon municipal autonomy normally associated with such a constellation, as was illustrated in the example of Lüneburg, did not exist for Osnabrück as

---

135 The treaty is discussed in detail by Stratenwerth, Reformation (note 126), 62s.

long as decisive resistance from the Catholic cathedral chapter united the city and the bishop. The Reformation of the territory, which likewise started at the beginning of the 1540's, was at no point directed against the independence of the Lutheran city church and the ecclesiastical authority of the city magistrate.[136]

Because of the special political constellation within the city (between the citizenry and the city council) and between the city and the territorial ruler, the position of the political elite was less exposed in Osnabrück than in other cities. The burgher Reformation movement ran relatively quietly without attacks upon the social or political status of the elite. This striking deviation from the majority of northwestern German urban Reformations had numerous causes including a favorable economic situation from which—as in Lüneburg—the majority of burghers probably benefited as well as a city constitution in which the guilds and the commons were given not simply representatives alongside of the city council, as in Brunswick, but they were a part of the city council circle itself. Some of these representatives were even members of the smaller council.[137] The absence of attacks by the territorial prince and state upon the rights of the burgher commune, which in many territorial cities provoked an additional radicalization of the burgher Reformation movement and protests against an ostensibly too compliant city council, also removed a potential source of conflict. A successful dissipation of (282) the anticlericalism that was previously especially strong in episcopal cities also resulted from this. The secondary barriers raised by a popular Reformation movement proceeding in a "revolutionary" fashion, which might have deterred the elite from accepting the new faith, were as a consequence hardly present in Osnabrück. On the other hand, there was also no outside pressure to force a quick restoration of an internal city consensus which had been destroyed by the spread of Lutheranism among the burghers. Everything points to a tension-free and at the same time natural turning of the political elite toward Protestantism. The small circle of adherents won by Klarenbach and Buthmann within the upper stratum in 1527

---

136 Ibid., 129.

137 0. Spechter, Die Osnabrücker Oberschicht im 17. und 18. Jahrhundert. Eine sozial- und verfassunggeschichtliche Untersuchung, Osnabrück 1975, 5ss., 15ss.

and 1532[138] was obviously able to expand itself during the second half of the 1530's. By the beginning of the following decade the city council as a whole had turned to Protestantism. No report has been preserved of a struggle between parties or of the banishment of a party loyal to the old faith. This does of course not eliminate the possibility, that individual city councillors remained Catholic.

The absence of a clear break-up of the city council into factions, and of the division of the political elite along confessional lines, is all the more striking because in Osnabrück the social recruitment of the political elite also had been subject to a remarkable change after the end of the fifteenth century. The medieval patriciate stepped down in favor of a new *Honoratiorentum* composed of academics and the economic elite of wealthy merchants and artisans.[139] The *Oberg* uprising, whose leadership belonged to the elite circle, demonstrates, that this process did not take place without friction.[140] However, during the Reformation such conflicts do not seem to have played a dominant role. As far as the prosopographical and genealogical information indicates, which for our question becomes more abundant only at the end of the century, all three groups—the patriciate, the rising economic elite and the academics—turned toward Lutheranism together.[141] Whether the shift of political importance (283) within these three elite groups was accelerated by the Reformation cannot be determined, because the first complete lists of city councillors appear only at the end of the century. The personnel composition of the Neustadt council, however, which has been preserved from the fourteenth century onward, shows no unusual changes between 1530 and 1550 that would suggest such an acceleration. Although it certainly shrank numerically, the patriciate had still an important part to play in Osnabrück's

---

138 Stratenwerth, Reformation (note 126), 48, 78, 123.

139 Spechter, Oberschicht (note 137).

140 Stratenwerth, Reformation (note 126), 32, note 13.

141 The patrician families of Osnabrück merged into the territorial nobility in the course of the sixteenth century when they did not die out altogether. The great majority of the territorial nobility became Lutheran. See Spechter, Oberschicht (note 137), 108s., 110, note 587; R. Renger, Landesherr und Landstände im Hochstift Osnabrück in der Mitte des 18. Jahrhunderts. Untersuchungen zur Institutionengeschichte des Ständestaates im 17. und 18. Jahrhunderts, Göttingen 1968, 71.

city government during the second half of the sixteenth century as well.[142]

The development that began during the 1540's, which amounted to the formation of a unified Protestant elite similar to those in Brunswick and Lüneburg,[143] was interrupted by the Interim and later modified on account of the enduring Catholic character of the bishopric. The burgher commune and by far the majority of the burgher elite remained Lutheran. A minority, even including members of the upper stratum, opted for Catholicism.[144] Until the beginning of the seventeenth century individual representatives of this Catholic group appeared in the city council. Later, however, after a transitory period when Osnabrück was forcibly re-catholicized between 1630 and 1632, they were unconditionally barred from city offices.[145] There were two clearly distinguished elites in the city during the late seventeenth and eighteenth centuries. One of them was Catholic, reckoned to be a part of the urban upper stratum but not a part of the political elite of the urban burghers. To the extent that they wished to hold political or administrative offices they were dependent upon the territory, i.e., the service of the territorial prince or of the cathedral chapter. The other elite was Lutheran, which as a rule held urban offices but sometimes also territorial ones.

If the closest political, confessional, and familial (284) connections between the urban elite and the earlier territorial civil servants can be observed in the case of Osnabrück during the Reformation period, it is consistent with the political constellation that we have described here.[146] Until the middle of the following century members of the Lutheran elite

---

142 See the lists of the burgomasters and councillors in: Spechter, Oberschicht (note 137), appendix 135ss., esp. 141.

143 With the introduction of the Protestant church ordinance the civic community did not of course immediately become excusively Protestant. Some families still went to Mass in the cathedral, occasionally including some members of the political elite, e.g. Karssenbrock, Heinrich Weichmann, the brother of the treasurer, and Johann Ertmann (see Berning, Bistum, note 126, appendix No. 9, Namenslisten katholischer Kommunikanten, 304s.). But the majority of Catholics were ordinary people, above all women.

144 Spechter, Oberschicht (note 137), 41, note 202, note 203 and 119, note 644.

145 Ibid., 11ss.

146 Stratenwerth, Reformation (note 126), 106. Dr. Jost Roland, then episcopal chancellor, married into the patriciate of Osnabrück, became a councillor in 1553 and later burgomaster. See Spechter, Oberschicht (note 137), 111.

appear—often one and the same person[147]—both as city councillors or as members of the urban magistrate and as civil servants employed by the episcopal territorial ruler. On account of
the specific confessional and constitutional structure of the bi-
confessional bishopric, introduced by a provision of the Peace
of Westphalia, there was at first no sharp distinction between
the urban burgher and the territorial elites. This division
occurred only during the second half of the seventeenth
century when Protestants increasingly restricted themselves to
urban offices and gave way in the territory to a Catholic circle
of civil servant families. This division cannot be regarded as a
direct expression of the conflicts of the confessional age, especially since Protestant and Catholic territorial princes alternately ruled in the episcopal territory of Osnabrück. However,
because they were based upon the marriage habits of both elite
groups, which remained confessionally influenced even during
the seventeenth and eighteenth centuries,[148] they were indeed a
consequence of the confessional age, exercising a lasting social
influence well into the Enlightenment and even later.

The contrasting courses of the Reformation in the neighboring cities of Osnabrück and *Münster*, where the preconditions were so similar and where the same person even ruled as
bishop at the decisive moment,[149] are among the most fascinating problems of early modern urban history in Germany.
Within the scope of our interpretation there are two closely
related major differences. *First*, in spite of favorable conditions, the city of Münster and its territorial prince were unable
to reach a tension-free relationship, to say nothing of an
alliance of interests.[150] In this context it must be (285) main-

147 In the first quarter of the seventeenth century Dr. Heinrich Schrader
became a senior offical for the bishop, but afterwards was a burgomaster of the
city; in the middle of the century Dr. Gerhard Schepeler first was a burgomaster,
afterwards a senior official for the bishop (ibid., 118; 114 note 618).

148 Ibid., 119.

149 Franz von Waldeck (1532-1553).

150 In Münster the relations between the bishop and the cathedral city were
never as good as those in the neighboring Hochstift of Osnabrück, either in the
Middle Ages or in later phases of the early modern period . Thus it is not surprising that the rulers' reaction to the disturbances of 1525 had far-reaching
consequences only in Münster, where the polarization between ruler and civic
communes occurred already in the second half of the 1520's. See Schilling, Aufstandsbewegungen (note 6), 193-238, esp. 206; U. Meckstroth, Das Verhältnis der
Stadt Münster zu ihrem Landesherrn bis zum Ende der Stiftsfehde, Münster 1962;
T. Klümper, Landesherr und Städte im Fürstbistum Münster unter Ernst und
Ferdinand von Bayern (1585-1650), Emsdetten 1940; H. A. Erhard, Geschichte

tained that the city[151] was far more responsible for provoking confrontation than the bishops. The anti-Protestant religious mandates[152] of the bishops must be understood more as demonstrations of good will toward the Catholic cathedral chapter and the Emperor than as the first steps taken against urban Protestantism. The city council did not pursue a policy of religious exclusion; this was the goal of the burgher opposition, as in Lemgo, but in sharp contrast to the situation in Brunswick. Hence the agreement made between the bishop and the magistrate through the mediation of Philipp of Hesse on February 14, 1533,[153] did not establish a strong Lutheran alliance between city and ruler such as existed in Osnabrück. In the wake of their strong policy against the territorial prince the burgher Reformation movement followed the theological turn made by Bernd Rothmann from Lutheranism to Anabaptism only too easily.[154] By following him the citizenry could confront the territorial prince on an even more radical level.[155]

The dynamic of the burgher Reformation movement consitutes the *second* difference with Osnabrück. After 1532—the same year that Protestant preachers were first called to be city pastors in Osnabrück as well as in Münster—the city council in Münster was no longer able to control the burgher movement. In Münster the burgher opposition developed both a communal and corporate self-understanding and a noticeable antagonism (286) toward the oligarchic government.[156] Due to the specific constitution of Münster the communal movement was in a position after only a short delay to "purge" governmental circles of its opponents, forcing the magistrate to follow the reli-

Münsters, Münster 1837; and A. Brand, Geschichte des Fürstbistums Münster. Ein Heimatführer im Rahmen der westfälisch-deutschen Geschichte, Münster 1925; Schröer, Reformation (note 125).

151 In December 1532 the citizens tried to kidnap the bishop. See Fischer, Reformationsversuche (note 128), 15.

152 For example, Erich von Braunschweig in his short rule in March/May 1532 and Franz von Waldeck in June 1532. For a detailed examination of the policy of Franz von Waldeck: Fischer, Reformationsversuche (note 128).

153 Ibid., 17.

154 The theological development of Rothmann and the specific character of the burgher movement were both decisive for the events in Münster.

155 K.-H. Kirchhoff, Die Belagerung und Eroberung Münsters 1534/35, in: Westfälische Zeitschrift 112, 1962, 76-170. esp. 159ss. It is typical that the Anabaptists included the municipal coat of arms of Münster in their seal (K.-H. Kirchhoff, Die Täufer in Münster 1534/35. Untersuchungen zum Umfang und zur Sozialstruktur der Bewegung, Münster 1973, 87).

156 Discussed in detail in Schilling, Aufstandsbewegungen (note 6).

gious position held by the majority of the citizens, first favoring the Lutherans and then the Anabaptists. The necessary
precondition for this domination of the magistrate was a
method of election to the city council that was completely
unique in the northwestern German cities. In Münster a group
of electors, over whose composition the members of the re-
signing council had little influence, were responsible for
electing the new city council, in stark contrast even to neighboring Osnabrück.[157] The result was that although the social
composition of the highest city governing bodies changed very
quickly in times of crisis, the religious position supported by
the councillors could not keep up with the quick and radical
religious shifts within the burgher movement—from Catholicism to Lutheranism, Zwinglianism and Anabaptism! Finally,
the city council lost authority because of its politically necessary dealings with the territorial prince.[158] All these were
important preconditions for the well-known special status of
Münster within the northwestern German urban Reformation.
Together with unique developments in the theological thinking
of the evangelical preachers—above all Bernd Rothmann—leading them to adopt Anabaptism, these factors were
essentially responsible for the fact that in the case of Münster
Lutheranism could not form the ideological basis for a new
Protestant harmony between citizenry and city council. As a
result the Reformation movement never reached the stage of a
magisterial Reformation.[159] (287)

Several rather firm conclusions can be drawn concerning the
social implications of this swift change within the city's
leadership groups.[160] To begin with we must note that also in
Münster the attitude of those who at that time were in charge
of the city's administration and foreign policy was
"conservative." Some of them—at first Catholics, then
Lutherans—were forced to abandon both their offices and the
city.[161] Under the circumstances to take this religious position

---

157 On the details of the election procedure see Spechter, Oberschicht (note
137), 17.

158 When the syndic of the city council, von der Wieck, started to negotiate
with the bishop and Philipp of Hesse to gain control over the Reformation in
Münster, the burgher movement immediately turned against its own city council.

159 The city council of Münster never succeeded in introducing a formal church
ordinance.

160 Kirchhoff, Täufer (note 155).

161 A list of Catholic burghers who returned to Münster after 1535 can be

meant at the same time to side with the territorial prince and
stand against an aggressive interpretation of the principle of
civic liberty. On the other hand, the Anabaptist government
publicly confessed its loyalty to the latter ideal through its
adoption of the old city seal.[162] This linkage of religious and
political choice applied above all to Catholics, and in a
weakened sense to Lutherans as well, who left the city in the
final period before the erection of the new Zion. In any case
these decisions, made during the crisis of the 1530's, meant
only in exceptional cases a long-term and fundamental renunciation of the urban burgher world in favor of the territorial
state. For the generation who had withdrawn before the Anabaptists, and then had been robbed both of its political rights
and autonomous right of self-government after the defeat of
the city by the territorial prince in 1535, experienced the
restoration of Münster to its old independence and "liberty"
after 1555. When this occurred the self-understanding of the
citizenry regained its old strength and the political elite of
Münster—now overwhelmingly, but not exclusively Catholic—kept its distance from the territorial prince, refusing to
serve as officials in his territorial bureaucracy.[163] (288) A fundamental change occurred only after the final conquest and
consequent integration of the cathedral city into the territorial
state in 1671.

When considering the Reformation years themselves, the
rapid changes in personnel within the city council did not
indicate a change in its social composition in the sense of
opening the political elite to the lower strata of the citizenry.
Social recruitment remained largely the same. The following
explanation seems most likely: In principle it was not impossible for members of the city council to carry out the religious
changes demanded by the burgher commune—first to Lutheranism and then to Anabaptism. Other members of the social
elite were, however, more important for the advance of the
new doctrine within the ruling elite. These were men who were

---

found in K.-H. Kirchhoff, Eine münsterische Bürgerliste des Jahres 1535, in:
Westfälische Zeitschrift 111 (1961).

162 Kirchhoff, Täufer (note 155), 87.

163 C. Steinbicker, Das Beamtentum in den geistlichen Fürstentümern Nordwestdeutschlands im Zeitraum von 1430-1740, in: G. Franz (ed.), Beamtentum
und Pfarrerstand 1400-1800, Büdinger Vorträge 1967, Limburg 1972, 121-148,
esp. 138ss. - R. Po-chia Hsia, Society and Religion in Münster 1535-1618, New
Haven and New York 1984.

still outside of the highest circles of political power, but were already aspirants for positions on the city council thanks to their takeover of political offices in the guilds, precincts, parishes and especially as city council electors (*Wahlmänner*).[164] Since members of these groups were carried into the city council directly through the two waves of the Reformation in Münster, a renewal of the narrower circle of the political elite occurred with personnel drawn from the reservoir of the broader elite circle. In a certain sense an acceleration of the elite replacement occurred here as well, which normally would have proceeded very slowly on the basis of the annual reappointment of previous city councillors.[165]

The example of Münster differs from the other cities not only by the speed and extent of the elite replacement. The processes at work within the elite were expressed at a different level of social development. At the time of the Reformation the withdrawal of the patriciate, the so-called *Erbmänner*, from the city and its governmental bodies had clearly advanced further than it had in other cities. A phase displacement can be demonstrated for the city of Münster in terms of the process of transformation of the urban burghers from a late medieval to an early modern elite discussed at the beginning of this essay when compared with Osnabrück and Brunswick, where the patriciate withdrew to the country only in the course of the seventeenth century. After the monopoly of power enjoyed by the hereditary patriciate had been broken already during the fifteenth century, they were still formally entitled to half of the city council offices and one of the burgomaster offices. After the beginning of the sixteenth century they were no longer interested in taking full advantage of this right.[166] The city council was recruited overwhelmingly (289) from guild burghers who experienced increasing economic prosperity, that is from among merchant-artisans active in long-distance trade, and distributors and merchants of the newer type. In contrast to the previously discussed cases, the processes at work within the Münster elite during the Reformation period already

---

164 See Schilling, Aufstandsbewegungen (note 6).

165 Kirchhoff, Täufer (note 155), 55.

166 K. Zuhorn, Vom Münsterschen Bürgertum um die Mitte des 15. Jahrhunderts, in: Westfälische Zeitschrift 51 (1939), 88-194; H. Lahrkamp, Das Patriziat in Münster, in: H. Rössler (ed.): Deutsches Patriziat 1430-1730, Büdinger Vorträge 1965, Limburg 1968.

represented battles for position *within* the new *Honoratiorentum*. The Reformation in Münster confronted a new, rising
political elite which on the one hand still lacked the integrative
power and stability which the presence of a patriciate or older
city council families supplied in other cities,[167] but on the
other already showed the normal tendency to reserve positions
of power for a narrow circle of privileged city council families
on the basis of the usual annual reelection. It is revealing for
the socio-political situation in early sixteenth century Münster
that the city council set up by bishop Franz von Waldeck in
1536 after the defeat of the Anabaptists again included twelve
Erbmänner and twelve additional burghers.[168] The territorial
prince obviously expected this strengthening of the patrician
element to result in quicker stabilization.

We can only devote cursory attention to *Paderborn*, the third
of the Westphalian episcopal cities. The Reformation[169] there
took a course that differed from every previous example, since
the Catholic territorial prince, in an alliance with the cathedral
chapter, succeeded in taking forcible control of the city and in
smothering the Protestant burgher movement.[170] (290) Beyond
this he was able to dictate a change in the urban constitution,
which was designed to consolidate the position of the territorial
prince over the burgher commune. He took back the right of
participation won by the commune not long before and established an oligarchic city government.[171] This victory of a territorial prince, which was very unusual within the setting of
northwestern German Reformation history, became particularly
obvious in a general proviso of the agreement forced upon the
city in 1532, which ceded to the bishop the right to "shorten,

167 The syndic, Dr. von der Wiek, who tried hard to stabilize and institu-
tionalize a Lutheran Reformation, came from a Münster patrician family (ibid.,
196).
168 Lahrkamp, Patriziat (note 166), 201.
169 L. Leineweber, Die Paderborner Fürstbischöfe im Zeitalter der Glaubenser-
neuerung. Ein Beitrag zur Reformationsgeschichte des Stiftes Paderborn, in:
Westfälische Zeitschrift 66 (1908), 75-158 and 67 (1909), 115-200; W. Richter,
Geschichte der Stadt Paderborn, 2 vols., Paderborn 1899 and 1903; R. Decker,
Bürgermeister und Ratsherren in Paderborn vom 13. bis zum 17. Jahrhundert.
Untersuchungen zur Zusammensetzung einer städtischen Oberschicht, Paderborn
1977; Schröer, Reformation (note 125), vol. 2, 41-69, 296-317.
170 Richter, Geschichte (note 169), 120ss.; Leineweber, Fürstbischöfe (note
169), 119ss.; Decker, Bürgermeister (note 169), 138ss.
171 See literature in note 170.

lengthen and to improve this agreement according to the common good and welfare."[172]

Apart from this extreme dominance of the non-city element of the three-way struggle, even in Paderborn the familiar basic pattern of social correlation present in the urban Hanseatic Reformation can be discerned—a burgher movement, whose decisive activities occurred here also between 1528 and 1532, the city council, and the wider political elite. There was a conservative city council which had many ties to Catholic institutions, above all economic ties.[173] On July 1, 1532 it acceded to the demands of the Protestant burgher movement by forming a union with the burgher commune,[174] which apart from the bishop's coup would doubtless have led, sooner or later, to a reestablishment of an internal city consensus under a Lutheran banner. A burgher movement was also present whose Protestant message was linked to economic and political demands, directed against the city council, and also against the territorial prince.[175] Finally, there was a group within the burgher movement, (291) which consisted of representatives of the artisan middle stratum and of members of the families of rising social prominence, who by contemporary standards could already claim the right to enter the city council.[176] In spite of the powerful attacks of the territorial prince against the Reformation and civic liberties, Lutheranism became widely accepted during the next decade, not only within the citizenry, but it even found entry into the city council.[177] Members of families who had lost all of their political influence because they had led the burgher opposition movement between 1524 and 1532 appeared during the second half of the century as Lutheran city councillors and burgomasters at the pinnacle of power within the city. Corresponding to the fundamentally defensive attitude which characterized Lutheranism in general

172 Richter, Geschichte (note 169), appendix 110, 79, esp. CXI.

173 Decker, Bürgermeister (note 169), 85.

174 Leineweber, Fürstbischöfe (note 169), 121s.

175 The citizens refused to pay homage to the new bishop, Hermann von Wied, and tried to destroy his castle in neighboring Neuhaus. Richter, Geschichte (note 169), 120.

176 Peter Schwertfeger, Jürgen Pamperlamp and Cyriacus Heidenreich. See Decker, Bürgermeister (note 169), 139, note 11; Richter, Geschichte (note 169), 124. Also Heinrich Hurlebut and Liborius Grude. See Decker, Bürgermeister (note 169), 139 note, 11.

177 Richter, Geschichte (note 169), 2nd vol., 15ss.; Leineweber, Fürstbischöfe (note 169), 115-200; Decker, Bürgermeister (note 169), 141.

after the middle of the century, this Lutheran takeover of the
Paderborn city council did not result in an aggressive policy
against the bishop.[178]

At the beginning of the seventeenth century another deepening crisis was provoked by the aggressive Counter-Reformation policy of the territorial prince. The basic constellation
between city and territorial state was the same as in neighboring Lemgo. However, the situation was complicated because
a politically occasioned antagonism had broken out between the
city council and the commune and because within a cathedral
city the position of the urban burghers was weakened by the
presence of the cathedral chapter and a number of other
Catholic institutions. These institutions employed many artisans
and purchased their wares and services. They were of considerable economic importance for specific burgher groups.[179]
(292)

The background of these processes, which are individually
quite confusing, cannot be reconstructed in detail. It is clear,
however, that within the overwhelmingly Protestant citizenry
there was a polarization between a group within the circles of
the Lutheran city councillors who were ready to compromise
with the bishop and the chapter and a radical burgher
movement led by Liborius Wichard, a man of rising social
prominence who had not been integrated into the circle of the
ruling city council families. With respect to internal affairs the
burgher opposition stood against governmental mismanagement;
with regard to external policy they fought the principle of the
territorial state which was linked to Catholic confessionalization, enforced by the territorial prince and the clergy.[180] Presumably inter-Protestant differences came into play as well.
Wichard and the radical opposition maintained ties with Landgrave Moritz of Hesse and thus with the Calvinist-Reformed
party in the Empire, which in contrast to the Lutherans advocated an aggressive policy.[181] Together with the superior position of the territorial prince militarily, politically, legally, and

---

178 The city council asked Lutheran jurists for their counsel and were advised
to obey the bishop because he was their princely ruler.

179 See the books and essays by Richter and Decker (note 169), L. Keller and
K. Honselmann (note 11).

180 Decker, Bürgermeister (note 169).

181 On Moritz of Hesse see G. Menk, Die "Zweite Reformation" in Hessen-
Kassel. Landgraf Moritz und die Einführung der Verbesserungspunkte, in: Schilling, Konfessionalisierung (note 39), 154-183.

ideologically, the conflicts among the burghers themselves made possible a renewed conquest of the city by the bishop as well as the destruction or break-up of the urban burgher elite, which at that time was mainly Protestant. It was replaced by a Catholic political elite—in part converts, but above all Catholic jurists who had hitherto been in the opposition[182]—which had a distinctly different social profile. They were no longer urban burghers, but rather were oriented toward the territory; they had close ties with the territorial bureaucracy and were dominated by jurists.

Before we leave Westphalia the situation in *Soest* should be examined because it has some special features. The political system of this city differed from the previous examples in several important respects. Internally it was characterized by a constitution which guaranteed the commune an unusually far-reaching right of political participation. (293) A successful division of power, between the artisans on the one hand and the patricians and the *Honoratiorentum* on the other, was based upon this right. The exterior territorial constitution was characterized by the very weak position of the territorial overlord and almost unlimited city autonomy, the latter resulting from a treaty concluded with the Duke of Kleve.[183] On this account some unique deviations are apparent within our basic pattern of a three-way struggle between city council, citizenry, and territory. They indicate that in Soest the pressure to conform with the citizenry was not felt as strongly by the political elite as in the majority of urban Reformations. The Catholic party within the city council was characteristically recruited only from the *Honoratioren* and the patricians, while the city councillors from the artisan party sided relatively quickly with Lutheranism.[184] The Catholic councillors were able to remain in power almost two years after the victory of the Reformation in 1531. They even formally directed the establishment of a Protestant church order. In the summer of 1533, however, the internal city pressure became so intense that the

---

182 Decker, Bürgermeister (note 169), 95ss., 143; Steinbicker, Beamtentum (note 163), 137.

183 Ehbrecht, Verlaufsformen (note 2), 34ss.; Schröer, Reformation (note 125), vol. 1, 353-411.

184 W.-H. Deus, Die Herren von Soest. Die Stadtverfassung im Spiegel des Ratswahlbuches von 1417-1751, Soest 1955.

sixteen leaders of the Catholic party had to leave the city.[185]
Apart from cases of a special nature[186] this did not mean, (294)
however, that these men became part of the territorial society
outside of the city, ceasing to be urban burghers. Both sides
recognized the duke as a mediator since his position in Soest
was far too weak to undertake a coordinated policy of territorialization. After the political and economic complaints of the
burghers were largely settled, the controversy between city
council and burgher commune focused on the questions of
what rights the Catholic minority should have within the
burgher corporation, and the status of the different ecclesiastical institutions in the city, particularly the venerable St.
Patroklus Stift. Finally agreement was reached, and all of those
who had abandoned the city returned. Some families within the
Soest patriciate remained Catholic. Their participation in the
government of the Protestant city was never questioned. They
could even hold office as burgomaster as early as the 1580's,
although this was an exception.[187]

Seen in a long-term perspective the Reformation in Soest did
not change the distribution of political power. By the middle of
the century at the latest the traditional elite was more firmly in
control than ever. The office of burgomaster, which became
even more important because of the early modern bureaucratization of the city government, was held exclusively by patricians between 1550 and 1600.[188]

---

185 The patricians had close social and familial ties with the members of the St.
Patroklus chapter.

186 The burgomaster Gropper is one of the exceptions; his family was totally
orientated toward offices in the church hierarchy of Cologne. His son, Cardinal
Johannes Gropper, is well-known. See W. Lipgens, Kardinal Johannes Gropper
(1503-1559) und die Anfänge der katholischen Reform in Deutschland, Münster
1951; H. Schwartz, Geschichte der Reformation in Soest, Soest 1932, 43ss., 165ss.,
216ss.; Ehbrecht, Verlaufsformen (note 2), 36s.

187 E.g. burgomaster Conrad Berswardt, who died in 1582 (Schwartz,
Geschichte, note 186, 23) as well as members of the patrician families Twifler,
Greve und Menge (Deus, Herren, note 184, 436, 443; H. Rothert, Zur Kirchenge-
schichte der "ehrenreichen" Stadt Soest, Gütersloh 1905, 153).

188 F. von Klocke, Alt-Soester Bürgermeister aus sechs Jahrhunderten, ihre
Familien und ihre Standesverhältnisse, Soest 1927, 181-183; idem, Patriziat und
Stadtadel im alten Soest, Lübeck 1927. - The Reformation in Dortmund, the only
imperial city in Westphalia which has been excluded in this essay, is discussed
seperately in H. Schilling, Dortmund im 16. und 17. Jahrhundert -Reichstädtische
Gesellschaft, Reformation und Konfessionalisierung, in: G. Luntowski and N.
Reimann (eds.), Dortmund 1100 Jahre Stadtgeschichte, Dortmund 1982, 151-202.

V

Finally, I will turn to a comparatively small group of cities,
where the communal-corporate activity that is demonstrable
everywhere in connection with the Reformation led either to a
formal change or significant modification of the constitution or
the method of electing the city council. Whether the position
and conduct of the elite in these cities was fundamentally different than in the previously discussed cases remains ques-
tionable. The best-known representative of this group is the
imperial city of *Hamburg*.[189] A permanent representation of
the (295) commune independent of the city council originated
there for the first time in connection with the Reformation.
Two representative bodies of the burgher commune succeeded
in establishing themselves as lasting institutions alongside of the
city council, anchored within the constitution—the burgher
committee, which had been commissioned by the burgher
Reformation movement for negotiating with the city council,
consisting of twelve officials in charge of poor relief and
twenty-four other burghers from each parish, and the smaller
committee of the so-called *Oberalten*. Lippstadt is another
example of this type of urban Reformation in Westphalia,
which in contrast to its sister city Lemgo had no representative
assembly of the commune outside of the city council at the end
of the Middle Ages. Here as well a permanent assembly of the
commune developed out of the Reformation burgher committee, which was first formed on February 22, 1531. It consisted
of two representatives each of the guilds and the commons, the
so-called *Richtleuten*.[190]

The Reformation history of the East Frisian port city of
Emden was an extreme case in this respect because at the end
of the Middle Ages it had no genuine urban constitution and
hence no burgher political elite. Both emerged only during the
religious and confessional battles of the sixteenth century.[191]
The first phase of the Reformation during the 1520's and

---

189 Lau, Bauernkrieg (note 1), 78, 88ss.; J. M. Lappenberg, Programm der
dritten Secularfeyer der bürgerlichen Verfassung Hamburgs, Hamburg 1828; R.
Postel, Die Reformation in Hamburg 1517-1528, Gütersloh 1986.

190 Niemöller, Reformationsgeschichte (note 33); Klockow, Stadt (note 33),
114s., 123s.

191 Discussed in detail in Schilling, Reformation (note 6), 128-161. See the
English translation in the book by H. Schilling, Civic Calvinism in Northwest
Germany and the Netherlands, Kirksville 1991.

1530's was less decisive than the events of the second half of the century. Emden, which experienced a rapid economic expansion, developed into a Calvinist civic republic while the territorial ruler, the Count of East Friesland, strove to erect an early absolutistic territorial domain under the banner of orthodox Lutheranism. In contrast to all the cases previously discussed, the Emden magistrate sided completely with the territorial prince. This was, however, not surprising because it was not a communal assembly, but rather one dependent upon the Counts. Led by an economically prosperous upper stratum, the Emden burghers fought for the right to ecclesiastical and political autonomy, which in the first instance meant transformation of the princely city government into a burgher city council in the true sense of the word. After a revolutionary coup in 1595 the city constitution was rewritten, providing a new foundation both for its internal order and its external relations with the territory. The princely, largely Lutheran, magistrate was replaced by a Calvinist (296) urban burgher elite which was oriented both spiritually and politically to the neighboring United Provinces. It drew its livelihood from mercantile trade, shipping, and increasingly from landholding in the surrounding, likewise Calvinist-influenced polder areas. This elite was clearly separated both socially and culturally from the mainly Lutheran early modern civil servant bourgeoisie of the territory.

I would like to discuss developments in the Brunswick-Kalenberg territorial city of *Göttingen* in somewhat more detail, because it is an especially fruitful example for our problem. The turbulent circumstances, which cannot be described in detail here,[192] reached a climax in October and November 1529 when the burgher movement, which there too was represented by committees known as the Sixty and the *Mittleren* respectively, succeeded in wringing from the city council both approval for the renewal of the church and a change in the constitution.[193] Apart from the years 1513-14, when the burgher

---

192 Lau, Bauernkrieg (note 1), 87; H. Volz, Die Reformation in Göttingen, in: Göttinger Jahrbuch 1967, 49-72; idem (ed.): Franz Lubecus, Bericht über die Einführung der Reformation in Göttingen im Jahre 1529, Göttingen 1967; B. Moeller, Die Reformation, in: D. Denecke and H.-M. Kühn (eds.), Göttingen, Geschichte einer Universitätsstadt, Göttingen 1987, vol. 1, 492-514.

193 H. Mohnhaupt, Die Göttinger Ratsverfassung vom 16. bis 19. Jahrhundert, Göttingen 1965; Denecke/Kühn, Göttingen (note 192), vol. 1: Von den Anfängen bis zum Ende des Dreißigjährigen Krieges.

commune failed in its first attempt to gain a share in the government, Göttingen was governed before the Reformation by a city council composed of life-long appointees who entered the council through cooptation, primarily from the prominent guild of merchants, while the other burghers were not eligible for councillor office. The governors of both the craft guilds and the non-guild commons were in principle part of the city government. Since, however, they were appointed by the city council and the guilds were under close magisterial supervision, they were in no way autonomous representatives of the commune.[194]

It was at this point that the burgher movement first acted to further its interests, when on October 21, 1529, they dismissed the governors appointed by the city council only ten days before and named their own guild and common representatives.[195] (297) In the end the city council had to accept this right of appointment formally and permanently. It also had to allow the participation of the guilds in the administration of the hospital and of the city finance department, i.e., in the area of fiscal administration, which had long been a focus of burgher criticism. All this was achieved through an agreement concluded with the burgher commune.[196] The process of increasing participation by the commune, i.e., by the guild burghers, in the city government that was set in motion by this agreement, continued after the Reformation independently of the evangelical burgher movement. It led to a new procedure for electing city councillors which revoked the right of cooptation and practically placed the annual election in the hands of the guild representatives in September of 1543.[197]

These processes within the city were able to run their course largely free of outside influence. This is all the more remarkable since only a few years earlier disagreements had led to serious clashes between the city and territorial prince. The commune and the city council had refused to swear their formal oath of allegiance to the prince.[198] Duke Ernst the Elder of Brunswick-Kalenberg, a convinced Catholic, issued decrees

---

194 Mohnhaupt, Ratsverfassung (note 193), 17.

195 ibid.; Volz, Lubecus (note 192), 26, and note 209.

196 Volz (note 192); Mohnhaupt (note 193); Moeller (note 192).

197 Mohnhaupt, Ratsverfassung (note 193), 44ss.

198 W. Havemann, Geschichte der Lande Braunschweig und Lüneburg, vol. 1, Göttingen 1853, 758s.

again and again opposing Protestantism in Göttingen.[199] In
stark contrast to his relatives in Wolfenbüttel and Lüneburg,
however, he never seriously attempted to use ecclesiastical and
confessional questions as a means of subjugating Göttingen. His
behavior toward Göttingen, the economically most important of
his cities, was dictated not by a desire to integrate it into the
territorial state,[200] but rather to make the fullest possible use of
its fiscal power. Just as after the earlier disputes already mentioned he had been willing to reach an accommodation with the
city in return for the payment of a large sum of money so he
finally accepted (298) the autonomous introduction of the
Reformation as well as an independent city church order after
similar financial concessions.[201] Similarly, Göttingen was spared
from the assaults of ecclesiastical institutions of the old church.
The superintendent of the archbishop of Mainz, Johann
Bruhns, was among the earliest followers of Martin Luther and
stepped forward as a supporter of the Protestant burgher
movement.[202]

In Göttingen it was not so much a pincer movement of
internal and external forces, but rather the radicalized policies
of the burgher Reformation movement which forced the city
council to act. With regard to the "archaic" structure of the
urban constitution the linkage of the demands for Reformation
with the demand of the burgher commune for political participation did not mean a mere revival of communal elements
within a bi-polar constitution composed of authoritarian and
communal elements, as was the case in Münster, Osnabrück
and Lemgo, or even in Brunswick. In Göttingen it was rather
the very first institution of political participation of the
commune by a more or less revolutionary reshaping of the city
constitution. Unlike Lüneburg where the burgher movement
was hindered from an unconditional struggle against the city
council patriciate, not least because of the common political

199 Volz, Reformation (note 192), 53, 64, 66, 68.

200 The first step toward the integration of Göttingen into the territorial state
was the attempt to control the city church. See J. Regula, Die kirchlichen Selbständigkeitsbestrebungen der Städte Göttingen, Nordheim, Hannover und Hameln
in den Jahren 1584-1601, in: Zeitschrift der Gesellschaft für niedersächsische
Kirchengeschichte 22, 1917, 123-152. But the ruler succeeded only in 1611. See
Mohnhaupt, Ratsverfassung (note 193), 57ss.

201 Havemann, Geschichte (note 198), 758; Volz, Reformation (note 192), 68.

202 Volz, Reformation (note 192), 65s.

front maintained against the territorial prince,[203] the Göttingen opposition could maintain its collision course against the autocratic government of the mercantile patriciate without interference and could keep up the internal struggle for participation until the very end.

It was no wonder that the city councillors were little inclined to turn to Lutheranism even after they had already surrendered politically and had agreed to the ecclesiastical changes.[204] (299) Between 1525 and 1530 no personnel changes had occurred in the city council. But then, although the council continued to exercise the right to appoint new members through cooptation, the years from 1530 until 1532 saw a thorough change in its personnel[205] resulting from the annual elections to the city council, an event which occurred every October. In at least one case a Catholic city councillor rejected his proposed reappointment.[206] Olaf Mörke concluded in his carefully quantified book in a *"Langzeitanalyse des politischen Personalkörpers des Rates"* that from a social perspective it was not the constitutional change of 1543, but rather the Reformation itself which produced a decisive change in favor of the artisans with respect to the recruitment of the city council. This change was measurable both quantitatively in the number of city councillors that they supplied and qualitatively with respect to the political offices that they held.[207]

Was there a religious polarization along the "class lines" dividing the mercantile patriciate from artisans or craftsman burghers? A concrete personnel classification of the burgher movement shows that such a interpretation would be incorrect. Even the extreme case of Göttingen requires no fundamental correction in our picture of the role played by the political elite within the Reformation process in northwestern German cities. The Reformation movement, initiated and largely sup-

---

203 At least the ruler prevented a shift to a radical "left wing" Reformation (ibid., 64).

204 Volz, Reformation (note 192), 66; Mohnhaupt, Ratsverfassung (note 193), 41s.

205 See the list of the members of the city council in: A. Hasselblatt and G. Kaestner (eds.), Urkundenbuch der Stadt Göttingen aus dem 16. Jahrhundert, 1500-1533, Göttingen 1881, 405s.

206 This was the fact in the case of Dr. jur. utr. Johann Winkelmann, a clergyman who was councillor in Göttingen since 1508, but then retired to his property close to the monastery of Weende. See Volz, Reformation (note 192), 67.

207 Mörke, Rat (note 44).

ported by the economically disadvantaged and socially
disunited artisans of the so-called "New Woolen Weavers"[208]
which met resistance at first from within the artisan
community itself,[209] above all from the (300) bakers, found a
noticeable number of leaders from within the wider elite circle
at the decisive moment, even in Göttingen. While some of these
individuals held communal offices, they were not at the time
excluded in principle from the city council. There were even
members of the mercantile guilds among them, the same group
which controlled the city council and whose members supported a decisively Catholic position.[210] It is striking that the
majority of these persons had either resided in the city for a
relatively short time or had recently received the right of citizenship.[211] If this suggests that Lutheranism held a particular
attraction for people of rising social prominence who had not
yet been sufficiently integrated within the wider elite circle,
then it must not be overlooked on the other hand that among
those city councillors who opted for Catholicism there were
also men of rising social prominence, together with members of
the older city council families. Either as native-born persons or
as emigrants, (301) they had achieved eligibility for councillor
office by purchasing membership in the guild of merchants at
the end of the fifteenth century.[212]

During the early phase the Catholic city council sought support repeatedly from the appropriate ecclesiastical officeholders
outside of the city and from the territorial prince. This did not
by any means indicate a renunciation of the urban burgher

---

208 W. Nissen, Die Göttinger Tuchmacher und ihr Einfluß bei der Einführung
der Reformation in der Stadt, in: Festschrift für Hermann Heimpel, vol. 1,
Göttingen 1971, 684-697.

209 The bakers planned to kill the Protestant minister (Volz, Lubecus, note
192, 21).

210 See the prosopographic data in note 200 of the German original of this
essay.

211 Of the twelve mediators at least Klaus Stenzel, Ludolf and Harmen Rusch-
platen, Martin Henkeln, Johannn Hund and Lorenz Hasfordt had only recently
immigrated to Göttingen.

212 Of the six Catholic councillors who withdrew in 1531 Hans von Dransfeld,
Heinrich Mundemann and Martin Weckenesel (as shown by A. Ritter, Die Ratsherren und ihre Familien in den südhannoverschen Städten Göttingen, Duder-
stadt und Münden, Oldenburg 1943, 121) were members of families that had
achieved eligibility for the city council only after 1514. Magister Jürgen Lendeke
as well as Dr. Johann Winkelmann, the former was a clergyman, the latter was
headmaster of a grammar school, became councillors as individuals but were not
members of councillor families.

world. Some city council families indeed had interests in the
territory, particularly agrarian ones. However, one does not
gain the impression that this fact decisively influenced their
religious choice.[213] Only in two very unusual cases did a city
councillor's choice of Catholicism result in him and his family
turning away from the city.[214]

Skepticism seems to me the appropriate response to the idea
that the clearly decisive break at the beginning of the 1530's
evoked a qualitative change in the social composition of the
Göttingen elite which would not have happened without the
upheavals of the Reformation. In any case it must be considered whether this "elite exchange" was not primarily a change
in the method of recruitment to the elite of *Honoratioren* which
was already open in principle before the Reformation. There
was apparently only a rather insignificant shift—from a political elite controlled by the guild of merchants, which allowed
people of rising social prominence from among the artisans to
purchase entry, to a new political elite consisting of an upper
stratum of artisan guilds, which also quickly displayed oligarchic tendencies.[215] The changes that occurred in connection
with the Reformation prove to be an acceleration of a long-
term process in this case as well, rather than a qualitative
jump. It cannot be overlooked that there is, however, a shift in
accent to the benefit of communal political participation. If
before 1529 the lines of decision and control ran from the city
council above to the guilds and commons below, then the
opposite principle was put into effect in the wake of the
Reformation movement. It was primarily a political and constitutional change which did not inevitably result in a forcible
change in the social composition of the city council. For the
rest, it is not unimportant that Göttingen at this point (302)
made up a developmental deficit. For in the majority of larger
cities of the northwestern region the political participation of
the commune had already become a constitutionally guaranteed
norm during the Middle Ages.

VI

For all their differences in dynamic and rhythm, the various

---

213 Ritter, Ratsherren (note 212), 119.
214 Volz, Lubecus (note 192), 248, 271.
215 Wiese-Schorn, Selbstverwaltung (note 126), 37.

reform movements active during the Reformation period in the
northwestern German Hanseatic cities had a great deal in common. These common factors include the degree and kind of
political and ecclesiastical presence of the territorial prince, the
recruitment, composition, and political/constitutional position
of the elite and their specific reactions to the advance of the
new faith. Therefore, it seems to me both defensible and
appropriate to formulate some summarizing theses delineating
the basic constellation. They are not designed to replace analyses of individual cases and of their specific character, but
rather to stimulate them.[216]

1. There were distinct primary barriers hindering acceptance,
both of the new doctrine and above all the institutional changes
within the church connected with it, by the political elite of
the cities. These existed first because of their close spiritual
and personal ties with the old ecclesiastical system, when compared with other burgher groups and strata. Their hesitation
also stemmed from the fact that the "egalitarian" principle of
sola fide took away their preferential treatment in securing
eternal salvation, since according to the late medieval piety of
works "salvation had become, so to speak, a purchasable com-
modity," protecting the wealthy.[217] To these factors we must
add the political pressures which were directed particularly
against the smaller circle of the elite who bore direct
"governmental responsibility" in the city council. Territorial
cities were in a weaker position than imperial cities to advocate
the Reformation against not only the Emperor, the Empire, and
the papal curia,[218] but also against the territory and the diocesan bureaucracy. Especially when the urban magistrates wished
to fulfil their obligation to secure peace for the city and independence against the territorial prince who aggressively sought
confrontation, they were forced to witness the worrisome
spread of a doctrine that was condemned by imperial law. It
could hardly be expected that the political elite as a social
group would ignore political responsibility in favor of a religious decision for Lutheranism. Such a decision became con-

216 In my opinion there must be a dialectical correlation between individual
case studies and generalizing conclusions.

217 G. Seebaß, Diskussionsbericht, in: Moeller, Stadt (note 1), 180.

218 K. Blaschke, Wechselwirkungen zwischen der Reformation und dem Aufbau
des Territorialstaates, in: Der Staat 9 (1970), 347-364, esp. 357; English translation in: J. Tracy (ed.), Luther and the Modern State in Germany, Kirksville 1986,
61-76.

ceivable, however, as the result of individual psychological processes, a decision as it were to leap over barriers raised by society and politics. Examples of such psychological processes can be found during the Reformation period just as they have been present in many other spiritual and ideological movements of earlier and later periods. The image of a "barrier" carries with it the possibilities of weakening or strengthening it, and of raising or lowering it. It is difficult to judge whether and in which direction the barriers would have changed in the long run if no pressure had been applied by the burghers or the territorial prince. In any case these pressures prevented the political elite and the city councils controlled by them from seizing the initiative in the ecclesiastical question.

2. Lutheranism, as a matter of necessity, had to clear a path from "below," that is from the broader burgher strata. The factors which stood in the way of a quick acceptance of the new doctrine by the elite either played no role for these groups or they worked in the opposite direction, encouraging quick acceptance of Lutheranism. The "normal burgher" felt little concern for political opportunities and dangers. He was only too willing to allow his anger free rein in a continuation of medieval riots and burgher protests against growing governmental pressure from within the city and from without. Thus a linkage was easily established between the communal theology of the Reformation and the communal tradition of urban constitutional and societal order. In contrast to the political elite, these groups of citizens had few links with the old church, but felt a natural affinity for the *sola fide* principle.[219]

On account of the communal and corporate accents that were present both in the Reformation and the burgher movement, secondary barriers were added to the primary barriers that separated the political elite from the burgher Reformation movement, which were discussed in the first paragraph. The communal character of the Reformation burgher movement made it more difficult for the political elite to accept Lutheranism, because of the threat it posed for their dominant position in government and the related challenge to the social and economic advantages which they derived from this dominance.

3. It is a hallmark of the particular situation of the Refor-

---

219 In my opinion this affinity existed not only among the lower strata (Seebaß, Diskussionsbericht, note 217) but also among the middle classes.

mation in the northwestern German territorial cities that the
lines of confrontation within the city overlapped with the
opposition of the city to the territorial state. The political elite
saw itself trapped in a kind of pincer movement which forced
them to make a decision. This was especially true when the
territorial prince supported the Catholic position, but also when
the possibility of a Protestant alliance between the burgher
commune and the territorial prince threatened. The
approaching danger from outside put pressure on the religious
parties to reconstruct the internal city consensus that had been
lost through the decision of the citizenry in favor of Lutheranism.[220] In the given situation this could only be attained if
the political elite accepted the religious choice of the burgher
commune. It is worth noting that younger members of the
political elite who had not yet themselves sat on the city council, as well as members of the elite from the artisan stratum,
were apparently able to make this change more quickly.
Finally, the plausibility of the Reformation ethos of a Christian
magistrate and the far-reaching rights of administration for the
political elite which grew together within the new church were
additional factors which tended to lower or even to sweep away
the primary barriers hindering an acceptance of Lutheranism
by the elite.[221]

    4. It is incorrect from the perspective of a social historian to
see the communal opposition in sharp confrontation with the
city council. According to the peculiar structure and dynamic
of the urban burgher world,[222] a part of the elite itself, or at
least the group closest to it when measured by wealth, emerged
as leaders of the opposition and advanced into the city council
if it succeeded. Accompanying the Reformation (305) there was
an acceleration of the normally slow[223] process of replacing the
elite. The question of whether it also meant a shift of political
importance among the different social groups within the ruling
circles, which were for the most part not socially homogeneous
groups, must be analyzed in each individual case. After the rise
of new groups from the merchant and artisan burgher circles,
the advance of academics must be considered as well.

---

220 Moeller, Stadt (note 1), Diskussionsbericht, 181.
221 Moeller, Deutschland (note 1), 112.
222 Schilling, Aufstandsbewegungen (note 6), esp. 230s.
223 Osnabrück is obviously an exception as there were no major changes in the
composition of the city council during the Reformation.

In general the changes which occurred within the city councils in connection with the Reformation are to be seen as one stage of greater or shorter length within long-term processes of social change, running from c. 1450-1650, rather than as a marked or even "revolutionary" break in the history of urban elites. New points of departure must be noted where the communal Reformation movement confronted comparatively archaic constitutional systems as occurred in Göttingen and Emden, but also in a weakened form in Lüneburg. Generally one gains the impression that the urban burgher elite of northwestern Germany was subjected to a more far-reaching transformation at the end of the sixteenth and during the first half of the seventeenth centuries than during the Reformation era.

Conversely, it cannot be said that the urban Reformations were decisively influenced by social and economic differences and divisions within the political elite. Münster was obviously an exception. Its particular path toward the Anabaptist kingdom of Zion was probably connected with, among other factors, the advanced state of estrangement of the *Erbmänner* patriciate from city affairs. In general it must be maintained that the religious lines separating Protestants and Catholics did not run along the social lines separating the upper stratum on the one hand from the middle and lower strata on the other hand. They also did not run along the line separating a newer from an older type or a rising from a declining group within the elite.[224]

5. During the Reformation period proper the urban elites regarded the rise of the early modern territorial state primarily as a threat. Only in a few cases was a burgher existence outside of the cities a viable alternative in the northwestern corner of the Empire. In the majority of the examples discussed the Catholic elite faction remained (306) exclusively oriented toward the city. The social break which occurred during the Reformation was not yet as a rule tied to the creation of different burgher elites, one oriented toward the city and one toward the territorial state. This was obviously the result of the specific situation in northern Germany which differed from that in southern Germany: Even in important principalities such as Brunswick-Wolfenbüttel the rise of an early modern

---

224 The imperial city of Aachen is an example of the opposite development—the polarization of two economically as well as socially opposing elite factions along the confessional lines. See Schilling, Bürgerkämpfe (note 6), 175-231.

bureaucracy run by learned burgher councillors was delayed by about half a century when compared with the Empire and the southern German territories.

This situation changed only in the course of the sixteenth century when the expansion of the princely civil service within the territorial state opened up a new career path for burghers. At the beginning of the seventeenth century a social and political division in the urban elites can often be recognized, reflecting the confrontation between city and territorial state. One faction sought to protect its interests within the urban burgher world and fought for the unity and independence of the burgher corporation. The other faction strove to make a new start within territorial society and was prepared to ally itself with the territorial prince. In those cities and territories where religious and confessional conflicts played a role during this period, confessional systems functioned as an important element of integration both for the old urban burgher elite and for the newer territorial burgher elite. The question of which factors were most decisive for each alternative must remain open for the present. Only two general observations can be made.

a) Only the members of the political elite, particularly academics who came overwhelmingly from the merchant segment of the citizenry, had a choice between two genuine alternatives. The broader artisan strata, and obviously also the majority of the groups who were not burghers, remained oriented toward the city in this early phase, having no other alternative in terms of their subjective evaluation of the situation. It was only later that this part of the urban population recognized the opportunities offered to them by the closer union with the territory, above all economic ones.[225]

b) In contrast to the elites of the imperial cities, who regarded city and territorial careers for officeholders as two possibilities which differed in their legal basis, but were not mutually exclusive and thus could be pursued simultaneously or

---

225 This was the case in Lüneburg at the end of the first third of the seventeenth century and in Brunswick at the end of the second third of the seventeenth century. See Friedland, Kampf (note 104); Heuer, Lüneburg (note 111); Querfurth, Unterwerfung (note 11). - Recently O. Mörke, Der gewollte Weg in Richtung "Untertan". Ökonomische und politische Eliten in Braunschweig, Lüneburg und Göttingen vom 15. bis ins 17. Jahrhundert, in: H. Schilling and H. Diederiks (eds.), Bürgerliche Eliten in den Niederlanden und in Nordwestdeutschland, Köln/Wien 1985, 111-134.

one after the other, their peers in the northwestern German
territorial cities regarded this choice as a fundamental parting
of ways. The choice of one (307) of the two "models of state
and society," the urban or the territorial one, usually meant
declaring war on representatives of the other way.[226] This
changed naturally at the moment when the city was completely
integrated into the territory, ending the conflict between the
urban and territorial burgher elites. Of all the examples
discussed here this development occurred only in Paderborn as
a direct consequence of the religious and confessional conflicts
of the sixteenth and early seventeenth centuries.

6. Finally, there are the long-term consequences of ecclesiastical innovation. An urban Reformation which was introduced independently of the territorial ruler usually
strengthened the position of the city against the territorial
state.[227] The winner was in the first instance the political elite
whose "autonomous rule of the city" was confirmed and
expanded by a widened jurisdiction, including oversight of the
the private lives of individual burghers. In this context the
marital courts and the general supervision of morals are most
important. With the consistories of the Protestant city churches,
the administration of poor relief and church property and
especially the appointment of pastors and teachers, the circle of
offices over which the urban elite had the right of disposal was
considerably enlarged and won greater attractiveness.[228] It must
be supposed that these were additional impulses in a social
process which can be observed in many northwestern German
cities independently of the Reformation. In its course the urban
elite restricted their economic activities and increasingly concentrated upon legal careers and urban offices, mostly supplemented by income accrued through land ownership in the surrounding countryside. Naturally the situation changed fundamentally at the moment when the city church was integrated
into the territorial church system and so was subjugated to the
territorial church government of the prince. In a number of

---

226 In this respect Osnabrück was also an exception (see above note 223).

227 H. Schilling, Der libertär-radikale Republikanismus der holländischen Regenten. Ein Beitrag zur Geschichte des politischen Radikalismus in der frühen
Neuzeit, in: Geschichte und Gesellschaft 10 (1984), 498-533. See also the essays
in: Schilling, Calvinism (note 191).

228 H. Schilling, Die Konfessionalisierung im Reich, in: Historische Zeitschrift 246
(1988), 1-45. English translation below pp. 205-245.

cities this occurred only in the course of the seventeenth century, in special cases even later.

CHAPTER THREE

THE RISE OF EARLY MODERN BURGHER ELITES DURING THE SIXTEENTH AND SEVENTEENTH CENTURIES*

Recent years have witnessed a propitious consolidation of West German research in social history. After initially focusing attention upon workers, the under-classes, and fringe groups, or—applied to the sixteenth and seventeenth centuries—the so-called "common man in the city and countryside" the world of scholarship has shown a renewed interest in the upper strata of urban society and the ruling elites. This development gives reason to hope that in the foreseeable future all social groups will be studied, at least in representative examples, providing us with a clearer picture of the entire spectrum of societal reality for that period. (122) We must keep in mind, however, that analyses covering the entire German Empire are sound only to a point and that concrete conclusions can only be drawn from geographically limited studies. In addition any attempt to describe simultaneously all of the ruling elites of the Holy Roman Empire, fragmented as it was by estate and territory, is subject to certain limitations. Such a synthesis must necessarily remain at the level of compilation and description and must largely dispense with any explicit discussion about the relationship of systematic and theoretical questions.[1]

---

* In translating this article into English, the problems of terminology were considerable: In keeping with the argumentation the expressions "burgher class" and "middle class" had to be eschewed, although they are commonly used in English for modern as well as early modern societies. For groups within the traditional urban society the term "burgher" is used—burgher upper stratum, burgher elites etc. For groups which became independent of early modern urban society by virtue of their economic or political-administrative activities within the territories the term "early modern bourgeoisie" has been used—early modern commercial bourgeoisie (Wirtschaftsbürgertum), early modern civil servant bourgeoisie or bureaucratic bourgeoisie (Beamtenbürgertum). In this case the qualification of "early modern" is crucial, since this Old European type of bourgeoisie must be distinguished from the bourgeoisie of the nineteenth century. "Class" is used in contexts which mark structures or developments toward modern, nineteenth century circumstances.

Consequently, it seems advisable to limit the study of the history of elites more narrowly both topically and geographically. The following discussion relates exclusively to the urban societies of western and northwestern Germany, that is to say the Rhineland north of Frankfort, and the regions of Westphalia and Lower Saxony, including the coastal trade centers of Bremen, Hamburg, and Lübeck. In view of the well-known shift of economic and political importance from southern to northwestern Germany,[2] this area can claim to be the fountainhead of an early modern economic and social dynamic, especially for the development of modern burgher classes (123) within German society.[3]

Thematically this essay should neither be regarded as an exhaustive survey, nor as a well-rounded description of individual groups, their special status or specific activities within the upper social strata.[4] It is, rather, an attempt to offer more than a narrow social historical analysis by describing the contours of developments significant for societal history. Hence the sixteenth and seventeenth centuries should be understood not as a more or less random period of time, but as a unified period of transition in the history of cities, or in the history of urban society. For the history of the upper strata of burgher society in northwestern Germany this period lasts from about 1450 to 1650. Alongside the traditional type of burghers, defined as citizens of towns (*Stadtbürgertum*), a new, early modern type of burgher group emerged, which will be described at greater length. In addition—as will be demonstrated in one of the theses to be discussed—important social changes

---

1 H.H. Hofmann and G. Franz (eds.), Deutsche Führungsschichten in der Neuzeit. Eine Zwischenbilanz, Boppard 1980, (articles by Volker Press, Rudolf Endres and Johannes Kunisch); H. Kellenbenz, Die Gesellschaft der mitteleuropäischen Stadt im 16. Jahrhundert, in: W. Rausch (ed.), Die Stadt an der Schwelle zur Neuzeit, Linz/Donau 1980, 1-20; Th. Brady, Ruling Class, Regime and Reformation at Strasbourg, 1520-1555, Leiden 1978.

2 Discussed in more detail by H. Schilling, Aufbruch und Krise. Deutsche Geschichte 1517-1648, Berlin 1988, 54-84.

3 Cf. Th. Brady, Patricians, Nobles, Merchants: Internal Tension and Solidarities in South German Urban Ruling Classes at the Close of the Middle Ages, in: M. Usher Chrisman and O. Gründler (eds.), Social Groups and Religious Ideas in the Sixteenth Century, Kalamazoo 1978, 38-45, 159-164.

4 W. Klötzer, Der Bankier und seine Stadt. Die öffentliche Verantwortung einer Führungsschicht am Beispiel der Stadt Frankfurt a.M., in: H.H. Hofmann (ed.), Bankherren und Bankiers, Limburg 1978, 1-26; G. von Lenthe, Das Patriziat in Niedersachsen, in: H. Rössler (ed.), Deutsches Patriziat, 1430-1740, Limburg 1968, 157-194.

took place that fulfilled preconditions which, in turn, made possible the later transformation of the Old European *societas civilis* into the middle class economic society of modern times.

The following presentation will examine the developments that were most important for this social transformation in varying degrees of detail under three headings:

—the antecedents of change and differentiation within the political elites, with respect to their composition, self-conception, authority and functions (Part I); (124)

—the new developments and shifts in function within the upper strata of burgher society resulting from the great migrations of the second half of the sixteenth century and the formation of an early modern "commercial bourgeoisie" (*Wirtschaftsbürgertum*) (Part II);

—and finally, some consequences of the Reformation and Counter-Reformation, as well as of confessionalization for the burgher elites (Part III).

To begin with, however, a short explanation of concepts is in order! The phrase "upper stratum" used in the title is understood to be a generic term. It designates that part of the urban or burgher population to which the majority of the social groups discussed in this paper may be assigned, and presupposes a division by strata of the city and its citizenry rather than by classes in the Marxist sense, based upon nineteenth century experience and thus anachronistic for early modern societies. In spite of weighty counter-arguments which have recently been put forward, the application of such a stratification model to the urban and burgher society of Old Europe, especially for the early modern period, is justifiable in my opinion.[5] This term must of course be understood in a multi-faceted way, i.e., in addition to property and wealth, other aspects of social status such as legal and constitutional status—particularly offices and participation in government—as well as prestige and positions of honor are considered. The term "elite," used primarily in part I, refers to the specific activities and accomplishments of these social groups;

---

5 Cf. E. Weyrauch, Über soziale Schichtung, in: I. Batori (ed.), Städtische Gesellschaft und Reformation, Stuttgart 1980, 5-58. H. Stoob takes a different approach in idem, (ed.), Altständisches Bürgertum, vol. 2, Darmstadt 1978, Introduction; W. Ehbrecht (ed.), Städtische Führungsschichten und Gemeinde in der werdenden Neuzeit, Köln 1980, IX.-For examples of sociological approaches, see H.P. Dreitzel, Elitebegriff und Sozialstruktur, Stuttgart 1961; K. v. Beyme, "Elite," in: Sowjetsystem und demokratische Gesellschaft, vol. 2, 103-128.

it defines elites according to their function and not by their own evaluation. The upper stratum of the medieval cities, which had previously been relatively unified in northwestern Germany, separated into several different elites responsible for various functions, only some of which remained oriented toward cities in the course (125) of the transformational processes described below. In the early modern period distinctions must be drawn between political, economic, and intellectual—either ecclesiastical and religious or profane and secular—elites within the citizenry. Parts of the burgher upper strata cannot be identified with any of these elites, because as pensioners or prebendaries they were obliged to refrain from exercising any public functions. The above-mentioned "functional elites" exercised authority in certain segments of society and so were sectorial ruling elites. By contrast only the political elite, that is the city council and magisterial circles within the cities as well as the territorial civil servants, can be included within the overarching category of ruling elites in the early modern period. Even within the urban burgher milieu of Old Europe, a share in political power or the exercise of authority still carried with it the highest prestige. Within this conceptual framework it is possible to speak with Theodor Schieder of an "elite pluralism" already during the early modern era, although not yet of a pluralism of equal ruling groups.[6] The peculiar transitional character of the period under discussion is revealed in this distinction. Finally, the spatially fragmented composition of the early modern social system should be kept in mind: the upper stratum, functional elites, and ruling groups within urban societies were organized within local or territorial units, irrespective of overarching familial and social connections. Nevertheless, it is possible to examine the history of elites structured in this way according to their common lines of development.

I. CHANGES WITHIN THE POLITICAL ELITES

The political elites of the urban centers of western and northwestern Germany—that is the portions of their upper strata which exercised governmental and administrative functions—went through a process of transformation (126) and

---

6 Th. Schieder, Theorie der Führungsschichten in der Neuzeit, in: Hofmann/Franz (eds.), Führungsschichten (note 1), 13-28.

differentiation between 1450 and 1650. This process affected both their social recruitment and self-understanding, as well as the status of these social groups within the society at large. Three developments can be distinguished, each closely related to the other.

1. The transformation, accomplished in different stages, of the elites of the late medieval Hanseatic cities—in most cities composed of a patriciate that had emerged from an older Hanseatic merchant elite—into a political elite of the early modern imperial and territorial cities on the basis of the shifts in social recruiting for magisterial groups.

2. The related advance of academics, primarily holders of law degrees, into the circles of the political elite of territorial as well as imperial cities during the fifteenth and sixteenth centuries. At first they were present only on the edges of these circles as advisors with legal expertise, but beginning in the sixteenth century they became increasingly important and by the seventeenth century they had reached the center of the magisterial and mayoral circles themselves, and so shared in the responsibility and authority of political decision-making.[7]

3. The entry of legal experts into these spheres was closely related to the establishment of a new sort of political elite within the citizenry which was no longer primarily oriented to the cities, but toward the territories and their rulers. The new elite often took positions on legal and constitutional norms, political functions, and frequently in city-territory conflicts that were in marked opposition to the older political elites of the urban burgher strata.

These transformations may be generalized only with such comparatively vague formulation. They were expressed differently in the various cities and rural areas ruled by cities, according to their stages of social development, the constitutional and economic structure of each city and especially

---

7 K. Wriedt, Das gelehrte Personal in der Verwaltung und Diplomatie der Hansestädte, in: Hansische Geschichtsblätter 96 (1978), 15-37; idem, Stadtrat-Bürgertum-Universität am Beispiel norddeutscher Hansestädte, in: B. Moeller et al. (eds.), Studien zum städtischen Bildungswesen, Göttingen 1983, 499-523; idem, Bürgertum und Studium, in: J. Fried (ed.), Schulen und Studium, Sigmaringen 1986, 487-525. W. Herborn, Der graduierte Ratsherr. Zur Entwicklung einer neuen Elite im Kölner Rat der frühen Neuzeit, in: H. Schilling and H. Diederiks (eds.), Bürgerliche Eliten in den Niederlanden und in Nordwestdeutschland, Köln/Wien 1985, 195-274.-For overviews of the problem: W. Trusen, Anfänge des gelehrten Rechts in Deutschland, Wiesbaden 1952; R. Schnur (ed.), Die Rolle der Juristen bei der Entstehung des modernen Staates, Berlin 1986.

its political status *vis à vis* the territorial state. The latter condition was especially important for territorial cities, but was
also significant under specific conditions for imperial cities.
Behind the differing situations and structures of particular
examples, however, some general lines of development can be
recognized to a certain degree. These will be the focus of the
following discussion. (127)

1. Changes in the Social Composition of City Councils.

Quantitatively there was a more or less comprehensive change
of families within the ruling councils in most cities of western
and northwestern Germany beginning at the end of the fifteenth century, and accelerating during the sixteenth century.
The Reformation, which was also in this region a movement of
urban burghers during its early period, caused a phase of swift
acceleration in this process of renewal within different cities.
A social revolutionary break in the composition of the magisterial circles did not, however, occur, even in Münster and
Lübeck, which through the rule of the Anabaptists and Jürgen
Wullenwever expressed the most extreme positions of the
Reformation within the Hanseatic cities.[8] The developments in
Lübeck make it especially clear how much the changes which
occurred followed the line of social development that had been
recognizable since the late Middle Ages. The much studied
coup of Jürgen Wullenwever brought to political power not the
artisans or even broader segments of the population, but rather
members of the wealthy, active merchant community
(*Kaufmannschaft*). In other cities of northwestern Germany,
above all in neighboring Hamburg, this social group was qualified for membership in the city council. In Lübeck, however,
it had been excluded from the political elite by an archaic
patrician constitution that recognized no institutional right of
participation for other burghers. This council of merchants was
able to retain power for only a few years and after the failure
especially of its foreign policy had to give way before a restoration of the patrician council.

The large Rhineland cities of Frankfort, Cologne and
Aachen must be excluded from this generalization regarding
the historical changes in elites that occurred during the Refor-

---

8 K.-H. Kirchhoff, Die Täufer in Münster 1534/35, Münster 1973; G. Korell,
Jürgen Wullenwever, Weimar 1980.

mation,[9] although in general they do not diverge from other lines of social development described below. (128) Aachen even made up a developmental deficit through this coupling of Reformation and changes in its elite during its later Calvinist-influenced Reformation.

The concrete social historical content of the changes is best illustrated by the example of Münster,[10] because the social developments clearly unfold there in chronological sequence, while in other cases they were complicated by unclear circumstances and transitional stages. The city council of this Westphalian episcopal city during both centuries under consideration was successively characterized by the following three types of burgher elites:

—until roughly 1460 by the so-called "hereditary patriciate," which had developed out of the merchant oligarchy of the early Hanseatic period beginning in the late fourteenth century;

—from the end of the fifteenth century by a *Honoratiorentum* of the guilds, composed of the newer merchants and including wealthy artisans, particularly from the "commercial crafts,"[11] while the patriciate increasingly withdrew from the council and city in order to live as landed nobility;

—finally, after the beginning of the seventeenth century, by the appearance of a legally educated civil service aristocracy (*Beamtenaristokratie*), oriented toward the territorial ruler, which actually took over the government within the city after the eminent and mighty Prince Bishop Christoph Bernhard

9 S. Jahns, Frankfurt, Reformation und Schmalkaldischer Bund, Frankfurt 1976; R. Scribner, Why was there no Reformation in Cologne?, in: Bulletin of the Institute of Historical Research 49 (1976), 217-241; F. Petri, Im Zeitalter der Glaubenskämpfe, in: Rheinische Geschichte, vol. 2, Düsseldorf 1976, 25ss.; H. Schilling, Bürgerkämpfe in Aachen zu Beginn des 17. Jahrhunderts. Konflikte im Rahmen der alteuropäischen Stadtgesellschaft oder im Umkreis der frühbürgerlichen Revolution?, in: Zeitschrift für Historische Forschung 1 (1974), 175-231.

10 Cf. H. Schilling, Die politische Elite nordwestdeutscher Städte in den religiösen Auseinandersetzungen des 16. Jahrhunderts, in: W.J. Mommsen (ed.), Stadtbürgertum und Adel in der Reformation, Stuttgart 1979, 235-308 (English translation above pp. 61-134). F. v. Klocke, Das Patriziatsproblem und die Werler Erbsälzer, Münster 1965; H. Mitgau, Geschlossene Heiratskreise sozialer Inzucht, G. von Lenthe, Das Patriziat in Niedersachsen, H. Lahrkamp, Das Patriziat in Münster, in: Rössler (ed.), Patriziat (note 4); I. Batori, Das Patriziat der deutschen Stadt, in: Zeitschrift für Stadtgeschichte, Stadtsoziologie und Denkmalpflege 1 (1975), 1-30; J. Lampe, Aristokratie, Hofadel und Staatspatriziat in Kurhannover, 2 vols., Göttingen 1963.

11 H. Reincke, Bevölkerungsproblem der Hansestädte, in: C. Haase, Die Stadt des Mittelalters, vol. 3, Darmstadt 1973, 256-302, here 287.

(129) von Galen forcibly incorporated his cathedral city, which up to this time had been relatively independent, into the territorial state in 1661.

The developments in Münster mark the main lines of elite history during the early modern period: from a medieval merchant oligarchy, which over the course of the fifteenth century in many cities developed increasingly into a Hanseatic patriciate, defined by birth and bound by marriage alliances, through a *Honoratiorentum* during the "long sixteenth century," consisting of artisans and merchants and, in part, wealthy retailers. These were forced to share power on the one hand with remnants of the patriciate and on the other with the lawyers. These gave way, finally, to a civil service aristocracy (*Beamtenaristokratie*) whose horizons lay beyond those of the urban burgher strata, and who controlled the fate of the cities during the last one hundred and fifty years of the *ancien régime* in agreement with, if not always completely dependent on, the territorial rulers. This same movement can be recognized in a number of other cities within our region, modified or perhaps limited by their size and their constitutional, legal, and economic relationships, as well as the political constellation of city and territory. In addition there are at least in some cases considerable shifts in the chronology of the phases.

The three types of elites drawn from the example of Münster will be used as ideal types, according to the definition of the term first given by Max Weber. A patriciate is characterized by an exclusivity of status through birth, and a narrow circle of marriage as well as by its "closure of status" (von Klocke) and homogeneity. A *Honoratiorentum* is characterized by its availability (in the Weberian sense of *Abkömmlichkeit von Berufspflichten*) both because its wealth was derived from direct economic activity and because of its relative openness to newcomers. A civil service aristocracy (*Beamtenaristokratie*) is characterized by officeholders exercising governmental and administrative powers which were delegated by a monopolistic holder of supreme power, by its specific qualifications for the exercise of authority, and by supervision and guaranteed remuneration, although this was limited in the case of the cities.

Similarities with the Münster model are most apparent in the neighboring episcopal cities of Osnabrück and Hildesheim, and to a certain degree also in Paderborn, even if there the Hanseatic patriciate was not so clearly developed. The similarities are also easily recognized in Brunswick and Lüneburg, as well as in Göttingen and Hanover.[12] The two latter cities lacked, however, a clearly defined patriciate, although the change in composition of their elites is unmistakable, in the case of Hanover forcibly compressed into the Reformation period. There was also a change of elites (130) in many of the middle-sized and smaller Hanseatic cities and in territorial cities, where on the one hand the medieval merchant oligarchy had not achieved the "closure of status" of a patriciate, and where on the other, beside the actual *Honoratiorentum* of the sixteenth century, lesser merchants, street pedlars, and even simple artisans could enter the circle of the political elite. In other words, there was a shift toward those with lower social standing at both levels. These groups did not attain genuine political importance, since the retailers and local artisans had too small a base of accumulated wealth at their disposal for long-term political involvement. As a consequence in such cases the real political elite consisted of the mayoral circle and the legally qualified members of the magistrate.

Given the individuality of Old European cities in constitutional and societal structure, there were also clear deviations and special developments. There is, for example, the salt city of Werl in the archiepiscopal territories of Cologne whose social history, especially its elite history, has received particular scholarly attention. Despite conflicts with the rest of the burghers, its hereditary salt patriciate was able to maintain its political hegemony until it withdrew from the city council after its collective elevation to the nobility in 1725.[13] In the East Frisian city of Emden, which experienced rapid economic growth during the second half of the sixteenth century thanks to the political and economic crises in the Netherlands, we encounter social and constitutional developments that usually took several centuries squeezed into a few decades at the end of the sixteenth and the beginning of the seventeenth centuries. The development here ran in the opposite direction, from an open *Honoratiorentum* during the sixteenth century to a quasi-patriciate during the seventeenth and eighteenth centuries, related to the pattern of development in the neighboring Dutch

---

12 Recently described by S. Müller, Stadt, Kirche und Reformation. Das Beispiel der Landstadt Hannover, Hannover 1987.

13 von Klocke, Patriziatsproblem (note 10).

cities with their regent-patriciate.[14] The third stage, the takeover of power by a civil service aristocracy, did not occur during this period in Emden, because the city was successful in resisting its integration into the territorial state of the Counts of East Friesland. Similarly, in the Hanseatic city Lemgo, located in the Westphalian County of Lippe, the sixteenth century *Honoratiorentum*, which had a rich medieval tradition, was able to (131) maintain its independence.[15] In both territories a civil service aristocracy in an especially pure form arose in nearby cities, which in both their traditions and their political and economic importance were subordinate to Emden and Lemgo. These were Aurich and Detmold, where the territorial rulers had withdrawn together with their courts and central administrations, after leaving the larger cities of Emden and Lemgo.[16]

The sociological pattern of elite development in the imperial cities must be distinguished from that of the Hanseatic cities under the jurisdiction of territorial states. By their very nature the imperial cities did not experience the third type of civil service aristocracy that was oriented toward a territorial prince. There is, however, a comparable development from the mid-seventeenth century in that legal experts entered the magisterial circles, although this was not in opposition to urban tradition. This phenomenon will be examined more closely in the following two sections. In the case of Cologne the transition from a medieval patriciate to an early modern *Honoratiorentum* was accomplished after the introduction of the guild or *Gaffel* constitution in the so-called *Verbundbrief* of 1396, a century earlier than the Hanseatic cities mentioned above. This constitution and the high degree of development already present in the medieval patriciate indicate that the Rhine metropolis followed the form of urban development common in southern and

---

14 H. Schilling, Reformation und Bürgerfreiheit. Emdens Weg zur calvinistischen Stadtrepublik, in: B. Moeller (ed.), Stadt und Kirche im 16. Jahrhundert, Gütersloh 1978, 128-161, esp. 153ss. (English Translation in H. Schilling, Civic Calvinism, Kirksville 1991).

15 Details in H. Schilling, Konfessionskonflikt und Staatsbildung, Gütersloh 1981, 259-291, 352-364, 376-378. English short version: H. Schilling, Between the Territorial State and Urban Liberty. Lutheranism and Calvinism in the County of Lippe, in: R. Po-chia Hsia (ed.), The German People and the Reformation, Ithaca 1988, 263-283.

16 W. Conring, Die Stadt und Gerichtsverfassung der ostfriesischen Residenz Aurich bis zum Übergang Ostfrieslands an Preußen im Jahre 1744, Aurich 1966; Geschichte der Stadt Detmold, Detmold 1953.

western Germany.[17] This is true for Aachen as well, although the transition there took place in the mid-fifteenth century.[18] In the Westphalian imperial city of Dortmund the change in composition of the elite was closely linked with the late victory of Lutheranism in the final third of the sixteenth century.[19] Frankfort had a special status, in that it never introduced a guild constitution which formally dissolved the patrician constitution (132), but instituted a three bench constitution. The patriciate, which dominated the city government until the end of the *ancien régime*, controlled the first and second benches, those of the *Schöffen* and the *Gemeinheit*. Artisans were represented through the third, the guild bench, which gave them a limited right of participation.[20] If council members of all three ranks are regarded as members of the political elite, which in the end is a question of definition, then it can be established that in Frankfort the "political elite" and "upper social strata" were no longer congruent circles of society in the early modern period. In Lübeck the medieval patriciate maintained its monopoly on power, as has been noted, after the coup by the mercantile *Honoratiorentum* during the Wullenwever episode and its subsequent failure to govern the city effectively, although the patriciate steadily became weaker through the intrusion of lawyers into magisterial circles which began toward the end of the sixteenth century. The *Honoratiorentum* of non-patrician merchant companies was able to achieve a genuine share in city government only in 1669.[21]

---

17 W. Herborn, Die politische Führungsschicht der Stadt Köln im Spätmittelalter, Bonn 1977; idem, Verfassungsideal und Verfassungswirklichkeit in Köln, in: W. Ehbrecht (ed.), Städtische Führungsgruppen und Gemeinde in der werdenden Neuzeit, Köln/Wien 1980, 25-52; F. Irsigler, Soziale Wandlungen in der Kölner Kaufmannschaft im 14. und 15. Jahrhundert, in: Hansische Geschichtsblätter 92 (1974), 59-78.

18 E. Meuthen, Der gesellschaftliche Hintergrund der Aachener Verfassungskämpfe an der Wende vom Mittelalter zur Neuzeit, in: Zeitschrift des Aachener Geschichtsvereins 74/75 (1962/63), 299-392.

19 H. Schilling, Dortmund im 16. und 17. Jahrhundert-Reichsstädtische Gesellschaft, Reformation und Konfessionalisierung, in: Dortmund-1100 Jahre Stadtgeschichte. Festschrift G. Luntowski and N. Reimann (eds.), Dortmund 1982, 151-202, esp. 186ss.

20 Cf. Jahns, Frankfurt (note 9); M. Meyn, Die Reichsstadt Frankfurt vor dem Bürgeraufstand von 1612 bis 1614, Frankfurt 1980; G. Soliday, A Community in Conflict. Frankfurt Society in the 17th and Early 18th Centuries, Hanover/N.H. 1974.

21 F. Bruns, Der Lübecker Rat, in: Zeitschrift des Vereins für Lübeckische Geschichte und Altertumskunde 32 (1951), 1-69; J. Asch, Rat und Bürgerschaft in Lübeck 1598-1669, Lübeck 1961; M.L. Pelus, Lübeck au milieu du 17e siècle:

The North Sea port cities of Bremen and Hamburg diverge the most from the model example of Münster. They were ruled during the Middle Ages and early modern period (during the latter with the participation of lawyers) by an open *Honoratio-rentum* of merchants which never evolved into a closed patriciate determined by birth. In Bremen, however, after the mid-seventeenth century there are traces of the more typical pattern in that it became normal for merchants who were active in the city council to give up active participation in the economic life of the city and live off their accumulated wealth as rentiers. This development is almost certainly related to the beginning of a contraction in the general economy of the city on the Weser.[22] By contrast, Hamburg continued to prosper greatly (133) from changes in the economic situation.[23] The merchants, who sat together with lawyers in the governing bodies of this port city during the early modern period, continued to participate actively in its trade and economic life. The city council members who were lawyers were tied closely to trade through their family relations, even if they themselves were not directly involved in trading ventures.

What is especially enlightening about Hamburg as a special case with a unique interrelation of social and economic structures or developments is, in my opinion, the particular stratification of early modern society in this city. Although a clear elite emerges that was to a large extent the sole executor of political as well as economic power, membership in it was not established or limited by status or stratum.[24] While in nearly all other cities during the early modern period, particularly in nearby Bremen,[25] wealth (134) and to an increasing degree the

Conflicts politiques et sociaux, conjuncture économique, in: Revue d'Histoire Diplomatique 92 (1978), 189-209; A. Grassmann (ed.), Lübeckische Geschichte, Lübeck 1988.

22 R. Prange, Die bremische Kaufmannschaft des 16. und 17. Jahrhunderts in sozialgeschichtlicher Betrachtung, Bremen 1963; H. Schwarzwälder, Geschichte der Freien Hansestadt Bremen, vol. 1, Bremen 1975; H. Kellenbenz, Der Bremer Kaufmann, in: Bremisches Jahrbuch 51 (1969), 19-49.

23 M. Reißmann, Die hamburgische Kaufmannschaft des 17. Jahrhunderts in sozialgeschichtlicher Sicht, Hamburg 1975; P.E. Schramm, Hamburg. Ein Sonderfall in der Geschichte Deutschlands, Hamburg 1964; H.-D. Loose, Hamburg. Geschichte der Stadt und ihrer Bewohner, 2 vols., Hamburg 1982-86.

24 Reißmann, Kaufmannschaft, 316; H. Reincke, Forschungen und Skizzen zur Hamburgischen Geschichte, Hamburg 1951, 221-240, esp. 229.

25 Prange, Kaufmannschaft (note 22), 118ss.-For the problem in general cf. E. Maschke, Unterschichten der mittelalterlichen Städte Deutschlands, in: Haase (ed.), Stadt (note 11), 345-454, here 352; idem, Die Schichtung der mittelalter-

possession of office, and above all, the status of burgomaster or councillor, counted as the most important criteria of social status, in Hamburg obviously vocation remained the most important factor for social classification, while a public office, private fortune and social origins were of only secondary importance.[26] On the tip of the societal pyramid stood the merchant, regardless of his actual capital. Obviously what was measured was not his concrete personal fortune, but rather his possibilities for profit. This situation is, in my opinion, of greatest importance both for the economic possibilities and for the recruitment of Hamburg's political elite. Economically this high social status opened up for every merchant, regardless of the actual extent of his wealth, the best possible economic opportunities, even for those with little capital or for those in business difficulties. This was because the credit-worthiness of individual merchants, which was of exceptional importance for trading practice during the early modern period, could not be limited by a classification according to categories of dress, established by a *Kleiderordnung*. For the political elite this vocation-oriented stratification model meant that the boundaries between orders could not harden, which could have served to ossify the given social and economic conditions at a certain time and stage of social development. The possibility remained for a continual addition of new members to the circles of political leadership. The political elite of Hamburg was thus clearly different from those of most other cities.

When we ask about the causes for the changes described in the composition of the urban burgher elite, the last-named example of Hamburg points us first to economy and the changing competitive situation both in general and in limited local areas. Economic reasons also take a prominent place in the historical development of elites in the other cities of the region under investigation. The penetration of artisans and merchants into the political elites after the middle of the fifteenth century is closely related to their increasing economic importance. The earliest economic impulse for this development

---

lichen Stadtbevölkerung, in: Méthodologie de l'Histoire et des sciences humaines, Toulouse 1973, 367-379; W. Ehrbrecht, Zu Ordnung und Selbstverständnis städtischer Gesellschaft im späten Mittelalter, in: Blätter für deutsche Landesgeschichte 110 (1974), 83-103; For an opposing position, see J. Ellermeyer, Sozialgruppen, Selbstverständnis, Vermögen und städtische Verordnungen, in: Blätter für Deutsche Landesgeschichte 113 (1977), 203-275.

26 Reißmann, Kaufmannschaft (note 23), passim, esp. 293-296, 308ss.

grew out of the general economic conditions of the late Middle Ages, which favored manufacturing. Hence, in the cities of our area, where the crafts were traditionally less developed than mercantile trade, the relative economic importance of crafts grew. The advance of leading artisans (135) into the political elites of the northwestern German cities is thus a parallel development, somewhat delayed, to the historical changes in elites which began in the southern and southwestern German cities in connection with the so-called "guild revolutions" or "burgher movements" (*Bürgerkämpfe*). However, it is typical of the pattern of development for the cities in the region under consideration that conditions remained at least somewhat favorable for profits in manufacturing, and hence also for a corresponding rise in the status of artisans, despite the changes in the economic situation as a whole during the sixteenth century, i.e., the change from an agricultural depression into an agricultural boom. This is especially true for the building trades, which due to intensive construction activity by the upper burgher strata and nobility—one need only consider the so-called Weser Renaissance—profited indirectly from the agricultural boom. The situation was similar for the so-called "commercial crafts," whose artisans not only produced their wares, but could also profit from related activities. Some, such as goldsmiths, were involved in financial activity and others, such as butchers and brewers, took part in long-distance trade in cattle and beer.

Among city dwellers the land-owning burgher upper stratum naturally profited the most from the agricultural boom. In our region these were usually families of the older Hanseatic patriciate who had invested their mercantile profits in land. Apart from their income from property rental, they also profited greatly from the grain trade, occasionally arousing the anger of their fellow citizens by their speculation in grain. From the end of the fifteenth century, however, newer families arose to prominence on the basis of mercantile activity, in part even from the retail activities of shopkeepers and pedlars. This development is related to the economic impulses generated by a spasmodic rise in trade and transportation activities first in the Baltic, and later also in the North Sea and the Atlantic. The merchants who were active in the hinterlands directly adjoining the coastal areas of western and northwestern Germany were indirectly involved in this economic expansion to the extent that they conveyed new goods from Holland and the German North Sea coast to the regions of lower Saxony and Westphalia and to a lesser degree also to Hesse and central Germany. In exchange, Westphalia, including the region of Osnabrück with its linen industry could offer a product in increasing demand, even outside of Europe. Since linen production took place exclusively in rural areas, the urban artisans could not profit much from it. By contrast it offered tradesmen of any field or any size, who were ready and in a position to take advantage of it, an excellent opportunity to become wholesalers and distributors. Apart from a few special exceptions, where non-local distributors, particularly those from the Wuppertal, (136) took over the linen trade, the inhabitants of the Westphalian cities were able to use this situation to their advantage. Consequently, alongside of the Hanseatic merchant of the older type arose both a newer type of long-distance merchant with new goods to sell and distributors of rural manufactured goods, who worked as intermediaries between the regions of production and sale.[27]

All of this demonstrates that if the crisis situation of the Hanseatic trade is overemphasized then a one-sided picture of the economic and social possibilities available in our region results. Such a crisis was decisive for the contraction of trade and general economic activity in the Baltic sea cities, particularly Lübeck, where accordingly the rise of the new *Honoratiorentum* was also very long delayed.[28] Already in other Wendish Hanseatic cities there were important new economic developments during the sixteenth century which offset the losses in the sectors of the older Hanseatic trade.[29] For lower

27 E. Geiger, Die soziale Elite der Hansestadt Lemgo und die Entstehung eines Exportgewerbes auf dem Lande in der Zeit von 1450 bis 1650, Detmold 1976; H. Schilling, European Crisis of the 1590s. The Situation in German Towns, in: P. Clark (ed.), The Crisis of the 1590s, London 1985, 135-156.

28 Recent research shows that even Lübeck did not decline in every respect. Cf. P. Jeannin, Die Rolle Lübecks in der hansischen Spanien- und Portugalfahrt des 16. Jahrhunderts, in: Zeitschrift des Vereins für Lübeckische Geschichte und Altertumskunde 43 (1963), 19-67 and 55 (1975), 5-40; E. Harder-Gersdorff, Lübeck, Danzig und Riga. Ein Beitrag zur Frage der Handelskonjunktur im Ostseeraum am Ende des 17. Jahrhunderts, in: Hansische Geschichtsblätter 96 (1978), 106-138; Pelus, Lübeck (note 21), 206ss. C. Meyer-Stoll, Die lübeckische Kaufmannschaft des 17. Jahrhunderts, Frankfurt 1989, discusses the situation of the late seventeenth century, i.e., economic decline and the late formation of a Honoratiorentum.

29 K.-P. Zoellner, Vom Strelasund zum Oslofjord, Weimar 1974; H. Langer, Stralsund 1600-1630, Weimar 1970.

Saxony and Westphalia the sixteenth century was simultaneously a period of crises and decline and also of new beginnings and positive economic impulses. Even the Rhineland
cities as far south as Frankfort profited from the new Atlantic
dynamism until the end of the sixteenth century. They became
intermediaries between the North Sea ports, above all in the
Netherlands, and the older economic centers of southern
Germany. Especially for Cologne, where until recently the
turning point in this development was considered to be (137)
the end of the sixteenth century, it has now been shown that
the local mercantile community was involved in important
trading ventures until well into the second half of the seventeenth century.[30]

The new impulses of historical development in manufacturing and commerce were the basis for the growing economic
importance of families that did not belong to the older Hanseatic merchants or the Hanseatic patriciate. Through the
Honoratiorentum of the "long sixteenth century" these families
also won a share of political power in the cities. Typical of the
economic possibilities of this epoch are the cases, by no means
rare, of families whose social rise can almost be described as
meteoric. The Dutch regent patriciate is a well-known example,
where within two generations a family could rise from obscure
social origins to the circles of the mighty Amsterdam ruling
families and hence to the very pinnacle of Dutch society.[31] In
attenuated form similar cases can be found in neighboring
German cities, not only among the Dutch exiles such as the van
der Meulen family in Bremen, which was already reckoned to
be a merchant family of high social status in the second generation after the arrival of its first member, a cobbler, but also
within the native burgher strata of so traditional a city as
Cologne, where Arnold van Brauweiler, Arnold van Siegen, and
Philipp Geil, the sons of an artisan, a sailor, and a "simple
shopkeeper" respectively, rose to the top of the political elite.[32]

---

30 A. Dietz, Frankfurter Handelsgeschichte, vols. 1 and 2, Frankfurt 1910/21;
H. Kellenbenz (ed.), Zwei Jahrtausende Kölner Wirtschaft, Köln 1975, esp. the
article by S. Gramulla.

31 Well-known examples are Frans Banning Kocq and Jacob Poppens. J.E.
Elias, De Vroedschap von Amsterdam, 1578-1795, 2 vols., Haarlem 1903.

32 R. van Roosbroeck, Niederländische Patrizier im Exil, in: Rössler (ed.),
Patriziat (note 4), 209-230, here 214; Prange, Kaufmannschaft (note 22), 235.
Köln: Herborn, Verfassungsideal (note 17), 46; H. Kellenbenz, Zur Sozialstruktur
der rheinischen Bischofsstädte in der frühen Neuzeit, in: F. Petri (ed.), Bischofs-

Unlike the shift from the Hanseatic patriciate to the *Hono-ratiorentum* of the sixteenth century, the transition to the civil service aristocracy did not occur for economic reasons, but for political and constitutional ones. It was in the best interest of the territorial rulers to have the governing bodies (138) of the cities under their jurisdiction staffed by men who no longer felt that their first allegiance was to the world of the cities. Certainly the territorial state also blazed new economic trails. It must be maintained, however, that the new civil service aristocracy (*Beamtenaristokratie*) was not bound to the economy to the same degree as the medieval merchant patriciate and the sixteenth century *Honoratiorentum*. And above all a mercantilistic view of the economy was only rarely the immediate reason for the shift to a new kind of elite within the cities. The end of municipal independence was the chief reason, and thus a political motive which the territorial prince and his civil servants pursued, if necessary even at the cost of a city's economic prosperity. The subjugation of Münster in 1661 serves as an example. The case of fortress cities such as Hameln, Minden, and Wesel shows an even more striking application of the same political principle. In these cities the political and military situation of their respective territorial states had absolute priority over the commercial and manufacturing interests of the burghers, which were in the truest sense of the word suffocated by a ring of fortifications.[33] As the case of Brunswick demonstrates, this weak or non-existent link between the civil service aristocracy and the economic sphere did not in principle prevent a city from deriving any economic advantages from its incorporation into a territorial state.[34] On the other hand, when the urban

---

und Kathedralstädte des Mittelalters und der frühen Neuzeit, Köln 1976, 118-145, here 126.

33 C. Haase, Die mittelalterliche Stadt als Festung, in: idem (ed.), Die Stadt des Mittelalters, vol. 1, Darmstadt 1975, 377-407; G. Eimer, Die Stadtplanung im schwedischen Ostseereich, 1600-1715, Stockholm (1961); G. Parker, The Army of Flanders and the Spanish Road, 1567-1659, Cambridge 1972.-Heimatchronik der Stadt und des Lankreises Hameln-Pyrmont, Köln 1961; V.U. Meinhardt, Die Festung Minden. Gestalt, Struktur und Geschichte einer Stadtfestung, Minden 1958; H.P. Dorfs, Wesel. Eine städtisch-geograpische Monographie mit einem Vergleich zu anderen Festungsstädten, Bonn 1972.-W. Kohl, Christoph Bernhard von Galen. Politische Geschichte des Fürstbistums Münster 1650-1678, Münster 1964; H. Eichberg, Militär und Technik, Düsseldorf 1978; H.W. Herrmann and F. Irsigler (eds.), Beiträge zur Geschichte der frühneuzeitlichen Festungs- und Garnisonsstadt, Saarbrücken 1983.

34 H.J. Querfurth, Die Unterwerfung der Stadt Braunschweig im Jahre 1671,

Honoratioren resisted subjugation by the territorial state, political goals—especially the preservation of municipal autonomy—were often set above considerations of economic utility as well.[35]

The importance of non-economic factors for the social history of the upper burgher strata is further revealed within our period of study by the fact that in many cities the older Hanseatic (139) patriciate could maintain a share in the government alongside the newer, socially mobile, economically more powerful *Honoratiorentum* through all the economic changes until well into the seventeenth century, in some cases even into the eighteenth century. The reason they could retain their political power was above all that—apart from the exception of Hamburg—the socio-economic criteria which were decisive for social prestige or membership in a political elite gave priority not to profession or economic function but to wealth and property, which were more permanent than success in active economic life. These criteria and reputation, which was so important in Old European society, as well as respect for the traditional law ensured both strong continuity within the circles of the political elite and that the replacement process usually occurred very slowly. In those places where the patriciate withdrew from the government it did so by its own will, as happened in Münster and Osnabrück as well as in Brunswick and Lüneburg. Lübeck is again a noteworthy exception. During the revolt of Jürgen Wullenwever the patriciate was forcibly removed from power and the mercantile *Honoratiorentum* seized exclusive control of the government. This radical deviation from the usual course of development within the history of elites, which can be observed even during the period of Anabaptist rule in Münster, could be partially responsible for the complete fiasco of Jürgen Wullenwever's rule in Lübeck during the 1530's.

In connection with the resistance of the older group within the political elite another interesting phenomenon should be noted that I can only allude to for lack of space: The families of the older merchant oligarchies which, apart from those of Cologne within our region, were, strictly speaking, not yet restricted by birth at the end of the fifteenth century, became

Braunschweig 1953; O. Mörke, Der gewollte Weg in Richtung Untertan, in: Schilling/Diederiks (eds.), Eliten (note 7), 111-134.

35 E.g. the case of Lemgo, cf. the literature in note 15 above.

increasingly closed at the same time as the younger *Honoratio-rentum* rose in power, and this resulted in a further weakening of the merchant oligarchy's own influence upon city government. Besides restricting marital possibilities, patrician societies were founded or developed into associations exclusively for those born into the proper order.[36] In Lüneburg the *Theodori-Gilde* of the salt producers (*Sülfmeister*) was founded in 1461 as a response to violent burgher unrest. After its founding, additions to the patrician circle, already very selective, ceased. In Brunswick the consolidation of patriciate families, already remarkably high when the so-called *Lilienvente* society was founded in 1384, achieved nearly complete social closure by founding the *Gelagebruderschaft* society in 1569.[37] There was a similar occurrence in (140) Soest with the patriciate society *Zum Stern*, first mentioned in 1517. In order to protect their remaining political rights as best they could from the *Honoratioren* and the guild masters, who themselves had recently founded the *Stalgadum-Gesellschaft* as a base for political activity on behalf of the crafts, the patriciate, already loosely united probably through the Schleswig brotherhood, closed themselves off more tightly in *Zum Stern*, in order to assure the most effective use of the political rights which remained to them.[38] In Lübeck the closure of the patrician circle, organized since 1379 as the *Zirkelgesellschaft*, was completed with the refounding of this society after the Reformation crisis.[39] And even in those places where institutionalization of this kind did not occur, for instance in Frankfort and Dortmund, there was a similar movement away from previously more open habits of acceptance over the course of the sixteenth century.[40] The

---

36 Cf. the literature in note 10 above.

37 W. Spieß, Der Stand der Geschlechter und der Stand der weißen Rose. Das Problem "Patriziat" und "Honoratiorentum" in der Stadt Braunschweig im 16. und 17. Jahrhundert, in: Braunschweigisches Jahrbuch 30 (1949), 65-80; O. Mörke, Rat und Bürger in der Reformation. Soziale Gruppen und kirchlicher Wandel in den Hansestädten Lüneburg, Braunschweig und Göttingen, Hildesheim 1983.

38 F. v. Klocke, Patriziat und Stadtadel im alten Soest, Lübeck 1927, 78ss.; idem, Die Honoratioren des Soester Stalgadums, in: Mitteilungen der Westdeutschen Gesellschaft für Familienkunde 1928, 430-436.

39 Bruns, Rat (note 21), 6.

40 L. v. Winterfeld, Die Dortmunder Wandschneider- und Erbsassengesellschaft, Dortmund 1920; A. Meininghausen, Vom Dortmunder Honoratiorentum, in: Mitteilungen der Westdeutschen Gesellschaft für Familienkunde 1928, 411-422; H. Voelcker (ed.), Die Stadt Goethes, Frankfurt 1932; F. Lerner, Die Frankfurter Patriziergesellschaft Alten-Limpurg und ihre Stiftungen, Frankfurt 1952;

CHAPTER THREE

example of Osnabrück shows the importance such patrician societies had for the social and political assertiveness of the older type of political elite within the cities of that time. There the old Hanseatic families remaining within the city did not create a formal association, and as a result the Hanseatic patriciate dissolved and entered the circle of the *Honoratioren* families.[41] Conversely, the tendency for closure among patrician families was partially responsible for the rapid rise of the *Honoratioren*, since in many cities the number of patrician families quickly decreased and the danger of extinction arose.

The institutional and societal formation of the older elite groups can be seen as a reaction to the rise of the *Honoratioren*. In the Middle Ages the political leadership of the Hanseatic merchants was as a rule undisputed because within the Hanseatic trading area craftsmen produced primarily for local markets and hence the guilds remained economically and politically relatively weak. The larger inland cities such as Brunswick, Dortmund, and Cologne were exceptions, and their upper stratum accordingly showed patriciate tendencies very early. In exceptional cases the merchant oligarchy could integrate newcomers who had made large fortunes through (141) manufacturing. This was particularly the case if those fortunes had been made by activity in the so-called "commercial crafts," because those newcomers from the artisan middle stratum had been engaged intermittently in mercantile activity, traditionally judged acceptable for the magistrate. This socio-economic situation reflected peaceful constitutional development. Very few of the Hanseatic cities had the same degree of civil strife as the southern German cities along with the accompanying constitutional revolution. Such conflicts occurred in Brunswick and Cologne and to a lesser extent in Hildesheim and Dortmund. The rule in the northwestern parts of the Empire was a constitutional modification without much use of force. In view of the relatively insignificant amount of social and political pressure exerted from below, it was unnecessary during the Middle Ages for the socially open mercantile oligarchy to transform itself into a legally and socially closed patriciate in the sense of an urban nobility. This changed after the mid-fifteenth century when, because of the

---

Klötzer, Bankier (note 4), 11ss.; Meyn, Frankfurt (note 20), 170ss., 218s.

41 v. Klocke, Patriziatsproblem (note 10), 45; v. Lenthe, Niedersachsen (note 4), 192.

changes described, it was no longer easily-integrated individuals who claimed a share of the political power, but rather competition arose from another group, the early modern *Honoratiorentum*. As their southern German social peers the families of the older Hanseatic elites now also chose to protect their social prominence and the remnant of their political rights by closing off entry into their social order. The chronological delay *vis à vis* the southern German region meant that its was far less probable that the newer urban elites would seek to emulate the patrician noble social standing and lifestyle.[42]

2. The Acceptance of Jurists into the Political Elite

The acceptance of jurists into governmental circles appears on the one hand to be a part of the processes of change in the political elites already described in the previous section, in that academics can be considered a further component of the new *Honoratiorentum* from the mid-sixteenth century onwards. On the other hand this process must be clearly differentiated from the advance of the merchant and artisan *Honoratioren* into governmental circles because it resulted in independent new developments. (142)

The basic outlines of this development are well-known. In the north it had already begun during the Middle Ages, but it occurred only after a long chronological delay when compared with southern Germany. The foundation was laid by an increasing number of educated personnel within the administration of the Hanseatic cities during the fourteenth and fifteenth centuries.[43] In the context of a history of political elites this can be considered a preparatory phase which lasted until about 1550. In the larger cities with a more diversified administration some academically educated jurists had already advanced into the city council. There were seven in Bremen's city council during the fifteenth century, the first in 1406; in Lübeck and Cologne they provided a few burgomasters; but in Hamburg and Frankfort there were only very few jurists in the city council, even until the end of the sixteenth century.[44] The

---

42 The similaries and differences between northern and southern German developments deserve further investigation, not only with regard to their urban social history, but at many other points as well.

43 Cf. the literature in note 7 above.

44 Prange, Kaufmannschaft (note 22), 161ss.; Bruns, Rat (note 21), 35; Reißmann, Kaufmannschaft (note 23), 344; W. Herborn, Zur Rekonstruktion der Kölner Bürgermeisterliste, in: Rheinische Vierteljahresblätter 36 (1972), 89-183,

actual field of activity for jurists lay during this period almost
entirely in administration outside the governing circles and in
providing legal advice in domestic, territorial, imperial, and
general diplomatic affairs for city council members and burgomasters who had no academic education.[45] This was true
particularly for the era of the Reformation, when the city
council secretaries and syndics of the Westphalian and lower
Saxon cities exercised a great, often decisive, influence upon
the ecclesiastical and general policies of the magistrates,
without themselves being able to make the decisions.[46] (143)
The acceptance of jurists with university degrees into the
political elite in the strict sense occurred on a wider front
toward the end of the sixteenth century. After about the
middle of the seventeenth century their status was secure in
nearly all cities and in many places they practically dominated
the magistrates. The chronological development in Cologne is
especially impressive: Before 1550 there is evidence of only
three educated jurists who were members of the city council,
and their numbers grew only slowly even during the next half
century (three doctors of law, ten masters). But in the time
between 1600 and 1649 the number grew more quickly to 42
(16 doctors, 26 masters) and reached 55 between 1650 and 1700
(36 doctors and 19 masters), with many of these jurists
becoming burgomasters after 1600.[47] A similar process can be
recognized in Bremen, where about half of the city council still
consisted of merchants in 1650. A century later it was only a
third. The last burgomaster who did not have a legal education
held office in 1665.[48] In Frankfort after 1612 several seats in
the city council were reserved for jurists. In Lübeck three of
the four burgomasters had to be jurists after 1665; in addition,

here, 128s.; idem, Ratsherr (note 7); Meyn, Frankfurt (note 20), 175.

45 Examples: G. Neumann, Lübecker Syndici des 15. Jahrhunderts in auswärti-
gen Diensten der Stadt, in: Hansische Geschichtsblätter 96 (1978), 38-46; Meyn,
Frankfurt (note 20), 180s.

46 Example: R. Stupperich, Dr. Johann von der Wyck. Ein münsterscher
Staatsmann der Reformationszeit, in: Westfälische Zeitschrift 123 (1973), 9-50.

47 Based on an analysis of the Ratsherrenlisten 1396-1700 done by Wolfgang
Herborn, (note 7). For a general discussion of the role of jurists in early modern
towns cf. H. Thieme, Le role des doctores legum dans la société Allemande du 16e
siècle, in: Travaux d'Institut pour l'Étude de la Renaissance et de l'Humanisme
(Université de Bruxelles) 3 (1965), 161-170; O. Brunner, Souveränitätsproblem
und Sozialstruktur in den deutschen Reichstädten der frühen Neuzeit, in: idem,
Neue Wege der Verfassungs- und Sozialgeschichte, Göttingen 1968, 294-321.

48 Prange, Kaufmannschaft (note 22), 161ss.

most of the normal city council members were jurists. After 1669 Hamburg followed a policy similar to Lübeck's with regard to burgomasters, and in addition half of the normal seats on the city council were reserved for jurists.[49] Beginning in the seventeenth century (144) middle-sized and smaller cities appear to have followed suit, even though as a rule no formal regulation was enacted.[50] Jurists enjoyed equality in rank and status not only with the older city council families, but most often directly with the burgomasters themselves, the highest social level within the citizenry.

Proceeding from the fact that in Frankfort, Hamburg and Lübeck the legal regulations concerning the participation of jurists in the city councils were enacted at the express wish of the citizenries, Otto Brunner characterized the acceptance of jurists into the city council as a "tendency toward bureaucratization and rationalization (*Versachlichung*)."[51] It can even justifiably be called a process of professionalization, since in comparison with the merchant councillors the appearance of jurist councillors meant that city government was run by specialists, according to academic standards.[52] Alongside of the merchant who had no particular education for governmental and administrative matters came the legally trained expert. In addition to the older way of entering the political elite, regulated through birth or wealth, a new, "modern" way was opened through academic education and technical expertise. To "qualification" in the older sense was added the (145) qualification of professional accomplishment of the modern burgher groups. As the demands of the citizenries for the

---

49 F. Bothe, Frankfurts wirtschaftlich-soziale Entwicklung vor dem Dreißig-jährigen Krieg und der Fettmilchaufstand, vol. 2, Frankfurt 1920, 383; Asch, Rat (note 21), 170; Bruns, Rat (note 21), 310; Brunner, Souveränitätsproblem (note 47), 310; K. Schwarz, Kompanien, Kirchspiele und Konvent in Bremen 1605-1814, Bremen 1969, 34, 48ss.

50 Lahrkamp, Patriziat (note 10), 206, note 18; J. Ketteler, Vom Geschlechter-kreis des Münsterschen Honoratiorentums, in: Mitteilungen der Westdeutschen Gesellschaft für Familienkunde (September 5, 1928), 421-429; O. Spechter, Die Osnabrücker Oberschicht im 17. und 18. Jahrhundert, Osnabrück 1975; R. Decker, Bürgermeister und Ratsherren in Paderborn, Paderborn 1977; W.-H. Deus, Die Herren von Soest, Soest 1955; D. Koch, Das Göttinger Honoratioren-tum, Göttingen 1958. An example of a medium-sized town: Schilling, Konfessi-onskonflikt (note 15), 96; K. Meier-Lemgo, Geschichte der Stadt Lemgo, Lemgo 1962, Bürgermeisterliste, 330s.

51 Brunner, Souveränitätsproblem (note 47), 312.

52 "Professionalisierung in historischer Perspektive", Geschichte und Gesell-schaft 6, Heft 3 (1980).

acceptance of jurists into the governmental circles illustrate, the new city council members also possessed a new basis of legitimation: not tradition, prestige or wealth, but rather professional accomplishment and provable competence.

Such an interpretation contains more than a grain of truth in so far as a new element came into play with the entry of jurists that, seen from a long-range perspective, and after a series of changes in society, politics, and mentality, advanced development in the way described. During the sixteenth and seventeenth centuries the process was anything but revolutionary. Two observations indicate that the jurists, characterized primarily by their education and specialized function, nevertheless remained largely tied to the older type of elite, which was predominantly characterized by property and birth.

1. Jurists were recruited to a large extent from the older city council families. This was less true during the Middle Ages, but increasingly the case for the sixteenth and seventeenth centuries, a development parallel to the general rise of status enjoyed by the legal profession. In Münster, for example, the first syndic, Johann von der Wieck, was not formally a part of the city council, but during the short period of Lutheranism before the Anabaptist takeover he practically dictated city policy. He belonged to an old family of the hereditary patriciate, which later supplied several jurists who worked both inside and outside the city council. Similar developments can be seen in Cologne, Lüneburg, and Frankfort.[53] In Bremen and Hamburg the traditional city council families divided during the seventeenth century (146) into one branch that continued to pursue mercantile activities, and another that pursued academic careers, especially law, to a noticeably smaller degree also medicine and the ministry.[54] But such family divisions were seldom permanent in the coastal cities, and heirs of the academic branch of families often shifted back to the mercantile activities of their ancestors and relatives. This development also occurred in middle-sized and smaller towns where from the

53 Stupperich, von der Wyck (note 46); Lahrkamp, Patriziat (note 10), 206; v. Lenthe, Niedersachsen (note 4), 178. U. Trumpold, Heinrich Kellner, 1536-1589. Frankfurt 1975, esp. 19ss.; H. Böhme, Frankfurt und Hamburg, Frankfurt 1968, 83; Meyn, Frankfurt (note 20), 63; Köln and Dr. Heinrich Sudermann: Wriedt, Personal (note 7), 17s., 29; W. Laufer, Die Sozialstruktur der Stadt Trier in der frühen Neuzeit, Bonn 1926, 199-213.

54 Reißmann, Kaufmannschaft (note 23), 268ss.; Prange, Kaufmannschaft (note 21), 85, 117.

second half of the sixteenth century families that undisputably belonged to the political elite allowed at least some of their sons to pursue a legal education. Persons who already possessed a claim to city council membership by their high birth thus earned a kind of supplementary qualification. In these cases entry into the city council was achieved through a double qualification—the traditional criteria of birth, prestige, and wealth and the "modern" qualification of expert academic competence. No break in social development can be adduced from these cases.

2. A not insignificant number of these jurists came, however, from the newer elite groups, in lesser numbers also from the middle level of small merchants and artisans or—especially in the marshy coastal areas with their large farms—even from the peasantry.[55] In the cathedral cities and other Catholic areas with aristocratic collegiate chapters, jurists were also recruited from among the bastards of clerics during the transitional period before the strict enforcement of the decisions of Trent. This was a social group that was dishonorable by older urban norms and under no circumstances suitable for membership in the city council.[56] Finally, another frequently encountered line of social development is the movement of a jurist from the upper stratum of a small or a very small town (147) to another somewhat larger city where he was immediately judged suitable for membership in the city council.[57]

These socially mobile jurists, coming from urban strata which were traditionally not considered eligible for city council membership because of their income and family background, were nevertheless accepted immediately into the older elites of the cities. Where there was no patriciate, this occurred most often through membership in the older, privileged corporations, in the Hanseatic cities above all in the merchant corporations (the *Kaufmannsämter*), as in Göttingen and Hanover,[58] or even

---

55 Wriedt, Personal (note 7), 29; Kellenbenz, Sozialstruktur (note 32), 127; Reißmann, Kaufmannschaft (note 23), 268s.; Prange, Kaufmannschaft (note 21), 89s., lists of immigrants e.g. from the Westphalian villages of Bramsche and Wellingholzhausen.

56 R. Decker, Bürgermeister und Ratsherren in Paderborn vom 13. bis zum 17. Jahrhundert, Paderborn 1977.

57 Example: The well-known Westphalian Derenthal family moved from Höxter to Lemgo and from there to Osnabrück.

58 v. Lenthe, Niedersachsen (note 4); D. Koch, Das Göttinger Honoratiorentum, Göttingen 1958.

in less traditional organizations such as the shopkeepers or
pedlars corporations, whose *Honoratioren* upper stratum had
become eligible for the city council by the end of the sixteenth
century on the basis of the changes described above. In cities
which had patriciates, jurists were usually directly accepted by
them, as happened in Lübeck, Brunswick, Lüneburg, and
Frankfort, since the patrician societies described above were
open to jurists.[59]

This process of "subjection" to the norms of the older political elite is especially clear in the case of the salt city of Lüneburg. Jurists who were accepted into the *Theodori-Gilde* and
into the city council not only married into the families of the
salt masters (*Sülfmeister*), but were often compelled to participate in the salt trade, in order to add to their qualification as
experts the older elite qualification, which had for centuries
determined suitability for city council membership within the
political elite of that salt city.[60]

In view of the circumstances described, the developments •
which allowed the entry of jurists into governmental circles
should not, in my opinion, be understood in the first instance
as a professionalization of the urban political elite. In order to
determine the structural changes within the political and societal system of the cities a specific characteristic of the new
jurist councillor must be taken into account. Abstractly
speaking, this characteristic was their mobility or flexibility, as
well as their many abilities and various services. The possibility
of changes between an academic and a mercantile, and in part
entrepreneurial (148) career, from one generation to another
has already been noted. In the earlier phase there were even
cases of such a professional change within individual lives, although they may not have been very common. More important,
however, is the flexible nature of academic employment itself,
above all again for jurists, but also for some theologians and
teachers as well as physicians, as we will show in section III. In
this connection Otto Brunner's observation should be remembered that in the conflicts between the citizenry and the magistrate during the early modern period, lawyers could be found

---

59 Spieß, Stand (note 37); Mitgau, Heiratskreise (note 10); idem, Ein Patrizischer Sippenkreis Braunschweigs um 1600, Braunschweig 1976; v. Lenthe, Niedersachsen (note 4), 176s.; Bruns, Rat (note 21), 35; Soliday, Community (note
20), 84ss. (Frauensteiner).

60 v. Lenthe (note 4); Mörke, Rat (note 37).

on both sides, so that it was always possible to change sides.[61] Of fundamental and far-reaching political and societal importance is the fact that jurists, in contrast to the medieval merchant elites, were not bound to the city but could find employment either in the city or the territorial state.

It was possible for jurists to reorient themselves toward the territorial state in two ways, although there were fundamental differences between territorial cities and imperial cities. In the first case jurists could remain within the city's governmental bodies, but could become increasingly open to the interests of the territorial ruler, even when these were directed against the political autonomy of the city. In the case of the territorial cities this development allowed a smooth transition between the two types of elites described above: from an autonomous city government ruled by the *Honoratioren* with a leading role for jurists to a burgher aristocracy of civil servants under the control of the territorial ruler. An example of this is Brunswick where according to the memorable phrase of Hermann Mitgau the jurists should be seen as the "place holders" of the territorial state from the end of the sixteenth century until the city's subjugation by the territorial ruler in 1671.[62] The other possibility was entering the service of the territorial ruler. This meant on the one hand a clear break with the urban civic tradition to which both the artisan and merchant *Honoratioren* and the Hanseatic patriciate felt committed, but which jurists, because of their education in Roman law, could only accept to a point. On the other hand it resulted in a very consequential widening of the circle of activity for the urban political elite.

3. The Rise of the Early Modern Civil Servant Bourgeoisie

The growth of the burgher political elite beyond the boundaries of the cities into the overarching political unities can justly be regarded as the most important transformation within the process of change (149) in the history of elites at the beginning of the early modern period.[63] In this connection special attention

---

61 Brunner, Souveränitätsproblem (note 47), 310. The same observation with regard to Humanist education and spirit: H. Neveux, Humanisme et élites urbaines à Caen, in: K. Malettke and J. Voll (eds.), Humanismus und höfisch-städtische Elite im 16. Jahrhundert, Bonn 1989, 181-193, here 190, 192.
62 Mitgau, Heiratskreise (note 10), 18.
63 Schilling, Elite (note 10); idem, Konfessionskonflikt (note 15), esp. 259-291, 376-378; H. Samse, Die Zentralverwaltung in den Südwelfischen Landen vom 15. bis zum 17. Jahrhundert, Hildesheim 1940; H.J. von der Ohe, Die Zentral- und

must be paid to the territories and the territorial rulers' administration, because in western and especially northwestern Germany the service for the Empire and the Emperor, apart from a few families in the imperial cities, was not considered an option. The concept "political elite" cannot be used for the burgher civil service in the same sense as it can be used for the urban burgher ruling groups that we have considered up to this point. For the latter, government and exercise of authority were an expression of original rights. They were derived from the autonomy of the commune and were rooted in the traditions and privileges of each respective city, and, according to a later theory advocated above all by the magistrates of the imperial cities, in the will of God himself. The ruling or administrative authority exercised by the burgher civil service, on the other hand, was clearly derived from the sovereign rights of the early modern territorial prince.

In western and northwestern Germany the great period of the burgher civil service as a support of the territorial rulers against the nobility and above all against that part of the urban burghers who resisted subjugation under the early modern state was the late sixteenth and early seventeenth centuries. After the Thirty Years' War the early modern civil servant bourgeoisie declined in significance *vis à vis* a nobility which was regaining its strength. It should be noted, however, that as a rule a number of burgher families which had risen to the nobility remained influential. The fall of the burgher civil service was especially abrupt in Hanover, where in the eighteenth century the government lay to all intents and purposes in the hands of the landed nobility after the personal union with England and the resulting absence of the territorial prince. The territorial nobility was not well-disposed toward the burgher families.[64]

The separation of the burgher civil service from the urban political elite occurred in various ways, depending primarily upon the respective relationships between the territorial princes and the cities. In particular, developments within the imperial cities and the territorial cities must be distinguished. With

Hofverwaltung des Fürstentums Lüneburg (Celle) und ihre Beamten, 1520-1648, Celle 1955; K.H. Schleif, Regierung und Verwaltung des Erzstifts Bremen, Hamburg 1972; Ch. van den Heuvel, Beamtenschaft und Territorialstaat, Osnabrück 1500-1800, Osnabrück 1984.

64 Lampe, Aristokratie (note 10).

regard to the imperial cities a similar picture emerges for those in the Rhineland and on the North Sea (150) as Volker Press recently sketched when he discussed the influence of the imperial cities and their inhabitants upon the confessional formation of the territories of southern and southwestern Germany.[65] The political elite of the imperial cities could seize political or career opportunities within the cities themselves yet enter the service of the territorial state in a local area or a wider region either simultaneously or successively without any significant problem of identity. For instance, during the sixteenth and seventeenth centuries members of the political elite of Cologne appeared repeatedly as councillors of neighboring princes and to a certain extent within the imperial administration as well. In spite of inherent civic opposition to the archiepiscopal chapter of Cologne, switches from urban to territorial offices or governmental positions usually took place without friction.[66] This was especially true for periods of common confessional opposition to Protestantism, for instance at the end of the sixteenth and the beginning of the seventeenth centuries. The same observation can be made about the political elite of Frankfort.[67] Among the coastal cities, by contrast, only Lübeck shows similar developments, while the political elites of Hamburg and Bremen were apparently less interested in territorial offices.[68] The case of the old imperial city of Aachen is especially complicated.[69] Until the second half of the sixteenth century the situation was similar to that of Cologne. After this a late Calvinistic Reformation caused a hardening of positions and divisions similar to what occurred in the territorial Hanseatic cities. At the end of the sixteenth and the beginning of the seventeenth centuries a Protestant faction within the political elite twice seized power, opposing the both neighboring territorial state of Jülich (151) and that

65 V. Press, Stadt und territoriale Konfessionsbildung, in: F. Petri (ed.), Kirche und gesellschaftlicher Wandel, Köln 1980, 251-296.

66 Kellenbenz, Jahrtausende (note 30), vol. 1, 334s.; idem, Sozialstruktur (note 32); Herborn, Rekonstruktion (note 44): Hardenrath, Gail and Sundemann families.

67 Soliday, Community (note 20), 81ss.; Trumpold, Heinrich Kellner (note 53), 20, 32s.

68 Prange, Kaufmannschaft (note 22); Reißmann, Kaufmannschaft (note 23); Schleif, Regierung (note 63), 252s., 257.

69 Examples: Schilling, Bürgerkämpfe (note 9); W. Schmitz, Verfassung und Bekenntnis. Die Aachener Wirren im Spiegel der kaiserlichen Politik (1550-1616), Frankfurt/Bern/New York 1983.

part of the burgher elite which held office in its civil service. Conversely, the remaining Catholic families of Aachen's upper social stratum, particularly of the patriciate, allied itself with the court in Düsseldorf during these years. The Protestant elite did also not restrict itself to the imperial city, and oriented itself toward the Protestant territories and their civil services, particularly toward the Electoral Palatinate.

For the political elites of territorial cities in the northwest, by contrast, the opposition between territory and city was decisive, at least during the earlier phases of the differentiation process. The Hanseatic cities in particular had won a high degree of autonomy from their rulers during the Middle Ages. At the turn of the sixteenth and seventeenth centuries they could still claim a special status between imperial cities and average territorial cities as so-called *civitates mixtae*.[70] The bitter struggle between the city of Brunswick and the Dukes of Brunswick-Wolfenbüttel which lasted well into the second half of the seventeenth century is well-known.[71] Similar conflicts occurred in a whole series of middle-sized and smaller Hanseatic cities.

The growth of the political elite beyond the city walls was shaped by that political confrontation, which in the period of confessionalization was very often religiously charged. During the sixteenth century, in a development parallel with the formation of a territorial civil service, which occurred very late in our area, new career possibilities outside the cities presented themselves to the burgher elite on a large scale. In view of the continuing opposition between the territories and cities the legally educated members of the urban elites felt obliged to make a decision.[72] They had to decide whether they should continue to defend the traditional autonomy of the cities and their independent urban elites, or take the new opportunities offered by the territorial civil service. At the beginning of the seventeenth century the confrontation between city and territorial state often caused a social and political division within the urban elite—one faction upheld the interests of the urban burgher world and fought for the unity and independence of

---

70 Schilling, Konfessionskonflikt (note 15), 331s.; articles in note 15 above.

71 Querfurth, Braunschweig (note 34).

72 In more detail: Schilling, Elite (note 10); idem, Konfessionskonflikt (note 15), 278ss. Cf. also v. Lenthe, Niedersachsen (note 4), 168s. (Hannover), 187 (Goslar), 191 (Hildesheim).

the commune, while the other faction, which aspired to make a new beginning within territorial society (152), was prepared to ally itself with the territorial state and seek its fortune as a part of the early modern civil servant bourgeoisie. In contrast to the political elites of the imperial cities who could simultaneously or successively pursue careers in urban and territorial offices as two opportunities which differed in their legal justifications but were not in principle mutually exclusive, the elites of the northwestern German territorial cities had come to a parting of ways. Choosing one of these two ways meant, as a rule, at the same time declaring war on that part of their own order which had decided to take the other way.

Unlike the situation in some southern and southwestern German territories, especially in Württemberg, where a united bourgeoisie encompassing both city and territory, had earlier been formed with the so-called *Ehrbarkeit*,[73] we are dealing with two antagonistic kinds of burgher elites in the northwest during the sixteenth and the greater part of the seventeenth centuries. This division at a social and prosopographical level reflects a process of conceptual differentiation recently formulated by Manfred Riedel which opposes the older urban conception of citizen, defined as men capable of political activities in an urban commune, with the newer territorial, absolutistic concept, defined in relation to the highest authority of the territorial prince.[74] Because of the proximity of their social origin the representatives of these two types of elites fought each other with particular bitterness, and they often formed the core of rival factions. Again and again it was councillors of urban origins who encouraged their territorial princes to take unrestricted action against the cities. And on the other hand the city councils were only too inclined to personalize the uncomfortable claims of the territorial states as the evil machinations of renegades directed against their own order.[75]

---

73 Cf. H. Liebel. The Bourgeoisie in Southwestern Germany, 1500-1789. A rising class?, in: International Review of Social History 10 (1965), 295s., based on the unpublished thesis of H. Decker-Hauf.

74 O. Brunner, W. Conze, R. Koselleck (eds.), Geschichtliche Grundbegriffe. Historisches Lexikon zur politisch-sozialen Sprache in Deutschland, Stuttgart 1972ss., articles "Bürger" (vol. 1, esp. 679s.) and "Gesellschaft, bürgerliche" (vol. 2, here 733s. and 737); D. Breuer, Gibt es eine bürgerliche Literatur im Deutschland des 17. Jahrhunderts?, in: Germanisch-Romanische Monatsschrift 61 (1980), 211-226.

75 Cf. examples given in Schilling, Konfessionskonflikt (note 15), esp. 266-271.

In a few cases this confrontation continued into the eighteenth century, in other cases coexistence developed in a peaceful way (153) as happened in the Westphalian episcopal city of Osnabrück.[76] In the vast majority of cases, however, the settlement was achieved by the forcible subjugation of the cities and by excluding from power the traditional urban burgher elite, which insisted on its independence and the autonomy of the town. It was replaced by a new political elite which governed the town on behalf of the territorial ruler.

The development described above has been examined in detail in a few cases—among others in Hanover and in the other Welfish territories—particularly with regard to circles of marriage and family.[77] These studies brought to light a web of family and kinship relations similar to that which Karl Demandt has shown for Hesse.[78] Seen from the perspective of social history it was particularly the ability to form and continue such family networks that distinguished the early modern bureaucratic bourgeoisie from the medieval clerical civil servants who came from burgher families. This was an essential condition for the swift consolidation of its position as well as for its ability to compete with the nobility over a relatively long period of time. However, in my opinion it is wrong to see this primarily as an imitation of the corresponding family politics of the nobility. At least in the area under discussion the early modern civil servant bourgeoisie continued a tradition of the medieval Hanseatic burgher elites. This medieval Hanseatic elite had already very early developed family networks, which encompassed not only individual cities, but often linked entire areas within the Hanseatic League. The urban burgher elite of the sixteenth and seventeenth centuries continued this tradition, producing a regional concentration that could only promote the cohesion of the social network. As long as the opposition between territorial and urban political burgher elites continued, two different family groupings also existed within the burgher upper strata of this region. Individual cases must be examined

---

76 Schilling, Elite (note 10), 278-284, esp. 283s.

77 Lampe, Aristokratie (note 10); von der Ohe, Zentral- und Hofverwaltung (note 63), 215ss.; Samse, Zentralverwaltung (note 63), 73ss.; Schleif, Regierung (note 63), 256ss.

78 K. Demandt, Amt und Familie. Eine soziologisch-genealogische Studie zur hessischen Verwaltungsgeschichte des 16. Jahrhunderts, in: Hessisches Jahrbuch für Landesgeschichte 2 (1952), 79-133.

to see whether the two circles fused together after the resolution of their antagonism.

The succession of the different types of burgher elites, and the specific expressions of their legal, constitutional, and social status, as well as their intellectual and cultural outlook, (154) i.e., their mentalities, described only in outline in the sections above, are topics that require further research from the perspective of societal history. Future study should not, however, be restricted exclusively to individual cities and urban groups. An important goal, which promises to be instructive for the further course of modern German history, would be to work out fully a typology of the development of the burgher elites specific to northwestern Germany, both with regard to its particular conditions and especially their consequences for the political and economic possibilities of the burgher elites, their status within the society as a whole, and their relationships with the nobility. In this context particular attention should be given to the dynamics at work when the *Honoratiorentum*, patriciate, and territorial nobility interacted. Concretely speaking, these would include burgher attitudes toward promotion to the nobility, and toward the life style and social interaction of the nobility as well as, in general, the extent and the type of burgher activities in rural areas. Presumably such studies would show that an "amalgamation of the urban merchants with the urban and rural nobles" could not have arisen in the northwest in the same way that Thomas Brady has recently described for southern Germany, using Strasbourg as an example.[79]

II. THE CONFESSIONAL MIGRATION AND THE RISE OF AN EARLY MODERN COMMERCIAL BOURGEOISIE

In conjunction with the rise of the *Honoratiorentum* as a new group within the political elite of the northwestern German Hanseatic cities, I have already referred to the replacement of the medieval Hanseatic merchants by a new stratum of merchant families as well as the rise of distributors and wholesalers of the rural spinning and linen crafts as a new kind of entrepreneur within the Hanseatic area. This process, which merits more detailed study, produced an important change in the formation and composition of the economic elites in

---

79 Brady, Patricians (note 3), 44.

northwestern Germany. Apart from particularly unusual cases such as the wholesalers from Barmen and Elberfeld in the Duchy of Berg,[80] the representatives (155) of this new type of merchant came from the native urban citizenry and remained, as a rule, connected with the traditional urban centers of Westphalia and lower Saxony, both through their residence and the location of their businesses, and through their interest in the government and administration of these cities. The situation was quite different for a second group of entrepreneurs and big merchants who appeared at the end of the sixteenth century, especially in the Rhineland. I am referring to the economic elites of the confessional and in part ethnic minorities, who, because of the migration of Calvinistically inclined exiles from the Netherlands, settled at first in the large and economically important cities of western and northwestern Germany. This was a very difficult experiment in settlement and integration, not only religiously and culturally, but also economically and socially. And while this uneasy situation existed, it generated developmental impulses that were extraordinarily significant from a societal history perspective, for they created a burgher society outside the urban civic society of the *ancien régime,* the center of economic activity. This phenomenon deserves closer examination.

1. Size and Geographical Distribution of the Dutch Confessional Migration

The general importance of the migration of exiles from the perspective of economic history cannot be discussed in detail here. It suffices to note the assessment of Carlo Cipolla that the diffusion of innovations in manufacturing and commerce took place in a different way during pre-modern times than it did in the nineteenth and twentieth centuries; it came not through technical literature but rather through the migration of workers and economic entrepreneurs.[81] In the sixteenth and

---

80 W. Köllmann, Die Sozialgeschichte der Stadt Barmen im 19. Jahrhundert, Tübingen 1960, 1-13; S. Murayama, Konfession und Gesellschaft in einem Gewerbezentrum. Das Wuppertal (Eberfeld-Barmen) von 1650 bis 1820, Tokyo 1990.

81 C. Cipolla, The Diffusion of Innovations in Early Modern Europe, in: Comparative Studies in Society and History 14 (1972), 46-52; idem, Before the Industrial Revolution, London 1976, 174ss.; H. Schilling, Innovation through Migration: The Settlements of Calvinistic Netherlanders in Sixteenth- and Seventeenth-Century Central and Western Europe, in: Histoire sociale-Social History 16, Nr.

seventeenth centuries, alongside of the Portuguese and the Italians, the Protestants who were driven out of the Netherlands were most important in this context, although it is beyond the limits of this study to estimate the relative proportion of religious and economic exiles.[82] The Catholic Italians, who emigrated especially to the Rhineland, were (156) as a rule quickly absorbed. Because they often engaged in crafts with few possibilities for development, such as chimney sweeping, they generated hardly any impulses for economic and social change.[83] The Portuguese colonies brought about a noticeable spurt of commercial development; however, because of their religious, cultural, and ethnic isolation their direct influence upon the social history of the western and northwestern German cities remained very limited.[84] By contrast, the Dutch immigrants[85] came from comparatively advanced economic regions and brought to the German cities a series of innovations in commercial and financial practices, manufacturing techniques, and organizational structures. On the one hand these Dutch immigrants were familiar enough to their host society in their language and manners that they soon appeared to be a more or less integrated part of the German towns. On the other hand the Dutch, particularly the Calvinist majority among them, remained separate enough from most of their German host societies, that they could not be totally absorbed by them. They were thus in a position to unleash an economic, social, and cultural dynamic that impressed itself deeply both upon the history of cities in general and upon their elites in particular. In the Catholic imperial cities of Cologne and Aachen the native Protestants fused with the Dutch in the

31 (1983), 7-33.

82 F. Petri, Die Ursachen der niederländischen Auswanderung im Zeitalter der Glaubenskämpfe, in: Westfälische Forschungen 21 (1968), 188-191.

83 J. Augel, Italienische Einwanderung und Wirtschaftstätigkeit in rheinischen Städten des 17. und 18. Jahrhunderts, Bonn 1971.

84 H. Kellenbenz, Sephardim an der unteren Elbe, Wiesbaden 1958; idem, Unternehmerkräfte im Hamburger Portugal- und Spanienhandel, Hamburg 1954; idem, Die Rodrigues d'Evora in Köln, in: Portugiesische Forschungen der Goerresgesellschaft, 1. Reihe, 6. Jg. (1966), 272-290.

85 H. Schilling, Niederländische Exulanten im 16. Jahrhundert. Ihre Stellung im Sozialgefüge und im religiösen Leben deutscher und englischer Städte, Gütersloh 1972; idem, Innovation (note 81); R. van Roosbroeck, Die Bedeutung der Emigranten aus den Niederlanden für die Neugestaltung der deutschen Wirtschaft, in: H. Helbig (ed.), Führungskräfte der Wirtschaft in Mittelalter und Neuzeit, 1350-1850, vol. 1, Limburg 1973, 121-148; idem, Brabanter Kaufleute im Exil, Köln 1974.

course of the sixteenth and early seventeenth centuries, so that the German Protestants must also be taken into consideration when discussing them.

Reflecting the political, ecclesiastical, and military events that occurred in the Netherlands, the different waves of emigration after the middle of the sixteenth century brought Dutch migrants to England, Scandinavia, Poland, Switzerland, and above all Germany, where, apart from southern and central Germany, they settled primarily in the cities and towns of the area between Frankfort and Aachen in the south and west and in Emden, Bremen, or Hamburg in the north. The social (157) composition of this stream of exiles was quite mixed, from penniless refugees and day laborers, through apprentices and master artisans to wealthy merchants, bankers, distributors, and entrepreneurs who were active in the newer luxury crafts. The representatives of the burgher upper stratum, in whom we are primarily interested, came after 1585, especially from Antwerp. Since the emigration of the Protestants was regulated by treaty, this wave of migrants was—from an economic standpoint—a relocation of businesses. For many economically powerful migrants the most desirable places to emigrate were the large cities of the Rhineland and the North Sea coast.[86]

The process of integration took place very differently in individual cities. The confessional factor was decisive: In Wesel, Emden, and Bremen,[87] cities whose official confession was Reformed, the foreigners—unless they resided there only temporarily—were quickly integrated after an initial period of tension, which was unavoidable given the large number of immigrants. This is true in particular for members of the elite who quickly established social and marital ties with their German peers and fused with the local population within a few generations. This occurred first of all with the so-called *"Nederduits,"* that is the Flemish or Dutch-speaking emigrants from the northern provinces, and then with the French-speaking Walloons. Taking a leading role from the very begin-

---

86 There were smaller settlements in the small towns of the Rhineland, in southern and eastern Germany: E. Bütfering, Niederländische Exulanten in Frankenthal, Neu Hanau und Altona: Herkunftsgebiete, Migrationswege und Ansiedlungsorte, in: H. Schilling and W. Ehrbrecht (eds.), Niederlande und Nordwestdeutschland, Köln/Wien 1983, 347-417.

87 Prange, Kaufmannschaft (note 22), 63, 69, 72; R. van Roosbroeck, Niederländische Glaubenflüchtlinge in Bremen (1585-1600) und ihr Briefwechsel, in: Bremisches Jahrbuch 52 (1972), 85-112; Schilling, Calvinism (note 14).

ning in the Calvinist presbyteries, as in Wesel and Emden, they won quick entry into the city councils as well, and thus belonged to the economic, social, ecclesiastical, and cultural as well as political elites of their new home cities. Apart from their large numbers, the immigration and integration of the Dutch into these cities can hardly be distinguished from the normal pattern of migration upon which Old European cities had always depended. For this reason these cases will not concern us further.

The relationships were quite different in the Lutheran cities of Hamburg and Frankfort as well as in Cologne and Aachen, which either unequivocally or after a difficult struggle remained faithful to the old church. Here more far-reaching societal consequences resulted from the immigration. In all four cases the absorption of the Dutch by the urban society was not possible because of confessional differences or could only comprise the smaller Lutheran portion. (158) The Lutheran and Catholic cities differed considerably in the degree of isolation that they imposed upon the "alien group." In Hamburg and Frankfort the Calvinist Dutch, after a period of initial uncertainty, could remain within the city as residents with a special legal, political, ecclesiastical, and cultural status. In Cologne and Aachen, on the other hand, they finally had to leave the city, with the exception of a few short periods. Hence in our consideration of the social consequences of the Dutch emigration we must draw a distinction between Lutheran and Catholic cities and regions.

2. The Rise of a New Type of Upper Stratum within the Lutheran Imperial Cities.

From the beginning of the seventeenth century there existed in Hamburg and Frankfort not only a Lutheran but also a Dutch Calvinist elite which was soon accepted as native. With regard to their economic power and wealth the two groups were of equal rank in Hamburg, because the Germans remained active in the economy and the favorable economic situation in the city on the Elbe paralleled that in the Netherlands. A certain difference existed only in so far as the Dutch, in contrast to the Germans who concentrated upon trade and shipping, were more active in the manufacturing crafts, which were not as strongly organized by guild. The situation was completely dif-

172CHAPTER THREE

ferent in Frankfort. Since the beginning of the sixteenth century the medieval merchants had been developing into a rentier patriciate, not involved in economic activity. This process was hastened in the last half of the century through the merchants' effort to separate themselves from the *homines novi* of the Calvinist colony. As a result there was soon a concentration of wealth and economic power in the hands of the Dutch, who became merchants, financiers, distributors, and entrepreneurs of the new exportable crafts, above all luxury items, thus constituting an almost monopolistic leading economic group within the social elite of Frankfort. In the case of Hamburg, there were increasingly loud complaints that the Dutchmen had to a large extent appropriated the fortunes of local people, as exhibited by the beautiful coaches with which they drove each Sunday to Calvinist services in Stade or Altona. This complaint reflected the hatred of foreigners felt by the lesser merchants and artisans rather than economic reality. In Frankfort, by contrast, there was actually a great shift of wealth in the form of house and property ownership within the city to the benefit of the Dutch as well as a concentration in their hands of other goods needed for an ostentatious lifestyle. And thus the descendants of the (159) sixteenth century Dutch exiles still struck the young Goethe in the mid-eighteenth century as a particularly prominent part of the Frankfort social elite. In *Dichtung und Wahrheit*, he noted, "As also in other places, the so-called Reformed *Refugiés* formed an outstanding class."[88]

In wealth and social standing—even if not in esteem—the Dutch could not be distinguished from the older established social elites of Hamburg and Frankfort, and they sometimes even surpassed the older elites in this regard. Apart from their special ecclesiastical and religious status, the essential difference between the two elites lay in the exclusion of the Dutch from the city councils and thus from the hitherto undisputed possibility for members of the upper strata of imperial cities to participate in the exercise of political authority, which was so decisive for social standing in Old European society.

---

88 4th volume, 17th book at the end.-Cf. W. Klötzer, Reichsstadt und Merkantilismus, in: V. Press (ed.), Städtewesen im Merkantilismus, Köln/Wien 1983, 135-155.

*3. The Rise of an Early Modern Commercial Bourgeoisie
Outside of the Cities*

After an initial period of instability which will not be discussed here, the religious and economic circumstances of both the Dutch colonies and the native Protestants in the Catholic cities of Cologne and Aachen[89] grew steadily worse from the beginning of the seventeenth century. The majority of the Cologne exile group, and above all their powerful social and economic elite, left the city already during the first decades of the seventeenth century. Most of them moved to Frankfort. However, a small minority of Protestant big merchants, entrepreneurs, and financiers could still be found in Cologne during the seventeenth and eighteenth centuries. They possessed a status similar to that of the Dutch Calvinists in Hamburg and Frankfort in that according to social standing and wealth they were reckoned a part of the upper stratum of this imperial city, but they were not a part of its leadership group because their entry into the political elite was barred. In addition there was a great deal of mobility between the city and the rural areas around it, particularly with regard to economic activities, but also as places of residence, since the oscillating religious and alien residency policies of the Cologne magistrates gave frequent cause for the departure of individual families or even for the entire community. (160)

This reorientation away from the city as the traditional center of commerce and manufacturing toward smaller places in the neighboring territories is more clearly illustrated in the nearby imperial city of Aachen. In this city a rather large part of the native upper stratum was included in this movement along with the Dutch.[90] This was because Protestantism, particularly Calvinism, had spread primarily through the *Honoratiorentum* of artisans and merchants, which grew more powerful during the sixteenth century, while the patriciate remained overwhelmingly faithful to the old church. The reason that Protestantism was so attractive to particular social strata was the traditionally close business and personal contacts of the economic elite of Aachen, in both the textile and the metal sectors, with the neighboring Netherlands, above all with Antwerp. The Dutch big merchants and entrepreneurs, in part

---

89 Schilling, Exulanten (note 85); idem, Innovation (note 81).
90 Schilling, Bürgerkämpfe (note 9), 175-231.

from families who had emigrated a generation earlier from Aachen to Antwerp for business reasons and had now returned to Aachen as religious refugees, were included in the native elite immediately upon arrival, whereby the sympathy for Protestantism that already existed quickly became stronger. After 1614, when Aachen was re-catholicized with the help of Spanish troops, one part of the Aachen big merchants and entrepreneurs emigrated to Holland, England, and Sweden. Another part tried to establish themselves in the closer or more distant vicinity of Aachen. This process of severance from the imperial city was very slow because of the customs privileges enjoyed by its residents, which were very important for mercantile activity, the dangers that arose from the Thirty Years' War, and surely also because of cultural and emotional ties, so that many of the Protestant families involved were still inhabitants of Aachen until the mid-seventeenth century.

At the initiative of this Protestant elite new economic centers arose in the course of the seventeenth century that were outside of the older manufacturing and mercantile cities and were characterized by newer manufacturing techniques and freer forms of organization.[91] Noteworthy examples include the

---

91 J. Hashagen, Der rheinische Protestantismus und die Entwicklung der rheinischen Kultur, Essen 1924; A. Müller-Armack, Genealogie der Wirtschaftsstile, in: idem, Religion und Wirtschaft, Stuttgart 1959, 46-244; B. Kuske, Der Einfluß des Staates auf die geschichtliche Entwicklung der sozialen Gruppen in Deutschland, in: Kölner Zeitschrift für Soziologie 2 (1949/50), 193-217, here 211ss.-On individual cases cf. H. von Asten, Die religiöse Spaltung in der Reichsstadt Aachen und ihr Einfluß auf die industrielle Entwicklung in der Umgebung, in: Zeitschrift des Aachener Geschichtsvereins 68 (1956), 77-197; idem, Wolfgang Wilhelm und Philipp Wilhelm von Pfalz-Neuburg und der Aufbau des Montangewerbes in den Herzogtümern Jülich und Berg (1614-1679), in: Annalen des Historischen Vereins für den Niederrhein 161 (1959), 146-231; idem, Religiöse und wirtschaftliche Antriebe im niederrheinischen Montangewerbe des 16. und 17. Jahrhunderts, in: Rheinische Vierteljahresblätter 28 (1963), 62-83; M. Barkhausen, Der Aufstieg der rheinischen Industrie im 18. Jahrhundert und die Entstehung eines industriellen Großbürgertums, in: Rheinische Vierteljahresblätter 19 (1954), 135-177; idem, Staatliche Wirtschaftslenkung und freies Unternehmertum im westdeutschen Raum bei der Entstehung der neuzeitlichen Industrie im 18. Jahrhundert, in: Vierteljahresschrift für Sozial- und Wirtschaftsgeschichte 45 (1958), 168-241; K. van Eyll, Die Kupfermeister im Stolberger Tal, Köln 1971; K. Schleicher, Geschichte der Stolberger Messingindustrie, Stolberg 1956; H. Pohl, Kupfer im Aachen Stolberger Raum von 1500-1650, in: H. Kellenbenz (ed.), Schwerpunkte der Kupferproduktion und des Kupferhandels in Europa 1500-1650, Köln 1977, 225-240; A. V. Schoeller, Geschichte der Familie Schoeller, Berlin 1894, 122ss.; J. Hashagen, Geschichte der Familie Hoesch, vol. 2, Köln 1916; H. Kisch, Das Erbe des Mittelalters, ein Hemmnis wirtschaftlicher Entwicklung: Aachens Tuchgewerbe vor 1700, in: Rheinische Vierteljahresblätter 30 (1965), 253-308; M. Barkhausen, Die Tuchindustrie in Montjoie, Aachen 1925; P.

cloth manufacturing and trade based in the Cistersian foundation of Burtscheid, immediately outside of the gates of the
imperial city, iron production in the Gemünd and Schleiden
valleys as well as brass manufacturing in the Vichttal, partially
in the territory of Jülich and partially in areas ruled by lesser
princes, above all in Stolberg, as well as in the domain of the
imperial abbey of Cornelimünster. In a wider sense and with
somewhat different origins this category also includes cloth
production in Monschau, which was especially important
during the eighteenth century, and the textile and paper
manufacturing industries in the area of Düren, which were also
founded and supported by the new Protestant mercantile and
entrepreneurial burgher classes, independently of the old
influential urban elites. In other parts of the Rhineland over
the course of the seventeenth century there were similar economic initiatives of Protestant economic elites, who still partially or from time to time resided in the large cities, but on
the whole had already renounced the urban burgher life to a
remarkable degree. I am not able to cite every single example
here but will mention only the especially striking example of
Krefeld because it shows a unique confessional constellation.
After the end of the sixteenth century within this commune,
which was monopolized politically by the Calvinists, a leading
economic group composed of immigrant Mennonite entrepreneurial families established itself (162), first within the linen
crafts, later above all in silk manufacturing (the firm of von
der Leyen).[92]
I refer to these well-known trends from economic history
because they are, in my opinion, important not only for the
social history of the upper burgher strata, but also more generally for the process of development from an Old European
societas civilis, shaped by status, honor and the exercise of
political power, to a modern economic society shaped by
wealth and participation in production. My thesis is that in the

---

Koch, Der Einfluß des Calvinismus und des Mennonitentums auf die nieder-
rheinische Textilindustrie, Köln 1928; F. Zunkel, Die Bedeutung des Protestantismus für die industrielle Entwicklung Stolbergs, in: Monatshefte für Evangelische Kirchengeschichte des Rheinlandes 29 (1980), 133-150.
92 G. von Beckerrath, Die wirtschaftliche Bedeutung der Krefelder Mennoniten
und ihrer Vorfahren im 17. und 18. Jahrhundert, Phil. Diss. Bonn 1951; Barkhausen, Wirtschaftslenkung (note 91); Koch, Einfluß (note 91); H. Kisch,
Prussian mercantilism and the rise of the Krefeld silk industry, Philadelphia 1968,
15ss.

course of the processes described above a new "early modern commercial bourgeoisie" was formed that in many respects was still part of the Old European society or feudal society, but in central elements had already broken out of this framework. Because it was substantially different from the traditional elites of the Old European cities, particularly the imperial cities, this new type of economic elite blazed a new trail, making it possible to go beyond the Old European type of urban society and constitution. The central criterion of differentiation is not the fact that they no longer settled in cities, specifically in what were at that time larger cities. The distinguishing feature is much more that this early modern commercial bourgeoisie, consisting of merchants, distributors, and entrepreneurs who lived in the countryside and small towns, no longer participated in the exercise of political authority. In addition to those groups that operated in the countryside, the Calvinist or Mennonite economic elites in the Lutheran cities (above all in Hamburg and Frankfort) together with the Protestant merchants, entrepreneurs, and bankers who repeatedly settled in the two great Catholic cities of the Rhineland[93] for longer or shorter periods of time must be included in this early modern commercial bourgeoisie that had no right to political participation. Thus toward the end of the sixteenth century there appeared for the first time in large numbers within and above all outside of the old urban centers a social elite that was native, and therefore not comparable to the Jews, and that was in principle disqualified from participation in urban government, hence was excluded from a share in the exercise of authority and power (*Herrschaft*), so important within the Old European society—in spite of their remarkable economic success and considerable wealth, the normal prerequisites for access to the city councils.[94] (163) The Mennonites may serve as a prototype of this early modern commercial bourgeoisie: They were prevented from participation in the exercise of political authority both by confessionally-expressed legal and constitutional barriers and by their own religious and ethical norms, which forbade them to accept public office, and their public activities were restricted exclusively to their church communities and the economy.

93 Kellenbenz (ed.), Jahrtausende (note 30), 334, 439.
94 W. Maschke, Die Unterschichten der mittelalterlichen Städte, in: Haase (ed.), Stadt (note 11), 345-454, here 351ss.; Ellermeyer, Sozialgruppen (note 25).

I would like to categorize the rise of the early modern commercial bourgeoisie along with the rise of the early modern
civil servant bourgeoisie described in the first section as a
further significant impulse in the early modern process of differentiation within the middle classes. No doubt this development was rooted in the late Middle Ages and can be observed
independently of the problems of religion and exile. The
expanding number of locations above all for the textile crafts
resulted from a process of development within the economy, as
recent investigations in economic history have shown.[95] The
wave of migration that was unleashed by the Reformation and
Counter-Reformation as well as the confessionalization of the
early modern society provided, however, a strong impulse and
therefore accelerated these processes. In addition, the release of
one part of the economic elite from its traditional orientation
toward political participation within the cities to a degree
significant for social history was first compelled by the constitutional requirements of the confessional age that restricted
political rights to the orthodox part of the elite and allowed
dissenters, apart from religion and church, to participate only
in the economy as a field of public activity. This circumstance
affected the cities and their surrounding countryside which
experienced the wave of Calvinist exiles, especially in the
Rhineland, by giving them a head start in economic and societal development within the German Empire during the seventeenth and eighteenth centuries.

I regard this social differentiation as a key process within
the rise of a modern bourgeois middle class, which at the same
time had far-reaching consequences for the further development of the early modern social system as a whole. In my
opinion, this was less a result of the new (164) points of departure for economic development in connection with the so-
called "manufacturing bourgeoisie."[96] Only when a significant
part of the wealthy citizenry was barred from city government
and hence from participation in the exercise of political power,

---

95 P. Kriedte, Spätfeudalismus und Handelskapital, Göttingen 1980, 49, 93ss.,
119ss.

96 Cf. e.g. G. Vogler, Probleme der Klassenentwicklung in der Feudalgesell-
schaft, in: Zeitschrift für Geschichtswissenschaft 21 (1973), 1182-1208; H. Hoffmann and I. Mittenzwei, Die Stellung des Bürgertums in der deutschen Feudal-
gesellschaft, in: Zeitschrift für Geschichte 22 (1974), 190-207; I. Mittenzwei, Zur
Klassenentwicklung des Handels- und Manufakturbürgertums in den deutschen
Territorialstaaten, in: Zeitschrift für Geschichte 23 (1975), 179-190.

which was assumed to be a right of the wealthy upper stratum
of the citizenry of medieval cities, were a significant number
of burghers removed from "feudal society." In a traditional
context the urban social elite, as measured by wealth, was
always at the same time the ruling elite. This was no longer the
case for the early modern commercial bourgeoisie described
above, who lived either outside of cities or remained in the
cities but were not considered eligible for councillor or other
political office on account of their confessional stance. This
commercial bourgeoisie profited from its status because it was
not obliged to observe the norms of the artisan guilds on the
one hand and did not feel compelled to fight for urban autonomy in opposition to the territorial princes on the other.
Consequently, it could seize upon economic opportunities that
offered themselves because of recent developmental impulses
within the territorial states.

A further aspect is also important: It is well-known that
when new social elites rose from within traditional urban civic
society, particularly during the Middle Ages, there were again
and again discrepancies between their economic power and
fortune on the one hand and their political participation on the
other. But these could always be settled through a process of
accommodation which all too often took place through the use
of force, but which was not revolutionary in the sense that it
broke up parts of the Old European constitutional and societal
system.[97] However, in the case of the early modern commercial
bourgeoisie, this was the only way that they could regain their
political rights lost during the sixteenth and early seventeenth
centuries.

The economic, social, and political process of transformation
from Old European society to the modern world, when seen as
a whole, was naturally much too complicated and was affected
by too many influences to be derived directly from the social
transformations within the burgher elites that I have described.
(165) In addition a more detailed description of the early
modern commercial bourgeoisie would reveal more traditional
characteristics, among others the patriarchal and semi-corpo-
rate, rather than individualistic methods of economic activity as
well as their subsidiary exercise of authority within the Prot-

---

97 Cf. the theoretical considerations in H. Schilling, Aufstandsbewegungen in
der stadtbürgerlichen Gesellschaft des Alten Reiches, in: H.U. Wehler (ed.), Der
Deutsche Bauernkrieg, Göttingen 1975, 193-238, here 230ss.

estant presbyteries, which were almost entirely composed of members of this commercial bourgeoisie. To this may be added family and kinship politics that were similar to those of the political elites in the cities and the territories. In my opinion the processes of change described here were, however, an important step in the direction of this process of transformation. At any rate, there was social continuity, for example, in the Rhenish families Hoesch, Palant, Ruhland, Prym, Peltzer, Schoeller, von Asten, Pastor, Klermondt, and Roemer who belonged both to the early modern Protestant commercial bourgeoisie and to the entrepreneurial bourgeoisie of the industrialization of the nineteenth century.[98]

III. Consequences of the Reformation and Counter-Reformation

Limits of space force me to restrict my remarks to a preliminary outline in the concluding discussion about the effects of the Reformation and Counter-Reformation as well as confessionalization upon the burgher elites of northern Germany. We have already been repeatedly confronted with the importance of religion or confession—for example in connection with the changes in the social composition of the urban political elite, the rise of an early modern civil service bourgeoisie and finally the process that severed the early modern commercial bourgeoisie from the political elite of the imperial cities. The societal function of the confessions[99] appears to have been both integrative, particularly important for the newly established groups of the early modern bureaucratic and commercial bourgeoisie, but it was also a mechanism for limitation and expulsion, clear above all in the (166) case of the Catholic elites of the Rhineland cities that maintained their traditionalism well into the nineteenth and twentieth centuries.[100] Confessional limitations upon marriage served to consolidate the early

---

98 J. Kermann, Die Manufakturen im Rheinland 1750-1833, Bonn 1972, appendix 620ss.; F. Zunkel, Der Rheinisch-Westfälische Unternehmer 1834-1879, Opladen 1962, 13ss., 20. J. Kocka, Familie, Unternehmer und Kapitalismus. An Beispielen der frühen deutschen Industrialisierung, in: Zeitschrift für Unternehmensgeschichte 24 (1979), 99-135.

99 Cf. the theoretical framework in Schilling, Konfessionskonflikt (note 15).

100 Most recently D. Ebeling, Bürgertum und Pöbel. Wirtschaft und Gesellschaft Kölns im 18. Jahrhundert, Köln/Wien 1987.

modern bourgeoisie elites, even long after the period under discussion.[101]

I would like to stress the functional interchangeability of the confessions within these processes—possible at least to a certain degree. The integration of the early modern territorial civil servant bourgeoisie was possible under all three of the larger confessions, Catholicism, Lutheranism, and Calvinism alike.[102] Moreover, the opposition between the older urban political elite and the early modern civil servant bourgeoisie was in principle supra-confessional.[103] Whether this was also true for the formation of the early modern commercial bourgeoisie is difficult to say because there was no comparable wave of migration of Catholics, at least not in the area under consideration. Within the Protestant early modern commercial bourgeoisie of the Rhineland at any rate, Lutherans could be found along with the more numerous Calvinists and Mennonites. And if the Rhenish Calvinists made a distinctive contribution to the origin and rapid success of the early modern commercial bourgeoisie, then, in my opinion, this did not derive from their doctrine of predestination, but rather from their particular constitutional model. The presbyteries and synods, which for generations were dominated by families (167) of the early modern commercial bourgeoisie, on the one hand encouraged the cohesiveness and far-reaching activity of the economic elite, and on the other softened the social opposition between entrepreneurs and workers or dependent artisans. Both made the process of separation from the traditional system of guilds within the large cities considerably easier, because the new way did not emerge in the form of individualistic economic striving, characterized by a pitiless competitive battle and harsh class conflict, but rather at an intermediate stage where economic leaders had a Christian corporative sense of obligation and they felt a patrician responsibility for the middling artisans, particularly for those of their own confession.

---

101 P. Schöller, Die rheinisch-westfälische Grenze zwischen Ruhr und Ebbegebirge, Münster 1953, 39ss., and map 6 in the appendix; Schilling, Bürgerkämpfe (note 9), 220ss.

102 Schilling, Konfessionskonflikt (note 15); idem, Die Konfessionalisierung im Reich. Religiöser und gesellschaftlicher Wandel in Deutschland zwischen 1555 und 1620, in: HZ 246 (1988), 1-46. (English translation below pp. 205-245).

103 With regard to poetic productivity, see the revealing discussion in Breuer, Literatur (note 74), 216ss.

The Reformation and confessionalization also affected the character of the urban upper strata of the sixteenth and seventeenth centuries in a completely different way. In the western and northwestern regions of the Holy Roman Empire where patronage rights for the nobility like those in eastern Germany remained unknown within the new ecclesiastical organization, the Reformation created a burgher church. This thesis sounds unusual against the well-known description of the Reformation process as a development from a "people's Reformation" to a "princely Reformation." Yet it is incontestable that as a result of the Protestant renewal of the church not only did the clergy disappear as a separate order but, apart from remnants in Protestant chapters and foundations, the nobility lost their prominence as holders of the highest positions within the church. This prominence of the nobility was typical above all of the Middle Ages and the Catholic territories of the early modern period.[104] (168)

1. The Status of Burgher Pastors

The social changes introduced by the Reformation constituted a part of the previously described process of differentiation within the burgher upper stratum. This is especially true for the Protestant clergy as a burgher estate.[105] According to the

---

104 B. Moeller, Pfarrer als Bürger, Göttingen 1972, 20; idem, Kleriker als Bürger, in: Festschrift für Hermann Heimpel, vol. 2, Göttingen 1972, 195-224, here 224.

105 K. Themel, Presbyteriologie und Genealogie, in: Der Herold, New Series 516 (1963/68), 57-85; E. Heydenreich, Handbuch der praktischen Genealogie, Leipzig 1913, vol. 1, 72ss., vol. 2, 136ss.; G. Franz (ed.), Beamtentum und Pfarrerstand, 1400-1800, Limburg 1972; P. Drews, Der evangelische Geistliche in der deutschen Vergangenheit, Jena 1905; B. Vogler, Le clergé Rhénan au siècle de la Réforme, Paris 1976; S.K. Boles, The Economic Position of Lutheran Pastors in Ernestine Thuringia 1521-1555, in: Archiv für Reformationsgeschichte 63 (1972), 94-125; von der Ohe, Zentral- und Hofverwaltung (note 63), 212; Liebel, Bourgeoisie (note 73) 283-307; H. Schnabel-Schüle, Distanz und Nähe. Zum Verhältnis von Pfarrern und Gemeinden im Herzogtum Württemberg vor und nach der Reformation, in: Rottenburger Jahrbuch für Kirchengeschichte 5 (1986); L. Schorn-Schütte, Prediger an protestantischen Höfen der Frühneuzeit. Zur politischen und sozialen Stellung einer neuen bürgerlichen Führungsgruppe in der höfischen Gesellschaft des 17. Jahrhunderts dargestellt am Beispiel von Hessen-Kassel, Hessen-Darmstadt und Braunschweig-Wolfenbüttel, in: Schilling/Diederiks (eds.), Eliten (note 7); eadem, "Gefährtin" und "Mitregentin". Zur Sozialgeschichte der evangelischen Pfarrfrau in der Frühen Neuzeit, in: H. Wunder and Ch. Vanja (eds.), Wandel der Geschlechterbeziehungen zu Beginn der Neuzeit, Frankfurt 1991, 109-153; L. Schorn-Schütte, Evangelische Geistlichkeit in der Frühneuzeit: Ihr Beitrag zur Entfaltung frühmoderner Staatlichkeit und Gesellschaft. Dargestellt am Beispiel Braunschweig-Wolfenbüttels, Hessen-Kassels und

distinction which was introduced in the first part of this article
the pastorate belongs partially to the early modern urban
burgher elite and partially to the early modern territorial civil
servant bourgeoisie. Particularly in the middle-sized and smaller territorial towns of the sixteenth century pastors belonged
to the burgher upper stratum. There was no social distance
worth mentioning between the pastors and the *Honoratioren*
families of the political elite.[106] This is true despite the fact
that especially during the century of the Reformation the social
origins of pastors were quite diverse and included, alongside
members of the upper stratum, also many sons of artisans and
peasants. The social status of a pastor was rarely determined by
birth or parental occupation, but rather by his office and
especially his university education, an attainment which became
more and more common in Protestant cities and territories,
placing pastors in the same (169) category as jurists, who were
then rising in social estimation. Both were typical criteria for
determining social status in the early modern period. This
societal status was consolidated to the extent that the pastor's
family itself became a significant base of recruitment for the
next generation of pastors.

As long as the territorial cities controlled appointments to
ministerial posts, something that was common during the sixteenth century and still occasionally the case afterwards, the
pastoral office seems to have been added to the established
circle of urban offices, providing new support positions which
were given to members of the burgher upper stratum. The
possibility of providing the office was not new, since pastors
and other benefice holders of the old church had often already
come from the burgher elites of the city. Much more
characteristic of the Protestant realm was the direct inclusion
of ecclesiastical office holders within the urban family
network. This is a topic which needs more exact prosopographical study that is based upon plentiful material, mostly
accessible in biographical dictionaries of pastors.

The successful formation of Protestant territorial churches,
which followed the urban Reformation after some delay, led to
the development of a territorial branch of the pastorate,
alongside of the urban burgher branch. Similar to what occur-

---

der Stadt Braunschweig, habilitation thesis Gießen 1991 (forthcoming).
106 Examples: Schilling, Konfessionskonflikt (note 15), 98ss., 114s., 130ss.,
180s., 271, 283ss.

red within the burgher political elite, these different types within the pastoral order often stood in more or less sharp opposition to each other during the sixteenth and seventeenth centuries. This antagonism became especially virulent when the urban churches were placed under the jurisdiction of the territorial ecclesiastical bureaucracy and hierarchy. For the urban pastor this meant a demotion comparable to that of the city council members under the supervision of the territorial officials. In any case it is unmistakable that the antagonisms within the pastoral burgher elite were not as sharply expressed as those within the political elite. This was related to the fact that the urban pastors, unlike the civic political elite, had never had an autonomous right to authority, but rather after the establishment of a civic church organization they were governed by the city council as employees of this body. Thus integration into the territorial church meant for pastors only a change in employer, not however, a difference in the legal quality of their office as was the case for members of the political elite who lost their independent urban magisterial offices to a territorial civil service under the sovereignty of the ruler. For the urban pastors such a reorientation was even attractive because they could easily enter leadership positions within the hierarchy of the territorial church thanks to their educational advantage over the rural pastors. Together with the ecclesiastical sovereignty of the Protestant territorial rulers, which was firmly established by the Peace of Augsburg, this (170) often gave the territorial church the chance to overcome the autonomy of city churches and to make them subject to the bureaucracy of the territorial state. In these cases the urban clergy were transformed into the advanced guard of the territorial civil servant bourgeoisie. The division of the pastorate into urban and territorial types that occurred in the course of the sixteenth century continued during the seventeenth century only in a few cases where there was a confessional difference between the city and the territorial church. These were the same cases in which the distinction between territorial and urban political elites was maintained.

The connection between the Protestant clergy and the early modern civil servant bourgeoisie existed from the very beginning within the villages. There the Protestant pastor was frequently the only burgher among the peasants and was thus especially suited to promote the interests of the territorial state

in the village. It is clear, however, that he occupied a lower
social station than the legally trained part of the burgher civil
service and there were, at times, social tensions between these
two groups of territorial burghers.

The same could be said about the pastors of the large imperial cities. In contrast to the small and middle-sized territorial
towns, there was from the beginning a clear social distance
between the clergy and the political and economic elites in the
imperial cities. This can be deduced from marriage restrictions
as well as from a series of other societal norms. For example,
in Lübeck the ceremonies accompanying the selection of a new
city council member included two to three weeks of banquets
for the social peers of the new city councillor. Only when no
more guests were expected, were the pastors invited; after they
had pronounced their blessing over the new city councillor "the
hospitalities were over" as a pithy contemporary report made
clear.[107]

This raises the question whether the pastors of these cities
should even be considered members of the upper stratum. In
any case they never belonged to it in the same way that academically trained jurists did. This may be the reason why the
pastors of the early modern period strove to place as much
social distance, both inside and outside of the church, between
themselves and the "uneducated" artisans.[108] The most decisive
reason why pastors enjoyed a lower social standing than jurists
is probably because the former stood in an employee relationship to the city council while jurists participated through the
city council in the exercise of authority, the distinguishing
characteristic of the burgher elite of an imperial city. (171)

2. The Burgher "Lay Groups" within the Protestant Church

"The creation of a burgher church by the Reformation" can be
interpreted in a wider sense, that is, through broader lay participation in the administration of the churches, among the Calvinists within its ruling bodies as well. (The term "lay" is understood in Protestant circles to be someone who is not or-
dained to pastoral office). In these lay bodies the upper stratum
was represented in great numbers, and in many cities they
alone comprised the lay leadership. As *Kirchendechen, Tempe-*

---

107 Bruns, Rat (note 21), 23.
108 Liebel, Bourgeoisie (note 73), 301ss.; Moeller, Pfarrer (note 104), 21.

liere, Provisoren, or *Kirchmeister*—the terminology varied from place to place—members of the burgher upper stratum administered the finances and properties that were seized by the city when the foundations and institutions that had belonged to the old church were secularized. Even though the wealth was usually not misappropriated, but was taken over by ecclesiastical successor institutions, these offices offered sufficient opportunities for the burgher upper stratum to skim off sums for both public and private purposes such as loans, leases, and grants.

On the other hand, it often became customary that the exercise of honorary ecclesiastical offices was in fact a prerequisite for assuming a position of political authority. For example, in Hamburg usually no one was given a place in the city council who had not first served in the church administration, above all in the *Juratenkollegium*, i.e., the board of laymen responsible for conducting the financial affairs of the church.[109] And in Bremen the *cursus honorum* of a city council member began as a rule with the position of deacon in one of the main urban parish churches, i.e., with an office administering a Calvinist form of poor and social relief.[110]

Even the Calvinist presbyteries themselves, which are often regarded as a model for a possible democratization of the burgher constitution, were dominated by the burgher upper stratum after an early phase characterized by broad social representation. There was thus an extensive overlapping of the ecclesiastical and the political circle of leadership. However, the presbyteries provided more than a wider field of activity for an already established political elite. To a lesser degree they also offered to many who were rising socially a first opportunity to exercise (172) public authority and served as a springboard for transition to the political elite. This has been proven in a prosopographically quantified way for the Dutch cities of Leiden and Groningen.[111] Other data indicate similar

---

109 H. Reincke, Aus der Geschichte der Hauptkirche St. Jacobi zu Hamburg und ihres Kirchspiels, in: 700 Jahre St. Jacobi zu Hamburg 1255-1955, Hamburg 1955, 37; R. Postel, Die Reformation in Hamburg, 1517-1528, Gütersloh 1986.

110 F. Petri, Unser Lieben Frau Diakonie. 400 Jahre evangelischer Liebestätigkeit in Bremen, Bremen 1925; Prange, Kaufmannschaft (note 22), 174.

111 H. Schilling, Calvinistische Presbyterien in Städten der Frühneuzeit-Eine kirchliche Alternativform zur bürgerlichen Repräsentation?, in: W. Ehbrecht (ed.), Führungsgruppen (note 17), 385-444; idem, Calvinism and Urban Elites, in: idem, Calvinism (note 14).

relationships in the urban Calvinist congregations of the Empire, for instance in Emden and for the dissident congregations of the lower Rhine, as well as in Hamburg and Frankfort. In these two cities activity within the Calvinist presbyteries could in some measure make up for the loss of political participation of the Calvinist burghers.

3. Post-Tridentine Catholicism

In the Catholic cities which in our area, apart from Cologne, were re-catholicized cities, there was likewise in the context of the Counter-Reformation or Catholic Reformation a reordering of the relationships between the burgher strata and the church. In contrast to the problems connected with the "urban Reformation" the "urban Counter-Reformation" as a whole has so far been little studied. This is true above all from the perspective of social history. One fundamental difference from the Protestant cities is obvious: In Catholic areas there was no corresponding domination of the church by burghers. The clergy remained a separate estate. Beyond that the Catholic church remained a church of the nobility at the upper levels, which thus remained beyond the reach of clerics who came from the burgher strata. The cathedral chapter in Münster offers a particularly striking example. For over a century it refused to accept members from the hereditary patriciate into the chapter even though the patriciate had long before outgrown burgher status.[112] As a whole the problem of "church and burgher upper strata" is quite different for Catholic cities than for Protestant ones. There the connecting links between the church and the burgher upper strata were not the pastors and lay groups, but rather the different religious orders—particularly the Jesuits, in Cologne above all the (173) Carthusians—as well as the confraternities which had changed considerably from their late medieval form.[113]

---

112 Lahrkamp, Patriziat (note 10), 195-207, here 201s.-For a comparative view: L. Schorn-Schütte, Die Geistlichkeit vor der Revolution, in: H. Berding et al. (eds.), Deutschland und Frankreich im Zeitalter der Französischen Revolution, Frankfurt 1989, 216-244.

113 There are only a few examples of research on this field: Cf. Petri (ed.), Bischofs- und Kathedralstädte (note 32) (Mauersberg, Kellenbenz, Bosl); H. Lepper, Reichsstadt und Kirche im späten Mittelalter und der frühen Neuzeit, in: W. Ehbrecht (ed.), Voraussetzungen und Methoden geschichtlicher Städteforschung, Köln 1979, 28-46, esp. 32ss.; J. Greven, Die Kölner Kartause und die Anfänge der katholischen Reform in Deutschland, Münster 1935; G. Schreiber (ed.), Das Weltkonzil von Trient, vol. 2, Freiburg 1951 (Franzen: Köln; Schröer: Münster;

I must limit myself to these very general observations. Nevertheless, it is clear that the church reforms were accompanied by a further differentiation within the burgher elites of early modern Germany; the burgher elite was divided into a Protestant part which was dominant in northern and western Germany particularly, and a Catholic part that could be found above all in southern Germany, in the Rhineland cities, and in the episcopal cities of Westphalia.

Stüwer: Paderborn); R. Decker, Bürgermeister und Ratsherren in Paderborn vom 13. bis zum 17. Jahrhundert, Paderborn 1977; H. Schoppmeyer, Der Bischof von Paderborn und seine Städte, Paderborn 1968; K. Hengst, Kirchliche Reform im Fürstbistum Paderborn unter Dietrich von Fürstenberg (1585-1618), München 1974; Th. Klümper, Landesherr und Städte im Fürstbistum Münster unter Ernst und Ferdinand von Bayern 1585-1650, Emsdetten 1940; W.E. Schwarz (ed.), Die Geschichtsquellen des Bistums Münster, vol. 7, Die Akten der Visitation des Bistums Münster aus der Zeit Johannes von Hoya, Münster 1913. Most recently, see R. Po-chia Hsia, Society and Religion in Münster, 1535-1618, New Haven/London 1984.

CHAPTER FOUR

THE COMMUNAL REFORMATION IN GERMANY:
AN UPPER GERMAN, ZWINGLIAN PHENOMENON
BEFORE THE "TURNING POINT OF THE
REFORMATION" IN 1525?

Heinz Maier-Leibnitz, President for many years of the Federal
Endowment for Research in the Sciences and Humanities
(*Deutsche Forschungsgemeinschaft*), recently made an impas-
sioned plea for a linkage of scholarship and rhetoric in the
public sphere. He justified his demand with the argument that
"anyone who speaks or writes today must perhaps take greater
pains to ensure that he expresses himself clearly and takes into
consideration what the public will understand or can understand."[1] Peter Blickle's *Gemeinde-Reformation*[2] is a brilliant
book when measured by this not unreasonable demand, to
which historians have lent a ready ear for some time. In style
and content it is a series of well-crafted books, beginning with
Die Revolution von 1525, and *Der Deutsche Untertan. Ein
Widerspruch*. Blickle, an early modern historian at the University of Bern, has submitted these books, written in quick
succession, with the goal of offering to the general public a
new interpretation of early modern German history, particularly of the Reformation era.[3]

Experts know that Blickle's position involves a very personal, particular point of view which he has developed on the
basis of his original research on Old European structural and
social history, particularly in the territories of southern Germany and Switzerland. In addition Blickle's book was shaped
by his knowledge of those fields in the history of the Refor-

---

1 H. Maier-Leibnitz, Beweisen ist nicht genug. Vernachlässigen Wissenschaft
und Technik die Rhetorik?, in: Frankfurter Allgemeine Zeitung, May 28, 1986,
No. 121, 33.
2 P. Blickle, Gemeindereformation.-Die Menschen des 16. Jahrhunderts auf dem
Weg zum Heil, München 1985.
3 P. Blickle, Die Revolution von 1525, 1st ed. München 1977, 2nd ed. Mün-
chen/Wien 1983; idem, Der Deutsche Untertan. Ein Widerspruch, München 1980.

mation and early modern theology which he studied in order to
write his paperback book *Die Reformation im Reich* and to
prepare his contribution to the Zwingli anniversary, an event
sponsored by the historical and theological faculties of the
University of Bern.[4] In 1985 he submitted a book that "argues
for the concept of a Communal Reformation" and claims to
offer "a new interpretation for the decisive years of the
Reformation in central Europe." According to the publisher's
note, the book contributes new insights by "drawing attention
to the salient importance of the upper German re-formers and
by supplying proof of a peasant Reformation, adding a large,
hitherto overlooked social group to the purview of Reformation
history and, as a result, placing the most recent research on
urban history into a new context." (326)

There is no need for us to add any further praise or recognition. Its organization, powerful presentation and dynamic,
well-ordered argumentation, quite suggestive at times, makes
reading the book an enjoyable experience both for non-special-
ists and specialists alike. It makes particularly stimulating reading, however, for the latter, above all for those who do not
share Professor Blickle's point of view. His commitment to
historical enlightenment with political and pedagogical intent is
also laudable. Only the scholar who must review the book is
faced with a dilemma: Phrases such as "scarcely arguable any
longer but still argued," (Blickle, p. 205) warn reviewers not to
question Professor Blickle's new vision of Germany's Reformation. Let us attempt, nevertheless, to enter into a discussion
with the author.

1. The model of a Communal Reformation as such hardly
seems controversial to me, since it has been well-known in
principle for years and has long been accepted by scholars of
the Reformation. The similarities between the theological and
ecclesiastical demands of the Reformation and the socio-political structure of society during the transition between the
Middle Ages and the early modern period as well as the communalization of the urban churches in the wake of the Reformation are generally accepted by urban and Reformation
historians. Blickle's contribution, the result of persistent and
largely convincing arguments, is to draw attention to the fact

---

4 P. Blickle, Die Reformation im Reich, Stuttgart 1982; P. Blickle, A. Lindt, A.
Schindler (eds.), Zwingli und Europa, Zürich 1984.

that the communal principle not only shaped public life in the cities and affected the mentality of the burghers but also played a salient role in rural areas, on a political level and within the religious mentality of the peasants. Karl Siegfried Bader, Dietrich Kurze, and Blickle himself have laid solid foundations for this linkage in their important, original research.[5]

There is something to be said for an attempt to place both phenomena under one roof, the concept of "communalism." However, Blickle's thesis becomes unnecessarily problematic, in my opinion, when he assigns the same level of importance to the rural and urban forms of these communal and corporate structures and mentalities, which in fact are among the key elements of Old European history. By doing so he welds them together in a way that hinders a historically necessary differentiation, if it does not make it altogether impossible.

There are very strong arguments, even after reading this book, for maintaining a qualified distinction between the forms of communalism present in the cities and those in the villages. Specialists in urban history argue convincingly for maintaining the distinction, since "the burgher commune of a city did not stand in the same kind of subordinate relationship to the city council as peasants did with respect to their lords."[6] This is not in any way to cast doubt upon the parallelism of the Reformation movement in town and countryside as Blickle has formulated it (above all, pp. 110-114). It seems evident to me, however, that peasant communalism was qualitatively inferior to the urban variety and as a consequence peasants had to make up a developmental deficit in both (327) the secular and ecclesiastical spheres. As a consequence of their relative backwardness in political communalism, peasants of the early sixteenth century were forced to raise questions that had already been settled by burgher communes in the cities generations before, although these solutions did not always work satisfactorily in everyday political and administrative affairs.

It also seems clear to me that the peasant "Communal

---

5 K.S. Bader, Studien zur Rechtsgeschichte des mittelalterlichen Dorfes, 3 vols., Weimar 1957-1973; D. Kurze, Pfarrerwahlen im Mittelalter. Ein Beitrag zur Geschichte der Gemeinde und des Niederkirchenwesens, Köln/Graz 1966.

6 E. Ennen and W. Janssen, Deutsche Agrargeschichte, Wiesbaden 1979, 200; H. Schilling, Bemerkungen zu Peter Blickles Interpretation des Bauernkrieges als Revolution des "gemeinen Mannes" in Stadt und Land, in: H.U. Wehler (ed.), Der deutsche Bauernkrieg, 1524-1526, Göttingen 1975, 237s.

Reformation" was stimulated by the cities and their burghers. The extent of their dependence remains to be clarified by the study of specific historical examples. This thesis could be verified through prosopographical analysis and by studies of communication between the representatives of the burghers and the peasants, through studies of the composition of their leadership and the origin of their programs. The case study of rural society in Alsace, analyzed by Blickle's student Franziska Conrad, which by Blickle's own admission "protects the flanks of the concept of a Communal Reformation (p. 10)," correctly emphasizes that "it was again and again the process of communication with *urban centers* (italics mine) that exercised an influence upon the actions and reactions of the rural communes."[7]

2. Regional differentiation is indispensable for the study of German history and crucially important for the subjects discussed in this book. The German Communal Reformation was a far more extensive phenomenon than Blickle implies when he restricts the use of the concept to only one region, namely the southern parts of the Empire. Above all Blickle's own arguments, drawn exclusively from the historical experience of southern Germany and Switzerland, illustrate the need to distinguish between different types and different regional groups of cities. To anyone familiar with the "town liberties" and "civic liberties" of the Hansa region, the form of communalism present in southern German territorial cities as Blickle describes it appears to be both stunted and short-lived, since it disappeared in 1525 according to Blickle. By contrast, the cities of the Rhineland, Westphalia, lower Saxony, Mecklenburg, and even numerous smaller towns displayed a fully developed form of communalism. They enjoyed far greater liberties even as late as the seventeenth century.

From a northern German perspective Blickle's sharp distinction between the political culture of imperial and territorial cities already during the 1520's is very problematic. For it was only the events of the sixteenth and early seventeenth centuries which first brought about important changes in the political culture of the large, privileged "territorial cities," which

---

7 See O. Mörke's review of F. Conrad, Reformation in der bäuerlichen Gesellschaft. Zur Rezeption reformatorischer Theologie im Elsaß, Stuttgart/Wiesbaden 1984, in: Blätter für deutsche Landesgeschichte 122 (1986), 627.

distinguished them from imperial cities.[8] In this context the political and ecclesiastical decisions codified in the Peace of Augsburg of 1555 were most important.

Should we account for these observations by saying that the amalgamation of urban communalism with peasant communalism, as Blickle describes it, occurred only in upper Germany because urban communalism there was comparatively undeveloped when compared with the urban communalism of non-imperial cities in the Hansa region? In this light Blickle's thesis that southern Germany was the only region where a breakthrough to a Communal Reformation took place experiences an interesting reversal: if we accept Professor Blickle's interpretation of the German Reformation, then we must change the geographical framework. Anyone who is familiar with the situation in northern Germany can demonstrate that it was in the Hansa region where urban communalism actually existed. It was in the Hansa cities that the Communal Reformation took the form of a powerful burgher movement not only during the early 1520's, but also during the 1530's. Blickle's distinction between a "communal" upper Germany (328) and a non-communal lower Germany cannot be maintained at all historically, even for the countryside and peasant communalism. The existence of peasant self-government in villages, not to speak of a full-fledged peasant estate, in those areas of Germany that were not affected by the "Revolution of the Common Man" must be acknowledged. In the north, e.g., in Friesland, Dithmarschen, and similar regions, rural communalism was strong despite their lack of participation in the Peasants' Revolt of 1525, a fact that drastically relativizes the significance of the year 1525 in the history of the Reformation and in early modern German history in general.

3. Profound regional differences are the Achilles' heel of any attempt to propose a general model for the Reformation as a societal change at the beginning of the early modern period in Germany. Unfortunately, Professor Blickle makes no effort to face this problem. Despite his claim to offer a new general

8 H. Schilling, Gab es im späten Mittelalter und zu Beginn der Neuzeit in Deutschland einen städtischen "Republikanismus"? Zur politischen Kultur des alteuropäischen Stadtbürgertums, in: H. Koenigsberger (ed.), Republiken und Republikanismus im Europa der Frühen Neuzeit, München 1988, 101-143 (English translation above pp. 3-60); idem, Konfessionskonflikte und hansestädtische Freiheit im 16. und frühen 17. Jahrhundert, in: Hansische Geschichtsblätter 97 (1979), 36-59.

interpretation of the German Reformation, Blickle presents his
readers with the concept of a Communal Reformation limited
geographically to upper Germany and theologically to Zwingli.
His position is essentially a modified version of the negative
view of the northern German urban Reformation presented in
Bernd Moeller's *Imperial Cities and the Reformation*, published
in 1962. This position has long since been refuted at every
point by intensive research both in urban history and in the
Reformation history of the central and northern German regions.[9]

At this juncture we must refer to a general historiographical
problem: Early modern historians in Germany, and in their
wake those in America as well, particularly specialists in Reformation and sixteenth century history, have drawn a peculiar, objectively unjustified contrast between southern and
northern Germany. When far-reaching interpretive theses are
developed on the basis of an intimate knowledge of only one
area, without considering the presence of contrasting structures
and also the occurrence of contradictory events in other areas,
it can lead to fatal conceptual errors.

In this context it is interesting that Blickle considers Switzerland to be part of the upper German zone and thus sharpens
the communal structures of southern Germany in an impressive
fashion, but he regards the Dutch experience with its "high
communal autonomy" as an expression of Burgundian-western
European rather than German imperial development (p. 205).
By leaving the Netherlands out of his consideration of the
history of the German Empire, Blickle can maintain his incorrect view of weak communal structures in the northern parts of
the Empire. From the perspective of structural history this
omission makes little sense. Thomas Brady's influential book
Turning Swiss,[10] which documents the influence that Switzerland had upon southern Germany, should and must be supplemented by a corresponding work treating the historical
interaction between northwestern German and Dutch regions—"Turning Dutch."

4. Is Blickle's premise of a unified religiosity of the common

---

9 See B. Moeller, Reichsstadt und Reformation, Gütersloh 1962, 62ss. The
second edition, Berlin 1987, 90-94, contains a revision of the earlier view in
accordance with this research on the Hansa region.

10 Th. Brady, Turning Swiss, Cities and the Empire, 1450-1550, Cambridge
1985.

man in town and countryside plausible historically and socio-
logically? The model of a homogeneous communalism of town
and countryside corresponds to the monistic concept of an
identical understanding of "God and the world held by both
peasants and burghers (p. 123)." Were the conceptions of God
and the world indeed essentially the same among the popula-
tions of rural and urban areas? (329) Prosopographical studies,
to which incidentally Blickle never refers, prove that members
of moderately and highly educated social strata played an important role in the burgher movements of the urban Reformation. Is it plausible to suppose that their religious and theological ideals were welded together with those of the rural population to form what is in my opinion a fictitious "religion of
the common man"? On the contrary, there is overwhelming
evidence (not least from the results of research on popular religion) indicating that peasants had completely different religious
needs than the vast majority of city dwellers. Magical exor-
cisms performed by the blessing of crops, and the ringing of
bells to protect them against hail storms and lightning were far
more important to farmers than was the conscious appropria-
tion of grace that was so important for burghers.

These arguments are not presented in order to cast doubt
upon Blickle's evidence but rather to raise concerns about his
interpretation and the methodological problem of whether the
evidence actually reflects the peasants' "understanding of God
and the world." Or are we hearing here "merely" an echo of
the urban burgher explanations of God and the world? Of
course this phenomenon attests to the willingness of the
peasants to accept urban ideas, particularly in "the atmosphere
of departure" during the early 1520's. This certainly does not
make the thesis of a unified religiosity of peasants and
burghers either historically or theoretically plausible. The
interconnections are more complex in my opinion.

Even the high value that both cities and villages placed upon
communal thinking is insufficient to vitiate the distinction
between urban and rural mentalities and to justify an understanding of the Reformation that was on the one hand a particular one, and on the other hand a common view shared by both
peasants and burghers. For the congregational ideal of the
Reformation was no more an appeal directed toward specific
social strata than were the doctrines of justification and the
other elements of the Reformation message. The congregational

and communal principle of the Reformation was also convincing to the nobility and motivated them to religious and
political action, as it moved the burghers and peasants. Examples of this include the imperial knights in the west and south
who, like the peasants, created a "Christian association," as did
the territorial nobility in the north and east. All of these congregational and corporate alliances and associations worked to
advance the Reformation. As in the case of the peasants these
alliances were both religious and political ones. Consequently,
the homogeneity of religious and ecclesiastical concepts on the
one hand and political and social concepts on the other was
typical not exclusively of burghers and peasants, but of all
groups, as might be expected given the fundamentally communal structures of Older European society. A different mentality
seems to have prevailed only among the princes and their civil
servants. Unfortunately, we still know little about the specific
reception of the Reformation communal principle by this
group.

    5. Was the year 1525 a "turning point in the Reformation"
(p. 204)? Skepticism seems warranted since the salient importance which Blickle has assigned to 1525—the defeat of the
common man—is based upon his social and geographical
reductionism, which we have already characterized as problematic. The "turning-point" thesis is more a logical consequence
of Blickle's premises and the direction taken by his arguments
than a convincing result of a genuine analysis of the historical
situation. (330) Both the concepts of a "Communal Reformation" and a "princely Reformation" represent interpretive tools
that provide insights into the prerequisites, goals, and consequences of historical processes and also the mentality and
interests of the different social groups supporting these processes. We must strictly maintain the epistemological and methodological distinction between analytical concepts of this kind
and historical reality in order to prevent them from assuming
an existence independent of the historical record as occurred
with the concept of the *"Frühbürgerliche Revolution."*

    In reality the "Communal Reformation" and the "princely
Reformation" were not separated from each other in chronological succession, divided by the year 1525. Had Luther and
his doctrine not been supported by princes before 1525 there
would have been no Reformation movement and the events of
1525 would never have happened. And if—the other way

around—there had been no "Communal Reformation" after 1525, many areas that are Protestant today would have remained Catholic after 1525. It is true that the "Communal Reformation" took place mainly in the north, and thus in a different part of the Empire than Blickle discusses, but if we are to speak of a "turning point in the Reformation," if that phrase has any meaning at all, then it must be valid for all of Germany, for the north as well as for Blickle's south.

The communal movement did not come to an end politically and socially in 1525 either. Testimony to its continued vitality is provided by burgher movements which arose in connection with the Reformation in northern German cities, phenomena which Blickle blithely ignores and constantly overlooks in his argumentation. For the sake of simplicity he deals only with the state of research present in the Lau article of 1959.[11] However, in the light of the voluminous research that has been published on the history of the early modern city in the decades since Lau's article, above all on northern Germany, it has become commonly accepted that urban burgher communalism or "republicanism," the term I prefer using to describe that phenomenon,[12] remained an active force throughout the sixteenth century, expressed in part by an unbroken tradition of burgher movements. The connection between urban communalism/republicanism and the Reformation was also maintained after 1525, even in its Lutheran (!) expression. And finally we know from the most recent research on absolutism that even the late seventeenth and eighteenth centuries witnessed more features of "communal" self-direction than had previously been assumed.[13] While all of these insights do not refute the thesis of communalism in principle, but apply it to other times and places, Blickle obscures them with his chronological fixation on 1525 and the geographical limitation of his study to upper Germany.

6. Blickle's theological premises and his understanding of the impact of religion upon early modern society are also prob-

---

11 F. Lau, Der Bauernkrieg und das angebliche Ende der lutherischen Reformation als spontane Volksbewegung, in: Luther Jahrbuch 26 (1959), 109-134, re-edited in: W. Hubatsch (ed.), Wirkungen der deutschen Reformation bis 1555, Darmstadt 1967, 68-100.

12 H. Schilling, Mittelalter (note 8); idem, Aufbruch und Krise, Berlin 1988, 162-183.

13 For a recent and very concise revisionist interpretation of the German history of that period: R. Vierhaus, Staaten und Stände, Berlin 1984.

lematic. The geographical (south/north) and chronological (before and after 1525) polarization of the German Reformation corresponds in Blickle's view to the theological rift between Zwingli and Luther. The author has familiarized himself thoroughly with the differences in their theological positions, as reported by the theological literature, and as a result has lost sight of the historical situation. Everything that has been said about the differences between Luther and Zwingli in terms of their theological assumptions and the further development of their thought, above all concerning the "social and ethical consequences," is illuminating not only for the theological orientation of both reformers, but also in a certain sense for a secular overarching typology regarding the social and political implications of Lutheranism and Reformed/Calvinist Protestantism. However, it has little to contribute toward an understanding of the early 1520's, if it does not draw attention away from the actual function of religious factors during these years.

At this point Blickle's new interpretive theory is again presented in conjunction with research positions that to my knowledge are no longer accepted or have at least been called into question by church historians. Is it indeed true that the spheres of influence of Luther and Zwingli can be distinguished so precisely before 1525? Or was it not the case (331)—as Martin Brecht among others has shown—that Luther's presence in upper Germany was stronger than Blickle allows? Were not the activists, above all peasants in 1525, convinced that they could draw arguments for their religious and social demands from Luther's theology just as much as from Zwingli's theology? And has it not been proved for northern Germany that the burgher movements, or if you wish the urban "communalism" of the Reformation period, appealed to Luther? That Luther did not expound upon "this community ... in its practical, visible form with a desirable degree of clarity" (p. 138) is evident *post factum* to Professor Blickle, but it was not at all evident to the activists of the early 1520's. The burghers of the Hansa cities were quite sure that urban communalism as they understood it[14] and Lutheran theology fit together very well, even during the 1530's. I assume that Luther's assessment was similar—at least until 1524/1525. The idea that "church congregation and political commune were identical" (Blickle, p. 154) is hardly an earth-shaking historical recognition of Zwinglian theology, but rather a general structural characteristic of the time, especially of the cities. "Civitas, burgher commune, means burgher unity, ... not only because it is surrounded by a wall, but because it is held together in desires and denials, by a single confession of faith (*eiusdem fidei symbolo*), by one bond of burgher law and rights, and—so to speak—because it has become one flesh."[15] This was how the ideal of communalism was expressed by Petrus a Beeck at the beginning of the seventeenth century in his history of Aachen, a witness for the Catholic communalism of the burghers and the churches in the lower German region, almost a century after the allegedly fateful year 1525.

The theological premises, above all the theological rift between Zwingli and Luther, upon which Blickle builds his thesis of the salient importance of upper Germany and the upper German Reformation, may reflect the state of research in current academic theology. When considering the historical situation that he has studied and wishes to explain, it is important for historians to recognize that these distinctions did not shape the mentality of the activists decisively, if they realized them at all. Even the two reformers themselves were well aware that their dispute resulted from differences in eucharistic doctrine, but not in social ethics.

As far as the social and political consequences for historical development during the modern period in general are concerned, the classical model offered by the sociology of religion has been refined and modified in the last few decades. The distinction made between a Lutheran "passion for obedience" and a Reformed (Zwinglian/Calvinist) "passion for liberty"

---

14 These questions are discussed in detail in H. Schilling, Alternatives to the Lutheran Reformation and the Rise of Lutheran Identity.-The Possibilities and Limitations of Religious and Social Differentiation at the Beginning of the Early Modern Period, in: A. Fix/S. Karant-Nunn (eds.), Germania illustrata: Essays presented to Gerald Strauss, (working-title), Kirksville 1991.

15 Petrus a Beeck, Aquisgranum, Aachen 1620: "Civitatem dictam aiunt ... quod eodem velle, eodem nolle, eiusdem fidei symbolo, earundem civilium legum acac iustiae nexu coalescere cives et velut inviscerasci debeant."

appears less and less persuasive to historians.[16] The issue of
resistance, which Blickle discusses in the context of Zwingli's
theology, (p. 153) is more complex, as Winfried Schulze has
recently demonstrated.[17] Actually more Lutheran thought than
Zwinglian informed the Calvinist doctrine of the Monarchomachians.

In those parts of Germany and Europe where Zwingli's
theology had a continuing impact it gave rise not to communalism but to statism or territorialism, i.e. the takeover of the
church by the state (332), in Blickle's parlance a
"decommunalization" (*Entkommunalisierung*) of church and
society. Thomas Erastus attempted this in the Electoral Palatinate as did the Arminians in the Netherlands. It was successfully realized in Anglicanism, even if "the identity of church
and state, as Zwingli understood it, ... was not the identity as it
was practiced in England."[18] Perhaps even more decisively than
the Lutherans, the Reformed were involved in the development
of the German territorial states under the absolutist or semi-
absolutist regime of princes with their authoritarian
(*obrigkeitlich*) praxis and use of social discipline.[19] Congregational structures were introduced within the major early
modern confessions not by Zwinglian, but by Calvinist
churches, but in a pure form only in Catholic or Lutheran
states where Calvinists were a minority and at times were
forced to form underground churches. Under these circumstances the Presbyterians were unable to form an alliance with
the state because of differences in their ecclesiological and
confessional positions. This constellation is a further example
of how social and political effects were not solely a result of
theological positions themselves, and most of the time were not
even primarily so. Often these social and political consequences
were also and most importantly a result of the historical cir-

---

16 Quotation from H. Heimpel, Der Mensch in seiner Gegenwart, Göttingen 2nd
ed. 1957, 156. See the discussion of the problem in H. Schilling (ed.) Die reformierte Konfessionalisierung in Deutschland. Das Problem der "Zweiten Reformation", Gütersloh 1986, passim, esp. 428ss., 459, 462, 464ss.

17 W. Schulze, Zwingli, lutherisches Widerstandsdenken, monarchomachischer
Widerstand, in: P. Blickle (ed.), Zwingli und Europa, Zürich 1985.

18 H. Kressner, Schweizer Ursprünge des anglikanischen Staatskirchentums,
Gütersloh 1953, 13.

19 See the essays and the discussions in Schilling (ed.), Konfessionalisierung (note
16).

cumstances in which the theological positions were introduced, adopted, and in which they were able to maintain themselves.

Blickle's *Gemeindereformation* is an important book because it stimulates the discussion of research and forces others to offer clearly argued opposing positions. Hopefully this important debate over "communalism" will take place without a hardening of positions whose premises are not open to discussion. Such unnecessarily inflexible and misleading positions include, in my opinion, especially the idea of a strict structural and mental identity of rural and urban communalism, the restriction of its scope to upper Germany and Switzerland, the conceptual shortening of early modern and modern German history stemming from this biased picture of the Reformation, and finally the chronological fixation on the "miracle year" of 1525. On a more general methodological and epistemological level we must recognize and keep in mind that the Reformation was much more than a result of social and political interests and forces, aspects which Blickle—as he has a legitimate right to do—concentrated upon in his book *Gemeindereformation*. It was a religious event and an event of far-reaching consequences for world history.

PART TWO

CONFESSIONALIZATION AND SECOND
REFORMATION

CONFESSIONALIZATION IN THE EMPIRE: RELIGIOUS AND SOCIETAL CHANGE IN GERMANY BETWEEN 1555 AND 1620

The Reformation period has always been strongly emphasized in German early modern research. This did not change after the Second World War when a new orientation emerged within German historical scholarship. Both in the Federal Republic and in the German Democratic Republic the Reformation era was stressed in the discussion of German social history at the beginning of the early modern period, in the GDR almost exclusively. By contrast the second half of this revolutionary period, called the "long sixteenth century" by structural and economic historians, remained hidden in the shadows. Already in the nineteenth and early twentieth centuries historical scholarship, concerned with the nation state, had little interest in the decades between 1555 and 1620—treating them as only a transitional period between the Reformation, the "highlight," and the Thirty Years' War, the "tragedy" of the German people at the beginning of the early modern period. This historiographical prejudice still affects the view held by contemporary research in early modern history. Even structural and societal[1] historians characterize the second half of the sixteenth century as a "period of decline, a boring interlude," (2) or they state that "any interest in this period can scarcely arise from the period itself."[2]

These comments are remarkable since a number of recent

---

1 "Gesellschaftsgeschichte" and "Gesellschaftshistoriker" are translated by "societal history/historians", "Sozialgeschichte" and "Sozialhistoriker" by "social history/historians". (See J. Kocka, Sozialgeschichte, Göttingen 1977, 97-111s.)

2 B. Vogler, Le monde germanique et helvétique à l'époque des Réformes, 1517-1618, vol. II, Paris 1981, 251; W. Schulze, Möglichkeiten der Reichspolitik zwischen Augsburger Religionsfrieden und Ausbruch des 30jährigen Krieges, in: Zeitschrift für historische Forschung (ZHF) 10 (1983), 253-256, esp. 253.

historians of the early modern period have written their significant works of original research on the second half of the
Reformation century rather than the first half.[3] Thus it appears
timely to reevaluate the importance of this epoch within German history from the perspective of general and developmental
history. In this context the inter-connections between religious,
political, and societal lines of development present during the
"long sixteenth century" must be examined more closely in
order to counteract its ossified division by the year 1555.
Whether the changes that began during the first half of the
sixteenth century continued during its second half, perhaps at a
quicker pace, (3) and whether they followed paths that were
indicative of the direction that would be taken during the later
period after the hiatus of the Thirty Years' War would also
repay closer study.

This shift in the focus of research toward the second half of
the sixteenth century described above is, upon further reflection, thoroughly consistent. After the transformation of method
and content within historical scholarship, which led to a general openness for posing questions about institutional and societal history, historians were almost forced to examine not only
the great religious, political and social upheaval at the beginning of the sixteenth century, but also the consolidation, solid-
ification, integration, and resulting new order of societies and
states, and thereby to consider German history after 1555. So a
new appreciation of individual features and trends of the
second half of the sixteenth century emerged "from below"

---

3 See e.g. M. Heckel, Staat und Kirche nach den Lehren der evangelischen
Juristen Deutschlands, in: Zeitschrift der Savigny-Stiftung für Rechtsgeschichte
(ZRG) 73 (1956), Kanonist. Abt. (KA) 42, 117-247; 74 (1957), KA 43, 202-308;
idem, Autonomia und Pacis Compositio. Der Augsburger Religionsfriede in der
Deutung der Gegenreformation, in: ZRG 76 (1959), KA 45, 141-248; H. Neuhaus,
Reichsständische Repräsentationsformen im 16. Jahrhundert. Reichstage, Reichs-
kreistage, Reichsdeputationstage, Berlin 1982; V. Press, Calvinismus und Territorialstaat. Regierung und Zentralbehörden der Kurpfalz, 1559-1619, Stuttgart
1970; W. Reinhard, Papstfinanz und Nepotismus unter Paul V. (1605-1621). Studien und Quellen zur Struktur und zu quantitativen Aspekten des päpstlichen
Herrschaftssystems, Stuttgart 1974; H. Schilling, Konfessionskonflikt und Staatsbildung, Gütersloh 1981; A. Schindling, Humanistische Hochschule und freie
Reichsstadt. Gymnasium und Akademie in Straßburg 1538-1621, Wiesbaden
1977; W. Schulze, Landesdefension und Staatsbildung, Wien 1973; idem, Reich
und Türkengefahr im späten 16. Jahrhundert, München 1978; G. Strauss, Luthers
House of Learning, Baltimore 1978; B. Vogler, Vie religieuse en pays rhénan dans
la seconde moitié du 16e siècle, Lille 1974; idem, Le clergé protestant rhénan au
siècle de la Réforme (1555-1619), Paris 1976.

without a general reevaluation of the period. Some individual vistas can indeed be seen within the landscape of present-day research that call for a reassessment of the time period in question. These include the new evaluation of the Peace of Augsburg, particularly in comparison with simultaneous developments in the history of France and England;[4] the related functional interpretation of the Empire as a political system based upon the territorial structure;[5] the studies of estate- and social history as well as political theory written by Gerhard Oestreich, which mostly deal with the half century after 1555;[6] the correlating recognition of the "altered meaning of social conflicts" such as the new interpretation of witch hunting;[7] and finally the thesis (4) that "confessionalization" constitutes the most important historical process of the epoch. The interpretive category of "confessional formation" (*Konfessionsbildung*), which sheds new light on the ecclesiastical and cultural history of this era, has been recast into a paradigm of societal history, i.e. "confessionalization."[8]

---

4 Heckel, Autonomia (note 3); idem, Deutschland im konfessionellen Zeitalter, Göttingen 1983.

5 P. Moraw and V. Press, Probleme der Sozial- und Verfassungsgeschichte des Heiligen Römischen Reiches, in: ZHF 2 (1975), 95-108; V. Press, Das Römisch-Deutsche Reich—ein politisches System, in: G. Klingenstein and H. Lutz (eds.), Spezialforschung und "Gesamtgeschichte". Beispiele und Methodenfragen zur Geschichte der frühen Neuzeit, München 1982, 221-242.

6 G. Oestreich, Geist und Gestalt des frühmodernen Staates, Berlin 1969; idem, Strukturprobleme der frühen Neuzeit, Berlin 1980.

7 W. Schulze, Die veränderte Bedeutung sozialer Konflikte im 16. und 17. Jahrhundert, in: H.U. Wehler (ed.), Der deutsche Bauernkrieg, 1524-1526, Göttingen 1975, 277-302; idem, Bäuerlicher Widerstand und feudale Herrschaft in der frühen Neuzeit, Stuttgart 1980; idem (ed.), Europäische Bauernrevolten der frühen Neuzeit, Frankfurt am Main 1982; idem (ed.), Aufstände, Revolten, Prozesse. Beiträge zu bäuerlichen Widerstandsbewegungen im frühneuzeitlichen Europa, Stuttgart 1983; P. Blickle (ed.), Aufruhr und Empörung. Studien zum bäuerlichen Widerstand im Alten Reich, München 1980; G. Schormann, article "Hexen", in: Theologische Realenzyklopädie, vol. 15, 297-304; W. Behringer, Hexenverfolgung in Bayern, München 1987, 96ss.

8 "Konfessionsbildung" was introduced by E.W. Zeeden, Die Entstehung der Konfessionen. Grundlagen und Formen der Konfessionsbildung, München/Wien 1965; idem, Konfessionsbildung (collected essays), Stuttgart 1985; P.Th. Lang, Konfessionsbildung als Forschungsgegenstand, in: Historisches Jahrbuch (HJb) 100 (1980), 480-493; idem, Die Ausformung der Konfessionen im 16. und 17. Jahrhundert, in: J.-M. Valentin (ed.), Gegenreformation und Literatur, Amsterdam 1979 (Beihefte zum Daphnis, vol. 3), 13-19.—The paradigm "confessionalization" was developed by Wolfgang Reinhard with regard to the Catholic world and by Heinz Schilling with regard to Calvinism and Lutheranism and finally as a universal paradigm of early modern European history. See W.

The following discussion will examine confessionalization within the German Empire. It is intended to advance the re-evaluation of the second half of the sixteenth century that is (5) still lacking, beginning with this central phenomenon.[9] The theoretical concept of confessionalization, which has already been adequately discussed, shall not be the point of our discussion, but rather its concrete historical out-working, that is, its concrete implications for the general- or societal history (*Gesamt- oder Gesellschaftsgeschichte*) of modern Germany.[10]

The concept of confessionalization, by way of reminder, is based on the fact that in pre-modern Europe, no differently during the Middle Ages than in the early modern period, religion and politics, state and church were structurally linked together, so that under the specific conditions of the early modern period the effects that religion and the church had upon society were not separate parts of a larger phenomenon, but rather affected the entire social system and formed the central axis of state and society. The connection was especially close during the Reformation era and in the subsequent confessional period.[11] Religion and politics were also not entirely

Reinhard, Gegenreformation als Modernisierung? Prolegomena zu einer Theorie des konfessionellen Zeitalters, in: Archiv für Reformationsgeschichte (ARG) 68 (1977), 226-252; idem, Konfession und Konfessionalisierung in Deutschland, in: idem (ed.), Bekenntnis und Geschichte. Schriften der Philosophischen Fakultäten der Universität Augsburg 20 (1981), 165-189; idem, Zwang zur Konfessionalisierung? Prolegomena zu einer Theorie des konfessionellen Zeitalters, in: ZHF 10 (1983), 257-277. Schilling, Konfessionskonflikt (note 3), part A; idem, Konfessionalisierung als gesellschaftlicher Umbruch. Inhaltliche Perspektiven und massenmediale Darstellung, in: S. Quandt (ed.), Luther, die Reformation und die Deutschen.—Wie erzählen wir unsere Geschichte?, Paderborn 1982, 35-51; idem, Town, Territorial State and the Reich in Early Modern Germany, in: R. Po-chia-Hsia (ed.), Society and Religion in Reformation Germany, New Haven 1987; idem, Die "Zweite Reformation" als Kategorie der Geschichtswissenschaft, in: idem (ed.), Die reformierte Konfessionalisierung in Deutschland.—Das Problem der "Zweiten Reformation", Gütersloh 1986 (English translation below, pp. 247-301.—With regard to popular religion: R. van Dülmen, Volksfrömmigkeit und konfessionelles Christentum im 16. Jahrhundert, in: W. Schieder (ed.), Volksreligiosität in der modernen Sozialgeschichte, Göttingen 1986, 14-30.

9 See W. Schulze, in: ZHF 12 (1985), 104-107, esp. 107, and the reply of H. Schilling, in: Historische Zeitschrift (HZ) 264 (1988), 5, note 9.

10 For "Gesamtgeschichte" see H. Lutz, in: Klingenstein/Lutz, (eds.), Spezialforschung (note 5), 279-299; for "Gesellschaftsgeschichte" see Kocka, Sozialgeschichte (note 1).

11 Discussed in detail in Schilling, Konfessionskonflikt (note 3), part A; idem, Nation und Konfession in der frühneuzeitlichen Geschichte Europas, in: K. Garber (ed.), Nation und Literatur, Tübingen 1989, 87-107; idem, Nationale Identität und Konfession in der europäischen Neuzeit, in: B. Giesen (ed.), Nationale und

separated during the later early modern period, even though
the modern separation of both spheres had already been theoretically worked out during the Enlightenment period. The
concept "confessionalization," (6) as I use the term, contains
this political and societal dimension. "Confessionalization"
signifies a fundamental process of society, which had far-
reaching effects upon the public and private life of individual
European societies. In most places this process ran parallel to,
though occasionally in opposition to, the rise of the early
modern state and the formation of an early modern society of
disciplined subjects. In contrast to medieval society the early
modern state was no longer fragmented and united primarily
through bonds of personal and feudal loyalty, but rather was
organized institutionally and by territory. There was also a
certain reciprocal interaction with the chronologically parallel
processes that gave birth to a modern capitalist economic
system.

One characteristic of confessionalization must be stressed
because it can easily be overlooked when it and early modern
state formation are described as "modernization":
confessionalization, as I understand it, was in principle ambivalent from a societal history perspective. It enabled states and
societies to integrate more tightly, an integration that could not
be achieved in any other way because of the specific form of
Old European society. But confessionalization could also pro-
voke confrontation with religious and political groups fundamentally opposed to this same integration of state and
society. The process of confessionalization took place between
the two poles of state-building and confessional conflict, both
within territories, and between the territories and the Empire
from 1555 until 1620. In the long run, however, it was the
integrative power of confessionalization that had a particularly
strong impact upon Germany.

I have drawn a conclusion regarding terminology from the
concept of confessionalization: instead of the Counter-Reformation, Lutheran Orthodoxy, and the "Second Reformation,"
we should speak of "Catholic confessionalization," "Lutheran

kulturelle Identität in der europäischen Neuzeit, Frankfurt 1991.—See also H.
Langer, Religion, Konfession und Kirche in der Epoche des Übergangs vom Feudalismus zum Kapitalismus, in: Zeitschrift für Geschichtswissenschaft (ZfG) 32
(1984), 110-124.

confessionalization," and "Reformed or Calvinist confessionalization."[12] By using linguistically parallel terminology it becomes clearer that these are three processes running parallel to
each other and that the concept of confessionalization includes
an over-arching political, social, and cultural change. This
stimulates the comparisons necessary for furthering knowledge.
It reveals both the functional and developmental historical
similarities, and the (7) theological, spiritual, and other differences between the three varieties of confessionalization. The
following reflections are to be understood as a contribution to a
comparative structural history of confessionalization in Germany and Europe. It is divided into three sections: A description of the functioning Religious Peace of Augsburg during the
first decades after its conclusion (section 1) followed by a
sketch of the phases and turning points marking the development of confessionalization (section 2), and finally a discussion
of their implications for the societal history of early modern
Germany (section 3).

1. THE FUNCTIONING RELIGIOUS PEACE

The period between the conclusion of the Peace of Augsburg
and the Thirty Years' War can be divided into two parts: A
period of functioning religious peace from 1555 until the end
of the 1570's, and the following decades when the swift
advance of confessionalization dominated a political and societal dynamic that unleashed forces capable of integrating societies or provoking conflicts. Of course these contradictory tendencies cannot be seen as absolute since confessional polarization
had already begun during the peaceful period. On the other
hand, political pragmatism was not completely lacking even
during the most dire confessional confrontations as both the
successful efforts to limit the conflicts in Donauwörth, Aachen
and Lippe, and the great supra-confessional peace plan of the
Humanist Heinrich Rantzau at the beginning of the 1590's
attest.[13] In the course of the Thirty Years' War the leading role

---

12 See Schilling (ed.), Konfessionalisierung (note 8), 7-10.

13 M. Lossen, Die Reichsstadt Donauwörth und Herzog Maximilian, München
1866; F. Stieve, Der Ursprung des dreißigjährigen Krieges 1607-1619, vol. II,
München 1875; R. Breitling, Der Streit um Donauwörth 1605-1611, in: Zeitschrift
für Bayerische Landesgeschichte (ZBLG) 2 (1929), 275-298; W. Schmitz, Verfassung und Bekenntnis. Die Aachener Wirren im Spiegel der kaiserlichen Politik

played by the various forms of confessionalization in political and societal history ended. The societal integration furthered by the confessions, however, continued to be an important factor for general history during the age of absolutism. (8)

The religious peace of 1555 was not the achievement of ideologically motivated advocates of peace, but rather of political pragmatists. It was a political and legal system of coexistence, not a religious and ideological one.[14] This pragmatic plan had flaws that could not be overlooked and in the end destroyed it. It would, however, be wrong to consider its short term success unimportant. This accomplishment can be illustrated with three examples that shed light particularly on concrete everyday coexistence.

The multi-confessional imperial cities with their ecclesiastical and municipal constitutions that ensured confessional parity are the first example. After years of bitter religious conflict during which old and new believers pursued the medieval ideal of a religiously united urban commune, a new phase that lasted until about 1580 began in Augsburg, Biberach, Ravensburg, and Dinkelsbühl, during which confessional conflict retreated into the background and the peaceful coexistence of Lutheran and Catholic burghers seemed to be at hand. Marriage bonds that reached over confessional boundaries were not uncommon. Likewise, the frequent changes from one confession to the other that occurred during this time were more commonly the expression of a relatively open exchange of opinion rather than the sign of an embittered struggle of two competing world views for the last of the lost souls, as later seemed to be the case. The problem of institutional and spatial coordination between the two churches, which could easily have resulted in friction even during a period of day to day calm, caused astonishingly few problems. This was true of

(1550-1616), Frankfurt am Main/Bern/New York 1983; Schilling, Konfessionskonflikt (note 3); R. Hansen, Der Friedensplan Heinrich Rantzaus und die Irenik in der Zweiten Reformation, in: Schilling (ed.), Konfessionalisierung (note 8), 359-372.

14 Heckel, Autonomia (note 3); idem, Parität, in: ZRG 80 (1963), KA 49, 261-420; idem, Deutschland (note 4), 33ss., 67ss., 198ss., 211s.; idem, Reichsrecht und "Zweite Reformation": Theologisch-juristische Probleme der reformierten Konfessionalisierung, in: Schilling (ed.), Konfessionalisierung (note 8), 11-43; U. Scheuner, Staatsräson und religiöse Einheit des Staates. Zur Religionspolitik in Deutschland im Zeitalter der Glaubensspaltung, in: R. Schnur (ed.), Staatsräson. Studien zur Geschichte eines politischen Begriffs, Berlin 1975, 363-405, esp. 376s.

school organization, social relief, and the sharing of church buildings. Few accounts of disturbances and incidents have been preserved from those places where, as in the Ravensburg Carmelite Church, the Catholic monks in the choir and the Protestant congregation in the nave conducted their church services at the same time. "Mutual allowance"—this is how Paul Warmbrunn, whose thorough study (9) I follow at this point, characterized the attitude of the 1550's, 1560's, and 1570's. Even the "intellectuals", who a little later led the way toward confrontation, cultivated contacts with the adherents of the other confessions as, for example, the teachers of the Latin schools did.[15]

As a second example I have chosen the bishopric of Münster from among the territorial states, and hence from among those places where the legal principle *cuius-regio-eius-religio* was in force. Even in the city of Münster, which had endured the shock of the Anabaptist disturbances, "after 1555, Lutherans could reside (though not worship) ..., and even the once-feared Anabaptists (now pacifist Mennonites) were no longer hunted down. ... Münster approached the model of a bi-confessional city." Daily work together in the artisan organizations and political corporations, a pre-confessional mentality that expressed itself in legal wills by generally Christian rather than specifically Catholic turns of phrase, and by syncretism in the liturgical forms of the old church (such as German hymns and communion in both kinds), and finally the willingness to accept new burghers on the basis of economic advantage rather than to ensure the religious purity of the urban burgher society convincingly prove that until well into the 1580's "a strong confessional identity was uncharacteristic of urban religious life" in Westphalia.[16]

Finally, as my third example, I have chosen a biographical

---

15 P. Warmbrunn, Zwei Konfessionen in einer Stadt. Das Zusammenleben von Katholiken und Protestanten in den paritätischen Reichsstädten Augsburg, Biberach, Ravensburg und Dinkelsbühl von 1548-1648, Wiesbaden 1983, esp. 217ss., 228, 268, 282, 287ss., 318, 358.—See also E. Francois, De l'uniformité à la Tolérance: confession et société urbaine en Allemagne, 1650-1800, in: Annales. ESC 37 (1982), 783-800; idem, Die Parität im reichsständischen Alltag: Abgrenzung, friedliche Koexistenz oder Toleranz?, in: Förderverein Augsburger Parität e.V., Jahresgabe 1984, Augsburg 1984.

16 R. Po-chia-Hsia, Society and Religion in Münster, 1535-1618, New Haven/London 1984, 199; A. Schröer, Die Kirche in Westfalen im Zeichen der Erneuerung (1555-1648), vol. I, Münster 1986, 439, 446s.

spotlight to show similar liberal circumstances even in the bishopric of Würzburg before the Counter-Reformation began to take effect there. The well-respected Frisian jurist Aggaeus von Albada,[17] a notorious Schwenckfeldian (10), who nonchalantly called the sacraments a hindrance on the way to salvation and stayed away from church services, had to give up his office as judge in the Speyer imperial chamber court in early 1571 after protests by the Jesuits and the Spanish crown. The bishop of Würzburg, Friedrich von Wirsberg, seized the opportunity to recruit a gifted jurist for his chancellery and named the Schwenckfeldian that same year to the council of his prince bishopric. It is true that this decision was made against a background of scarcity of learned jurists, as is correctly noted in the most recent literature.[18] Further, it is possible that the well-known aversion of the German princes toward the Spanish also played a role in Albada's appointment. And finally, it is also correct that the spiritualists did not confront the dominant churches in a militant way, but rather practiced the quietism that Schwenckfeld recommended. Nevertheless, Albada's activities in Würzburg are convincing evidence that the archiepiscopal territory, soon to be in the vanguard of Catholic confessionalization, was during the 1570's still far from such an ideological, political, and societal transformation. Albada received a formal dispensation from the obligation to attend Catholic services and, besides his professional activities, he maintained a wide correspondence and travelled often. In this way he spiritually held together the Diaspora of the "pious friends," spiritualists and Schwenckfeldians, who were spread all over the Empire. At first nothing changed when Julius Echter von Mespelbrunn succeeded to the episcopal throne of Würzburg in 1573. Only in 1576 did the continual pressure to conform, set in motion by Echter and the Jesuits, reach a point where Albada was forced to choose between joining the Catholic church and attending Mass, or leaving the archiepiscopal territory. But even then the intellectual exchange between "heretic" and "Counter-

---

17 W. Bergsma, Aggaeus van Albada (c. 1525-1587), schwenckfeldiaan, staatsman en strijder voor verdraagzaamheid, Groningen 1983.

18 N. Hammerstein, Universitäten—Territorialstaaten—Gelehrte Räte, in: R. Schnur (ed.), Die Rolle der Juristen bei der Entstehung des modernen Staates, Berlin 1986, 687-735.

Reformer" did not end. At the beginning of the 1580's Albada still corresponded with Echter von Mespelbrunn in order to level harsh criticism against the German prince bishop for the cruel deeds that were inflicted upon his homeland by the Spanish military dictatorship in the name of Catholic renewal.[19] (11)

In all three cases, to which others could be added even from rural areas,[20] the period of a more or less problem-free coexistence among adherents of different religions ended during the late 1570's or the early 1580's. The increasing confessional polarization, which in rapid succession seized control of nearly every area of private and public life, replaced coexistence, and cut the ground from under the political and legal pragmatism of the system that originated in the Peace of Augsburg.[21] A period began that was both a time of intellectual and religious reshaping, and also of political and societal formation. The agents of this upheaval were theologians, jurists, and the princes. It was a process that ran from above to below. Communal movements or associations, such as those that affected the Reformation during the first third of the century, played a role only in resistance movements. Only in particularly exceptional situations did they take the initiative. What can be said of the so-called "Second Reformation" is true of all three kinds of confessionalization: they were princely confessionalizations.[22]

Within the shortest possible time—in a few years, even months—this movement passed through the entire Empire from Salzburg to Hamburg, from Aachen to Dresden, changing fundamentally the intellectual and material conditions of life. The rapid spread of this movement is related to the fact that two fundamental processes merged with it, adding to the strength

---

19 Bergsma, Aggaeus (note 17), 112, 194; letter of 22 May 1582 from Cologne. On Protestant civil servants in the Catholic bishopric of Münster, see Schröer, Kirche (note 16), 34.

20 See e.g. H. Schilling, Niederländische Exulanten im 16. Jahrhundert, Gütersloh 1972; J. Whaley, Religious Toleration and Social Change in Hamburg, 1529-1819, Cambridge 1985; Ph. Denis, Les églises d'étrangers en pays Rhénans, 1538-1564, Paris 1984; O. Mörke, Integration und Desintegration. Kirche und Stadtentwicklung in Deutschland vom 14. bis 17. Jahrhundert, in: N. Bulst (ed.), Stadt—Bürgertum—Staat (12. bis 18. Jahrhundert). La ville, la bourgeoisie et la genèse de l'état moderne (12—18 siècles), Paris 1988, 297-321.

21 Warmbrunn, Konfessionen (note 15), 280s., 358s., 388; Hsia, Society (note 16), 67ss., 72, 116, 129ss., 132ss., 163s.

22 Schilling (ed.), Konfessionalisierung (note 8), passim.

of its dynamic: The theological and religious dynamic that broke into the Empire from Geneva and from Trent joined with the secular dynamic of the early modern state, which in Germany received another forceful thrust during the final third of the century (12). After the end of the Middle Ages and the acceleration of changes that took place during the Reformation, the Peace of Augsburg served as a foundation upon which even the numerous smaller territories could begin an internal restructuring of state and society in a systematic and continual fashion.[23] Within the long-term process of transformation, which Theodor Rabb characterized as a "struggle for stability,"[24] only a temporary stopover point had been reached. It was upon this foundation that an attempt was made to end the first phase of the process. This was true both for the establishment of Protestant and Catholic territorial churches and for the formation of the modern political elites in the cities and territories.[25] The changes that had begun in the late Middle Ages and had accelerated during the Reformation period could be used at the end of the "long sixteenth century" as a building block in the construction of new forms of state and society. If one takes, for example, the need of the rising territorial states for experts, that is in the first instance learned, legally trained councillors, but also pastors, superintendents, and theological (13) consistorial councillors—the demand far outweighed the

---

23 This is proved by the quick expansion of the number of civil servants in the territorial bureaucracy, see Hammerstein, Universitäten (note 18), 728ss., 732.

24 Th. Rabb, The Struggle for Stability in Early Modern Europe, New York 1975.

25 R. Endres, Die deutschen Führungsschichten um 1600, in: H.H. Hofmann and G. Franz (eds.), Deutsche Führungsschichten in der Neuzeit. Eine Zwischenbilanz, Boppard 1980, 79-109; Th. A. Brady, Ruling Class, Regime and Reformation at Strasbourg, 1520-1555, Leiden 1978; I. Bátori and E. Weyrauch, Die bürgerliche Elite der Stadt Kitzingen. Studien zur Sozial- und Wirtschaftsgeschichte einer landesherrlichen Stadt im 16. Jahrhundert, Stuttgart 1982; O. Mörke and K. Sieh, Gesellschaftliche Führungsgruppen, in: G. Gottlieb (ed.), Augsburg von der Römerzeit bis zur Gegenwart, Stuttgart 1984, 301-311. See also the two articles H. Schilling, Die politische Elite nordwestdeutscher Städte in den religiösen Auseinandersetzungen des 16. Jahrhunderts, in: W.J. Mommsen (ed.), Stadtbürgertum und Adel in der Reformation, Stuttgart 1979, 232-308 (English translation above, pp. 61-134); idem, Wandlungs- und Differenzierungsprozesse innerhalb der bürgerlichen Oberschichten West- und Nordwestdeutschlands im 16. und 17. Jahrhundert, in: M. Biskup and K. Zernack (eds.), Schichtung und Entwicklung der Gesellschaft in Polen und Deutschland im 16. und 17. Jahrhundert, Parallelen, Verknüpfungen, Vergleiche, Wiesbaden 1983, 121-173 (English translation above, pp. 135-187).

supply for decades.[26] Only at the end of the sixteenth century, considered to be the century of the first educational revolution, did a change apparently take place. Only then were enough qualified personnel available, a precondition for realizing the long-attempted consolidation of the state and the accompanying reshaping of society. Still clearer was the opportunity for fresh approaches in the field of political theory. In the great works of Bodin and Lipsius conceptual, legal, and ethical tools were offered for the first time—concentrated in the doctrines of "sovereignty" and "discipline"—with which the early modern state could articulate and legitimize succinctly its political and societal claims.[27]

In this historical constellation confessionalization became a catalyst for societal change. Domination of the church and religious life by the confessional state became a key monopoly within the process of early modern state-building, which has been tellingly described as a multi-stage process of monopolization.[28] This politically and socially explosive situation received an additional psychological charge as news of the Paris "Blood Marriage" penetrated the relatively peaceful world of the Augsburg religious compromise, and as thousands of Dutch exiles sought refuge in the Empire from the fury of Spanish military and religious persecution.[29]

(14)   2. THE PHASES OF CONFESSIONALIZATION

Since I understand the confessionalization of German cities and territories to be an internally consistent process resulting in the

26 Hammerstein, Universitäten (note 18).

27 H. Quaritsch, Staat und Souveränität, vol. 1, Frankfurt 1970; W. Quint, Souveränitätsbegriff und Souveränitätspolitik in Bayern, Berlin 1971; Schilling, Konfessionskonflikt (note 3); H. Wiemann, Materialien zur Geschichte der Ostfriesischen Landschaft, Aurich 1982, 150-160.

28 Norbert Elias, Über den Prozeß der Zivilisation, 2 vols., 4th edition, Frankfurt am Main 1977; see the commentary in: Schilling, Konfessionskonflikt (note 3), esp. 365ss.

29 A. Soman (ed.), The massacre of St. Bartholomew, Reappraisals and Documents, Den Haag 1974 (L.W. Spitz, 71-95); Actes du Colloque "L'Amiral de Coligny et son temps", Paris 24th - 28th October 1972, Paris 1974 (B. Vogler, 175-190, R.M. Kingdon, 191-204); G. Menk, Landgraf Wilhelm IV. von Hessen-Kassel, Franz Hotmann und die hessisch-französischen Beziehungen vor und nach der Bartholomäusnacht, in: Zeitschrift des Vereins für Hessische Geschichte und Landeskunde 88 (1980/81), 55-82, esp. 67ss.

theological, ideological, and political formation of the three large confessional churches as well as their corresponding power blocs, which appeared independently of each other within a relatively short period of time, it must be possible to identify distinct phases and their corresponding turning points, which are equally valid for all three developments. For the intra-Protestant differentiation this is easy to observe, since it resulted directly in controversies between Calvinism and Lutheranism, characterized by brotherly hatred.[30] Yet Catholic confessionalization also occurred at about the same time, although strict year-for-year parallels cannot be expected.

First phase: The beginnings of confessionalization, from the late 1540's to the 1560's. I place the beginning of this societal, one could also say general historical (*gesamtgeschichtlich*),[31] process of confessionalization shortly before the middle of the century, which I see followed by a preparatory phase lasting until the end of the 1560's and taking place within a society that was largely pre-confessional. Naturally I am not denying that from a narrowly theological perspective the path toward confessional formation was already present in the early Reformation period—between the Catholic and the Protestant churches as much as between the Lutheran and the Reformed churches.[32] One must only remember the personal and conceptual rifts that occurred during the Marburg eucharistic controversy, the Augsburg Confession, the *Confutatio* and *Variata* as well as the Tetrapolitan Confession. It can hardly be ignored, however, that the Reformed branch of Protestantism, which was legally branded as "Sacramentarian" along with the Anabaptists by the Diet of Speyer in 1529, was not able to maintain itself as an independent element at the beginning of the 1530's (15) against the forcible "territorialization of the German Reformation and the development of the Lutheran confession in the context of the Schmalkaldic League."[33] Even from the perspective of historical theology a new phase must

---

30 Schilling, Reformation (note 8), esp. 401ss.

31 See Lutz in: Klingenstein/Lutz (eds.), Spezialforschung (note 5), esp. 279ss.; see also Blätter für deutsche Landesgeschichte (BlldtLG) 119 (1983), 493-501.

32 See B. Lohse and W. Neuser in: C. Andresen (ed.), Handbuch der Dogmen- und Theologiegeschichte, vol. 2, Göttingen 1980.

33 J.F.G. Goeters, Genesis, Formen und Hauptthemen des reformierten Bekenntnisses in Deutschland. Eine Übersicht, in: Schilling (ed.), Konfessionalisierung (note 8), 44-59, esp. 44.

have begun during the 1540's to account for the renewed outbreak of the antagonisms that were previously only latent in
Germany.

Decisive for my periodization is the thesis that the theological differences which surfaced during the Reformation era
developed their social and political dynamic only during the
period of confessionalization that followed at the end of the
sixteenth century and so attained a new importance for state
and society in general. This began at the end of the 1540's. I
maintain emphatically that another periodization may be more
accurate from the specific perspectives of church history and
historical theology as separate disciplines.

As the Lutherans after the death of the reformer lapsed into
their struggle of succession, Switzerland became the cradle of a
revival of non-Lutheran Protestantism which took its direction
from the *Variata* of the Augsburg Confession.[34] The most
important events and indicators of change were the First
Helvetian Confession of 1549, the second eucharistic quarrel
that was unleashed by the western European exile theologians
and reached its peak in 1559 at Bremen and Heidelberg, and
finally the Second Helvetian Confession of 1566. These events
sharply differentiated Reformed theology in Germany from
Lutheran theology.[35] At the same time the revival of non-
Lutheran Reformed Protestantism within the Empire was
strengthened by the Dutch exile congregations, the calvinistically ordered urban reformations of Metz, Trier, and Aachen at
the end of the 1550's, and finally through the first movement
toward Calvinism in the Electoral Palatinate where in December of 1561 Elector Friedrich III celebrated the Lord's Supper
by breaking bread, steering his territorial church into a new
channel with the Heidelberg catechism. (16)

The crucial years for nascent Reformed confessionalization
and Lutheran confessionalization, which developed in response
to it, were 1561 and 1566.[36] In 1561 the Reformed exile congregation was driven out of Frankfurt for the first time and at
the same time Elector Friedrich III of the Palatinate successfully argued at the princely convention of Naumburg for
recognition of the *Variata* as a confessional basis for German

---

34 P. Blickle, A. Lindt, A. Schindler (eds.), Zwingli und Europa, Zürich 1985.
35 Goeters, Genesis (note 33).
36 Ibid., 45s.; Heckel, Reichsrecht (note 14).

Protestantism. This soon provoked a Lutheran reaction, first in Ernestinian Saxony and in the lower Saxon circle and then in the entire Empire, which emphasized in confessional polemics the differences between the two Protestant movements. In 1566, at the Diet of Augsburg, the Palatinate succeeded in preventing its ejection from the Augsburg Confession, and thus its exclusion from the religious peace, without having to concede any point of theological content affecting the independence of its confessional policy.

The decades between the late 1540's and the early 1570's also represent a preparatory phase for Catholic confessionalization. Even more pronounced than among Protestants, this period of time was characterized among Catholics by its contradictions. On the one hand theology, ecclesiastical politics, and especially the mentality of the clergy were still expressed in traditional, pre-Tridentine forms and structures, while on the other hand the will for renewal expressed by the Tridentine system gained ground step by step.[37] In (17) this situation the following milestones on the road to Catholic confessionalization are visible. In 1549 the first Jesuit establishment on German soil was founded in Ingolstadt. From there these agents of the Counter-Reformation and Catholic renewal wove a continually tighter web of colleges, residences, and stations throughout the entire Empire. In their gymnasia and universities the future supporters of Catholic confessionalization were educated. These institutions included Ingolstadt (1566; in 1588 the Jesuits took over

---

37 Basic literature: G. Schreiber (ed.), Das Weltkonzil von Trient. Sein Werden und Wirken, 2 vols., Freiburg 1951; Zeeden, Entstehung (note 8); idem (ed.), Gegenreformation, Darmstadt 1973; J.M. Valentin (ed.), Gegenreformation (note 8); H. Molitor, Kirchliche Reformversuche der Kurfürsten und Erzbischöfe von Trier im Zeitalter der Gegenreformation, Wiesbaden 1967; J. Krasenbrink, Die Congregatio Germanica und die katholische Reform in Deutschland nach dem Tridentinum, Münster 1972; J. Bücking, Frühabsolutismus und Kirchenreform in Tirol (1565-1665), Mainz 1972; F. Flaskamp, Die große Osnabrücker Kirchenvisitation an der oberen Ems. Ein Beitrag zur Geschichte der Gegenreformation, in: Jahrbuch der Gesellschaft für niedersächsische Kirchengeschichte 70 (1972), 51-105; 71 (1973), 155-196; E.M. Buxbaum, Petrus Canisius und die kirchliche Erneuerung des Herzogtums Bayern 1549-1556, Rom 1973; K. Hengst, Kirchliche Reformen im Fürstbistum Paderborn unter Dietrich von Fürstenberg (1585-1618). Ein Beitrag zur Geschichte der Gegenreformation und katholischen Reform in Westfalen, München/Paderborn/Wien 1974; B. Jäger, Das geistliche Fürstentum Fulda in der Frühen Neuzeit, Marburg 1986.—Th. P. Becker provides a very detailed analysis of the grass roots process in: Konfessionalisierung in Kurköln, Untersuchungen zur Durchsetzung der katholischen Reform in den Dekanaten Ahrgau und Bonn anhand von Visitationsprotokollen 1583-1761, Bonn 1989.

the chairs of theology and liberal arts at the university), Dillingen in the Augsburg region (1563), Würzburg (a *gymnasium
illustre* in 1567; a university in 1582), and Fulda (a *gymnasium
illustre* in 1572).[38] In 1565 and 1566 Petrus Canisius, the father
of the German Jesuit establishments and Provincial of the
upper German province, travelled throughout the Empire on
behalf of the Pope in order to urge the German bishops to
accept the Tridentine decrees. At the Diet of Augsburg in 1566
the papal legate obliged the Catholic estates to accept the
Council of Trent, even if he received only oral assent at first.[39]
Finally in 1567 the first sign of a change within the German
clergy appeared when, for the first time, two high German
prelates, Bishop Johann von Hoya of Münster (1566-1574) and
the Archbishop of Trier, Jakob von Eltz (1567-1581), declared
themselves ready to accept the *Professio fidei Tridentina*,
obliging themselves under oath to conform their personal lives
to the dictates of Trent and to reform their dioceses accordingly.[40] (18)

Until well into the 1570's the decisions of the Council of
Trent remained to a large extent legal claims and theoretical
concepts. The clergy, led by the bishops, were overwhelmingly
opposed to the Tridentine reforms, which demanded a far-
reaching, thoroughgoing, and disciplined transformation of the
clergy themselves. They refused to take the confessional oath,
so that its spread throughout the Empire was accomplished not
from above by the bishops, but rather from below. It was
prescribed above all in the Jesuit universities. The bishops saw

---

38 B. Duhr, Geschichte der Jesuiten in den Ländern deutscher Zunge, 4 vols.,
Freiburg im Breisgau 1907-1928; E. Schubert, Zur Typologie gegenreformato-
rischer Universitätsgründungen: Jesuiten in Fulda, Würzburg, Ingolstadt und
Dillingen, in: H. Rössler and G. Franz (eds.), Universität und Gelehrtenstand
1400-1800, Limburg an der Lahn 1970, 85-105; R. van Dülmen, Die Gesellschaft
Jesu und der bayerische Späthumanismus. Ein Überblick, in: ZBLG 37 (1974),
358-415; K. Hengst, Jesuiten an Universitäten und Jesuitenuniversitäten, Paderborn 1981.

39 W. Hollweg, Der Augsburger Reichstag von 1566 und seine Bedeutung für
die Entstehung der Reformierten Kirche und ihres Bekenntnisses, Neukirchen-
Vluyn 1964, 293ss., 317ss., 380s.

40 Molitor, Reformversuche (note 37), 26; idem, Die Generalvisitation von
1569/70 als Quelle für die Geschichte der katholischen Reform im Erzbistum
Trier, in: Zeeden (ed.), Gegenreformation (note 37), 175-189; V. Conzemius,
Jakob III. von Eltz, Erzbischof von Trier 1567-1581. Ein Kurfürst im Zeitalter
der Gegenreformation, Wiesbaden 1956, esp. 208, note 116; Schröer, Kirche (note
16), 97, 282.

no reason to introduce the decrees of the council, the Roman
breviary, published in 1568, or the new Missal of 1570, into
their dioceses. Apart from a few exceptions, such as Cardinal
Otto Truchsess von Waldburg (1543-1573), bishop of Augsburg,[41] as well as the archbishops of Trier and Salzburg, the
German episcopate was composed of men until well into the
1570's who resisted Protestantism in order to protect their own
hold on power, but used the traditional means rather than those
of confessionalized Tridentine Catholicism.[42] Canisius himself
stated soberly in his final report that everything depended
upon which men would succeed to the episcopal thrones of
individual dioceses. Therefore energetic measures were necessary first of all at the upcoming Diet of Augsburg. In Canisius'
opinion the Catholic cause rested on the edge of a knife at
Augsburg. For influential circles were prepared to force new
decisions allowing freer choice in the area of religion.[43] This
referred, of course, to Palatine Calvinism whose success or
failure Canisius saw in a direct relationship with his own cause.
Here one can grasp the acceleration of confessionalization as a
competitive race for influence and political power and as a
confrontation with the opposition that was deliberately ar-
ranged.

At the Diet itself a memorable encounter occurred when
Elector Friedrich of the Palatinate made a courtesy visit to the
papal legate Commendone.[44] On this occasion the leaders of
two ecclesiastical systems with differing world views joined
hands. Although neither had as yet a large following in Germany, both sides had made significant progress in that direction. The prelate succeeded in moving the Catholic estates to
recognize the Tridentine changes, at least in principle. The

---

41 F. Zoepfl, Kardinal Otto Truchsess von Waldburg (1514-1573), in: Lebensbilder aus dem Bayerischen Schwaben, vol. 4, München 1955, 204-248; idem, Das
Bistum Augsburg und seine Bischöfe im Reformationsjahrhundert, München
1969; F. Siebert, Zwischen Kaiser und Papst. Kardinal Truchsess von Waldburg
und die Anfänge der Gegenreformation in Deutschland, Berlin 1943; V. Press,
Schwaben zwischen Bayern, Österreich und dem Reich, in: P. Fried (ed.), Probleme der Integration Ostschwabens in den bayerischen Staat. Bayern und Wit-
telsbach in Ostschwaben, Sigmaringen 1982, 17-78.

42 For details regarding the Westphalian bishoprics: Schröer, Kirche (note 16).

43 Petrus Canisius to the General of his order Franciscus de Borgia, 27 January
1566, Beati Petri Canisii, Societatis Jesu, Epistulae et Acta, ed. by O. Braunsber-
ger, vol. 5, Freiburg 1910, 169s.

44 Hollweg, Reichstag (note 39), 81.

Calvinist Elector secured the decisive legal and political freedom of maneuver that allowed, during the next phase, a withdrawal from Lutheranism in order to form a separate
Reformed confessional church.[45]

Second phase: Transition to confessional confrontation, the
1570's. The 1570's had a transitional character, particularly for
Reformed and Lutheran confessionalization, which in many
places took the form of an agonizing struggle between es-
tranged brothers. The catastrophes of western European Protestantism that spilled over into the Empire where the religious
peace was in force—the stream of refugees from the Netherlands and the Massacre of St. Bartholomew in
France—awakened in numerous Protestant courts a traumatic
fear that the Catholic offensive would overrun Germany
next.[46] As a result both wings of Protestantism began to close
their ranks still more tightly. The Lutherans pursued this goal
through the exclusion of heterogeneous opinions, in order to
make the defense of the peace more certain for themselves.
Among the Reformed the wish became stronger (20) to lead the
Reformation to its logical conclusion, as they understood it, by
eliminating the last vestiges of Catholic tradition in order to
make it unassailable by newly strengthened Catholicism. For
some partisans of the Palatinate seizing the Bohemian crown
was an action dictated by the need for self-defense, a need
born during the 1570's. This sentiment was expressed in the
following aphorism, published by the Palatine poet Julius Wilhelm Zincgref in 1623 in his *Quodlibetische Weltkefig*: "As
long as a single spark from the Council of Trent glimmers (...)
judgement has already been passed on heretics, the staff long
ago broken/ and the Pope previously lacked only executioners
(...). As geese have their St. Martin's Eve and the French their
St. Bartholomew's Night/ so the Germans have ... their
appointed day of massacre and slaughter."[47]

---

45 Heckel, Reichsrecht (note 14).

46 See note 29.

47 "So lange ein Füncklein vom Concilio Tridentino glimmet (...) ist das Ur-
theil den Ketzern schon gefellet, der Stab vorlengst gebrochen/und hat nur biß-
hero gemangelt an des Bapst Executoren. (...) Wie die Gense ihre Mertens Nacht
und die Franzosen ihre Bartels Nacht haben/Also die Teudschen ... ihre gewisse
Schlacht- und Metzeltage", quotation from K. Garber, Zentraleuropäischer Calvinismus und deutsche "Barock"—Literatur. Zu den konfessionspolitischen Ursprüngen der deutschen Nationalliteratur, in: Schilling (ed.), Konfessionalisierung

The polarization within Protestantism, which spread rapidly under this real or imagined threat, destroyed the pre-orthodox, mediating party of upper German, early Reformed, Philippist, and Humanist provenance. The blow against the so-called crypto-Calvinists in Electoral Saxony during 1574 and the restoration of Lutheranism in the Palatinate two years later deprived the Philippists of their most important strongholds.[48] In the Protestant territories pre-orthodox churches were reshaped according to the standards of Reformed or Lutheran confessionalism. Where more than one ruler was responsible for the confessional position, special tensions ensued, above all in Hesse which had been considered a moderating influence among Protestants since the days of Landgrave Philip the Magnanimous. When pressured to decide, his sons—Wilhelm in Kassel, Ludwig in Marburg, and Georg in Darmstadt—chose different confessional directions, so that during the 1570's the first quarrels broke out at the university of Marburg, which was supported as a collective institution by all three territorial princes.[49] (21) The Formula of Concord of 1577 and the Book of Concord of 1580-1581 together served as a boundary marker and a catalyst.[50] Here Lutheranism rallied itself around the *Confessio Augustana* In*variata*. The battles over doctrine that had broken out after Luther's death had ended and the way toward Lutheran confessionalization was clear. Not everyone who signed the concordat did so with a joyful heart. For example, the Lutheran Elector Ludwig VI of the Palatinate, who succeeded his Calvinist father Friedrich III in 1576, would have gladly avoided the final step toward confessionalization.

(note 8), 317-348, esp. 329s.; E. Koch, Der kursächsische Philippismus und seine Krise in den 1560er und 1570er Jahren, in: ibid., 60-78.

48 V. Press, Die "Zweite Reformation" in der Kurpfalz, in: ibid., 104-129: "Eine solche 'altmodische' Position entsprach nicht den heraufziehenden 1580er Jahren" (112).

49 A. Friedrich, Die Gelehrtenschulen in Marburg, Kassel und Korbach zwischen Melanchthonismus und Ramismus in der zweiten Hälfte des 16. Jahrhunderts, Darmstadt/Marburg 1983; V. Press, Hessen im Zeitalter der Landesteilung (1567-1655), in: W. Heinemeyer (ed.), Das Werden Hessens, Marburg 1986, 267-332; G. Menk, Die "Zweite Reformation" in Hessen-Kassel. Landgraf Moritz und die Einführung der Verbesserungsvorschläge 1605, in: Schilling (ed.), Konfessionalisierung (note 8), 154-183.

50 See M. Brecht and R. Schwarz (eds.), Bekenntnis und Einheit der Kirche. Studien zum Konkordienbuch, Stuttgart 1980.

In 1582 he was forced to do so because the intense confessional polarization left him no choice.[51]

Corresponding to Lutheran developments, the process of Reformed confessionalization also gained momentum as a result of opposition to the *Formula concordiae*. Some princes, who had kept their distance from Lutheran orthodoxy without already having entered the opposing camp, felt compelled to decide. For example, Margrave Friedrich of Baden-Durlach and the Dukes of Palatinate-Zweibrücken brought their territorial churches into the Calvinist camp in reaction to the Lutheran concord movement.[52] Also in the Prussian cities of Danzig, Thorn, and Elbing the defense of concordial Lutheranism was a decisive factor in the sudden spread of Reformed/Calvinist currents within the ruling elites.[53] (22)

By the end of the 1570's it was irrevocably determined that henceforth within the Empire two separate Protestant confessional churches would exist, and they would begin to compete with each other, struggling to contain the other as fiercely as either did individually against Catholicism. That a third variant, Philippist territorial churches with the *Confessio Augustana Variata* as their confessional statement, could maintain themselves, distancing themselves both from concordial Lutheranism and also from Calvinism, was on the whole considered to be of marginal importance. This does not weaken the main impression of an increasing "pressure for confessionalization."[54]

Catholic confessionalization, after the fundamental decisions at the Council of Trent and the Diet of Augsburg, did not require any similar turning points or milestones. Corresponding to its organization and its confessional concept of the universal church, all that was required was a practical implementation of the decisions that had already been made. On another level, however, the 1570's marked a decisive break that at the beginning of the 1580's would result in swiftly advancing intellectual, institutional, and political developments. The papal diplo-

---

51 Press, Reformation (note 48), 112.

52 G.A. Benrath, Baden-Durlach, in: Theologische Realenzyklopädie, vol. 5, 97-103; W.-U. Deetjen, Das Ende der Entente cordiale zwischen den Bruderkirchen und Bruderdynastien Pfalz-Zweibrücken, Württemberg und Pfalz-Neuburg, in: Blätter für württembergische Kirchengeschichte 82 (1982), 38-217.

53 M.G. Müller, Zur Frage der "Zweiten Reformation" in Danzig, Thorn und Elbing, in: Schilling (ed.), Konfessionalisierung (note 8), 251-265, esp. 256s.

54 W. Reinhard, Zwang (note 8), 257-277.

matic corp was expanded. Alongside of the greater nuncios of the first rank, so important for international politics, came the so-called lesser, second rank of nuncios who were not diplomats in the first instance, but were active in religious and confessional politics. They were based in Graz for Inner Austria, in Luzern for Switzerland, and in Cologne for northern and western Germany.[55] It was these legates and nuncios of the Holy See who paved the way for Catholic confessionalization during the 1570's and 1580's among the German princedoms and archiepiscopal territories.[56] At the same time more and more clergy attainted high office and rank who had received their schooling in theology, (23) ecclesiastical politics, and law, based completely on the new Tridentine Catholicism. Many of them had been educated in Rome at the *Collegium Germanicum*.[57] Bishops and suffragan bishops who were completely loyal to Trent entered the leadership of dioceses—from Würzburg and Hildesheim in 1573 (Julius Echter von Mespelbrunn and Ernst von Bayern) to Cologne and Münster in the years 1583 and 1585. Similar developments can be observed among the princes and their political advisors, above all the Hapsburgs in Tyrol and Inner Austria as well as the Bavarian Wittelsbachs.[58]

Since exactly the same processes were at work on the Prot-

---

55 H.J. Mezler-Andelberg, Erneuerung des Katholizismus und Gegenreformation in Innerösterreich, in: Südostdeutsches Archiv 13 (1970), 97-118; J. Rainer, Papst Gregor XIII. und die Gründung der Grazer Nuntiatur, in: Bericht über den zehnten österreichischen Historikertag in Graz 1969, Wien 1970, 71-79; R. Pfister, Kirchengeschichte der Schweiz, vol. 2, Zürich 1974, 315ss.; K. Unkel, Die Errichtung der ständigen apostolischen Nuntiatur in Köln, in: Historisches Jahrbuch der Görresgesellschaft 12 (1881), 505-537.

56 See e.g. the evaluation in: Schröer, Kirche (note 16), 444; H. Molitor, Gegenreformation und kirchliche Erneuerung im niederen Erzstift Köln, in: Kurköln, Land unter dem Krummstab, Kevelaer 1985, 199-207, esp. 204s.

57 H. Lutz, Das Ringen um deutsche Einheit und kirchliche Erneuerung: von Maximilian I. bis zum Westfälischen Frieden (1490 bis 1648), Berlin 1983, 324; Mezler-Andelberg, Erneuerung (note 55), 100; Peter Schmidt, Das Collegium Germanicum in Rom und die Germaniker. Zur Funktion eines römischen Ausländerseminars (1552-1914), Tübingen 1984.

58 E. Schubert, Julius Echter von Mespelbrunn, in: G. Pfeiffer (ed.), Fränkische Lebensbilder, vol. 3, Würzburg 1969, 158-193; idem, Gegenreformation in Franken, in: Zeeden (ed.), Gegenreformation (note 37), 222-269; F. Merzbach (ed.), Julius Echter von Mespelbrunn und seine Zeit, Würzburg 1973; E. Soder von Güldenstubbe, Die Bischofsweihe des Julius Echter von Mespelbrunn, in: Würzburger Diözesangeschichtsblätter 42 (1980), 245-294; Max Braubach, article "Ernst von Bayern", in: Neue deutsche Biografie (NDB), vol. 4, Berlin 1959, 614s.

estant side, a change of generations took place between 1570 and 1585 throughout the Empire. In place of men who had protected the religious peace as a hard-won political compromise there appeared theologians and politicians who actively sought to reshape, delimit, and revise. They were prepared to gamble with the existing political and legal compromise for the sake of an additional internal consolidation of their churches as well as an expansion of their sphere of influence, which would also contribute to their personal reputation. Emperor Maximilian II,[59] a pre-confessional mediator of Humanist thought, died in 1576 and his son Rudolf II (24) succeeded to the imperial throne. He was the first in a long series of Hapsburgs who attained the imperial throne and took a strong stand on behalf of their confessional church; with him a transition toward Catholic confessionalization took place at the pinnacle of the Empire.

Third phase: the apogee of confessionalization, from the 1580's to the 1620's. The changes that occurred were conspicuous, even spectacular, in those places where, for all practical purposes, a third confessional church was introduced into the Empire with the Reformed/Calvinist confession. Although it claimed legal status as church adhering to the Augsburg Confession this had long been, of course, "a theological hypocrisy, a purely legalistic claim for protection."[60] After the first step of the Palatinate, where a relatively open Calvinist church order was introduced, a long series of territories and cities confessionalized their churches according to a Reformed or Calvinist standard, beginning in 1578 with the counties of Wetterau, Sayn-Wittgenstein, and Nassau-Dillenburg. In the 1580's followed the city of Bremen (1581), the Rhenish minor domain of Moers (1581), the second and final calvinization of the Palatinate (1583), the Wetterau County of Solms-Braunfels

---

59 O. Helmut, Kaiser Maximilian II. und der Kompromißkatholizismus, München 1895; V. Bibl, Maximilian II. Der rätselhafte Kaiser, Hellerau 1929.

60 Heckel, Reichsrecht (note 14), 31.—Reformed confessionalization is discussed in detail in Schilling (ed.), Konfessionalisierung (note 8) with articles by K. Blaschke on Saxony, W.U. Deetjen on Zweibrücken, V. Press on the Palatinate, G. Menk on Hesse-Kassel, G. Schmidt on the Wetterau, H. Klueting on Westphalia, R. von Thadden on Brandenburg-Prussia, M.G. Müller on the cities of Danzig, Thorn and Elbing. Recently on the counts of the Wetterau: G. Schmidt, Der Wetterauer Grafenverein, Marburg 1989; B. Nischan, Reformation or Deformation?, in: K.C. Sessions and P.N. Bebb (eds.), Pietas et Societas, Kirksville 1985, 203-214.

(1582), a part of Isenburg (1584) and Wied (1589), Bentheim-
Tecklenburg in Westphalia (1587/1588), Palatine-Zweibrücken
(1588) as well as a short phase of Calvinism in Electoral Saxony
(1586-1591). The movement, which continued without pause
until the eve of the Thirty Years' War, saw a renewed wave
during the decade between 1595 and 1605 with Hanau-Münzenberg (1595), a second part of Isenburg (Büdingen 1596),
Saxony-Anhalt (1596), the upper Palatinate (1595-1598), Lin-
gen (1597), Palatine-Simmern (1598), Baden-Durlach (1599),
(25) Hesse-Kassel, Lippe and Sayn (both 1605). After 1605 a
break occurred: In Germany the Reformed church "made no
further territorial gains as a whole ... . It was reduced to
growth within the residences and castles of territorial princes."[61] These included the Hohenzollern family of Brandenburg, which was of far-reaching importance, and, temporarily,
the ruling family of Mecklenburg-Güstrow. The Silesian Duchy
of Brieg (1619) followed along with other areas ruled by the
Bohemian crown. Particularly unusual cases included the rigid
calvinization of the church of Emden together with the surrounding countryside, which had long maintained a pre-confessional Reformed stance,[62] as well as the movements, ultimately unsuccessful, in some German communities beyond the
imperial frontier, particularly in Danzig, Thorn, and Elbing. In
addition to the Palatinate and Hesse-Kassel a bloc of smaller
Reformed territories emerged, mostly imperial counties, which
were concentrated in the center of western Germany and had
outlying territories in the north and east.

Lutheran confessionalization occurred at the same time, if in
a less spectacular way, since it took place on the basis of a
recognized confessional stance whose legitimacy was not disputed by imperial law. The decisive dynamic began with the
concordial movement that passed through Germany from 1573
until 1582.[63] About fifty territories—among them both the traditional and aspiring leading powers of Protestantism within
the Empire, that is Electoral Saxony and Württemberg, and for

61 Goeters, Genesis (note 33), 55.
62 See H. Schilling, Civic Calvinism, Kirksville/Mo 1991.
63 W.U. Deetjen, Concordia Concors—Concordia Discors. Zum Ringen um das
Konkordienwerk im Süden und mittleren Westens Deutschlands; I. Mager, Aufnahme und Ablehnung des Konkordienbuches in Nord-, Mittel- und Ost-
deutschland, both in: Brecht/Schwarz (eds.), Bekenntnis und Einheit der Kirche
(note 50), 303-349, 271-302 respectively.

a short time the re-Lutheranized Palatinate under Elector Ludwig VI (1576-1583), together with at least three dozen imperial
cities—formed themselves into a separate Lutheran confessional
bloc, "whose confessional standard was clearly established."[64]
Even in those Lutheran territories that had not formally (26)
accepted the Book of Concord, a rigidity set in that was
intellectual and theological in nature as well as political, institutional, and social, as occurred within the Lutheran territorial
churches of East Friesland and in Brunswick-Wolfenbüttel.
Both cases will be examined in the final part of this article.

Finally during the 1580's and 1590's the decisive
breakthrough of Catholic confessionalization also occurred.
After Bavaria, Inner Austria, Tyrol, and Salzburg stepped forward as the advanced guard of the Tridentine renewal[65]—as
the Palatinate had for the Calvinists and Württemberg for the
Lutherans—a long series of Catholic territories adopted new
ecclesiastical policies at the end of the 1570's. In quick succession Tridentine confessionalization was instituted in the bishoprics of Constance, Strasbourg, and Basel, with further
expansion in Catholic Switzerland,[66] in Fulda, (27) in the

64 Deetjen, Concordia (note 63), 336. The names of the territories and towns
are listed in: Bekenntnisschriften der evangelisch-lutherischen Kirche, 4th
edition, Göttingen 1959, 15-17.

65 W. Goetz and L. Theobald (eds.), Beiträge zur Geschichte Herzog Albrechts
V. und der sogenannten Adelsverschwörung von 1563, Leipzig 1913; W. Goetz,
Die bayerische Politik im Jahrzehnt der Regierung Herzog Albrechts V. von
Bayern (1550-1560), München 1896; G. Pfeiffer, Bayern, in: Theologische
Realenzyklopädie, vol. 5, 361-387; H. Lutz, Das konfessionelle Zeitalter, in: M.
Spindler (ed.), Handbuch der bayerischen Geschichte, vol. 2, München 1977, 297-
350; idem, Ringen (note 57), 328-334; Buxbaum, Canisius (note 37); B. Sutter, in:
NDB, vol. 11, Berlin 1977, 240s.; F. Hurter, Geschichte Kaiser Ferdinands II. und
seiner Eltern, 2 vols., Schaffhausen 1850; Mezler-Andelberg, Erneuerung (note
55); J. Hirn, Erzherzog Ferdinand II. von Tirol. Geschichte seiner Regierung und
seiner Länder, 2 vols., Innsbruck 1885-1888; F. Steinegger, in: NDB, vol. 5, Berlin
1961, 91s.; Bücking, Frühabsolutismus (note 37),; idem, Das Tridentinum in
Tirol, in: Zeeden (ed.), Gegenreformation (note 37), 204-221; H. Widmann,
Geschichte Salzburgs, vol. 3, Gotha 1914; F. Martin, Salzburger Fürsten in der
Barockzeit, 1587-1812, 3rd edition, Salzburg 1966; R.R. Heinisch, Die bischöfli-
chen Wahlkapitulationen im Erzstift Salzburg 1514-1688, Wien 1977, esp. 36
(1554), 46 (1580), 58ss. (1587); F. Ortner, Reformation, katholische Reform und
Gegenreformation im Erzstift Salzburg, Salzburg/München 1981.

66 A. Schindling, Die Universität Dillingen und die katholische Schweiz im
konfessionellen Zeitalter, in: Schweizerisch-deutsche Beziehungen im konfessionellen Zeitalter. Beiträge zur Kulturgeschichte 1580-1650, Wiesbaden 1984, 253-
259; idem, Die katholische Bildungsreform zwischen Humanismus und
Barock—Dillingen, Dole, Freiburg, Molsheim und Salzburg, in: H. Maier and V.
Press (eds.), Vorderösterreich in der frühen Neuzeit, Sigmaringen 1989, 137-176.

Eichsfeld, a region ruled by the Archbishop of Mainz with its center in Erfurt, in the Franconian bishoprics of Würzburg and Bamberg and in the archbishopric of Trier. As a result of the "conquest" of Cologne by the Bavarian Wittelsbachs similar changes occurred in the key ecclesiastical territories of the Rhineland and Westphalia—Hildesheim, Cologne, Münster, and Liege—and, in the wake of these developments, also in Paderborn and in a series of secular territories of this area.[67] The adroit use of dynastic politics, in which the Bavarian Wittelsbachs played a crucial role, served to open a path for Catholic confessionalization. Within two decades this path ran from southeast to southwest and then toward the northwest, passing through the most important territories that had remained loyal to the old faith.

In place of the pragmatic protection of peace now there was more readiness to gamble with peace. Politics was dominated by a willingness to use every possible means, legal and coercive, even including military force, to gain personal advantage. The leaders of the confessional parties would soon charge each other with paying little heed to alliances or legal agreements, or even with urging their ruling authorities to break the law when only confessional opponents were affected.[68] The Calvinists above all were convinced that they were engaged in an eschatological culminating battle, taking place throughout the Empire and Europe, between the children of light and the children of hell, between the powers of light, gathered in the Reformed church, and the powers of hell led by the Pope and his blind accomplices in orthodox Lutheranism.[69] At the end of (28) the sixteenth century Germany was overwhelmed by a veritable flood of controversial theology in the form of pamphlets and combative works using every po-lemical tool, which sought to close confessional ranks and to destroy the intellec-

---

67 See bibliographical references in note 37.

68 See e.g. the pamphlet edited in Bremen in 1592: "Missive oder Sendbrieffe etlicher Guthertzigen ... Studenten ... aus Rom ... darinnen die Fürnembsten Geheimniß des Antichristischen Bapstumbs ... offenbaret, 48.

69 H. Schilling, Calvinism and Civic Liberties, in: idem, Civic Calvinism (note 62), p. 69-104. In contrast to the Calvinists, the Lutherans insisted on maintaining the illusion of a working religious peace, which meant at the same time sharp attacks on Calvin-ism. See e.g. B. Mentzer, Examen Eilshemianum: Darinnen D.B. Eilshemii ... Beständige Verthädigung ... widerlegt, Frankfurt a.M. 1622, 165.

tual and moral position of those who were loyal to the other confessions. When one adds this to the political and social conflicts that were going on at the same time in numerous territories and cities,[70] the contours of an enormous battle for public opinion emerged, which shook the Empire and many of its territories. The well-known political conflicts within the Empire—over permission for Protestant residence within bishoprics, the visitation commission for the chamber court, the Strasbourg chapter dispute, and the Four Monastery conflict—were only the most spectacular expressions of confessionalization. It was also taking root during these decades within German society in the cities and villages, and even within individual households and families.

Fourth phase: The end of confessionalization under the conditions of war and on the basis of the Peace of Westphalia; Irenicism and the weakening of confessionalization. Should we wish to write a complete history of German confessionalization, then we would have to describe the final phase, which took place between the 1620's and the early eighteenth century, in more detail. This fourth phase, during which the significance of confessionalization for general history decreased over time, is characterized by clearly pronounced contradictory tendencies. On the one hand the connection between (29) confessionalism and absolutism, conceived in the sixteenth century, finally came to full fruition—partially because of the confessional reshaping that took place under martial law during the 1620's and 1630's, which occurred first in Bohemia and Austria, as well as through the final consolidation of the territorial confessional churches that resulted from the Peace of Westphalia.[71] On the other hand confessional fixation slowly decreased,

---

70 See Schilling, Calvinism and Civic Liberties (note 69); idem, Gab es in Deutschland im späten Mittelalter und in der frühen Neuzeit einen Stadt-Republikanismus?—Zur politischen Kultur des alteuropäischen Stadtbürgertums, in: H. Koenigsberger (ed.), Republiken und Republikanismus, 15. bis frühes 17. Jahrhundert, München 1987 (English translation above, pp. 3-60; R. Kniebe, Der Schriftenstreit über die Reformation des Kurfürsten Johann Sigismund von Brandenburg seit 1613, Halle 1902. For general observations on the origin and function of polemical style within Lutheranism, see: R. Kolb, Perilous Events and Troublesome Disturbances. The Role of Controversy in the Tradition of Luther to Lutheran Orthodoxy, in: K.C. Session and Ph. Bebb (eds.), Pietas et Societas, Kirksville/Mo, 1985, 181-201.

71 E. Tomek, Kirchengeschichte Österreichs, 3 vols., Innsbruck/Wien 1935-1959; A. Careth, Pietas Austriaca. Ursprung und Entwicklung barocker Fröm-

so that irenical and undogmatic supra-confessional forms of piety—pietism among the Protestants, Jansenism among the Catholics—had room to develop.[72] The roots of this theological and religious development can be traced back to the sixteenth century. But at the high point of confessionalization irenical impulses were untimely and could not develop. Irenical thought became, not uncommonly, a vehicle of confessionalization. For example, irenical edicts *de non calumniando* promulgated by territorial princes, which forbade Lutherans and Calvinists to engage in polemics from the pulpit, often opened a path for a "Second Reformation," which meant the change from a Lutheran to a Calvinist confessional stance.[73] What began as an appeal for peace, and could have from a subjective viewpoint been quite sincerely meant, perforce degenerated into an instrument of confessionalization under the conditions of an unlimited competitive battle between opposing political and religious systems (30). Only when the "pressure for confessionalization" was relaxed, because confessional unification and formation were complete or because the politicization of religion, and with it confessionalism, had been abandoned, could irenicism and an inner "piety of the heart" return to themselves. Not uncommonly it was Humanist groups on the fringes of the confessional churches who stepped forward, now freed from the goals of state and ecclesiastical politics, with irenical ideas. At the high point of the confrontation they had submitted to confessionalization without giving up the wish for an undogmatic free piety and for inter-confessional exchange.

---

migkeit in Österreich, Wien 1959; E. Winter, Der Josephinismus. Die Geschichte des österreichischen Reformkatholizismus 1740-1848, Berlin 1962; P. Hersche, Der Spätjansenismus in Österreich, Wien 1977; J. Karniel, Die Toleranzpolitik Kaiser Josephs II., Gerlingen 1985; G. Klingenstein, Staatsverwaltung und kirchliche Autorität im 18. Jahrhundert. Das Problem der Zensur in der theresianischen Reform, Wien 1970.

72 H. Lehmann, Das Zeitalter des Absolutismus, Gottesgnadentum und Kriegsnot, Stuttgart/Berlin/Köln/Mainz 1980 gives further literature.

73 H. Leube, Kalvinismus und Luthertum im Zeitalter der Orthodoxie, Leipzig 1928, reprint Aalen 1966; U. Stutz, Kurfürst Johann Sigismund von Brandenburg und das Reformationsrecht, Berlin 1922; Schilling, Konfessionskonflikt (note 3), 244ss.; Goeters, Genesis (note 33), 52ss.; G.A. Benrath, Irenik und Zweite Reformation, and R. Hansen, Der Friedensplan Heinrich Rantzaus und die Irenik in der Zweiten Reformation, both in: Schilling (ed.), Konfessionalisierung (note 8), 349-358 and 359-372; B. Nischan, John Bergius: Irenicism and the Beginning of Official Religious Toleration in Brandenburg-Prussia, in: Church History 51 (1982), 389-404.

Irenicism and pietism gained ground all the more quickly as
confessionalism proved its own absurdity in the horrors of a
religious war.[74]

3. THE CONSEQUENCES OF CONFESSIONALIZATION FOR SOCIETY AND POLITICS

The differences of the three varieties of confessionalization in
theology and spirituality as well as in their legal and institutional forms were less important than their functional and
structural similarities when their impact upon state and society
is considered. This can be demonstrated both in the details of
ecclesiastical measures and in their direct effects upon society
and politics. Visitations[75] were used by the confessional
churches with grim determination to shape the personal, (31)
theological, and intellectual character of their charges, and to
purge themselves of heretics and even "unreliable elements"
who still adhered to pre-confessional standards. Confessional
school and university policies[76] had as their goal the

---

74 See the shifts in pamphleteering and its illustrations during the Thirty
Years' War, documented by W. Harms (ed.), Illustrierte Flugblätter des Barock.
Eine Auswahl, Tübingen 1983; J.R. Paas, The German Political Broadsheet.
1600-1700, 2 vols., Wiesbaden 1985-1986; H. Wäscher, Das deutsche illustrierte
Flugblatt, Dresden 1955, 49 reproduces an impressive illustration with "Suffering
Christ among politicians and church men" from the 1640's.

75 P.Th. Lang, Die Bedeutung der Kirchenvisitation für die Geschichte der
Frühen Neuzeit. Ein Forschungsbericht, in: Rottenburger Jahrbuch für Kirchengeschichte 3 (1984), 207-212.—Fundamental information is given by the volumes
of the Repertorium der Kirchenvisitationsakten aus dem 16. und 17. Jahrhundert
in Archiven der Bundesrepublik Deutschland: vol. I: Hessen, ed. by Chr. Reinhardt and H. Schnabel-Schüle, Stuttgart 1982; vol. II: Baden-Württemberg, part
1: Der katholische Südwesten, die Grafschaften Hohenlohe und Wertheim, ed. by
P.Th. Lang, Stuttgart 1984; vol. II: Baden-Württemberg, part 2, ed. by H.
Schnabel-Schüle, Stuttgart 1987.—See also R. Reinhardt, in: ZHF 13 (1986),
350-353; E.W. Zeeden and H. Molitor (eds.), Die Visitation im Dienst der kirchlichen Reform, Münster 1977; E.W. Zeeden and P.Th. Lang (eds.), Kirche und
Visitation, Stuttgart 1984.

76 P. Baumgart and N. Hammerstein (eds.), Beiträge zu Problemen deutscher
Universitätsgründungen in der frühen Neuzeit, Nendeln 1978; A. Schindling, Die
Universität Gießen als Typus einer Hochschulgründung, in: P. Moraw and V.
Press (eds.), Academia Gissensis. Beiträge zur älteren Gießener Universitätsge-
schichte, Marburg 1982, 83-114; N. Hammerstein, The University of Heidelberg in
the Early Modern Period, in: History of Universities 6 (1986), 105-133; idem,
Schule, Hochschule und Res publica litteraria, in: Res publica litteraria, Wolfenbüttel 1987, 93-110; idem, Vom "Dritten Genf" zur Jesuiten-Universität: Heidelberg in der frühen Neuzeit, in: Die Geschichte der Universität Heidelberg. Studium Generale 1985/86, Heidelberg 1986, 34-44; idem, Universitäten (note 18),

"ideologically correct" education of the next generation in religious, intellectual, and political terms, in order to unite the faith and thoughts of subjects and to provide ideologically reliable office holders for church and state. Similar efforts were made to control marriage, the family (32) and household, the poor, sick, and aged.[77] This historical similarity is particularly clear in the measures instituted for church discipline.[78] Their concrete expressions were quite different, above all with respect to the division of responsibility between church and state. However, they performed, more unwanted throughout than wanted, the same social function of obliging the people of the church, and hence all subjects, to observe the religious and ethical standards of their respective confessional systems, which were at the same time the norms of the disciplined, rationally organized modern society. In the end it is unmistakable that the

---

687-735, esp. 702ss.; G. Menk, Territorialstaat und Schulwesen in der frühen Neuzeit. Eine Untersuchung zur religiösen Dynamik in den Grafschaften Nassau und Sayn, in: Jahrbuch für Westdeutsche Landesgeschichte 9 (1983), 177-220; G. Schormann, Zweite Reformation und Bildungswesen am Beispiel der Elementarschulen, in: Schilling (ed.), Konfessionalisierung (note 8), 308-316; A. Schindling, Humanistische Reform und fürstliche Schulpolitik in Hornbach und Lauingen. Die Landesgymnasien des Pfalzgrafen Wolfgang von Zweibrücken und Neuburg, in: Neuburger Kollektaneenblatt 133 (1980), 141-186.

77 Th. M. Safley, Let No Man Put Asunder. The Control of Marriage in the German Southwest: A Comparative Study, 1500-1600, Kirksville 1984; L. Roper, Going to Church and Street: Weddings in Reformation Augsburg, in: Past and Present 106 (1985), 62-101; eadem, Discipline and Respectability: Prostitution and the Reformation in Augsburg, in: History Workshop Journal 19 (1986), 3-28; F.P. Lane, Johannes Bugenhagen und die Armenfürsorge der Reformationszeit, in: Braunschweigisches Jahrbuch 64 (1983), 147-186; R. Jütte, Obrigkeitliche Armenfürsorge in deutschen Städten der frühen Neuzeit, Köln 1984.

78 H. Schilling, "History of Crime" or "History of Sin"—Some Reflections on the Social History of Early Modern Church Discipline, in: E.J. Kouri and T. Scott (eds.), Politics and Society in Reformation Europe, London/München 1986; J. Estèbe and B. Vogler, La genèse d'une société protestante: étude comparée de quelques registres consistoriaux languedociens et palatins vers 1600, in: Annales. ESC 31 (1976), 362-388; P. Münch, Zucht und Ordnung. Reformierte Kirchenverfassungen im 16. und 17. Jahrhundert (Nassau-Dillenburg, Kurpfalz, Hessen-Kassel), Stuttgart 1978, (Spätmittelalter und Frühe Neuzeit, vol. 3); idem, Kirchenzucht und Nachbarschaft. Zur sozialen Problematik des calvinistischen Seniorats um 1600, in: E.W. Zeeden and P.Th. Lang (eds.), Kirche (note 75), 216-248 (Spätmittelalter und Frühe Neuzeit, vol. 14); H. Schilling, Reformierte Kirchenzucht als Sozialdisziplinierung?—Die Tätigkeit des Emder Presbyteriums in den Jahren 1557-1562 (Mit vergleichenden Betrachtungen über die Kirchenräte in Groningen und Leiden sowie mit einem Ausblick ins 17. Jahrhundert), in: W. Ehbrecht and H. Schilling (eds.), Niederlande und Nordwestdeutschland, Köln/Wien 1983, 261-327; idem, Calvinism and the Making of the Modern Mind, in: idem, Calvinism (note 62), 11-40.

structures and institutions of the confessional churches in Germany functioned, as a rule, in conformity with the early tendencies toward absolutism shown by the princely territorial states, not least among the Reformed territorial churches.[79] Only in a few (33) exceptions resulting from special conditions were there alliances between Calvinism and estates or republican and constitutional movements.[80]

All of these tendencies were bound together by the oath of allegiance sworn by the servants of church and state. The Lutherans and Catholics had definitive texts or collections of texts in the Formula of Concord and the Tridentine Confession of Faith. Even Reformed confessionalization, which produced nothing comparable to these *formulae*, did not dispense with the confessional oath, which became a part of the oath of citizenship in some places such as Emden. Besides narrower theological goals, these confessional oaths fulfilled "the function of a fundamental value that served to build a social consensus, which in turn justified recourse to legal compulsory measures. The unity of faith, produced by legal compulsion, corresponded to a need for integration within state and church." —*Religio vinculum societatis* was the justification for confessionalization given by theologians and politicians of all three large Christian churches.[81]

At first glance this seems to be a return to a medieval conception, particularly when this principle was formulated for a city. At the high point of confessionalization during the early seventeenth century, Petrus a Beeck, chronicler of a re-catholicized Aachen, defined a city as a *"civium unitatem, non modo quod uno aggere vel vallo circumagatur sed quod eodem velle, eodem nolle, eiusdem fidei symbolo ... coalescere."*[82] Just as the

---

79 Discussed in detail by the contributions to Schilling (ed.), Konfessionalisierung (note 8).

80 G. Menk, Die politische Kultur in den Wetterauer Grafschaften, in: Hessisches Jahrbuch für Landesgeschichte 34 (1984), 77-100, esp. 98; H. Schilling, Calvinism (note 62).

81 K. Schreiner, Rechtgläubigkeit als "Band der Gesellschaft" und "Grundlage des Staates". Zur eidlichen Verpflichtung von Staats- und Kirchendienern auf die Formula Concordiae und das "Konkordienbuch", in: Brecht/Schwarz (eds.), Bekenntnis (note 50), 341-379, quotation on page 375.

82 Petrus a Beeck, Aquisgranum, Aachen 1620. German translation by P.St. Käntzeler, Petrus a Beeck, Aquisgranum oder Geschichte der Stadt Aachen, Aachen 1874, 329.

medieval (34) "conception of secular-spiritual unity"[83] was
preserved in all early modern peace treaties between the confessions, so also the medieval conception of the city as a sanctified community was retained—among Catholics no differently
than among Calvinists.[84] However, the medieval corporate
ideal, or—following Peter Blickle—Old European communalism, did not stand behind this, but rather a new reality. It
was in the first instance the early modern state that made use
of the older conceptions of unity. In the confessionally and
politically fragmented world of the Empire it was not possible
for these conceptions of unity to contribute to the idea of an
imperial or national state. They became, rather, the motive
power behind secular and ecclesiastical integration within the
individual territorial states, powerfully advancing the consolidation of princely states. Confessionalization served to consolidate the territorial structure of the Empire.[85] Under the conditions of the "long sixteenth century" it was also impossible that
the assumption of harmony and unity, retained from the
Middle Ages, would lead to peace in the long run.[86] On the
contrary, the linkage of the secular interests of these territorial
states with the dynamic of differentiation set in motion by the
confessional orthodoxies led, as a logical consequence, to an
unlimited confrontation between the military alliances, representing opposing world views, hurling the tri-confessional,
multi-territorial Empire into the chaos of an enormous war,
which was both a religious and civil war at the same time.

In recent years theoretical discussions have drawn attention
to the logical link between confessionalism and early modern
state-building within the context of both Catholic and Calvin-
ist/Reformed states. The "Counter-Reformation as modernization" has been understood to mean the rise of an absolutist
state that monopolized all power and authority. Reformed
confessionalization has been regarded as a fundamental conflict
between the fragmented older estates on the one hand and the
early modern conception of a disciplined state and society of

---

83 Heckel, Reichsrecht (note 14), 14.

84 This is even true for the Netherlands apart from the specific situation within
the province of Holland. For the unity policy of the Calvinists in the city of Groningen see Schilling, Civic Calvinism (note 62).

85 See Schilling, Identität (note 11).

86 This underscores my argument in the discussion with Th. A. Brady. See
Schilling, Konfessionskonflikt (note 3), 376, note 17 a.

subjects on the other hand.[87] The concrete experience of Catholic as well as Protestant confessionalization has been described in several fundamentally important books.[88]

For Reformed confessionalization the connecting link between ecclesiastical and theological changes and political and social ones was forged through the assumption that the "Reformation of Doctrine" should be complemented by a "Reformation of Life." This was the distinctive feature of a so-called "Second Reformation," which was at the same time, by definition and self-interpretation, a religious, political, and social event.[89] Catholic confessionalization lacked such a programmatic linkage. In its place came a pragmatic alliance of interests between the universal church, which had been on the defensive for almost five decades, and the early modern state, which first guaranteed protection for the former and then, beginning in the mid-sixteenth century, supported a counter-offensive using political coercion and even military power. This pragmatic alliance of interests permitted a confluence between the policies of ecclesiastical and theological renewal adopted by the Council of Trent and the secular goals of political and social change sought by the princes and their early modern bureaucracy. In both cases the state assumed the leading role, so that in Catholic as well as Reformed territories the governance of the church by the territorial prince, a practice that had already begun during the late Middle Ages, was strengthened in very real terms.[90] This occurred no matter how strongly theologians of both confessions advocated a constitution guaranteeing autonomy of church or congregation. (36)

These connections between religious and social change have gone largely unnoticed with reference to Lutheran confessionalization because it was assumed that the political and social changes within Lutheran states had already been completed

---

87 See the books and articles by Reinhard and Schilling (note 8); with regard to Catholic confessionalization: J. Bossy, The Counter-Reformation and the People of Catholic Europe in: Past and Present 47 (1970), 51-70.

88 Press, Calvinismus (note 3); R. Glawischnig, Niederlande, Kalvinismus und Reichsgrafenstand 1559-1584. Nassau-Dillenburg unter Graf Johann VI., Marburg 1973; Münch, Zucht (note 78); Schilling, Konfessionskonflikt (note 3). On Catholic confessionalization see note 37 above.

89 The slogan "Reformation of Life" is discussed in detail in: Schilling (ed.), Konfessionalisierung (note 8).

90 Lutz, Ringen (note 57), 323ss.; Bücking, Frühabsolutismus (note 37), 235.

during the Reformation itself. This assumption is valid, if at all, only for a few territories. Usually a decisive ideological and social reshaping took place, even within Lutheran areas, in the course of confessionalization.[91] For example, in East Friesland, Lutheran confessionalization, supported by the ruler who sought to establish an early modern state with princely sovereignty, confronted Reformed confessionalization, which had allied itself with the estates and civic republicanism in Emden. Recently, Manfred Rudersdorf has argued convincingly that the motive power of Lutheran confessionalization contributed to "general territorial modernization," as he terms it, using the examples of Hesse-Marburg and Württemberg.[92] Similar developments occurred also during the confessionalization of Brunswick-Wolfenbüttel, upon which Luise Schorn-Schütte has shed new light in the course of her analysis of the early modern clergy as members of the burgher estate.[93] For our (37) topic the conditions in Brunswick merit further attention for several reasons. The confessional motive power for the consolidation of state and society came first of all from commitment to a renewed Lutheranism. The Brunswick church distanced itself, however, step by step from the Book of Concord, which, although it was treasured within the church during the 1580's and 1590's, was never elevated to a legally binding standard.[94] The unwavering, progressive formation of

91 See my very first remarks on this fact in: H. Schilling, Neue Gesichtspunkte zur ostfriesischen Ständegeschichte, in: Emder Jahrbuch 55 (1975), 80-89 and idem, Konfessionskonflikt (note 3), 42, 368. Meanwhile, Lutheran confessionalization has been discussed at another symposium of the VRG. See H.Ch. Rublack (ed.), Lutherische Konfessionalisierung, Gütersloh 1991 (forthcoming).

92 M. Rudersdorf, Lutherische Erneuerung und zweite Reformation—Hessen und Württemberg als Beispiele, in: Schilling (ed.), Konfessionalisierung (note 8), 130-153.

93 L. Schorn-Schütte, Prediger an protestantischen Höfen der Frühneuzeit. Zur politischen und sozialen Stellung einer neuen bürgerlichen Führungsgruppe in der höfischen Gesellschaft des 17. Jahrhunderts, dargestellt am Beispiel von Hessen-Kassel, Hessen-Darmstadt und Braunschweig-Wolfenbüttel, in: H. Schilling and H. Diederiks (eds.), Bürgerliche Eliten in den Niederlanden und in Nordwestdeutschland, Köln/Wien 1985, 275-336; eadem, "Papocaesarismus" der Theologen? Vom Amt des evangelischen Pfarrers in der frühneuzeitlichen Stadtgeschichte bei Bugenhagen, in: ARG 78 (1987), 230-261; eadem, contribution to H.Ch. Rublack (ed.), Konfessionalisierung (note 91); H. Ch. Rublack, "Der wohlgeplagte Priester." Vom Selbstverständnis lutherischer Geistlichkeit im Zeitalter der Orthodoxie, in: Zeitschrift für Historische Forschung 16 (1989), 1-30.

94 Mager, Aufnahme (note 63), 278-286, esp. 282; J. Beste, Geschichte der braunschweigischen Landeskirche, Wolfenbüttel 1889; K. Krüger and E. Jung,

an early modern state and church governance was accomplished at the end of the sixteenth and the beginning of the seventeenth centuries in conflict with concordial Lutheranism. For in the meantime the latter had become the ideological basis for the resistance both of the nobility, who were allied with the court preacher Sattler, and of the urban burgher estates of Brunswick, Göttingen, Hanover, and Northeim, who sought to defend their rights to political and ecclesiastical autonomy against the early modern state.[95] The territorial government distanced itself officially from the Lutheran orthodoxy that it originally supported, and allied itself with the post-orthodox theology of its university in Helmstedt. Under the theological leadership of Georg Calixt the Book of Concord was formally removed from the canon of confessional documents accepted in Brunswick.[96] (38)

The distinctive course of church history in Brunswick-Wolfenbüttel, which seems to contradict the thesis of an internal connection between confessionalization and early modern state-building, demands that we systematically summarize the political and societal functions of confessionalization and inquire into its specific effects upon the modern history of Germany.

1. Seen as a whole the aspects of confessionalization that were dominant in Germany were its disciplinary, centralizing, and integrative impulses, both political and social; indeed they were much stronger in Germany than was the case in most European countries. The territorial structure of the Empire, already established before the Reformation, was not the least important factor in this connection. Its tri-confessional and multi-territorial character, each factor reinforcing the other,

Staatsbildung als Modernisierung. Braunschweig-Wolfenbüttel im 16. Jahrhundert, in: Braunschweigisches Jahrbuch 64 (1983), 41-68; H.W. Krumwiede, Geschichte der evangelischen Kirche von der Reformation bis 1803, in: H. Patze (ed.), Geschichte Niedersachsens, vol. III, 2, Hildesheim 1983, 1-216.

95 Mager, Aufnahme (note 63), 285ss.; J. Regula, Die kirchlichen Selbständigkeitsbestrebungen der Städte Göttingen, Northeim, Hannover und Hameln in den Jahren 1584-1601, in: Zeitschrift der Gesellschaft für niedersächsische Kirchengeschichte 22 (1917), 123-152.

96 H. Dreitzel, Protestantischer Aristotelismus und absoluter Staat. Die "Politica" des Henning Arnisäus (ca. 1575-1636), Wiesbaden 1970; P. Baumgart and E. Pitz (eds.), Die Statuten der Universität Helmstedt, Göttingen 1963; P. Baumgart, Universitäten im konfessionellen Zeitalter: Würzburg und Helmstedt, and idem, Die Gründung der Universität Helmstedt, both in: Baumgart/Hammerstein (eds.), Beiträge (note 76), 191-216, 217-242.—J. Wallmann, article "Calixt", in: Theologische Realenzyklopädie, vol. 7, 552-559.

resulted in the peculiarly German combination of confessionalization and early modern state-building. The differences
between Catholic, Lutheran, and Calvinist confessionalization
were of a contingent, not an essential nature; all three supported the early absolutist territorial princely state.

2. This insight should not, however, obscure the fact that in
Germany confessionalization also acted as a catalyst for religious, political, and societal opposition, particularly within territories. So as confessional pressure was applied in order to
unify state, church, and society, it was confessional loyalty, on
the other hand, which continually stirred up a fundamental
opposition to the presumptions of the ruling authority, impel-
ling individuals and social groups—not least among whom were
the theologians[97]—to resist (39) the early modern autocratic
state as it strove to abolish traditional liberties in order to build
a uniform society of subjects. Besides state-building, in many
territories confessional conflict took the form of a political
battle between opposing models of state and society—between
the newer ideal of a unitary state focused in the sovereignty of
the prince, and the opposing estate and libertarian understanding of the state, which supported the decentralized medieval pattern, characterized by liberties and graduated
privileges.

3. Even when considering the function that confessionalism
performed in legitimizing conflict and opposition, there was no
fundamental difference between the large confessions—at least
not between the two Protestant confessions. In the northwest in
East Friesland, and in the southeast in Bohemia and Austria,
Calvinism was the confession of the oppositional estates. In
Brandenburg-Prussia and in many other territories, which were
to become Calvinist by governmental decision, it was Lutheranism that allied itself with the resistance in urban and rural
areas. As has been shown, concordial Lutheranism played this
role for a time in Brunswick-Wolfenbüttel. This observation
does not in principle deny differences in political practice, political theory, or—broadly conceived—political culture between

---

97 A typical figure of the age of confessionalization was the clergyman who
went into exile for religious reasons and who moved from territory to territory
without showing consideration for himself and his family. H. Schieckel, Pfarrer
aus (Kur)Sachsen in Norddeutschland, in: Herbergen der Christenheit, Jahrbuch
für Deutsche Kirchengeschichte (1967), 55-75; Schilling, Konfessionskonflikt
(note 3), 180, 204, 234, 245, 283.

the three confessions. Yet scepticism seems warranted against
any attempt to explain these difference by quick recourse to
the distinctive theologies or specific "spirits" (Max Weber) of
the respective confessional churches. Instead attention should
be focused upon the historical context within which Lutheran,
Calvinist or Catholic confessionalization took place. Within the
German Empire circumstances differed significantly from those
in other European countries. The German situation was
characterized by state-building that took place in small areas,
and was therefore more intensive; by a political constellation in
which the confessions found it more advantageous to ally
themselves with the princes than with the people; and finally,
by the legal and political solution of the confessional problem
through the Religious Peace of Augsburg,[98] by which the
confessions were bound still more firmly to the secular authorities, above all to the territorial princes and their jurist
councillors. (40)

Still more remarkable is the appearance of an early modern
doctrine of resistance on German soil. In the history of political thought it is now undisputed that the doctrine of resistance
formulated by Lutheran theologians during the siege of Magdeburg, which took place during the Interim crisis, laid the
theoretical and theological groundwork which later entered
Reformed/Calvinist resistance theory through Beza and the
monarchomachs.[99] That the Calvinist theory of resistance had a
much broader impact upon the history of Western Europe is
hardly a consequence of Calvin's specific theology. It was a
result of the political, societal and, above all, ecclesiastical
circumstances of Reformed confessionalization in Germany on
the one hand, and in France, the Netherlands, and England on
the other.

4. On the level of relations between territories and in imperial politics confessionalization served both to integrate and to
produce conflict. This is well-known and does not need to be
discussed in detail here. The history of the confessional allian-

---

98 See note 14 above.

99 W. Schulze, Zwingli, lutherisches Widerstandsdenken, monarchomachischer
Widerstand, in: P. Blickle, A. Lindt and A. Schindler (eds.), Zwingli und Europa,
Zürich 1985; W. Reinhard, Vom italienischen Humanismus bis zum Vorabend der
Revolution, in: H. Fenske et al., Geschichte der politischen Ideen, Königstein
1981, 203-316, esp. 225ss.; A. Laube, Widerstandspflicht um 1530, in: Zeitschrift
für Geschichtswissenschaft 37 (1989), 976-983.

ces and the confessional wars, the Schmalkaldic as well as the
Thirty Years' War, has long been well-known. It must be
pointed out, however, that the old contrast between politically
active Calvinism and Catholicism on the one hand, and a politically idle or even unpolitical Lutheranism on the other is no
longer tenable in the light of the results achieved through a
comparative approach to the structural history of confessionalization. The fact that the first two confessions were particularly active politically in the Empire during the half century
between 1570 and 1620 had more to do with their particular
initial political situtations, and in the case of Calvinism above
all its legal situation, than with an especially politicized theology. Lutheranism was certainly in a position to participate in
imperial and alliance politics. These occurred necessarily in a
less spectacular fashion.[100] The supra-territorial integrative (41)
power of confessionalization was of long term significance for
imperial history beyond the confessional age to the extent that
the confessional alliances of the sixteenth and seventeenth
centuries were a step toward the right to form alliances
(*Bündnisrecht*) given to the imperial estates by a provision of
the Peace of Westphalia. Thus the religiously-guided alliance
policies of the "confessional states" opened the way for the
German territories to become members of the early modern
international community.[101]

5. The triumph of confessionalization in Germany can be
described, employing an emphatic tone, as a path away from
the political and juristic accomplishment of religious peace and
toward a surrender to the pressures of religious and ideological
systems, and thus toward a collective failure that led to the
catastrophe of self-mutilating civil war and international war,
which remained unsurpassed in its ferocity and destructiveness

100 This becomes evident by comparing the policies of Lutheran Hesse-Darmstadt and Calvinist Hesse-Kassel during the Thirty Years' War, see Press, Hessen
(note 49), 267.

101 Discussed in more detail in two recent publications: H. Schilling, Formung
und Gestalt des internationalen Systems in der werdenden Neuzeit—Phasen und
bewegende Kräfte, in: P. Krüger and K. Malettke (eds.), Stabilität und Wandel in
der internationalen Ordnung der Neuzeit. Beiträge zur Geschichte des internationalen Systems vom 16.—20. Jahrhundert, Marburg 1991; idem, Konfessionalisierung und Formierung eines internationalen Systems während der frühen
Neuzeit, in: H. Guggisberg and G. Krodel (eds.), The Reformation in Germany
and Europe: Interpretations and Issues, Actes of the joined conference of the SRR
and the VRG, Washington 1990, Gütersloh 1992.

until the wars of the twentieth century. This raises the question of how much individuals, especially theologians and politicians, contributed to this failure and what proportion should be attributed to the objective factors of structural and historical development.

Let us carefully note that on the subjective side a large amount of blind zeal and indeed moral guilt can be ascribed to the men who after the 1570's gambled with the religious peace, seeking confrontation. They marched into confrontation with their eyes wide open because they believed that by a change in the status quo they could win an advantage for themselves, their confession, their state, and their alliance. They formulated and pursued legal policies where earlier generations would have ignored insoluble conflicts of interest for the sake of a peaceful compromise. Instead of pragmatic considerations of peace the new generation practised the dialectical rhetoric of polemics which drove opponents into a corner in order to convict them of heresy or of apostasy from the true, pure word of God.[102] Naturally there were warning voices—such as Heinrich Rantzau's peace plan mentioned earlier—expressing the readiness for super-confessional dialogue of the Humanists, or—this already a partisan viewpoint—the adherence of Lutheran theologians and politicians to the good, old religious peace.[103] But these voices could not (42) stop the dynamic of confrontation. In 1617 the Reformation anniversary became a festival of demarcation and delimitation, of polemics and defamation.

More important than these subjective failures, however, were factors, even pressures, which resulted from the structural linkage between religion and politics that characterized the early modern type of society. In its organizational phase the early modern state was dependent on the confession as a *vinculum societatis*.[104] The presence of conflict, already inherent

---

102 See e.g. the pamphleteering analysed in Schilling, Calvinism (note 69).

103 See e.g. the treatises of the Lutheran theologians of the university of Giessen, esp. of Balthasar Mentzer (1565-1627): "Evangelische Prob/Deß Ost-Frieslándischen Kleynods ... Darin die zwischen der Augsburgischen Confession und den Calvinisten/streitige Lehrpuncten erkläret" (Gießen 1618) and "Examen Eilshemianum" (Frankfurt 1622), 165, in which Mentzer rejects political alliances for the sake of religion.—See also F. van Ingen, Das Kaiserbild bei den protestantischen Dichtern des 17. Jahrhunderts, in: H. Zeman (ed.), Die österreichische Literatur, Graz 1986, 1035-1054.

104 Dreitzel, Aristotelismus (note 96); Schreiner, Rechtgläubigkeit (note 81).

in the process of state-building itself, became more frequent because of this linkage and was intensified by confessionalization, resulting in a total confrontation of opposing world views. This is not a peculiarly German excess of implacability or hatred,[105] since the same attitudes could be found in France and England. That the confessional civil war in the Empire became a great power conflict was a consequence of medieval developments which had, in turn, resulted in state-building within individual German territories and not on a national level.

6. An alarming mixture of subjective guilt, blindness, indifference, fanaticism, and indeed diabolical implacability on the one hand, and a fatal accumulation of structural circumstances on the other blocked political stabilizing mechanisms and encouraged confrontation. The explosive result becomes fully apparent when we take into account the simultaneous crisis in the demographic, economic, and even climatic situation, together with the radical changes in the concrete world of political experience within the cities and villages. (43) At the same time as this confessional polarization took place there were crises of inflation and provision, plagues and the demographic pressure that occurred during the later phase of the "long sixteenth century," made more acute by the "little ice age."[106] To this must be added the rapid, progressive loss of "communal" political authority, which had remained a vital force until the end of the sixteenth century, at least in the cities.[107] These symptoms of comprehensive upheaval and crisis determined the everyday circumstances of contemporaries and fostered a long-term change in mentality, so that it can be argued in some respects that the upheavals of the confessional age influenced

---

105 This is the opinion expressed by Lutz, Ringen (note 57), 32ss.

106 H. Lehmann, Frömmigkeitsgeschichtliche Auswirkungen der "kleinen Eiszeit", in: Schieder (ed.), Volksreligiosität (note 8), 31-50.

107 H. Schilling, The European Crisis of the 1590s: the Situation in German Towns, in: P. Clark (ed.), The European Crisis of the 1590s, London 1985; idem, Deutschland (note 70); P. Blickle, Deutsche Untertanen. Ein Widerspruch, München 1981; idem, Kommunalismus als Gestaltungsprinzip zwischen Mittelalter und Moderne, in: Gesellschaft und Gesellschaften, Festschrift für Ulrich Im Hof, Bern 1982, 95-113.—See the general description of the situation at the turn of the sixteenth century in the chapters "Politischer und gesellschaftlicher Wandel. Das späte 16. Jahrhundert als Vorsattelzeit der Moderne" and "Krise und Krieg", in: H. Schilling Aufbruch und Krise, Deutsche Geschichte 1517-1648, Berlin 1988, 313-396.

the modern history of Germany in a more enduring way than
the actual Reformation.

7. I will emphasize only some of the socio-psychological
consequences that resulted from confessionalization and state-
building when they were linked with a narrowing of the socio-
economic horizon of expectations, a subject that has hardly
been exhaustively studied. Individuals and social groups saw
themselves overpowered by the modern "apparatus" of the
early modern states and in equal measure by the confessional
churches. Legally educated civil servants and magistrates
argued on the basis of Roman law or the new doctrine of
sovereignty, radically questioning older political and legal
thought and actions, which were based upon concrete legal
agreements and liberties. In the cities and villages people had
the impression, which became increasingly stronger, that an
inescapable influence from "above" had been unleashed upon
them. As numerous uprisings in the cities and several peasant
disturbances show, these people, who had long possessed a
right of political participation through the "communes," felt
compelled to respond violently to this provocation. In all three
confessional churches pastors and other ministers (44) attended
to the salvation of man with an intensity previously
unknown—through catechisms, commentaries, books of edifi-
cation, sermons, pastoral care, and also through social relief for
the poor, sick, and feeble. The biting polemics of controversial
theological pamphlets, however, which sought to annihilate the
intellectual and moral existence of those who held opposing
religious convictions, and the thundering barrage of complaints
that so many pastors shot off from the pulpit each Sunday
created within the horizon of the everyday religious experience
of the people an awareness of a total confrontation of astrin-
gent religious, political, and societal parties that was going on
above their heads. Insecurity and fear, which were fed by
many sources, were not checked or reduced by religion, but
rather were placed into a confessionally explained context. It
was an eschatological struggle between good and evil, the
powers of light and darkness, between the children of God and
hell, a struggle that they perceived as encroaching upon them
and for which they were to be armed with a sanctified willing-

ness for enmity.[108] Famine, plague, insurrection, and military campaigns were experienced as the afflictions of God, as scourging for a depraved world.[109] Neither political action aimed at limiting conflict nor a spiritual and intellectual victory over the antagonism of the opposing world views were regarded as adequate countermeasures, but rather repentance and the endurance of suffering.

8. Finally one further remark concerning the core of the syndrom of crises and upheaval, the linkage of confessionalization and early modern state-building. The anti-libertarian price that was paid for an integration of the state led by a confession is clear within German history and can be shown above all in the practice of the confessional oath—not least in the scholarly pursuits of the universities.[110] To complain about it or even to declare the politicians and theologians of the confessional era guilty (45) would be unhistorical. Only after the mighty exertions that propelled these political, societal, and cultural changes had run their course—as the example of Brunswick-Wolfenbüttel noted above shows—could other forces finally prevail. They recognized that it was not an absolute unity of the symbols of faith, as cited in the chronicle of Aachen, that guaranteed civic harmony, but rather "the freedom guaranteed to all burghers."[111] In contrast to England or the Netherlands, in Germany it was not societal forces from below that brought this principle to the forefront, but rather decrees issued from above, by the confessionally neutral state. It had learned during the difficult crises of the late sixteenth and early seventeenth centuries that political dealings, in the modern sense of the word, presupposed a decoupling of confession and politics.

---

108 See note 101 above.

109 Hsia, Münster (note 16), 197; H. Lehmann, Die Kometenflugschriften des 17. Jahrhunderts als historische Quelle, in: W. Brückner, P. Blickle and D. Breuer (eds.), Literatur und Volk im 17. Jahrhundert, Wiesbaden 1985, 683-700. For several striking examples see: Hans Heberles "Zeytregister" (1618-1672), Aufzeichnungen aus dem Ulmer Territorium, Ulm 1975.

110 Schreiner, Rechtgläubigkeit (note 81); idem, Disziplinierte Wissenschaftsfreiheit. Gedankliche Begründung und geschichtliche Praxis freien Forschens, Lehrens und Lernens an der Universität Tübingen (1417-1945), Tübingen 1981.

111 This maxim was coined by a Humanist author at the apogee of the confessional era, and is quoted in R. Schnur, Die französischen Juristen im konfessionellen Bürgerkrieg des 16. Jahrhunderts. Ein Beitrag zur Entstehungsgeschichte des modernen Staates, Berlin 1962, 71, 67, note 5.

CHAPTER SIX

THE SECOND REFORMATION —
PROBLEMS AND ISSUES

"Irreducible diversity and abundant contrasts give Germany its charm." This loving characterization of our history, made by the former director of the French *Mission Historique* in Germany is especially pertinent for the present topic.[1] Experts in the field realize that the concept of a "Second Reformation" covers a complex variety of contrasting movements which had themselves developed over a long period of time, each passing through different stages. Even the theology underlying the Second Reformation was varied and complex. Zwinglians, Calvinists, and Philippists—the students and adherents of Philipp Melanchthon, who were not a homogenous group--disagreed about the doctrine of the Eucharist, church organization, and church-state relations, to give only the most obvious examples.[2] The political circumstances under which the Second Reformation--or the movements which led to it—emerged and grew were also very different. The processes that led to a Second Reformation were significantly affected by factors such as the size and importance of the political units involved, their status as imperial estates, (388) their internal organization and the degree to which they experienced early modern state-building. The political units affected included urban communes, both imperial (Bremen) and territorial cities (Emden); small territo-

---

1 E. François, Immigration et société urbaine en Allemagne à l'époque moderne XVIIe—XVIIIe siècles, in: M. Garden and Yves Lequin (eds.), Habiter la Ville, XVe—XXe siècles, Lyon 1985, 37.

2 W. Neuser, Dogma und Bekenntnis in der Reformation: Von Zwingli und Calvin bis zur Synode von Westmünster, in: C. Andresen (ed.), Handbuch der Dogmen- und Theologiegeschichte, vol. 2, Göttingen 1980, 167-352; J.F.G. Goeters, Genesis, Formen und Hauptthemen des reformierten Bekenntnisses in Deutschland. Eine Übersicht, in: H. Schilling (ed.), Die reformierte Konfessionalisierung in Deutschland—Das Problem der "Zweiten Reformation", Gütersloh 1986, 44-59.

ries whose dependence upon feudal overlords could be politically explosive (for example, the counties in Westphalia and the
Wetterau, Neuenahr-Moers in the Rhineland and the Silesian
principalities); territories that were split among different
branches of the ruling dynasty (such as Hesse-Kassel, Holstein-
Gottorf, Baden-Durlach, Mecklenburg-Güstrow); and finally
no less than three of the seven Electoral territories. Even
among the Electoral territories the confessional situation and
the political and legal starting points were very different. The
large integrated Lutheran territorial states of Saxony and Brandenburg were located in an area distant from the Emperor's
base of power, while the Electoral Palatinate, which was associated with Lutheranism only for a short time, had a tense and
ambivalent relationship with the Emperors because of its
history and its geographical position as a bridge between the
Empire and the countries of southern and western Europe.[3] As
a consequence it developed into a compact, institutionalized
state only with great difficulty.

The Second Reformation was obviously concentrated in the
middle of western Germany with offshoots in the west and
northwest: the Palatinate, the Wetterau, Hesse, and the Westphalian counties. Southern and northern German territories
(Baden, Gottorf) and territories east of the Elbe and Saale
rivers (Anhalt, Saxony, Brandenburg, Güstrow) were also

---

3 H. Schilling, Konfessionskonflikt und Staatsbildung. Eine Fallstudie über das
Verhältnis von religiösem und sozialem Wandel in der Frühneuzeit am Beispiel
der Grafschaft Lippe, Gütersloh 1981, 45-53, 380-391; H.J. Cohn, The Territorial
Princes in Germany's Second Reformation, 1559-1622, in: M. Prestwich (ed.),
International Calvinism 1541-1715, Oxford 1985, 135-165. See the case studies in
Schilling, Reformierte Konfessionalisierung (note 2) and R. Joppen, Anhalt, in:
Theologische Realenzyklopädie, vol. 2, 734-742; G.A. Benrath, Baden, in: Theologische Realenzyklopädie, vol. 5, 97-103; O. Rudloff, Bremen, in: Theologische
Realenzyklopädie, vol. 7, 153-168; Schleswig-Holsteinische Kirchengeschichte ed.
by the Verein für Schleswig-Holsteinische Kirchengeschichte, vol. 4, Neumünster
1984, esp. 11-63; K. Schmaltz, Kirchengeschichte Mecklenburgs, vol. II, Schwerin
1936, 210-219; G.C.F. Lisch, Über des Herzogs Johann Albrecht II. v. Güstrow
calvinistische Bilderstürmerei und die Altäre in den Klosterkirchen zu Dargun
und Doberan und der Schloßkirche zu Güstrow, in: Jahrbücher des Vereins für
Mecklenburgische Geschichte und Alterthumskunde 16 (1851), 199-202; G.
Hecht, Schlesisch-kurpfälzische Beziehungen im 16. und 17. Jahrhundert, in:
Zeitschrift für die Geschichte des Oberrheins 81 (N.S. 42), (1929), 176-222. The
case study on the Second Reformation in Saxony in: Schilling, Reformierte Konfessionalisierung (note 2) by K. Blaschke provoked an interesting revisionist
article by S. Hoyer, Staat und Stände und Konfessionen in Kursachsen Ende des
16. Jahrhunderts—Das Experiment Christians I., in: H. Timmermann (ed.), Die
Bildung des frühmodernen Staates, Saarbrücken 1989, 175-192.

affected, as were territories on the fringes of the Empire and
German communes outside of it (Silesian duchies, Danzig,
Thorn, Elbing). Similar developments also occurred in the
Scandinavian kingdoms (389) of Denmark and Sweden, which
were closely related to the Empire in their confessional history
and politics, and also—on a different confessional and political
basis—in Bohemia and Moravia.[4] These non-German countries
and territories will not be considered, especially since their
confessional processes never developed into a real Second
Reformation. Despite the geographic dispersal of the German
territories in question one fact is clear: none of them lay within
the direct sphere of influence either of the Emperor or of the
Hapsburg dynasty. Most of them had close relations with
Switzerland, France, or the northern Netherlands—the western
European cradles of Reformed or Calvinist theology. Despite
their different situations these countries were flash points of
political and confessional conflict within Europe, and they
were all uncompromising enemies of Spain.

The diversity and degree of internal differentiation among
the processes within the German territories concerned have
made it difficult to develop a common conceptual vocabulary
to describe them and to integrate them into both church history
and the more general history of this period. The much-la-
mented lack of a satisfactory monograph on the history of the
German Reformed church is also a consequence of the complex, internally differentiated political and theological background of the Second Reformation. The movements towards a
reformed type of Protestantism within Germany (390) simply
cannot be written as a history of Calvinism as it could be for
example in the case of Scotland. Nevertheless, while acknowledging the diversity of the individual examples, historians cannot evade their responsibility to organize and delimit evidence,
to offer a conceptual vocabulary that is both systematic and

---

4 I. Montgomery, Die cura religionis als Aufgabe des Fürsten. Perspektiven der
Zweiten Reformation in Schweden, in: Schilling, Reformierte Konfessionalisierung
(note 2), 266-290; P.G. Lindhardt, Skandinavische Kirchengeschichte seit dem
16. Jahrhundert, Göttingen 1982. On similar movements in Denmark see J.G.
Moller, Socialetiske aspekter af Niels Hemmingsens forfatterskab, in:
Kirkehistoriske Samlinger 1979, 7-56; in Bohemia: J. Burian, Philipp
Melanchthon, die Confessio Augustana und die tschechischen Länder, in: Archiv
für Reformationsgeschichte 73 (1982), 255-284, esp. 269ss., 278ss. Some Scottish
church historians interpret Andrew Melville's reform of John Knox's system as a
"Second Reformation."

analytical in character, and to formulate general models
without restricting themselves strictly to the terminology found
in the sources. In this sense I will attempt to draw together
some facts that I think are pertinent to the history and character of these processes and that justify the research paradigm of
a "Second Reformation."[5]

The question of perspective is as crucial for this paradigm as
it is for the formulation of historical terminology and models
in general: I am arguing backwards from the result, that is to
say, from either a successful or unsuccessful attempt to adopt a
Reformed/Calvinist confessional stance. When earlier theological and dogmatic currents such as Philippism are examined
from this perspective, they appear much differently than they
would in a dogmatic history that reflects Lutheran interests. I
am also arguing from the viewpoint of a secular historian who
wishes to place the events and developments of church history
and the history of theology within the context of more general
historical trends and structures. As I have argued elsewhere I
assume that within this syndrome of social, political, religious,
ecclesiastical and other factors all of them are equally important in principle, but I assign a certain leading role to religious
and theological structures and tendencies when examining the
Confessional Age. This role derives from a particular structural
characteristic of the early modern social system and from the

---

5 Schilling, Konfessionskonflikt (note 3), esp. 15-39, 365-375; idem, Konfessionalisierung als gesellschaftlicher Umbruch. Inhaltliche Perspektiven und massenmediale Darstellung, in: S. Quandt (ed.), Luther, die Reformation und die Deutschen, Paderborn 1982, 35-51; idem, Between the Territorial State and Urban
Liberty: Lutheranism and Calvinism in the County of Lippe, in: R. Po-chia Hsia
(ed.), Society and Religion in Reformation Germany, New Haven 1987; idem, Die
Konfessionalisierung im Reich—Religiöser und gesellschaftlicher Wandel in
Deutschland zwischen 1555 und 1620, in: Historische Zeitschrift 246 (1988), 1-45
(translation above 205-245); idem, Nation und Konfession in der frühneuzeitli-
chen Geschichte Europas. Zu den konfessionsgeschichtlichen Voraussetzungen der
frühmodernen Staatsbildung, in: K. Garber (Hg.), Nation und Literatur im
Europa der frühen Neuzeit, Tübingen 1989, 87-107; idem, Nationale Identität und
Konfession in der europäischen Geschichte der Neuzeit, in: B. Giesen (Hg.),
Nationale und kulturelle Identität in der europäischen Neuzeit, Frankfurt 1991.
On the historiographical side of the problem see idem, Konfessionsbildung, Kon-
fessionalisierung und konfessionelles Zeitalter—ein Literaturbericht, in: Geschichte
in Wissenschaft und Unterricht 42 (1991).—For a Marxist interpretation see: H.
Langer, Religion, Konfession und Kirche in der Epoche des Übergangs vom
Feudalismus zum Kapitalismus, in: Zeitschrift für Geschichtswissenschaft 32
(1984), 110-124.—Excellent, stimulating contribution for continuing the
discussion: W. Sparn, Zweite Reformation und Traditionalismus. Die
Stabilisierung des Protestantismus im Übergang zum 17. Jahrhundert, in:
Pirckheimer Jahrbuch 6 (1991), 117-131.

stage of historical development during the second half of the
sixteenth century: the Old European concept of politics, which
integrated religion and church, allowed historical processes in
the church, especially extraordinary events such as the Reformation and confessionalization, to affect politics and society
directly. The process of confessionalization developed in the
mid-sixteenth century from the previous period of the Reformation, affecting societal development throughout Europe, but
having particularly complex and powerful effects upon the
German Empire because of its multi-confessional character.
The Second Reformation was one of the most marked expressions of confessionalization. (391) In order to be historically
accurate in describing the Second Reformation, as well as
Lutheran and Catholic confessionalization, we must begin with
a societal syndrome—to use a concept from the natural sciences. This syndrome includes the specific events; political,
social, and prosopographical factors (e.g., supporters
[*Trägergruppen*] and social networks); institutional and legal
aspects (e.g., early modern state-building and "communalism");
religious and ecclesiastical developments, and changes in
mentality. All of these factors worked together and constantly
influenced each other, and their consequences for territorial,
national, and world history are correspondingly complex.

This essay cannot offer a complete discussion of the problem
under consideration, much less provide a history of German
"Calvinism." My purpose is to offer a problem-oriented sketch:
After a short characterization of the present state of research
(I), I will propose a periodization that, on the one hand, is
flexible enough to accommodate differences in timing and
circumstances, as well as regional variation, between the individual cases of the Second Reformation and on the other
reveals the salient characteristics of the general phenomenon
(II). I will then assess the historical significance of the Second
Reformation, both from the perspective of church history and
general history (III). My discussion of the supporters of the
Second Reformation and the channels of communication that
they employed, (IV) and of the introduction and reception of
the Second Reformation by different social groups (V) examines factors that I think are crucially important for understanding and interpreting the processes in question. Building
upon these elements I will sketch my own interpretation of the
"Second Reformation" in Germany (VI). In the epilogue I

discuss the terminological consequences of confessionalization for the confessional movements and the epoch in general (VII).

I. THE STATE OF RESEARCH

The historiography of the Second Reformation in Germany has a long tradition, beginning with contemporaries of the Reformation itself who wrote partisan accounts of it in support of their own positions.[6] An excellent example of this genre is *Die Geschichte der kursächsischen Kirchen- und Schulreformation*, written by Urban Pierius (1546-1616), a work rightly rescued from obscurity by Thomas Klein. Since the nineteenth century the problem has been treated in numerous studies of local and regional history, so it is possible to assemble a considerable (392) bibliography concerning the "Second Reformation." However, research on the Second Reformation has not achieved the standard of Reformation research either in number of studies or their level of analysis.

Leaving aside the interest in Calvinism generated by Max Weber which is only tangentially related to our topic, the importance of these processes, especially for political and social history, first became apparent to researchers in 1931 through an article by Otto Hintze entitled *Kalvinismus und Staatsraison in Brandenburg-Preußen zu Beginn des 17. Jahrhunderts.*[7] This study, however, was understood almost exclusively within the "Rise of Prussia" paradigm and was ill-suited to call attention to other cases of the "Second Reformation." The discussion only began after the Second World War with Jürgen Moltmann's study of the introduction of Calvinism in Bremen from the perspective of historical theology and Thomas Klein's study of the Second Reformation in Electoral Saxony. Shortly after these works were published two seminal essays appeared, one by church historian Franz Lau and the other by Marxist historian Gerhard Zschäbitz, which opened a general discussion on

---

6 Th. Klein (ed.), Geschichte der kursächsischen Kirchen- und Schulreformation von Urban Pierius, Marburg 1970, esp. 55ss.; B. Nischan, Reformation or Deformation? Lutheran and Reformed Views of Martin Luther in Brandenburg's "Second Reformation", in: K.C. Sessions and P.N. Bebb (eds.), Pietas et Societas, Kirksville 1985, 203-214; R. Kniebe, Der Schriftenstreit über die Reformation des Kurfürsten Johann Sigismund, Halle 1902.

7 O. Hintze, Die Epochen des evangelischen Kirchenregiments in Preußen, in: idem, Gesammelte Abhandlungen, ed. by G. Oestreich, vol. 3, 2nd edition Göttingen 1967, 56-96; idem, Kalvinismus und Staatsräson in Brandenburg zu Beginn des 17. Jahrhunderts, in: idem, Abhandlungen (o.c.), 255-312.

the character and significance of the conversion of German princes to the Reformed confession.[8]

Despite their differing presuppositions both Lau and Zschäbitz emphasized the political and societal background of these events, i.e. the interest of the territorial princes and states in supporting the Second Reformation (Lau) and the "driving force of socio-economic or political factors" (Zschäbitz). Zschäbitz rejected Thomas Klein's judgement that a simple "change of *course*" had taken place in the theological, humanist-pedagogical, and foreign policies of the princes; instead he postulated a fundamental "marked process of transformation in the (393) policies" of those territories. To him the events occurring in connection with the Second Reformation were a subcategory of the "Princely Reformation." I myself have adopted the paradigm of a "Second Reformation" in my book *Konfessionskonflikt und Staatsbildung* and have tried to formulate it as a consistent model of social and mental change.[9] In contrast to the Marxist approach of Zschäbitz, I have reconstructed the social and political meaning of the Second Reformation by pointing out the Old European system-specific connection between religion and society, between state and church. At the same time I have retained the quality of a "marked process of transformation" that Zschäbitz rightly observed. In addition I have tried to connect these events with the long-term historical process that constitutes the historical and theoretical context of the Reformation and confessionalization, as well as with the political and societal events of the "long sixteenth century." Historians have traditionally split the sixteenth century into two parts with the year 1555 as its dividing point, a periodization that incorrectly separates these contexts. To correct this traditional approach further research on the Second Reformation must be done with the historical continuity of the "long sixteenth century" in mind so that the historical factors at work during the second half of the six-

---

8 J. Moltmann, Christoph Pezel und der Calvinismus in Bremen, Bremen 1958; Th. Klein, Der Kampf um die Zweite Reformation in Kursachsen 1586-1591, Köln/Graz 1962; F. Lau, Die Zweite Reformation in Kursachsen. Neue Forschungen zum sogenannten sächsischen Kryptocalvinismus, in: Verantwortung. Festschrift für G. Noth, Berlin 1964, 137-154; G. Zschäbitz, Zur Problematik der sogenannten "Zweiten Reformation" in Deutschland, in: Wissenschaftliche Zeitschrift der Karl-Marx-Universität Leipzig, Gesellschafts- und sprachwissenschaftliche Reihe 14 (1965), 505-509.

9 Schilling, Konfessionskonflikt (note 3), 45-53, 387-391.

teenth century and the beginning of the seventeenth century can be interpreted against the background of this long-term development. On the basis of these theoretical and historical assumptions I consider the Second Reformation, illustrated by the example of the County of Lippe, to be part of an established historical paradigm, i.e. "early modern state-building," whereby "confessionalization" was part of the first, premature phase, characteristic of German history of the sixteenth and early seventeenth centuries.

Like the works of Moltmann and Klein my own model of a "Second Reformation" has not gone unchallenged.[10] (394) Most of the objections have focused on my formulation of terms in a narrow sense, and they have been raised by Reformed theologians and historians of Pietism.[11] Considering only the use of the term "Second Reformation," it appears that Catholic *church historians* have the fewest objections.[12] It has also been used by Lutheran *church historians* such as Werner Ulrich Deetjen without being tied to a specific historiographic interpretation.[13] Most *social and political historians* have accepted the concept (395) of a Second Reformation. They have not found persuasive the counter-arguments advanced during the first stage of the debate, above all by Ernst Walter Zeeden. In his introduction to the social history of the Reformation Rainer Wohl-

---

10 E.W. Zeeden, Zeitalter der Glaubenskämpfe (Literaturbericht), in: Geschichte in Wissenschaft und Unterricht 15 (1964), 106; A. Wiedeburg, in: Historisches Jahrbuch 84 (1964), 166. In contrast to these scholars H.A. Oberman obviously does not see any problem with the analytical terminology of "first", "second", and even "third" Reformation. See e.g. H.A. Oberman, Die Reformation. Von Wittenberg nach Genf, Göttingen 1986, 283-299.

11 Contra: W. Neuser, Review of Schilling, Konfessionskonflikt (note 3), in: Zeitschrift für Kirchengeschichte 94 (1983); idem, Die Erforschung der "Zweiten Reformation". Eine wissenschaftliche Fehlentwicklung, in: Schilling, Reformierte Konfessionalisierung (note 2), 379-386._Pro: H. Faulenbach, Hermann, Graf zu Neuenahr und Moers, in: 400 Jahre Bedburger Synode, Bedburg 1971, 72-88, here 83.

12 B. Gassmann, Ecclesia Reformata. Die Kirche in den reformierten Bekenntnisschriften, Freiburg/Basel/Wien 1968, 231-268; A. Schröer, Die Reformation in Westfalen, Münster 1979, here 428-481; E. Iserloh, Die deutsche Fürstenreformation, in: H. Jedin (ed.), Reformation, Katholische Reformation und Gegenreformation, Freiburg/Basel/Wien 1967, 420-427.

13 W.U. Deetjen, Das Ende der Entente cordial zwischen den Bruderkirchen und Brüderdynastien Pfalz-Zweibrücken-Württemberg und Pfalz-Neuburg. Deutungsversuche und Dokumente zur Vorgeschichte des zweibrückischen Konfessionswechsels (1575-1580), in: Blätter für württembergische Kirchengeschichte 82 (1982), 49, 215; W. Bellardi, Die Geschichte der "Christlichen Gemeinschaft", Straßburg/Leipzig 1934 with regard to Bucer and Strasbourg.

feil stated that the term "Second Reformation" was ideally
suited "not only to encompass conceptually the origins and
diversity of specific circumstances, but also to incorporate
them into a comprehensive understanding of the Reformation."[14] By contrast, in spite of Zschäbitz' early reaction the
discussion initiated by the works of Moltmann and Klein had
little or no effect upon *Marxist research*. This must be attributed in part to the lack of interest in the second half of the
sixteenth century shown by historiography (396) in the German
Democratic Republic.[15] However, the concept has become established in foreign historiography, especially within the
Anglo-Saxon world, where both detailed studies and general
overviews of the "Second Reformation" have been published.[16]
Reflecting the syndrome-like character of the events, the
processes of interest to us have been examined not only in
monographs on the Second Reformation within the Empire and

---

14 V. Press, Die Grafen von Erbach und die Anfänge des reformierten
Bekenntnisses in Deutschland, in: H. Bannasch and H.-P. Lachmann (eds.), Aus
Geschichte und ihren Hilfswissenschaften. Festschrift für Walter Heinemeyer zum
65. Geburtstag, Marburg 1979, 656; idem, Stadt und territoriale Konfessionsbildung, in: F. Petri (ed.), Kirche und gesellschaftlicher Wandel in deutschen und
niederländischen Städten der werdenden Neuzeit, Köln/Wien 1980, 283s.; P.
Münch, Zucht und Ordnung. Reformierte Kirchenverfassung im 16. und 17. Jahrhundert, Stuttgart 1978, 14; G. Schormann, Aus der Frühzeit der Rintelner Juri-
stenfakultät, Bückeburg 1977, 17; idem, Simon VI. und seine Bibliothek. Ein Beitrag zur Zweiten Reformation in Lippe, in: Jahrbuch des Vereins für westfälische
Kirchengeschichte 70 (1977); R. Wohlfeil, Einführung, in: Reformation oder frühbürgerliche Revolution?, München 1972, 62; H. Klueting, Gab es eine "Zweite
Reformation"? Ein Beitrag zur Terminologie des Konfessionellen Zeitalters, in:
Geschichte in Wissenschaft und Unterricht 38 (1987), 261-279; idem, Das Konfessionelle Zeitalter 1525-1648, Stuttgart 1989.
15 S. Looß, Bürgerliche "Modernisierungskonzeptionen" am Beispiel der städ-
tisch-reformatorischen Bewegung Anfang des 16. Jahrhunderts, in: Jahrbuch für
Wirtschaftsgeschichte 3 (1982), 184; K. Czok, Der "Calvinistensturm" 1592/93 in
Leipzig—seine Hintergründe und bildliche Darstellung, in: Jahrbuch zur
Geschichte der Stadt Leipzig, 123-144; E. Koch, Zwingli, Calvin und der Calvi-
nismus im Geschichtsbild des Marxismus, in: Zwingliana 14 (1974/75), 61-88;
Hoyer, Staat (note 3).
16 Cohn, Princes (note 3); Nischan, Reformation (note 6); idem, The "Fractio
Panis": A Reformed Communion Practice in Late Reformation Germany, in:
Church History 53 (1984), 17-29; idem, The Second Reformation in Brandenburg:
Aims and Goals, in: The Sixteenth Century Journal 14 (1983), 173-187; idem,
John Bergius: Irenicism and the Beginning of Official Religious Toleration in
Brandenburg-Prussia, in: Church History 51 (1982), 389-404; idem, The Exor-
cism Controversy and Baptism in the Late Reformation, in: The Sixteenth Cen-
tury Journal 18 (1987), 31-50; idem, The Schools of Brandenburg and the
"Second Reformation": Centers of Calvinist Learning and Propaganda, in: R.
Schnucker (ed.), Calviniana, Kirksville 1988, 215-233.

in individual territories,[17] but also in studies that focus on particular issues that were important during the sixteenth and early seventeenth centuries. These include intensive research on humanism, (397) education and universities[18] and biographical, prosopographical, and other studies in social history, focusing above all on the social networks of princely dynasties, the nobility, and the burgher academics,[19] including (398) the

17 V. Press, Calvinismus und Territorialstaat. Regierung und Zentralbehörden der Kurpfalz 1559—1619, Stuttgart 1970; see also the many essays of G. Menk on Hesse and the Wetterau published in the journals: Zeitschrift für hessische Geschichte und Landeskunde, Hessisches Jahrbuch für Landesgeschichte, Jahrbuch für westdeutsche Landesgeschichte. R. Glawischnig, Niederlande, Kalvinismus und Reichsgrafenstand, Marburg 1973; Schleswig-Holsteinische Kirchengeschichte, ed. by the Verein für schleswig-holsteinische Kirchengeschichte, vols. 2 and 3, Neumünster 1982 and 1984; Schröer, Reformation (note 12).

18 G. Menk, Die Hohe Schule Herborns in ihrer Frühzeit, 1584-1660. Ein Beitrag zum Hochschulwesen des deutschen Kalvinismus im Zeitalter der Gegenreformation, Wiesbaden 1981; A. Schindling, Humanistische Hochschule und freie Reichsstadt. Gymnasium und Akademie in Straßburg 1538-1621, Wiesbaden 1977; G. Schormann, Academia Ernestina. Die schaumburgische Universität zu Rinteln an der Weser (1610/21-1810), Marburg 1982; G. Menk, Territorialstaat und Schulwesen in der frühen Neuzeit. Eine Untersuchung zur religiösen Dynamik in den Grafschaften Nassau und Sayn, in: Jahrbuch für westdeutsche Landesgeschichte 9 (1983), 177-220; idem, Konfessionelle Haltung im Konflikt. Eine Fallstudie am Beispiel des Pfarrers Johannes Croll, in: Monatshefte für Evangelische Kirchengeschichte des Rheinlandes 33 (1984), 229-273; A. Friedrich, Die Gelehrtenschulen in Marburg, Kassel und Korbach zwischen Melanchthonianismus und Ramismus in der zweiten Hälfte des 16. Jahrhunderts, Darmstadt/Marburg 1983; N. Hammerstein, Schule, Hochschule und Respublica Litteraria, in: Res Publica Litteraria, Wiesbaden 1987, 93-110; idem, The University of Heidelberg in the Early Modern Period, in: History of Universities 6 (1986), 105-133.

19 F.H. Schubert, Ludwig Camerarius 1573-1651, Kallmünz 1955; G. Menk, Landgraf Wilhelm IV. von Hessen-Kassel, Franz Hotmann und die hessisch-französischen Beziehungen vor und nach der Bartholomäusnacht, in: Zeitschrift des Vereins für hessische Geschichte und Landeskunde 88 (1980/81), 55-82; idem, Philipp Ludwig I. von Hanau-Münzenberg (1553-1580). Bildungsgeschichte und Politik eines Reichsgrafen in der zweiten Hälfte des 16. Jahrhunderts, in: Hessisches Jahrbuch für Landesgeschichte 32 (1982), 127-163; idem, "Qui trop embrasse, peu estreind." Politik und Persönlichkeit Graf Johannes VI. von Nassau-Dillenburg 1580-1606, in: Jahrbuch für westdeutsche Landesgeschichte 7 (1981), 119-157; Press, Grafen von Erbach (note 14); idem, Graf Otto von Solms-Hungen und die Gründung der Stadt Mannheim, in: Mannheimer Hefte 1 (1975), 9-23; idem, Die Landschaft aller Grafen von Solms. Ein ständisches Experiment am Beginn des 17. Jahrhunderts, in: Hessisches Jahrbuch für Landesgeschichte 27 (1977), 37-106; idem, Die Ritterschaft im Kraichgau zwischen Reich und Territorium 1500-1623, in: Zeitschrift für die Geschichte des Oberrheins 121 (N.S. 82) (1974), 35-97; H. Faulenbach, Hermann von Neuenahr (1520-1578), in: Rheinische Lebensbilder, vol. 8 (1980), 105-123; R. Rübel, Graf Arnold von Bentheim-Steinfurt, in: Westfälische Lebensbilder, vol. 9 (1968), 18-33; W. Baumann, Ernst Friedrich von Baden-Durlach, Stuttgart 1962; H. Richter, Johann von Münster, in: Westfälische Lebensbilder, vol. 4 (1933), 112-125.

SECOND REFORMATION 257

newly emerging Protestant pastoral families.[20] Other relevant
research includes studies on the late urban Reformation,[21] the
origin of a German national literature at the end of the sixteenth century,[22] the history (399) of political thought,[23] early
modern poor relief,[24] and finally, of course, histories of theology and dogma. Interestingly enough histories of dogma tend
to focus on the second half of the sixteenth century, especially
upon Lutheran orthodoxy,[25] but in so doing they also devote

20 R. v. Thadden, Die brandenburgisch-preußischen Hofprediger im 17. und 18.
Jahrhundert, Berlin 1959; L. Schorn-Schütte, Prediger an protestantischen Höfen
der Frühneuzeit. Zur politischen und sozialen Stellung einer neuen bürgerlichen
Führungsgruppe in der höfischen Gesellschaft des 17. Jahrhunderts. Dargestellt
am Beispiel von Hessen-Kassel, Hessen-Darmstadt und Braunschweig-Wolfenbüttel, in: H. Schilling and H. Diederiks (eds.), Bürgerliche Eliten in den Niederlanden und Nordwestdeutschland, Köln/Wien 1985, 275-336.

21 K. v. Greyerz, The late City Reformation. The case of Colmar, 1522-1628,
Wiesbaden 1980; idem, Basels kirchliche und konfessionelle Beziehungen zum
Oberrhein im späten 16. und frühen 17. Jahrhundert, in: M. Bircher, W. Sparn
and E. Weyrauch (eds.), Schweizerisch-deutsche Beziehungen im konfessionellen
Zeitalter. Beiträge zur Kulturgeschichte 1580-1650, Wiesbaden 1984, 227-252; H.
Schilling, Bürgerkämpfe in Aachen zu Beginn des 17. Jahrhunderts. Konflikte im
Rahmen der alteuropäischen Stadtgesellschaft oder im Umkreis der frühbürger-
lichen Revolution?, in: Zeitschrift für historische Forschung 1 (1974), 175-231;
idem, Dortmund im 16. und 17. Jahrhundert—Reichsstädtische Gesellschaft,
Reformation und Konfessionalisierung, in: G. Luntowsky and N. Reimann (eds.),
Dortmund—1100 Jahre Stadtgeschichte, Dortmund 1982, 151-202; idem, Innovation through Migration: The Settlements of Calvinistic Netherlanders in Six-
teenth- and Seventeenth-Century Central and Western Europe, in: Histoire
sociale—Social History 16, No. 31 (May 1983), 7-33.

22 K. Langvik-Johannessen, Die Rolle der Kalvinisten in der ästhetischen Ent-
wicklung der deutschen Literatur, in: Dikt og idé, Festskrift til Ole Koppang, Oslo
1981, 59-72; K. Garber, Der deutsche Sonderweg—Gedanken zu einer calvinistischen Alternative um 1600, in: A. Schöne (ed.), Kontroversen, alte und neue.
Akten des VII. Internationalen Germanistenkongresses, Göttingen 1985, vol. 9,
Tübingen 1987, 165-172; idem, Zentraleuropäischer Calvinismus und deutsche
"Barock"-Literatur. Zu den konfessionspolitischen Ursprüngen der deutschen
Nationalliteratur, in: Schilling, Reformierte Konfessionalisierung (note 2), 317-
348.

23 G. Menk, Die politische Kultur in den Wetterauer Grafschaften am Ende
des 16. und zu Anfang des 17. Jahrhunderts, in: Hessisches Jahrbuch für
Landesgeschichte 34 (1984), 67-100.

24 R. Jütte, Andreas Hyperius (1511-1564) und die Reform des frühneuzeitlichen Armenwesens, in: Archiv für Reformationsgeschichte 75 (1984), 113-138.

25 R. Kolb, Nikolaus von Amsdorf (1483-1565): popular polemics in the preser-
vation of Luther's legacy, Nieuwkoop 1978; idem, The Flacian Rejection of the
Concordia. Prophetic Style and Action in the German Late Reformation, in:
Archiv für Reformationsgeschichte 73 (1982), 196-216; idem, Dynamics of Party
Conflict in the Saxon Late Reformation. Gnesio-Lutherans vs. Philippists, in: The
Journal of Modern History 49 (1977), 1289-1305.; Andresen, Handbuch (note 2);
H. Leube, Kalvinismus und Luthertum im Zeitalter der Orthodoxie, Leipzig 1928;
P. Tschackert, Die Entstehung der lutherischen und der reformierten Kirchen-
lehre samt ihren innerprotestantischen Gegensätze, 1st edition 1910, reprint Göt-

some attention to its opponents and thus to the stream of tradition that led to the Second Reformation.

Taken as a whole the Second Reformation and its historiography can be compared to an iceberg in that it, and the
studies referring to it, constitutes only the smallest, visible part
of the entire phenomenon. Future research must take this fact
into consideration. Restricting research on the Second Reformation to the few cases where it was successful (400) would
narrow the field considerably and would give a false impression of the broad stream towards a reformed type of Protestantism present during the preparatory phase. In the County of
Waldeck, for example, there were humanist and Philippist currents in addition to the Calvinist inclinations of the count,
although no Second Reformation ever took place there.[26] Similar processes can be detected in the histories of Emden, Wesel,
and Duisburg, and also incidentally in Basel, even if these
cities cannot be included among the most important examples
of the Second Reformation.[27]

As a result of this review of research I propose that a history
of the "Second Reformation" in Germany is a goal worth
striving for. The deeper insight into German history which this
would provide outweighs terminological reservations, particularly since the reservations raised by historians of theology can
easily be addressed. The "Second Reformation" paradigm is
especially well suited to serve as the organizational core for the
modern history of the Reformed confession in Germany that is
still lacking. Moreover, this concept makes it clear why such a
history, in contrast to the history of the expansion of reformed
Protestantism in western Europe, most obvious in the case of
Scotland, cannot be written simply as a history of Calvinism. It
provides conceptual advantages even for the history of dogma
and of theology to the extent that dogmatic attribution is flexible and the most important stages of theological development
and regional variations can be described and labeled. Use of
the term emphasizes (401) the unity of the processes at work in
church history from the beginning of the Reformation through

tingen 1979.

26 Friedrich, Gelehrtenschulen (note 18), 129-170, esp. 160-163; Schilling,
Konfessionskonflikt (note 3), 335, note 226; G. Menk, Rechtliche und staatstheoretische Aspekte im waldeckischen Herrschaftskonflikt 1588-1624, in: Geschichtsblätter für Waldeck 72 (1984), 45-74.

27 Schilling, Konfessionskonflikt (note 3), 48-50, Klein (ed.), Geschichte (note
6), Introduction.

confessionalization on the one hand, and the differing concepts
of the "Reformation" that were espoused during the first and
second halves of the sixteenth century on the other. Finally it
links the processes of church history with those of social and
constitutional history in the sense described above, a linkage
that can only benefit the history of dogma and theology.

II. Phases in the History of the Second Reformation

At the outset it seems wise to provide an organizing structure
for the processes of the Second Reformation by dividing its
history into several stages or phases. This will prevent the
sharply defined limits of our topic from being obscured by the
broad range of examples.[28] The entire process can be divided
into several coherent parts. In comparatively few cases did the
process result in an attempted Second Reformation, let alone its
successful introduction, and therefore the phases must take into
account not only the events themselves, but also especially the
preparatory changes in the theological and dogmatic discussion.

*First Phase: the pre-confessional phase, late 1540's to the
early 1570's.* During the first phase, which extended from
Luther's death to the beginning of a pervasive change of political and religious climate within the Empire and in Europe
during the first half of the 1570's, the most important factors
at work within the Empire were those that emerged from the
insoluble conundrums of the Reformation period. These were
the differences between Zwinglian upper German theology and
Erasmian Dutch theology on the one hand and Lutheranism on
the other, the struggles for succession surrounding the preservation of the Lutheran inheritance, aggravated by questions of
political ethics in connection with the Interim crisis, and
finally the problem of humanism or the humanists.[29] This latter
factor was on the one hand a subsidiary aspect of the first two
(402) conflicts, but on the other hand it developed its own

---

28 Goeters, Genesis (note 2).

29 To name only a very few works on the debate on humanism: G.A. Benrath,
Die Lehre des Humanismus und des Antitrinitarismus, in: Handbuch der Dog-
men- und Theologiegeschichte, vol. 3, Göttingen 1984, esp. 39s.; J.F.G. Goeters,
Die evangelischen Kirchenordnungen Westfalens im Reformationsjahrhundert, in:
Westfälische Zeitschrift 113 (1963), 111-168; W.F. Dankbaar, Hervormers en
Humanisten, Amsterdam 1978; H.R. Guggisberg, Basel in the Sixteenth Century,
St. Louis 1982; W. Kaegi, Humanistische Kontinuität im konfessionellen Zeitalter,
Basel 1954.

historical dynamic during this time, because the emerging trend of confessionalization clashed with the hope which some humanists still cherished for a mediatory Christianity independent of the dogmatic fronts. In the end the humanists were forced to choose in favor of one of the three confessions present in the Empire and thus to recognize the inevitability of identifying with one of the confessional churches as the only concrete and inescapable expression of public Christianity in their time. On the Protestant side it appears that a comparatively large number of these humanists, above all non-theologians, finally joined the Reformed movement, some of them forced to do so by Lutheran orthodoxy. Few of these Reformed humanists, however, became fierce partisans of the Reformed confession. On the contrary, they were advocates of tolerance and irenicism. By ignoring humanism as a factor some historians have falsely attributed certain currents of tolerance and liberalism within Reformed countries to Calvinism itself whereas they actually emerged from the humanist tradition.

The humanists, many of them students of Melanchthon although some of them were influenced primarily by Erasmus, were concentrated in upper Germany, especially in the imperial cities, in Electoral Saxony, in the lower Rhine area, and in the adjoining northwestern German region. They initially tried to steer an unorthodox and non-confessional course on the basis of Lutheran or upper German Reformed theology. Melanchthon and the Philippists pursued this goal in Electoral Saxony, as did Polish reformer John a Lasco and Dutch burgomaster Petrus Medmann in Emden, Albert Rizaeus Hardenberg in Emden and Bremen, and Jacob Schöpper and Johannes Lambach in the humanist Reformation of Dortmund. Basel can also be included in this group. The Calvinist principle won out in the city church there as the "memory of Erasmus," which had endured for a particularly long time, finally faded. In some cases, such as Nuremberg, the development could be stopped at the Philippist stage, so that Reformed/Calvinist confessionalization never had a chance to succeed.[30] (403)

---

30 H. Klugkist-Hesse, Leben und Wirken des Petrus Medmann, geheimen Rates des Kurfürsten Hermann von Wied, in: Monatshefte für Rheinische Kirchengeschichte 26 (1932), 321-348; E. von Reeken, Die Marginalien des Petrus Medmann (1507-1584), in: Lias 7 (1980), 151-181; A. Rauhaus, Untersuchungen zur Entstehung, Gestalt und Lehre des kleinen Emder Katechismus von 1554, Diss.

The Second Reformation in the Palatinate, which was so significant for broader developments, emerged from this kind of environment. The new ecclesiastical and religious policies that were introduced by Friedrich III had been formulated by the influential counts of Erbach together with a group of learned burgher councillors who came primarily from southern German imperial cities. These men had been influenced by Philippist or upper German Reformed and humanist thought and supported a pre-orthodox concept of church reform.[31] Volker Press has shown that the counts of Erbach maintained this middle course in their territory until the Palatinate became irrevocably Calvinist at the beginning of the seventeenth century. The counts then broke with the Palatinate and shifted into the orthodox Lutheran stream, aligning themselves politically with Württemberg. This small territory in Odenwald must be numbered with those cases where the Philippist phase did not lead to a Second Reformation.

Philippism, however, was a position that stemmed from an older phase of the Reformation, and Friedrich III of the Palatinate quickly abandoned it. His policy of church reform in the Palatinate is among the earliest evidence of an internal developmental dynamic which entered Germany along with the new variety of Protestantism that had originated in Geneva under the conditions of the Confessional Age. The Palatine reform created a new situation within the Empire, especially through the promulgation of the Heidelberg Catechism, its confessional manifesto.[32] (404) The confessional Calvinist model gradually

Göttingen 1977; M. Smid, Johannes a Lasco, in: Neue Deutsche Biographie, vol. 13, Berlin 1982, 657; B. Spiegel, D. Albert Rizaeus Hardenberg, Bremen 1869; H. Engelhardt, Der Irrlehreprozeß gegen Albert Hardenberg 1547-1561, phil. Diss. Frankfurt 1961; Schilling, Dortmund (note 21), 159ss.; Schubert, Camerarius (note 19); Press, Ritterschaft (note 19); Kaegi, Kontinuität (note 29), 18; v. Greyerz, Basel (note 21); K. Leder, Die religiöse Entwicklung Nürnbergs nach dem Augsburger Religionsfrieden, in: Nürnberg—Geschichte einer europäischen Stadt, München 1971, 279-283, esp. 279; R. van Dülmen, Orthodoxie und Kirchenreform. Der Nürnberger Prediger Johannes Saubert, in: Zeitschrift für bayerische Landesgeschichte 33 (1970), 636-786, esp. 636ss., 674ss.

31 Schubert, Camerarius (note 19); W. Seeling, Der sogenannte Calvinismus in der Pfalz. Versuch einer Klärung, in: Blätter für Pfälzische Kirchengeschichte und religiöse Volkskunde 37/38 (1970/71); Press, Grafen von Erbach (note 14), 679-682; idem, Stadt (note 14).

32 W. Henss, Der Heidelberger Katechismus im konfessionspolitischen Kräftespiel seiner Frühzeit, Zürich 1983; Rauhaus, Untersuchungen (note 30), esp. 210s., 217; Press, Calvinismus (Note 17); E. Sehling (ed.), Die evangelischen Kirchenordnungen des 16. Jahrhunderts, vol. 14, Kurpfalz, edited by J.F.G. Goeters, Tübingen 1969.

attracted new followers within the Empire itself. As a result it
became more and more difficult to maintain a Philippist stance
within Lutheranism, a position that was older, preorthodox,
and thus increasingly anachronistic. The Palatinate became a
point of entry for new Protestant streams that originated
outside of the Empire and which increasingly overwhelmed the
older movements.

In a smaller and less important context similar events took
place in the lower Rhine area at the same time as those in the
Palatinate: When Wesel came under the influence of the
Gnesio-Lutheran Heshus at the beginning of the 1560's and the
city council planned to steer the hitherto humanist-Philippist
city church into the orthodox Lutheran stream, it was prevented from doing so by a burgher movement. Its demand that
the preachers "teach according to the Bible alone" led step by
step to a weakening of the humanist-Philippist tradition and to
the city church becoming Calvinist in character. The presence
of a Dutch exile church helped to tip the balance in this direction as well.[33] The early shift to Calvinism in both places was a
result of special conditions: in the case of the Palatinate a personal decision by the Elector, in Wesel the introduction of
Reformed or Calvinist theology by Dutch and Walloon refugees
and its acceptance by the German burgher commune. In both
cases these specific conditions resulted in a breach of the legal
and political barriers against Calvinism that had been erected
by the Peace of Augsburg in 1555.

The early decision for Calvinism in the Palatinate and the
publication of the Heidelberg Catechism in 1563 constituted an
important milestone on the road to the Second Reformation.
Whether the Palatine reform can itself be described as a Second
Reformation in the strict sense of the term requires further
discussion. However, there are a number of apparent differences between the processes at work in the Palatinate and those
which took place between 1580 and 1620. First of all, there
was no systematic purge of the clergy and bureaucracy. Philippists were able to exercise an important influence alongside of
the strictly Calvinist party within the church, state, and
schools. Elector Friedrich acted very cautiously and defensively
in his foreign and imperial policies, in stark contrast to his

---

33 Schilling, Niederländische Exulanten im 16. Jahrhundert. Ihre Stellung im
Sozialgefüge und im religiösen Leben deutscher und englischer Städte, Gütersloh
1972, 90.

Calvinist successors at the end of the sixteenth century.[34] Finally, the "ideology" of the Second Reformation (405) as a fulfillment of the Lutheran Reformation apparently played no role as yet during the 1560's.

Cases in which the Philippist "transitional phase" was much longer are far more typical of the Second Reformation than those where the entire process was squeezed into a few short years as occurred in the Palatinate and in Wesel. The example of Hesse is particularly illuminating in that Landgrave Wilhelm IV never questioned the pre-confessional Lutheran stance of the Hessian territorial church. Despite his sympathy for the new Genevan theology and intensive contacts with French Huguenots, he maintained his father's traditional policy. Some of the Wetterau counts maintained a similar policy at first,[35] until the dominant influence of Nassau spurred them to adopt Reformed confessionalization and the Second Reformation connected with it. Even during the final phase, when a Second Reformation had already been introduced in a number of places throughout the Empire, there were usually explicitly Philippist intermediate stages. This occurred in Lippe, for example, where Johannes von Exter, a student of Melanchthon, became superintendent of the territorial church during the late 1570's and organized it according to Philippist principles.[36] Martin Schalling actively promoted a Philippist position in the Upper Palatinate, giving rise to the hope that this eastern territory, which was ruled by the same dynasty as the Rhenish-Palatinate, could escape the Second Reformation on this theological basis even as late as the early 1590's.[37] There was, however, little chance that the pre-confessional stance of Philippism could hold its own during the late phase against the

---

34 Schubert, Camerarius (note 19), 22; W. Hollweg, Der Augsburger Reichstag von 1566 und seine Bedeutung für die Entstehung der reformierten Kirche und ihres Bekenntnisses, Neunkirchen-Vluyn 1964.

35 S. Schulz, Wilhelm IV., Landgraf von Hessen-Kassel, phil. Diss. München 1941; Menk, Landgraf Wilhelm IV. (note 19); idem, Philipp-Ludwig I. (note 19); see also the essays of G. Menk and G. Schmidt on Hesse and the Wetterau in: Schilling (ed.), Reformierte Konfessionalisierung (note 2), 154-183, 184-213.

36 Schilling, Konfessionskonflikt (note 3).

37 V. Press, Das evangelische Amberg im 16. Jahrhundert, in: Ausstellungskataloge des Stadtarchives Amberg, No. 1, Amberg 1983, 7-28; idem, Das evangelische Amberg zwischen Reformation und Gegenreformation, in: Amberg 1034-1984—Aus tausend Jahren Stadtgeschichte, Amberg 1984, 119-136; idem, Die "Zweite Reformation" in der Kurpfalz, in: Schilling, Reformierte Konfessionalisierung (note 2), 104-129.

advance of confessionalization and the virulence of the Calvinist church system that had been established in Geneva,
Western Europe, and in many imperial territories, most importantly in the Rhenish-Palatinate and the Wetterau region.

*Second Phase: The Crisis of Philippism and the Pressure for
Confessionalization, the 1570's.* The 1570's were an intermediate stage and a transitional phase during which the pre-
orthodox mediating party of upper German Reformed, Philippist, and humanist provenance went through a crisis and was
destroyed. At the same time decisive shifts took place that
worked in favor of the Second Reformation, preparing the way
for its smooth introduction during the next phase. During this
transitional phase, impulses from outside of (406) the Empire
and internal German developments had effects that were
equally important. The renewal of Catholicism achieved at
Trent and the expansion of Genevan Calvinism resulted in
increasing polarization throughout Europe. Accordingly the
period of functioning religious peace, i.e. the coexistence of
Protestantism and pre-Tridentine Catholicism, came to an end
within the Empire. The confessionalization of church, state,
and society had begun.[38] In social terms a generational change
had occurred: in the place of the theologians, politicians, and
princes who valued the religious peace of 1555 as a hard-won
political compromise, men rose to power on both sides who
actively sought to reshape, demarcate, and revise. They were
prepared to gamble with the Augsburg compromise in order to
gain new territory, expand the authority of their states, and to
further their reputations.

The first blows suffered by the religious peace came from
outside of the Empire: the experience of a flood of refugees
fleeing the militant Counter-Reformation imposed by Spain
upon the Netherlands and the St. Bartholomew's Day Massacre
aroused Protestant princely courts to take action.[39] The fear of
a Catholic assault within the Empire born of these traumatic

---

38 Case study: Po-Hsia, Society (note 5); Schilling, Konfessionalisierung im
Reich (note 5).

39 Ph. Denis, Les églises d'étrangers en pays rhénans, 1538-1564, Paris 1984;
B. Vogler, Huguenots et protestants allemands vers 1572, in: Actes du Colloque
l'Amiral de Coligny et son temps, Paris 1974; L.W. Spitz, Imperialism, Particu-
larism and Toleration in the Holy Roman Empire, in: A. Soman (ed.), The Massacre of St. Bartholemew. Reappraisals and Documents, Den Haag 1974; Menk,
Landgraf Wilhelm IV. (note 19); R.M. Kingdon, Myths About the St. Bartholomew's Day Massacres, 1572-1576, Cambridge, Mass. 1988.

events that occured during the western European Counter-Reformation awakened a will among German Protestants to close their own ranks and a desire for a formal, confessional orthodoxy. Lutherans had an additional motive: since imperial law protected only the pure Lutheran form of Protestantism, it was obviously to their advantage if they could exclude heterodox opinions from the Lutheran camp, ensuring that they alone enjoyed the protection of the Augsburg religious peace. Within Reformed and Calvinist circles, on the other hand, political and theological leaders quickly became convinced that Protestantism could protect itself only by becoming more dynamic and aggressive and that further dogmatic and organizational changes in the church were necessary to achieve this end. In their opinion the Reformation could only be completed and the churches made invulnerable to assaults by newly strengthened Catholicism if the Protestant churches eliminated the last vestiges of Catholicism from both their doctrine and life. Thus Lutherans and Calvinists not only responded in different ways to the pressures of the Counter-Reformation, but they inevitably attacked each another and so became irreconcilable enemies.

In this situation the Philippists suffered two blows in quick succession that were both a signal and a foretaste of things to come. They were deprived of their most important strongholds by the purge of the church, bureaucracy, and court of Electoral Saxony during 1574, (407) which removed the strong Philippist influence previously present there, and by the re-Lutheranization of the Palatinate in 1576 by the new Elector Ludwig.[40] Their position as mediators between the various Protestant doctrines no longer had any political backing worth mentioning within the Empire. The diaspora of Philippist exiles, dozens of professors, clergymen, and bureaucrats who were forced to leave their positions because of the orthodox Lutheran purge in Saxony and the Palatinate, meant at the same time a wider sowing of seeds which could germinate into Second Reformations in the territories that gave refuge to them. In addition about the same number of exiled ministers from the Netherlands were pursuing similar goals, particularly in the western territories of the Empire.

At present we have only a bare outline of how these pro-

---

40 E. Koch, Der kursächsische Philippismus und seine Krise, in: Schilling, Reformierte Konfessionalisierung (note 2), 60-78; Press, Calvinismus (note 17).

cesses of transformation worked. More exact prosopographical studies of specific areas are needed to determine how and to what extent territorial churches that later entered the concordial Lutheran camp were affected at an earlier stage by Philippist movements. This occurred, for example, in the case of Brunswick-Wolfenbüttel, where Philippist/Crypto-Calvinists were strongly entrenched for several decades. In any case it is clear that nearly every territory that later experienced a Second Reformation had taken in a greater or lesser number of exile theologians—above all Nassau and Bremen, but also Hesse, Lippe, and Anhalt.[41] The example of Emden shows strikingly how confessionalization advanced at the expense of older traditions during these years. During the late 1570's the Dutch exile minister Menso Alting, who came to Emden via the Palatinate, played a crucial role in reshaping the pre-orthodox Reformed church organized by John a Lasco into a genuinely Calvinist confessional church, thus in a certain sense introducing the Second Reformation.[42]

On the other hand the concord movement pushed the Lutherans into confessionalization as well, further isolating and excluding the Philippist faction within pre-orthodox Lutheranism.[43] Accordingly the Philippists gradually became a genuinely Crypto-Calvinist diaspora. The same is true for some princes who kept their distance from the movement of concord. (408)

Third Phase: Confessionalization and the Introduction of the Second Reformation, ca. 1580-1619. Lutheran confessionalization ended successfully in the efforts for concord and the publication of the *Book of Concord* with the signatures of princes and theologians in 1580. The other side also moved step by step along the path of confessionalization. On the one hand,

41 Moltmann, Pezel (note 8), H. Schieckel, Pfarrer aus Kursachsen in Norddeutschland, in: Herbergen der Christenheit, Jahrbuch für deutsche Kirchengeschichte 1967, 55-75; Schilling, Konfessionskonflikt (note 3), 171ss., 180, 245s.; Menk, Politik (note 19); idem, Territorialstaat (note 18).

42 H. Klugkist-Hesse, Menso Alting. Eine Gestalt aus der Kampfzeit der calvinistischen Kirche, Berlin 1928; M. Smid, Ostfriesische Kirchengeschichte, Pewsum 1974; H. Schilling, Reformation und Bürgerfreiheit. Emdens Weg zur calvinistischen Stadtrepublik, in: B. Moeller (ed.), Stadt und Kirche im 16. Jahrhundert, Gütersloh 1978, 128-161. (English translation in: H. Schilling, Civic Calvinism, Kirksville 1991.)

43 M. Brecht and R. Schwarz (eds.), Bekenntnis und Einheit der Kirche: Studien zum Konkordienbuch, Stuttgart 1980; E. Koch, Aufbruch und Weg: Studien zur lutherischen Bekenntnisbildung im 16. Jahrhundert, Stuttgart 1983.

as has already been emphasized, the *Formula of Concord* exerted pressure, especially where the Philippist tradition and the new Reformed/Calvinist impulse had to hold its own within a Lutheran environment. It is possible to speak here of a struggle provoked by the efforts for concord, most evident in case of Palatinate-Zweibrücken, which lay within Württemberg's sphere of influence and where the Second Reformation grew out of a "crisis of concord," or in Baden-Durlach, where Margrave Friedrich introduced the Second Reformation in the so-called *Staffortschen Buch* of 1599, which contained his personal theological critique of the efforts for concord.[44]

On the other hand confessional consolidation unmistakably followed its internal logic within the Reformed or Calvinist churches, most clearly in regions that had close contact with western Europe. Nassau and the Wetterau counties, for example, were open to influences from Germany and from western Europe, especially from the Netherlands. Bremen was also affected by these currents, apart from the role that the Saxon exile Christoph Pezel played there. Besides other external factors such as the accession of a new prince (1583 in the Palatinate, 1586 in Electoral Saxony, and 1592 in Hesse-Kassel) the combination of an internal logic of development and the external pressure for confessionalization seems to have determined the rhythm of events which resulted in a Second Reformation. Chronologically Nassau was the first to take this step, followed by the Wetterau counties, by Bremen, and by Bentheim, all of them situated in areas that were exposed to the direct influence of Calvinism, above all from the Netherlands. This was most obvious in the case of Nassau, which even adopted the Middelburg church ordinance of the Dutch Reformed church. By contrast there was an attempt in Anhalt to combine Lutheran and Reformed elements, illustrated by the draft proposal for a new liturgy composed in 1599.[45]

Dynastic and other personnel networks had a dynamic effect linking particularly the Palatinate, Hesse, and the Netherlands with the different German territories: the calvinization of Anhalt, where the dynasty was linked both to the ruling house of the Palatinate and to the house of Orange, was accelerated in this way. The same is true in the case of Lippe and Hol-

44 Deetjen, Ende (note 13), S. 98ss., Gassmann, Ecclesia Reformata (note 12), 252.
45 Joppen, Anhalt (note 3), esp. 737.

stein-Gottorf, where the (409) ruling houses were in close contact with the Calvinist court of Hesse-Kassel.[46] Brandenburg,
which in chronological terms is usually regarded as the last
instance of a Second Reformation, was connected with this
network too, particularly with the Netherlands. However, since
the public conversion of Elector Johann Sigismund during
December 1613 did not result in a confessional change within
the territorial church no Second Reformation took place there
in the strict sense of the word. This exceptional development
was a result of an earlier policy which had been instituted to
solve the problem of concord in Brandenburg:[47] the clergy, and
hence the territorial church, were obligated to uphold the
Formula of Concord. However, individual nobles, members of
the upper bureaucracy, and of the court were free to choose.
Elector Johann Friedrich (1598-1608) rejected the *Formula of
Concord* for himself personally. The later religious partition of
Brandenburg-Prussian Protestantism into Lutheran subjects,
including a majority of the nobility, and a Calvinist dynasty,
together with that part of the political elite (nobles and
bureaucrats) who were committed to the ruling house, was
presaged in the way that the work of concord had been instituted a generation earlier.

The actual course of the Second Reformation was different
in each case, reflecting the chronological duration of the process and the constellation of ecclesiastical and other conditions
present in each locale. Where the Philippist tradition was strong
it was usually a slow process with many stages. By contrast it
was quick and decisive in places that were exposed to direct
Calvinist impulses from western Europe. The Second Reformation was introduced through the following measures: the
publication of confessional documents, composed either by the
territorial prince or a leading theologian (usually under Calvinist influence); the imposition of church visitations; the
introduction of a new catechism, usually the Heidelberg Catechism or one of its variants;[48] the selective replacement of

---

46 E. Feddersen, Der Kryptocalvinismus am Gottorfer Hofe unter Herzog
Johann Adolf, in: Schriften des Vereins für Schleswig-Holsteinische Kirchengeschichte, 2nd series, vol. 8 (1926-28), 344-391; Schleswig-Holsteinische Kirchengeschichte (note 3), vol. 4, esp. 29ss.; Schilling, Konfessionskonflikt (note 3), 173-
176.
47 G. Heinrich, Brandenburg II, in: Theologische Realenzyklopädie, vol. 7, 11-
128.
48 Above note 32; W. Neuser, Die Einführung des Heidelberger Katechismus in

pastors holding the most important positions in the church, especially of church superintendents; the organization of academic disputations among the clergy and also at court, including the central bureaucracy; the "cleansing" of church buildings together with changes in the liturgy and in the communion ceremony, in most cases publicized by the attendance (410) of the prince and his entourage at its first celebration,[49] and finally the systematic introduction of these changes both in the towns and countryside by ordinances of the territorial government, supervised by the ecclesiastical bureaucracy of the territorial church. Symbolically the most important elements were the breaking of bread in the eucharist ceremony, the introduction of church discipline, and the elimination of exorcism from the baptismal ceremony.

This phase of confessionalization, when the Reformed territories were bound most tightly by mutual influences and interdependence (for example between Nassau and Hesse), resulted in at least a relative confessional unity among the new Reformed churches as it did among the Lutherans. The Heidelberg catechism assumed a leading role in this process, and thus its adoption at the Synod of Dordrecht in 1619 seems to be an appropriate milestone marking the end of this crucial phase of the Second Reformation.[50] On the one hand its acceptance signalled attainment of that stage reached within Lutheran confessionalization with the publication of the Lutheran *Book of Concord* in 1580. On the other hand it underscored the historical connection which had developed between the German areas that adopted the Second Reformation and western European Calvinism.

Fourth Phase: After Confessionalization. For an adequate appraisal of the significance of the Second Reformation some remarks about events occurring after the era of confessionalization are in order. During the process of confessionalization, German Protestantism faced an insoluble dilemma when confronted by the confessional dialectic of internal integration and external demarcation. The confessional formulations, whose adoption had been spurred by fears of Counter-Reformation

---

Lippe im Jahre 1602 und der Kampf um seine Beibehaltung im 19. Jahrhundert, in: Jahrbuch für Westfälische Kirchengeschichte 74 (1981), 57-78.

49 Schilling, Konfessionskonflikt (note 3), 183, note 183.

50 J.P. van Dooren, Dordrechter Synode (1618/19), in: Theologische Realenzyklopädie, vol. 9, 140-147, here 146.

onslaughts, had the effect of weakening the Protestant position
by dividing it theologically, organizationally, and politically
into two hostile camps. The Reformed side especially tried to
counteract this division through endeavors towards a union,
reflecting a continuation of the older, fundamentally irenic
stance of the Philippists. Such a position was untimely and had
no chance of success as long as the trend for confessionalization dominated, particularly because of secondary obstacles
such as the latent claim to superiority made by the Reformed.[51]
Only after the processes of integration and demarcation had
run their course within both Protestant confessional systems
could irenic and unionist undercurrents again emerge and gain
strength in the wake of Pietism's lack of emphasis on dogma.

This was the historical context for the union theologies of
the universities of Helmstedt and Rinteln, as well as the
impressive (411) union initiatives of Calixt and Durie. These
efforts were supported above all by Brandenburg-Prussia and
Hesse-Kassel, two Reformed governments which linked their
state interests with the theological and ecclesiastical political
goal of union.[52] However, I think that corresponding developments within the spheres of private, social, and political life
are no less important than these well-known trends within
theology and ecclesiastical politics. Apparently there was a
praxis of irenic, trans-confessional coexistence and of spiritual
and intellectual interchange in some places already during the
early seventeenth century, particularly within the Reformed
sphere. Examples of this include the imperial city of Dortmund
and some south German imperial cities.[53] This humanist tradition maintained its identity by accepting Reformed confessionalization when it came under confessional pressure at the end
of the sixteenth century. From Dutch history, however, we
know that this humanist line was able to develop into an independent type within the Reformed tradition (Remonstrants),
and was distinctly different from the confessional Calvinist

---

51 Koch, Zwingli, (note 15), 85s.

52 C.H.W. van den Berg, Durie, John, in: Theologische Realenzyklopädie, vol.
9, 242-245; J. Wallmann, Calixt, in: Theologische Realenzyklopädie, vol. 7, 552-
559; L. Mayer, Hermann Conring als theologischer Schriftsteller—insbesondere in
seinem Verhältnis zu Georg Calixt, in: M. Stolleis (ed.), Hermann Conring (1606-
1681), Berlin 1984, 55-86; G.A. Benrath, Irenik und Zweite Reformation, in:
Schilling, Reformierte Konfessionalisierung (note 2), 349-358.

53 Schilling: Dortmund (note 21) 178, 195; Dülmen, Johannes Saubert (note
30).

type (Counter-Remonstrants). The markedly different effects that these two groups within Dutch Protestantism had upon the state, political life, academic and cultural trends, and social life is well-known. We must also distinguish these different currents in the history of the Second Reformation in Germany. The irenical and humanist undercurrents especially deserve further attention, particularly because of their continuing impact during the seventeenth and eighteenth centuries and the related consequences for historical development in general.

III. THE HISTORICAL SIGNIFICANCE OF THE SECOND REFORMATION: REFORMED CONFESSIONALIZATION

In the following discussion events grouped together under the rubric of the Second Reformation are illustrated retrospectively from their results, i.e., the third phase described above. A historical appraisal of the Second Reformation must begin with its two central characteristics: the movement's specific theology with its distinctive (412) understanding of "Reformation"[54] and the Second Reformation as an expression of confessionalization, a phenomenon that is understood to be, on the one hand, the emergence of a confessional church whose theology is defined by a formal confession and, on the other, a process affecting all of society. This confessional and organizational strengthening of the church spearheaded a campaign to reshape both political life and society as a whole. The Second Reformation took place at the same time as the Counter-Reformation and the Lutheran renewal in the movement of concord, and its pervasive religious, political, and social effects are comparable to theirs. The most important task of a history of the Second Reformation would be to identify the structural and functional similarities and differences of these parallel processes, providing a theoretical tool for a synthetic analysis of confessionalization in Germany, i.e. encompassing all three confessions. My book *Konfessionskonflikt und Staatsbildung* is a first step in this direction. Comparing the political and social consequences of the Second Reformation in Lippe with those of Lutheran confessionalization in East Friesland, I have found a functional similarity in the political, institutional, and social

---

54 This important aspect is covered by the expression "Second Reformation", which thus needs to be used as an explanatory addition to "Reformed Confessionalization."

effects of Calvinism and Lutheranism—a position that conflicts
with the classical theory of Weberian sociology of religion.[55]
Recent historical comparisons of Hesse-Marburg and Württemberg (Rudersdorf), and also Brunswick-Wolfenbüttel and
Hesse-Kassel (Schorn-Schütte) have confirmed this interpretation. Manfred Rudersdorf has even proposed the concept of a
"Lutheran Second Reformation" on the basis of this parallelism.[56]

In addition to the historical justification there is also a
theological justification for using the term "Second Reformation" to denote a second step after the first Lutheran Reformation. The Second Reformation (413) can be distinguished
from the confessional reshaping of Lutheranism through the
concord movement by its specific theology and its particular
concept of a "Reformation." It is precisely this specifically
theological concept of a second step in the process of the
Reformation that justifies the concept of a "Second Reformation." Consequently the term must be reserved for Re-
formed/Calvinist confession-building and for the changes in
state, church, and society that accompanied it—if the term is
not to emptied completely of its theological content.[57]

Without overlooking the numerous theological differences
between Lutherans on the one hand and Erasmians, Philippists,
Zwinglians, and Calvinists on the other or disputing the internal differentiation of the lines of tradition which led toward
the Second Reformation, there is one element that is characteristic of the theology of the Second Reformation—the programmatic turn toward "life," an emphasis upon the
"external," public aspect of human life in the church, state,
and society which, it was felt, should be rationally organized
and shaped. In its essentials this point illustrates the difference

55 Schilling, Konfessionskonflikt (note 3), 40-44, 380-391.

56 M. Rudersdorf, Der Weg zur Universitätsgründung in Gießen. Das geistige
und politische Erbe Landgraf Ludwigs IV. von Hessen-Marburg, in: P. Moraw
and V. Press (eds.): Academia Giessensis—Beiträge zur älteren Gießener Univer-
sitätsgeschichte, Marburg 1982; L. Schorn-Schütte, Evangelische Geistlichkeit in
der Frühneuzeit. Ihr Beitrag zur Entfaltung frühmoderner Staatlichkeit und
Gesellschaft. Dargestellt am Beispiel des Fürstentums Braunschweig-Wolfenbüttel, der Landgrafschaft Hessen-Kassel und der Stadt Braunschweig (16._18.
Jahrhundert), Habilitationsschrift Gießen 1991 (forthcoming).

57 H. Leube, Die Reformidee in der deutschen lutherischen Kirche zur Zeit der
Orthodoxie, Leipzig 1924; v. Dülmen, Johannes Saubert (note 30); H.-Ch.
Rublack (ed.), Lutherische Konfessionalisierung. Wissenschaftliches Symposion
des Vereins für Reformationsgeschichte, 1988, Gütersloh 1991.

between Luther and Erasmus which in the course of the Reformation era widened into a theologically and historically differentiated syndrome. On account of his almost monomaniacal concentration upon the fundamental problem of how individuals receive divine grace, Luther focused exclusively on the internal religious core of the Reformation. The shaping of the world, and even the shaping of the visible church, he left to the princes and also in a certain sense to Melanchthon. Without blaming the "theologian of the first hour" of the Reformation, the theologians of the Second Reformation regarded this as a deficiency of Luther's theology, as Zwingli had already argued in principle. They categorized Luther's achievement as the "Reformation of Doctrine" and advocated its completion through a "Reformation of Life."[58] In so doing they did not deny the Lutheran tradition, but rather regarded themselves as legitimate disciples of Luther. However, there was no question that they wanted to go beyond Luther and that they considered an additional Reformation to be necessary. Among Calvinists this second step was even considered to be necessary for salvation, since Calvin had taught that a presbyterian church structure was a mark of the true church. Thus the movements favoring a Calvinist or Reformed type of Protestant church did not seek a "Second Reformation" in the sense of another "Copernican transformation" in theology, but rather in the sense of a completion of the first Reformation. Such a "Second Reformation" had to be qualitatively different not in its theological core but in its results, affecting broader dimensions of life in accordance with the Reformed concept of the church and world, influenced strongly by humanist thinking.

The conviction that a Second Reformation was necessary rested in part upon very pragmatic considerations and a realistic, pessimistic evaluation of the concrete success of the Reformation: "We have preached for years, but has such preaching borne fruit?" asked John a Lasco, referring to the tenacity with which Catholic institutions and forms of faith

---

58 Koch, Zwingli (note 15), 85. This is not denied by the critics of the terminology of "Second Reformation". See Neuser, Erforschung (note 11); H. Klueting: "Zweite Reformation" oder reformierte Konfessions- und Kirchenbildung? Zum Problem von Politik und Religion im konfessionellen Zeitalter, in: Monatshefte für Evangelische Kirchengeschichte des Rheinlandes 34 (1985), 19-40; idem, "Zweite Reformation"? (note 14).

were maintained in East Friesland.[59] In addition there was a deeper theological justification for the necessity of a second attempt at reform. It emerged from the particular worth that the theological systems of Melanchthon, Zwingli, and Calvin attached to other aspects of life apart from the religious core discussed by Luther. Calvin's theology in particular advocated a systematic concept of the church and world that placed a special religious and theological emphasis upon organization and activity within the world, e.g., the biblical foundation of the presbyterial organization of the church or the doctrine of the "third use of the law," according to which political and social activities were godly works and a fulfillment of the Lord's commands.[60]

All of this gave the Second Reformation an eminently political and social character. In contrast to the Lutheran Reformation, the "Reformation of Life" was not directed primarily toward the lives of individuals but focused upon communal and social life in both church and state. The "Social History of Criminality" misrepresents church discipline in a fundamental way when it assumes that church discipline, like the state's punishment of criminals, was directed against individual subjects. In its theological origin church discipline was first and foremost (415) concerned not with individuals, but with protecting the purity of the fellowship of those receiving the Lord's Supper.[61] The individual was looked upon as a member of the ecclesiastical or burgher community, and neighborhood associations and the family functioned as intermediary groups.

---

59 Letter from September 1545 to the East Frisian secretary Hermann Lentius: A. Kuyper (ed.), Johanni a Lasco Opera, vol. 2, Amsterdam / Den Haag 1866, 596, letter No. 31.

60 J. Plomp, De kerkelijke tucht bij Calvijn, Kampen 1969, 328; P.M. Hoyer, Law and Gospel: With Particular Attention to the Third Use of the Law, in: Concordia Journal 6/5 (1980), 189-201.

61 H. Schilling, "History of Crime" or "History of Sin"?_Some Reflection on the Social History of Early Modern Church Discipline, in: E.J. Kouri and T. Scott (eds.), Politics and Society in Reformation Europe. Essays for Sir Geoffrey Elton on his 65th Birthday, London/München 1986; idem: Reformierte Kirchenzucht als Sozialdisziplinierung?_Die Tätigkeit des Emder Presbyteriums in den Jahren 1557-1562 (mit vergleichenden Betrachtungen über die Kirchenräte in Groningen und Leiden sowie mit einem Ausblick ins 17. Jahrhundert), in: W. Ehbrecht and H. Schilling (eds.), Niederlande und Nordwestdeutschland, Köln/Wien, 1983, 261-327; idem, Sündenzucht und frühneuzeitliche Sozialdisziplinierung. Die calvinistische, presbyteriale Kirchenzucht in Emden vom 16. bis 19. Jahrhundert, in: G. Schmidt (ed.), Stände und Gesellschaft im Alten Reich, Stuttgart 1989, 265-302. (English translation in: idem, Civic Calvinism, Kirksville 1991).

This feature helps to explain one fact that is at first rather perplexing, indeed paradoxical: among the theological writings of the Second Reformation devotional works are comparatively rare, and Reformed theologians had great difficulty popularizing their theology.[62] The religious and pastoral priority of aiding individual Christians in their religious needs was typical of Lutheranism. By contrast the theologians of the Second Reformation sought to change institutions and the socio-political framework, in a continuation of the humanist tradition, in order to ensure the proper socialization and education of individuals. One of the consequences of this presupposition was the special role that the political and academic elite played in the introduction of the Second Reformation. This was especially true of the highly regarded academic disputations, which—in contrast to the great urban disputations of the Reformation period that took place among Zwinglians and Lutherans alike—were conducted during the Second Reformation without the involvement of the broader social strata. They were intended for the schooling of the members of the academic elite in church and state, who were appointed to take responsibility for a process of education that was to be imposed upon the subjects in the form of a Reformation from above. Consequently the Second Reformation became to a great extent a "process of acculturation."[63] (416)

I do not need to emphasize that these differences in theology and spirituality were blurred to a certain extend in everyday life. Lutherans as well as the Tridentine reformers, were naturally also concerned with social institutions such as schools and universities, whereas the Reformed quest for changes in public life included the private sphere as well. However, the three confessions differed in their understanding of humanity, the world, and history, and such differences in particular had historical consequences. In Lutheran territories a powerful process of consolidation in state and society took place in the wake of confessionalization as the examples of East Friesland, Württemberg, and Brunswick-Wolfenbüttel demonstrate. Lutheran governments too showed political cunning, for example in their dealings with the Emperor (compare the policies of

---

62 Koch, Philippismus (note 40); H. Lehmann, Das Zeitalter des Absolutismus, Stuttgart 1980, 114-135.

63 Examples in Schilling, Konfessionskonflikt (note 3), 183s; see also Garber, "Barock"-Literatur (note 22).

Hesse-Darmstadt and Hesse-Kassel). The disparaging judgment, often found in older historical works and in the sociology of religion, that Lutheranism during the Age of Orthodoxy was apolitical, stagnant, and undynamic, is no longer tenable. Nevertheless, the direct justification of this reshaping and restructuring of state, church, and society by a distinctive theology with a unique concept of "Reformation" is characteristic of the Second Reformation and of the traditions of Reformed theology which prepared the way for it. Which of the historical consequences can actually be traced back to this distinction and how pervasive they were can only be answered after a systematic comparison between the political and social consequences of confessionalization in orthodox Lutheranism on the one hand, and that of the Second Reformation on the other.[64]

At this point, however, we must discuss differing conceptions of worldly activism within the Reformed camp which affected its political and social character and also its tangible effects. These differences emerged from differing conceptions of social organization and of the division of responsibilities in the ordering of political and social life.[65] Following late medieval humanist ideals concerning the duties of a good prince (*Fürstenspiegel*), Zwinglians and Philippists were inclined to assign these functions in the first instance to the territorial princes (417) or to city governments. Thomas Erastus went the furthest in this direction.[66] Whereas Luther had simply accepted this development, it became an essential part of the theological program and agenda of the Second Reformation. The religiously and theologically based sphere of responsibilities belonging to the government was much broader in the humanist-Zwinglian tradition than in the Lutheran one. In contrast, the Calvinist position on these issues emphasized the rights and duties of inferior magistrates in the church and state for reasons that cannot be further discussed here. They were responsible for most public duties, ideally working together with their princes and city governments, but working independently of them or even against them if necessary. Clearly these

64 Rublack, Konfessionalisierung (note 57).

65 I. Montgomery, Värjostånd och lärostand. Religion och politik i meningsutbytet mellan kungamakt och prästerskap i Sverige 1593-1608, Uppsala 1972.

66 G.B. Lechler, Thomas Erastus, in: Realencyklopädie für protestantische Theologie und Kirche, vol. 5, Leipzig 1898, 444-446.

two positions assume fundamentally different models of church and society. Although these distinctions tended to blur in practice, there is no question that they could have an effect upon the political and social changes that took place in the course of individual instances of the Second Reformation. Without wishing to prejudice further research on the question, it is safe to suggest that the Reformed territories and cities of the Empire were on the whole more strongly affected by Erastian thought than by Calvinism. This was especially true of its influence upon scholarship and the universities.[67]

IV. SUPPORTERS AND CHANNELS OF COMMUNICATION

An examination of supporters and channels of communication is instructive both for the origins of the Second Reformation and for its social importance. Some work has been done on these topics, but it has largely been restricted to examinations of individual territories, persons, and groups of persons.[68] By contrast we do not know enough about the supraterritorial social network as a whole, particularly during its formative phase, and about the changes that took place during the different stages of the Second Reformation. Consequently we can only discuss the bare outlines of this social network.

The strong participation of non-theologians is the most important characteristic of this communications network. Lay persons were also involved in the Lutheran Reformation; the jurists of Electoral Saxony, such as Chancellor Georg Brück, are prominent examples. Much the same can be said of the Counter-Reformation. (418) However, the extent of lay involvement was even greater in the Second Reformation, both in the number of laymen who were involved and in the influence they had upon the reshaping of theology and of ecclesiastical policies. Most importantly, the spectrum of professions involved in such activities was broader: besides learned jurists other academics—physicians, professors of all faculties, Latin school teachers—participated as well as many intellectuals who were not employed in one of the academic professions.[69] The

---

67 Hammerstein, Schule (note 18).

68 Klein, Kampf (note 8); Press, Calvinismus (note 17); idem, Ritterschaft (note 19); Schilling, Konfessionskonflikt (note 3); Moltmann, Pezel (note 8); Schubert, Camerarius (note 19); Menk, Haltung (note 18), Schieckel, Pfarrer (note 41).

69 E.g. the Dortmund patrician Kaspar Schwarz (see Schilling, Dortmund, note

CHAPTER SIX

extent to which big merchants and financiers were involved has yet to be examined. This pattern of recruitment was on the one hand a consequence of the broad range of interests represented within a theology informed by humanism, which was concerned with more than theology proper.[70] Furthermore it was also a consequence of the rational style (Doctrine of the Lord's Supper) and the relative dogmatic openness of the Second Reformation. Finally the programmatic turn toward the public duties of church and state described in the previous section was important: for everyone who played a leading role in the Second Reformation—laymen and theologians alike—theology was both a point of theoretical integration and a justification for their concepts of order, their models, and the goals they set for their public activities. However, despite the strong participation of laymen, the communication system of the Second Reformation was dominated by theologians, i.e. by the clergy, superintendents, and university professors.

Originally the principal nodal points of this clerical personnel network were located on the one hand in Zürich, Basel, and in the upper German imperial cities, and on the other with Erasmian circles located in the Netherlands, in the lower Rhine area, and in northwestern Germany, with important offshoots in Hesse and in the imperial city of Frankfort. In addition during the 1540's and 1550's there was a strong connection with the settlements of Dutch and Walloon exiles in England. Electoral Saxony entered the network when the Philippists gained control, and with the rise of Calvinism, Geneva, the strongholds of the Huguenots in France, and the universities of Paris, Orléans, and Bourges were added. After its switch to Calvinism the Palatinate quickly became the most important center of communication within the Empire. Spanish intervention in the Netherlands, the St. Bartholomew's Day Massacre, the Augustinian purge of Philippists in Electoral Saxony, and the return of the Palatinate to the Lutheran camp destroyed those nodal points within the network. At the same time by exiling proponents of the Second Reformation they effectively increased the number of smaller centers, even down to the level of towns and villages.

Exiled theologians played an active role even during the first

21, 178), and in certain respects also the Westphalian noble Johann von Münster, see Richter, Johann von Münster (note 19).

70 See Koch, Philippismus (note 40).

phase of the Second Reformation. Prominent examples include Caspar Olevian[71] at Trier and Petrus Dathenus and Valérand Poullain who led the Dutch and Walloon exile churches in England. After they were expelled from England during the Marian Counter-Reformation they sought new havens on the continent. During the 1570's and 1580's expelled refugee theologians were numerous and influential figures all over Germany, constituting a recognizable social grouping. (419) In addition to those who had been driven out of Saxony and the Palatinate, the systematic purges conducted by orthodox Lutherans in the wake of the concord movement unleashed a new wave of exiles who had been forced to leave their pastoral positions. Much research on these phenomena remains to be done, both in church history and social history. Not only should the fates of individual exiles with their successes and failures be examined, but there must also be an attempt to establish a typical pattern for the lives of such exiles during the Confessional Age.

During the second half of the sixteenth century a marked social and geographical shift took place within this network of personnel and communication, away from professors and church leaders at the universities and in the "Cathedral cities" of Reformed theology (Zürich, Basel, Geneva)—although they did not entirely lose their function—toward the territorial princes with their courtly noble and learned burgher entourage in the residence cities, and the bureaucrats of the central and local administrations. In contrast to the older network of clerics, this new component of the Second Reformation communication network reflected fields and mechanisms of recruitment that were typical and to a certain extent traditional for particular territories. This is especially clear in the case of the Palatinate but was also apparent in other places such as the Westphalian counties with their traditional orientation toward Hesse. These older territorial patterns were broadened by their linkage with the Reformed system of communication, a complex network consisting of personal contacts made by individuals during their education in schools or at court, at the university, during academic grand tours, or during military service. They

---

71 On Olevian most recently see the articles on his vita and oeuvre by W. Holtmann, K. Müller, G. Menk, C. Walton, H. Eßer and J.F.G. Goeters, in: Monatshefte für Evangelische Kirchengeschichte des Rheinlandes 37/38 (1988/89).

took these links into the territorial service and continued to cultivate them.

This personnel network was supraterritorial, and even European in scope, concentrated around institutional centers such as Latin schools, universities, princely courts (including circles of pages), the garrisons of the Huguenots, and especially the house of Orange in the Netherlands. Personal contacts were a crucial element in Old European society, important not least for professional advancement. The exchange of ideas through forums such as theological and philosophical lectures and colloquia are also more typical of the Second Reformation. For instance, Johann Jacob Grynaeus' lectures on history at Heidelberg in 1584 had to be moved to a larger lecture hall because they were attended by university students as well as a host of Electoral councillors and other "*Literati*."[72] Other forums included discussions of the new drill regulations in military circles and the debates over poetic forms within literary circles.[73] The flow of communication between major centers and smaller "outposts" took place through intensive correspondence, official publication of pamphlets, polemical works, and memoranda, and also extended journeys either for private reasons or purposes such as diplomacy. (420) In this way it was easy to maintain regular communications not only among the universities, "Cathedral cities," and the larger residence cities, but also with the second rank of residences in lesser territories, middle-sized and smaller territorial towns, particularly if they had Latin schools, and even with the study rooms of parsonages in remote Frisian villages.[74]

There was a great deal of social intermingling, particularly during university studies and the academic grand tours made by the nobility in the company of burgher tutors. The connections between nobles and non-nobles in particular stabilized the network and allowed it to function smoothly. It opened "career opportunities" for burgher academics at a time when the overproduction of academics in the wake of the "educational revolution" of the sixteenth century made it difficult for jurists,

---

72 G.A. Benrath, Reformierte Kirchengeschichtsschreibung an der Universität Heidelberg im 16. und 17. Jahrhundert, Speyer 1963, 11.

73 Garber, Calvinismus (note 22).

74 See e.g. H. Brugmans and F. Wachter (eds.), Briefwechsel des Ubbo Emmius, 2 vols., 1911/23; K. Wolf, Aus dem Briefwechsel Christoph Pezels mit Graf Johann dem Älteren von Nassau-Dillenburg, in: Archiv für Reformationsgeschichte 34 (1937), 177-234.

theologians, physicians, and teachers to earn a living. This personnel network crossed lines of social status and estate even within individual territories. It extended from the territorial princes and their families through the imperial and territorial nobility (the counts of Erbach and the numerous Wetterau counts in the Palatinate, the von Donop family in Lippe, and the von Dohnas in Brandenburg) and the highest burgher officials (Ehem, Zuleger, Camerarius, Krell) to the middle and lower levels of the central and local administrations, including some notables in town and countryside who were not government officials. The territorial networks, assuming the form of a vertical structure of local and regional political elites and factions, were typical for early modern society. In the case of the Second Reformation these territorial networks were also linked to the supra-regional network described above. It is also typical for Old Europe in general that social change took the form of a conflict between two antagonistic factions. During the Confessional Age this traditional type of social conflict escalated into a confrontation between two irreconcilable views of the world (*Weltanschauungssysteme*). The victory of the Second Reformation was at the same time the victory of the Reformed faction of the territorial social network whereas the victory of the Concord movement was the victory of the Lutheran one.

Although not incorrect in and of itself, the position that the Second Reformation was imposed from above by the territorial princes and their bureaucracy must be modified in light of the specific functions of this multi-level personnel and communications network. The communications system existed before governments adopted the Second Reformation, and it developed independently of them. At times it almost seems that the territorial princes were, so to speak, "the horse that pulled the cart" of their own academic (421) Reformed clientele. This was especially evident during the early phase when Philippist/Crypto-Calvinist movements emerged in individual locales, independent of the territorial governments and often against their will, and established contact with one another by means of the channels described above. Examples of this include the circle around Pastor Johann Pincier in the northern Hessian territorial town of Wetter and the circle of Justus Vultejus and Wilhelm Roding who were teachers at the *Pädagogium* in

nearby Marburg during the 1560's and 1570's.[75] Similar cells
emerged at almost the same time in Korbach (County of Waldeck), led by Lazarus Schöner, and in Lemgo and Detmold
(County of Lippe), led by Bernhard Copius, Lazarus Schöner,
and Nikolaus Thodenus.[76] Gerhard Menk has traced the formative influence that such an intellectual circle had upon the life
of Johannes Croll, a theologian born in Wetter, as well as its
role in opening up professional opportunities for him.[77] This
individual case shows how the initiative came from circles of
pastors, professors, and teachers and that state authorities, the
territorial princes and their governments, did not play a leading
role, apart from the fact that they made official appointments
to the offices sought by aspirants.

   These observations show that there were also independent
movements within the Second Reformation, not sponsored by
the state yet present among its subjects, even though they
existed in a different milieu and were never as deeply rooted
socially as the popular Reformation movements of the first half
of the sixteenth century. Of course these preparatory activities
of the social network do not change the fact that the final
decision concerning the formal introduction of the Second
Reformation was made by princes and their governments. This
simply reflected the imperial constitution and at the same time
reflected changes that had taken place in political organization
and in the political process since the first half of the century.
The Second Reformation can only be identified as a *"Princely
Reformation"* in the same way that the Counter-Reformation
or the Lutheran renewal are. Within the social and constitutional structure in Germany after 1555, everything was determined by the personal choice of confession made by the territorial prince. The abrupt changes in Saxony, the Palatinate, and
the less spectacular struggles of smaller territories such as
Sayn-Wittgenstein or Mecklenburg-Güstrow all reflect this
reality. In Mecklenburg-Güstrow the territorial estates were
finally able to limit Calvinism to the immediate entourage of
Duke Johann Albrecht. In Baden-Durlach (421) and in Hol-

   75 On Vultejus: Friedrich, Gelehrtenschulen (note 18), 38-49; on Pincier:
Menk, Haltung (note 18), 235; idem, Hohe Schule (note 18), 40s, F.W. Schellen-
berg, Die Gelehrten-Familie Pincier, in: Allgemeines Nassauisches Schulblatt
1856, 321s.
   76 Schilling, Konfessionskonflikt (note 3), 173, 180, 182; Friedrich, Gelehrtenschulen (note 18), 129ss.
   77 Menk, Haltung (note 18).

stein-Gottorf the Second Reformation ended abruptly with the
deaths of Margrave Ernst Friedrich (1604) and Duke Johann
Adolf (1616) respectively.[78] Hence, the princely and dynastic
core within the personnel and communication network determined the course of the Second Reformation through the
Empire in a very special way. The rulers of Electoral Palatinate
played a key role in nudging Wittgenstein, Anhalt, Baden-
Durlach, Zweibrücken, and Brandenburg toward a Second
Reformation, as did Nassau in Wied, Solms, Hanau, Isenburg,
and Hesse. If Duke Johann Adolf of Holstein-Gottorf had not
had dynastic connections with Hesse-Kassel—Landgrave Wilhelm was his uncle—and had not been acquainted with Count
Johann of Nassau, there probably would have been no attempt
at all to institute a Second Reformation in Holstein-Gottorf, to
name only one example.[79]

V. INTRODUCTION AND RECEPTION OF THE SECOND REFORMATION

Despite these modifications to the picture of reforms instituted
by the magistrate it must be stressed that the Second Reformation and every movement that led to it was essentially an elite
phenomenon. The independent emergence of Philippist and
Reformed intellectual circles in Wetter, Lemgo, and Korbach
did not lead to a Reformed burgher movement, let alone
transform the cities into Reformed communes. Whereas during
the first half of the sixteenth century intellectuals and citizens
worked together in Reformation movements, the demands of
Reformed intellectuals for a Second Reformation usually
evoked a strong defensive reaction among the citizenry during
the second half of the century. The "civic reaction" against the
Second Reformation was particularly strong in Lemgo, but was
also apparent in Dortmund where the humanist reform of

---

78 Mecklenburg-Güstrow: Schmaltz, Kirchengeschichte, vol. II (note 3), 213-
219; Holstein-Gottorf: Kirchengeschichte (note 3), 32s; Sayn-Wittgenstein: Menk,
Haltung (note 18), 249; Baden-Durlach: W. Baumann, Ernst Friedrich von
Baden-Durlach. Die Bedeutung der Religion für Leben und Politik eines süd-
deutschen Fürsten im Zeitalter der Gegenreformation, Stuttgart 1962; F. Merkel,
Geschichte des evangelischen Bekenntnisses in Baden von der Reformation bis zur
Union, Karlsruhe 1966.

79 It would be interesting to sketch genealogical "family trees" of the "Second
Reformations" in the German territories. Most of them, however had more than
one "father" or "mother", and besides the German dynasties or territories
impulses from abroad—France, Switzerland, the Netherlands—would have to be
considered, too.

Lambach was swept away by a Lutheran burgher movement. If
indeed there was a process of acculturation—i.e., the systematic, more or less forcible imposition of a new system of norms
by political and cultural elites from above upon their subjects
in the sense proposed by Robert Muchembled—anywhere in
the wake of the early modern reshaping of state, society, and
church, then it occurred in the case of the Second (423) Reformation, especially since its theological system had a wholly
intellectual character.[80]

Another characteristic element distinguishes the second
Reformation from the first: the Second Reformation was
usually not sustained by a communal and corporate movement
of the broader strata in town and countryside as was typical for
the Reformation during the first decades of the sixteenth century, for the Lutherans no less than for the Zwinglians. There
were only a few cities in the western part of the Empire, particularly Emden, Wesel, and Duisburg,[81] where burgher
movements sought a shift from Lutheranism to the Reformed
confession or, as occurred in the case of Emden, sought to
introduce Calvinist confessionalization to replace the older,
pre-orthodox humanist-Zwinglian form of Reformed theology.[82] This change was based upon special and exceptional
circumstances—above all on the stream of Dutch Calvinist
immigrants and the specific confessional policy pursued by the
territorial princes. In East Friesland the rulers abruptly adopted
a rigorous policy of Lutheran confessionalization, and in
response the burghers of Emden, who strove for political (424)

---

80 R. Muchembled, Lay judges and the acculturation of the masses (France
and the Southern Low Countries, Sixteenth to Eighteenth Centuries), in: K. v.
Greyerz (ed.), Religion and Society in Early Modern Europe, 1500-1800, London
1984, 56-65, together with the replication of J. Wirth, ibid., 66-78.

81 Emden: Schilling, Reformation (note 42); Wesel: idem, Exulanten (note 33);
Duisburg: H. Averdunk and W. Ring, Geschichte der Stadt Duisburg, Essen 1927,
181ss., esp. 184; G. v. Roden, Geschichte der Stadt Duisburg, Duisburg 1970, vol.
1, 267s.

82 Critical remarks on the idea of "Reformation from above" by Goeters,
Genesis (note 2), 444. In my opinion the cities mentioned (Metz, Trier and
Aachen) are examples of "Late City Reformations", not of Second Reformations.
See e.g. Schilling, Exulanten (note 33), 167ss; J. Ney, Die Reformation in Trier
1559 und ihre Unterdrückung, Halle/Leipzig 1906/1907; R. Laufner, Der Trierer
Reformationsversuch vor 400 Jahren, in: Trierer Jahrbuch 11 (1960), 18-41;
J.F.G. Goeters, Der Trierer Reformationsversuch von 1559 im Rahmen der deut-
schen Reformationsgeschichte, in: Monatshefte für Evangelische Kirchenge-
schichte des Rheinlandes 37/38 (1988/89), 267-286.

and economic independence, followed Menso Alting, an exile theologian, on the path to Calvinism.

Events took a different turn in neighboring Bremen. It is true that in 1562 a burgher movement opposed the turn toward orthodox Lutheranism ordered by a minority of city councillors, and the citizenry made common cause with Hardenberg and the Philippists led by burgomaster Daniel von Büren. However, the actual introduction of the Second Reformation took place only during the 1580's through the joint efforts of burgomaster von Büren and the exile theologian Christoph Pezel without any burgher involvement.[83] The result was more apparent in the territories. Despite careful organizational preparation, spirited educational efforts, and the intensive use of propaganda explaining the need for a further Reformation instituted by ecclesiastical and governmental organs, there was seldom even a spark of religious enthusiasm for such a reform within church congregations in the towns and countryside. In the long run the Reformed churches encountered many perplexing difficulties in popularizing the new liturgical forms and in promoting the new religiosity in general, for example through a form of popular piety.[84] In this sense the Second Reformation contrasts markedly even with the Counter-Reformation whose introduction was likewise at first ordered by state and governmental agencies.[85] This constitutes a significant

---

83 Moltmann, Pezel (note 8),; Rudloff, Bremen (note 3), 158s.

84 See the very interesting comment on popular culture and Calvinism by Samuel Pufendorf in his famous "Severini de Monzambano Veronensis, de statu imperii Germanici ad Laelium fratrem ... liber unus, Geneva 1667, chapter 8, §7. (On the character of the protestant confessions).—Scholarly interest in the topic "early modern piety" has grown, see e.g. D. Breuer (ed.), Frömmigkeit in der frühen Neuzeit. Studien zur religiösen Literatur des 17. Jahrhunderts in Deutschland, Amsterdam 1984.

85 See H. Hörger, Die "Ulrichsjubiläen" des 17. bis 19. Jahrhunderts und ihre Auswirkungen auf die Volksfrömmigkeit in Ulrichspfarreien, in: Zeitschrift für bayerische Landesgeschichte 37 (1974), 309-357; idem, Dorfreligion und bäuerliche Mentalité im Wandel ihrer ideologischen Grundlagen, in: Zeitschrift für bayerische Landesgeschichte 38 (1975), 244-316; W. Brückner, Erneuerung als selektive Tradition. Kontinuitätsfragen im 16. und 17. Jahrhundert aus dem Bereich der konfessionellen Kultur, in: Der Übergang zur Neuzeit und die Wirkung von Tradition, Vorträge gehalten auf der Tagung der Joachim Jungius-Gesellschaft ... am 13. und 14. Oktober in Hamburg, Göttingen 1978, 55-78, esp. 63ss.; P. Münch, Volkskultur und Calvinismus. Zur Theorie und Praxis der "reformatio vitae" während der "Zweiten Reformation", in: Schilling, Reformierte Konfessionalisierung (note 2), 291-307. Most recently P. Münch, Reformation of Life. Calvinism and Popular Culture in Germany around 1600. The Paradigm of Nassau-Dillenburg, in: L. Laeyendecker et al. (eds.), Experiences and Explanations. Historical and Sociological Essays on Religion in Everyday Life, Leeu-

difference (425) between the Second Reformation in Germany and the Puritan movement in England, which otherwise had a number of common characteristics.

The lack of popular involvement in the Second Reformation cannot be traced to a general weakening of the political and social strength of communes in the cities and countryside. In many places communal and corporate movements emerged at the end of the sixteenth and the beginning of the seventeenth centuries much as they did during the first half of the sixteenth century.[86] However, apart from the exceptions mentioned above these communal movements never sought a further extension of the Reformation. They fought rather to preserve their original Lutheran confession, and in so doing they sometimes tried to steer church policy away from a moderate Philippist position toward an orthodox Lutheran one. Examples of such movements can be found in nearly every territory that experienced a Second Reformation. The flash points of confrontation were cities such as Leipzig, Lemgo, Marburg, the town of Eschwege in northern Hesse, Amberg in the upper Palatinate, Pforzheim in Baden-Durlach, and Berlin.[87] However, there were acts of both passive and active resistance even in villages and in country areas. I need only refer to the circumstances surrounding the removal of the high altar from the parish church of Sonnenborn in Lippe. Peasant resistance in particular must be examined more carefully, especially the peasants' need for magical protection that was disregarded by the spirituality of the Second Reformation, a *sensibilité religieuse* (B. Vogler) that was alien to them. (426) The

---

warden 1990, 37-57.

86 Ch. F. Friedrichs, German Town Revolts and the Seventeenth-Century-Crisis, in: Renaissance and Modern Studies 26 (1982), 27-51. For a general discussion of the problem see H. Schilling, Gab es im späten Mittelalter und zu Beginn der Neuzeit in Deutschland einen städtischen Republikanismus?, in: H. Koenigsberger (ed.), Republiken und Republikanismus im Europa der frühen Neuzeit, München 1987, 101-144 (English translation above pp. 3-60).

87 On Hesse and the Palatinate see Menk, Landgraf Wilhelm IV. (note 19); Press, Calvinismus (note 17). For more general observations: Schilling, Konfessionskonflikt (note 3) 370, 380s; Siegen: K. Wolf, Zur Einführung des reformierten Bekenntnisses in Nassau-Dillenburg, in: Nassauische Annalen 66 (1955), 186ss.; Amberg: J.B. Götz, Religiöse Wirren in der Oberpfalz 1576-1620, Münster 1937, 127ss.; Pforzheim: F. Merkel, Geschichte des evangelischen Bekenntnisses in Baden von der Reformation bis zur Union, Karlsruhe 1960, 116ss.; Berlin: E. Faden, Der Berliner Tumult von 1615, in: Jahrbuch für brandenburgische Landesgeschichte 5 (1954); Leipzig: Czok, "Calvinistensturm" (note 15); Hoyer, Staat (note 3).

attempt to impose a new form of spirituality took place at a
time when peasants felt compelled by economic and climatic
changes ("the little ice age") to rely upon the older forms of
magical and semi-magical rituals.

Popular rejection of the Second Reformation was both
unanimous and vehement, suggesting the existence of deeply
rooted conflicts. Statements made by dissenters under state
interrogation, the forms of resistance employed, and the course
of the pro-Lutheran burgher movements indicate a number of
theological and religious, individual, socio-psychological, and
legal-constitutional causes. In general, however, it can safely be
assumed that neither the urban burghers nor the peasants, nor
even a majority of the nobility, felt the need for a Second
Reformation, in contrast to their strong support for the
Lutheran and Zwinglian Reformations during the first half of
the sixteenth century. There was clearly no argument which
touched individuals, congregations, or communes in the same
way that the *sola fide* principle had affected personal and
collective conceptions of salvation. In contrast to the territorial
princes, bureaucrats, and intellectuals, their subjects felt no
need for a "Reformation of Life." Their daily experience gave
them no cause to wish for a continuation of the Reformation in
the direction that the intellectuals and authorities wished;
instead the governmental pressures for a new Reformation gave
them reason to think that their traditional way of life and religious forms were threatened.

When asked by church and state officials to give reasons for
their opposition at Eschwege, the Hessian subjects answered:
"once a tree has been grafted, it cannot be changed without
harm" (*wenn ein Baum einmal gepfropft wäre, könne er mit
Nutzen nicht wohl anders gemacht werden*)," or "the pot has the
good flavor of the first dish (*der Topf schmecket gern nach der
ersten Brühe*)." These and similar expressions demonstrate the
strong identification of many individuals with the religious
forms that grew out of the first Reformation. In some cases
citizens, peasants, or the guilds joined together to form corporate unions (*Einungen*), demonstrating how deeply rooted in the
communal and corporate intellectual tradition Lutheranism had
become.[88] In many places Lutheranism was practically regarded

---

88 K.A. Eckhardt (ed.), Eschweger Vernehmungsprotokolle von 1608 zur
Reformatio des Landgrafen Moritz, Witzenhausen 1968, interrogation of Celiax
Ziegenbach 6, No 92, of Hanß Spillner 6, No. 93, 94s.

as an historical manifestation of the strength of the communal and corporate principle and its victory during the first half of the sixteenth century.

Moreover we can identify genuinely religious and theological factors that were responsible for popular identification with Lutheranism. The academic understanding of the church and world (427) and the rational spirituality that informed the Second Reformation frightened the broader strata of burghers and peasants. It is not "demanding too much of the guilds-men"[89] to assume that the Lutheran doctrine of communion was better suited to their needs than that of the Second Reformation: communicants experienced the differences between the two positions directly. Burghers and peasants forcefully objected to the simplicity of the Calvinist communion rite, to the abolition of the high altar, and to the use of communion tables and leavened bread instead of communion wafers. In general they attempted to protect their churches against the "cleansing" promoted by Second Reformation theology. They rejected all of these innovations because they thought that they "took away power from the Lord" as the Westphalian peasants of Sonnenborn in the County of Lippe expressed it. Another important factor in favor of Lutheranism was the intensive pastoral care provided by Lutheran theologians, especially their devotional activities mentioned above. This considerably strengthened the identification of broader strata with Lutheranism and enhanced their ability to make religious and theological judgments.

Popular resistance had a directly political dimension as well: burghers and peasants rejected the Second Reformation because it was not rooted in the will of the church congregation and the commune, in contrast to the first Reformation, but rather was imposed upon city and village from the outside. Everywhere it is clear that pastors, superintendents, and secular officeholders who wished to introduce a Second Reformation were rejected as foreigners, agents of a new principle; indeed they were hated and persecuted. This occurred, for instance, in the village of Sonnenborn and in the Hessian town of Eschwege, where the superintendent Georg Reimann and all who had accepted the Second Reformation practically became social outcasts.[90] Clearly the resentment felt by residents both

89 Th. Klein, Review of Schilling, "Konfessionskonflikt und Staatsbildung", in: Hessisches Jahrbuch für Landesgeschichte 32 (1982), 344.

90 Eschweger Vernehmungsprotokolle (note 88), IX, X, and the information on

of the towns and countryside against the swift social rise of the academic stratum in the state and church during the course of the sixteenth century also played a role. The artisans and peasants regarded these men, who had been appointed to offices in the state and church, as unprincipled opportunists and willing tools of the early modern state.[91] (428)

VI. ON A SOCIETAL INTERPRETATION OF THE SECOND REFORMATION

Reflecting the broad historical dimension of confessionalization, the religious, social, and political conflicts that underlay the struggles between agents of the Second Reformation and their opponents corresponded to two irreconcilably views of the world and of political and social organization. Using the example of the Second Reformation in Lippe, I have interpreted these lines of conflict typologically as a conflict between the early modern territorial state with its principle of sovereignty and its inherent desire to reshape society and to discipline its subjects on the one hand, and on the other a model of state and society that was characterized by a relative autonomy of social and political subunits, including officeholders (pastors and secular officials alike), with a communal and corporate foundation for public and political life in village, city, and territory.[92]

Two questions emerge from this typology concerning the general history of the Second Reformation. First, is the model derived from the case of Lippe valid for the Second Reformation movement in general? This question concerns the outlines of the problem. Variations in the expression of particular structures and processes are as much to be expected as differences in focus (internal state-building or foreign policy activism). The second question concerns the *proprium*, the distinctive elements of Reformed confessionalization, i.e. the Second Reformation, compared with the Lutheran or Counter-Reformation type of confessionalization. Since confessionalization in general appears to be linked with early modern state-building, the conflict between two competing models of state

---

Superintendent Reimann (index, s.v. Reimann).

91 Some observations in Schilling, Konfessionskonflikt (note 3); idem, Urban Elites (above 61-134); idem, Early Modern Burgher Elites (above 135-187).

92 Schilling, Konfessionskonflikt (note 3), 365-391.

and society was common to all three types. It remains to be
determined whether there are characteristics that can be identified as unique to the Second Reformation within this fundamental similarity. I will close my discussion with a few general
observations concerning both sets of problems.

Regarding the general applicability of the pattern of social
confrontation in the battle over the Second Reformation, the
description of supra-territorial networks of personnel and
communication provides the basis for an answer. The supporters of the Second Reformation were usually those persons
and groups for whom the early modern territorial state promised a measure of personal, political, social, and perhaps even
economic advancement or who felt that the rise and consolidation of the state would be advantageous for their churches.
(429) These included officials in the service of princes, the
faction of the nobility which was ready to take advantage of
the opportunities offered by the early modern state instead of
defending their feudal privileges and independence, the civil
service burghers—including pastors and preachers—who were
oriented toward the territorial state, and professors at universities supported by territorial states. They also included human-
ist-educated intellectuals, whatever their profession, who hoped
for a renewal of state and society, including the church, and
felt that these goals would be most quickly realized through the
Christian princes whom they advised. A final group of supporters included entrepreneurs and big merchants, although
their numbers were small and they did not play an important
role either in preparing the way for a Second Reformation or
its introduction. Their activities had grown beyond a purely
"urban economy" and they wished to seize the opportunities
offered by a territorial economy. The alliance between these
"modern" social groups[93] as supporters of the Second Reformation and the early modern princely state appears to be a
supra-territorial constant of the Second Reformations.

This social conflict reflects a difference in ideals of state,
political, and social order. The Second Reformation appears
throughout to have been a movement seeking a sovereign, pervasive state directed against Old European "communalism."
There is one serious exception to this, although it cannot be
considered a typical case of the Second Reformation: the social

---

93 Discussed in detail ibid., 259-282.

and constitutional polarities were reversed during the calvinization of Emden due to its unusual political and confessional
constellation, i.e. opposition to a territorial ruler's policy of
Lutheran confessionalization.[94] In the case of Nassau and the
Wetterau counties the social and political consequences of the
Second Reformation are still disputed. However, it is clear that
even there an ecclesiastical renewal accompanied early modern
state-building. Gerhard Menk, who focuses on these processes
in great detail, has advanced the theory that this form of state-
building differs from what was usual elsewhere in the Empire
and did not follow the model of a centrally directed territorial
state centered on the sovereign will of the prince. Instead it
followed the principle of a "limitation of power through
regents, professors, and bureaucrats." This "limitation of
power" was achieved not through semi-autonomous cooperation
in a medieval sense (430) but through "strikingly modern
forms" of constitutionally guaranteed participation of the political and intellectual elite. This explanation has not gone
unchallenged, and Georg Schmidt has a somewhat different
view of the political culture of early modern Wetterau.[95]
Whichever interpretation is adopted, the events in the Wetterau
counties fit into the pattern of the Second Reformation as a
process of early modern state-building. Even taking Menk's
remarks into account there is no deviation from the general
pattern either in theory or history. For the social groups
working with the princes were very influential in the everyday
shaping of politics even in the semi-absolutist and absolutist
states. Nevertheless if the resistance of subjects in town and
countryside to the Second Reformation that was present almost
everywhere else was absent in the case of Nassau and the
Wetterau counties because of the particular style of ecclesiastical, governmental, and social renewal, then it provides an
interesting test for the adequacy of our characterization of the
Second Reformation.

The political consequences of the Second Reformation included an expansion of state authority and the internal integra-

---

94 Schilling, Reformation (note 42); idem, Konfessionskonflikt (note 3), 41s.

95 Menk, Kultur (note 23); G. Schmidt, Die "Zweite Reformation" im Gebiet
des Wetterauer Grafenvereins. Die Einführung des reformierten Bekenntnisses im
Spiegel der Modernisierung gräflicher Herrschaftssysteme, in: Schilling, Reformierte Konfessionalisierung (note 2), 184-213; idem, Der Wetterauer Grafenverein. Organisation und Politik einer Reichskorporation zwischen Reformation und
Westfälischem Frieden, Marburg 1989.

tion of territorial society. Despite differences in their political organization and in theoretical foundations, this is true both for the County of Nassau and for the Palatinate where the "Electors had long preferred informal, i.e. medieval forms, of sovereignty" and where the "turn towards a territorial polity was completed very late and only after (431) a Reformed church structure had been established."[96] The consolidation of states as a consequence of the Second Reformation took place even in small territories that were directly comparable to the County of Lippe in their level of development and in their legal status within the Empire. The initial situation was different in Hesse-Kassel, Saxony, and Brandenburg because in these territories the process of early modern state-building had already reached an advanced stage when the Second Reformation began. Nevertheless ecclesiastical renewal clearly ushered in a new stage in the rise of the early modern state even in these polities, not least through changes in church organization and structure that consolidated the position of the secular authorities in the church. In Hesse-Kassel, for example, in the wake of the Second Reformation the consistory was used as a political tool to end the relative autonomy which the Hessian church had enjoyed under its synodal structure.[97]

The assault upon the alliance of Lutheranism and semi-autonomous social powers (urban burghers, nobles, estates) which had formed during the course of the Lutheran Reformation seems to be especially important. This is particularly apparent in the case of Brandenburg and likewise in Sweden, where the Lutheran bishops could pursue a policy independent of royal power as a fourth political estate. This made Duke Karl von Södermanland, later King Karl IX, predisposed to favor a Second Reformation as he strove to concentrate state power in his own hands.[98] States frequently pursued an external policy of demarcation with their neighbors as a complement to this internal consolidation and expansion of authority. Apart from Lippe, the antagonism of Hesse-Kassel and Hesse-Darmstadt is the most prominent example. In a certain sense the victory of the Reformed confession at Basel also illustrates this process since it drew a line of demarcation, separating the city from

---

96 Press, Grafen von Erbach (note 14), 680.
97 Schorn-Schütte, Prediger (note 20).
98 Montgomery, Värjostand (note 65).

the neighboring Lutheran Markgrafschaft of Baden-Durlach.[99] Hence it played a role, at the same time, in establishing the modern border between Germany and Switzerland.

Finally another common feature—expressed in different ways—of states that adopted the Second Reformation was their pursuit of an energetic foreign policy both within the Empire and outside of it that paralleled the internal reshaping of church and state. This aspect of the Second Reformation has always been strongly emphasized because of its political consequences, particularly the foundation of the Protestant Union and the Thirty Years' War. When we consider both this activism in foreign policy and the internal territorial consolidation described above, the dialectical quality of the political consequences of the Second Reformation becomes apparent. (432) On the one hand the confrontational foreign policy pursued by the German territorial states was an integral part of their general strengthening in the wake of confessionalization. When the imperial estates were granted the right to form alliances, a right approved by imperial law in 1648, it was not least a result of the politicization of confessional territorial states generally and particularly of the Reformed territories. On the other hand it was precisely this activism in foreign policy that often led to their defeat, if not to their destruction. The discrepancy between a small territorial power base and involvement in imperial or international politics can almost be considered as another characteristic of Second Reformation states. In cases such as the Palatinate, Hesse-Kassel, and the Wetterau counties this is obvious, but it can also be seen in Electoral Saxony when its foreign policy became dangerously over-extended by its involvement in confessionally based imperial politics. Some smaller territories such as the County of Lippe pursued a more moderate policy and emerged undamaged from the political catastrophe of the German Calvinists during the first phase of the Thirty Years' War. The only true counter-example is Brandenburg-Prussia, where the foreign policy and the international dynamic of the Second Reformation was wisely directed by the state. This resulted in a rather prudent consolidation of Brandenburg's position within the Empire and the rising European power system. However, even

---

99 v. Greyerz, Basel (note 21), 239, 243.

the course adopted by Brandenburg-Prussia came perilously close to disaster only too often.

Finally, let us turn our attention to the place of the Second Reformation within confessionalization as an overarching process of societal change. First of all, we must again stress that the connection between confessionalization and state-building, with its political, structural, and social implications that were expressed to a greater or lesser degree, is also characteristic of both the Lutheran renewal and the Counter-Reformation. This is clear from the internal consolidation of Bavaria that made it "the first Catholic confessional state in central Europe."[100] It is also reflected in the participation of the early modern, territorial elite under the leadership of chancellor Thomas Franzius in the course of the Lutheran confessionalization of East Friesland,[101] and in the foreign policy of Württemberg in the wake of the concord movement, which had Empire-wide repercussions.[102] When seeking to identify the unique features (433) of Reformed confessionalization or the Second Reformation within this context, a distinction must be drawn between features of a contingent nature resulting from the particular historical circumstances of its introduction and spread, and those of an intrinsic nature resulting from its distinctive theology.

The particular intensity of foreign policy activity must be assigned to the first category. But it must also be considered a special characteristic of the Second Reformation even if Lutheran and Catholic confessionalization were accompanied by a certain activism in foreign policy as well. The generally observable trans-territorial power politics of the territorial states were especially apparent in the case of the Second Reformation territories because of the historical and legal position of the Reformed church in the Empire. While the other confessions sought to protect or to improve their own positions that were protected by imperial law, the Reformed newcomers,

---

100 H. Lutz, Bayern und Deutschland seit der Reformation—Perspektiven, Bilder und Reflektionen, in: A. Kraus (ed.), Land und Reich, Stamm und Nation. Festschrift für M. Spindler zum 90. Geburtstag, München 1984, vol. 2, 1-19, here 7.

101 H. Schmidt, Politische Geschichte Ostfrieslands, Leer 1975; H. Wiemann, Materialien zur Geschichte der ostfriesischen Landschaft, Aurich / Leer 1982.

102 M. Rudersdorf, Lutherische Erneuerung und Zweite Reformation? Die Beispiele Württemberg und Hessen, in: Schilling, Reformierte Konfessionalisierung (note 2), 130-153.

who did not participate in the Religious Peace of Augsburg, had to fight in order to achieve legal recognition. In addition the marked estrangement and hostility towards the Emperor and the House of Hapsburg shown especially by the Reformed lent their supra-territorial offensive a particular virulence from the very beginning. Finally, the ties of the Reformed to other western European countries must also be considered. Although the "internationalism" of Calvinists often seems to be nothing more than an historical cliché,[103] the Second Reformation had an international flavor that distinguished it from the Reformation of the first half of the century. While the Lutheran Reformation of the 1520's and 1530's spread throughout the Empire as a movement of spiritual renewal and only entered into political alliances under unusual circumstances (such as the Treaty of Chambord), the Second Reformation was part of an international movement with both religious and political significance by the time the German Philippists became allied with Calvinism in western Europe.

These connections meant that the Reformed bloc in the Empire shared directly in the alarming experience of the west European Calvinists with the Counter-Reformation and, accordingly, it organized itself politically and militarily. By contrast the Lutherans were always more concerned with the German situation and eagerly sought to preserve the Religious Peace of Augsburg. The major opponent of Calvinist internationalism, which included to a greater or lesser degree all of the German territories that adopted the Second Reformation, was Spain. At least in the case of the Reformed counts of the house of Nassau this anti-Spanish feeling was even more deeply rooted than their antagonism against either Catholicism or the Emperor.[104]

Turning to the distinctive intrinsic features of the Second Reformation, its first characteristic was the importance it placed upon providing theological justification for the linkage of confessional renewal and the public duties of the state, church, and society, based upon the concept of a "Reformation of Life."[105] The Second Reformation gave theological justifica-

---

103 Menk, Haltung (note 18), 231.

104 K.E. Demandt, Das Siegerland im Widerstreit vom Glauben, Recht und Politik, in: Hessisches Jahrbuch für Landesgeschichte 32 (1982), 176-206, here 181-183.

105 S.H. Hendrix, Luther's Impact on the Sixteenth Century, in: The Six-

tions for practices that were usually linked pragmatically by
the other confessions. This distinction is significant, even if in
such an important field as educational policy its actual success
was either modest or completely lacking.[106]

The theological rationalism of the Reformed theologians was
paralleled by a new rationalism in politics. This was Otto
Hintze's point when he identified "the spiritual intensity and
rationalism of religious and political life" as elements common
to both Calvinism and modern *raison d'état*.[107] In addition a
humanist undercurrent affected both the social recruitment and
the spirituality of the Second Reformation. In a later phase,
especially after the Thirty Years' War, this strong representation of humanism enabled the separation of politics and confession to proceed in a relatively quick and uncomplicated way
in the Reformed territories of the Empire, eventually leading
to the secularization of state and society. (435)

Finally it must be determined whether the Second Reformation was connected with particular conceptions of political,
governmental, and ecclesiastical organization or even with a
specific theory of politics and society that did not appear either
within the spheres of Lutheran or of Catholic confessionalization in Germany.[108] Not least because of their own understanding, the Reformed are usually portrayed as promoters of
democracy, in contrast to the Lutherans. This view was
obviously already a commonplace among intellectuals in early
modern times as Pufendorf noted in his well known work *De
statu imperii Germanici* of 1667: "the spirit of this religion
(Calvinism) encourages the emergence of democratic free-
doms."[109]

Historians must disagree with this conclusion in light of the
connection between the Second Reformation and territorial
state-building. Obviously even in this context German Re-

teenth-Century-Journal 16, No. 1, 1985, 3-14.

106 G. Schormann, Zweite Reformation und Bildungswesen am Beispiel der
Elementarschulen, in: Schilling, Reformierte Konfessionalisierung (note 2), 308-
316; Menk advocates the opposite position in Territorialstaat (note 18).

107 G. Oestreich, Geist und Gestalt des frühmodernen Staates, Göttingen 1964,
33.

108 The differences between Lutheran and Reformed political theory are mini-
mized by recent research. See e.g. W. Schulze, Zwingli, lutherisches Widerstandsdenken, monarchomachischer Widerstand, in: P. Blickle, A. Lindt and A. Schindler (eds.), Zwingli und Europa, Zürich 1985, 199-216.

109 Pufendorf, De statu imperii (note 84), chapter 8, §7.

formed positions were clearly dependent upon the historical circumstances in which they were espoused.[110] Analogous to the exceptional pedagogical success of the Calvinists in the Rhenish territories of Kleve and Berg related by Gerhard Schormann's contribution to the "Second Reformation" symposium, the democratic tendencies observed by Pufendorf and others can probably be considered valid for the few cases of a Reformed minority within a multi-confessional environment. In the Reformed (436) territories with a territorial church structure, its political and social consequences were of quite a different kind. In such states the Second Reformation usually strengthened authoritarian structures in both church and state, even if it retained elements of presbyterian and synodal organization. This was true in Lippe as much as in the important territories of Hesse-Kassel and Brandenburg and in the port city of Bremen, whose church government was tightly controlled by the city council. This type of state praxis was obviously a consequence of humanist political thought and of the Zwinglian-Erastian type of state-church relationship. In this humanist and Zwinglian tradition, the secular and ecclesiastical commonwealth was understood to be a unity, and consequently the state was given responsibility for ensuring proper order in every sphere of public and private life. This duty was justified both in moral and theological terms. As a result the church actually became part of the state, subjugated to the will of the ruler and his early modern bureaucracy. Paul Stein, the Reformed court preacher at Kassel, left no doubt in his funeral sermon for Landgrave Moritz that it was the duty of the Christian government to be involved with the internal affairs of the church in order to advance the true religion. The "monarchic principle of rule" was adopted in Hesse-Kassel together with the Second Reformation.[111] Only a few traces of monarchomachian political theory remained, and they were not a threat to the status quo as long as the government and the theologians were in accord. It is true that the right of princes to regulate church affairs had to be exercised for the benefit of the people; otherwise the regent would have to give up his

---

110 F.W. Wibbeling, Die beiden Typen reformierter Kirchen, in: Reformierte Kirchenzeitung 85 (1935), 332-333; Gassmann, Ecclesia reformata (note 12) 11ss., 253ss.; Münch, Zucht (note 14), 25-34; Klueting, "Zweite Reformation" (note 58).
111 Schorn-Schütte, Prediger (note 20).

office. However, the "common good" was not determined in
detail by democratic or semi-democratic institutions, but by
the Reformed theologians and the political elite. Accordingly
the Reformed ideal of a Christian commonwealth was no less
effective as a theological justification for authoritarian government than the well-known and often criticized alliance between
Lutheranism and princely territorialism.

By contrast the genuine Calvinist position, which supported
an autonomous congregational church and established the
church-state relationship upon quite different principles than
the Zwinglian and Erastian one, and which sought a strengthening of inferior magistrates and a limitation of princely power
in the political sphere, and supported a corporation of subjects
whose modern integration and reshaping would be accomplished from below, was very weakly represented in the
Empire. Within the German Second Reformation this kind of
political thought made headway in only a few places, chiefly
those that were strongly influenced by the Netherlands. The
most prominent example is the "Emden Revolution" of 1595,
though its theoretical justification was influenced to a considerable extent by the pre-Calvinist, communal and republican
tradition of German cities.[112] Calvinism found its most effective academic home in the Gymnasium of Herborn, whose
influence extended far beyond its immediate region in its hey-
day. This influence was due not least to (437) Johannes Althusius, the most productive of its professors in the area of political theory.[113] However, the influence of his works was the
strongest outside of Germany where the historical conditions
differed from those present under the territorial structure of
the Empire.[114] The same can be said of the political effects of
federal theology, which is of special interest for the political
theory of the Second Reformation. Spreading from its early
centers in Herborn and Marburg, federal theology influenced

---

112 Schilling, Republikanismus (note 86).

113 The "democratic" interpretation of Althusius' political theory is denied
recently by M. Behnen, Herrscherbild und Herrschaftstechnik in der "Politica"
des Johannes Althusius, in: Zeitschrift für historische Forschung 11 (1984), 417-
472.

114 K.O. Frhr. von Aretin and N. Hammerstein, Reich, Frühe Neuzeit, in: O.
Brunner, W. Conze and R. Koselleck (eds.), Geschichtliche Grundbegriffe. Historisches Lexikon zur politisch-sozialen Sprache in Deutschland, vol. 5, Stuttgart
1984, 456-486, here 468.

political developments in the Netherlands, England, and Scotland.[115]

The history of the Second Reformation, given here in broad outlines only, must be approached as a comparative territorial history of confessionalization in Germany and must be analyzed in connection with the history of confessionalization in Europe.

VII. EPILOGUE: A TERMINOLOGICAL MODIFICATION, BUT NO "CONVERSIO."

To conclude, I think it appropriate to reappraise the historiographic implications of terms that have been traditionally used to discuss the Confessional Age. The fifth symposium of the *Verein für Reformationsgeschichte* (October 2-5, 1985) was held at Reinhausen to discuss "The Problem of the 'Second Reformation' in Germany." It was concerned with two issues: an analysis of the historical process of transition from Lutheranism to the Reformed confession observable in several German territories and cities, and the problem of nomenclature for these events, which is at the same time a problem of interpretation. The result of the symposium is reflected in the title of the congress volume, *Die reformierte Konfessionalisierung in Deutschland*. The reasons for this terminological modification are given in the final discussion. The arguments recorded there and in this essay show that no painful "conversion" was necessary to make this modification. Subsequently a number of early modern historians (including Notker Hammerstein and Winfried Schulze) have argued strongly for the continued use of the term "Second Reformation" despite objections that have been raised against it. Since I share their view, I have not abandoned all use of the term. It is crucially important, however, to recognize its "ideological character" as an element of Calvinist propaganda in its struggle with Lutheranism. We must also recognize that the program of a "Reformation of Life" as a second stage following the "Reformation of Doctrine" was also known among Lutherans and probably among Tridentine Catholic Reformers too. This makes the historical and theoretical parallelism between those processes denoted as "Second Reformation" and the Lutheran renewal associated with the

---

115 J.F.G. Goeters, Föderaltheologie, in: Theologische Realenzyklopädie, vol. 11, 246-252.

movement of Concord set out in my paper even more clear. This parallelism should be expressed terminologically—as "Lutheran confessionalization" and "Reformed confessionalization." Both processes have the same dignity. The claim to superiority made by sixteenth century Calvinists must not be preserved in the analytic concept of a Second Reformation.

The "neutral" terminology "Reformed confessionalization" and "Lutheran confessionalization" should simplify the historians' task of identifying the distinctive features of each kind of confessionalization. However, it seems justified to qualify Reformed confessionalization in Germany additionally as a "Second Reformation" in order to designate the self-understanding of the actors, as well as to denote its distinctive political dynamic and its explicitly public character as a "Reformation of Life."

The new nomenclature should not be restricted to processes within Protestantism but should also be used to describe corresponding phenomena on the Catholic side. These processes belong together historically and theoretically, and so after the two symposia on Reformed and Lutheran confessionalization[116] during the summer of 1993 a third "confessionalization" symposium will take place on the theme of "Catholic Confessionalization." The conceptual unification of "Reformed Confessionalization," "Lutheran Confessionalization," and "Catholic Confessionalization" shows that they are parallel processes. It also clarifies the concept of confessionalization itself as an overarching political, religious, and social transformation which had a lasting impact especially on German history. The academic neutrality of the new terminology has an additional advantage over the previous terms "Lutheran orthodoxy" or "Concordial Lutheranism," "Counter-Reformation" or "Catholic Reformation," and "Second Reformation" in that it eliminates the emotional and subjective connotations that are connected with this older terminology. The neutral, unbiased terminology is important not only to those committed to a religious or confessional point of view but also to those outside the church who have great difficulty understanding the history of the confessional quarrels adequately. Last but not least the paradigm of "confessionalization" will stimulate research. It

---

116 The papers are published in H. Schilling (ed.), Die reformierte Konfessionalisierung in Deutschland, Gütersloh 1986, and H.Ch. Rublack (ed.), Die lutherische Konfessionalisierung in Deutschland, Gütersloh 1991.

encourages necessary historical comparisons because it focuses attention upon similar historical and developmental conditions, but at the same time it allows us to see the distinguishing features of the responses made by the individual confessions to these conditions. The epoch should no longer be called the "Age of the Counter-Reformation," but the "Confessional Age," or even more precisely the "Age of Confessionalization." This expression emphasizes the dynamic and revolutionary character of the period as well as the political and social implications of its religious and ecclesiastical change.[117]

---

117 As the reader might be interested in the adoption of the ideas and the research programm outlined in this essay a list of the more substantial reviews of the Second-Reformation volume seems appropriate: R.M. Kingdon, in: Archiv für Reformationsgeschichte 79 (1988), 358-362; H.R. Schmidt, in: Zwingliana 1990, Fasc. 3, 280-286; H. Frost, in: Zeitschrift für evangelisches Kirchenrecht 34 (1989), 311-317; N. Hammerstein, in: Historische Zeitschrift 247 (1988), 421-423; J. Langhoff, in: Jahrbuch für Regionalgeschichte 16 (Weimar, DDR, 1989), 311-314; B. Nischan, in: The Sixteenth Century Journal 19 (1988), 288-289; J. Backus, in: Bibliothèque d' Humanisme et Renaissance 1988, 227-229; G. Chaix, in: Francia 17,2 (1990), 257-259.

PART THREE

THE NETHERLANDS — THE PIONEER SOCIETY
OF EARLY MODERN EUROPE

CHAPTER SEVEN

THE HISTORY OF THE NORTHERN NETHERLANDS AND MODERNIZATION THEORY

I. FORMULATION OF THE PROBLEM

The concept of modernization, which is an offshoot of the historical and evolutionary thinking of Max Weber and Otto Hintze, is used by historians to examine the paths which led to the more or less pluralistic and democratic industrial society of the nineteenth and twentieth centuries. This process of modernization and transformation is thought to be characterized by the following distinctive features: significant economic growth together with both specialization and differentiation within the economy and a free capitalistic form of business and labor organization; the emergence of a pervasive state structure as well as greater political participation for citizens; and secularization, the separation of church and state, of religion and society. Further elements of the theory, which are important for the following discussion, include the concepts of pioneer and follower societies within this process and the measurement of degrees of social modernity with the help of social-demographic indices such as literacy and urbanization.[1] (476)

---

1 There are dozens of articles and books on modernization theory and processes. The following were especially helpful for this essay: R. Bendix, Modernisierung in internationaler Perspektive, in: W. Zapf (ed.), Theorien des sozialen Wandels, Köln 1971, 505-512; D. Lerner and J.S. Coleman, Modernization, in: International Encylopaedia of the Social Sciences 10 (1968), 386-402; J. Brode, The Process of Modernization: An Annotated Bibliography on the Sociocultural Aspects of Development, Cambridge 1969; W. Zapf, Modernisierungstheorien, in: Prismata. Dank an Bernhard Hanssler, Pullach 1974, 302-317; H.U. Wehler, Modernisierungstheorie und Geschichte, Göttingen 1975; idem, Vorüberlegungen zu einer modernen deutschen Gesellschaftsgeschichte, in: Industrielle Gesellschaft und politisches System, Bonn 1978, 3-20; D.C. Tipps, Modernization Theory and the Comparative Study of Societies: A Critical Perspective, in: Comparative Studies in Society and History 15 (1973), 199-226; H. Schissler, Theorien des sozialen Wandels, in: Neue Politische Literatur 19 (1974), 155-189; F. Eberle, Bemerkungen zum Stand der Diskussion um die Modernisierungstheorie, in: C. Pozzoli (ed.), Jahrbuch der Arbeiterbewegung, vol. 4: Faschismus und Kapitalismus, Frankfurt 1976, 242-258; J. Wallerstein, Modernization: requiescat in pace, in:

The concept of a general European-Atlantic process of development, which can be understood as a unified process in spite of pronounced differences at specific points, still remains heuristically fruitful for historians and ought not be rejected. When undogmatically and flexibly applied it offers historians important advantages. These include the opportunity to reduce complex societal patterns to their central structural elements and to follow their development over the course of centuries, (477) an analytical perspective that is by nature comparative, and a salutary pressure to recognize how the concrete historical experiences of individual nations relate to the general course of development in European history. This inherent pressure for comparison is particularly helpful since it tends to counter both unreflective adherence to ideological agendas and chauvinistic blindness. Another point in favor of the modernization concept is that it is based upon historical data, in contrast to a number of other theories of the social sciences. Although the data used to formulate these generalizations are drawn almost exclusively from English and American history, I think they can be modified easily to the extent that hypotheses derived in this way can appropriately serve as an heuristic tool for the analysis of different historical processes of development within Europe.[2] Although modernization theory has traditionally been applied in a biased manner, it can more easily be adjusted to actual historical development and to specific cases than is possible with purely rational constructs and social scientific models that are subject only to the formal laws of logic and cannot be adjusted to reflect historical reality.

Among all of the suggestions for modifying the theory that have been advanced since the beginning of the debate the work of Talcott Parsons and others seems particularly promising. These scholars have sought the antecedents of the processes of

idem, The Capitalist World-Economy. Essays, Cambridge 1979, 132-137.-Among the few historical studies employing modernization theory the following are of special importance: E.A. Wrigley, The Process of Modernization and the Industrial Revolution in England, in: The Journal of Interdisciplinary History 3 (1972), 225-259; H.Ch. Schröder, Die neuere englische Geschichte im Lichte einiger Modernisierungstheoreme, in: R. Koselleck (ed.), Studien zum Beginn der modernen Welt, Stuttgart 1977, 30-67; F. Krantz and P.M. Hohenberg (eds.), Failed Transitions to Modern Industrial Society: Renaissance Italy and Seventeenth Century Holland, Montréal 1974; J. de Vries, On the Modernity of the Dutch Republic, in: Journal of Economic History 33 (1973), 191-202.

2 See M. Walzer, The Only Revolution. Notes on the Theory of Modernization, in: Dissent 11 (1964), 432-443.

modernization in the period before the American and French revolutions at the end of the eighteenth century, ascribing part of the preparatory transformation to the *ancien régime* and devoting renewed attention to cultural factors.[3] By considering the early modern roots of modernization, which varied dramatically from country to country in the variegated political and social landscape of pre-modern Europe, historians are confronted with realities that prevent them from assuming a unilinear pattern of development, a charge rightly leveled at earlier modernization theorists. The process of transformation that occurred in the early modern Netherlands is a particularly good test case for illustrating the need to modify modernization theory in order to allow for greater diversity and variety in the process of early modern societal development.

The Dutch Republic displays an independent path of development[4] that differs both from the English and from the absolutist-continental models, (478) which provided the basic historical information for modernization theory. The pattern of bureaucratization and centralization within modernization theory was derived from the absolutist-continental model while the elements of participation were derived from the English model.

During the seventeenth century contemporary observers described the northern Netherlands as a pioneer society and the other European states as follower societies, i. e., using similar categories expressing these ideas, as modernization theorists do today. The English, the Swedes, the Germans, and the French were aware of their relative backwardness during the seventeenth century and regarded the Dutch Republic as the forerunner of a development that should be introduced as

---

3 See T. Parsons, The System of Modern Societies, Englewood Cliffs, N.J., 1970, chapter 4.

4 On a general introduction to the history of the Netherlands see the articles of J.J. Woltjer and J. Schöffer, in: Th. Schieder (ed.), Handbuch der Europäischen Geschichte, vols. 3 and 5, Stuttgart 1971, 1968; J. Huizinga, Holländische Kultur im 17. Jahrhundert, 3rd ed. Frankfurt 1977; F. Petri, Die Kultur der Niederlande, Frankfurt 1964; T. Wittmann, Das Goldene Zeitalter der Niederlande, Leipzig 1975; P. Geyl, The Netherlands in the 17th Century, 2 vols., 2nd ed. London 1966 and 1968; K.H.D. Haley, The Dutch in the 17th Century, London 1972; L. Price, Culture and Society in the Dutch Republic During the 17th Century, London 1974; J.S. Bromley and E.H. Kossmann (eds.), Britain and the Netherlands, London 1960ss.; Acta Historiae Nederlandicae 1 (1966)ss, since 1978 (vol. 11) called The Low Countries History Yearbook; G.A.M. Beekelaar et al. (eds.), Vaderlands Verleden in Veelvoud, Amsterdam 1980.

quickly as possible into their own lands, patterning them
directly after the Dutch model. Not only the economic structures but also the social conditions, that is, the capacity for
toleration and the integrative power of the political system,
were mentioned in this context.[5] The status of Dutch society as
a model for others was limited to the seventeenth century; in
the following century the situation was reversed. Seen as a
whole the Republic at that time no longer exemplified modern
tendencies. When compared with the pervasive power of centralized, absolutist states it appeared to be "a smaller, old-
fashioned merchant state in a pre-modern but durably con-
structed house."[6] After 1670 (479) a progressive decline took
place, marked by economic stagnation, if not contraction, and a
political withdrawal from world power status to that of a
second- or third-rate power travelling in the wake of England.

   This is indeed a contradictory finding: at first the position
of a pioneer society, then stagnation and even backwardness.
By itself this hardly seems remarkable to historians who are
used to the rise and fall of states and cultures. It only becomes
a problem if we realize that the seventeenth century Netherlands can be characterized as "modern" not only in the impre-
cise definition of the word, i. e., the extent of relative development present in the time period under consideration, but
also according to the more rigorous definition of modernization
theory. During the seventeenth century Dutch society already
displayed features of modernity in this specific sense and it
fulfilled those criteria that modernization theorists consider to
be signs either of a successful breakthrough to a modern
society marked by democracy, individualism, and a capitalist
economy, or of a society on the threshold of such a
breakthrough. These criteria are measured by a series of socio-

---

5 See Schröder, Englische Geschichte (note 1).-Sir William Temple, Observations upon the United Provinces of the Netherlands (1673), ed. by G. Clark,
London 1972, 107, 112; J. Thirsk (ed.), Seventeenth-Century Economic Documents, Oxford 1972, 69ss.: Josiah Childe's statement before the Council of Trade
that the lead of the Netherlands is based on "the education of the children, ... the
well-providing of their poor and employing of them, ... the freedom makes the
nation valiant, ... liberty of religion". On a similar statement concerning Sweden
see E. Hassinger, Wirtschaftliche Motive und Argumente für religiöse Duldsamkeit, in: Archiv für Reformationsgeschichte 49 (1958), 226-245, here 241ss.

6 Schöffer, in: Schieder (ed.), Handbuch (note 4), vol. 4, 654. On the economic
side see J. de Vries, De economische achteruitgang der Republiek in de achtiende
eeuw, Amsterdam 1959; J.L. Price, Culture and Society in the Dutch Republic
During the 17th Century, London 1974, 211-229.

demographic indices.[7] The urban literacy rate in Holland, the province I am focusing upon in the following discussion together with the other maritime provinces (Zeeland, Utrecht, Friesland and Groningen), was 60% for men during the seventeenth century, and reached 85% by the end of the eighteenth century. In rural areas reading ability was relatively common already during the sixteenth century and increased dramatically, above all during the seventeenth century.[8] Widespread literacy was reflected in the printing industry by production of the first series of pocket-sized books. In 1645 ten different newspapers could be purchased each week in Amsterdam.[9] The urbanization rate in Holland was 50% at the beginning of the sixteenth century, and during the eighteenth century it reached 63%.[10] Geographic mobility was extremely high not only in the cities but also between villages. The same can be said for upward social mobility in these years.[11] The maritime provinces of the northern Netherlands also scored high on other indices of development toward societal and political modernity such as a closely knit transportation network, the frequency of regular freight and passenger service, the introduction of new technology, and the consumption of energy, measured by peat cutting.[12] In Friesland, one of the mainly agricultural regions, the

7 D. Lerner, Die Modernisierung des Lebensstils: eine Theorie, in: Zapf (ed.), Theorien, 362-381; Wehler, Modernisierungstheorie, 22ss. (both note 1).

8 S. Hart, Geschrift en Getal, Dordrecht 1976, 115ss.; idem, in: Amstelodamum 55 (1968), 3-6; H.A. Enno van Gelder, Nederlandse Dorpen in de 16 eeuw, Amsterdam 1953, esp. 14, 32, 38s., 87.

9 D.W. Davies, The World of the Elzeviers, Den Haag 1957; G.C. Gibbs, The Role of the Dutch Republic as the Intellectual Entrepôt of Europe in the 17th and 18th Century, in: Bijdragen en Mededelingen betreffende de Geschiedenis der Nederlanden 86 (1971), 323-349; F. Dahl, Amsterdam—Earliest Newspaper Centre of Western Europe, in: Het Boek 25 (1938-39), 161-197.

10 J. de Vries, The Dutch Rural Economy in the Golden Age, 1500-1700, New Haven 1974, 115; J.A. Faber et al., Urbanisering, industrialisering en milieuaantasting, in: Afdeling Agrarische Geschiedenis van de Landbouwhogeschool Wageningen, Bijdragen (abbreviation: A.A.G. Bijdragen) 18 (1973), 251-271, here 254ss.; Schöffer, in: Schieder (ed.), Handbuch (note 4), vol. 4, 642.

11 Many examples are documented in J. Elias, De vroedschap van Amsterdam, 1578-1795, 2 vols., Haarlem 1903 (see e.g. Gerrit Witsen, the son of a peasant who became a well-to-do merchant and burgomaster of Amsterdam). As far as the villages are concerned see de Vries, Economy (note 10), 112.

12 de Vries, Economy (note 10), 93, 165, 173, 123, 205-209; idem, Barges and Capitalism. Passenger Transportation in the Dutch Economy, 1632-1839, Wageningen 1978, = A.A.G., Bijdragen 21, 32-398. Temple, Observations (note 5), 77: "And by this easie way of travelling an industrious man loses no time from his business, for he writes, or eats, or sleeps while he goes." Ch. Wilson, Transport as a Factor in the History of Economic Development, in: Journal of European Eco-

pattern of employment was closer to that of modern societies than to Old European feudal ones: the labor force was distributed almost equally between the three sectors of the economy—agriculture, industry, and commerce.[13] While about 80% of the population were still employed in agriculture in large parts of the rest of Europe, the maritime regions of the Netherlands had already clearly left Old European agrarian civilization behind them.

Dutch society presents an ambivalent, even a contradictory situation: on the one hand social modernity was unmistakable even during the seventeenth century, and there was no fundamental regression while the economy stagnated during the eighteenth century. On the other hand the Republic showed an inability to accommodate endogenous change at the end of the eighteenth century. The process of transformation to an industrial and democratic society was slow and suffered many setbacks when it finally did occur under external pressure during the nineteenth century.[14] This contradiction confirms that modernity, as measured by socio-demographic indices, is not necessarily connected with an institutionalized ability to sustain growth and change, and to develop free—in the sense of democratic—and rational institutions and political orientation.[15] In order to take the critique of the evolutionist strain within modernization theory—the assumption that modernization occurs as a linear and synchronous process—a step further, I would like to offer the following thesis: In the case of the Dutch Republic the inability to accommodate en-dogenous change during the eighteenth century and the further difficulties occasioned by the process of transformation during the nineteenth were ultimately a consequence of its pioneer status during the sixteenth and seventeenth centuries. In a dialectic setback the forerunner became the rear guard because its partial modernity blocked any substantial further development. In order to verify this assertion (481) I will consider in succession the *economy*, the *state*, *society*, and the *ecclesiastical* and *cultural situation* of the early modern Republic.

---

nomic History 2 (1973), 320-330.

13 de Vries, Economy (note 10), 125, 130.

14 J. Mokyr, Industrialization in the Low Countries, 1795-1850, New Haven 1976; J.A. de Jonge, De Industrializatie in Nederland tussen 1850 en 1914, Amsterdam 1968.

15 S.N. Eisenstadt, in: S.N. Eisenstadt and S. Rokkan (eds.), Building States and Nations, vol. 1, Beverly Hills 1973, 42s.

II. THE ECONOMY

A clear distinction must be drawn between commerce and industry on the one hand and agriculture on the other. Commerce and industry were characterized by an unusual breadth of activity, by an optimal concentration of supply and demand at the famous Amsterdam Bourse, and by increasing rates of production and tonnage that had hardly ever been reached previously. The northern provinces became the major transshipment point for northwestern European, Mediterranean, and colonial trade, driving the commercial revolution of the sixteenth century and transferring it to the northern and eastern European regions. Thus the European-Atlantic division of labor between regions of manufacturing, agriculture, and production of raw materials was strengthened.[16]

Apart from the genuinely brilliant and innovative invention of a new merchant vessel, the so-called *Fluitschip*, which was inexpensive to build and economical to use since it was faster and required a smaller crew but had a large freight capacity, this expansion of industry and commerce rested not upon fundamental innovations but upon a "highly developed traditionalism."[17] Free trade was dominant both in economic theory and economic policy. Industries were organized by craft guilds, although in a flexible form that took into account the interests of the merchants.

The source of developmental impulses is a key question in the modernization paradigm. According to the theory based upon English experience, economic growth appears initially to be a consequence of endogenous impulses, generated from within a given society. In the case under investigation, however, the expansion of trade and manufacturing which occurred during the decisive phase (482) of the 1580's and 1590's resulted primarily from *exogenous* impulses. These included:

1. The existing inter-regional division of labor, not so much

---

16 J.G. van Dillen, Van rijkdom en regenten, Den Haag 1970; J.H. van Stuijvenberg (ed.), De economische Geschiedenis van Nederland, Groningen 1977; J. de Vries, The Economy of Europe in an Age of Crisis, 1600-1750, Cambridge 1976; J.A. van Houtte, An Economic History of the Low Countries 800-1800, London 1977.-H.P.H. Jansen, Hollands Voorsprong, Leiden 1976 (English translation: Acta Historiae Nederlandicae 10 (1977), 1-20); K. Spading, Holland und die Hanse im 15. Jahrhundert, Weimar 1973.

17 de Vries, Europe (note 16) , 251; V. Barbour, Capitalism in Amsterdam, Baltimore 1950.

on the level of the global economic system as within Europe itself, was between the agricultural regions in the east and the areas dependent upon grain imports in western and southern Europe. The need for large scale transportation resulting from this division of labor could only be satisfactorily met by the northern Netherlands because they were in the most advantageous position geographically and they practically had a monopoly on freight transportation.

2. A second series of impulses for growth resulted from the military and political situation. The immigration of specialists and entrepreneurs from the southern provinces, which had been highly developed both commercially and industrially for generations, contributed significantly to economic development in the north.[18] The northern Netherlands also prospered through their well known "trade with the enemy," i. e., by providing Spain with materials necessary for war, for example, ship-building materials, copper, and copper goods including cannons.[19] In light of the controversy unleashed by Sombart and Nef over the possibility or impossibility of economic growth impulses being generated by war,[20] the northern Netherlands are clearly an example of its stimulating effects. This was recognized by a contemporary English pamphleteer when he angrily asserted, "Of all the world they are the people that thrive and grow rich by warre, which is the world's ruine and their support."[21] Nothing illustrates the power of these impulses for growth better than the trade and manufacturing empire of the Amsterdam cannon kings Louis de Geer and Elias Trip—both immigrants from the south—which extended as far as the iron and copper mines of Sweden. Since de Geer

---

18 J. Briels, De Emigratie uit de zuidelijke Nederlanden omstreeks 1540-1621/30, in: Opstand en Pacificatie in de Lage Landen, Gent 1976, 184-220, esp. 198ss. For a wider perspective see H. Schilling, Innovation through Migration: The Settlements of Calvinistic Netherlanders in Sixteenth- and Seventeenth-Century Central and Western Europe, in: Histoire sociale-Social History 16, No. 31 (May 1983), 7-33.

19 J.H. Kernkamp, De handel op den vijnd, 1572-1609, 2 vols., Utrecht 1932 and 1934.

20 J.M. Winter, The Economic and Social History of War, in: idem (ed.), War and Economic Development, Cambridge 1975. F. Snapper, Oorlogsinvloeden op de overzeese handel van Holland, 1551-1719, Amsterdam 1959; G. Parker, War and Economic Change: The Economic Costs of the Dutch Revolt, in: idem, Spain and the Netherlands, Glasgow 1979, 178-204.

21 Pamphlet "Dutch Drawn to the Life" (1664), quoted by Ch. Wilson, Queen Elizabeth and the Revolt of the Netherlands, London 1970, 19; see also Snapper, Oorlogsinvloeden (note 20), 285-292.

(and others) through his entrepreneurial activities helped to build Sweden's infrastructure, thereby supplying an important element necessary for its development from an agricultural state into a northern European great power, integrated into the European network of trade and manufacturing, the dynamic emerging (483) from the Netherlands served at the same time to reshape the entire European economic system.[22]

During the first half of the seventeenth century, this set of circumstances resulted in the concentration of European mercantile wealth and both manufacturing and entrepreneurial skills in the Dutch Republic, above all in Holland.

A completely different picture emerges when we examine the agricultural sector[23] with respect to both its antecedents and to the high degree of development that it achieved in the course of the sixteenth century. The concepts that best describe Dutch agricultural development are not exogenous impulses or highly developed traditionalism, as in the trade and manufacturing sectors, but rather an endogenous rhythm of development and fully developed modernity. The conditions responsible for this early transition to modernity are to be found in special structural features which already during the Middle Ages distinguished this part of the northwestern European cultural zone, located north of the great rivers (Rhine and Meuse), from the rest of Europe.[24] Feudalism never existed there or only in a very imperfect and weakened form. Control over land by the nobility was restricted to a few areas and

22 O. Johannsen, Louis de Geer, Berlin 1933; J. Romein, Louis de Geer der König der Kaufleute, in: idem, Ahnherren der holländischen Kultur, Bern n.d., 178-205; E.F. Heckscher, Economic History of Sweden, 3rd ed. Cambridge 1968; M. Roberts, Gustavus Adolphus, 2 vols., London 1958.

23 de Vries, Economy (note 10); See also the following articles in A.A.G. Bijdragen, Wageningen, esp. B.H. Slicher van Bath, Yield Ratios, 810-1820, 10 (1963); idem, Agrarische Geschiedenis van de Veluwe, 11 (1964); idem, Economic and Social Conditions in the Frisian Districts, 13 (1965); A.W. van der Woude, Het Noorderkwartier, Een regional historisch onderzoek etc., 16 (1972); J.A. Faber, Drie eeuwen Friesland, 17 (1972); H. van der Wee and E. van Cauwenberghe, Productivity of Land and Agricultural Innovation in the Low Countries (1250-1800), Leuven 1978; H.A. Enno van Gelder, Nederlandse dorpen in de 16e eeuw, Amsterdam 1953.

24 Petri, Kultur (note 4); idem, Zum Problem der herrschaftlichen und genossenschaftlichen Züge in der mittelalterlichen Marschensiedlung an der flämischen und niederländischen Nordsee, in: Historische Forschungen für Walter Schlesinger, Köln 1974, 226-241; H. van der Linden, De Cope, Bijdragen tot de rechtsgeschiedenis van de openlegging der Hollands-Utrechtse laagvlakte, Assen 1955; B.H. Slicher van Bath, Herschreven Historie, Leiden 1948; J.J. Kalma et al. (eds.), Geschiedenis van Friesland, Drachten 1968.

even there remained weak both because the region had been only imperfectly integrated—or had never been incorporated—into the Roman and Frankish empires, and also because of the particular necessities of the settlement process there. Even in those places, such as Holland, where settlement was directed by princes and overlords, they were forced to give far-reaching freedom of self-government to the settlers because of the special difficulties involved in preparing and maintaining farmland in these marsh regions where the danger of flooding was ever present. The peasants were free and usually possessed at least part of their land as a freehold. The remaining land they rented—sometimes from members of their own estate—for set periods of time, regulated by legal agreement. A money economy was introduced early in Friesland because of the farmers' participation in trading ventures. During the late Middle Ages these capitalistic structures were expanded through a large, freely operated land market—(484) dealing mostly in individual plots of land—and by the rental agreements mentioned above. Publicly owned fields and common lands were either abolished or their size was greatly reduced. The position of the nobility and clergy was very weak at the beginning of the sixteenth century with the exception of Utrecht and the interior provinces of the east, the latter being excluded from consideration in this essay. The nobility of Friesland first appeared in the late Middle Ages. In Holland there were quite a few nobles, but their relationship to the peasants was scarcely of a personal, feudal character, but rather an objective, legal one. The right of nobles to exercise various kinds of authority in this province was from the beginning very limited, and comprised, for the most part, only the lower justice, church patronage and a few other lesser jurisdictional rights. In addition the ties binding the nobility and peasants ceased to be personal and became increasingly pragmatic ones as a result of the repeated division of noble districts, the so-called *Ambachtsheerlijkheden*, and the absenteeism of their noble occupants. Individual nobles, who acted as shareholders in a whole series of *Ambachtsheerlijkheden*, limited themselves to the collection of monies and participation in the appointment of office holders, particularly for bailiffs (*schouten*), who accepted their office by means of a lease agreement.[25]

As a result of these factors the Dutch peasantry developed strong individualist tendencies.[26] This individualism was augmented by their familiarity with complicated arrangements, an ability to comprehend contexts other than the local one, and by a wealth of experience in communal public activities.[27] These qualities were the result of a long tradition of peasant involvement in communal affairs, above all in the formidable duties of coastal protection and drainage, as well as in agricultural trade and sea travel. These constitutional and socio-economic structures, which emerged during the Middle Ages and remained vital during the early modern period, contained within them a potential for endogenous development which enabled Dutch agriculture to achieve a quick and optimal adjustment to the new opportunities offered by the commercial revolution and rapid population growth of the sixteenth century.[28]

Until the end of the sixteenth century these economic and social circumstances created a situation which, in contrast to the traditionalism of the industrial and commercial sectors in the Dutch economy, exhibited the characteristics of modernity in significant ways. (485) The decisive breakthrough that made it possible for farmers to adopt modern, capitalistic forms came when Dutch agriculture outgrew subsistence farming. Farmers gave up non-agricultural activities, typical of subsistence farming, and began to specialize in raising those agricultural products that were best suited to their soil, and thus would give them the best possible harvest of crops that were at the same time most in demand at the market. Grazing and the cultivation of industrially important plants, vegetables, and flowers replaced the older unprofitable grain farming. The relatively small, non-specialized, and unproductive subsistence farms grew into commercial enterprises that employed laborers on a contract basis. These farms were capital-intensive and

---

25 Enno van Gelder, Dorpen (note 23); S.J. Fockema Andreae, De nederlandse Staat onder de Republiek, 7th ed. Amsterdam 1975.

26 de Vries, Economy (note 10), 55.

27 Petri, Kultur (note 4); idem, Problem (note 24); Enno van Gelder, Dorpen (note 23); the essays of J. Alberts and J.M. van Winter, in: Th. Mayer (ed.), Die Anfänge der Landgemeinde und ihr Wesen, vol. 1, Stuttgart 1964.

28 See note 23.

produced high yields of crops intended for the supra-regional market. Sizeable businesses appeared in grazing areas especially. Their methods of production were characterized by the use of machines, above all windmills, but also horse-powered butter churns, by heavy and continual fertilization, made possible by trade in dung and fertilizers, and by new methods of animal breeding and feeding.

This conformity to market conditions was only possible because the farmers were freeholders, subject to no cultivation restrictions from either the nobility or their fellow farmers on the basis of communal tradition. The specific contractual terms for the ownership and leasing of land stimulated intensive investment of manpower and capital.

As a consequence of these agricultural changes the number of non-agricultural specialists in freight shipment, transportation, energy, and crafts increased in villages and rural areas. These workers supplied goods and services which the farmers could no longer provide for themselves. Considerations of profitability motivated farmers to enlarge and adjust the boundaries of their farms by buying appropriate parcels of land. A "landless semi-proletariat," such as the *Kötter* of Westphalia, could not take root and hence no rural manufacturing or proto-industrialization developed in this part of the northern Netherlands. The excess rural population streamed into the cities because the large agricultural firms with their huge pasture areas and the non-agrarian trades of the villages and small towns offered only limited employment opportunities. The profitability of agricultural products created favorable investment opportunities for the urban elite. Land was no longer purchased by the wealthy to enhance prestige, but to make a profit.

The economy of the Republic, thus characterized at the same time by both a "highly developed traditionalism" in industry and commerce and by early modernity in agriculture, entered a period of decline beginning in the 1660's. Only in the second half of the nineteenth century did a recovery occur, characteristically enough beginning in the agricultural sector. Exogenous factors were responsible to a considerable degree for the decline, particularly mercantile competition from the larger states, which had in the mean time achieved a level of economic development similar to the Netherlands. Involvement in the wars at the end of the seventeenth and beginning of the eight-

eenth centuries also burdened the Republic financially without
bringing (486) economic advantages of the kind present at the
end of the sixteenth century. Endogenous barriers to economic
growth cannot, however, be disregarded. The Republic by and
large followed general European economic cycles as numerous
regional studies now illustrate, despite its remarkable deviations
in some respects. After 1660 the Netherlands too were affected
by the general European crisis of the seventeenth century,
experiencing slackened or stagnating population growth and a
plunge in agricultural prices.[29] Despite their modern agricultural sector the northern provinces had not escaped the pre-
modern linkage of economic and social development with
agricultural cycles. The general fall of agricultural prices was
particularly devastating for the Netherlands because high agricultural productivity could be maintained only by regular
capital investment to cover high business costs, including dike
protection, drainage, and high taxation. This level of investment could no longer be maintained because of shrinking profit
margins. The reclamation of polder lands for farming ceased in
some places and intensive cultivation became less commonly
practiced.

The degree to which this fall from the heights of the golden
century was caused by endogenous economic barriers to growth
became clear when the European economy as a whole entered a
period of growth after the middle of the eighteenth century.
The once-successful Netherlands were hardly affected by this
new economic dynamism. The most important barriers to economic growth inherent within the system itself resulted from
the following set of inter-related factors, which in turn were
created by the earlier state of partial modernity——a significant
point for my thesis:

1. The delay in demographic recovery was a consequence of
a continuously high degree of urbanization and also migration
from rural areas, which was a result of specialization and differentiation within the agricultural economy. Migration to the
cities continued even during the period of demographic
decline. These processes resulted in a shrinking population
since mortality rates were higher in the cities than in rural
areas. Until the middle of the eighteenth century the state of

---

29 van de Woude, Noorderkwartier (note 23); Faber, Friesland (note 23); K.W.
Swart, Hollands Bourgeoisie and the Retarded Industrialization, in:
Krantz/Hohenberg (eds.), Failed Transitions (note 1), 44-49.

medical knowledge and hygiene practices were not sufficient to ensure good conditions of life and health in the cities.[30] (487)

2. In areas where at least part of the excess population remained within the rural setting the situation developed in one of two ways. Either the type of proto-industrial worker appeared, alongside the regular peasant, who engaged in cottage manufacturing using new forms of business organization and methods of production, as occurred in Westphalia, or—as a consequence of many subdivisions—peasants were left with small holdings that were insufficient to support them, as occurred in Belgium. During the nineteenth century these small holders provided the manpower necessary for industrialization. In the maritime provinces of the northern Netherlands these demographic conditions led to a strengthening and consolidation of the conservative urban craft guilds and hence raised endogenous barriers against modernization. Since the craft guilds were by no means able to incorporate all newcomers, particularly during the eighteenth century, a large number of urban unemployed workers resulted. However, these formed no reservoir of inexpensive labor in the maritime provinces because of their fine social relief system. Both mass unemployment and a labor shortage in poorly paid and lower status occupations thus hindered growth in the industrial sector of the economy. The eastern, non-maritime regions, especially the province of Brabant, the Veluwe (the plain in the border area between Gelderland and Utrecht) and Overijssel, formed a special case which followed a pattern of development similar to neighboring Westphalia.[31]

3. The commercialization of agriculture brought about a marked change in the the consumption habits of the peasants and thus created a demand for certain kinds of manufactured products. Peasant consumer demand was not well suited, however, to stimulate a significant expansion of the internal market and to encourage the mass production of goods. It was met above all by goods fulfilling higher order needs, such as fur-

---

30 van der Woude, Noorderkwartier (note 23); J.A. Faber et al., Population Changes and Economic Developments in the Netherlands: A Historical Survey, in: A.A.G. Bijdragen 12 (1965), 47-113.

31 K.H. Roessingh, Beroep en bedrijf op de Veluwe in het midden van de achttiende eeuw, in: A.A.G. Bijdragen 13 (1965), 181-274 (English translation in: Acta Historiae Nederlandicae 4 <1970>, 105-129); B.H. Slicher van Bath, Een samenleving on der spanning Geschiedenis van het platteland in Overijssel, Assen 1957.

niture, clocks, jewelry, tea, coffee, spices, sugar, even books and pictures.[32] These facts highlight an important cultural and mental proclivity of economic modernization. Obviously peasants as a social group were unsuited to bring about a fundamental change in consumption habits that would make mass production possible. In this case they demonstrably copied the habits of their (488) burgher contemporaries.[33] Even though the Frisian clothing ordinances of the sixteenth century charged that the peasants were as vain as peacocks and that they had their clothing cut from expensive English cloth,[34] the stimulus for a rapid change in clothing fashions—the foundation for sustained mass production of textiles—could only come from an urban burgher milieu. However, in the case of the northern Netherlands this burgher milieu was unsuited to create a demand for fashionable clothing because of the notorious frugality of the Dutch regents and the purism of influential Calvinist preachers. In addition the state did not stimulate consumption, but suppressed it through high excise taxes.

4. Another barrier to industrial growth, which can hardly be emphasized too strongly, resulted from the investment habits of early modern capitalists. As has already been noted the well-to-do regents of the large Dutch cities invested to a large extent in agriculture, including the reclamation of land, during the sixteenth and seventeenth centuries. As a consequence not only was the proportion of investment available for manufacturing reduced, but the economic slump evoked a security consciousness among the economic elite which had important long term effects. When agricultural profit margins sank after the end of the seventeenth century burghers purchased bonds and lent to the government rather than investing in domestic industries. What has often been described as the regents' "rentier mentality" during the eighteenth century cannot simply be characterized as traditionalism. It was at least partially shaped by the opportunities that were offered by modern agriculture during the boom of the seventeenth century. To this can be added the increasing absorption of the entire burgher elite with governmental affairs as well as the generally low

32 de Vries, Economy (note 10).
33 A. and J. Romein, De Lage Landen bij de zee, Amsterdam 1934, 335ss.; Amsterdam in de zeventiende eeuw, 6 vols., Den Haag 1897ss.
34 See the statement of Eggerik Beninga (d.1562) quoted in E.J.H. Tiaden, Das gelehrte Ostfriesland, vol. 1, Aurich 1785, 104ss.

esteem enjoyed by industrial entrepreneurs.[35] These factors guided the aspirations of those rising in social prominence both in the cities and countryside. As a consequence there was a lack of entrepreneurial initiative in the northern Netherlands during the nineteenth century.

5. This development was reinforced by the fact that wage levels remained, or had to be maintained, at a comparatively high level even during the economic slump of the eighteenth century. This occurred because most crafts were organized by guild and also because of the industrial actions and strikes of the laborers in the few large-scale industries such as textile production in Leiden. High salaries were also retained because of the high levels of taxation levied upon the broader strata of society. (489) As a result this sector of the economy could not grow in the face of English competition,[36] further discouraging investment in manufacturing.

6. The sophisticated Old European technologies worked very well until the early nineteenth century. This was true of the high standard of development and efficiency of the old mill wheel technology, the use of peat as an energy source, and a transportation system based upon canals. Consequently the Dutch economy did not experience those bottlenecks, which according to Wrigley's theory[37] constituted the decisive challenge that provoked a shift to completely new technologies in England during the industrial revolution. Even during the nineteenth century the transition to the alternative methods—such as steam engine technology, coal, and railways—was very difficult for the Dutch economy. Adopting the new technologies required that certain mental barriers be overcome in order to replace proven, workable technologies that were not as efficient as the newer ones. In addition to that, their introduction required enormous imports of raw materials that were not available in the Netherlands.[38]

---

35 See Th. van Tijn, Pieter de la Court, Zijn leven en zijn economische denk-beelden, in: Tijdschrift voor Geschiedenis 69 (1956), 304-368.

36 Krantz/Hohenberg (eds.), Transitions (note 1), 46s., 56s., 58s., 65s.; Ch. Wilson, The Decline of the Netherlands, in: idem, Economic History and the Historian, London 1969, 22-47.

37 Wrigley, Process of Modernization (note 1).

38 J. Romein, De Dialektiek van de vooruitgang, in: idem, Historische lijnen en patronen, Een keuze uit de essays, Amsterdam 1972, 40-89; de Vries, in: Krantz/Hohenberg (eds.), Transitions (note 1), 56s.; de Vries, Barges (note 12), 217-250.

7. Finally the relatively high standard of living and educational level of the broader social strata had a restrictive effect. The suffering experienced during industrialization in England and later in neighboring Belgium could only serve to deter the relatively affluent Dutch from making the same transition to an industrial economy.

The Dutch themselves did not feel obliged to seek new ways and means at the end of the eighteenth century, but believed—this is the general impression—that they could restore an economic system that was both proper and effective by breaking down barriers which were imposed by foreign powers. This opinion was tellingly illustrated by the revealing slogan with which King William I closed his proclamation of November 17, 1813: "The good old times are returning."[39]

III. THE STATE

Social scientists consider the most important aspects of modernization of the state and politics to be the building of a national or unified state, the expansion of participation, i. e., the participation of broader strata of society in the process of political decision making, an increasing rationality and predictability of government resulting from a legal, bureaucratic civil service, the movement toward a constitutional state, and finally, a change in the conditions and the institutional forms of political activities (490) through the formation of modern political parties.[40] How does the historical situation of the northern Netherlands appear in light of these criteria?

1. *State-building*. Dutch state-building did not occur either according to the pattern of an absolutistic state or according to the English model. Even the extent to which one may speak of a "State of the Republic" is a matter of debate.[41] The early

39 Petri, Kultur (note 4), 162.

40 See literature note 1 and G.A. Almond et al. (eds.), Crisis, Choice and Change, Historical Studies of Political Development, Boston 1973; R. Bendix, Nation-building and Citizenship, New York 1964; R. Braibant (ed.), Political and Administrative Development, Durham/N.C. 1969 (esp. contribution of C.J. Friedrich); Eisenstadt/Rokkan, States (note 15); Ch. Tilly (ed.), The Formation of National States in Western Europe, Princeton/N.J. 1975.

41 See literature note 4 and R. Fruin and H.T. Colenbrander, Geschiedenis der staatsinstellingen in Nederland, Den Haag 1922; Fockema Andreae, nederlandse Staat (note 25); J.Ph. de Monté Ver Loren and J.E. Spruit, Hoofdlijnen uit de ontwikkeling der rechterlijke organisatie, 5th ed. Deventer 1972; C.W. van den Pot, Bestuurs- en rechtsinstellingen der nederlandse provincien, Zwolle 1949; J.V.

modern Republic was a federation of seven largely autonomous provinces whose estates, not the people, possessed sovereignty. Central institutions, the so-called "generality," were kept to a minimum and their responsibilities were narrowly limited. Apart from the house of Orange, a relic of the pre-revolutionary princely period, the following institutions of the "generality" can be noted: the *Estates General* was a permanent congress of delegates from the individual provincial estates—not a directly representative body whose members came from individual districts like the English parliament. It made foreign policy and defense policy decisions. The *Admiralty Board* and the publicly-owned overseas companies—the *United East India Company*, and the *United West India Company*—were responsible for maritime policy and for colonial policy. The *State Council* oversaw national taxation, which amounted to no more than a fraction of the provincial taxes. Finally, the *Coinage Office* ensured a unified monetary system. There were no all-union offices for supervising legal affairs, church administration, social and educational policies, or even for economic policy apart from the limited measures already mentioned. A state administrative structure and a modern state civil service were present only in embryonic form.[42] General and provincial bodies existed in the first instance to guarantee internal order for the local authorities, i. e., the cities, through policies that were mutually agreed upon in their fundamentals. (491) With regard to external policies, national institutions existed to guarantee local authorities freedom of action by setting military, diplomatic, and trade policy.

To summarize: when measured by the standards of contemporary absolutistic states or even when compared with the level of centralization and bureaucracy present in its Burgundian predecessor state[43] which was defeated by the Dutch Revolu-

---

Ripperda Wierdsma, Politie en justitie. Een studie over de hollandschen staatsbouw tijdens de Republiek, Zwolle 1937; G. Durand, États et institutions, 16e-18e siècles, Paris 1969, 189.

42 W. Prevenier, Ambtenaren in stad en land, Socioprofessionele evoluties 14-16. eeuw, in: Bijdragen en Mededelingen betreffende de Geschiedenis der Nederlanden 87 (1972), 44-59 (Acta Historiae Nederlandicae 1974, 1-17); Tijdschrift voor Geschiedenis 90 (1977), 301-536.

43 M. Baelde, De Collaterale Raden onder Karel V. en Filipp II. 1531-1578, Brüssel 1965; idem, Financial Policy and the Evolution of the Demesne in the Netherlands under Charles V and Philipp II, in: H.J. Cohn, Government in Reformation Europe, 1520-1560, London 1971, 203-224. See also W. Prevenier and W. Blokmans, Die burgundischen Niederlande, translated by R. Erdorf,

tion, the Dutch state would be characterized as "regressive" according to the categories of modernization theory. However, the yardstick of bureaucratic, centralized state-building chosen by modernization theorists, and incidentally assumed in most historical treatments as well, obscures the special conditions affecting political and state development within the federal Republic. As a result those theories over-simplify the numerous, complicated historical paths between the Old European *societas civilis* and the modern centralist and unified state of the nineteenth century. The example of the Dutch Republic forces modernization theorists to recognize a higher degree of variation between regions and different phases in political, structural, and legal developments, particularly at two points.

a. The reciprocal effects of state-building and economic development in the Dutch Republic during the sixteenth and seventeenth centuries run counter to the assumptions of modernization theory. Economic growth occurred not only despite the absence of a unified state, but to a large degree *because* of it. Federalism and local autonomy fostered an optimal flexibility and encouraged multi-faceted mercantile and entrepreneurial initiatives, as contemporary observers had already noted.[44]

b. Even the development of the political system itself cannot be accurately described as "regressive." Despite its lack of bureaucratization and unitary, homogeneous structures, the "State of the Republic" displayed progressive characteristics. They are responsible for the fact that the Netherlands became one of the most thoroughly stable democracies after the middle of the nineteenth century. In the early modern history of the Netherlands we are dealing with the development of a unitary state, paving the way for a national state without the erection of a bureaucratic administrative staff and without (492) centralization. The Netherlands are even a better representative than England of this kind of non-absolutistic or even anti-absolutistic development. A sampling of the evidence for this includes the early origin of a nation by a revolutionary abolition of its peripheral status (with respect to the Spanish center of the Hapsburg Empire), and also the consolidation of state boundaries, and reduction of the population to a largely unified ethnic substratum, which occurred as parallel developments

Weinheim 1986.

44 See Temple, Observations (note 5) and the political theory of Pieter and Johan de la Court.

during the late sixteenth and first half of the seventeenth centuries. A national language came into being and cultural unification occurred, both emanating from the province of Holland. Finally, the social group fostering national integration was not the military or the bureaucracy, but the urban elites of the cities in the province of Holland through their economic activities, which extended across provincial borders. This fact resulted in the achievement of a very early national integration through autonomous social forces and not because of governmental coercion.[45] Above all the latter factor reveals a peculiarity which was crucial for the developmental process of Dutch society during the nineteenth and twentieth centuries. The fact that the United Provinces renounced great power policies in the mid-seventeenth century, not least because of its ostensibly under-developed state structure, spared them from paying the internal political price of militarism.[46] As a result the Dutch successor state of the nineteenth century was able to maintain a nationalism that was comparatively free from distortions and encumbrances. (493)

Thus in the northern Netherlands an early modern nation and state were built on the basis of a decentralized federation. Since the resultant social integration was considerable the Republic was able to dispense with enforcing religious conformity at a moment when such conformity was considered to be a central requirement for solidarity within the early modern societies that were being formed throughout the rest of Europe.[47] Further it must be emphasized that rationality and predictability of government definitely increased in the

45 H. Wansink, Holland and Six Allies: the Republic of the Seven United Provinces, in: J.S. Bromley and E.H. Kossmann (eds.), Britain and the Netherlands, vol. 4, Den Haag 1971, 113-155; J.C. Boogman, Die holländische Tradition in der niederländischen Geschichte, in: Westfälische Forschungen 15 (1962), 96-105; J.A. van Houtte, in: Algemene Geschiedenis der Nederlanden, vol. IV, 187-194, esp. 190s.; van Dillen, Rijkdom (note 16), 225ss., 233-238; Barbour, Capitalism (note 17), passim; Kalma et al. (eds.), Geschiedenis (note 24), 605ss.; de Vries, Economy (note 10), 214-224; J. Huizinga, How Holland became a Nation, in: Beekelaar et al. (eds.), Verleden (note 4), 1-16, esp. 11ss.; P. Geyl, Opkomst en verval van het Noord-Nederlandsch nationaliteitsbesef, in: ibid., 17-33.

46 G. Oestreich, Geist und Gestalt des frühmodernen Staates, Berlin 1969, 155ss.; H. Schilling, Der libertär-radikale Republikanismus der holländischen Regenten. Ein Beitrag zur Geschichte des politischen Radikalismus in der frühen Neuzeit, in: Geschichte und Gesellschaft 10 (1984), 498-533.

47 T. Parsons, The System of Modern Society, Englewood Cliffs, N.J., 1970, chapter 4. For more details see H. Schilling, Religion and Society in the Northern Netherlands (See below pp. 353-410).

Netherlands. Careful studies of the Dutch type of early modern bureaucracy have revealed that even within the traditional, i.e., largely non-professionalized, government a rational, legal administration developed.[48] Despite the retention, in principle, of the old statute law—partially uncodified—a certain harmonization with Roman law took place in the legal system.[49] There is some evidence which suggests that the transition to a state under the rule of law was largely complete. In any case the privileges of particular groups within state and society were guaranteed, and there were instances when arbitrary administrative actions underwent judicial review.[50]

This federal decentralized model of the state was in theory quite capable of further development. As the reform plans submitted by Simon van Slingeland at the second great state assembly of 1716-1717 reveal, an expansion of the governmental boards of the Estates General, and a broadening of participation, resulting in a truly democratic mandate for the deputies of this supra-provincial assembly of the estates could have been possible without inevitably starting down the road to a centralized, unified state.[51]

2. *Forms and conditions of political activity.* Similar to statebuilding, important changes can be noted within the sphere of political activity (494) that encouraged development toward modern forms of political organization. Already in the early seventeenth century two groupings similar to parties had been organized—the "Orange" and "Regent" parties—which governed the Republic by turns. Although both "parties" show traditional patterns of social composition and "organization" with their factions and client networks, their differing programs, by contrast, display an element of modernity. Emerging from the great confessional controversies of the truce period, the parties concentrated increasingly upon their differing conceptions of state and government and their disagreements over trade and foreign policy. This form of political discourse reveals a decisive step away from the complete loyalty to confessional parties with their opposing, mutually exclusive ways

48 A. van Braam, Bureaucratiseringsgraad van de plaatselijke bestuursorganisatie van Westzaahndam ten tijde van de Republiek, in: Tijdschrift voor Geschiedenis 90 (1977), 457-502.
49 de Monté Ver Loren/Spruit, Hoofdlijnen (note 41), 207ss.
50 Fockema Andreae, Staat (note 25), 103ss.
51 Schöffer, in: Schieder (ed.), Handbuch (note 4), 653.

of understanding the world toward groupings based upon common interests commanding only rela-tive loyalty. It was introduced by units of political organization on a level higher than
the local one.[52]

Political activity within the Republic was no longer restricted to the forms and conditions characteristic of the Middle
Ages and the early modern period. It was not limited to disputes between cliques which had no basis in ideology or content; nor were the ideological components within the political
program of the parties and factions based upon transcendental
elements as in case of the many confessional parties all over
Europe at that time which would have made modern political
tendencies toward pragmatism and compromise impossible.
Characteristics of the modern type of confrontation and cooperation between government and opposition can be recognized at particular times in the role that both of the groupings
played in the political life of the Netherlands. There were periods when the Republic was led according to the principles of
the "Orange" party and other times when the principles of the
"Regents" and their party prevailed. What is important is that
despite the deep-seated differences of opinion separating the
two factions both parties shared a common set of values. The
opposition never acted in a fashion calculated to destroy the
state as confessional parties did in France and England.[53] At
the same time politics became a concern of the general public.
The pressure for legitimization felt by those who governed and
the need to recruit followers (495) felt by the opposition gave
rise to an intensive use of propaganda which, in turn, resulted
in a spirited, wide-spread discussion of domestic and foreign
policy decisions in taverns, at the market, and in the sitting
rooms of burgher houses.[54]

In the Netherlands these political groupings did not continue
to change along evolutionary lines into fully developed forms

52 D.J. Roorda, Partij en factie, Groningen 1961; J. van Vucht Tijssen, De
politieke partij, Een onderzoek naar haar functie en structuur sedert hat midden
van de zestiende eeuw, Assen 1941.

53 On the character and function of confessional parties in early modern Europe
see H. Schilling, Konfessionskonflikt und Staatsbildung, Gütersloh 1981, introduction.

54 Bibliography of the pamphlet literature: W.P.C.Knuttel, Catalogus van de
Pamflettenversameling berustende in den Koninklijke Bibliotheek, 9 vols., Den
Haag 1889-1920. See P. Geyl, Pennestrijd over Staat en Historie, Groningen
1971; Schilling, Republikanismus (note 46).

of modern bourgeoisie party organizations as occurred in England. On the one hand it is unmistakable that the framework of political action in the Republic stimulated the founding and early success of the Patriot party during the 1780's, the first Dutch party organization in the modern sense of the word. The rise of the Patriot movement occurred within the context of the traditional mechanism for changing the ruling party of government, hitherto an exchange between the Orangists and the Regents. On the other hand, the channelling of political and social controversies through the established system of early modern factions and parties hindered the transition to newer forms of organization and activity.[55] The modern Dutch parties of the nineteenth and twentieth centuries are only a result of the post-revolutionary situation.[56]

3. *Political participation.* The Dutch experience also presents similar problems for modernization theory with respect to political participation and its development from an Old European form to modern forms. When measured by the yardstick of suffrage, political participation in the northern provinces was not nearly as high as in England, which stood in the forefront of European states during the early modern period. After the revolution and separation from Spain political decision-making lay in the hands of about two thousand regents, i.e., members of the estate assemblies (496) in the seven prov-inces and the magistrates and city council committees of the fifty-seven cities with electoral rights. These regents made up about one half of one percent of the adult male population. The governmental activities of the regents themselves reflect a remarkably high degree of participation when we consider that all of them participated more or less directly in the exercise of govern-

55 H. Maier, Demokratie, in: O. Brunner et al. (eds.), Geschichtliche Grundbegriffe, vol. 1, Stuttgart 1972, 839-861; R.R. Palmer, The Age of Democratic Revolution, 2 vols., Princeton, N.J., 1959-64; C.H.E. de Wit, De Nederlandse Revolutie van de achtiende eeuw, Oirsbeek 1974; S. Schama, Patriots and Liberators, Revolution in the Netherlands 1780-1813, London 1977; E.H. Kossmann, The Crisis of the Dutch State 1780-1813, in: Beekelaar et al. (eds.), Verleden (note 4), Den Haag 1975, 435-452; C.H.E. de Wit, De Nederlandse revolutie, in: ibid., 380-401; E.H. Kossmann, The Low Countries 1780-1940, Oxford 1978; M. Prak, Civil disturbances and urban middle class in the Dutch Republic, in: Tijdschrift voor sociale Geschiedenis 15 (1984), 165-173.
56 W. Verkade, Democratic Parties in the Low Countries and Germany, Origins and Historical Development, Leiden 1955; J. van de Giessen, De opkomst van het woord democratie als leuze in den Nederlanden, Den Haag 1948; Th. van Tijn, The Party Structure of Holland and the Outer Provinces in the 19th Century, in: Beekelaar et al. (eds.), Verleden (note 4), Den Haag 1975, 560-589.

mental authority. However, this involvement quotient appears
in an altogether different light when the proportion of voters is
considered. Since the city council (*vroedschap*) was appointed
through cooptation, the circle of voters in the Dutch cities was
to a large extent identical with those in the government of the
magistrate.[57]

Only in Friesland, where hereditary farmers (*herenboeren*)
sent deputies to the estate assembly, was the proportion of
voters much higher. The participation rate there was between
ten and seventeen percent (varying between localities), a quotient that far surpassed the English level, estimated to be about
four percent.[58]

a. However, in this context as well, it is clear that theorizing
on the basis of a single course of development—in the present
case upon the growth of voter participation in England—leads
to an inadmissible oversimplification of the historical process
of modernization. The problem does not arise because particular phenomena have been lost through a legitimate process of
abstraction, but because an important variant of modernization
has been ignored. In the fragmented society of Old Europe the
exercise of governing authority and the right to elect representatives to an estate assembly—the parameters of the theory
derived from England—was only *one* aspect of political and
social involvement. This type of early modern participation was
not very highly developed in the northern Netherlands. After a
high point at the end of the sixteenth century, when for a
short time the guild burghers of the Dutch cities and the free
peasants of the Frisian marsh areas shared in political participation, these groups were continually subjected to a process of
exclusion. On the other hand, the pattern of participation in
regional and local autonomy, and participatory administration
on a cooperative basis did not necessarily correspond to possessing the right to vote and to being represented at the provincial
level. These forms of non-voting political participation were
particularly strong in the northwestern European marsh regions
as has been noted. This principle reached its fullest development in the early modern period. The public responsibilities
fulfilled by provincial assemblies included participation in the
administration of church property by church wardens (*kerk-*

---

57 Figures from Fockema Andreae , Staat (note 25), 37.

58 Kalma et al. (eds.), Geschiedenis (note 24), 308ss.; Fockema Andreae, Staat
(note 25), 59s.

meesters), i.e. parish officers appointed by parishioners or patron, responsible for church buildings and parochial endowments, and dike and water authorities. After the Reformation Calvinist presbyteries, concerned with the internal affairs of the established church, were added to this system.[59] (497) This meant, to be sure, participation in decisions that had only a limited effect upon the Republic as a whole. Nonetheless it resulted in a high degree of integration and can be described as a "pattern of interacting relationships for the making of public policy and the pursuit and achievement of societal goals" according to the formulations of modernization theory.[60]

The specifically Dutch path of political development can be seen in the intensification of communal and corporate administration and government. It did not occur either as a process of organic expansion of suffrage, as in the case of England, or as the leveling of an estate society into a uniform society of subjects, the prerequisite for creating a general national citizenry in the absolutist states. It was rather the communal and corporate education of a relatively high number of persons for responsibility and for seeking the "common good." If this path did not in fact merge with the modern democratic road it created a solid basis upon which democratic participation could easily be built during the nineteenth century. Already at the end of the eighteenth century delegates from the French revolutionary convention recognized this, observing Dutch conditions with great interest. They reported back to Paris with amazement that a large number of persons with experience in dealing with public affairs could easily be found in the Dutch

---

59 There was a great variety of those non-voting forms of political and social participation. See the literature in notes 24 and 27 together with Fockema Andreae, Staat (note 25), 49ss., 181ss.; de Monté Ver Loren/Spruit, Hoofdlijnen (note 41), 164; C. Dekker, De vertegenwoordiging van de geerfden in den wateringen, in: Bijdragen en Mededelingen betreffende de Geschiedenis der Nederlanden 89 (1974), 345-374; S.J. Fockema Andreae, Het hoogheemraadschap van Rijnland, Leiden 1934; idem, Studien over waterschaps geschiedenis, 8 parts, Leiden 1950-1952; idem, L' eau et les hommes de la Plaine Maritime, in: Tijdschrift voor Rechtsgeschiedenis 23 (1960), 181-195; A.A. Beekmann, Dijk- en Waterschapsrecht in Nederland voor 1795, 2 vols., Den Haag 1904-1907.-On the presbyteries: A. van Ginkel, De Ouderling, Amsterdam 1975; H. Schilling, Calvinistische Presbyterien in Städten der Frühneuzeit, in: W. Ehbrecht (ed.), Städtische Führungsgruppen und Gemeinde, Köln 1980, 385-444; idem, Civic Calvinism, Kirksville, Missouri 1991, chapter V: Calvinism and Urban Elites.-The Social Profile of the Presbytery of Groningen from the Sixteenth to the Nineteenth Century.

60 Lerner/Coleman, Modernization (note 1), 400.

Republic for every important responsibility,[61] an important prerequisite for a workable democracy and a condition that was utterly unknown in their own homeland.

This finding, which cannot be attributed to an improper romanticizing of traditional conditions in the Dutch Republic since it was made by delegates of the French Revolution, deserves particular attention when compared with social and political developments in England, particularly in rural areas, and the conclusions that can be drawn from them regarding the prerequisites of the process of political modernization. (498) In England the commercialization of agriculture occurred in conjunction with the elimination of an independent peasantry, a process which began in the late Middle Ages and had particularly intense effects during the first half of the eighteenth century. In his well known study of the *Social Origins of Dictatorship and Democracy*,[62] Barrington Moore argued that its elimination was the most important prerequisite for a relatively smooth process of political and economic modernization in the British Isles. In the Netherlands, by contrast, it was the independent peasantry who introduced and supported modernization in agriculture, using both their own land and property leased on a capitalistic basis. This was, incidentally, a form of rationalized, capitalist, agricultural structure that Max Weber overlooked. The peasantry was at the same time the social group most heavily involved in administrative activities of the communal and corporate type within rural districts. It must be conceded that these peasants—among whom the *herenboeren* of Friesland, so-called because of their direct participation in the rural estates, constituted a minority—did not fight either for full political rights or even for an expansion of political rights to the landless social strata in town and countryside. Still the case of the Netherlands makes plain that, contrary to Moore's assumption, the establishment of a stable democracy did not in any way require the elimination of an independent peasantry.[63]

---

61 Quoted by P. Geyl, De Bataafse Revolutie, in: Bijdragen voor de Geschiedenis der Nederlanden 11 (1956), 177-199, esp. 189; for a similar judgement see Temple, Observations (note 5), 69s.

62 American original 1966, German translation Frankfurt 1969. Moore's thesis that the history of "small nations" is irrelevant for his problem is absurd with regard to the early modern period.

63 This Old European type of participation was revitalized by the Dutch jurist and politician Johan Rudolf Thorbecke. See W. Verkade, Overzicht van de

b. My second remark on the problem of participation deals with the relationship between a high degree of participation and economic growth as it is represented in the literature of modernization theory. At first glance the situation during the "Golden Century" of the Republic seems to support this linkage. The Republic had a level of political participation which can be considered relatively high, regardless of its backwardness when compared to England, and an extraordinary economic boom occurred at the same time. Doubtless this linkage of factors was not accidental since the circle of political decision-makers (499) was largely identical with the commercial citizenry who vigorously stimulated both the commercial expansion and the modernization of agriculture.[64] A further limiting factor that hindered economic development in other countries was removed on the basis of this governmental structure. This barrier was the Renaissance princely state itself with its cumbersome civil service apparatus, its costly power and military policies, and its need for princely and noble representation at court.[65] The frugality of the Dutch regents, which contrasted sharply with princely lavishness, was repeatedly cited by foreign diplomats as an important reason for the political and economic success of the Republic.[66]

Nevertheless it seems inappropriate to speak of a close causal connection between economic growth and an expansion of political participation when referring to the Netherlands.[67] Economic growth and tendencies toward democratization did not occur as parallel phenomena. Political participation was at its broadest during the beginning phase of the Revolution and the first years of independence and was a result of political and religious conditions, not an expression of economic necessity. Immediately after the seizure of power by the Calvinist part of the burgher elite, political participation was drastically reduced in the cities. Even some of the rights of democratic participation enjoyed by the guilds, which had been recognized

---

staatskundige denkbeelden van R. Thorbecke (1798-1872), Arnheim 1935; Petri, Kultur (note 4), 194.

64 This was already obvious to the contemporaries: Temple, Observations (note 5), 5, 107; A. Smith, Der Wohlstand der Nationen, trans. H.C. Recktenwald, München 1978, 781. English 5th edition, London 1789, part 2, 197.

65 See the essays of H. Trevor-Roper, in: T. Aston (ed.), Crisis in Europe, 1560-1660, London 1965.

66 See note 87 below.

67 H.Ch. Schröder, Geschichte (note 1) argues similarly with regard to England.

since the Middle Ages and were present in only a few northern
Dutch cities such as Utrecht, were abolished. The rural areas of
Friesland later followed the lead of urban areas. Thus it is
obvious that—contrary to the assumptions of modernization
theory—the economic boom of the seventeenth century did not
produce an increase in political participation. It took place on
the basis of restricted political participation.[68]

At this point a further observation should be made: the relatively high degree of participation that was still present during
the seventeenth and early eighteenth centuries when compared
with the absolutist states, even after the oligarchic concentration of power, could not guarantee either enduring economic
growth or even an ability to make qualitative innovations.
After the end of the eighteenth century industrialization in
neighboring Belgium (500), where medieval rights of participation had been largely abolished and the mercantile bourgeoisie
was excluded from participation in government, made rapid
progress. In the northern Netherlands it was precisely those
groups who could participate in politics who opposed economic
change.[69] A generally applicable conclusion can be derived
from this: The ability to fulfill political and communal responsibilities is not always and in every place connected with the
ability or willingness to introduce economic innovations. This
can also be deduced from the process of modernization in
Germany: the political and administrative innovations of the
early modern period were introduced into the territories and
imperial cities by that segment of the burgher elite who served
in the territorial civil service or as city councillors. This elite
group became increasingly detached from the economy. New
economic impulses were generated, on the other hand, by an
economic bourgeoisie that was often no longer based in the
cities and hence was excluded from political participation.[70]
Even during the first half of the nineteenth century economic
modernization and political liberalization were not parallel
processes. These cases all run contrary to the assumptions of
modernization theory which suggests that in principle such

---

68 J.J. Woltjer, Dutch Privileges, Real and Imaginary, in: Britain and the
Netherlands, vol. 5, Den Haag 1975, 19-35; Kalma et al. (eds.), Geschiedenis
(note 24), 303-312, 369s.

69 Mokyr, Industrialization (note 14).

70 See H. Schilling, The Rise of Early Modern Burgher Elites during the Sixteenth and Seventeenth Centuries, above pp. 135-187.

developments went in the same direction and occurred at the same time within the different sectors of the societal system, particularly within politics and the economy.

  c. Finally, in connection with the aspect of participation, we will make a few references to political theory and to both the cycles of political unrest and the kinds of political movements accompanying them, which reveal so much about early modern societies. Monarchism, which until the middle of the seventeenth century had dominated Dutch political theory, was replaced by a radical republicanism after the conclusion of the Peace of Westphalia and the defeat of Stadholder William II's politically ill-fated coup, which was directed against the province of Holland and the city of Amsterdam. An analysis of the republicanism of the Dutch regents party demonstrates that the specifically Dutch pattern of change, which we have discovered when examining the economy and political participation, was present in their political theory and political culture as well. Here too modern and progressive forces grew from a traditional mentality and medieval concepts of social and political order. Historians usually assume that the regents were conservatives, and that this was the basis of their struggle against monarchism and centralism—normally considered to be standards of modernity. Their conservatism, however, was no more than a veneer concealing the progressive aspects of their understanding of state and society. This is the judgement of E. H. Kossmann, the most knowledgeable expert on Dutch political theory in the seventeenth century. Taken as a whole the constituent elements of regent republicanism can almost be described as a kind of "fashionable modernism," as Kossmann put it.[71] (501) This form of "modernism" reached its most thorough development in the political and economic writings of the de la Court brothers, particularly the elder of the two, Johan de la Court (d.1660). Spinoza based the political passages in both of his treatises upon their thought.[72] The de la Court brothers were perhaps the most decisive advocates of liberty out of all of the political and economic thinkers before the time of Adam Smith, arguing that liberty is the fundamental principle of social and political coexistence. In the present

---

71 E.H. Kossmann, Politieke theorie in het zeventiende-eeuwse Nederland, Amsterdam 1960, esp. 30ss.
72 Tractatus theologico-politicus; Tractatus politicus, esp. chapter XI. Best edition: B. de Spinoza, The Political Works, ed. by A.G. Wernham, Oxford 1965.

context, however, their ideas concerning participation in political decision making are particularly important. In the book
Consideratie van Staat, ofte Politike Weeg-schaal they advocated a broadening of the basis of participation to include "all
inhabitants of the country, who it can be assumed have the
abilities necessary to pursue their own interests (*welvaaren*)."
This meant in fact an extension of the right to vote to all males
who were not servants; the latter restriction was supported even
by the Levellers, the political radicals of the English Revolution. At the same time the de la Courts and Spinoza praised
democracy as the best and freest form of state.[73]

It is important for our examination of the "potential for
modernization" in the Republic to note that the theoretical
positions mentioned above did not stem from academic tradition, where the question of the ideal form of state had been
discussed back and forth for centuries, as is well known, with
few effects if any upon political praxis. The demand made by
both the de la Courts and Spinoza for a broadening of participation and their high opinion of democracy, quite unusual for
the period, were rather the result of the pragmatic type of
political theory that began with an analysis of reality and
whose primary aim was to reshape reality, i. e., political, social
and economic praxis. Both the de la Courts and Spinoza saw
their political conclusions as a logical development of the
Dutch system and justified them with trade interests and the
generally liberal needs of their own society. Whether their ideas
would have had a chance of realization through an organic
process of further development during the de Witt Regency
administration cannot be (502) discussed here. Since Johann de
Witt was murdered in 1672 by the *Oranje gepeupel*, the Orange
party mob, he did not have the time to take up such experiments even if he had wanted to. The Regents of the eighteenth
century no longer worried about these theoretical possibilities
that might open the way for democratic experiments, but continued in their traditional oligarchic ways.

In the case of the Dutch Republic there is a recognizable
line of development even in the political practices of the
popular movements opposing the ruling regime, manifested by
periodic outbreaks of unrest of the Old European sort, and the

---

73 See Weeg-schaal, Amsterdam 1662, 675.-The political theory of the Dutch
regents is discussed in more detail in H. Schilling, Republikanismus (note 46).

demands of the broader strata of the population for a right of co-determination and/or participation in government, justified primarily on the basis of communal and corporate ideals. They point ahead to modern political movements that proceed from the assumption of a general and equal state citizenship, and not from an array of corporative, exclusive groups possessing a variety of special rights and privileges not enjoyed by other groups. We must not, however, imagine that this line was all that clearly drawn. The conditions were very complicated, and the aspect of transformation that interests us here has not been adequately studied. However, this much is clear: in the two centuries of its existence the Dutch Republic experienced six periods of intense political activity in town and countryside, pursued by popular groups who normally were completely excluded from direct political participation by the established constitution. These social and political movements emerged during the following periods: during the 1570's and 1580's in connection with the "revolutionary Reformation;" in 1617/1618 on the periphery of the Remonstrant crisis; in 1672 during the fall of the Regent government and the return of the Stadhoulder of the house of Orange, William III; between the years 1702-1708 in response to the misuse power by Orange clients after William III's death; during the years 1747-1748, when the pendulum swung the other way and popular opposition to the Regent oligarchy again brought a Stadhoulder of the house of Orange to power; and finally the Patriot movement during the 1780's, a political grouping whose left wing fought against both the house of Orange and the regent aristocracy.[74]

The most important Old European elements of these political movements become clear even in this simple enumeration: linkage with religious positions (up to 1672), and the prominent (503) role of disputes between elite groups, and the client- and faction-ridden structures in general. Even the battles fought by broader strata of the population for political participation that occurred in conjunction with these elite conflicts belong to the Old European type of political movement, both with respect to

---

74 H. de Buck presents numerous case studies in Bibliographie der Geschiedenis van Nederland, Leiden 1968. Of special importance are A.H. Wertheim-Gijse Weenink, Demokratische Bewegingen in Gelderland 1672-1795, Amsterdam 1973; Geschiedenis van Gelderland, vol. 2, Zutphen 1975; eadem and W.F. Wertheim, Burgers in verzet tegen regenten-heerschappij, Onrust in Sticht en Oversticht (1703-1706), Amsterdam 1976; and the same authors in Plooierijen te Zutphen, Zutphen 1977.

its institutional setting and the kinds of argumentation employed by them. In the cities (I must limit my discussion to them), the institutional basis for such movements was formed by guilds and burgher committees, by financial commissions,[75] or, in those places such as the cities of Holland where the guilds had had no rights of political participation during the Middle Ages, the shooting societies (*Schuttersgilden*).[76] These groups demanded corporate participation for the citizenry and, in part, also achieved it for short periods of time. What we have here is the type of Old European burgher movement based upon the communal and corporate ideal,[77] which was little suited to develop into a modern democratic, individualistic ideal of participation. A second Old European component of Dutch popular movements, different both in terms of its institutional expression and political theory, resulted from the ties of the broader strata in the cities and countryside with the house of Orange and the Calvinists. These ties were especially important for the popular movements of 1618 and 1672, when opposition to the government of the regents was legitimized by the Calvinist and monarchomachic principle of popular sovereignty. However, since this idea was conceived in corporate and not individual terms, and particularly because emphasis was placed on the ties of the people to God and through God to the princes of Orange who were sent by him for the welfare of the people, a "caesaric concept of democracy" resulted that effectively excluded the people from participation.[78] Consequently the popular movements of 1672 and 1747, which were organized by the Orangist middle class, resulted in a semi-monarchic position of power for the Stadhoulder.

In spite of this endogenous barrier there is evidence suggesting that the Old European tradition of uprisings at least

---

75 Especially in Middelberg, Utrecht, Nimwegen, Arnheim, Zutphen and the cities on the river Ijssel. Wertheim, Bewegingen (note 74); J. Vijlbrief, Van anti-aristocratie tot democratie (Utrecht), Amsterdam 1950.

76 N.J.J. de Voogd, De Doelistenbeweging te Amsterdam, phil. diss., Utrecht 1914; Roorda, Partij (note 52). The political movement of 1797/98 is called "doelisten"-movement because it started in the "doelen", i.e. the houses of the shooting guilds in Dutch cities.

77 H. Schilling, Aufstandsbewegungen in der Stadtbürgerlichen Gesellschaft des Alten Reiches, in: H.U. Wehler (ed.), Der deutsche Bauernkrieg, Göttingen 1975, 193-238, esp. 230ss.

78 1618: A.Th. van Deursen, Bavianen en Slijkgeuzen, Assen 1974; 1672: Roorda, Partij (note 52); "caesareaanse democratie" coined by P. Geyl, Demokratische tendenties in 1672, Amsterdam 1950.

helped prepare the ground for modern democratic movements in the case of the Netherlands.[79] The experience of the uprising of 1747/1748 was particularly important. The Stadhoulder, who had achieved power not least through a popular movement in the cities of Holland—the *Doelisten* movement—once in power flatly rejected all the political demands made by the movement. (504) This defeat opened the way for a fundamental change to occur within the political principles of the broader strata. They became aware that political participation was open to them only by opposing the Orange Stadhoulder, not by making an alliance with him. At the same time they were forced to abandon the traditional pattern of political argumentation and to seek an alternative to the traditional form of political organization based upon clientele and factional structures, which had been dominated by the Orangists and the Regents. Certainly this awareness was shared only by an intellectual minority even during the 1780's. Thus the early success of the Patriot party resulted from the traditional methods of opposition.[80] The basis of mass support for a radical change was so small that the radical democratic movement within the Patriot uprising could hardly have succeeded, even had Prussia not intervened. Yet the thesis still appears to be justified that endogenous impulses for fundamental political change were present in the Netherlands during the eighteenth century, based upon the tradition of popular political movements during the early modern period. The northern Netherlands was in any case the best prepared of all European countries for modern democratic ideas when these were powerfully spread by the American Revolution. Both the theoretical discussions[81] accompanying the various early modern revolts and the fact that there was a socio-psychological discrepancy between the high expectations aroused during each period of revolt and the bitter disappointment that resulted when the most important demands were rejected fundamentally alienated at least part of the population with political interests from supporting the political system. The modern

79 To prevent a misunderstanding: I have said "helped to prepare." There was no direct transition into actual modern democratic movements.

80 See the literature given above in note 55.

81 P. Geyl, De Witten-oorlog, een pennestrijd in 1757, in: idem, Pennestrijd (note 54), 130-273; J.L. Leeb, The Ideological Origins of the Batavian Revolution, Den Haag 1973.

democratic part of the Patriot party took full advantage of this legacy.

The base of power of the burgher-democratic left wing of the Patriot party was by no means located in the economically and socially most developed areas of Holland, but in the non-maritime provinces and in Friesland as well as in cities such as Utrecht, Zutphen, and Nimwegen which appear to have been more traditional or pre-modern in social and economic terms. This fact is worth noting when considering the close relationship between economic and political processes of change presumed by modernization theory.[82] Particularly within the urban context attention should be directed toward political lines which ran relatively independent of economic and social conditions. Within these lines of political development older urban burgher-democratic and more recent state citizen-democratic elements merged and blended with each other.

If the political system of the early modern Republic shows tendencies towards endogenous development both in state-building and in the questions of participation and (505) citizens' rights in general, how can the difficulties that actually occurred during the transition to modern democratic and state structures be explained? According to my assessment they were in the first instance a consequence of the conservative characteristics of this type of burgher society as it first appeared in the northern Netherlands during the sixteenth century, within the early modern framework.

IV. SOCIETY

I have suggested in parts II and III that the political system of the northern Netherlands retained important progressive elements, regardless of its decentralized form, its rudimentary bureaucracy and the resulting awkwardness of the state, and its limited political participation, but that the development of these elements was hindered by a conservative social structure. In a certain sense this thesis stands the current evaluation of Dutch society on its head. In contrast to the negative judgment concerning the Dutch state already mentioned, most historians characterize the society of the Republic as highly developed

---

82 However it can be taken for granted that the non-maritime province of Overijssel was the only one of all Dutch provinces which expanded demographically during the 18th century.

and modern, as a bourgeois society or a class society because of the dominance of the burgher elite. This opinion is held by historians representing completely different perspectives such as Russian Marxist historians and the French historian Roland Mousnier.[83]

I wish to oppose this position by arguing that an early modern society, which was strongly influenced by the Old European urban bourgeoisie, must not be regarded per se as modern and not even as necessarily striving toward the modern bourgeois capitalist economic society of the nineteenth century. With respect to Dutch society much can be said for the view that the obstacles to further changes within state and society that were present during the eighteenth century were a consequence of the early "seizure of power" by an Old European type of bourgeoisie. This social group, which had dominated the Republic since the end of the sixteenth century, was not a modern, individualistic economic bourgeoisie, but a bourgeoisie which must be characterized as a *Bourgeoisie d'ancien régime*.[84] Its prosperity was based upon long distance trade and investment income. Its ambitions were not focused primarily upon economic success, but upon public offices and the authority and prestige that they imparted. (506)

A considerable number of chronological shifts must be taken into consideration when discussing the type of society present in the Republic. Development did not occur in a "progressive" fashion from a society of estates to a society of classes, but often in the opposite direction. In the first decades of the Republic stratification according to class[85] was much further developed than in the period after 1670. Thus Ivo Schöffer speaks of a "society of classes" when referring to the early modern Netherlands, which reverted to a society divided

---

83 A.N. Cistozvonov, Über die stadialregionale Methode, in: Zeitschrift für Geschichtswissenschaft 21 (1973), 31-48; idem, Die Rolle des Calvinismus in der niederländischen bürgerlichen Revolution, in: Weltwirkungen der Reformation, Berlin 1959, 104-129. R. Mousniers (ed.), Problèmes de stratification sociale, Paris 1968, esp. 135.

84 See the terminology of R. Robin, La Société française en 1789: Semur-en-Auxois, Paris 1970; P. Goubert, L'Ancien Régime, vol. 1, Paris 1969. Quite similar is the suggestion of "altständisches Bürgertum" by H. Stoob, Altständisches Bürgertum, 2 vols., Darmstadt 1978.

85 I. Schöffer, La stratification sociale de la République des Provinces Unies au 17e siècle, in: Mousniers (ed.), Problèmes (note 83), 121-135, here 130s.; de Vries, Economy (note 10), 67.

according to caste or estate in the course of the seventeenth century.[86]

However, it is important to emphasize that the presence and even the periodic advance of stratification according to class was not unusual even during the *ancien régime* and can be demonstrated in nearly every large city of Old Europe.[87] It must further be maintained that this did not in any way express a social situation comparable to those of the modern economic societies (*Wirtschaftsgesellschaften*) of the nineteenth century. The novelty of early modern Dutch society was expressed by the fact that the specific social structures, social norms, and mentality of the urban burgher elite spread beyond the narrow sphere of the cities, affecting many rural areas and their inhabitants. This was a first step in the direction of a "national" or, more precisely, a "territorial" expansion of the early modern bourgeoisie. The clergy as an estate had been abolished by the Protestant Revolution. In the dominant province of Holland the nobility were economically and socially meaningless. In the remaining provinces they mostly submitted to the bourgeois (507) standards and norms held by the regents.[88] It must be noted, however, that even this early modern "bourgeois" society of the Dutch Republic before 1670 exhibited traditional characteristics alongside of its class-like features. In my opinion they were the determining factor for the character of the entire system. Let me enumerate the most important points:

1. The high correlation between economic activity and political power cannot hide the fact that social prestige was deter-

---

86 Schöffer, Stratification (note 85).

87 See the numerous essays by E. Maschke, esp.: Die Schichtung in der mittelalterlichen Stadtbevölkerung, in: Mélanges en l'honneur de Fernand Braudel, Toulouse 1973, 367-374; Die Unterschichten der mittelalterlichen Städte Deutschlands, in: C. Haase (ed.), Die Stadt des Mittelalters, vol. 3, Darmstadt 1973, 345-454, here 351-354.-G.L. Soliday, A Community in Conflict, Frankfurt Society in the 17th and Early 18th Centuries, Hanover/N.H. 1974; Th.A. Brady, The Themes of Social Structure, Social Conflict, and Civic Harmony in Jacob Wimpheling's Germania, in: Sixteenth Century Journal 3 (1972), 65-76.-For a comparative view on Dutch and German "middle-class" development during the early modern periode see H. Schilling, Vergleichende Betrachtungen zur Geschichte der bürgerlichen Eliten in Nordwestdeutschland und in den Niederlanden, in: H. Schilling and H. Diederiks (eds.), Bürgerliche Eliten in den Niederlanden und in Nordwestdeutschland, Köln-Wien 1985, 1-32.

88 See e.g. Temple, Observations (note 5), 55, 69ss., 86; J. and A. Romein, De Lage Landen bij de Zee, Utrecht 1940, esp. 329s., 344ss.; Roorda, Partij (note 52), 40.

mined to a large degree by the possession of a public office
and the exercise of authority even during the first years of the
Republic. The regents constituted the highest stratum of Dutch
society when measured by this standard and not only by
economic factors. The distinction regarding their social
rankings drawn between city councillors and magistrate office
holders on the one hand, and common burghers on the other,
no matter how wealthy the latter were or what place within the
economy they held, became fixed immediately after the
conclusion of the first phase of the war of independence. In
Holland this distinction became socially far more important
than it did in the German imperial cities in the course of the
early modern period. It also hardened the divisions of the citizenry according to estate. This is expressed by the meaning of
the word "burgher." In contrast to the German term *Bürger* the
Dutch word *burgerij* in the eighteenth century no longer
referred to inhabitants of a city who possessed the right of
citizenship, but was used pejoratively to refer to the social
strata beneath the regents.[89] In Marxist parlance *burgerij* means
petit bourgeoisie.

2. Despite broad toleration, religious dissenters were largely
or completely excluded from political influence and public
office, and hence from the highest social rank and prestige.

3. Even within the early modern "bourgeois" society of the
northern Netherlands, relative social prestige was determined
by the fundamental division between those occupations which
were close to and those distant from physical labor. This was a
general feature of early modern estate society. The norm in the
Netherlands was not the indulgent leisure of a noble, but rather
the rentier or merchant whose (508) business was conducted
without any physical labor on his part and was not in direct
contact with the world of work, in contrast to the less prestig-
ious manufacturing entrepreneur.[90] By general consensus, even
in the broader segments of the population—provided that these

---

89 Romein, Lage (note 88), 347; On a differentiation expressed by funeral
customs see P. den Boer, Naar een geschiedenis van de dood, in: Tijdschrift voor
Geschiedenis 89 (1976), 161-201, esp. 178s.

90 In general see W. Mager, Diskussionsbeitrag, in: J. Kocka (ed.), Theorien in
der Praxis des Historikers, Göttingen 1977, 48-51. On the Dutch situation, especially the social position of the enterpreneurs see N.W. Posthumus, De geschiedenis van de Leidsche lakenindustrie, 3 vols., Den Haag 1903-1939; Th. van Tijn,
Pieter de la Court, in: Tijdschrift voor Geschiedenis 69 (1956), 304-368, esp.
337s.

did not give precedence to noble reputation and the charisma of the house of Orange—members of this merchant elite were thought to be best suited to govern the destiny of the commercial Republic because of their broad perspective, their world-wide connections, and their availability (*Abkömmlichkeit*). This elite thought it necessary to prepare for their governmental duties through learning and education—through literary circles in rural regent houses or by the study of law, above all in Leiden. Since the late seventeenth century most regent families withdrew from active involvement in trade and lived as rentiers from investment income derived from shares in the overseas companies, state debt, and landholding. They turned their back on the world of work and increasingly developed into a patrician estate with some caste characteristics, whose authority they sought to secure through so-called *contracten van correspondentie*. These were formalized agreements in treaty form between regent families, granting each other positions within the city councils or offices within the magistracy. Some of these *contracten* extended to the year 2000.[91]

4. A remarkable variant of the much discussed "self-betrayal of the early modern bourgeoisie" appeared in the Netherlands, not least as a consequence of the hierarchy of social prestige mentioned above, which was to a large degree obligatory also for the elites growing up outside of the regent patriciate.[92] It took place not through a weakening of the entire estate by the defection of its best parts to the nobility, but by a weakening of its most modern part (entrepreneurs, financiers and—in the eighteenth century—enlightened intellectuals) either through their ambition to achieve membership in the traditional regent group or by their identifying with the Orangists and their court society. Leiden textile entrepreneur Pieter de la Court is an example of the first type. He achieved political influence not because he fought for the introduction of a broadened base of political involvement as he advocated in his political theory, (509) but through his marriage and business connections with Amsterdam regent and merchant circles. These connections

---

91 J. de Witte van Citters, Contracten van Correspondentie, Den Haag 1873; Temple, Observations (note 5), 82-86: Those merchants who gained a fortune were eager " (to) introduce their Families into the way of Government and Honour, which consists not here in Titles, but in Publique Employments" (85).

92 F. Braudel, La méditerranée et le monde méditerranéen, 6th ed. Paris 1966, vol. 2, 68-75; for a critical appraisal, see: H. Soly, The "Betrayal" of the Bourgeosie, in: Acta Historiae Nederlandicae 8 (1975), 31-49.

together with a belated study of law gave him the social and
professional qualifications necessary for to become an office-
holder in the court of justice of Holland.[93] Examples of the
second type, the Orangist partisans among the burgher
intellectuals, include Constantijn Huygens, a well-known poet
and private secretary to the Princes of Orange during the
seventeenth century, and Eli Luzac, an enlightenment figure
and Leiden newspaper publisher during the eighteenth century.[94]

To this a further factor must be added: in contrast to the
monarchs and princes of the early modern national or territorial states, the Dutch regents needed no bureaucratic staff of
civil servants to support their rule. On the contrary, they did
their utmost to hinder the rise of a group of potential compe-
titors. Already in connection with the Dutch Revolution the
bureaucratic and administrative apparatus had been partially
trimmed, and partially frozen at its current level, as occurred
with the courts of justice. The regents opposed all attempts to
expand the governmental circle of the Stadhoulders. As a result
an important move toward further differentiation of the political and administrative system was blocked. Similarly the rise
of a modern bureaucratic bourgeoisie, a group which spearheaded the transformation of the *ancien régime* in other places,
was hindered.

Those groups within the elite, composed of the modern
burgher elite and parts of the nobility and the clergy that in
other states, above all France, unleashed both economic and
political impulses for modernization were very weakly represented in the Dutch Republic. They failed to formulate their
own claims to authority as a threat to the system, and were
unable to challenge seriously the power of the two different
branches of the traditional political elite, the regents and the
clients of the house of Orange. Consequently in the Netherlands the *Bourgeoisie d'ancien régime* remained the crucial barrier upon which each wave of endogenous change broke until
the end of the eighteenth century. It was violently shaken for
the first time by the entry of the French army.

5. Added to this lack of a serious opposition within the
burgher elite itself there was yet another social barrier to polit-

---

93 Tijn, De la Court (note 90), 326-331.
94 Geyl, De Witten-oorlog (note 81), esp. 186-256.

ical modernization. The broad middle and lower strata in the towns and countryside were hindered from supporting modern democratic tendencies and remained tied to the established order above all by the Orangists and the myth of the house of Orange—whose stabilizing function within the system I can only refer to in passing—and by the Calvinist public church. (510)

It was thus the specific structure of Dutch society, and here I take up again the thesis formulated above, a burgherly world in the sphere of the Old European corporative states, that hindered possible political changes from taking place. Intense political opposition had arisen repeatedly in the northern Netherlands, as noted in part III, but the dead weight of social circumstances hindered further development of these opposition groups into movements capable of destroying the system. Similar to the economic sphere the desire for political renewal, repeatedly articulated in the course of the eighteenth century on account of the increasingly oligarchic exclusiveness of the regent elite, was restorative in its historical expression, i.e., directed toward a revival of the lost corporate participation of the burghers and free peasants. The new ideas of individual democracy, which included political participation by religious dissidents, found by contrast only a limited following, that was too limited in the end.

V. SUMMARY AND RESULTS

It seems appropriate to begin my concluding arguments regarding the process of modernization in the northern Netherlands with a further look at its ecclesiastical and cultural circumstances, factors that have been left out of the preceding discussion; any examination of the problem of modernization would be incomplete without them. As we have already discussed the basic structures in greater detail elsewhere,[95] we can confine ourselves here to the salient features. They can be summarized as follows:

—At the end of the sixteenth century a modernizing impulse made possible the much praised coexistence of several denominations, securing a state guarantee for individual free-

---

95 H. Schilling, Religion und Gesellschaft in der calvinistischen Republik der Vereinigten Niederlande, in: F. Petri (ed.), Kirche und gesellschaftlicher Wandel, Köln 1980, 197-250 (English translation below, pp. 353-410).

dom of conscience and also made it possible to distinguish between the civil and ecclesiastical community both in theory and practice, most clearly expressed in the possibility of civil marriage.

—However, despite numerous structural changes, central elements of an early modern "confessional church" were retained in the Calvinist public church. Individual magistrates regarded themselves as *tutores religionis* in the traditional sense and the Republic as a whole was hardly the type of a religiously neutral state, as it emerged after the French Revolution. Dutch society was multi-confessional but not pluralistic in a modern sense. The Calvinist church, although it did not represent the majority of Christians except in certain cities and regions, was not reduced to the status of one social group among many equals (511) but was regarded as the central social axis whose existence was indispensable for the stability of the state and for the common good. Dutch republican liberties, regarded by contemporaries as an element of modernity, were not based upon the anticipation of nineteenth century liberalism and a secular state, but were conditioned by the presence of a "state confession," i.e., Calvinism, and by the institutional axis of the public church.

—Even in the sphere of state-church relations and in the fields of culture and education this mixture of traditional and modern elements raised barriers against change. The alternative of a strict separation between religion and society, between church and state, first offered by the Enlightenment and the French Revolution, had anticlerical and atheistic overtones. This meant a worsened situation not only for the Calvinists but also for the position attained by confessional dissidents in the Republic.[96] Even among the free thinkers, found above all in regent circles, there was no strong party in favor of imposing a fully developed form of secularization. By so doing their own freedom of thought would hardly have been fundamentally enhanced, and an important means for exercising a moral and religious influence upon the people would have been lost, an influence that even they still considered necessary. The protracted struggles over the building of a national state school system during the nineteenth century are typical for the social

---

96 P. Geyl, De patriottenbeweging, Amsterdam 1947, esp. 83; idem, Revolutie (note 61), 178.

and cultural transitional difficulties experienced in the Netherlands. They led to the unique solution of *verzuiling*: the coexistence of three different educational systems—Catholic, Protestant and secular humanist—each financed by the state and each subject to mandatory school attendance laws.[97] In the course of time this *verzuiling*, as it is called in Dutch, became typical for nearly all relevant public institutions.

Taking the latter socio-cultural developmental rhythm into account, the course of northern Dutch history yields these results which shed light upon the problems of modernization:

1. The Dutch example serves to emphasize that scholars must look back further than the narrow phase of industrialization and the French Revolution and examine early modern or Old European conditions and developmental (512) points of departure in order to understand the European-Atlantic process of transformation and its consequences for the political, social, and cultural situation, as well as its influence upon popular mentalities, during the nineteenth and twentieth centuries. Such studies may have to include not only the early modern period, but even the Middle Ages in some cases. Only in this light can the differing places occupied by individual European societies within the accelerated demographic, economic, cultural, and political changes of the second half of the eighteenth century be understood. These changes appeared at first only in some regions, above all England, but within a generation included the entire European-Atlantic area.[98]

It is crucially important that any analysis of the Old European pre-history of modernity consider the whole range of social, political, economic and cultural frameworks present within early modern European societies. Old European society—as the Dutch example shows—must not be measured by a single standard as it is when developmental types such as "bureaucratic centralized state-building" and "increasing voter participation" are used normatively. And finally cliche-ridden contrasts between a modern world that is dynamic and a premodern world that is per se static must be abandoned since they make it difficult, if not impossible, to identify and eval-

---

97 Bendix, Nation-Building (note 40), 87-93; Petri, Kultur (note 4).

98 The consequences of the early modern pre-history of modernization are present even today in the Netherlands. See the analysis of political scientist A. Lijphart, The Accomodation. Pluralism and Democracy in the Netherlands, Berkeley 1968.

uate older processes of change and preparation for the transformation of the late eighteenth and early nineteenth centuries.

2. The actual developmental path followed by the northern
Netherlands was characterized by a powerful impulse at the
beginning of the early modern period which was uniform
neither in its causes nor effects. In the case of agriculture its
causes can be found primarily in an endogenous potential for
development, while growth in the industrial and commercial
sectors was stimulated by exogenous forces. As a consequence
this early modern dynamism of change created contradictory
structures: when measured by at least some indices of modernization, the agricultural sector was characterized by modern
forms of production, and in its wake modern socio-demographic circumstances were fostered in the maritime provinces
and in a few other regions. In the industrial and commercial
sectors, by contrast, a "highly developed traditionalism"
resulted.

Even the ecclesiastical and cultural changes were partially a
result (513) of special conditions. In the late Middle Ages and
during the sixteenth century there were already individual
forms of piety present in the Netherlands, and an especially
broad social foundation of humanist studies and humanist spirituality had been built up there. Dutch ecclesiastical and cultural conditions were also in part a result of the acute crisis of
the last decades of the sixteenth century, in which the religious
fragmentation of society and political success both required a
commitment to toleration.

In the political sphere after the revolutionary break with the
monarchic, princely tradition of the Middle Ages, traditional
institutions were adapted to the new republican structure. A
corporate-federal type of early modern state emerged, as did
national integration, on the basis of communal and corporate
self-government and estate representation. The character of
such a structure cannot be evaluated accurately if it is categorized per se as "traditional" or "regressive." The possible
accomplishments of such an early modern tradition in creating
an environment that allowed modern democratic forms to take
root quickly and in providing a secure foundation for them to
build upon during the nineteenth and twentieth centuries are
obscured when the most important indicator of modernization
during the late Middle Ages and early modern period is considered to be the advance of absolutist elements at the expense

of federal and communal ones. The example of the Netherlands shows the advantages of a process of development that was not driven by a state apparatus, separate from and with higher authority than society, but was determined by a continued limitation of state authority, imposed by the society itself in the context of an Old European *societas civilis*. A far more solid foundation was created for a modern democratic political order in the Netherlands than emerged in many of those states which developed in this direction by means of a princely, absolutistic reshaping of Old European society during the eighteenth century. This preparation occurred despite the fact that Dutch society displayed no democratic tendencies in the modern sense of the phrase and accomplished its transformation to more modern forms not by a process of endogenous development but only under exogenous pressure and by revolution.

The development of a capacity for toleration is an essential element of social and cultural change. By referring to the Dutch experience Richard Saage has recently rejected the one-sidedness of the thesis, advocated particularly by Roman Schnur, that the best way toward toleration was through a strengthening of the early modern state.[99] (514) The same can be said of the emergence of a general democratic national citizenry and the formation of national states. There was no ideal road toward political modernity. The absolutistic, princely, centralized state was the dominant way, but there was also another based upon communal and corporate institutions, upon estate and often federative principles. Both routes must be noted in discussions of modernization. A careful enumeration of the advantages and costs of each path appears necessary. Examples of the second, non-absolutistic way can be found not only in the Netherlands, in some Scandinavian states, and in Switzerland, but also in some imperial cities and territories of western and southwestern Germany whose traditions have often been overlooked by historians fascinated by the absolutistic paradigm.

It is correct to note the importance of the doctrine of *raison d'état* and the development of an absolutism of the estates within republican political theory in the northern Netherlands.

99 R. Saage, Widerstandsrecht und Toleranzprinzip im Aufstand der Niederlande, in: Neue Politische Literatur 24 (1979), 318-344; For a similar point of view see Schilling, Religion (note 95), 248-250.

It is also true that in Holland as well as in absolutistic princely states "it was regarded as fully responsible to perceive a sin in every good deed if it harmed the state and on the other hand to regard a sin as a pious work provided that it served the common good."[100] However, these formal similarities must not divert attention from the fundamental differences, which resulted from different kinds of linkage between state and society in each system. The ways of defining and enforcing the "common good" were very different within the two systems. At the latest after the end of the sixteenth century the tendency for governments in princely states to determine the concrete meaning of the "common good" and to place both its realization and the supervision of the moral behavior of their subjects in the hands of the princely civil service is unmistakable. Regardless of the fact that similar attempts at usurpation were made both by the urban magistrates and the provincial estates of the Netherlands, it remained the responsibility of broader segments of the population to determine and pursue the common good, as is clear from the report of the French revolutionary delegation cited above. In princely absolutistic states the "common good" was enforced from above; in states like the Dutch Republic it was rooted in the interest of society or at least in that of the broader strata.

Thus a special type of modernization took place in the northern Netherlands because of the early impulse of development at the beginning of the early modern period, and the unique hybrid structure of the early modern Republic that emerged as a result. The Dutch model has hardly been noticed in theoretical discussions of European-Atlantic modernization until now. It must particularly be stressed that, despite the historically mixed character of the Republic, the state, economy, and society, as well as church and religious order (515) functioned together in a very stable fashion. Neither a progressive expansion of modern circumstances resulted, nor did old and new, "traditional" and "modern" forces remain locked in perpetual conflict, forcing movement toward a new level of development. The social change that took place during the sixteenth century did not set in motion a process of self-sustaining change and of transformation. On the contrary, the inability of the Republic to transform itself during the eight-

100 R. Koselleck, Kritik und Krise, Frankfurt 1973, 17.

eenth century and the transitional difficulties experienced by
the newly created kingdom of Holland during the nineteenth
century stand in a direct causal relationship with the early
changes of the sixteenth century and the Republic's forerunner
position during the seventeenth century.

3. Several conclusions can be drawn from the example of the
Netherlands that are relevant for the theoretical framework of
the modernization discussion. First, the Dutch example supports
those scholars who criticize modernization theory because it
characterizes social transformation as primary an endogenous
process that is stimulated by internal differentiation. Both an
endogenous potential for development and exogenous stimuli
played a role in the Netherlands during the sixteenth century
and both were necessary. This can be confirmed by comparing
the Dutch Republic with early modern Switzerland, where
social and political structures were quite similar to those of the
Dutch maritime provinces, but which received no exogenous
stimuli in the form of a commercial Revolution, or a political
or military crisis. Describing modernization as a unified process
in all three sectors of the economy also appears to be incorrect
in light of the Dutch experience. Modernization can be introduced separately into one or more sectors of the economy,
resulting in a situation characterized by the presence of dispa-
rate levels of development at the same time, at least when
measured by the standards of modernization theory. The Dutch
experience shows further that a preliminary modernization of
agriculture is not necessarily a condition favorable to modernization in industry, as the example of England might suggest.
The archaic agricultural forms present in Belgium or the mixed
forms of Westphalia were far more favorable for encouraging
modernization in industry during the early modern period.
When considering the most appropriate subject for historical
analysis, it is clear that the unit whose economic processes
during the early modern period can most profitably be investi-
gated is neither the national state nor another sizeable political
grouping, but rather individual regions, characterized by economically favorable conditions and distinguished by their social
structure, transportation connections, and other kinds of economic infrastructure.

Finally when discussing political modernization, the question
of stable modern democratic structural and state forms, the
Dutch example reminds us to consider more fully those mecha-

nisms of "national integration" which functioned independently of the emergence of a bureaucratic, centralized state. It also forces theorists to devote more attention to traditional elites instead of measuring political involvement only by the standard of voter participation. (516)

Beyond these individual points a modification of the model of modernization itself seems necessary. It seems particularly important to me that the chronological and thematic limitation of the theory to the problem of transition be removed. The *chronological* restriction of modernization theory to the late eighteenth and nineteenth centuries has already been removed thanks to an increasing interest of social scientists in the sixteenth and seventeenth centuries, noticeable above all in the work of Parsons. Overcoming the *thematic* limitation of modernization theory is more important still. This limitation is a result of focusing only upon those mechanisms of transformation which were at work at the end of the eighteenth century. As a result the accomplishments of the princely states have come to the fore, particularly bureaucratic state centralism, toleration imposed from above, a uniform society of subjects who were largely without rights, and free, unbound labor and property relationships. By highlighting the perceived or actual advantages resulting from state intervention for the transformation from "traditional" to "modern" societies, their acute and long-term costs have remained outside of the purview of modernization theory and research guided by it. In addition those traditional structures and mechanisms have been overlooked which did not by themselves promote a change in the system (perhaps even hindering change) but served in the long term to prepare a stable foundation for modern structural and social forms. Such were the communal and corporate traditions of self-government in the cities and villages, and the social and economic solidarity of a strong urban guild structure that were present in the early modern Dutch Republic.

It might also be necessary to reassess the modalities of the great processes of change from the "pre-modern" world to modernity. In the case of the Netherlands the impulses of economic and social modernity, resulting from the early spurt of development during the sixteenth and seventeenth centuries, were directly responsible for delaying further development during the eighteenth century. It seems appropriate to replace the continual, progressive conception of modernization with one that has been described by Jan Romein as a "dialectic of progress."[101] This dialectic rests upon the supposition that a country which is heading toward a new stage of social development reaches barriers at a particular point in time beyond which further change is extremely difficult. They can be overcome only under pressure, particularly exogenous pressure upon the society to accommodate itself to other societies which had in the meantime assumed a leading role. The probability is great that such a reshaping can only be achieved when the traditional forms, which had by and large been considered adequate, were destroyed either by direct, violent (517) attack or were weakened in another way. Alongside of the evolutionary route to modernity that the Netherlands took at the beginning of the early modern period and which England followed at the end, the emergence of the modern world was necessarily also accompanied by violent, revolutionary thrusts which destroyed old structures to make room for new ones. In light of this, the evolutionary component of modernization theory must be supplemented by elements of the theory of revolution which make it possible to determine the function and significance of each violent break with traditional structures. It seems to me that a combination of modernization theory, freed from its traditional preoccupation with the chronologically and thematically narrow problem of transition, with an undogmatic and flexibly applied theory of revolution comprises the most suitable analytical tool for historians. Such a combination offers the measure of flexibility necessary to do justice to the diversity of each historical era in which alongside of the newer elements, traditional features are also present in varying degrees of strength and effectiveness. They did not function only as barriers, but could also smooth the process of change and transformation in certain respects, and by so doing could encourage acceptance of the new structures and help to stabilize them.

---

101 J. Romein, Dialektiek (note 38), 40-89.

CHAPTER EIGHT

RELIGION AND SOCIETY
IN THE NORTHERN NETHERLANDS
"Public Church" and Secularization,
Marriage and Midwives, Presbyteries
and Participation.

The following essay examines the function of religion and the specific type of state-church relations present in the early modern Republic of the United Netherlands. It is one of a series of articles which describe and analyze the Dutch experience as a distinct type within early modern European history.[1] The early modern Netherlands were unique because of their republican and federal constitution, the bourgeois scope of their society, the dynamism and partly—in agriculture—the modern structure of their economy, their social diversity and liberal spirit in culture and the sciences, and last but not least their solution to the confessional problem and ecclesiastical life within the Republic.[2] To understand the specifics of early

---

1 See H. Schilling,"The History of the Northern Netherlands and Modernization Theory" above pp. 305-352, idem., Civic Calvinism in Northwestern Germany and the Netherlands (16th to 19th century), Kirksville 1991, idem, Der libertär-radikale Republikanismus der holländischen Regenten. Ein Beitrag zur Geschichte des politischen Radikalismus in der frühen Neuzeit, in: Geschichte und Gesellschaft 10 (1984), 498-533; idem, Calvinistische Presbyterien in Städten der Frühneuzeit—eine kirchliche Alternativform zur bürgerlichen Repräsentation? (Mit einer quantifizierenden Untersuchung zur holländischen Stadt Leiden), in: W. Ehbrecht (ed.), Städtische Führungsgruppen und Gemeinden in der werdenden Neuzeit, Köln/Wien 1980, 385-444.—Note on the translation: The very extensive additional commentaries in the notes have been removed from the translated version. Readers who are particularly interested in special aspects of the problems discussed should consult the notes of the original German version.

2 There is ample literature on Dutch society during the "Golden Age", except for the impact of religion and ecclesiastical institutions on society. See Rapport over de huidige stand en toekomstige planning van het wetenschappelijk onderzoek der Nederlandse geschiedenis, ed. by the Historisch-Wetenschappelijke Commissie der Koninklijke Nederlandse Akademie van Wetenschappen, Amsterdam 1974, 31; for a precise and well-written church history: O.J. de Jong, Nederlandse kerkgeschiedenis, 3rd ed., Nijkerk 1985.—See also A. Duke, Reformation and Revolt in the Low Countries, London 1990 (collected essays) and, in response to this article: O. Mörke, Konfessionalisierung als politisch-soziales Prinzip? Das

modern Dutch history and its resulting type of development it
is helpful to discuss the Dutch experience in general and our
present topic in particular within the context of the debate of
the past few decades concerning modernization, especially
among American sociologists and political scientists, which has
brought forth a number of new theories. These theories seek to
identify milestones and turning points on the paths that led to
the pluralistic and democratic industrial society of the late
nineteenth and twentieth centuries by means of macro-socio-
logical analysis.[3] While most modernization theorists have concentrated their attention upon industrialization and the
democratic revolutions that took place at the end of the eighteenth century or later, some have considered the preparatory
changes in Old European societies and have devoted more
attention to cultural aspects of the problem. Talcott Parsons,
for example, (199) has appealed to other scholars to recognize
that the "beginning of the system of modern societies" can be
found in "certain seventeenth-century developments in the
societal community," i.e. in decisive religio-sociological
changes, above all the emergence of an "internal religious pluralism."[4]

Modernization theory could become more useful to historians
if its chronological scope were extended and its purview
expanded in this way. New perspectives have emerged through
the application of this theoretical tool to the Dutch Republic
and the developmental lead that it enjoyed over other European
countries that was so often remarked upon by contemporaries.[5]

Verhältnis von Religion und Staatsbildung in der Republik der Vereinigten
Niederlande im 16. und 17. Jahrhundert, in: Tijdschrift voor sociale Geschiedenis
16 (1990), 31-60; G.J. Schutte, Het Calvinistisch Nederland, Utrecht 1988.

3 On "modernization theory" and its application to early modern history see
Schilling, History (note 1).

4 T. Parsons, The System of Modern Societies, Englewood Cliffs, NJ 1971, 50s.,
68-92, esp. 68s. and 73ss.

5 H.-Ch. Schröder, Die neuere englische Geschichte im Lichte einiger Modernisierungstheoreme, in: R. Koselleck (ed.), Studien zum Beginn der modernen Welt,
Stuttgart 1977, 30-65.—On the cultural side of Dutch early modern modernity we
have an interesting statement of Josiah Childe, a member of the London Council
of Trade in 1669. In his opinion the Netherlands were effective and successful in
consequence of the "education of the children, ... the well-providing for their poor
and employing of them, ... the freedom makes the nation valiant, ... liberty of
religion"; see J. Thirsk, Seventeenth-Century Economic Documents, Oxford 1972,
69ss.; see also several similar statements by Sir William Temple, Observations
upon the United Provinces of the Netherlands (1673), ed. by G. Clark, London
1972, 107, 112; and by Swedish business men: E. Hassinger, Wirtschaftliche
Motive und Argumente für religiöse Duldsamkeit im 16. und 17. Jahrhundert, in:

In any case historians must formulate Parsons' very general pronouncements on the cultural and religious changes that occurred during the early modern period far more precisely and measure their importance for societal modernization both empirically and theoretically.

We proceed from the assumption that a fundamental change in the relations between the political and social system on the one hand and the religious and ecclesiastical system on the other was an essential element of the overall process of modernization. Associated with this change was a redefinition of the societal function of church and religion.[6] This aspect of modernization was characterized by the following elements:

1. The dissolution of the unified political and ecclesiastical world in which "a particular religion was the compulsory foundation of the political order,"[7] either under the leadership of the church, as was the case from time to time during the Middle Ages, or of the state, as during the first phase of the early modern period. (200)

2. The emergence of freedom of conscience as the principal result of changes in the theoretical legitimation of the state and the self-understanding of society. Tolerance and confessional pluralism were no longer social realities which had to be *endured*, as occurred during the sixteenth century in many areas of central and northwestern Europe where the population included adherents of several different confessions, but were regarded and *accepted* as generally recognized fundamental social principle by both state and society.

3. The desacralization of the aims of state policy and their restriction to the concerns of this world. The state and the civic magistrate renounced responsibility for establishing God's will on earth and for insuring the eternal salvation of its subjects. Instead the state committed itself to pursuing the temporal happiness of its citizens, seeking to perfect earthly coexistence through ameliorating or even eliminating social needs.

4. Dismissal of church and religion from a *general* social

Archiv für Reformationsgeschichte 49 (1958), 226-245, 241s.

6 This is covered by the paradigm "confessionalization", discussed in the articles of part II of this volume.

7 E.-W. Böckenförde, Zum Verhältnis von Kirche und Moderner Welt. Aufriß eines Problems, in: R. Koselleck (ed.), Studien zum Beginn der modernen Welt, Stuttgart 1977, 154-177, 155. ("Eine bestimmte Religion (ist) verbindliche Grundlage der politischen Lebensordnung.")

responsibility, limiting them to *specific* functions and interests,[8] and restricting them to spiritual and religious "core
duties." Their previous "peripheral" responsibilities in the
areas of marriage, family, education, poor relief, and care for
the sick were increasingly administered by civic and secular
institutions and authorities, who now also set the social norms
associated with them.

5. The result of these processes was a liberal, tolerant, pluralistic society in which it was possible for several confessions
to coexist as equals in legal terms. The church was no longer a
privileged institution encompassing in principle the entire
society but only one among many societal groups or groupings,
and the religious values and norms that it espoused belonged to
the private sphere.[9] This was also true in those cases where as a
consequence of their special status during the Old European
epoch the churches enjoyed a distinct legal status as so-called
"corporations under public law" (*Anstalten des öffentlichen
Rechts*) as they do today in Germany.

Placing our investigation within the context of modernization
theory yields two interpretive advantages: first, it employs a
comparative perspective that draws attention to the unique
characteristics of the Dutch Republic;[10] second, it links the
theme of "church and city," (201) which usually concerns only
a small group of experts in ecclesiastical and legal history, to a
discussion that is of broader interest to historians and other
social scientists. Incidentally, the debate over a possible linkage
between the ecclesiastical upheavals of the sixteenth and the
seventeenth centuries and the modern world is hardly a new
one. With regard to the older debate in the classical sociology
of religion dominated by Max Weber, however, let me emphasize that I have not placed my topic in the context of modernization because we are dealing with *Calvinism*, but in order
to examine the situation in the larger *commercial* and

---

8 T. Rendtorff, Zur Säkularisierungsproblematik. Über die Weiterentwicklung
der Kirchensoziologie zur Religionssoziologie, in: Internationales Jahrbuch für
Religionssoziologie, vol. II: Theoretische Aspekte der Religionssoziologie I,
Köln/Opladen 1966, 51-72, esp. part III.

9 See Böckenförde, Verhältnis (note 7), 176s.

10 F. Krantz and P.M. Hohenberg, Failed Transitions to Modern Industrial
Society: Renaissance Italy and Seventeenth Century Holland, Montreal 1975; J.
de Vries, On the Modernity of the Dutch Republic, in: Journal of Economic
History 33 (1973), 191-202, and idem, Economy of Europe in an Age of Crisis,
1600-1750, Cambridge 1976, esp. 251ss.; Schilling, History (note 1).

manufacturing cities of Holland together with Calvinism. By framing my topic in this way I disclaim the use of any single element to provide a comprehensive explanation for social transformation. In contrast to the Weber school, which was fascinated by Calvinism, I do not expect to uncover the umbilical cord of the modern period and modernity with this topic. An analysis of the changing structure and the social functions of churches and confessions during the early modern period serves to illuminate *one* element—albeit an important one—within a broader complex of questions that are important for the discussion of modernization. Such an investigation can, however, reveal much about both the structure and stage of development of a given early modern society as a whole.

In the following study I will examine the extent to which (or at which points) Dutch society in the northern Netherlands—particularly urban society in the larger cities of Holland—exhibited characteristics of modernity, in the sense defined above, between the end of the sixteenth and the end of the eighteenth centuries. Let me emphasize that my remarks here should be considered only a preliminary approach to a very complicated, multi-faceted historical problem. In particular, it is impossible within the scope of a single article to provide an analysis that takes into account every aspect of Dutch society, including provincial and local differences and nuances, desirable as this might be for such a complex society.

From the wider framework of interaction between ecclesiastical-religious and social change, I have selected three individual themes which I consider particularly significant for illustrating the situation of the post-Reformation Republic:

I. The "public church" (*puplieke kerk*) as a distinct model for solving the early modern problem of confessionalization together with its social and political consequences.

II. The institution of civil marriage and changes in the role of midwives as indices for the limitation of the social responsibilities of the church in Dutch society.

III. The political and societal implications of the synodal-presbyterian structure of church government.

I. THE "PUBLIC CHURCH" MODEL AND THE PROBLEM OF SECULARIZATION

Any discussion of the status of church and religion within the social system of the early modern period must proceed from the problem of confessionalization which emerged with the Reformation. Finding a solution to this problem was one of the most important tasks of the sixteenth and seventeenth (202) centuries. The character and concrete structures assumed by early modern states and societies were determined to a considerable degree by the point in time when they solved the problem and the modalities that this solution finally took.[11] When considering the Republic of the United Netherlands, this question can be answered to a large extent by examining the position and importance of the Calvinist church within the Dutch commonwealth, which was born at the time of the revolution.

Dutch historical research has provided no generally accepted answer to this question. This is particularly apparent when consulting Dutch legal and constitutional histories, since most of the older works in this field were written from the perspective of the confessional traditions of the seventeenth century. As a rule these works emphasize the connections of the Dutch state and Dutch society to Calvinism.[12] By contrast general historians and more specialized studies of Dutch cultural and intellectual history tend to relativize or even question the influence of Calvinism and the Calvinist church.[13] It appears that the latter viewpoint will dominate the field in the foreseeable future. This position can enlist the authority of the influential Dutch historian Enno van Gelder, who in his final work under the title *Getemperde Vrijheid*[14] offered an impressively detailed study of the relationship between church and state in the Republic of the United Netherlands. This book

---

11 For a magisterial discussion of this problem, see: R. Koselleck, Kritik und Krise, Frankfurt/M. 1973.

12 J.Th. de Visser, Kerk en staat, 3 vols., Leiden 1926/27; S.J. Fockema Andreae, De nederlandse staat onder de Republiek, Amsterdam 1961.

13 J.L. Price, Culture and Society in the Dutch Republic During the Seventeenth Century, London 1974; F. Petri, Die Kultur der Niederlande, Frankfurt/M. 1972, 134s.; F. Petri and W.J. Alberts, Gemeinsame Probleme deutsch-niederländischer Landes- und Volksforschung, Groningen 1962, 4ss.; H. Brugmans, Geschiedenis van Amsterdam, 8 vols., Amsterdam 1930-1933, here vols. 3 and 4.

14 H.A. Enno van Gelder, Getemperde vrijheid. Een verhandeling over de verhouding van Kerk en Staat in de Republiek der Verenigde Nederlanden en de vrijheid van meningsuiting in zake godsdienst, drukpers en onderwijs gedurende de 17e eeuw, Groningen 1972; idem, Vrijheid en Onvrijheid in de Republiek, Geschiedenis der vrijheid van drukpers en godsdienst van 1572 tot 1798, vol. I, Van 1572 tot 1619, Haarlem 1947.

impresses the reader both by its sharp-eyed analysis of the legal status of the Calvinist public church and also by its evaluation of the evangelical and Catholic dissenters. It must not be overlooked, however, that by emphasizing the constant friction between reformed preachers and libertine regents van Gelder tended to force objective data into a particular interpretive framework. As a result, Calvinism and the Calvinist church are portrayed in the end as a relic of the pre-liberal epoch, enjoying only a purely historical legitimacy. The church's role is reduced to a kind of anachronistic clericalism of the *dominees*, whose loud claims, tirelessly advanced, were nullified by the fundamentally liberal and tolerant stance of the regents.[15] (203) According to this kind of interpretation Dutch society was characterized by an early secularism; the situation within the Republic is thus portrayed as one approaching a pluralism familiar to us today.

By contrast, the Republic appears in a completely different light in studies which seek to portray the religious and social life of cities and villages, drawing upon the sources of ecclesiastical and communal archives. One need only mention the important multi-volume study that Pastor Evenhuis dedicated to his Calvinist congregation under the evocative title, *Ook dat was Amsterdam* (This too was Amsterdam).[16] Another such work is Theodor van Deursens' book, which traces the struggle between *Bavianen* and *Slijkgeuzen*, the Arminian *Paviane* and Gomarian *Mudgeusen* in the first decades of the seventeenth century. He sketches a colorful, true-to-life portrait of churches and churchmen in their struggles for pure doctrine and a godly way of life.[17]

This juxtaposition shows the extent to which an evaluation of the influence of Calvinism in the northern Netherlands depends upon the questions posed and upon underlying historiographic interests. In the following study I am not interested in substantiating either the liberal or the clerical, Calvinist

---

15 In a certain respect van Gelders view stands in the tradition of early modern anticlericalism of the Dutch regents. See H. Schilling, "Afkeer van domineesheerschappij"—ein neuzeitlicher Typus von Antiklerikalismus?, in: H.A. Oberman (ed.), Anticlericalism in the Middle Ages and Modern Times, Leiden 1991.

16 R.B. Evenhuis, Ook dat was Amsterdam, 5 vols., Amsterdam 1965-1978; most recently: H. Roodenburg, Onder censuur. De kerkelijke tucht in de gereformeerde gemeente van Amsterdam, 1578-1700, Hilversum 1990.

17 A.Th. van Deursen, Bavianen en Slijkgeuzen, Kerk en kerkvolk ten tijde van Maurits en Oldenbarnevelt, Assen 1974.

tradition, but in examining the functional connection between the Dutch state and republican society on the one hand, and the Reformed church and the Calvinist confession on the other.

To what extent had state and church already separated in the northern Netherlands during the seventeenth century? What was the degree of secularization present in the political and social order? Was the Republic, praised by so many contemporaries as being especially progressive,[18] still a part of the unified religious and political world of the Middle Ages and the confessional age, in which a particular religion or confession served as a foundation for state and society? Or can the Republic already be considered part of the modern era, in which the state no longer pursues spiritual and religious goals because it is dominated by pluralistic—religious and non-religious—social forces?

1. The Emergence and Character of the Public Church

The legal foundations of the public church can be described relatively easily.[19] The new settlement of ecclesiastical affairs lay within the jurisdiction of the provincial estates,[20] (204) so that the circumstances and problems experienced by the churches varied greatly from province to province, even from city to city and among rural areas of comparable size. In the following discussion I will refer primarily to the province of Holland because it occupied the position of a forerunner and model. No single self-consistent church ordinance, in the strict sense of the word, was ever drafted there.[21] Two ordinances

---

18 See the literature given in note 5.

19 H. Edler von Hoffmann, Das Kirchenverfassungsrecht der niederländischen Reformierten bis zum Beginn der Dordrechter Nationalsynode von 1618/19, Leipzig 1902; J. Bohatec, Das Territorial- und Kollegialsystem der holländischen Publizistik des 17. Jahrhunderts, in: Zeitschrift der Savigny-Stiftung für Rechtsgeschichte 66, Kanonistische Abteilung 35 (1948), 1-150; E. Conring, Kirche und Staat nach der Lehre der niederländischen Calvinisten in der ersten Hälfte des 17. Jahrhunderts, Neukirchen 1965; de Visser, Kerk (note 12); Th.L. Haitjema, Nederlands hervormd Kerkrecht, Nijkerk 1951.

20 Paragraph 13 of the Union of Utrecht allowed each of the provinces to decide upon the confession and order of the provincial church for itself. See R. Fruin and H.E. Colenbrander, Geschiedenis der Staatsinstellingen in Nederland, Den Haag 1901, 381.—Later on, in 1583, the Provinces obliged each other to accept Calvinism, but ecclesiastical matters remained the business of provincial authorities. See Kerkelyk Plakaat Boek, Behelzende de Plakaaten, Ordonnantien, Ende Resolutien, Over de Kerkelyke Zaken, collected by N. Wiltens, 4 vols., Den Haag 1722-1798, here vol. I, 2-4.

21 Consequently there was no Dutch equivalent to the great discussion on

passed by the estates of Holland during the first half of the 1570's constituted a "legal framework" which served to direct the changing relationship between church and state on a case-by-case basis.

1. On July 20, 1572, during the first "revolutionary" assembly of the estates at Dordrecht, a decision was made at the request of William of Orange to allow "freedom of religion both for the Reformed and the Roman Religion" and to leave practical matters, especially the allotment of church buildings, in the hands of the local authorities.[22]

2. A reordering of the administration of church property also took place during the first half of the 1570's. Lay ecclesiastical officials assumed responsibility for some of this property, especially funds for church maintenance and social relief. These officials were appointed by the civic community and not by the magistrate. The remainder of the church property came under the direct control of the magistrate, particularly church lands, buildings, and estates, parsonages, endowments, and monastic property, which were collected together into a kind of trust. The magistrates also had the right to oversee the lay administrators of church property. In addition, they were generally responsible for the material well-being of the churches, particularly for the remuneration of those pastors who were not paid by income derived from church property set aside for such purposes.[23] (205)

Further events, above all the successful conclusion of the "revolutionary Reformation"[24] which led to a takeover of the magistrates by the Calvinist party, nullified the parity ruling of 1572. Catholics were forced to give up all rights to church property and after 1576 every form of Catholic worship was

---

state-church relations by German jurists. See M. Heckel, Staat und Kirche nach den Lehren der evangelischen Juristen Deutschlands in der ersten Hälfte des 17. Jahrhunderts, in: Zeitschrift der Savigny-Stiftung für Rechtsgeschichte 71 and 74, Kanonistische Abteilung 42 and 43 (1956 and 1957), 117-247; 202-308.

22 Edited in Documenta Reformatoria, ed by. J.N. Bakhuizen van den Brink et alii, vol. I, Kampen 1960, 155; see Enno van Gelder, Vrijheid (note 14), 51s. ("Vrijheit der religien, zoowel de Gereformeerde als de Roemsse religie.")

23 Kerkelyk Plakaat Boek, vol. I (note 20), 213ss.; Enno van Gelder, Vrijheid (note 14), 52ss.; D.G. Rengers Hora Siccama, De geestelijke en kerkelijke goederen onder het canonieke, het gereformeerde en het neutrale recht, vol. I, De canonieke en de gereformeerde bedeeling, Utrecht 1905.

24 H.A. Enno van Gelder, Revolutionnaire reformatie, De vestiging van de Gereformeerde Kerk in de Nederlandse gewesten, gedurende de eerste jaren van de Opstand tegen Filips II, 1575-1585, Amsterdam 1943.

prohibited in Holland and Zeeland, and in the remaining provinces after the mid-1580's.[25] Calvinist congregations inherited the older parishes, without of course assuming the position of the medieval *ecclesia universalis*. In a decision confirmed by all of the provincial estates, the *Gereformeerde Kerk* received the status[26] of a public church (*puplieke kerk*)[27] which it maintained until the end of the Republic. As public church, it could expect state financial support out of funds derived from medieval church property[28] as well as additional (206) financial allocations.[29] Officially only Calvinist worship was permitted and only Calvinist doctrine could be taught in any state or quasi-state institution, including schools and universities, poor houses and orphanages, the army and navy, and the overseas companies.[30]

The numerous points of contact between the public church and secular institutions are illustrated particularly well by the important office of church warden (*kerkmeester*). These officials were responsible for administering parish churches, which included maintaining church buildings and the grave sites located within them. They were appointed not by the Calvinist congregation but by the parishioners—that is, the men who lived within the district of the medieval parish—and by the community. Thus they were "civic" officials,[31] whose conduct

---

25 See paragraph 15 of the Union of Utrecht, Kerkelyk Plakaat Boek (note 20), vol. I, 1s. and 515ss. On the Catholic church see J.D. Tracy, With and Without the Counter-Reformation: The Catholic Church in the Spanish Netherlands and the Dutch Republic, 1580-1650, in: The Catholic Historical Review 71 (1985), 547-575.

26 Kerkelyk Plakaat Boek (note 20), vol. I, 4.

27 In my opinion the literal translation "public church" is more precise than "ruling church" (Regierungskirche) as is suggested in A.N. Cistozvonov, Über die stadial-regionale Methode bei der vergleichenden historischen Erforschung der bürgerlichen Revolutionen des 16. bis 18. Jahrhunderts in Europa, in: Zeitschrift für Geschichtswissenschaft 21 (1973), 31-48, esp. 41.

28 In general on subventions given to a church by the state see J. Heckel, Kirchengut und Staatsgewalt, Ein Beitrag zur Geschichte und Ordnung des heutigen gesamtdeutschen Staatskirchenrechts, in: Rechtsprobleme in Staat und Kirche. Festschrift für R. Smend, Göttingen 1952, 103-143, 104s.

29 The concrete reality of the early modern Dutch "state" was very complex. See Schilling, History (note 1).

30 Van Deursen, Bavianen (note 17), 13ss. and 18ss.; Kerkelyk Plakaat Boek (note 20), vol. I, 66, 71, 213; vol. II, 411; vol. III, 85-88; C.R. Boxer, The Dutch Seaborn Empire, 1600-1800, London 1965, 132-154.

31 See Kerkelyk Plakaat Boek (note 20), vol. I, 213; Th.van Deursen, Kerk of parochie? De kerkmeesters en de dood ten tijde van de Republiek, in: Tijdschrift voor geschiedenis 89 (1976), 531-537, correcting P. den Boers, Naar een geschie-

in office, accordingly, was supervised by the secular magistrates. The same was true for directors of hospitals, poorhouses, and orphanages and for supervisors of poor relief. They were all "civic" officeholders who were, however, obliged to be Calvinists by the duties of their offices.

The Calvinists also had, at first, a monopoly on public worship services, but this legal barrier was soon broken down by the Anabaptists, Lutherans, and Remonstrants. These dissenters met at first in private assemblies in a number of cities but in the course of the seventeenth century received permission to erect their own church buildings. Jews were allowed to worship in their own synagogues in many cities on the basis of a special, formal indulgence granted by the magistrates.[32] Only the public church, however, had the right to magisterial support in the administration of its internal affairs and in upholding its doctrinal positions as well as the possibility of affecting state policies to support a christianization, as the Calvinists saw it, of society as a whole, including the non-Calvinist part.[33] The basic law that all officeholders should be members of the Reformed church, which was effective until the end of the Republic, was of particular political importance even if in reality it was not always enforced.[34] (207)

2. Modern Aspects of the Public Church

2.1 Structurally Ensured Tolerance

In what respects did the Dutch model of a "public church" differ from the type of state or territorial church present in the German territories, a type which dominated the European nation states of the early modern period? The Dutch model, first of all, did not assume the principle of confessional unity in the state and the identification of the ecclesiastical and civic

denis van de dood, ibid., 161-201.

32 L.J. van Aken, De Remonstrantsche Broederschap in verleden en heden, Arnheim 1947; J.W. Pont, Geschiedenis van het Lutheranisme in de Nederlanden tot 1618, Haarlem 1911; W. Bergsma, Marnix and the Schwenkfeldians: some general remarks, in: Mennonite Quarterly Review LXVII (1988), 236-248.

33 On "christianization" according to Calvinist standards see H. Schilling, Calvinism and the Making of the Modern Mind, in: idem, Civic Calvinism, Kirksville 1991. On the officeholders see the mandates of the provincial governments in: Kerkelyk Plakaat Boek (note 20), vol. I, 34-113.

34 Kerkelyk Plakaat Boek (note 20), vol. I, 598ss.; J.C. Naber, Dissenters op't kussen. Een bijdrage tot de staatkundige geschiedenis der Vereenigde Neederlanden, in: Tijdspiegel II, Amsterdam 1884, 45-57.

community. In reality, this fundamental principle was frequently violated in other places too during the sixteenth century, even in territories which had state or territorial churches, but apart from the Netherlands it did constitute a norm and a structural principle.[35] Religious groups whose beliefs differed from the state confession were considered to be special cases whose right to religious expression required a special and explicit legal foundation in the form of a privilege granted by the magistrate. The confessional dissidents of foreign churches in trade centers, especially the large port cities, were typical of the conditional, exceptional nature of these groups because they were *foreign* churches. This situation only changed when these "exceptional cases" became much more important because of changes in territorial boundaries during the seventeenth century and because of the deconfessionalization of state and society that was introduced with the Enlightenment.

Already at the end of the sixteenth century the situation was markedly different in the Republic of the United Netherlands. (208) The presence of confessional dissidents, who were after all such a large part (nearly half) of the population, did not depend upon a special dispensation of the government, established in the form of statute law, but rather reflected a certain freedom of conscience which was also expressed in the structure of the public church.

Until the middle of the seventeenth century the existence of dissenting religious communities was allowed by dint of necessity in regions with state churches or territorial churches. It was impossible, or at least it appeared unfeasible, either to drive religious dissidents into exile or to pay the price of a civil war in order to impose a unitary constitutional or ecclesiastical law. Religious tolerance was above all a result of calculated political and economic policies[36] and accordingly could be changed at any time, as occurred in France, without

---

35 M. Heckel, Lehren der evangelischen Juristen Deutschlands, in: Zeitschrift der Savigny-Stiftung für Rechtsgeschichte 74 (1957), 272ss.; U. Scheuner, Staatsräson und religiöse Einheit des Staates. Zur Religionspolitik in Deutschland im Zeitalter der Glaubensspaltung, in: R. Schnur (ed.), Staatsräson. Studien zur Geschichte eines politischen Begriffes, Berlin 1977, 363-406. See the remarks on the principle of religio-vinculum-societatis in the articles on confessionalization in section II of this volume.

36 Hassinger, Motive (note 5); U. Scheuner, Staatsräson (note 35); H.R. Guggisberg, Veranderingen in de argumenten voor religieuze tolerantie en godsdienstvrijheid in de zestiende en zeventiende eeuw, in: Bijdragen en Mededelingen betreffende de Geschiedenis der Nederlanden 91 (1976), 177-196.

destroying the foundations of state and society. Of course economic arguments were also used in the Netherlands, but they were only concerned with how broadly or narrowly the principle of tolerance should be interpreted, since tolerance itself was widely accepted. In contrast to a state church, the structure of the public church made a special legitimation of religious tolerance unnecessary. Despite every specific restriction, individual freedom of conscience, as formulated for Holland in 1572 and for the other provinces in the thirteenth article of the Union of Utrecht, remained one of the pillars of the state. Indeed, it was one of the fundamental values in the self-understanding of Dutch society. The Dutch Republic was based upon the conviction that a stable state and well-ordered society do not automatically presuppose a uniformity of faith.[37] "The principle of unified (209) religious worship as a foundation of state order," which only "gradually lost its axiomatic validity" in the rest of early modern Europe,[38] had never been accepted in the Republic of the United Netherlands. The Dutch state and society were "modern" in this respect.

A comparison with the absolutistic solution to the problem of confession and toleration favored by Thomas Hobbes, which became the foundation of a reorganization of the absolutist European states during the late seventeenth and eighteenth centuries, clarifies the extent to which the structurally guaranteed tolerance in the northern Netherlands broke with early modern religio-sociological norms.[39] Starting with a recognition of the fact that faith and conscience are always able to escape external pressure in the end, the English state theorist postulated freedom of conscience. However, because his Leviathan, in contrast to the Dutch Republic, was based upon the foundation of an identity of society and the worshipping community, he was forced, on the other hand, to maintain the existence of a public church to which all subjects had to belong. The citizen found himself in a kind of schizophrenic dilemma: his religious convictions were a private matter and he was forced to conceal them in public, yet he had to satisfy publicly the ritual

---

37 See Emanuel van Meteren, Historien der Nederlanden en haar Naburen Oorlogen tot het Jaar 1612, Amsterdam 1647, book XIV, 250ss.; J.L. Motley, History of the United Netherlands, vol. 2, New York 1876, 226.

38 Guggisberg, Veranderingen (note 36), 178.

39 See Leviathan, chapters 12 and 31 (ed. by M. Oakeshott, Oxford 1960, 69ss., 232ss.); Koselleck, Kritik (note 11), 18ss.

demands of the civil religion. By contrast, in the northern
Netherlands the individual conscience was not banished to a
purely private sphere. The principle of freedom of conscience
was translated into political and social reality, which allowed
Protestant dissidents public religious expression within certain
limitations.

The situation was quite different, however, for Catholics.
They were tolerated but were officially forced to refrain from
any form of public worship until the end of the Republic.
Strictly speaking, even the private exercise of religion
(*exercitium domesticum*) was forbidden, a practice which in the
case of the German territories opened the way toward equal
legal status for confessional minorities. This limitation of the
rights of Catholics does not vitiate our evaluation as a whole,
for the restrictions were not directed against religious forms
deviating from Protestantism or even against the religious convictions of individual Catholics, but rather against Catholicism
as a political force, which sought to overturn the Protestant
"Revolution" against Spain and to dissolve the union treaty.[40]
Already in that document, with which they committed themselves to Calvinism forever, the united provincial estates had
held their alliance open for the entry of Catholic provinces and
cities.[41] Hence they were, in principle, capable of granting full
toleration for Catholics, with the proviso that they could plau-
sibly share the political goal of the union in opposing Spain.
The fact that Catholic worship was prohibited in the Dutch
Republic cannot be advanced as evidence to prove that at least
a weakened form of the traditional conception of confessional
unity remained in force even in the Netherlands, and that, as a
result, the state considered religious nonconformity as such to
be a threat. Moreover, the restrictions were in reality loosely
applied, so that the existence of private Catholic services was
never seriously threatened.[42] (210) On the contrary, there was a
continual improvement of the situation for Catholics after the
beginning of the seventeenth century. This degree of toleration
for Catholics is an indication of the remarkable stability of the

---

40 This was the main point even in the argumentation of Calvinist theologians,
see Bohatec, Territorial- and Kollegialsystem (note 19), 44.

41 Kerkelyk Plakaat Boek (note 20), vol. I, 4.

42 L.J. Rogier, Geschiedenis van het katholicisme in Noord-Nederland in de
16e en 17e eeuw, 2 vols., Amsterdam 1947, esp. chapter VI, 4: "De Katholieken
als bijwoners", 457-475; Tracy, Counter-Reformation (note 25).

young Republic even as it fought for survival against the might of the Counter Reformation. At the same time it demonstrates the determination felt not only by the regents but by a majority of Dutch society to uphold the principle of freedom of conscience, that had been laid down at the birth of the new polity. Granted, there were restrictions upon the religious practice of dissidents in the northern Netherlands. There was not, however, an Inquisition.

Statistics of the confessional communities show that the Republic had always been a multi-confessional society and remained one. The Swiss military chaplain Stouppe estimated in 1672 that a third of the population was actively Calvinist, a third Roman Catholic, and the remaining third was composed of dissident Protestants and of the indifferent, or of free-thinkers, the majority of the latter belonging officially to the public church.[43] A modern study which evaluated the communicant lists of the Holland Mission established that for the year 1656 the percentage of Catholics was as high as 47%, although by 1726 the number had shrunk to 34%.[44] Apart from the inexactitude of these numbers, an inevitable problem stemming from the particular, (211) non-verifiable presumptions that guided their collation as well as the general vagueness of figures gathered before the advent of statistics in a modern sense, these values are not very revealing, referring as they do to the Netherlands as a whole. Dramatic regional variations are the

---

43 S.J. Fockema Andreae, De staat onder de Republiek, Amsterdam 1961, 149.

44 J.A. de Kok O.F.M., Nederland op de breuklijn Rome-Reformatie. Numerieke aspekten van Protestantisering en Katholieke Herleving in de Noordelijke Nederlanden 1580-1880, Assen 1964. The percentage of Catholics in de Kok's opinion was as follows (J.A. de Kok, o.c., table 40, 248):

	1656	1726	1775	1809
South-Holland	29	15	18	22.64
North-Holland	45	20	22	25.84
Utrecht	55?	30?	?	39.06
Zeeland	10?	9?	13?	±20.0
Friesland	13 á 16	11.5?	10.5?	9.42
Groningen	11	8?	8?	7.73
Drenthe	3?	?	?	0.73
Overijssel	43	40	37	34.36
Gelderland	50?	40?	35?	36.32
North-Brabant	-	-	-	87.58
Limburg	-	-	-	98.26
The Netherlands	47	34	36	38.10

On the methodological problems see the review of H.J. van Xanten in: Revue d'Histoire Ecclesiastique 60 (1965), 906-909.

most striking feature of Dutch confessional statistics. The
generality territories along the border of the Spanish provinces
were always overwhelmingly Catholic, probably over 80%. For
Utrecht, Overijssel, and Gelderland the study mentioned above
estimates that the Catholic segment of the population was 55%,
43%, and 50% respectively. By contrast, only 11% of Groningen
was Catholic, and the figures were 10% in Zeeland, 13% in
Friesland, and only 3% in Drenthe. The first statistics, collected
in 1796, show that in Friesland 81% of the population was Calvinist, 8% were Anabaptist, 10% were Catholic and 1% were
not members of any confession. The corresponding figures for
the Frisian cities are 74%, 6.5%, 16.5% and 3%, indicating that
the Catholic population was concentrated in the cities.[45] The
figures for the province of Holland are particularly interesting,
especially for the large cities. Mission reports indicate that the
population was 37% Catholic in 1656 and 17.5% in 1726, and
the numbers are clearly higher for cities in northern Holland
than in the southern part of the province. Pastor Trigland estimated in 1615 that only a third of the population of Amsterdam was Calvinist. A new study estimates that 22% of Amsterdam was Catholic in 1656 and in 1726 the proportion was
18%.[46]

---

45 J.A. Faber, Drie eeuwen Friesland, Wageningen 1972, table II, 29, part II,
428.

46 Holland: de Kok, Nederland (note 44), 227, table 38.—Amsterdam: J. Trig-
landius, Kerckelijcke geschiedenissen begriipende de geschillen in de Vereenichde
Nederlanden voorgevallen. De Kok's (note 44, table 34, 203) percentage figures of
Catholics within Dutch cities are as follows:

	1656	1726	1775	1809
Amsterdam	±22	18	±21	20.9
Haarlem	±20	16	±30	33.3
Hoorn	±25	12	±20	26.5
Enkhuizen	±5	4	±10	14.2
Alkmaar	±45	15	±30	37.0
Towns of North-Holland	±25	17	±20	23.3
The Hague	±25	28	±28	26.0
Delft	±35	30	±30	32.1
Rotterdam	±27	12	±18	26.9
Schiedam	±16	12	±15	34.8
Vlaardingen	±13	8	±13	14.8
Dordrecht	±13	5	±6	11.3
Gouda	±45	22	±25	25.8
Leiden	±15	10	±15	22.8
Towns of South-Holland	±25	14	±18	24.9

These figures are impressive from the perspective of confessional history and confessional sociology even if the individual estimates should be received with some skepticism, and the percentages for the seventeenth century must be discounted accordingly. Apart from particularly exceptional cases, such as the German imperial cities which followed a policy of confessional parity or European border territories (212) which were in danger of Turkish conquest (Hungary), no any other early modern states had such a confessional mixture. The strength and diversity of religious dissent was without question a structural characteristic of Dutch society during the seventeenth century. This was particularly true of the province of Holland which had a number of villages with large Catholic majorities in addition to its large multi-confessional cities.[47]

Despite the repeated synodal pronouncements against non-Calvinist worship, especially against the mass, the religious freedom of dissidents was recognized in the end even by the majority of Calvinists.[48] We can get some idea of the extent of individual freedom of conscience in Holland, if we consider that it was quite possible to live there as a non-Christian or an atheist without any formal connection to a Christian congregation. There was neither a legal requirement to baptize children nor any other mechanism to ensure that individuals belonged to one or another of the existing religious communities.[49] Even if such an atheistic existence during the early seventeenth century was more hypothetical than real, it does indicate the potential for a genuine freedom of conscience. This spiritual freedom had an enduring effect upon social and political coexistence within the Republic as a whole, which was clearly influenced by Holland. The first traces of an open society had appeared. This particular solution to the (213) problem of confessionalization was a basic component of the alternative that Dutch society presented to the surrounding absolutistic world. The Dutch solution to confessionalization served to enhance the reputation of the United Provinces, which many contemporaries praised as a model society,[50] and which even some present

47 De Kok, Nederland (note 44), 183-193.

48 Bohatec, Territorial- und Kollegialsystem (note 19), 47ss.

49 For a discussion about children who were not baptized see Kerkelyk Plakaat Boek (note 20), vol. III, 470: 1578 and 535: 1586; vol. I, 124, 137: 1618 and 831: 1656.

50 See note 5.

day historians consider to be an early example of a liberal, modern society.

2.2. Distance between Church and State

A second characteristic element of the Dutch model of a public church, closely related to the structurally ensured tolerance that distinguished it from state or territorial churches, was its strict distinction between the ecclesiastical and civic community and between state and ecclesiastical institutions, each remaining independent of the other. This separation of church and state was not only present in theory, but to a large extent was also observable in practice, both of which are important for our problem. It was most evident in the relationship of the state to the Protestant churches and associations outside of the public church. In the German territories, despite every theoretical distinction that had been made between church and state, after the mid-seventeenth century dissenting religious congregations were made subject to the ecclesiastical law of the territories and hence to the supremacy of the state. A similar form of state oversight for dissident Protestant churches never emerged in the Dutch Republic. Already during the first half of the seventeenth century their status was approaching that of largely private associations and thus the position which all Christian churches would have within the modern liberal state. The Remonstrants, who had to withdraw from the public church after all provincial and local magistracies had passed into the hands of counter-remonstrant Calvinists, provided a theoretical justification for this situation, advancing a solution formulated by Episcopius. He argued that "the government had the right to oversee the affairs of the public church only and it could not interfere in the affairs of private or "private-public" (i.e., Remonstrant) religious assemblies and congregations that had separated from the state church."[51]

The position of the public church was different. On account of its importance for state and society it possessed a status which was not compatible with the legal form of a private association. We will refer to this difference later in our discussion. At this point it must be maintained that there was a clear distance between state authority and the public church despite its special status, the assistance it received from the govern-

---

51 Bohatec, Territorial- und Kollegialsystem (note 19), 21.

ment, and the fact that the magistrate had an interest in supporting Calvinism. This distance narrowed or grew as the internal political constellation of forces changed, but it never disappeared. A logical consequence of the model of a public church which had special privileges and was backed by the magistrates was the introduction of the *commissarissen politiek*, that is the practice of sending representatives of the state to attend synods, (214) and even meetings of local presbyteries in some cities, in order to advance the interests of the magistrate and the state.[52] The Reformed public church was always able, however, to protect its institutional and spiritual autonomy. The local and synodal churches remained independent corporations, and the presbyteries and synods remained their organs of autonomous government. In contrast to German state and territorial churches, the Dutch public church was never a tool of the state but rather an independent political and social force. As such it was always taken seriously by politicians and, at times, was also feared for the power it had over broad strata of the population. As a rule the church used its political influence for the benefit of the Stadhoulders of the house of Orange. At times when the princes of Orange were strong and the distance between state and church correspondingly narrowed, the danger was greatest that the church would become an institution like a German territorial church.[53]

The breaking of institutional ties between the church and political order, which in theory took place during the Reformation but in the reality of a confessional state tended to be partially reestablished, was realized to a great extent in the Dutch Republic.[54] The reasons for the success of this "Reformation" are not to be found either in specific socio-economic and political structures or in spiritual or theological traditions alone. It was, rather, the result of a fortuitous conjunction of a number of factors, arising from material and intellectual realities that coincided and complemented each other. The most important *structural* factors were:

---

52 Kerkelyk Plakaat Boek (note 20), vol. I, 114s. and vol. III, 131-133; Bakhuizen van den Brink (ed.), Documenta (note 22), 368, No. 224; Evenhuis, Amsterdam (note 16), vol. I, 314ss.

53 On the attitude of the Calvinists towards the house of Orange see the analysis of the pamphlets in P. Geyl, Democratische tendenties in 1672, Amsterdam 1950. More recently H. Schilling, Afkeer (note 15); idem, Regentenrepublikanismus (note 1).

54 Cf. Böckenförde, Verhältnis (note 7).

—the social and religious consequences of a late Reformation, which could no longer encompass all members of a society and which fostered almost necessarily a large number of dissidents, composed of both the indifferent and those holding different beliefs;

—the fact that the Dutch Reformation was one which was instigated "from below." It involved a revolt against the state power of the Hapsburgs and never led to a "princely Reformation," in contrast to Germany, England, and Scandinavia;

—the origin of what later became the Dutch public church as a "free church under the cross." These churches had to contend with unfriendly or indifferent governments in German and English exile in order to maintain their autonomy. In this situation the Reformed understanding of church and ecclesiastical order changed, and its practical result was the presbyterian synodal form of the Dutch exile churches; (215)

—the absence of any central state authority seeking deliberate expansion of its bureaucracy. Within most early modern states the church served as a means of achieving political and administrative goals. Such policies served in practice to block the dissolution of the union of church and state which theoretically had taken place during the Reformation;

—the strength and homogeneity of a political elite which was most interested in maintaining its political and spiritual freedom of choice together with unhindered opportunities for trade and transportation. In this respect it was unimportant whether they were more committed to Calvinism or to the Erasmian-humanist tradition;

—the exigencies of the life-and-death political and military struggle to maintain a governmental system that was born through revolution, which simply could not afford the political costs that were inevitable when a religious consensus was imposed.

The decisive *intellectual* force was the ecclesiology and correlated legal theory of rigid counter-remonstrant Calvinism. It must be noted, however, that this concept of the church and church-state relations was never uncontested either with respect to its internal structure or its practical mechanisms even if its hegemony could no longer be threatened seriously after 1618. On the one hand, it faced a nationally and internationally strengthened Catholicism, which threatened the Dutch Calvinists because of the exposed position of the Republic more directly than it did the theologians and jurists of the German territories who were preoccupied with questions of state church law. On the other hand, the Calvinists had to ward off the Erastian-humanist positions advanced by the Remonstrant opposition emerging from their own ranks. Caught up in a perpetual struggle with a religious tradition that—in the case of Catholicism—was unwilling to accept the abolition of a unified world of church and society, or—in the case of the Erastian Remonstrants—was committed to reestablish it by state sovereignty in ecclesiastical matters, the theologians of the Dutch public church were continually forced to reformulate the legal relationship between the secular-political and spiritual-ecclesiastical realms on the basis of their own genuinely Calvinist position.

Dutch theologians could refer to the decisions made at the national Synod of Dordrecht, in which the delegates of international Calvinism, with the support of the Estates General, repudiated the Erastian doctrine of the Remonstrants. In contrast to Remonstrant thought on state-church relations, which went back to Zwingli, counter-remonstrant legal scholarship began with the Calvinist distinction between two different kingdoms of God on earth: the spiritual kingdom (216) of the church and the secular kingdom of the civil order. In this basic position there was complete agreement with Luther and German Lutheranism. For the relationship between church and state, however, the Lutheran and Calvinist positions had markedly different consequences in theory and practice. This difference can primarily be traced to the fact that in contrast to Germany the church law theories of the Dutch theologians never had to compete with a sophisticated legal doctrine of state-church relations drawn up by secular jurists, whose work was formulated in a different way and pursued different goals. Ecclesiastical law within German Protestantism, particularly in its central doctrine of the three estates and the magistrate as *membrum praecipuum ecclesiae*, was originally also intended to protect the church from state supremacy, or at least to restrict the latter. This idea quickly lost its impetus, however, since ecclesiastical law was absorbed into the secular law of the territorial state. In the Netherlands, by contrast, counter-remonstrant church law continued to develop largely without such interference and could clarify the relationship of church and state in the context of a systematic treatment of the

internal order of the church.[55] Church-state relations in the
province of Holland had almost no foundation in statute law, as
we have noted above. Thus the bias in favor of state interests
that was present in Germany as a result of the great imperial
codifications enacted by the treaties of Augsburg and Mün-
ster/Osnabrück was absent in the Netherlands. The theological
positions of important Calvinist pastors or professors such as
Wilhelm Appollonius, Jacobus Trigland, and Gisbert Voetius
could be maintained in their purest form without compromise.
Ecclesiastical law could play an effective role in helping to
determine the arrangement of relations between state and
church. Unlike the jurists whose doctrines set trends in Germany, these Dutch theologians did not begin with the interests
of the state and the necessity of political coexistence for the
different confessions, but with the character and interests of
the religious congregation and the need for a "civilizing" of
society according to Christian principles. The foundation of
their ecclesiastical and political thought consisted neither of
natural nor of positive law, but a doctrine of society derived
from the Bible.

It remained an urgent task for these Calvinist theoreticians
to provide theological justification for the distinction between
church order and ecclesiastical law on the one hand and the
political and secular order and secular law on the other. The
decisive criterion for the independence of each sphere was for
these theoreticians "the difference of life and community" in
each of them: within the church there was a confession of
faith, unity around the sacraments, and the subjection of its
members to church discipline, which was understood to be the
judgment of a spiritual and pastoral court. The secular order
rested largely upon submission to authority, compulsion, and
liability to punishment (217) through the sanctioned order of
the secular government.[56] Dutch church law discussions were
preoccupied with establishing the "correct" church order, i.e.,
with structuring the visible church according to biblical norms.
Since Calvinism, in contrast to Lutheranism, regarded a proper

---

55 Conring, Kirche (note 19).

56 Ibid., esp. 152, 189; Bohatec, Territorial- und Kollegialsystem (note 19),
44ss. On this distinction with regard to the resulting different types of discipline
see H. Schilling, "History of Crime" or "History of Sin"?—Some Reflections on
the Social History of Early Modern Church Discipline, in: E.J. Kouri und T. Scott
(eds.), Politics and Society in Reformation Europe. Essays for Sir Geoffrey Elton
on his 65th Birthday, London 1987, 289-310.

ordering of the visible church as necessary for salvation, these
theorists erected a further barrier against an improper tutelage
by the state. This was an important development, which helps
to explain why church-state relations followed divergent paths
in the northern Netherlands and in Germany.

Besides internal ecclesiastical problems, the Dutch counter-
remonstrant theologians were preoccupied with the question of
a "correct," i.e., divinely sanctioned, ordering of the secular
world. The magistrates bore primary responsibility for working
toward this end. According to Calvinist doctrine, they were
rulers of a realm that stemmed directly from God in the same
way that the church did. As a consequence the government was
obliged to use every legal means at its disposal to institute
God's will on earth. A dilemma resulted from this position
which is important for our investigation: on the basis of this
theocratic ideal and its dynamic effects, there was always a
danger within a Calvinist commonwealth that the theoretical
distinction between the spiritual and secular spheres would
become untenable in reality, i.e., that either the Christian-Cal-
vinist government could take over the church, or the theologians could usurp the power within the state, depending upon
the actual balance of power between the two. This, in turn,
would amount to a renewal of the medieval unified spiritual
and political world. Apart from chronologically and geographically limited phenomena, such a theocratic dynamic
could never develop in the Netherlands because of the structural and ideological counterweights mentioned above. The
Republic was in this respect, together with colonial America
and Cromwell's England, one of the few countries in which the
Calvinist theological distinction between the secular and spiritual spheres was in fact preserved. If one maintains that the
liberalism of Dutch society in the seventeenth century rested
"upon the defeat of Calvinism,"[57] then it can be added that if,
in the first instance, it was the defeat of a certain aspiration
for political power harbored by the *dominees*, its defeat was
also, paradoxically, a victory and resulted in the preservation
of an ecclesiastical structure that was genuinely and traditionally Calvinist in nature. Apart from the Netherlands and the
Anglo-Saxon examples, only the free churches "under the
cross" (218), which existed as underground churches in western

---

57 Position advanced by J.J. Woltjer.

parts of Germany under Catholic governments, were able to do
the same. Other Reformed churches, particularly those in the
Reformed territories of the Empire, adopted a Zwinglian-
Erastian solution.[58]

2.3. Focusing the Aims of State Policy upon the Concerns of this World

Perhaps the most important consequence of the development
described above for our topic was a remarkable shift of
emphasis in the way that state policy was set. Most importantly, it resulted in a new definition of the highest and
supreme duty of the secular magistrates: within the confessional
states dominant in Europe until the mid-seventeenth century
the highest good was to ensure the eternal salvation of their
subjects. By contrast in the Dutch Republic it became accepted
very early that the church alone was responsible for sanctifying
the people of the church and leading them to eternal life.
Freed of transcendental responsibilities, it became the "genuine
responsibility of secular government . . ., to create earthly
happiness, peace and quiet."[59] This division of responsibility,
which had already been established by the first half of the
seventeenth century, was an ideal mechanism for freeing the
state from any restraint that could result from having to pursue
policies dictated by transcendental considerations. This meant
greater freedom of action for the magistrate in both political
and social affairs, which over the long term could not fail to
have consequences for the structure and character of society. In
the second part of our essay we will return to this point.

3. Traditional Features of the Public Church

3.1 The Christianization of Society in this World and the Promotion of the Calvinist Religion as Duties of the State

Is it justifiable to understand our findings as an anticipation of
a modern liberal separation of church and state and a progressive secularization of society and political authority according to the definition of modernity that was discussed at the

---

58 On the "underground churches" see E. Simons, Niederrheinisches Synodal-
und Gemeindeleben "unter dem Kreuz", Freiburg and Leipzig 1897; on the
Erastian solutions in the German territories see the articles and the discussion in:
H. Schilling (ed.), Die reformierte Konfessionalisierung in Deutschland. Das Problem der "Zweiten Reformation", Gütersloh 1986.
59 Conring, Kirche (note 19), 149.

outset?——Weighty counter-arguments can be advanced against such an interpretation as it is encountered particularly in older German analyses of Dutch ecclesiastical law[60] and also those which follow the interpretive line of the American sociologist Talcott Parsons. First of all, there is the fact that the Dutch magistrates, despite their lack of obligation for the eternal salvation of their subjects, worked to promote a christianization of life in the northern Netherlands. This responsibility was even more distinct in the Calvinist Republic than it was in most other early modern (219) states. It was theoretically based upon the direct derivation of the secular realm from God himself. The civic government was instituted by God directly just as the governing bodies of the church had been. Its duty was to guarantee the domination of God's word in the *regnum universale* by passing laws and, if necessary, by compulsion and force. A variety of laws and ordinances attest to the fact that both local and provincial governments in the Republic labored zealously for a christianization of life in both the public and private spheres. They paid special attention to the so-called "crying sins,"[61] among which were Sabbath-breaking, prostitution, drunkenness, gambling, dueling, blasphemy, cursing, and acts of violence.

It would be incorrect to regard these efforts as the expression of a general Christian cultural norm, as is still present even in the secular societies of Europe and the Americas. What we see here is a much more traditional ideal. This becomes especially apparent when state reports linked the redemption or damnation of the polity with the obedience or disobedience of society to such Christian norms. This idea was, for example, expressed by an ordinance passed against prostitution in 1666 by the estates of Zeeland. The frequency of this vice was said to have provoked "God's wrath, punishments, and plagues." The warning of divine punishment was not a commonplace, but rather seen——as was stated in the mandate——as "stalking the land openly," an empirical reality. The traditional nature of such arguments becomes even clearer when we remember that what is referred to as divine "punishments and plagues" were clearly consequences of the second English-Dutch naval war.

60 Bohatec, Territorial- und Kollegialsystem (note 19); Edler von Hoffmann, Kirchenverfassungsrecht (note 19); Conring, Kirche (note 19), esp. 10-13.
61 Kerkelyk Plakaat Boek (note 20), vol. I, 694-802.

This conflict caused general impoverishment, especially in Zeeland.[62]

3.2. Calvinism as a State Ideology

Many of the state decrees that have been mentioned can be traced back to admonitions of Calvinist presbyteries or synods. Even if, as a rule, they were concerned with norms that were common to all Christian confessions, the sincerity and intensity of these cooperative efforts between theologians, elders, and politicians must be considered an expression at least of the deep influence that the spirit and ethos of Calvinism, if not its specific dogmatic content, had upon political powers.

The significance of Calvinism and the Calvinist public church cannot be judged from confessional statistics alone, since barely half of the Dutch population was Calvinist. Calvinism also did not have the legal status of a state confession, nor was the Dutch public church a state church. It was rather—and this is a second argument against the modern-secular interpretation of the Republic—a part of the official historical and national self-conception of the politically, culturally, and socially dominant segment of the population, almost an integral part of the (220) official state ideology held by Dutch society as a whole.[63] The regents could not have changed this reality, a consequence of the leading role played by Calvinism in the early phase of the revolt, even if all of them had embodied the anti-clerical, liberal type described by Enno van Gelder. An episode in connection with the marriage of Cornelius Pietersz Hooft, the free-thinking mayor of Amsterdam, illustrates this. When Hooft let it be known that he was planning to dispense with a church wedding ceremony some of his magisterial colleagues objected: "You are an old patriot . . . it would be inappropriate for you not to marry in the church."[64] Even those regents who could not be characterized as overly committed to the church felt that Calvinism

62 Ibid., 848.

63 De Visser, Kerk (note 12), vol. II, 281s.; J.C. Breen, Gereformeerde populaire historiographie in de zeventiende en achttiende eeuw, in: Christendom en historie, Lustrumbundel uitgegeven vanwege Het Gezelschap van Christelijke Historici in Nederland, Amsterdam 1925, 213-242.

64 Evenhuis, Amsterdam (note 16), vol. II, 66; H.A. Enno van Gelder, De levensbeschouwing van Cornelis Pietersz Hooft Burgermeester van Amsterdam, 1547-1626, Amsterdam 1918, 6. ("Ghij zijd een oude patriot ... ten zoude nyet wel passen, dat ghij niet in de kerck soudet trouwen.")

was the "true Reformed religion" which had to be defended under all circumstances.[65] The provincial estates and the Estates General repeatedly expressed this view. In its statement accepting the decisions made at the Synod of Dordrecht, the Estates General described "the true Reformed Christian religion" as "the foundation and bond of unity of the United Netherlands."[66] The official account of the Synod, which was sent to friendly governments together with copies of the synodal records, maintained that "as long as we live the church can hardly be separated from the Republic."[67] In the great assembly of 1651, which inaugurated the first period without a Stadhouder, every province was again enjoined to uphold the exclusive claims of the true, Christian Reformed religion.[68] Despite a readiness to show genuine toleration to non-Calvinists, there was a broad consensus among the political elite of the Republic that Calvinism and Calvinism alone must retain the status of a publicly sanctioned and privileged religion. Even Pieter de la Court, who demanded that all denominations should have the right to exercise their religion freely, supported the maintenance of a dominant, state-supported church in the interest of peace and order. He even agreed that its members alone should have the right to hold a public office.[69]

3.3. The Lack of a non-Christian Component

A third observation casts doubt upon a modern, secular interpretation of our findings. When the adherents of the public church and dissident Christian groups are added together they account for nearly all of Dutch society during the seventeenth century, even though it was possible in theory to live as an atheist or as a non-Christian. The Jews had a special status and were not regarded as true members of Dutch society. Early modern Dutch society was not at all pluralistic in the modern

---

65 See e.g. F. van Vervov, Enige gedenckvverdige geschiedenissen, tot narichtinge der nakomelingen, sommarischer wijze beschreven, ed. Provinciaal Friesch genootschap, Leeuwarden 1842.

66 Enno van Gelder, Vrijheid (note 14), 10. ("De ware Gereformeerde religie is het fondament ende de bant van de eenicheyt der Vereenichde Nederlanden.")

67 Kerkelyk Plakaat Boek (note 20), vol. I, 176. ("De Kercke, soo langh als wy hier leven, naeuwlijcks van de Republijcke gescheyden kann worden.")

68 Bakhuizen van den Brink, Documenta (note 22), 377; cf. also D.J. Roorda, Partij en factie, Groningen 1961, 69s.

69 Hassinger, Motive (note 5), esp. 329; Schilling, Regentenrepublikanismus (note 1).

sense of coexistence of Christians, adherents of other religions, agnostics, and atheists, all of whom enjoy full rights of citizenship. Even Christians who belonged to no church or congregation, whom the Polish philosopher Kolakowski characterized as "Christians without a church" and to whom he rightly ascribed a key role in the history of philosophy,[70] are actually not an indicator of modern pluralism, but rather of the limits of tolerance within Dutch society. This is particularly true of Socinians and Anti-Trinitarians who could not be accepted and integrated into the northern Netherlands, the most "liberal" society of early modern Europe. There as everywhere else in Europe denial of the Holy Trinity, a fundamental dogma of the Christian faith, was considered to be a very dangerous and pernicious form of rebellion against the foundation of society.

3.4. The Absence of a Strong, Bureaucratic, Centralized State

Finally, a fourth factor must be considered: the ideal of a separation of church and state, stemming from the nineteenth century, distorts the actual circumstances of the northern Netherlands because it assumes the existence of a powerful state with strong institutions whose omnipresent power permeates every area of social life. The "State of the Dutch Republic" did not in any way reflect this ideal. It was much more a complex and loose amalgamation of local, regional, and general state magistrates and office holders, whose interests and governing maxims could diverge in many ways. Many phenomena that give the Dutch situation a modern, secular appearance actually resulted from the weakness of the state. This weakness made it impossible either to use the church as a vehicle to pursue state goals or to enforce religious conformity upon the population. The weakness of the state was the best guarantee of a multi-confessional, genuinely tolerant society. The fact that the law requiring that all officials be Calvinists was repeatedly ignored in certain areas and even Catholics served as church wardens, and as such bore responsibility for maintaining the buildings of the parish church now in the hands of the Calvinists, can also be attributed primarily to the decentralized, fragmented nature of state authority. Where one part of the community, or of the elite which determined the

---

70 L. Kolakowski, Chrétiens sans église. La conscience religieuse et le lien confessionnel au 17e siècle, Paris 1969.

choice of church wardens in villages, was secretly Catholic, the appointment of a non-Calvinist member of the community was quite possible and there was little that higher officials could do to hinder it. Since this was a direct consequence of the specific political and constitutional structure of the Republic, it can hardly be considered an appropriate indication of the advance of secularization within the state or progress toward a confessionally neutral state. (222)

After the end of the Middle Ages an expansion and consolidation of the centralized, bureaucratic state took place in most European countries. An essential part of this process was the subjection of the church to the authority of the state and its institutional inclusion, or at least addition, to the state administrative apparatus, which in the long run became an essential prerequisite for the secularization of state and society. In contrast to this, after the struggle for freedom against the early absolutism of the Hapsburg government,[71] the northern Netherlands built upon traditional forms of government that were based upon the principle of regionalism and the constitutional and administrative autonomy of communal and corporate structures. Both the autonomy of the public church, which according to its self-understanding was likewise established by "contracts" between God and man individually and the fellowship of believers corporately,[72] and religious liberty for dissidents were expressions of this state structure in religious life. To understand the religious policies of the northern Netherlands as an expression of the separation of church and state or as advanced secularization in the sense of the nineteenth century is to misunderstand the Dutch situation in a fundamental way.

II. CIVIL MARRIAGE AND CHANGES IN THE RESPONSIBILITIES OF MIDWIVES AS EXAMPLES OF EARLY SECULAR ELEMENTS IN THE REPUBLIC.

I will now turn from our discussion of the place of religion and church within the whole social system to its status within certain sectors of society that were understood by contemporary theorists to be *res mixtae*. The church shared responsi-

---

71 On this interlude see the penetrating study by J.D. Tracy, Holland under Habsburg Rule, 1506-1566, Berkeley 1990.
72 Bohatec, Territorial- und Kollegialsystem (note 19), 48ss.

bility with the secular magistrates for the administration of
these areas and could exercise influence through religious
norms. By the end of the Middle Ages there was a general
trend toward secularization, i.e., the partial or complete abolition of ecclesiastical authority over certain affairs and the
transfer of oversight to burghers or burgher institutions. But
occasionally the opposite happened, as in the case of the introduction of the early modern wedding ceremony, which gave
the church expanded influence in all of Europe except the
Netherlands. Secularization took place primarily in the areas of
poor relief, social welfare, care for the sick, and schools and
education. It need not be expressly stated that this process was
not a phenomenon unique to Dutch history or that it was only
partially a result of the Reformation. Nonetheless the process
of secularization made impressive advances in the Calvinist
Republic whose network of poor houses, orphanages, schools,
and universities was praised so highly by visitors from abroad.
This development was also reflected in the Calvinist/counter-
remonstrant doctrines of ecclesiastical law, to the extent that
(223) these *res mixtae* were considered to be *extrinseca* of the
church and thus were placed under state authority.[73]

At this point some general remarks should be made concerning both marriage, particularly the practice of solemnizing
marriages, and the status of midwives. They will serve to draw
attention to two spheres in which the Republic adopted secular
solutions more radically and much earlier than other European
countries.

*1. Civil Marriage as a Secular Variant of the Early Modern
Wedding Ceremony*

The doctrine of the sacramental character of marriage, which
was generally recognized by the second half of the twelfth
century at the latest, allowed the church to gain increasing
influence over marriage during the course of the Middle Ages,
a state of affairs reflected in its sole jurisdiction over marital
matters. The Council of Trent confirmed the sacramental character of marriage and the exclusive jurisdiction of the church
and thus the legal competence of the church for marital matters
was ensured for generations in Catholic countries during the

---

73 Esp. in the teaching of the theologian Gisbertus Voetius, see ibid., 40.

early modern period.[74] Its position was further strengthened
because it finally received a decisive role in the legal act that
solemnized a marriage, a matter which during the high Middle
Ages had been the responsibility of the extended family.[75] This
development was due to social and political changes, particularly in the decline of the clan structure which in turn raised
doubts about its ability to secure inheritance rights,[76] and in
the rise of the early modern state with its bureaucratic and
administrative interests. Strictly speaking, a church wedding
did not bestow any additional sacral quality upon the union.
Despite this theoretical distinction, however, a far-reaching
transformation accompanied these changes: in Catholic areas
the idea that weddings should occur in a church and that the
church shared responsibility with the state in marital and
family matters spread rapidly.

Luther's removal of marriage from the list of sacraments
created an important spiritual and theological pre-condition
within the Protestant world that would allow for a complete
transfer of all competence for marital law to civil authorities.
At first the consequences of this change were evident only in
the Netherlands, in some North American colonies, and in
Cromwell's England.[77] Other Protestant states adopted the
Catholic practice of wedding ceremonies. Under the banner of
Lutheran orthodoxy especially a thorough-going restitution of
the the marital provisions of canon law took place.[78] As a

---

74 Overviews: E. Friedberg, Das Recht der Eheschließung in seiner geschicht-
lichen Entwicklung, Leipzig 1865, (reprint Aalen 1965); G.E. Howard, A History
of Matrimonial Institutions, Chiefly in England and the United States, 3 vols.,
Chicago/London 1904.

75 Howard, History (note 74), vol. I, 308-320.

76 See e.g. H. Schilling, Bürgerkämpfe in Aachen zu Beginn des 17. Jahrhunderts. Konflikte im Rahmen der alteuropäischen Stadtgesellschaft oder im
Umkreis der frühbürgerlichen Revolution?, in: Zeitschrift für historische Forschung 1 (1974), 175-231, esp. 221s. To prevent chaos in matrimonial matters
and to secure inheritance rights Johann Eberlin von Günzburg suggested that
couples who married without the public ceremony should be drowned. See the
quotation in St.E. Ozment, The Reformation in the Cities, The Appeal of
Protestantism to Sixteenth-Century Germany and Switzerland, New
Haven/London 1975, 100.

77 Howard, History (note 74), 404ss.; Friedberg, Recht (note 74), 478ss.; D.
Schwab, Grundlagen und Gestalt der staatlichen Ehegesetzgebung in der Neuzeit,
Bielefeld 1967.

78 H. Dietrich, Das protestantische Eherecht in Deutschland bis zur Mitte des
17. Jahrhunderts, München 1970; R. Schäfer, Die Geltung des kanonischen
Rechts in der evangelischen Kirche Deutschlands von Luther bis zur Gegenwart.
Ein Beitrag zur Geschichte der Quellen, der Literatur und der Rechtsprechung

Protestant churches also assumed a key role both in administering and in establishing norms for marriage, particularly
through marital courts, either independently from the state or
in cooperation with it.

Developments in the northern Netherlands followed a completely different path. The option of civil marriage was offered
by the provincial estates of Holland at the end of the sixteenth
century and by the Estates General by the middle of the
seventeenth century.[79] In view of the fact that the church wedding ceremony was a relatively recent development during the
sixteenth century it would not be entirely correct to speak of
(225) secularization in this context.[80] Nevertheless at the beginning of the early modern period both Holland and later most of
the other Dutch provinces followed a secular path, or at least
provided a secular alternative to the obviously uneasy question
of formalizing a marriage, in contrast to nearly all other Christian states. They dispensed not only with the church's role of
administrative and bureaucratic oversight, but also with the
compulsory religious and sacral sanction of such a central social
institution as marriage and family. I consider the latter aspect
to be particularly noteworthy for our investigation.

Here we are dealing with a phenomenon that was itself a
consequence of the general characteristics of the state-church
relationship in the Republic. Civil marriage is a corollary,
indeed almost a necessary consequence of freedom of conscience and the toleration of dissident Protestant minorities. In
view of the fact that a large part of the population could only
be moved to solemnize their marriages in the public church by
the threat of serious legal sanction, there was little else that
could be done except to make it possible to solemnize a marriage outside of this church, if society was unwilling to dispense completely with any kind of formalization. However, this
would have been an unacceptable solution for any government

---

des evangelischen Kirchenrechts, in: Zeitschrift der Savigny-Stiftung für
Rechtsgeschichte, Kanonistische Abteilung 5 (1915), 165-413.

79 Matrimonial act of the province of Holland from April 1, 1580, see Kerkelyk
Plakaat Boek (note 20), vol. I, 804-812; matrimonial act of the province of Zee-
land from February 3, 1583, see ibid., 812-817. Basic literature on the problem:
L.J. van Apeldoorn, De historische ontwikkeling van het recht omtrent de huwe-
lijkssluiting in Nederland, in: Lustrumbundel (note 63), 67-182; L. Knappert, De
Gereformeerde Kerk in haren strijd om het wettig huwelijk, in: Nederlands
Archief voor Kerkgeschiedenis, N.S. 2 (1903), 217-275, 359-396.

80 See the edict from October 4, 1540, by Charles V, Kerkelyk Plakaat Boek
(note 20), vol. I, 803s.

during the early modern period. An orderly registration of marriages was indispensable for the mercantile Dutch Republic, above all because of questions of parentage and inheritance. The marriage ruling, passed by the province of Holland on April 1, 1580, mentions these very necessities: it referred to the difficulties and irregularities which had arisen in the recent past because of the war and the lack of a generally recognized authority in marital matters, and emphasized the necessity of an order "with which each can be satisfied in his own heart and mind, and which can make it possible for property and inheritances to be transferred to their rightful owners without complications and legal disputes." Those married couples who in the past had gotten married without observing legal formalities would have the opportunity to legalize their relationship by registering it with the local authorities. The law stipulated that henceforth "either the magistrates or the clergy in each locality" were required to solemnize marriages.[81]

Consequently the early modern Republic had no form of obligatory civil marriage; that was first introduced in 1795 by the Batavian Republic. During the seventeenth and eighteenth centuries there were two possible ways to formalize a legal marriage: civil marriage before representatives of the state or a marriage ceremony performed by a Calvinist minister. This can be regarded as an inconsequential and half-hearted solution, especially since the estates of Holland (226) obviously yielded to pressure from the Calvinists. The ruling was fully consistent, however, with the model of an officially recognized public church with special privileges as discussed in the first part of this essay. It is worth noting that the Calvinists with their claim to the legal validity of a church ceremony fell back to a more restrictive position than their own synodal decision of 1572, in which they had called upon the secular government "to assume all responsibility for marital matters, relieving the church of this obligation."[82] Both civil magistrates and Calvinist ministers had the same legal status to the extent that both had the right to examine qualifications for marriage and to publish banns. In addition, the marital ordinance of Holland

---

81 Ibid., 804.

82 For Art. 3, § 3 of the Synod of Edam from August 8, 1572, see: J. Reitsma and S.D. van Veen (eds.), Acta der provinciale en particuliere Synoden, gehouden in de Noordelijke Nederlanden gedurende de Jaren 1572-1620, 8 vols., Groningen 1892-1899, here vol. 1 (1892), 3.

recognized that marriage belonged within a sacral context by stipulating that government officials should use a religious formula similar to the "formulas that are used in the church" when conducting civil wedding ceremonies.[83]

These concessions to the public church lost much of their significance in practice after civil marriage was introduced. This was certainly the case in Amsterdam. All those who wished to marry in Amsterdam were to appear before the civic *Commissie voor de huwelijkse zaken*, composed of city officials who were empowered to examine the qualifications of each couple. Then their names were written down either in the civil or in the public church marriage register, depending upon whether the marriage was to be solemnized by a civil or church ceremony; both registers were governmental documents. Only after approval was obtained from this city commission could banns be published three times, either in the church by the so-called "announcer" of the Reformed congregation[84] or on market days from the front steps of the city hall, the *Pui*.[85] (227) Afterwards the wedding took place either in the church or in the presence of the *schepenen*. The specifically religious formula provided by the marriage ordinance passed by the provincial estates of Holland was not used for civil marriages.[86] During the seventeenth century there was one civil marriage for every three church marriages; in the eighteenth century it was reduced to a one-to-two ratio.[87]

The traditional church courts lost their importance because of the transfer of marital affairs to the oversight of the secular authorities. But in the context of church discipline the presbyteries and synods of the public church continued to be involved with marital matters. They also discussed the question of degrees of consanguinity, which incidentally were little

83 Kerkelyk Plakaat Boek (note 20), vol. I, 807. ("Ordonnantien die in de Kercken gebruyckt worden.")

84 Evenhuis, Amsterdam (note 16), vol. I, 64.—Recently D. Haks, Huwelijk en gezin in Holland in de 17de en 18de eeuw, Assen 1982, esp. 114ss.; Roodenburg, Censuur (note 16), 90ss.

85 Evenhuis, Amsterdam (note 16).—On the iconographic programme of the rooms in the new Amsterdam town hall set aside for this ceremony see K. Fremantle, The Baroque Town Hall of Amsterdam, Utrecht 1959, 74, 78; on the registers see I.H. van Eeghen, De Doop-, Trouw- en Begraafboeken te Amsterdam, in: Nederlands Archievenblad 52 (1947/48), 123-132.

86 Evenhuis, Amsterdam (note 16), vol. II, 64.

87 S. Hart, Statistische gegevens inzake analfabetisme te Amsterdam, Amstelodamum 55 (1968), 3-6.

changed from those prescribed by canon law. In both cases, however, the final decision was made by civil authorities: the courts and the city magistrates or provincial estates. Disciplinary oversight of marital and sexual matters was common to all confessions in the early modern period.[88] It can be assumed that the division of authority in marital matters between the church and state was the reason that such oversight appeared only in a weakened form in the Netherlands and that it was more liberal than in other states.[89] In any case it is obvious that official investigations of an inquisitorial character, intended to reveal whether the first child of a couple who had been married for several years had been conceived before or after the church wedding ceremony, were unknown in the Republic. Such investigations were known to have occurred in other places, even in Protestant countries where church courts continued to function as marriage courts with a mixed judiciary of representatives from both church and state. Nevertheless, adultery remained a criminal offense in the Netherlands as well. If no complaint was filed by the injured party, however, the claim was often settled out of court by paying compensation. The amount of the payment was settled by the judges and the guilty parties.[90]

The changes in Dutch marital law described above might seem to be rather insignificant and of little importance for the character of society as a whole. Jurists usually stress the continuity of marital law in the Netherlands from canon law to the new republican law, which they regard as "Reformed marital law" despite the desacralization of marriage itself.[91] Historians, however, must insist that (228) the possibility of civil marriage, which the Calvinists also allowed for their own parishioners, and the abolition of clerical jurisdiction over marriages, which encompassed all members of the national populace, could not

---

88 A similar problem is discussed in W. Reinhard, Gegenreformation als Modernisierung? Prolegomena zu einer Theorie des konfessionellen Zeitalters, in: Archiv für Reformationsgeschichte 68 (1977), 226-252.

89 On the astonishingly small amount of sexual and matrimonial discipline see H. Schilling, Reformierte Kirchenzucht als Sozialdisziplinierung? (Emden, Groningen, Leiden), in: W. Ehbrecht and H. Schilling (eds.), Niederlande und Nordwestdeutschland, Köln/Wien 1983, 261-327, especially the graphs on p. 300 and 304, and text on 316ss. Recently Roodenburg, Censuur (note 84), 230ss.

90 See the mandate of the Estates of Holland from December 11, 1677, Kerkelyk Plakaat Boek (note 20), vol. I, 867s.

91 Apeldoorn, Ontwikkeling (note 79).

fail to have an impact upon the collective attitude toward marriage and the spheres of life associated with it. The desacralization of marriage, which had in theory accompanied the Reformation, was able to penetrate the consciousness of society much more easily in the Netherlands than in other Protestant areas, where marriages had to be solemnized in the church, although in theory marriage had lost its sacramental character. A detailed study of marriage in the Republic would in any case be necessary in order to draw these distinctions more clearly and to formulate detailed conclusions concerning the Dutch advances in this area. Such an investigation should devote particular attention to the institution of marriage within the different confessions and the question of which social strata limited themselves to civil marriage.[92] However, it should be noted that Protestant dissenters had an additional church ceremony and so were free to participate in the sacral act voluntarily; Catholics too had secret church weddings.[93]

2. Relieving Midwives of Ecclesiastical and Religious Duties

Our second example of an early secular structure within an important social subsystem might seem rather far-fetched at first glance. Midwives and their professional responsibilities are significant for our study not so much because of the institutional and legal changes that affected their work, but rather because these structural adjustments might reflect changes in Dutch society's attitude toward the process of birth and finally toward life itself. The regulation of obstetrics, particularly the level of professionalization demanded of the midwives, could be an important indicator of the level of rationalization and differentiation present in society. Both prenatal and postnatal care of mother and child were almost exclusively in the hands of midwives during the early modern period. The aid of physicians became generally accepted only after a number of tenaciously held prejudices were overcome, including some that were based upon religious and magical beliefs.[94] It might then

92 Meanwhile Haks, Huwelijk (note 84), has done substantial work on this field, though he scarcely discussed the questions raised above.

93 Knappert, kerk (note 79), 362.

94 J. Donnison, Midwives and Medical Men. A History of Inter-Professional Rivalries and Women's Rights, London 1977; W. Gubalke, Die Hebamme im Wandel der Zeiten. Ein Beitrag zur Geschichte des Hebammenwesens, Hannover 1964; E. Haberling, Beiträge zur Geschichte des Hebammenstandes, vol. I: Der Hebammenstand in Deutschland von den Anfängen bis zum 30jährigen Krieg,

be a matter of importance both for the actual reproductive possibilities (229) of a pre-modern society[95] and for the opportunities to improve medical care whether the professional activities of midwives were unambiguously linked to the church and to the sacral sphere, partially connected with it, or had no ties to it at all. The activities of midwives are also important to the extent that they touched upon the nature and extent of social oversight of sexual behavior. However, before discussing obstetrical practices in the early modern Netherlands I think that an overview of the situation throughout Europe during the late Middle Ages and early modern period would be appropriate.

The supervision of obstetrics and midwives was among those social matters over which the medieval church had assumed responsibility and for which ecclesiastical regulatory activity provided an important developmental impulse. It is not our task here to trace the consequences that resulted from ecclesiastical oversight and the related effects that Christian ethics and anthropology had upon the midwife profession.[96] The fundamental attitude behind such supervision, however, is important: the principal motive of all ecclesiastical regulation of midwives was the concern to preserve human life from eternal damnation.[97] To this end it was necessary to struggle against life-threatening conditions before or during birth or—if that proved impossible given the limited medical means of that period—to baptize the child promptly. The church had to ensure that the midwives knew the baptismal formula and that they led moral lives which guaranteed their conscientious use of the sacrament. As a second task, the church assigned midwives the responsibility of overseeing compliance with Christian marital and sexual norms, to the extent that breaking them led to pregnancy. In medieval Germany midwives were highly regarded but feared witnesses in the episcopal court. These courts were also an important means of institutional oversight

---

Berlin 1940.—G. Burckhard, Die deutschen Hebammenordnungen von ihren ersten Anfängen bis auf die Neuzeit, Leipzig 1912 is a important sources.

95 According to the calculation of an English midwife approximately 6,000 mothers and 18,000 children died within 20 years, two thirds of them because the midwife lacked ability or care. (Petition of Elisabeth Cellier from 1687 quoted by Th.R. Forbes, The Regulation of English Midwives in the 16th and 17th Centuries, in: Medical History 8 (1964), 235-244, here 235s.)

96 Haberling, Beiträge (note 94), 16.

97 Donnison, Midwives (note 94), 3ss.

for the church, both for selecting midwives according to the
criteria mentioned above, and for supervising them in the performance of their medical and religious duties.[98]

Corresponding to the general trend of the late Middle Ages,
particularly in the cities, the ecclesiastical oversight of midwives was supplemented by a secular form of oversight,[99] and
state and civic institutions took their responsibility (230) for
overseeing them more seriously. Civil regulations emphasized
the professional qualifications that a midwife should possess.
The removal of midwives from the circle of ecclesiastical and
religious responsibility and the related professionalization of
the occupation was hindered in many places by a policy of
confessionalization, which was pursued by state and society
during the sixteenth and early seventeenth centuries. In those
regions where Catholicism could be maintained only by a
supreme effort, the midwives were given additional, more precise religious responsibilities in the wake of Catholic confessionalization. Strictly speaking they only then became, for the
first time, a means of religious oversight and social discipline.
In contrast to the Middle Ages, ecclesiastical and state institutions usually worked together closely. The imperial city of
Aachen can serve as an example of the situation of midwives
in *Germany*.[100] The obligations of midwives to the episcopal
court were renewed there during the middle of the sixteenth
century in connection with the defensive struggle against a
powerful and growing Protestant movement. Before midwives
were granted permission to practice their profession, a process
in which civic magistrates probably also played a role, they
were required to swear before the archpriest (the highest clerical authority within the city) and the members of the church
court that they would report the birth of all illegitimate children or those born to "heretical" parents, that they would take
the children exclusively to the central baptismal chapel of
Aachen, St. Johannis vor dem Münster, and if necessary perform an emergency baptism using the proper Catholic formula.
With respect to their professional performance midwives were

---

98 Haberling, Beiträge (note 94), 19-22.

99 See the chapter: "Die Städte und der Hebammenstand", in: ibid., 27-66.

100 L. Frohn, Das Sendgericht zu Aachen bis zur Mitte des 17. Jahrhunderts,
Aachen 1913, 34-37, 121; A. Brecher, Die kirchliche Reform in Stadt und Reich
Aachen von der Mitte des 16. bis zum Anfang des 18. Jahrhunderts, Münster
1957, 56, 59ss., 65s., 219, 415.

under oversight of the episcopal court, which annually checked their knowledge of the baptismal formula, and also of the papal nuncio in Cologne.

A similar development occurred in *England* during the time of the Catholic Queen Mary: the bishops sought the aid of midwives in their struggle against heretics.[101] (231) They made use of a statute passed in 1512 that transferred the responsibility for examining members of the medical profession and providing them with licenses to ecclesiastical authorities—i.e., the Bishop of London and the Dean of Saint Paul's cathedral.[102]

This statute—which was also almost certainly applied to midwives—remained in force after the triumph of the Reformation. Apart from the years 1642-1660 when a college of physicians took over, the Anglican church bore almost exclusive responsibility for supervising midwives. After discussing the prospective candidates with the church warden and the leading women of his church congregation, the parish minister submitted the name of a woman to the church hierarchy who was, in his opinion, suitable to serve as a midwife. Professional supervision lay in the hands of the ecclesiastical court of the diocese, which could excommunicate any midwife in case of irregularities.[103] In contrast to Catholic areas, the church hierarchy was not primarily interested in ensuring that emergency baptism was available to all infants.[104] The Anglican church was primarily concerned with (232) suppressing Catholic dissent and also with stamping out magical practices which were still widely accepted.[105] As religious and political

---

101 See Forbes, Regulation 16th/17th Centuries (note 95), 238s.; idem, The Midwife and the Witch, New Haven 1966, esp. chapter 10, 139ss.; idem, The Regulation of English Midwives in the 18th and 19th Centuries, in: Medical History 15 (1971), 352-362.

102 Forbes, Regulation 16th/17th Centuries (note 95), 237; idem, Midwife (note 101), 148; Donnison, Midwives (note 97), 12.

103 Forbes, Regulation 16th/17th Centuries (note 95), 236.

104 On the Anglican opinion concerning emergency baptism see the chapter "The Ministration of Private Baptism of Children in Houses", in: Book of Common Prayer, 1662. See also Forbes, Regulation 16th/17th Centuries (note 95), 236; P.E More and F.L. Cross (eds.), Anglicanism. The Thought and Practice of the Church of England, Illustrated from the Religious Literature of the Seventeenth Century, London 1962, 438ss.; Book of Oaths, 1648, quoted by Forbes, Regulation 16th/17th Centuries (note 95), 238.

105 Forbes, Regulation 16th/17th Centuries (note 95), 238; idem, Midwifery and Witchcraft, in: Journal of the History of Medicine and Allied Sciences 17 (1962), 264-283.

structures became more secure on the island, the confessional motive for ecclesiastical supervision became less important. The church continued to oversee midwives in more or less the same way that state authorities would. Nevertheless, religious orthodoxy and a pious manner of life remained central qualifications for midwives.[106] Every attempt made during the seventeenth century to abolish the system of episcopal oversight in favor of secular institutions such as a guild of physicians or a specially incorporated guild of midwives failed, although ecclesiastical supervision was repeatedly attacked and its professional and practical utility as a means of recruiting midwives disputed. Even when the system had practically broken down on account of the increasing secularization of English society—in the area of London, for example, hardly any midwives sought an episcopal license during the 1720's—the ordinance officially remained in force. Civil regulation of midwives was instituted for the first time in England during the early twentieth century.[107]

The history of obstetrics in *Catholic France* is to some degree difficult to compare with the previous examples. By the sixteenth century a scientific practice of gynecology had emerged there and served as a model for other European countries. In France doctors had assumed a leading role at the bedside instead of midwives.[108] In addition secular efforts for improving the professional standards of midwifery resulted in important successes, especially in Paris, despite the interests of the Catholic state church whose confessional conflict with the Huguenots had already reached its climax.[109] Nevertheless (233) post-Tridentine Catholicism continued to have influence over midwives and ensured that baptism remained a central concern,

---

106 Forbes, Regulation 18th/19th Centuries (note 101), 241s.

107 See Donnison, Midwives (note 97), 13-15, 19s., 20s.; Forbes, Regulation 18th/19th Centuries (note 101).

108 Donnison, Midwives (note 97), 16, 22. On the influence of the French system on other European countries see: A.J. van Reeuwijk, Vroedkunde en vroedvrouwen in de Nederlanden in de 17e en 18e eeuw, Amsterdam 1941.

109 J. Gelis, La formation des accoucheurs et des sages-femmes aux 17e et 18e siècles, Evolution d'un matériel et d'une pédagogie, in: Annales de démographie historique 1977, 153-180; idem, Sages-femmes et accoucheurs: L'obstétrique populaire aux 17e et 18e siècles, in: Annales E.S.C. 32 (1977), 927-957; R.L. Petrelli, The Regulation of French Midwifery during the Ancien-Régime, in: Journal of the History of Medicine and Allied Sciences 26 (1971), 276-292; J.-P. Goubert, Malades et médecins en Bretagne 1770-1790, Paris 1974, 161-172.

which was both recognized and encouraged by the state.[110]
This was important as the birth of a child with a physician in
attendance was a process that affected only certain groups
within French society; the broader social strata in both the
cities and the villages continued to depend almost entirely upon
the services of midwives. In the larger cities midwives were
under the oversight of state and city officials and the church's
regulatory role was very limited. The situation was quite different in smaller provincial towns and especially in the villages.
The influence of ministers and bishops was dominant there
until the end of the *ancien régime*, and the decisive criteria for
a good midwife were not her medical knowledge and practical
experience but her exemplary religious and moral character and
her reliability with respect to the sacrament.[111]

In *Lutheran regions* the distinction between secular and
ecclesiastical oversight of midwives was more clearly preserved
than in Anglican or Catholic states. This is true at any rate for
the Lutheran cities and territories of the *German Empire*.
Secular authorities were responsible both for the selection and
appointment of midwives.[112] Theologians were only involved to
the extent that it was their duty to exhort the Christian
government to do its duty by providing the best possible organization for the Christian commonwealth, especially care for
the poor and sick.[113] (234) Bugenhagen mentioned midwives in
the church ordinances that he wrote for Brunswick and Hamburg because their profession, even more clearly than other
Christian occupations, involved work that pleased God, and the
midwives together with the women bearing children encountered God's "incomprehensible glory."[114] His high esteem for
the profession of midwives as a "calling" (*Beruf*) also served as
a model for a number of other church ordinances.[115] Bugenha-

110 Goubert, Malades (note 109), 284, 292.

111 See Petrelli, Regulation (note 109), 290, quotation from D.A. Leblanc (ed.),
Le rituel Romain pour l'usage du diocèse du Sarlat, Sarlat 1729; L.A. de
Grimaldi, Rituel de diocèse du Mans, Paris 1774, 63s., quoted by Petrelli,
Regulation (note 109), 291.

112 See the chapter "Van den heveammen" in Bugenhagen's church ordinance
for Brunswick, in: E. Sehling, Die evangelischen Kirchenordnungen des 16. Jahrhunderts, vol. VI, part I, fasc. I, Tübingen 1955, 359. G. Burckhard provides a
collection of ordinances on midwives in his Studien zur Geschichte des Hebammenwesens, vol. I, 1: Die deutschen Hebammenordnungen, Leipzig 1912.

113 Bugenhagen (note 112), 359.

114 Ibid.. ("Unbegripliken hehrlichkeit")

115 See the chapters and paragraphs on midwives in the church ordinances of

gen pointed out that these lay women were "servants of the church" who served not only the secular commonwealth but also the church in the performance of their office. In order to be properly equipped for their profession they were to be licensed by the secular authorities and then to receive instruction from the church superintendent or another pastor, "so that they might learn what God's word teaches about their calling."[116]

There were essentially two sets of duties for which pastoral instruction was necessary: *first*, pastoral care for the mother, in order to make clear to her the working of God's grace both in pregnancy and birth and also the compassion of God when the life of mother or child was in danger. *Second*, the proper administration of emergency baptism to a dying child according to Lutheran norms. In this context it is important to note that Lutheran emergency baptism had a distinctly different emphasis from that present in the medieval or Catholic understanding. This is especially apparent in that it applied exclusively to babies after, not during delivery, and that even babies who (235) had died before baptism could in principle be buried in the churchyard, that is, alongside of baptized Christians, and thus could hope for eternal salvation. A reevaluation of the most urgent tasks of midwives accompanied these changes. Medical "assistance to preserve physical life" for mother and child could now be clearly separated from the "assistance for salvation," which chronologically came after the former.

By giving the magistrates exclusive responsibility for appointing and supervising midwives and by removing the process of birth from religious considerations in a narrow sense, Lutheran areas established important precedents, despite

---

Brunswick in Sehling, Kirchenordnungen (note 112), 348ss., 359-362; church ordinance of Hamburg: E. Sehling, Evangelische Kirchenordnungen, vol. V, Leipzig 1913, 488ss., 513; church ordinances of Soest, Bremen, Schleswig-Holstein, Land Hadeln, Hildesheim, Lüneburg: A.L. Richter, Die evangelischen Kirchenordnungen des 16. Jahrhunderts, Urkunden und Regesten, Weimar 1846, vol. I, 166, 244, 357; vol. II, 74, 81, 286; of Brandenburg-Nürnberg (1533): Richter, o.c., vol. I, 199. It is characteristic that the Calvinist church ordinance of Emden in East Friesland does not give any regulation on midwives: Sehling, Evangelische Kirchenordnungen, vol. VII, 1, Tübingen 1963, 480ss. In Emden only the civic magistrates oversaw the work of midwives (City Archives, Emden, 1st Registratur, No. 776).

116 Sehling, Kirchenordnungen (note 112), 359. ("Dat se leren, wat Gades wort bedrept in orer sake.")

their formal maintenance of emergency baptism and the strengthened pastoral role of midwives. This had enduring consequences not only because it allowed for a potential improvement of the professional performance of midwives but also because it influenced their position in society and the collective attitude toward birth and life. While in Germany this was a long-term process which could only make substantial progress with the advance of secularization throughout society as a whole, the situation was different in the northern Netherlands.[117] There the effects of such changes began to be felt even by the end of the sixteenth century because of the more radical break the Dutch had made with medieval tradition.

The reordering of the activities of midwives that took place in the *Dutch Republic* stood in stark contrast to the previous examples. This is the more noteworthy because only a generation earlier, by the mid-sixteenth century midwives in the Netherlands were obliged to perform duties similar to those required in Catholic and Anglican areas, particularly when the government of the Duke of Alba had enlisted them in the service of the Counter Reformation.[118] Consequently the Spanish southern provinces maintained a system of oversight and licensing for midwives by ecclesiastical authorities in the sense described above, even during the seventeenth century.[119] (236)

By contrast, in the northern provinces a decisive change took place after their separation from Spain and the introduction of the Reformation. This change, indeed, went much further than the Lutheran policy in German cities and territories. In the Republic the oversight of midwives lay exclusively within the jurisdiction of state institutions and midwives were no longer expected to fulfill religious or ecclesiastical duties.[120] This

---

117 It is of special interest in the present context, that the Dutch system of midwifery served as an exemple for German territories. See e.g. E. Dietrich, Das Hebammenwesen in Preußen, Merseburg 1896; O. Walter, Das Hebammenwesen im Großherzogtum Mecklenburg-Schwerin, Güstrow 1883.

118 A. Hallema, Vroedvrouwen in stad en dorp in het westen van Noord-Brabant, in: Bijdragen tot de Geschiedenis der geneeskunde 35 (1955), 85-92, here 88s.; J.G.W.F. Bik, Vijf eeuwen medisch leven in een Hollandse stad (Gouda), Assen 1955; J. Ter Gouw, Geschiedenis van Amsterdam, part IV, Amsterdam 1884, 391s.

119 M. Cloet, Het Kerkelijk Leven in een landelijke dekenij van Vlaanderen tijdens de 17e eeuw, Tielt van 1609 tot 1700, Leuven 1968, 294ss.; Th.B.W. Kok, Dekenaat in de steigers, Kerkelijk Opbouwerk in het Gentse Dekenaat Hulst, 1596-1648, Tilburg 1971, 360-367.

120 See van Deursen, Bavianen (note 17), 138; A.C. Drogendijk, De verloskun-

situation was doubtless a consequence of the legal status of the
public church discussed earlier, which gave to individuals, i.e.,
in the seventeenth century to the individual family, a measure
of freedom to make their own decisions of conscience and to
provide for the religious education of children. In addition, the
fact that the removal of midwives from the ecclesiastical sphere
of authority occurred with the consent of the public church
and happened so quickly was due to the Calvinist understanding of baptism. In contrast to Anglicanism and Lutheranism, Calvinists not only rejected the necessity of emergency
baptism for salvation; they completely repudiated the practice
of emergency baptism. Only after much discussion did the
synod of exile churches held in Wesel allow for the possibility
of baptism in private homes, a provision which for security
reasons could not entirely be avoided among the "churches
under the cross."[121] In 1574, the first provincial synod of Holland and Zeeland on Dutch soil ruled succinctly, referring to
Calvin's teaching,[122] that "baptism performed by women is no
baptism at all."[123] (237) Finally the national Synod of Dordrecht in 1618 issued a prohibition against any baptism "outside
of the congregational assembly," which from a Reformed perspective was the only appropriate setting for baptism.[124] In
contrast to Catholicism and Lutheranism the Reformed Dutch
public church did not identify its members by baptism but by
participation in the Eucharist[125] and the consequent acceptance
of church discipline. Dutch Calvinists did not depend upon the
help of the midwives to provide pastoral care for mothers
giving birth and for their children because they had established
a special office of *Ziekentroosters* (visitors of the sick) to care
for the sick.

Since the public church was willing to dispense with the
religious responsibilities of midwives, a rapid professionaliza-

---

dige voorziening in Dordrecht, Amsterdam 1935, 49; A.J. van Reeuwijk, Vroedkunde en vroedvrouwen in de Nederlanden in de 17e en 18e eeuw, Amsterdam
1941, 67.

121 Kerkelyk Plakaat Boek (note 20), vol. III, 397.

122 Institutio IV, 15, 20-22.

123 Kerkelyk Plakaat Boek (note 20), vol. III, 443. ("Vrouwen doopen geen
Doopen is") See also vol. I, 703.

124 Ibid., vol. III, 126. ("buyten de Vergaderingh"). See van Deursen, Bavianen (note 17), 135-144.

125 Van Deursen, Bavianen (note 17), 135, 200; Duke, Reformation (note 2),
291.

tion of midwifery could occur fairly easily. The appointment
and oversight of Dutch *vroedvrouwen* (midwives) lay entirely in
the hands of secular authorities, specifically local magistrates in
the cities and villages, a state of affairs corresponding to the
political structure of the Republic.[126] According to the doctrine
of Calvinist theologians, these magistrates were responsible
exclusively for temporal affairs, to promote happiness on earth.
Accordingly, providing the civic commune with the best possible midwives was a purely temporal duty, performed exclusively with reference to medical and hygienic concerns. Direct
reference to the works of God and the assignment of a particular ecclesiastical dignity to midwives, or to the corresponding
regulatory activity of the magistrates as in Lutheran regions,
was lacking in the Netherlands. (238)

It was possible to build an exemplary form of birth help
upon this foundation in the Netherlands during the seventeenth
century.[127] The only criteria considered when appointing a
midwife were her knowledge of anatomy, her psychological
and physical abilities,[128] and her practical experience at childbirth which had to be acquired during an apprenticeship to a
fully qualified midwife. In addition candidates in the cities,
and later in the villages as well, had to pass an examination
administered by a council of physicians.[129] The procedures
used and decisions made during the process of birth were
solely concerned with the physical well-being of the mother

---

126 Apart from the literature given in notes 118 and 120 I consulted the following writings of historians of medicine: C.R. Post, De Amsterdamse vroedvrouw
uit de 18e eeuw, in: Bijdragen tot de geschiedenis der geneeskunde 36 (1956), 1-8;
J.J. Haver Droeze, Het Collegium Medicum Amstelaedamense 1637-1789, Haarlem 1921.—On the situation in the countryside see: L. van Hommerich, Een
geschiedkundige bijdrage over de pharmaceutisch-medische verzorging in het
Land van Herle, in: Het Land van Herle 21 (1971), 33-36, 106-111, 152-173; M.J.
Elzinga, Catharina Geertruid Schrader 1655-1745, in: It Beaken, Tijdschrift fan
de fryske Akademy 16 (1954), 192-196; B.W.Th. Nuyens, Het dagboek van vrouw
Schraders, in: Bijdragen tot de geschiedenis der geneeskunde 6 (1926), 93-104;
E.D. Baumann, Uit drie eeuwen nederlandse Geneeskunde, Amsterdam n.d.; G.A.
Lindeboom, Geschiedenis van de medische Wetenschap in Nederland, Bussum
1972.

127 On the "apprenticeship" of midwives see H. Noordkerk (ed.), Handvesten;
ofte Privilegien ende Octroyen ... der stad Amstelredam, vol. II, Amsterdam 1748,
967-970; earlier sources are given by J.G. van Dillen, Bronnen tot de geschiedenis
van het bedrijfsleven en het gildewezen van Amsterdam, vol. I, Den Haag 1929,
25; vol. II, Den Haag 1933, 424.

128 The candidates had to be able to read and write and their hands had to
have the "right" anatomical shape. See Noordkerk, Handvesten (note 127), 969s.

129 Haver Droeze, Collegium (note 126).

and child, and the midwife's chief concern for the newly born child was not the salvation of its soul but that it receive appropriate medical care.[130]

Within the public church moral discipline was the responsibility of the presbyters, who were usually responsible for individual streets or quarters. Thus the Calvinists were able to dispense with the help of midwives in this area as well. This did not mean, however, that the Dutch *vroedvrouwen* were released from all responsibility for moral supervision. Apart from submitting weekly lists of newborns, in which they had to record all familial relationships, they were obligated by city and state regulations to administer the so-called "paternity oath" to single mothers, which was the normal practice for such cases already in the Middle Ages. Should a single mother refuse to name the father, then the midwife was not allowed to give any kind of help under threat of punishment.[131] Clearly the procedure of the "paternity oath" was a result of Christian teaching on marriage and sexuality.[132] But the reason for its enforcement was less the wish to punish "sinners" than to clarify obligations for child support and to reduce the size of the city's budget allotment for orphans.[133] (239)

As with civil marriage it is not easy to assess the practical consequences of these new policies. Did the changes that were adopted in the northern Netherlands only amount to the replacement of ecclesiastical oversight with supervision by the secular magistrate without any perceptible social consequences? A separate study would be necessary to answer this question, especially regarding changes in mentality. Above all, it would be necessary to look for sequential sources over a long period of time that would indicate possible long-term changes which could be quantitatively analyzed.[134] Such a study should also take into account the fact that social reality did not correspond

---

130 Noordkerk, Handvesten (note 127), 969, § VIII.

131 Ibid., §§ XII, XIII, 969; J.G. van Dillen (ed.), Bronnen tot de geschiedenis van het bedrijfsleven en het gildewezen van Amsterdam, vol. II, = RGP, No. 78, Den Haag 1933, 81.

132 Kerkelyk Plakaat Boek (note 20), vol. I, 817-842.

133 See e.g. Bik, eeuwen (note 118), 350.

134 An interesting study of this type is: P. den Boer, Naar een geschiedenis van de dood, Mogelijkheden tot onderzoek naar de houding ten opzichte van de dode en de dood ten tijde van de Republiek, in: Tijdschrift voor Geschiedenis 88 (1976), 161-201.

with the official regulations at every point.[135] However, it is
possible to offer several preliminary observations and hypotheses concerning the activities of midwives. When considering the
effects these changes had upon the professionalization of midwives we must recognize that the remaining religious obligations of midwives in Catholic, Lutheran, and Anglican areas,
within the German Empire, in France, and in England, did not
in any way preclude the possibility of a theoretical or practical
improvement of their profession.[136] And on the other hand the
new theoretical understanding of midwifery did not inevitably
result in a substantial improvement of the practice. Indeed,
there were constant complaints especially from physicians about
the low educational level of the midwives during the seventeenth century in the Netherlands as well.[137] Nevertheless there
is no doubt that the level of midwife care for the broader
strata of the urban population, and especially in rural areas,
was relatively higher in the Republic than it was in other
European states. In part this can surely be attributed to the
higher degree of urbanization and the generally high standard
of civilization present in the northern Netherlands. However,
releasing the midwives from ecclesiastical responsibilities might
not have been entirely without importance either. It is at least
reasonable to assume that in the villages religious or moral
considerations were more important when the pastor played a
crucial role in selecting a midwife, but medical considerations
were paramount when secular magistrates chose a midwife. The
quality of Dutch midwives living in rural areas was dependent
upon how distant these areas were from the nearest city, since
most physicians still lived in urban areas; those in England and
France were dependent upon the educational level of the clergy
making the selection. In the Republic it was rather unlikely
even during the seventeenth century (240) that a matron would
be selected as a midwife who had never been present at the
birth of a child and whose only qualification consisted of her

---

135 Forbes, Regulation 18th/19th Centuries (note 106); Cloet, Leven (note
119), 287; Kok, Dekenaat (note 119), 362ss.

136 Gubalke, Hebamme (note 94), 80; Forbes, Regulation 18th/19th Century
(note 106); Petrelli, Regulation (note 109). On the medical training of midwives
in the German imperial city of Aachen see Brecher, Reform (note 100), 65.

137 Bik, eeuwen (note 118), 353; Drogendijk, voorziening (note 120), 24; Hallema, Vroedvrouwen (note 118), 90.

piety, as was still possible in France at the end of the eighteenth century.[138]

I consider the relationship between changes in the activities of midwives and changes in mentality, that is possible shifts in collective attitudes and the changes in social behavior resulting from them, to be almost as important as the effect of medical care upon the population. It is indeed the crucial difference between the married women of a village choosing a midwife together with the pastor as occurred in France, or the *schout* (local sheriff) and the *schepenen* (judges) making the selection as in the Netherlands.[139] The two processes also differed in that the former followed an ecclesiastical ritual, in which the assembly declared that the candidate was "free of all suspicion of heresy, evil magic, superstition, and every other sort of crime, and exhibits a pious and moral life." The midwife then swore an oath to the priest, whose central point concerned the administration of the sacrament of baptism.[140] In the Netherlands, by contrast, the appointment process took place in the business-like atmosphere of a meeting of *schepenen* and was only one point of business on the agenda. Letters of application, examinations of medical competency, and recommendations were checked and the annual salary was determined. At the end the midwives swore an oath to the community, represented by the *schout*, to assist each woman to the best of her ability and to provide her with medical care.[141] The two conceptions of midwifery differ above all in their response to life and death crises, one considering the eternal salvation of the child to be of paramount importance while the other concentrated on the physical well-being of mother and child. Not only did the degree of discretion that midwives had to exercise their professional judgement differ,[142] but there was also a sharp contrast in the collective attitude toward birth and life that they represented: in one case magical and sacral conceptions were encouraged and reinforced, in the other—the Netherlands—secular and rational ones. (241) It must also be

---

138 G.J. Witkowski, Histoire des accouchements chez les peuples, Paris 1887, 663.

139 Petrelli, Regulation (note 109); Hallema, Vroedvrouwen (note 118), 90.

140 Petrelli, Regulation (note 109), 129, based on Catholic ritual manuals of the 18th century.

141 Hallema, Vroedvrouwen (note 118), 90ss.

142 In cases of emergency the Dutch midwives were allowed to take care of the mother's life first. See Elzinga, Schrader (note 126), 195s.

remembered that during early modern times complications frequently arose during childbirth and that these were more or
less directly experienced by the family since the birth of
children took place at home. That this new attitude toward
birth was in fact a change that required a major shift in mentality, is made evident by the fact that the Calvinists were able
to enforce their prohibition on emergency baptism only with
great difficulty, meeting stiff resistance from their own
parishioners even in the Netherlands.[143]

Removing midwives from ecclesiastical supervision of
Christian sexual norms had a similar effect. The practice of
midwives reporting the names of illegitimate children was no
longer maintained for the benefit of ecclesiastical courts. The
reporting procedure was maintained for the benefit of secular
courts and was used only when the injured party was not
prepared to withdraw charges. This, however, occurred only
when child support was guaranteed without the threat of liti-
gation. The activities of secular institutions, i.e., midwives and
the courts, were directed solely toward providing for "human"
needs. They sought to care for the newborn child and to provide for its integration into society, not to perfect the "ethical
nature" of the citizenry.[144] Congregational disciplinary authorities within the public church and in other religious groups[145]
were responsible for fulfilling this role; their activities were
restricted, however, to their own parishioners. Those who were
unwilling to recognize the ethical norms of the public church
could evade the jurisdiction of ecclesiastical boards and were
not forced to demonstrate repentance in public, wearing a
white robe, holding a burning candle and condemning their
past deeds, as occurred in German territories, particularly in
Calvinist ones.

III. PRESBYTERIAN AND SYNODAL CHURCH GOVERNMENT AND SOCIO-POLITICAL PARTICIPATION.

In the third and final part I will discuss the political and social
implications of the presbyterian and synodal order of the Dutch

---

143 The Calvinist public church was often forced to make concessions, see e.g.
van Deursen, Bavianen (note 17), 140.

144 Böckenförde, Verhältnis (note 7), 2.

145 In the Netherlands Lutheran congregations too were normally supervised
by presbyteries.

public church. In comparison with the two preceding sections, the third deals with very concrete social facts. When considering (242) the problem of religion and society in the Dutch Republic, however, they are of fundamental importance. The Reformed presbyter embodied the intersection between the ecclesiastical and secular spheres in a way that ensures a significant place for him and his social circle in the early modern history of religion and society. This reality has not received adequate recognition either among Dutch historians or those from other Reformed countries. As a result I will again have to be satisfied with a preliminary analysis that raises questions and problems without being able to provide definitive answers for them at every point. Detailed answers can only be obtained with the help of prosopographical methods, by attempting to correlate the personal and institutional networks of individual presbyteries with other social groups and political corporations.[146]

This particular question has a long tradition of scholarship, since the connection between Calvinism and democratic development has been discussed repeatedly since Georg Jellinek raised the issue for the first time. In the wake of Max Weber's sociological studies of religion the debate has focused increasingly upon "ideal factors," i.e., the influence that particular elements of Calvinist theology and ethics had upon the development of democratic political theory and the emergence of democratic behavior and structures.[147] By contrast I intend to concentrate primarily upon the political and societal conse-

146 Schilling, Presbyterien (note 1); H. Schilling, Calvinism and Urban Elites (Groningen), in: idem, Civic Calvinism, Kirksville 1991.

147 G. Jellinek, Die Erklärung der Menschen- und Bürgerrechte, 1st ed., Heidelberg 1895; C.B Hundeshagen, Calvinismus und staatsbürgerliche Freiheit ed. A. Frey, Zürich 1946; J. Staedtke, Calvins Genf und die Entstehung politischer Freiheit, in: W.B. Fuchs (ed.), Staat und Kirche im Wandel der Jahrhunderte, Stuttgart 1966, 100-114; H. Vahle, Calvinismus und Demokratie im Spiegel der Forschung, in: Archiv für Reformationsgeschichte 66 (1975), 182-212; J.M. Lochman and J. Moltmann, Gottesrecht und Menschenrecht, Studien und Empfehlungen des reformierten Weltbundes, Neukirchen 1977.—On the Netherlands see: J.C. Baak, Het Calvinisme oorsprong en waarborg onzer constitutioneele vrijheden? Bijdrage tot het vraagstuk van de verhouding van de Christelijke vrijheid tot de politieke vrijheden, Amsterdam 1945; for the opposite opinion see: M. Walzer, Puritanism as a Revolutionary Ideology, in: History and Theory 3 (1964), 59-90; idem, The Revolution of the Saints, A Study in the Origins of Radical Politics, London 1966.

quences of the Calvinist form of church organization, that is to examine its institutional and social context.[148]

I think that modernization theory, which I discussed at the outset, provides a sensible theoretical framework for discussing this topic as well, because it is ideal for analyzing central structures and developments in history and because it enables us in the present context to pose central questions regarding the relationship (243) between religious and political change. However, by analyzing the impact of presbyterian synods we are addressing a different level of theoretical analysis than the interpretation of changes in the relationship of the ecclesiastical and secular systems in general, which was the focus of both previous sections. This section concerns political modernization as a part of the overarching process of societal modernization. Modernization theorists consider political modernization to include among other things, an increase in participation, i.e., involving broader segments of the population in political decision-making, or more generally and more importantly for our purposes, greater popular involvement in "societal activities."[149] This process was in general linked to the process of economic growth.[150] These elements will not be considered in the following discussion. We will focus on the connection between particular changes in the structure of the church, specifically the introduction of the presbyterian and synodal model of church governance and administration, and an increase in societal participation, and also the consequences of these changes for the social and political life of the Republic, which contrasted so sharply with absolutistic states.

The decisive characteristics of the presbyterian and synodal model are its markedly anti-hierarchical structure for protecting church unity above the level of individual congregations

---

148 This problem is briefly touched upon in: I. Schöffer, La Stratification sociale de la République des Provinces-Unies au 17e siècle, in: Problèmes de stratification sociale, Actes du Colloque International (1966), ed. by R. Mousnier, Paris 1968, 121-135, here p. 124.

149 Introductory literature: J.S. Coleman, "Modernization: Political Aspects", in: International Encyclopedia of the Social Sciences, vol. 10, New York 1968, 395ss.; S.P. Huntington, Political Order in Changing Societies, New Haven 1968; L.W. Pye, Aspects of Political Development, Boston 1966; C. Tilly (ed.), The Formation of National States in Western Europe, Princeton N.J. 1975, and the two essays by G.A. Almond and S. Rokkan, in: W. Zapf (ed.), Theorien des sozialen Wandels, 3rd ed., Köln 1971, 211ss. 228ss., 518ss.; Schröder, Geschichte (note 5), 53ss.

150 Discussed in detail in: Schilling, History (note 1).

and the involvement of the congregation and its representatives in the governance of the church.[151] With its rejection of hierarchical elements and its balance of power between local autonomy and regional or provincial governing bodies, the organizational structure of the Reformed church fit in especially well with the secular structure of the Republic, which was also built from lower levels of government, from the urban and rural communities, to higher ones and which was permeated by the principle of communal (244) and corporate self-government.[152] Against this background the presbyteries must be regarded as a further variant of the numerous political and societal corporations present in the Republic. Since the majority of ecclesiastical offices were annual appointments, there was a significant expansion of participation, already at a a relatively high level in the Republic.[153] It is also important to note that, in contrast to Calvinist city states such as Geneva or Emden, this system had a territorial, temporarily even a "national" dimension in the Netherlands from the very beginning, despite the importance of city and village government. Most evident, however, were changes in the cities: here a second institution with far-reaching official duties—the circle of elders and deacons who represented the public church—existed alongside of the city council and the burgher committees as representatives of the commune.[154]

151 See the first article of the 1571 Synod of Emden in J.F.G. Goeters, Die Akten der Synode der Niederländischen Kirchen zu Emden vom 4. bis 13. Oktober 1571, Neukirchen 1971, 14-54, 72-87.—On Calvinist synods in general: H. Forst, Die Synode zu Bedburg am 3. und 4. Juli 1571. Voraussetzungen, Ablauf und kirchengeschichtliche Bedeutung, in: Monatshefte für evangelische Kirchengeschichte des Rheinlandes 20/21 (1971/72), 33-82; idem, Der Konvent von Wesel im Jahre 1568 und sein Einfluß auf das Entstehen eines deutschen evangelischen Kirchenverfassungsrechts, in: Zeitschrift der Savigny-Stiftung für Rechtsgeschichte, Kanonistische Abteilung 56 (1971), 325-387; Weseler Konvent 1568-1968. Eine Jubiläumsschrift, Düsseldorf 1968; D. Nauta (ed.), De Synode van Emden, Kampen 1971; Introduction to Simons, Synodal- und Gemeindeleben (note 58); J.H. Garrels, Die Entwicklung der reformierten Presbyterial- und Gemeindeverfassung, Leipzig 1920; van Deursen, Bavianen (note 17), esp. 5ss.—The northwestern German-Dutch tradition of presbyteries and synods is in part independent from the Genevan one, described in the books and articles of R.M. Kingdon. See the introduction by H. Schilling, Die Kirchenratsprotokolle der reformierten Gemeinde Emden, vol. 1, Köln 1989.
152 Fockema Andreae, staat (note 12).
153 Ibid., 37; Schilling, History (note 1).
154 On the social background of the elders of the Dutch presbyteries see Schilling, Presbyterien (note 1); Schilling, Calvinism (note 146) and van Deursen, Bavianen (note 17), 83s.

To identify the political and ecclesiological forms of participation, however, would be to misunderstand the character and
function of Calvinist presbyteries in a fundamental way. Elders
and deacons were of course not involved directly in the exercise of political authority. Yet the prohibitions that were
repeatedly issued by the magistrates against any interference by
church officers in political matters provides evidence that it
was not possible to draw a clear demarcation line between the
two spheres. Deacons and presbyters in the large cities of Holland were above all responsible for overseeing the faith and
moral life of the official church community and for providing
care for the sick and the poor. While their oversight seldom
affected more than half of the population, it comprised the
most important segments of the population, including the
majority of the middle stratum and—at least nominally—the
regents. In addition it was never questioned that they bore a
measure of responsibility for the commonwealth as a whole, for
the city, province, and Republic.[155] Important spheres of
public life within the Republic were open to their activity
because of the Christian ethos of Dutch society. (245) As the
agendas of synods and meetings of church councils illustrate,
the presbyters' concerns extended from marriage and family to
the educational system and schools. They discussed how best to
regulate Sundays and holidays, the economic life of the Republic, and the problem of how the church could promote a general civilizing of society.[156]

These problems were usually discussed in close cooperation
with the magistrates, who also had the final responsibility for
formulating and passing laws. The policy decisions that they
made were only too often passed over the opposition of con-

155 The church ordinance of Dordrecht entitled the Calvinist elders to oversee
not only the members of their own church, but also non-members ("oock andere
tot de Christelycke Religie te vermanen"): Kerkelyk Plakaat Boek (note 20), vol.
I, 157, § 23; cf. vol. III, 532, § 21).

156 W.P.C. Knuttel (ed.), Acta der Particuliere Synoden van Zuid-Holland,
1621-1700, 6 vols., s'Gravenhage 1908-1916, (= RGP, KS, 3, 5, 8, 11, 15, 16); F.
Rutgers, Acta van de Nederlandsche synoden der zestiende eeuw, s'Gravenhage
1889; Reitsma and van Veen (eds.), Acta (note 82); Livre Synodal contenant les
articles résolus dans les synodes des églises wallones des Pays-Bas, vol. I, 1563-
1685, Den Haag 1896.—Records of presbyteries of city churches include e.g.:
Th.W. Jensma (ed.), Uw rijk kome, Acta van de Kerkeraad van de Nederduits
Gereformeerde Gemeente te Dordrecht, Dordrecht 1981; H. Schilling (ed.), Die
Kirchenratsprotokolle der Reformierten Gemeinde Emden 1557-1620, 2 vols.,
Köln/Wien 1990/91. (Emden is regarded as the "moeder kerk", the mother
church, of the Dutch churches.)

sistories and synods. Nevertheless it seems possible to speak of a kind of participation in the state and societal decision-making process and to interpret the activity of presbyters as a form of societal participation. Characteristically the magistrates, who were already turning back toward an anti-communal posi-tion at the beginning of the 1580's,[157] never questioned the right of congregational representatives to have a voice in deci-sions affecting the church, even if they tried to keep it under tight control through the appointment of state commissioners. It must be assumed that this kind of ecclesiastical participation had some significance for the sphere of decisions regarding state and church concerns in the narrow sense, which in turn affected societal and political coexistence as a whole. It also gave a relatively large number of persons the opportunity to be trained in administrative and governing responsibilities, seeking the common good.[158] Only further research can show which social strata could take advantage of this opportunity, and most importantly, what its consequences were for individual and collective social mobility. It is safe to assume, however, that among the persons who benefited from holding lay ecclesiasti-cal offices were always some members of those groups and social strata who were excluded from magisterial offices and hence from genuine political participation on account of the (246) oligarchic structure of the Republic's political elite. In addition, a church administration staffed by laymen that was in principle independent of the magistrate was perfectly suited to make the population aware of the limitations of state admi-nistration and authority, while in the German territories, by contrast, the activities of the ecclesiastical bureaucracy tended to confirm the omnipresence and omnipotence of the state. It is noteworthy that contemporary observers were fully aware of these realities: a theorist of the mid-seventeenth century advanced the opinion that "the Calvinist office of elder gives

---

157 On March 23, 1581, a mandate of the Estates of Holland prohibited urban magistrates from consulting guilds and shooting guilds in provincial matters, J. Wagenaar, Vad. Hist. vol. VII, 432. See also J.J. Woltjer, Dutch Privileges. Real and Imaginary, in: J.S. Bromley and E.H. Kossmann (eds.), Britain and the Netherlands, vol. V, Den Haag 1975, 19-35; 30-32.

158 The French ambassador informed his government in 1790, that in the Netherlands many people were experienced in managing public affairs; quoted by P. Geyl, De Bataafse revolutie, in: Bijdragen voor de Geschiedenis der Nederlan-den 11 (1956), 177-199, here 189; see also Schilling, History (note 1). This was among other factors, a result of the participation of so many elders in the public affairs of the Calvinist church.

the common people a characteristic element of liberty" and
that "through this method of internal church government . . .
the people of the Netherlands remain free both ecclesiastically
and politically."[159]

It goes well beyond the bounds of our present topic to
discuss whether this ecclesiastical participation was already an
element of modern, democratic representation or whether it
only prepared the soil for such developments. Such a discussion
would require not only an analysis of the political and societal
system of the Dutch Republic as a whole but also a detailed
description of the complicated problem of its transition to the
modern world. A few comments may suggest, however, the
directions in which to seek an answer. First of all the distribution of power within the church's governing bodies themselves must be examined. Critics of the Calvinists repeatedly
charged that they wished to establish a theocracy
(domineekratie), that is domination of the church government
by the clergy. Of course this would have been a fundamental
violation of the ecclesiological theory of Calvinism. This charge
was not completely baseless, however, as can be inferred from
the ratio of preachers to presbyters present in meetings of the
classes and synods, in which theologians outnumbered laymen
by three to one.[160] In addition the moderators of such con-
ferences (247) were clergymen as a matter of principle. The
clergy in general enjoyed more social prestige than presbyters.
The predominance of the clergy at classis and synodal meetings
naturally relativizes to a large degree the significance of a congregational right of participation, even allowing for the fact
that the synods met only occasionally, while laymen always
outnumbered clergymen in the weekly presbytery meetings.
Ecclesiastical participation was further relativized by the
method used to select presbyters. Despite the possibilities for
variation in choosing individual presbyters, the congregation
itself did not generally choose them: new office holders were

---

159 Ludovicus Gerardus van Renesse (1599-1671), Van het Regeer-Ouder-
linghschap, dat ist Bewijs dat het Ampt der Regeer-Ouderlingen een Goddelijck
ende dienvolgende noodtsaeckelijck / ende deftich beroep is in Godes Kercke, 2
vols., Utrecht 1659/64, 277, quoted by A. van Ginkel, De Ouderling, Oorsprong
en ontwikkeling van het ambt van ouderling ... in de Gereformeerde Kerk der
Nederlanden in de 16e en 17e eeuw, Utrecht 1975, 294, 264.

160 Ibid., 212; Schilling Afkeer (note 15).

selected by cooptation, a process which was usually overseen by the magistrate.[161]

In my opinion it is inappropriate to interpret both the dominance of the clergy and the absence of congregational election of presbyters as a case of harmonization with the oligarchic structural and social model of a burgher commonwealth and thus to understand it as a perversion of an originally democratic concept of church government.[162] It is much more the result of a unique type of ecclesiastical representation which differed in principle from the secular kind of representation. For the presbyters were in principle not only representatives of the congregation, but were at the same time, even preeminently, God's representatives, and it was through them that he worked in his church. This transcendental legitimation of the presbyters precluded their direct responsibility to the congregation and gave their recruitment a sacral dimension that went beyond an earthly act of selection.[163] Caution should be exercised when drawing a direct connection between ecclesiastical congregational representative bodies and democratic structures and attitudes in the secular sphere, between the presbyterian model and modern, representative democracy. With regard to the Netherlands (248) there is a serious question whether the Calvinist model of representation hindered the victory of a modern democratic system rather than fostered it. After the mid-seventeenth century the Calvinists became more and more closely tied to the party of the *Stadhoulder* and the House of Orange. In their struggle against the oligarchy of the Regents they were more than willing to use democratic arguments and to claim that they supported popular sovereignty. What they had in mind, however was, in the words of Pieter Geyl, a "caesaric democracy."[164] The monarch appeared to the people as the executor of God's will and thus was not answerable to any earthly authority. This concept of divinely delegated authority was clearly similar to that present in the internal model

---

161 Van Ginkel, Ouderling (note 159), 226ss.

162 This is the interpretation of Ginkel, ibid., 195.

163 This is reflected in a penetrating essay by the former west German president Gustav Heinemann, himself for years a member of the protestant synod of the present-day Rhineland. See G. Heinemann, Das Verhältnis von Synode und Parlament, in: E. Lomberg (ed.), Emder Synode, 1571-1971, Beiträge zur Geschichte und zum 400jährigen Jubiläum, Neukirchen 1973, 285-294.

164 P. Geyl, Democratische tendenties in 1672, Amsterdam 1950, 5s., 15s., 31ss.; Wansink, Holland (note 2), 154.

of representation and democracy present in the presbyterian organization of the public church.

IV. SUMMARY

Let us summarize: In general, the unique form of mediation between the state and the political system on the one hand and the ecclesiastical and religious system on the other that was present in the early modern Dutch Republic cannot be regarded as "modern" in the strict sense of modernization theory. Both the status of the public church within the state and also the function of the Calvinist confession within Dutch society show traditional characteristics at crucial points. On the one hand, the state of the Republic guaranteed freedom of conscience; as a result it never felt compelled to force all subjects to adhere to a single confession as the French state of Louis XIV did. Nevertheless it was also a *tutor religionis* in the traditional sense, and it supported not an abstract religion but the Reformed confession which officially was accepted as the only true form of religion. Even the Dutch Republic, which during the seventeenth century represented the most advanced society in Europe, was still far from a confessionally neutral state as later emerged with the coming of the French Revolution. Dutch society was multi-confessional but not pluralistic in a modern sense. The Calvinist church was not one societal group among many others which in principle enjoyed equal rights. As a public church it was much more a central pillar of society, upon whose presence both the existence of the state and the societal order were dependent. In this sense it exercised the function of a "state confession" which was evidently indispensable despite the relatively modern church—state relations of the Dutch *ancien régime* society. It might not be an exaggeration to assert that the freedom present in the Republic, so much admired by contemporary observers, was only possible because it had such a "state confession." Although by no means all Dutch people were Calvinists, (249) the public church represented an especially important stone in the foundation of the commonwealth of the northern Netherlands. The existence of a privileged public church was evidently crucial for the diversification of the cultural and religious life of the Republic. If this supposition is correct then it is unwarranted to understand the freedom of the Republic, which suffered heavy setbacks from time to time and decreased considerably during the eighteenth century, as an early form of modern political liberalism.

Apart from this fundamental evaluation, however, important individual elements were present very early in the northern Netherlands which played a significant role in the process of modernization. The most important of these were tolerance and the guarantee of individual freedom of conscience, which constituted fundamental principles of the Republic. The same can be said for the distance between church and state, which was not only a theoretical distinction but was actually maintained in many areas when compared with other European countries. In both of these areas the Republic of the seventeenth century had made a developmental leap forward. In most other European countries tolerance was introduced in the face of stiff resistance and was guaranteed by means of exceptional case rulings which were mostly based upon political or economic interests.[165] Despite the fact that the ideal of a unified political and religious world had been abandoned in theory or that it had retreated into the background with the triumph of the Reformation, in reality both spheres continued to be closely interwoven, even in Protestant countries. These distinctions persist even when the dominance of the state, which included all connections between church and state during the early modern period, is understood to be the driving force behind the process of secularization and hence modernization as well.

As a consequence of the freedom of conscience and the distancing of the state from the church within certain sectors of Dutch society secular solutions to problems could emerge in areas where the pre-modern world generally allowed the church a voice in decision-making and where the support of religious sanctions was still necessary. Examples of such secular solutions include civil marriage and changes in the handling of marital matters in general, as well as the abolition of ecclesiastical oversight for midwives. In one respect this regulation is especially interesting: during the sixteenth and seventeenth centuries there was an increase in the restriction and oversight of sexual life within every confession. Since in the Netherlands the church was either hindered or forbidden to impose social

---

165 I have discussed Brandenburg-Prussia in considerable detail in H. Schilling, Höfe und Allianzen, Berlin 1989, 378-385.

norms or to enforce compliance with them in both of these central societal institutions this pan-European development was only reflected there after some delay. In this respect too the Republic was more liberal than other states.

A comparative viewpoint is crucially important for our topic. We must evaluate the Dutch conditions described above against the backdrop of the rest of Europe, which during the first hundred and fifty years of the early modern period was characterized by confessionalization as a fundamental societal process[166] and by an increasingly important role for the churches. There are indications that the northern Netherlands[167] were not as strongly affected as other European countries by this process, which strengthened and renewed state and society and instituted more pervasive social discipline (250), of which sexual oversight was only one aspect.[168] Dutch humanism, which has not previously been mentioned here, may be significant in this context.

At this point, however, another fundamental problem arises, which I would like at least to mention: the relationship between continuity and change, and the character of the European process of modernization. Jan de Vries has demonstrated that the modernity of the Republic in the agricultural sector of its economy was a result of continuity with medieval social and structural forms and did not involve a radical break at the beginning of the modern period. From this de Vries concluded that the path to economic modernity followed by the northern Netherlands was different than the course followed by neighboring states.[169] Our own observations concerning the fields of church and religion can be interpreted in a similar way: in addition to the weakness of the early modern process of confessionalization in the Netherlands and a corresponding continuity of late medieval elements of religious and cultural life generally, a centralized, authoritarian (*obrigkeitlich*) church

---

166 See the essays in part II of this volume.

167 Discussed in more detail by O. Mörke, Konfessionalisierung (note 2).

168 On the situation in other countries see Reinhard, Gegenreformation (note 88), 231ss. John Bossy holds that during the 16th century "an obsession with individual sexuality" did not yet dominate "the social universe of sin" within Catholicism. J. Bossy, The Social History of Confession in the Age of the Reformation, in: Transactions of the Royal Historical Society, 5th series, 25 (1975), 21-38, esp. 37s.

169 J. de Vries, On the Modernity of the Dutch Republic, in: Journal of Economic History 33 (1973), 191-202.

government, which was the typical pattern of church structure
during the early modern period, never emerged in the northern
Netherlands and this peculiar situation was closely connected
with the absence of an early modern centralized bureaucratic
state. Even the presbyterian and synodal model of church
structure was by no means a new or "revolutionary" principle
but rather an adequate structural element within church organization that fitted very well into the medieval conceptions of
communal and corporate self-government and political participation which survived in the Republic until the end of the
ancien régime. With respect to the ecclesiastical and religious
sector it also seems that the process of "modernization" in the
northern Netherlands differed fundamentally from its course in
other European societies, where the emergence of tolerance and
freedom of conscience and the separation of the ecclesiastical
and secular spheres accompanied the strengthening of a centralized bureaucratic state which subjugated the church or
churches and, in turn, advanced the process of secularization.
This finding of a specific type of early modern modernization
in the northern Netherlands has consequences both for the
place of the Republic of the United Netherlands within early
modern European history and for modernization theory more
generally which, however, I cannot discuss here.

CHAPTER NINE

DUTCH REPUBLICANISM IN ITS
HISTORICAL CONTEXT

I

This essay will discuss the rise of republican theory in the Netherlands during the last decade of the Thirty Years' War and its subsequent triumph over monarchical concepts.[1] The theory was developed for the Regents' Party, the party of well-to-do merchant patricians of the economically prosperous urban centers, mainly in the provinces of Holland and Zeeland. They were opposed politically as well as in their concepts of state and society to the party of the Orange Stadhouders. On a *political* level the parties disagreed whether the center of power in the young republic should be at the court of the Stadhouders or in the town halls. On a *theoretical* level they espoused two different concepts of the state, the Orange party favoring the monarchic principle and the Regents' Party advancing an anti-monarchical and radically republican agenda. During their struggles both sides developed distinct bodies of political theory and sophisticated propaganda to influence public opinion.

In 1650 when Johan de Witt was elected to the office of *Ratspensionaris*, a sort of Prime Minister, and the baby prince Wilhelm, posthumous son of the last Stadhouder Prince Wilhelm II, was rejected as hereditary Stadhouder, the Regents' Party triumphed. The fundamental laws as well as the most important institutions were modified along republican lines. This first republican period within Dutch history ended in 1672, when de Witt was murdered by an Orange mob, Prince Wilhelm was

---

1 This paper was delivered at the symposium "Critical Theories of Quentin Skinner", April 5-7, 1990, Madison, Wis., organized by the Institute for Research in the Humanities of the University of Wisconsin—Madison. Readers who wish to consult the sources and literature should read my article "Der libertär-radikale Republikanismus der holländischen Regenten. Ein Beitrag zur Geschichte des politischen Radikalismus in der frühen Neuzeit," in: Geschichte und Gesellschaft 10 (1984), 498-533.

declared Stadhouder, and the constitution was once again altered in a more monarchical direction.

By introducing my research on Dutch Regents' republicanism
in a symposium on the "Critical theories of Quentin Skinner",
I will offer an example of how a historian seeks understand
political theory. I hope that this will provide theorists of the
study of political ideas with an interesting example which
illustrates two advantages of an historical approach: It will
demonstrate how historians cope with the problems of "context
and meaning," without being explicitly concerned with
linguistic theories. It will also give an impression of the
different types of texts that may be studied to gain an
historically adequate understanding of the structure and the
meaning of a given political theory.

It is my understanding that the history of political ideas has
two complementary goals: to reconstruct political theories and
to evaluate their contributions to the general development of
thinking on the state and society. To understand the body of
political theory developed during the seventeenth century in
the Netherlands, I first must reconstruct this theory within the
historical context of early modern European societies at the end
of their "confessional" period. Then I will evaluate its meaning
within the Old European tradition of political theory, starting
in ancient Greece, mainly with Aristotle, and reaching its
turning point at the end of the 18th century, with the Enlightenment and the revolutionary transition to modern political
thought.

Applying this approach to our present example, we can formulate two methodological assumptions. *First*: The political
theory of the Regents' Party must be studied and evaluated in
the context of the general shape and structure of political
thought of the period. In spite of the changes brought by the
Reformation, this structure was still one based on an Aristotelian view of state and society, combined with an Old European
political culture and mentality that was stamped by the
"feudal" values of honor and reputation which assumed aristocratic or at least oligarchic institutions in state and society.
Second: The republicanism of the Regents must be studied
together with the political, social, religious and, to a certain
extent, even the economic structures and struggles within the
Netherlands. For in contrast to Switzerland and Venice the
republican and middle-class character of the Dutch state was

never unchallenged. On the contrary, strong monarchical and aristocratic attitudes and even institutions flourished in the Dutch republic. They were all linked together with the House of Orange: with the office of Stadhouder-governorship, held by Orange Princes in all the seven provinces on a semi-hereditary basis; with the fact that the house of Orange actually symbolized the union of the seven provinces and also provided the strongest ties of *generaliteit* in everyday politics; with the predominant position of the House of Orange within the calvinistic *publieken kerke*, comparable to the *praecipuum membrum ecclesiae* position of the German princes within their territorial churches; with the office of commander-in-chief of the Dutch army and navy; and last but not least with the dynastic and diplomatic significance of a princely family within the European international system dominated by kings and princes. These latter functions created especially strong arguments for a monarchical interpretation of the Dutch constitution: A strong commander-in-chief was needed because of the continuing wars with Spain. A princely dynasty was necessary, because in absolutistic Europe the reputation of a state and its success in international affairs depended to a considerable degree upon dynastic connections and princely representation. In 1641, when Prince William, the eldest son of Stadhouder Fredric Hendric was married to Mary Stuart, princess of England, the quasi-monarchical character of Dutch "Stadhoudership" was strengthened considerably. This created a real challenge to all groups with anti-monarchical feelings.

This political and constitutional conflict was linked to social and economic interests. The Orange Princes supported the interests of the nobility and advocated a strong position of power for the Netherlands within the international arena. The Regents and the town magistrates under their control were interested primarily in commerce and industry and consequently favored peace rather than war. The conflicts reached a climax at the end of the 1640's, when the peace talks at Münster succeeded and the Netherlands had to define their postwar position—with respect to internal organization as well as to external politics. Ultimately the Regents' Party came to power in 1650 after the failure of an Orange coup d'état in Amsterdam, the stronghold of republican opposition, and the sudden death some weeks later of the Stadhouder Prince William II, in his early twenties, who had been deeply dis-

credited by this failure. Within a year the Regents took all of
the legal and institutional steps necessary to impose their
republican concepts of state and society, especially in the province of Holland. But theoretical debates continued nevertheless,
as the Orange family remained in The Hague, to claim the
office of Stadhouder for young Prince William. Both parties
produced and published dozens of texts to influence public
opinion in favor of their respective theories.

As the contest of political theories was at the same time a
conflict of institutions and political power, a great variety of
texts should be taken into consideration if we are to reconstruct the meaning of the Regents' republicanism. At least
three different types of propaganda can be distinguished by
their style and literary genre as well as by an elaboration of
their contents and intended readers. The *first* type were mass-
produced pamphlets. They were written by the dozen and
distributed systematically to influence public opinion in the
cities. To understand the political debates adequately we must
keep in mind that the audience for whom these texts were
intended were mainly members of the civic middle class in the
towns of Holland and Zeeland.

The *second* type were declarations and petitions drafted by
the respective parties. They also contain important remarks on
political theory. These documents were issued in order to bring
the points of view of these parties to town councils and, above
all, to the provincial and general estates. They addressed the
political elite in order to influence their votes. Since most of
the time they discussed decisions concerning day-to-day politics, the principles of political theory they contain appear
usually in the form of answers to concrete individual problems
or questions. Only seldom do they take the form of basic or
fundamental statements. A summary of these republican
statements are to be found in the great acts of the early 1650's
concerning the change of the constitution.

The *third type* of text is the most elaborate, though not
necessarily the most enlightening for the historian: the philosophical treatises, especially those of the de la Court brothers
and of Baruch de Spinoza. As several of these writings were
directly influenced by Johan de Witt, they are not free from
propagandistic features. Mainly, however, they are philosophical, theoretical, and historically-based reflections as well as
a more or less systematic explanation of the republican model

for state and society. The de la Courts and Spinoza were followers, even admirers, of Johan de Witt. Nevertheless, they cannot be regarded as mere members of his Party. Spinoza, especially, kept his distance from everyday politics. His political writing spells out the logical conclusions of the political culture and the political practice of the Regents' Party. In so doing, it develops a system of full republicanism, with consequences that neither de Witt nor the de la Courts would have been willing to accept. Spinoza's unique achievement was to create a republican model for state and society founded upon the ideal of equality for all individuals. For the seventeenth century, particularly for the aristocratic Dutch regents, this was a vision that was directed far into the future and so was, de facto, for the moment uncompelling.

II

According to my argument on the importance of historical context, a reconstruction of the Regents' theory cannot be reduced to the question of the specific form of government. It must also include arguments concerning everyday domestic and foreign policy decisions as well as those affecting the economy, society, religion, and the church. We must examine the main issues that lay at the heart of the public debates, as well as certain key terms that served to define them.

1. The Three Cardinal Topics

Let me start with the key topics of the controversy. There were three cardinal problems that lay at the heart of the discussion: *First*, the historical role of the Orange princes in the foundation of the state during the war of independence against Spain. *Second*, military organization, particularly the question of whether the office of a supreme commander was sufficient for a republic. *Third*, ecclesiastical and religious organization within the Netherlands, especially striking the right balance between the confessional foundation of the community and the individual's claim to freedom of conscience, which the regents supported, thereby upholding a humanist concern of the sixteenth century. We must examine these debates to show how the texts issued by the Regents' Party gradually developed their liberal, republican interpretation of state and society.

The historical role of the Orange princes was discussed in

several pamphlets. With their attacks on the historical importance of the contributions of the Orange princes, the Regents'
pamphlets destroyed the Orange myth and by doing so presented their own antagonistic version of the history and present
character of the state. The idea that martial ability and noble
bravery were the cornerstones of Dutch independence—as
argued by Orangist propaganda—was rejected and replaced by
a liberal, middle-class interpretation. Royal and martial values
and behavior, allegedly the crucial ingredients for the victory
over Spain, were reexamined by tracing them back to the people and institutions that made them possible. The first precondition of victory was the property and blood of the people who
had suffered to help the Orange princes win their fame as
generals. A second was the financial power of the Dutch towns,
without which none of the princes would have been able to
finance his wars. Without denying the military achievements of
the house of Orange, the republican regents removed Orange
military glory from the sphere of a royal or noble identity and
put it instead into the context of officials and functionaries
who are appointed, paid, and above all controlled by the state.
Thus the fame of the House of Orange shrank from a monarchical magnitude to a civic, republican size.

The second debate, concerning the *form of the military
establishment*, provided an opportunity to launch a fundamental
attack on one-man-rule in general. In confronting the argument of the Orange court that the security of the state required
the office of a captain general, and that it be a hereditary
office of the House of Orange, the Regent's Party drew up the
theoretical foundations for a liberal, republican organization of
the army, based on the principle that in a republic the highest
authority always had to be held by the magistrates. These
principles were deduced from the law of nature and illustrated
with many examples out of the Bible and history. The model of
a republican army emerged. It was not to be as large as the
Orange Army, separated from society and threatening the independence and freedom of the middle-class to make their own
decisions, serving dynastic and autocratic state interests rather
than bourgeois economic ones. It was rather to be a military
force controlled by the states, principally the towns and their
Regent magistrates. This army and navy were to be instruments
of the commercial interests of the middle-class instead of
instruments of the state and the dynastic interests of the nobil-

ity, eager to advance their personal reputation and not to support the commonweal. Thus the republican army would not endanger trade or individual and commercial liberties, but rather strengthen and serve them.

The third key debate, concerning *religion and ecclesiastical organization*, gave the Regents' Party an opportunity to extend their platform for a liberal society by including a demand for tolerance and freedom of conscience. By contrast, the Orange Party in alliance with the Calvinist clergy stood for confessional conformity and discipline. It was not a modern, pluralistic and secular concept, but rather an early modern one that did not question the general importance of church and religion for a well-ordered society.

Starting from the question of economic profit, Pieter de la Court saw freedom of religion and conscience within these limits as the essence of social freedom and thereby as the best poosible guarantee for the growth of Holland. Spinoza moved more consciously toward a modern, liberal point of view: his system was based on the natural equality of all human beings, and so freedom of opinion and equal rights for all religions were already seen as individual, fundamental rights.

2. "Freedom" and "republic" as key words in the linguistic and theoretical context

Examining the linguistic context of the three debates outlined here only very roughly, we repeatedly encounter two key words: "freedom" and "republic." An analysis of their meaning will give us information necessary to understand the significance of the political theory of the Regents, within its contemporary context as well as its place within the development of modern political theory in general.

"Freedom" is a fundamental category in the pamphlets, the official decrees and statute-books, and in the philosophical treatises. It even became the official label of the Regents' regime between 1654 and 1672, characterizing itself as *"vrije regeeringe," "ware vrijheid"* and *"Vrije Vereenigde Provinzen."* When examined more closely, the different uses of the term "freedom" and its specific relation to "republic" display an ambiguity that is revealing for the character of the Regents' theory.

On the one hand, *"freedom / vrijheid"* is used in the traditional medieval sense of *"jura et libertates,"* that is privileges and specific rights laid down by positive law. Even in its more general sense, referring to the "freedom of the Batavians," it did not really go beyond tradition. In the Middle Ages there had always been an abstract idea of freedom apart from the concrete liberties of the estates—as *libertas christiana*, *Romana* or *Naturalis*. But there were still other elements within the concept of "freedom" that in my opinion served to shift the discussion from traditional to modern ways of understanding it. Most crucial was the direct connection of the concept of freedom with the legal question of the nature of the Dutch consitution. This connection was important because it paved the way for a new concept of freedom, defined and understood in modern terms.

This can be illustrated by the pamphlet *Hollands Praatje*, a dialogue between two craftsmen, one from Brabant, hence a subject of the King of Spain, the other from Holland, now under the regime of the Regents. Despite his traditional liberties, especially strong in Brabant because of the famous *Joyeuse entrée*, the man from Brabant was characterized as *"verheerde,"* that is "dominated," "ruled over," "un-free," because he was subject to a monarch. In contrast, the Dutch craftsman is characterized as a *"vrije Hollander,"* free because he lived with a constitution that guaranteed his "true freedom" by two fundamental achievements. First, it permanently abolished the last remnants of the old monarchical form of government as well as the newly created elements of one-man-government, which were regarded as conflicting with freedom in principle, while the republican—in the sense of non-monarchic form of government was seen as identical with "true freedom." Second, the constitution established the autonomous governmental and administrative power of the town councils as basic units of the state which were to have the unrestricted right of assembly and cooptation as well as the right to dispatch deputies to the provincial estates without hinderance.

At this point in our analysis the historian of early modern political thought can draw an important conclusion based on the reconstruction of the Regent's political theory from these texts and its interpretation within the context of early modern European societies: The essential message of the political theory of the Regents' Party was evidently the explicit and emphatic identification of "freedom" with the federative "republic" in the sense of a specific form of government. That is to say, "republic" in the context of the political theory of the Regents' party no longer meant "commonweal" in the sense of any state producing the common good. Even Macchiavelli regarded those monarchies which secured the common good as "republics." In the Dutch context by the mid-seventeenth century the concept of "republic" was in principle opposed to monarchy and to any other kind of one-man or one-woman rule. Furthermore, the Dutch republican theorists claimed that only this specific form of republican government could support the common good. This was a clear shift in political thinking, the more so since at that time, apart from England, political theory as well as political reality all over Europe was dominated by an emphatic monarchism. The theory of the Regents' Party was innovative in two other respects: First, because it connected the republican ideal to political practice, whereas earlier republic theories had been largely a matter of academic discussion. Second, it served as the theoretical foundation for a national state in the form of a federation. Up to that time the term "republic" had usually been applied to city-states only, above all to those of the German Empire and of Italy, or to communities like Geneva.

The Dutch regents succeeded in making republicanism into a working model for organizing both state and society by claiming a natural and necessary identification of liberty with republican government. In France and Germany, by contrast, the term "republic" became politically relevant as a model for the state in general (not merely for a town) only at the end of the eighteenth century. The Regent's success also contrasts sharply with the failure of republicanism in England, which was discredited after the Commonwealth had become a military dictatorship. It was so attractive a concept that the republican theory survived the "caesaro-monarchical regime" (Pieter Geyl) of William III, installed in 1672. A revived Republican Regents' government came to power in the early eighteenth century.

3. Dutch Regents' republicanism as connecting link between the early-modern and traditional political thought, and the modern type of political theory

The next, even more important step towards an interpretation and understanding of Dutch Republicanism and its contribution to the history of political ideas must be to evaluate the meaning and significance of the innovation just described. We

must pose and answer the following question: Did this early
actualization of the republican model in any respect display
manifestations of the modern type of republican theory, which
in general did not become established until the American and
French revolutions? Or was Dutch Regents' republicanism only
a variation upon traditional political thinking?

There are two crucial qualifications that distinguish the traditional and modern concepts of both key words, "republic"
and "liberty/freedom." That is the *dynamic* and *universal* character of their modern meaning. In the traditional context they
were only relative and static, relevant only to specific individuals, groups, or countries. Did the political theory of the
Dutch Regents, we must ask, show elements that were able to
transform both 'republic' and 'freedom' from concepts with
only relative and partial applicability into categories of fundamental value for every political and social order, as is
characteristic of the modern use of the terms 'freedom' and
'republic'?—This question once again must be adressed on
different levels and within different contexts. The answer once
again will be ambiguous.

On the one hand the context of political and social reality
gave meaning to the theory under consideration. There is no
doubt that "liberty" as well as "republic" retained their traditional, that is restricted scope. The de Witt regime of the 1650s
and 1660s and its republican successor in the first half of the
eighteenth century were both oligarchic and not democratic.
They never tried to bring republican forms of government to
other countries as the French Republic did at the end of the
eighteenth century. In this respect Dutch republicanism of the
seventeenth and eighteenth centuries was not a forerunner "of
today's democratic republics" but rather the sign "of an effort
by the trading patricians, the heirs of medieval trade capital, to
defend their economic and social privileges in monarchical
Europe." The Regents' ideal of republicanism and liberty de
facto legitimized and established the government of a minority,
that is the big merchants, especially in the Dutch cities. In
socio-economic terms "true freedom" meant a government in
which a coalition of loosely connected groups of merchants
preserved their freedom to respond quickly to economic opportunities revealed by markets without the restrictions likely to
result from a central government that imposed its economic
policies upon the entire country. When read within its social

and economic context, the political theory of "true freedom" developed by the Regents' Party appears in an ideological light. And this makes it possible for most scholars concerned with Dutch history to characterize the Regents' republicanism as old-fashioned and traditional.

But there is still another context which must be considered in order to understand the theory and its contribution to modernizing political thinking. In this second context the Regents' republicanism appears to be an important link between early modern and modern conceptualizations of state and society. To show this I will summarize a more detailed argument in the following three statements:

First: The Regents' republicanism already marked a shift from the Old European civic republican format, typical even for advanced civic humanism in Italy, to a modern republican constitution valid for a *"Flächenstaat"* (territorial state). Although de Witt could not accept the idea of a *respublica in singulari numero* for his fatherland he was eager to stress that the Dutch constitution was more than just an assembly of "municipal republics" as in Italy, but *respublicae federatae et unitae in plurali numero*. The Regents' concept of a republican constitution was no longer merely an urban one but it was not yet a unitarian one. It was the ideal of a composite republic, integrating the city republics into provincial republics and these, in turn, into the federal "unified republic"—a principle of organization that still dominated the American republic at the end of the eighteenth century when France experienced a breakthrough and became a centralized republic. In his *Tractatus politicus* Spinoza provided an elaborated justification for this decentralized, federal solution, claiming that it was superior when compared with the centralized type of the aristocratic republic as it had existed in ancient Rome, and did exist in Venice and Geneva. For Spinoza the decisive advantages were better protection from the danger of the despotism of a minority and a healthy obligation to discuss political decisions, thus increasing the chances of finding the best answer in every situation. Since the social and economic advantages of the ruling Regents elite, mentioned earlier, were consistent with the general philosophical preconditions of liberty, Spinoza, the most outstanding representative of the Regents' republicanism, was able to formulate a political theory that broke away from the restrictions of oligarchical reality.

Second: This break is even more obvious in my second argument, which concerns the progressive character of the concept of participation. Despite its limitations, Regent's republicanism had within it a logical dynamism which, in theory, allowed a considerable expansion of participation. If de la Court, as well as Spinoza, argue that "freedom" and the "interest" of the individual are unchangeable preconditions for the prosperity of the commonwealth, and that in a republic, contrary to absolutistic societies, this identity should be based upon free consent, the theory inevitably makes room for an ultimately individualistic concept of a socially enlarged, far-reaching right of participation. Spinoza therefore moves from the idea of an aristocratic republic to that of a democratic one, in which participation is an inherited, individual right of all men descended from citizens (*ex parentibus civibus*) and of all others born within the fatherland who have served the republic well and have not lost the right to vote because they have committed a crime or lost their financial independence.

This quantitative widening of participation coincided with a similar significant re-definition of the principle of qualification. It was an essential characteristic of "true freedom" that, when public offices, honorary posts, or other "high dignities" were distributed, they were handed out not on the basis of birth and family reputation, but for personal efficiency and ability as well as for individual achievements for the common good. This was theoretically all the more important, since this new modern principle of qualification by ability and achievement appeared in an anti-monarchical and anti-noble context, that was basic to the Regents' self-interpretation.

Third: Even with regard to the question of the traditional relativism and modern universalism of republican concepts, the political theory of the Dutch Regents displayed early elements of modernity, though once again the texts are ambiguous. On the one hand, and especially in de la Court's works, "republic" appears as a specific constitutional model of certain nations in countries with a special geographical and material background. In the case of Holland, fishing, commerce, and shipping required a liberal, not an absolutistic framework. This relativism corresponds to an almost isolationist attitude, that is, the renunciation of any attempt to "export" the republican form of government. The Dutch republican Regents were inclined to support hereditary monarchies in other countries instead of challenging them ideologically and politically, as the English Commonwealth had on occasion. You will remember in this context Admiral Blake's propagandistic statement at Cadiz in the early 1650's, announcing that republican principles would soon overthrow all the monarchies of Europe.

Besides its relativism and isolationism, there was one aspect of Dutch republican writing which gave the republican concept a universal dimension. This can be illustrated by the following reference in a republican pamphlet of 1650 that appeared only a short time after the death of Prince William II: *"Want de text (i.e., of the Bible, H.Sch.) is klaer dat Republycken Godt behaechlycker syn als Monarchien."* ("The Bible has clear evidence that God is in favor of a republican form of government"). Therefore, the Dutch should not endanger the "golden freedom" God granted them by striking against the house of Orange. If in this situation the Dutch did not honor the republican form of government, "He (i.e. God) would say, they have rejected me, and in His wrath give us a king." In line with the thought expressed in the pamphlet, Pieter de la Court and Johan de Witt earnestly argued that a republic was the only form of government under which people could be led to the "promised land."

Despite this eschatological perspective, it is no less clear in the works of de la Court and de Witt than in those of Spinoza that it is *secular rationality* that made a republic superior to all other forms of government. With Spinoza, its superiority consisted in its power to foster social integration and its ability to come to reasonable decisions by discussion. With de Witt and de la Court, it was its rationality and predictability in both domestic and foreign policy.

A contextual analysis of the use of the term "freedom," which cannot be discussed in detail here, would show the same differences between traditional and modern meanings that we have demonstrated with the term "republic." Thus, the analysis of the two most important key-words within the texts under consideration confirms our initial hypothesis: the republicanism of the de Witt era was a liberal and radical form of political theory that must be considered an important connecting link between early-modern, traditional, and modern ideas on state and society, or the between the early-modern and modern types of political theory. The most advanced position then expressed was that of Spinoza who argued that the liberal—ultimately democratic—republic was not only the best form of government in terms of its success but actually the only one that was adequate for reasonable human beings. This was not, however, the position that the Regents accepted as their party program. Rather it was a philosophical deduction from that position developed by a small circle of intellectuals whose statements on this subject were either not published—in the case of Spinoza—or appeared in a considerably weakened form—in the case of the de la Courts.

With regard to the general development of political theory in Europe and its precursors, our finding confirms that it was in the northwestern, maritime zone of Europe that political theory gained its modern dynamism in parallel with economic and social modernization. It is well-known that this was also true of England and Scotland, especially in the late seventeenth century. If our observations and interpretations are correct, then the northern Netherlands or, more precisely, their western, maritime parts, dominated by the cities and the early modern bourgeoisie or middle-class, must be considered an additional important center for this development. That fits in with the well-known picture of Holland, already held by contemporaries, as a society that set social, cultural, and economic trends for all of early modern Europe. Holland in its "Golden Century" also set intellectual trends in political theory with its analysis of state and society. This body of thought supplied a crucial mediating connection between the Renaissance ideal of a "civic humanism," developed in Florence and Venice, and the modern liberalism that emerged in the last quarter of the seventeenth century in England.

III

I hope my presentation demonstrates that historians of political theory who are not familiar with linguistic theories are not necessarily methodologically naive but can provide their own kind of contextual interpretation—in fact, offering interpretations within two distinct contexts: the context of the texts themselves and the context of political, social, and economic structures. To provide an adequate interpretation on both the textual and the structural level, an understanding of the long-term development of the meaning of words, concepts, and theories as well as of historical reality is crucial. Concepts which have been helpful for my own understanding include those of modernization, elaborated by Max Weber and his students, and of *"Begriffsgeschichte,"* elaborated by the German scholars Brunner, Conze, and Koselleck. The most important idea associated with the latter school of thought is the so-called *"Sattel-Zeit,"* from roughly 1750 to 1820 which was the decisive period of change for the meaning of key words in political context, as they lost their Old European meanings and acquired modern ones. This fundamental change is documented in the volumes of the encyclopedia *Geschichtliche Grundbegriffe*, which provides scholars of early modern political theory with an indispensable tool for understanding the meaning of terms and texts. Finally, I would like to underscore the interpretative and unavoidable subjective character of both the formulation and interpretation of political theory. In my opinion, this cannot be overcome by theories of texts and knowledge, however sophisticated and well-established they might be. It is very important to keep this relativism both of understanding and of interpreting historical texts in mind, because pretensions of scientific objectivity can do even more harm to the meaning of the texts than an interpretation without any concern for the historical context.

INDEX

This index includes the names of persons mentioned in this book, historical as well as contemporarian, and all places, except of names of countries ("Germany," "England," "the Netherlands" etc.) The territories of the Holy Roman Empire and of the dutch provinces are included.

STUDIES IN MEDIEVAL
AND REFORMATION THOUGHT

EDITED BY HEIKO A. OBERMAN

Prospectus available on request

E.J. BRILL — P.O.B. 9000 — 2300 PA LEIDEN — THE NETHERLANDS